THE OFFICIAL®
PRICE GUIDE TO

AMERICAN INDIAN ARROWHEADS

THE OFFICIAL
PRICE GUIDE TO
AMERICAN INDIAN ARROWHEADS

JOHN L. STIVERS

FIRST EDITION

House of Collectibles
Ballantine Books · New York

Important Notice. All of the information, including valuations, in this book has been compiled from the most reliable sources, and every effort has been made to eliminate errors and questionable data. Nevertheless, the possibility of error, in a work of such immense scope, always exists. The publisher will not be held responsible for losses that may occur in the purchase, sale, or other transaction of items because of information contained herein. Readers who feel they have discovered errors are invited to write and inform us, so they may be corrected in subsequent editions. Those seeking further information on the topics covered in this book are advised to refer to the complete line of Official Price Guides published by the House of Collectibles.

© 1994 by John L. Stivers

All rights reserved under International and Pan-American Copyright Conventions.

℔ This is a registered trademark of Random House, Inc.

Published by: House of Collectibles
                201 East 50th Street
                New York, NY 10022

Distributed by Ballantine Books, a division of Random House, Inc., New York, and simultaneously in Canada by Random House of Canada Limited, Toronto.

Manufactured in the United States of America

ISSN: 1073-8622

ISBN: 0-876-37913-7

Cover design by Kristine Mills

Line illustrations used with the permission of Amy Annette Smith

First Edition: December 1994

10 9 8 7 6 5 4 3 2 1

CONTENTS

ACKNOWLEDGMENTS

There were so many individuals who contributed their time and cooperation to help me compile and complete this work. I thank you all!

Particular thanks and mention, however, is greatly deserved by the following individuals. Thanks to my editor at Ballantine Books, House of Collectibles, Stephen Sterns. His persistence and confidence helped to get this work off the ground. Strangely enough, he and I created the precepts of the work over casual conversation. I have been supported and backed honorably.

I want to complement Amy Annette Smith for the fine illistrations in the <u>Introduction</u>, "How to use this Guide".

I give a great deal of thanks to Cherry Weiner, my agent, who negotiated with Ballantine on my behalf. Cherry kept me working through the good times and the bad. Thank you, Cherry, for your moral support and confidence.

I give special thanks to the man I call my mentor in my adventure into artifact collecting, Les Grubbe, of southern Illinois, Les's time, knowledge, patience and persistence, massive collection, and his contacts were virtually indispensable to the compilation of this guide. In addition I need to mention three other individuals, John Harris, Dr. Alex Shaw, and my little lady. Without John's and Alex's expertise in computers and computer software, the project would have taken a year longer to complete. I must also thank my family, who put up with my strange, long hours and my frequent trips from home.

Notable mentions:

Southern Illinois University, Carbondale, Illinois

Joe Lift	Fred Suite
Charles McCorkle	Tim Rubbles
Tony Clinton	Tim Crawford
Randall Kimbell	David Zinkie
Bob Maples	Tommy Bryden
Loney Hall	Don May
	Bob Cox

Once again I thank all of the individuals and groups that gave me time to compile my photographs and listings.

To the author's knowledge the pieces represented in this guide are authentic. If there is proof of any discovered fakes or pieces questionable enough to be investigated please notify the author. Mistakes made in this edition will be corrected in the next edition.

Part One:

Points and Blades

INTRODUCTION

The collection of Amerind (American Indian) artifacts was born when the first European set foot in the lands that were to become known as the Americas. The stone tools of the Americas are some of the finest and certainly the most materially diverse on the globe. They span in size from the monolithic to minute translucent flakes.

The focus of this identification and price guide is on those tools commonly referred to as arrowheads, consisting of arrowheads, atlatl points, spear points, and knives. There is also a small section of the guide on other stone tools.

We can reasonably speculate that the size and quality of tools and points were environmentally affected. Simply visualize the diversity in size for a point fashioned for hunting mammoth and one for rabbits or squirrels.

Virtually every family in the Americas, the United States, Canada, South and Central America has one or more items deemed an Amerind collectible or artifact. Throughout the United States nearly every small town citizen or farmer has a piece of human worked stone.

Projectile points and stone tools are the first type of humankind's durable machines. They are objects created with a specific purpose in mind: ceremonial, hunting, farming, or even repairing the original tool.

Most artifacts are found simply by accident, or handed down from one generation to the other. Yet there are an increasing number of artifacts that are sought out in the most rigorous manner. The stone tools (including arrowheads) of the indigenous people of the Americas are plentiful and widely dispersed and of a nearly unbelievable diversity. It seems that the Amerind was very adept at utilizing the most abundant as well as the best material on hand.

Until a hundred or so years ago simple stone tools and projectiles were rarely viewed as having any value outside of the

academic pursuits of anthropologists and archaeologists. Today
there is an increasing awareness and appreciation of the
uniqueness and beauty of Amerind tools. With this increase in
interest, the number of artifacts is decreasing while their value is
steadily increasing. Today many of the finest pieces of stone
work are in the hands of private collectors, not the museums. The
reason for this phenomenon is not the greed of collectors, but
instead the fact that universities and museums today are not
receiving the funding they did in the past to investigate potential
and proven archeological sites.

It is an exhilarating and amazing feeling to hold a point
or stone tool in one's hand and contemplate—even imagine its
ancient user and use. You hold in your hand a part of prehistory
as well as a piece of the prehistory of a particular individual.
Someone fashioned, designed, and adapted the piece you hold to
sustain a way of life. Possibly the piece you hold passed through
generations of users' hands. Regardless, you have in your hand a
key, one of many, to the evolutionary survival and adaptation of
the indigenous people of the Americas.

Welcome to the world of collecting American Indian
artifacts; in particular arrowheads and stone tools. This book is
not solely a price guide. A price guide is virtually useless unless
it is also an identification guide. The objective of this work is to
give the reader and collector the best of both pricing and
identification when collecting Amerind stone artifacts.

THE AMATEUR ARCHAEOLOGIST

Having been formally educated in the field of
anthropology, I had been told the horror stories of the crimes of
the Amateur Archaeologist. These crimes and horrors were
paramount in my mind when I first began this work. I began with
a variety of preconceived ideas that were unabashedly negative
toward the amateur archeologist and/or collector of Amerind
artifacts.

I quickly discovered that there are those who are
unethical in their approach to the collection of artifacts. Just as
quickly I discovered they are few and far between and are looked
upon more harshly by the average collector and amateur
archeologist than by the educated professionals in the field of

archaeology.

There are a number of beneficial attributes possessed by amateur archaeologists that are both impressive and educational. I was greatly impressed by the care paid to private collections. I was also impressed by the diligence and persistence of private collectors in obtaining and identifying their pieces.

In every endeavor one seems to need a mentor; for me that individual was Les Grubbe of southern Illinois. While working and traveling with Les I learned a great deal about amateur archaeologists. I learned that though their objectives differ from those of professional archaeologists, in many ways they are more demanding concerning the identification, usage, and preservation of the artifacts they collect. Les, who has collected artifacts for well over 20 years, had a personal research library more extensive than most university libraries I have visited.

Amateur archaeologists have a code of their own that overlaps with that of professionals in many ways. They truly strive to be the best at what they do: identifying and preserving the artifacts they collect. I met very few that had become interested in Amerind artifacts solely for profit. The vast majority were into collecting for the love of the pieces and the mystery surrounding them.

The vast majority of collectors as well as amateur archaeologists made every effort to contact the professionals at the universities in their areas before even making surface collections in their own plowed fields. There was a great deal of respect for the prehistorical and historical value of the artifacts they discovered and a great deal of effort was put into trying to register their finds with the professionals.

Individuals such as Les Grubbe would no sooner desecrate a grave site or attempt a dig without contacting professionals than murder his own mother. Like Les, nearly every collector focused on surface collections or previously disturbed sites of confirmed insignificant value to the professional archaeologist.

Working with individuals like Les Grubbe, Tom Bryden, Fred Suite, Joe Flint, and Charles McCorkle I quickly began to respect the individuals I met as well as their love for Amerind artifacts.

FOCUS AND DIMENSIONS OF THIS GUIDE

There were a multiplicity of factors that helped the author in developing this guide. I was impressed by the demands of collectors for specific information concerning their pieces. The major concerns were the time period of the artifact's manufacture and use; the chert, flint, or stone type of the artifact; a more simplified and consistent means of identification; the known history of a particular piece if possible; and a degree of more specific identification.

Whereas professionals might be satisfied with the identification of an artifact as Archaic, Woodland, or Paleo-archaic, for example, the amateur seems to demand more.

This was brought home to me as Les and I sat examining three particular points on a Friday afternoon. We could have relatively easily identified two of the points as Adena Dickson, and the third as an E-notch. Yet such a simple and reasonably sufficient identification of the pieces was not acceptable. It was amazing to watch journals and identification guides spanning decades grabbed from shelves and boxes in the quest for more specific information.

The E-notch was brown chert, but there was a name for the chert on the tip of our tongues that would lead us to the history and site location of the piece. After several days of checking and cross checking the identification was pinned down; we were dealing with a Gram Cave E-notch, of Dover chert, a particular type of chert almost exclusively from a specific area in Tennessee.

Over the 18 months it took to gather the information and photos for this guide I experienced this type of fervor and devotion in identifying particular pieces time after time. Often the so-called final identification was begun all over again just to make sure that no mistakes had been made.

It gave me a sense that, to the collectors, their pieces were not just stone with a monetary value. Instead, I began to understand that each particular piece had a personality; it had a home, a particular style, an age, a use, and a specific place in the pre-historical record of the indigenous Amerind culture that was respected, cherished, and enjoyed by their possessors.

THE COLLECTOR

The collector of Amerind artifacts is a difficult breed to describe. The oldest collector I met was over 80 years old, the youngest was only 10 years old. The collector may be a professional, a farmer, a computer technician, even a biker. To identify a collector by sex or age is little less than ridiculous. There are as many grandmothers as grandfathers collecting, and there was no gender difference in any age group. So who is a collector of Amerind artifacts? The collector is simply an individual who, through hunting or purchasing, collects Amerind artifacts.

Many collectors overlook the less recognized or coveted pieces, such as scrapers, hammer stones, and heating stones. Keep in mind that these too are artifacts and are of considerable value to the collection and preservation of Amerind prehistory. It is also important that these items are identified and have a value.

The reason artifacts are collected seems to vary as much as the individuals who collect them. One thing I was inspired by was the number of families that were involved. It was very apparent that wives and husbands and their children collected for recreation and educational reasons. Something that I found surprising was seeing families involved in something together that was both relaxing, entertaining, recreational, and educational.

Contrary to the horror stories I was told about in academic circles, I must say that the average collector could pass any non-graduate archaeology class. For those who had been at it for more than a decade, graduate classes certainly would not have been difficult.

A large number of collectors had done considerable work as voluntary assistants on professional digs and many of the more experienced collectors, such as Les Grubbe, were published in the field.

There are a number of ways to collect artifacts, and often it is best to combine several methods. There is always the simplest way, and that is to go to shows and exhibitions and "attempt" to buy collections and pieces. I say attempt, because at least half of the material at a given display is there not be sold, but to be enjoyed, even marveled at.

Regardless, there are always plentiful artifacts for sale at reasonable and negotiable prices, either as single pieces or as collections. In addition there are several experts in identification and authenticity always on hand—use them!

Then there are the less conventional and little more physically exacting means of collecting artifacts. I became well acquainted with a number of individuals, couples, and families that spend a day or so of their weekend searching flea markets and swap meets for artifacts. They generally fared well and were able to find authentic pieces at good prices. Then there are those a little more physical who walked freshly plowed fields, river banks, and known or suspected mounds and building sites.

If you are searching in the natural sources for artifacts there are a few simple rules that should be followed. First and foremost, ask the owner of the property you wish to investigate for permission. If at all possible consult the nearest archaeology department at your closest university to determine the significance of a particular site. One thing all collectors need to understand is that once an artifact is removed from its original resting place, unless it is properly documented it is lost to the archaeological field of study forever.

If an artifact is actually removed from the ground by nature or collector (from elow the surface), it has no place in the professional's chronological excavation of a site. Such a piece may be an important element to the entire dig. There are so many fine pieces available in surface collections that digging is rarely necessary and not desired.

A freshly plowed field or a stream or river bank after a good rain in a site area will offer the collector more than enough beautiful and interesting artifacts. Surface collection in disturbed areas, plowed fields, construction sites, and the like can turn up numerous pieces that are of very little scientific value. Still, it is always a good idea to report the location of surface finds to the nearest university.

It is also a good idea to check into the state and federal laws concerning artifact collection in your area. On private property there is rarely if ever a problem, yet it is still a good idea to check. And once again, don't forget to get the land owner's permission.

The final advice for the collector, novice, or expert is to get the best available research material that you can. I hope that this guide will offer such a tool to both the novice and expert.

GETTING THE REAL THING

The most reliable means of collecting arrowheads and stone tools is to find them in their natural state. It is extremely unusual for someone to be malicious enough to go through the trouble of knapping their own artifacts and distributing them in a field or other site.

It is not as unusual to find modern-made artifact replicas at flea markets, yard sales, or swap meets. Occasionally an individual will sneak a replica into one of the thousands of amateur club and public gatherings. However, individuals who do sneak in fakes are generally quickly discovered and either asked not to come back to an association display and gathering or given a reputation when deserved, and potential buyers of their collections and pieces are forewarned. The Central States Archaeological Assoc., its peer regional organizations, and other associations go through a great deal of trouble to assure that the artifacts on display and for sale at their meetings are authentic. If in doubt seek out an expert, who will be readily recommended at such association meetings, and get their advice.

Always be careful of that deal that sounds too good to be true; usually it is. However, also try to remember that many large and very valuable collections were begun by individuals buying a bucket or box of interesting rocks from someone's garage, barn, or yard sale.

There is a simple test that can be done to help check the authenticity of your points. Over time an artifact collects a patina. An authentic piece placed in water will usually cause an oily rainbow on the water's surface. This rainbow of oil is representative of the oils the artifact has collected since it was fashioned.

PRICING STONE ARTIFACTS

I am often asked why there is such a wide range of value assessments for a particular piece. The answer is not a difficult one, although it is somewhat confusing unless a few elements are understood.

Arrowheads and stone tools are much like paintings and sculptures, yet are nowhere near as volatile to public opinion.

There are many considerations in establishing a value for artifacts. Unquestionably the top consideration is workmanship. Categorizing a piece as museum quality signifies that the piece is rare, of excellent to good quality workmanship, unique within the classic design of a certain style and usually of quality material. Excellent, average, and poor quality identifications relate to the level of deterioration from the standards of workmanship, material, and damage.

The material used plays a significant role in the quality and aesthetic view of a particular piece. Still, there is a wide variety in workmanship from one region to another and from one time period to another. Amerind artifacts date from in excess of 40,000 years in the past to less than one hundred years. The tools and points of 40,000 years ago are certainly cruder than those made in the last 10,000 or so years. In the archaeology of the Americas, Paleo refers to the cultural period from 48,000-16,500 B.P.; Late Paleo from 16,500-12,000 B.P.; Paleo Transitional from 12,000-8,500 B.P. Determinations concerning workmanship are made up of several factors. Factors considered, for example, are symmetry, personal style, craftsmanship with difficult materials, classic representation, uniqueness, and form. The second major consideration is simply usage. Of course, some of these determinations are unquestionably subjective. Regardless, although a point or tool was made more recently, this does not assure that it will be a better worked or more aesthetic piece than one twice its age.

One factor that is taken into consideration throughout this guide is the age of a particular piece. As well, the rarity of the piece in workmanship and material is highly considered. Although a piece worked in obsidian or jasper is certainly more appealing to the eye, this doesn't necessarily mean that it is more valuable than a piece made of hematite, granite, or a cruder chert.

Thus, the main factors taken into consideration in this guide in pricing artifacts are quality of workmanship, material used, age of the piece, rarity, uniqueness, and size. The size factor can work both ways; a large or small piece may be more highly valued considering the other factors mentioned above and noted throughout the guide. These are the primary factors that are taken into consideration, and a great deal of time and energy has been spent in convincing collectors and auctioneers always to consider these factors. Very little argument exists in this matter, and there is a general agreement among all concerned.

The main sources of obtaining artifact values in this guide were gathered from Midwestern archaeological societies. In addition, great attention was given to museum, public, and private price offers. This, coupled with dealers', auctioneers', and collectors' prices, greatly aided in this guide's artifact pricing.

Piece condition categories are museum quality, excellent, average, or poor. There are few poor pieces pictured in this guide. Determinants of piece condition are workmanship, material, and craftsmanship with difficult materials. These factors add to or subtract from the value of the piece.

Museum quality pieces that are rare are very difficult to place a value on. Yet, using the resources and methods mentioned above, a reasonable estimate of value can be determined.

Individuals familiar with other guides will not see a particular piece dropping in value. There are only a limited number of artifacts and their value can only increase. On the other hand, there are a variety of artifacts that will display an appreciable increase in value.

HOW TO USE THIS GUIDE

Following are point and blade charts to demonstrate points of consideration and recognition on points and blades. It would also be helpful to familiarize yourself with the glossary.

<u>IDENTIFYING MARKS:</u>

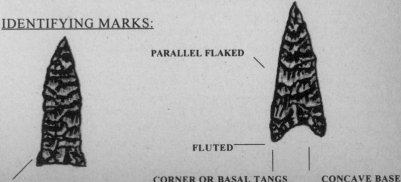

PARALLEL FLAKED

FLUTED

RANDOM FLAKED

CORNER OR BASAL TANGS   CONCAVE BASE

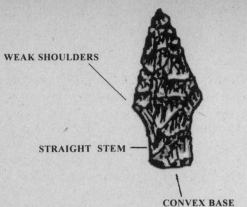

WEAK SHOULDERS

STRAIGHT STEM

STRAIGHT BASE

CONVEX BASE

SHOULDER BARBS

BEVELED EDGE

EDGE SERRATIONS

FLARING TANGS

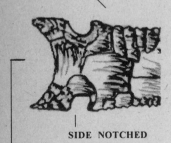

SIDE NOTCHED

CORNER NOTCHED

DEEP CONCAVE BASE

BASAL NOTCHED

SNAPPED TANGS

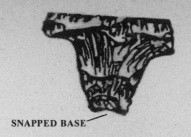

SNAPPED BASE

DOVETAIL

TURKEYTAIL

FISH TAIL BASE

ROUND BASE

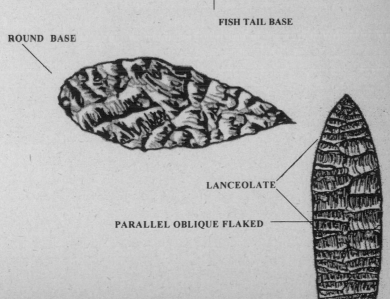

LANCEOLATE

PARALLEL OBLIQUE FLAKED

CHAPTER I
ABASOLO-AUTAUGA

Abasolo: 8,000-5,000 B.P. Early to Mid-Archaic

The blade points of the Abasolo are characterized by their leaf shape dimensions. They are found from the midwestern U.S. into Mexico. Many points and blades are beveled with the parallel flaking of the early Archaic period.

♦ Abasolo point from southeastern MO. Point 2 1/2 in. long, 1 1/2 in. wide, 1/4 in. thick. This particular blade has been dated at 6,500 B.P. Made of pebble chert.

Priv. col., average quality, valued $15-20.

• Abasolo leaf blade from eastern OK. Blade 2 5/8 in. long, 1 1/16 in. wide, 5/8 in. thick. Light brown quartz grained pebble chert. *Priv. col., average quality, valued $8-12.*

• Abasolo leaf blade from southern UT. Blade 3 5/8 in. long, 1 1/2 in. wide, 5/8 in. thick. Beveled predominantly on the right side, upper half of the blade parallel flaked. Unidentified light gray banded or marbled chert. *Priv. col., excellent quality, valued $35-65.*

• Abasolo leaf blade from northwestern TX. Blade 3 in. long, 1 in. wide, 3/4 in. thick. Beveled on both sides with parallel flaking. Gray Texas chert.
Priv. col., museum quality, valued $75-100.

• Abasolo leaf blade from Dagget co., UT. Blade 4 5/8 in. long, 1 1/4 in. wide, 1/2 in. thick. Beveled predominantly on the right side, blade parallel flaked. Narrow, symmetrical, round base. Made of gray chert.
Priv. col., excellent quality, valued $35-65.

• Abasolo leaf blade from Andrews co., TX. Blade 3 3/4 in. long, 1 in. wide, 3/4 in. thick. Thick, heat treated, beveled on both sides, parallel flaked, rounded base. Made of light gray chert.
Priv. col., museum quality, valued $55-80.

• Abasolo leaf blade from Juab co., UT. Blade 4 1/8 in. long, 1 1/4 in. wide, 3/8 in. thick. Narrow, beveled, parallel flaked, round base. Made of light gray chert.
Priv. col., average quality, valued $35-45.

• Abasolo leaf blade from Dagget co., UT. Point 2 3/4 in. long, 1 1/3 in. wide, 1/4 in. thick. Wide, thin, beveled on both sides, parallel flaked, round base. Made of white to tan marbled chert.
Priv. col., average quality, valued $30-40.

• Abasolo leaf blade from Dagget co., UT. Blade 3 7/8 in. long, 1 1/8 in. wide, 1/2 in. thick. Thick, symmetrical, heat treated, beveled on one side of each face, blade parallel flaked. Made of white to tan marbled chert.
Priv. col., excellent quality, valued $45-65.

• Abasolo leaf blade from Dagget co., UT. Blade 3 1/2 in. long, 1 in. wide, 3/4 in. thick. Thick, narrow, steeply beveled on both sides with parallel flaking. Made of white to tan marbled chert.
Priv. col., excellent quality, valued $55-70.

• Abasolo leaf blade from Jaub co., UT. Blade 5 5/8 in. long, 2 1/2 in. wide, 5/8 in. thick. Large, symmetrical, sharp tip, steeply beveled on one edge of each face. Heat treated, random flaked, typical rounded base. Made of light gray chert.
Priv. col., excellent quality, valued $65-85.

• Abasolo leaf blade from Baylor co., TX. Blade 3 5/16 in. long, 1 in. wide, 1/4 in. thick. Thin, symmetrical, finely serrated. Beveled on both sides with parallel flaking. Gray Texas chert.
Priv. col., museum quality, valued $85-110.

• Abasolo leaf blade from Deuel co., SD. Blade 3 5/8 in. long, 1 in. wide, 1/8 in. thick. Extremely thin, narrow, heat treated, good workmanship. Beveled predominantly on the right side, blade parallel flaked, round base. Made of multi-tone gray marbled chert.
Priv. col., museum quality, rare, valued $95-125.

• Abasolo leaf blade from Deuel co., SD. Blade 5 in. long, 3 1/8 in. wide, 3/4 in. thick. Long, wide, thick, heat treated. Steeply beveled on all four sides, parallel flaked. Made of a local multi-tone gray marbled chert.
Priv. col., museum quality, valued $75-100.

• Abasolo leaf blade from Seminole co., OK. Blade 4 5/16 in. long, 1 1/3 in. wide, 5/16 in. thick. Symmetrical, heat treated, quality workmanship. Beveled on one side of each face, parallel flaked. Made of oily gray chert.
Priv. col., excellent quality, valued $55-75.

• Abasolo leaf blade from Seminole co., OK. Blade 5 in. long, 1 in. wide, 1/3 in. thick. Symmetrical, long, very narrow, round base. Steeply beveled on both sides, unevenly serrated, random flaking. Made of oily gray chert.
Priv. col., average quality, valued $25-40.

• Abasolo leaf blade from Seminole co., OK. Blade 3 7/8 in. long, 2 in. wide, 3/8 in. thick. Steeply beveled, sharply serrated, heat treated. Rounded base, parallel flaked. Made of oily gray chert.
Priv. col., excellent quality, valued $45-65.

• Abasolo leaf blade from Seminole co., OK. Blade 4 3/16 in. long, 1 1/32 in. wide, 3/4 in. thick. Long, narrow, symmetrical, top half heat treated. Steeply beveled on both sides, parallel flaked. Made of oily gray chert.
Priv. col., museum quality, valued $65-80.

• Abasolo leaf blade from Seminole co., OK. Blade 3 3/8 in. long, 1 1/2 in. wide, 7/16 in. thick. Wide, asymmetrical, sharply serrated. Beveled steeply on one side of each face. Good workmanship, parallel

flaked. Made of oily gray chert.
Priv. col., excellent quality, valued $55-65.

• Abasolo leaf point from northwestern TX. Point 3 in. long, 1 2/3 in.
wide, 3/4 in. thick. Wide, symmetrical, steeply beveled on all four
edges. Nearly straight base, parallel flaked, pointed tip. Made of Gray
Texas chert.
Priv. col., museum quality, valued $75-100.

Adena: 3,000-1,000 B.P. Woodland

*Adena refers to a Woodland culture of the Ohio and
Mississippi valleys in the United States. The period was noted for its
large houses and extensive mound building.*
*The Adena artifact identifies a cultural period from 3,000
years B.P. to 950 B.P.*
*The Adena were a Woodland culture characterized by large
houses and complex entombing practices involving the construction of
burial mounds. In the later part of the period (1,500 to 900 B.P.), in
the southern Woodland area, numerous effigy mounds were built.*
*The Adena have become well recognized as practicing a high
level of workmanship. Like other Woodland cultures, their Archaic
culture was predominantly agricultural and adapted to forest and
waterway environments. In particular they were recognized, as were
the Hopewell, for their pottery decorated with cord or fabric
impressions. A number of the Woodland traditions continued until the
historical period. Many of the tribes encountered by Europeans were
ancestrally Woodland.*

♦ Adena blade found in northwestern Lawrence co., IL. Blade 5 1/4 in.
long, 1 5/8 in. wide, 1/8 in. thick. A photograph of this piece appeared
in the April-June 1993 issue of the *Central States Archaeological
Journal.* Made of an unidentified chert.

Bob Cox col., museum quality, valued $650-850.

◆ Adena blade from south central MO. Blade 4 1/2 in. long, 1 7/8 in. wide, 3/8 in. thick. Made of pebble chert.

Priv. col., excellent quality, valued $145-205.

◆ Adena beveled blade from Union co., IL. Blade 6 in. long, 2 in. wide, 3/8 in. thick. Adena blade and tooth handle, cache find, Union co., IL. Blade 5 1/2 in. long, 2 3/8 in. wide, 3/4 in. thick. Made of Mill Creek chert.

Les Grubbe col., average quality, valued $75-100.

◆ Adena Dickson 2,500-1,600 B.P. Woodland: Adena point found in Adams co., IL. Point is 3 1/8 in. long, 1 1/4 in. wide, 1/4 in. thick. The point displays very fine edges, is light gray chert with a 1/48 in. thick line of golden brown chert down the length of the point.

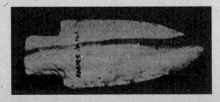

Charles McCorkle col., excellent quality, valued $145-185.

◆ Adena Dickson blade found in southern IL. Blade 5 1/4 in. long, 1 3/4 in. wide, 1/4 in. thick. The tail is 2 3/4 in. wide with a concave center. Made of Mill Creek chert.

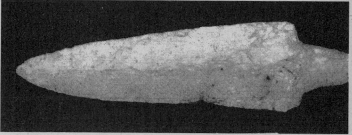

Les Grubbe col., excellent quality, valued $125-185.

◆ Adena Dickson point from Johnson co., IL. Point 3 1/2 in. long, 2 1/16 in. wide, 5/32 in. thick. Fine edge, thin blade. Made of Mill Creek chert.

Les Grubbe col., excellent condition, valued $85-125.

◆ Adena Dickson point from Union co., IL. Point 3 1/8 in. long, 1 1/4 in. wide, 1/4 in. thick. The point has been heat treated. Color: white top, pink bottom. Made of Cobden chert.

Les Grubbe col., excellent quality, valued $85-115.

• Adena Dickson from Union co., IL. Blade 5 in. long, 2 in. wide, 1/4 in. thick with a fine 21/32 in. bevel from point center. The blade does not display a true anchor (possibly Knappers signature).
Les Grubbe col., museum quality, valued $275-360.

• Adena Dickson blade from Madison co., IL. Blade 5 5/8 in. long, 2 in. wide, 5/8 in. thick. Made of heat treated Mill Creek chert. *Priv. col., excellent quality, valued $100-140.*

♦ Adena Dickson point from Union co., IL. Point 3 1/4 in. long, 1 1/2 in. wide, 1/4 in. thick. Point is of very fine workmanship. Made of 3-tone gray Cobden chert.

Les Grubbe col., museum quality, valued $250-325.

♦ Adena Dickson from Fulton co., IL. Blade 3 1/4 in. long, 11/16 in. wide, 3/16 in. thick. Classical design, high quality workmanship. Blade has long, sharp tip. Made of marbled pink beige chert.

Priv. col., museum quality, rare, valued $350-400.

♦ Adena Dickson from northeastern AR. Point 2 in. long, 1 1/8 in. wide, 1/4 in. thick. Made of false jasper.

Grover Bohannon col., excellent quality, valued $120-160.

• Adena beveled blade from Union co., IL. Blade 5 1/3 in. long, 2 in. wide, 3/8 in. thick. Adena blade, roughly serrated, cache find, Union co., IL. Blade narrow, thin, heat treated. Made of Mill Creek chert. *Priv. col., average quality, valued $100-125.*

• Adena Dickson from Adams co., IL. Point 2 3/8 in. long, 1 in. wide, 1/4 in. thick. Finely serreated edges and tip, classical Dickson. Made of beige pebble chert.
Priv. col., excellent quality, valued $125-150.

• Adena Dickson from Pope co., IL. Blade 5 1/2 in. long, 1 1/4 in. wide, 1/4 in. thick. Symmetrical, narrow, sharply serrated edges. Made of Mill Creek chert.
Priv. col., excellent quality, valued $100-125.

• Adena Dickson from Johnson co., IL. Point 3 1/8 in. long, 2 1/16 in. wide, 1/8 in. thick. Fine serrated edges, thin, wide, symmetrical. Made of Mill Creek chert.
Priv. col., excellent condition, valued $85-100.

• Adena Dickson point from Union co., IL. Point 2 3/8 in. long, 1 in. wide, 1/4 in. thick. Symmetrical, thin, heat treated, classical Dickson. Made of Cobden chert.
Priv. col., museum quality, valued $200-250.

♦ Adena Gary point from Jasper co., IL. Point 3 in. long, 1 in. wide, 3/8 in. thick. Very fine grade Dover chert.

Priv. col., museum quality, valued $250-325.

♦ Adena Gary point from Adams co., IL. Point 3 1/8 in. long, 1 3/4 in. wide, 1/4 in. thick. Fine edge on point, sharply serrated edges. Made of Mill Creek chert.

Priv. collection, average quality, valued $75-100.

• Adena Gary from Johnson co., IL. Point 2 3/4 in. long, 1 1/8 in. wide, 5/32 in. thick. High quality workmanship, finely serrated edges, heat treated. Made of Mill Creek chert.
Priv. col., excellent quality, valued $150-200.

• Adena Gary point from Adams co., IL. Point 3 in. long, 1 1/4 in. wide, 1/4 in. thick. Finely sharpened edges. Made of Mill Creek chert.
Priv. col., excellent quality, valued $175-200.

◆ Adena Gary from Jackson co., IL. Point 3 1/2 in. long, 2 1/8 in. wide, 5/32 in. thick. High quality workmanship, fine thin edge serrations. Made of Mill Creek chert.

Priv. col., excellent quality, valued $150-200.

• Adena Gary from Johnson co., IL. Blade 3 3/4 in. long, 1 1/8 in. wide, 5/32 in. thick. High quality workmanship, finely serrated edges, heat treated. Narrow, thin, symmetrical. Made of Mill Creek chert.
Priv. col., excellent quality, valued $200-250.

• Adena Gary from Johnson co., IL. Blade 3 7/8 in. long, 1 1/2 in. wide, 1/4 in. thick. Finely sharpened edges, heat treated, narrow, thin, symmetrical. Made of Mill Creek chert.
Priv. col., excellent quality, valued $225-275.

• Adena Gary from Johnson co., IL. Blade 4 1/2 in. long, 2 in. wide, 3/16 in. thick. High quality workmanship, fine thin edge serrations. Very thin and symmetrical for an Adena Gary. Made of Mill Creek chert.
Priv. col., excellent quality, valued $200-250.

◆ Adena Ledbetter point from Clark co., IL. Point 2 7/8 in. long, 1 1/2 in. wide, 5/8 in. thick. White to pink pebble chert.

Priv. col, average quality, valued $85-115.

• Adena Ledbetter from Clark co., IL. Point 2 3/8 in. long, 1 1/16 in. wide, 5/8 in. thick. Thick, narrow, finely serrated edges. Made of white to pink pebble chert.
Priv. col., excellent quality, valued $150-175.

• Adena Ledbetter blade from Madison co., IL. Blade 5 1/4 in. long, 2 3/4 in. wide, 1/4 in. thick. Very fine heat treated tail with concave center. Made of Mill Creek chert.
Les Grubbe col., museum quality, valued $450-600.

• Adena Ledbetter from Clark co., IL. Point 2 5/8 in. long, 1 1/3 in. wide, 3/8 in. thick. Thin, symmetrical, poorly serrated. Made of white to pink pebble chert.
Priv. col., average quality, valued $75-100.

• Adena Ledbetter from Clark co., IL. Blade 4 7/8 in. long, 3 1/2 in. wide, 5/8 in. thick. Unusually wide, yet symmetrical, sharply serrated. Made of white to pink pebble chert.
Priv. col., excellent quality, valued $150-175.

• Adena Ledbetter blade from Madison co., IL. Blade 5 in. long, 2 1/4 in. wide, 1/2 in. thick. Thick, symmetrical, fine workmanship, heat treated. Made of tan pebble chert.
Priv. col., museum quality, valued $350-400.

◆ Adena Ledbetter point, Union co., IL. Point 3 1/2 in. long, 1 1/2 in. wide, 3/8 in. thick. This is an exceptionally fine edged piece, good workmanship. Beautiful symmetry throughout the flaking of the piece. Made of Dover chert.

Priv. col., museum quality, valued $750-1,000.

◆ Adena Morhiss point from Union co., IL. Point 2 1/2 in. long, 1 3/8 in. wide, 1/4 in. thick. Made of Mill Creek Chert.

Priv. col., average quality, valued $65-85.

♦ Adena Morhiss point from central TN. Point 2 1/4 in. long, 1 1/8 in. wide, 1/4 in. thick. Made of 3-tone brown Dover chert.

Priv. col., average quality, valued $65-80.

♦ Adena Morhiss point from northern Arkansas. Point 2 1/8 in. long, 1 1/2 in. wide, 3/8 in. thick. Uniquely, yet lightly serrated, with fine tan lines through the center. Made of dark brown Arkansas chert.

Priv. col., excellent quality, valued $125-175.

• Adena Morhiss point from Hamilton co., TN. Blade 3 1/8 in. long, 1 in. wide, 1/2 in. thick. Heat treated, with heavy field patina, soft shoulders, concave base. Made of Mill Creek chert.
Grover Bohannon, excellent quality, valued $125-185.

• Adena Morhiss from Pike co., IL. Point 2 11/16 in. long, 1 1/8 in. wide, 1/4 in. thick. Sharply serrated, lightly beveled opposing edges. Made of brown pebble chert.
Priv. col., excellent quality, valued $150-200.

• Adena Morhiss from Pike co., IL. Blade 3 1/8 in. long, 1 3/16 in.
wide, 1/2 in. thick. Heat treated, thick, wide, poor workmanship,
roughly serrated edges. Weak shoulders, concave base. Made of brown
pebble chert.
Priv. col., average quality, valued $65-85.

• Adena Morhiss from Searcy co., AR. Point 2 5/8 in. long, 1 1/4 in.
wide, 3/8 in. thick. Symmetrical, thin, fine, long, serrations. Made of
dark brown Arkansas chert.
Priv. col., excellent quality, valued $150-225.

• Adena Morhiss from Searcy co., AR. Blade 3 5/8 in. long, 1 in. wide,
1/3 in. thick. Heat treated, good field patina, weak shoulders, concave
base. Made of dark brown Arkansas chert.
Priv. col., excellent quality, valued $125-175.

• Adena Morhiss from Searcy co., AR. Point 1 5/8 in. long, 3/4 in.
wide, 3/8 in. thick. Unique, short, symmetrical, finely serrated. The
concave base is heat treated. Made of dark brown Arkansas chert.
Priv. col., excellent quality, valued $175-225.

• Adena Morhiss from Searcy co., AR. Blade 4 3/8 in. long, 1 1/4 in.
wide, 3/16 in. thick. Long, narrow, thin, good workmanship. Heat
treated, some field patina, concave base. Made of dark brown Arkansas
chert.
Priv. col., excellent quality, valued $185-235.

♦ Adena Robbins blade from central TN. Blade 4 7/8 in. long,
1 7/8 in. wide, 1/4 in. thick. Made of multi-tone Dover chert.

Priv. col., excellent quality, valued $25-40.

♦ Adena Robbins blade from central TN. Blade 3 1/4 in. long,
1 7/8 in. wide, 5/8 in. thick. Finely serrated, with tan band across blade
above stem. Made of Dover chert.

Priv. col., museum quality, valued $65-85.

• Adena Robbins from Grundy co., TN. Blade 5 1/8 in. long, 2 1/8 in. wide, 3/8 in. thick. Finely serrated, sharp tip, thin and symmetrical. Concave base beveled on one side of each face. Made of yellow tan chert.
Priv. col., excellent quality, valued $35-45.

• Adena Robbins from Grundy co., TN. Blade 3 7/8 in. long, 1 3/8 in. wide, 1/4 in. thick. Finely serrated, crudely flaked, long concave stem. Made of yellow tan chert.
Priv. col., average quality, valued $25-35.

• Adena Robbins from Grundy co., TN. Blade 4 1/8 in. long, 1 1/2 in. wide, 1/4 in. thick. Heat treated, sharp edges, concave base. Made of yellow tan chert.
Priv. col., excellent quality, valued $45-60.

• Adena Robbins from Grainger co., TN. Blade 3 3/4 in. long, 1 in. wide, 5/8 in. thick. Finely serrated, narrow, thick, steeply beveled on all four sides. Made of Dover chert
Priv. col., museum quality, valued $75-85.

• Adena Robbins from Grainger co., TN. Blade 5 3/8 in. long, 1 5/8 in. wide, 1/4 in. thick. One of the longest, most symmetrical, and most finely worked Adena Robbinses I have seen. Made of Dover chert.
Priv. col., excellent quality, valued $30-40.

• Adena Robbins from Grainger co., TN. Point 2 3/4 in. long, 1 1/2 in. wide, 3/8 in. thick. Finely serrated, wide, asymmetrical, thin, random flaked, concave base. Made of Dover chert.
Priv. col., museum quality, valued $75-95.

• Adena Robbins from Grainger co., TN. Point 2 7/8 in. long, 3/4 in. wide, 3/16 in. thick. Thin, narrow, finely worked for Adena Robbins.

Short stem, point heat treated with concave base. Made of Dover chert.
Priv. col., excellent quality, valued $25-40.

• Adena Robbins from Grainger co., TN. Blade 2 1/4 in. long, 7/8 in.
wide, 5/8 in. thick. Steeply beveled, serrated edges, sharp tip. Made of
Dover chert.
Priv. col., museum quality, valued $60-80.

Agate Basin: 9,500-8,000 B.P. Paleo to Early Archaic

*Agate Basin transition pieces, Paleo to early Archaic, are
medium to large points and blades. The bases are generally ground
either concave, convex, to straight. Agate Basin blades are of excellent
quality.*

◆ Agate Basin blade from LaSalle co., IL. Blade 5 in. long, 1 1/4 in.
wide, 1/4 in. thick. Beautiful signature piece. Made of multi-colored
quartz, veined red and white with areas of tan, blue, and a variety of
browns represented.

Tim Crawford col., museum quality, valued $575-850.

◆ Agate Basin knife from WI. Blade 4 1/4 in. long, 1 1/4 in. wide,
3/8 in. thick. Blade translucent, knife very slim and light. Made of
rosy quartz.

Tim Crawford col., museum quality, valued $800-1,100.

◆ Agate Basin blade from AR. Blade 5 1/4 in. long, 1 1/2 in. wide,
1/4 in. thick. Made of a dark brown Arkansas chert.

Tim Crawford col., average quality, valued $125-175.

• Agate Basin blade from Johnson co., IL. Blade 4 3/8 in. long,
1 1/8 in. wide, 1/4 in. thick. Fine transverse percussion flaking, square
base. Made of Mill Creek chert.
Priv. col., excellent quality, valued $285-365.

• Agate Basin from Green Lake co., WI. Blade 4 in. long, 1 1/16 in.
wide, 1/4 in. thick. Narrow, thin, symmetrical, transverse percussion
flaked, straight base. Made of greenish chert.
Priv. col., museum quality, valued $850-1,000.

• Agate Basin from Green Lake co., WI. Blade 5 1/4 in. long, 1 1/4 in.
wide, 1/4 in. thick. Typically narrow, thin, sharply serrated and angular.
Made of greenish chert.
Priv. col., excellent quality, valued $425-575.

• Agate Basin from Green Lake co., WI. Blade 5 3/8 in. long, 1 1/4 in.
wide, 1/4 in. thick. Transverse percussion flaked, straight, square base.
Thin, narrow, sharply serrated edges. Made of greenish chert.
Priv. col., museum quality, valued $750-850.

• Agate Basin from Green Lake co., WI. Blade 4 1/2 in. long, 1 3/4 in.
wide, 1/4 in. thick. Blade thin, wide, sharply serrated, straight base.
Made of greenish chert.
Priv. col., museum quality, valued $800-875.

• Agate Basin from Prairie co., AR. Blade 5 1/2 in. long, 1 1/2 in.
wide, 1/4 in. thick. Classical design, slight tip break. Made of multi-
toned tan brown chert.
Priv. col., average quality, valued $100-150.

• Agate Basin blade from Johnson co., IL. Blade 4 1/32 in. long,
1 3/8 in. wide, 1/4 in. thick. Transverse percussion flaked, slightly
concave base. Made of Mill Creek chert.
Priv. col., excellent quality, valued $250-325.

• Agate Basin blade, Union co., IL. Blade 4 3/4 in. long, 1 3/8 in.
wide, 5/8 in. thick. Concave base, well-defined horizontal transverse
percussion flaking, with very fine edge work. Made of Kaolin chert.

Priv. col., museum quality, rare, valued $450-250.

• Agate Basin from Lucas co., OH. Blade 2 7/8 in. long, 1 1/8 in. wide, 5/8 in. thick. Base converse edges not noticeably fine nor excessively worn. Unlike most Agate Basin type blades the flaking of the blade face is nearly random, certainly not horizontally transverse. Made of Coshocten chert.
Priv. col., poor quality, valued $25-40.

• Agate Basin from Iowa co., WI. Blade 4 1/2 in. long, 1 3/4 in. wide, 3/8 in. thick. Blade translucent, thin, symmetrical, slightly concave base. Knife very slim and light. Made of rosy quartz.
Priv. col., museum quality, valued $650-800.

• Agate Basin from Iowa co., WI. Blade 5 in. long, 1 1/2 in. wide, 3/8 in. thick. Translucent, narrow, thin, symmetrical. Made of rosy quartz.
Priv. col., excellent quality, valued $425-575.

• Agate Basin from Johnson co., IL. Blade 5 3/8 in. long, 1 3/8 in. wide, 1/4 in. thick. Heat treated, transverse percussion flaking, square base. Made of Mill Creek chert.
Tim Rubbles col., excellent quality, valued $375-450.

• Agate Basin knife from Jackson co., IL. Blade 5 1/4 in. long, 1 1/2 in. wide, 3/8 in. thick. Fine edge serrations, thin, symmetrical, concave base. Made of Cobden chert.
Jim Smith col., museum quality, valued $875-1,000.

• Agate Basin from Alexander co., MO. Blade 4 1/2 in. long, 1 1/16 in. wide, 1/4 in. thick. Transverse parallel flaked, thin, narrow, symmetrical, good workmanship. Point is thin and sharp, square base. Made of lightweight white chert.
Priv. col., excellent quality, valued $325-375.

• Agate Basin from Johnson co., IL. Blade 4 5/8 in. long, 1 1/8 in. wide, 1/4 in. thick. Fine transverse percussion flaking, thin and narrow. Highly serrated square base. Made of Mill Creek chert.
Priv. col., excellent quality, valued $350-450.

<u>Agee: 1,100-500 B.P. Mississippian</u>

Small points, needle sharp, narrow, barbed and corner

notched. Found throughout the midwestern United States.

◆ Agee point from southern AR. Point 1 in. long, 3/8 in. wide, 1/32 in. thick. Uneven notches, asymmetrical point, with a very sharp tip. Made of jasper.

Priv. col., excellent quality, valued $45-75.

• Agee point from western MS. Point 1 1/8 in. long., 5/8 in. wide, 1/32 in. thick. Finely made blade, symmetrical percussion flaking on each face, horizontally transverse, with deep corner notches. Made of rosy quartz.
Priv. col., museum quality, valued $125-175.

• Agee point from Madison co., IL. Point 1 5/32 in. long, 5/16 in. wide, 1/16 in. thick. Symmetrical point, fine horizontally transverse percussion flaking. Deep corner notches, one side slightly higher than the other. Made of heat treated Mill Creek chert.
Priv. col., excellent quality, valued $35-50.

◆ Agee from Monroe co., TN. Point 5/8 in. long. 1/4 in. wide, 1/8 in. thick. Classical Agee design, good field patina. Made of quartzite.

Grover Bohannon col., average quality, valued $8-12.

• Agee from Rankin co., MS. Point 1 3/8 in. long, 5/8 in. wide, 1/32 in. thick. Very thin, high quality workmanship, symmetrical percussion flaked, horizontally transverse, with deep, wide corner notches. Base is slightly convex. Made of milky pink quartz.
Priv. col., museum quality, valued $75-125.

• Agee from Rankin co., MS. Point 1 11/32 in. long, 1/4 in. wide, 1/16 in. thick. Symmetrical point, fine horizontal transverse percussion flaking, extremely thin point. Deep corner notches, bottom half heat treated, concave base. Made of milky pink quartz.
Priv. col., excellent quality, valued $65-80.

- Agee from Monroe co., TN. Point 5/8 in. long, 3/8 in. wide, 1/8 in. thick. Classical Agee design, wide, thick, yet symmetrical. Made of light gray chert.
Grover Bohannon col., excellent quality, valued $45-60.

- Agee from Monroe co., TN. Point 1 7/8 in. long., 5/8 in. wide, 3/32 in. thick. Finely made point, long for an Agee. Symmetrical percussion flaked, horizontally transverse, deep corner notches. Made of light gray chert.
Grover Bohannon col., museum quality, valued $100-125.

- Agee from Pope co., IL. Point 1 13/32 in. long, 1/2 in. wide, 1/8 in. thick. Symmetrical point, horizontally transverse percussion flaked. Deep corner notches, heat treated point, straight base. Made of tan to gray chert.
Priv. col., excellent quality, valued $55-70.

- Agee from Pope co., IL. Point 1 1/8 in. long, 1/3 in. wide, 1/8 in. thick. Wide, symmetrical, good field patina. Heat treated, sharp edges and tip, straight base. Made of tan to gray chert.
Priv. col., excellent quality, valued $35-45.

- Agee from Covington co., MS. Point 1 1/4 in. long., 11/16 in. wide, 1/32 in. thick. Fine workmanship, thin, symmetrical percussion flaking, horizontally transverse, deep corner notches. Made of grainy quartzite.
Priv. col., average quality, valued $12-25.

- Agee from Covington co., MS. Point 1 15/32 in. long, 9/16 in. wide, 1/16 in. thick. Extremely thin, symmetrical point, fine horizontally transverse percussion flaked. Wide, shallow corner notches, straight base. Made of grainy quartzite.
Priv. col., excellent quality, valued $45-60.

- Agee from Franklin co., MS. Point 7/8 in. long. 1/2 in. wide, 1/8 in. thick. Short, wide, thick, symmetrical, good field patina. Made of quartzite.
Grover Bohannon col., average quality, valued $15-25.

- Agee from Amelia co., VA. Point 2 1/16 in. long, 1 3/8 in. wide, 5/32 in. thick. Large, wide, thick, symmetrical, horizontally transverse flaked. Straight base with deep corner notches. Made of tan to brown chert.
Priv. col., excellent quality, valued $85-115.

• Agee from Amelia co., VA. Point 1 3/16 in. long, 1/2 in. wide, 1/16 in. thick. Very thin, narrow, symmetrical point, horizontally transverse flaked. Deep corner notches, slightly concave base. Made of tan to brown chert.
Priv. col., museum quality, valued $125-150.

• Agee from Amelia co., VA. Point 1/2 in. long, 5/16 in. wide, 1/8 in. thick. Small, very wide, good workmanship, percussion horizontal flaked. Heat treated, concave base, said to be part of a burial find. Made of tan to brown chert.
Priv. col., excellent quality, valued $45-55.

• Agee from Craig co., VA. Point 1 in. long, 7/8 in. wide, 7/32 in. thick. Low quality workmanship, nearly as wide as long. Shallow uneven corner notches, straight base. Made of quartzite.
Priv. col., average quality, valued $12-20.

• Agee from Craig co., VA. Point 1 19/32 in. long, 7/16 in. wide, 1/8 in. thick. Symmetrical point, fine horizontal transverse percussion flaked. Deep, uneven corner notches, staight base. Made of quartzite.
Priv. col., excellent quality, valued $45-60.

• Agee from Craig co., VA. Point 2 5/8 in. long. 1/4 in. wide, 1/8 in. thick. Long, thin, symmetrically narrow. Horizotal transverse flaked, concave base. Made of quartzite.
Priv. col., excellent quality, valued $30-40.

• Agee from Craig co., VA. Point 1 5/8 in. long, 5/16 in. wide, 1/16 in. thick. Thin, sharp tip, symmetrically narrow, percussion flaked, deep corner notches. Made of gray chert.
Priv. col., average quality, valued $25-40.

• Agee from Madison co., IL. Point 1 1/2 in. long, 1/2 in. wide, 1/16 in. thick. Very thin, classical Agee, symmetrical angular point, fine horizontal transverse percussion flaking. Deep corner notches, straight base. Made of Mill Creek chert.
Priv. col., excellent quality, valued $25-35.

• Agee from Madison co., IL. Point 1 3/8 in. long, 3/4 in. wide, 1/8 in. thick. Classical Agee design, horizontal transverse percussion flaked. Heat treated, shallow corner notches, straight base. Made of Mill Creek chert.
Priv. col., excellent quality, valued $40-50.

Alba: 2,000-350 B.P. Mississippian

A small to medium point found from the Midwest to the
northwestern U.S. Points have prominent tangs; some are serrated or
bulbous stemmed.

◆ Alba from Monroe co., TN. Point 5/8 in. long, 3/16 in. wide, 1/8 in.
thick. Very sharp, random flaked point, with deep side notches. Made of
gray pebble chert.

Grover Bohannon col., excellent quality, valued $35-60.

◆ Alba point from AR. Point 2 1/2 in. long, 1 1/16 in. wide, 1/4 in.
thick. Prominent tangs with bulbous stem. Made of an Arkansas pebble
chert.

Priv. col., museum quality, valued $85-100.

• Alba point from northern LA. Point 1 1/4 in. long, 1/2 in. wide,
3/32 in. thick. Serrated point with definitive tangs. Made of a dark
pebble chert.
Priv. col., excellent quality, valued $25-35.

• Alba point from central IA. Point 1 3/8 in. long, 5/8 in. wide, 1/4 in.
thick. Distinctive slanted tangs, non-serrated. Made of a pink green
grained quartzite.
Priv. col., average quality, valued $15-25.

• Alba point from Madison co., IL. Point 1 3/4 in. long, 7/8 in. wide,
3/8 in. thick. The point is unusually thin with very sharp and well-
defined serrations the length of the point. Point has a long, bulbous
stem. Made of Kaolin chert.

Priv. col., museum quality, rare, valued $100-125.

• Alba from Madison co., IL. Point 1 1/2 in. long, 5/8 in. wide, 1/4 in. thick. Unusually thin, very sharp, distinct sharp serrations the length of the point. Long, bulbous stem, convex base. Made of Kaolin chert.
Priv. col., museum quality, rare, valued $80-100.

• Alba from Madison co., IL. Point 1 3/8 in. long, 1 in. wide, 3/8 in. thick. Thin, nearly as wide as long, sharp, deep, wide serrations the length of the blade. Point has a classical long bulbous stem. Made of Kaolin chert.
Priv. col., museum quality, rare, valued $90-115.

• Alba from Madison co., IL. Point 1 5/8 in. long, 7/8 in. wide, 1/2 in. thick. Thick, symmetrical, sharp, wide, well-defined serrations, sharp pointed tip. Heat-treated point, short bulbous stem. Made of Kaolin chert.
Priv. col., museum quality, rare, valued $85-100.

• Alba from Butler co., KY. Point 2 3/4 in. long, 1 1/8 in. wide, 3/8 in. thick. The point is thin with very sharp and well-defined serrations, heat-treated. Point has a long, bulbous stem, convex. Made of tan pebble chert.
Priv. col., excellent quality, valued $60-85.

• Alba from Butler co., KY. Point 2 1/4 in. long, 7/8 in. wide, 1/4 in. thick. Thin, narrow, heat-treated, symmetical, sharp edge serrations. Point has a short bulbous stem, slight tip break. Made of tan pebble chert.
Priv. col., average quality, valued $30-45.

• Alba from Butler co., KY. Point 2 in. long, 5/8 in. wide, 3/8 in. thick. The point is unusually narrow, thin with very sharp and well defined serrations, heat-treated. Point has a bulbous stem, convex base. Made of local tan chert.
Priv. col., excellent quality, valued $60-85.

• Alba from Randolf co., MO. Point 1 in. long, 3/8 in. wide, 1/8 in. thick. Thin, fine workmanship, with very sharp tip and serrations. Extremely symmetrical point, long bulbous stem. Made of gray white chert.
Priv. col., museum quality, valued $85-100.

• Alba from Randolf co., MO. Point 1 3/4 in. long, 1/2 in. wide, 3/16 in. thick. Point is thin, narrow, heat-treated with sharp and well-defined serrations typical of this particular site. Symmetrical point, long bulbous stem, convex base. Made of gray white local chert.
Priv. col., museum quality, valued $100-125.

• Alba from Randolf co., MO. Point 2 1/2 in. long, 5/8 in. wide, 5/32 in. thick. The points of this site are unusually thin, narrow and symmetrical, with very sharp and well-defined serrations. Point has a long bulbous stem, pointed tip. Made of local gray white chert.
Priv. col., museum quality, valued $100-125.

• Alba from Butler co., MO. Point 2 3/4 in. long, 1 in. wide, 3/8 in. thick. Typical of this site, heat-treated, thin, narrow, symmetrical, fine serrations. Point has a long, bulbous stem. Made of local gray white chert.
Priv. col., museum quality, valued $130-160.

• Alba from Butler co., MO. Point 1 2/3 in. long, 1/2 in. wide, 1/4 in. thick. This point is the finest from this particular site. Thin, narrow, heat-treated, with very sharp and well-defined serrations. Exceptional workmanship. Point has typical long, bulbous stem. Made of local gray white chert.
Priv. col., museum quality, valued $150-175.

• Alba from Lake co., TN. Point 1 3/8 in. long, 7/8 in. wide, 1/2 in. thick. Point wide, thick; sharp, wide serrations; long, thin pointed tip. Point has a long, unique concave stem. Made of tan to white Bullseye chert.
Priv. col., museum quality, valued $125-150.

• Alba from Lake co., TN. Point 2 3/4 in. long, 1 1/16 in. wide, 5/8 in. thick. Thick, yet symmetrical; thinned tip; sharply serrated edges. Point has a long, concave stem. Made of tan to white Bullseye chert.
Priv. col., museum quality, valued $100-125.

• Alba from Greene co., IL. Point 1 1/4 in. long, 5/8 in. wide, 3/8 in. thick. Thin, narrow, good workmanship, with very sharp and deep serrations. Point has short, bulbous stem, slightly convex. Made of white pebble chert.
Tim Rubbles col., excellent quality, valued $50-65.

• Alba from Greene co., IL. Point 2 1/32 in. long, 7/8 in. wide, 1/2 in. thick. Point is thick, narrow, symmetrical; fine, sharp serrations, several nicks on one edge. Point has a long, bulbous stem, convex base. Made of white pebble chert.
Tim Rubbles col., average quality, valued $30-45.

• Alba from Greene co., IL. Point 1 7/8 in. long, 5/8 in. wide, 3/8 in. thick. The point is thin, very symmetrical and narrow, sharply serrated edges and tip. Long bulbous stem, convex base. Made of white pebble chert.
Tim Rubbles col., excellent quality, valued $70-85.

• Alba from Carrol co., OH. Point 1 3/4 in. long, 1 1/8 in. wide, 3/8 in. thick. Point nearly as wide as long, thick, symmetrical, sharp edges. Point has squat stem, straight base. Made of white pebble chert.
Priv. col., excellent quality, valued $50-65.

• Alba point from Franklin co., IL. Point 2 3/4 in. long, 1 1/8 in. wide, 1/4 in. thick. Thin, symmetrical, good workmanship, sharp serrated tip and edges. Point is heat-treated, bulbous stem, convex base. Made of Mill Creek chert.
Priv. col., excellent quality, valued $70-85.

• Alba from Franklin co., IL. Point 2 3/16 in. long, 1 in. wide, 3/8 in. thick. Point is thin, wide, sharp, well-defined serrations, slight tip break. Point has a bulbous stem, convex base. Made of Mill Creek chert.
Priv. col., average quality, valued $50-65.

• Alba from Franklin co., IL. Point 1 1/4 in. long, 5/8 in. wide, 1/8 in. thick. The point is unusually thin with very sharp, wide, and well-defined serrations, bulbous stem. Made of Mill Creek chert.
Priv. col., excellent quality, valued $80-100.

• Alba from Pike co., IL. Point 1 7/8 in. long, 5/8 in. wide, 1/4 in. thick. The point is thin, sharply serrated. Point has a bulbous stem, convex base. Made of Cobden chert.
Priv. col., museum quality, valued $90-105.

• Alba from Pike co., IL. Point 1 1/8 in. long, 1 in. wide, 3/8 in. thick. Point thick, wide, with very sharp and well-defined serrations. Point has a bulbous stem, covex base. Made of Cobden chert.
Priv. col., museum quality, valued $100-125.

<u>Angostura: 10,000-7,000 B.P. Paleo to Mid-Archaic</u>

Angostura are found predominantly in the Southeast. Still, the occasional Angostura is found in the midwestern Mississippi Valley. It is a medium to large point or blade with all range of flaking techniques. One consistent factor of the Angostura and other similar points is their thinned, unground bases.

♦ Angostura transitional point from northern TN. Point 2 7/8 in. long, 3/4 in. wide, 3/8 in. thick. The point is beveled on both sides of right edge. Point randomly flaked with a thinned concave base. Made of Kaolin chert.

Priv. col., excellent quality, valued $250-315.

• Angostura blade from Roll co., MO. Blade 5 1/2 in. long, 1 1/2 in. wide, 1/4 in. thick. Thin base, deeply concave notched. The blade has striking oblique parallel flaking on both blade faces. Made of dense, oily white chert.
Priv. col., museum quality, valued $400-600.

• Angostura blade from southeastern MO. Blade 6 in. long, 1 1/4 in. wide, 3/8 in. thick. Straight base, fine oblique parallel flaking, delicately serrated. Made of a grainy, dull white quartzite.
Priv. col., museum quality, valued $550-800.

• Angostura from Bollinger co., MO. Blade 4 1/2 in. long, 1 2/3 in. wide, 1/4 in. thick. Thin, symmetrical, parallel oblique flaked, sharp edges. Concave base, deep notches. Made of oily tan chert.
Priv. col., museum quality, valued $350-450.

• Angostura from Bollinger co., MO. Blade 6 1/3 in. long, 1 1/2 in. wide, 1/4 in. thick. Oblique parallel flaking, sharp and finely serrated. Made of oily tan chert.
Priv. col., museum quality, valued $450-600.

• Angostura from Bollinger co., MO. Blade 5 5/8 in. long, 1 1/4 in.

wide, 1/4 in. thick. Thin, sharp serrated edges, parallel oblique flaked, long pointed tip. Deeply concave, notched base. Made of oily tan chert.
Priv. col., museum quality, valued $400-600.

• Angostura from Bollinger co., MO. Blade 6 1/32 in. long, 1 1/4 in. wide, 3/8 in. thick, Thin, narrow, symmetrical, oblique parallel flaking, finely serrated. Made of oily tan chert.
Priv. col., museum quality, valued $600-750.

• Angostra from Boone co., MO. Blade 4 1/2 in. long, 1 7/32 in. wide, 1/4 in. thick. Thin, narrow, symmetrical, sharply seerated edges. Thin base, deeply concave, shallow notched. Parallel oblique flaked on one blade face. Made of lightweight, cream white chert.
Priv. col., excellent quality, valued $250-400.

• Angostura from Rolla co., MO. Blade 6 3/8 in. long, 1 1/2 in. wide, 3/8 in. thick, Thin, narrow, symmetrical, high quality workmanship. Straight base, oblique parallel flaking, sharply serrated. Made of a grainy white quartzite.
Priv. col., excellent quality, valued $350-500.

• Angostura from Rolla co., MO. Blade 6 1/2 in. long, 1 1/2 in. wide, 1/4 in. thick. Blade oblique parallel flaked. Thin, narrow blade, base deeply concave, wide notched. Made of grainy white quartzite.
Priv. col., excellent quality, valued $400-500.

• Angostura from St. Clair co., MO. Blade 5 3/32 in. long, 1 1/3 in. wide, 13/32 in. thick, Thick, narrow, oblique parallel flaked, finely serrated. Made of white pebble chert.
Priv. col., average quality, $150-200.

• Angostura from St. Clair co., MO. Blade 5 3/4 in. long, 1 1/8 in. wide, 1/4 in. thick. Thin, narrow, parallel flaked. Thinned base, deeply concave notched. Made of white pebble chert.
Priv. col., excellent quality, valued $300-350.

• Angostura from St. Charles co., MO. Blade 4 1/4 in. long, 1 in. wide, 1/4 in. thick, Symmetrical, concave edges, straight base, oblique parallel flaking, sharply serrated. Made of white local chert.
Priv. col., museum quality, valued $500-650.

• Angostura from St. Charles co., MO. Blade 5 1/4 in. long, 1 1/3 in. wide, 1/4 in. thick. Thin, narrow, angular, symmetrical blade. Oblique

parallel flaked on both blade faces. Made of local white chert.
Priv. col., excellent quality, valued $300-450.

• Angostura from Barton co., MO. Blade 6 3/4 in. long, 1 1/4 in. wide,
3/8 in. thick, Straight base, fine oblique parallel flaking, delicately
serrated, heat-treated. Made of tan pebble chert.
Priv. col., museum quality, valued $750-850.

• Angostura from Barton co., MO. Blade 5 1/4 in. long, 1 1/3 in.
wide, 1/4 in. thick. Parallel flaking on both blade faces, deeply
notched, heat-treated. Made of tan pebble chert.
Priv. col., museum quality, valued $475-550.

• Angostura from Barton co., MO. Blade 5 in. long, 1 1/3 in. wide,
3/8 in. thick. Heat-treated, straight base, oblique parallel flaked, finely
serrated. Made of tan pebble chert.
Priv. col., excellent quality, valued $350-500.

• Angostura from Barton co., MO. Blade 6 1/2 in. long, 1 1/4 in. wide,
1/4 in. thick. Heat-treated blade, oblique parallel flaking, sharp edge
serrations. Made of tan pebble chert.
Priv. col., excellent quality, valued $275-400.

• Angostura from Boone co., MO. Blade 6 3/8 in. long, 1 3/4 in. wide,
3/8 in. thick. Symmetrical, good workmanship, parallel flaked, straight
base, rough serrated edges. Made of local gray white chert.
Priv. col., average quality, valued $250-300.

• Angostura from Boone co., MO. Blade 5 1/8 in. long, 1 1/2 in. wide,
1/4 in. thick. Thin, narrow, symmetrical, base deeply concave and
notched. The blade has oblique parallel flaking on both blade faces.
Made of local gray white chert.
Priv. col., excellent quality, valued $300-450.

• Angostura from Boone co., MO. Blade 6 in. long, 1 1/2 in. wide,
1/8 in. thick. Very thin, narrow, symmetrical, straight base, oblique
parallel flaking, delicately serrated. Made of gray white chert.
Priv. col., excellent quality, valued $350-500.

• Angostura from Rolla co., MO. Blade 4 1/2 in. long, 1 2/3 in. wide,
1/4 in. thick. Thin, wide, convex edges, highly serrated. Base, deep
concave notching. The blade has striking parallel flaking. Made of
dense, oily white chert.
Priv. col., excellent quality, valued $300-450.

- Angostura from Randolf co., MO. Blade 4 in. long, 1 1/16 in. wide, 3/8 in. thick. Oblique parallel flaking, roughly serrated, straight base. Made of quartzite.
  Priv. col., average quality, valued $250-300.

- Angostura from Randolf co., MO. Blade 5 1/8 in. long, 1 1/32 in. wide, 3/16 in. thick. Thin base, deeply concave and notched. Oblique parallel flaking on both blade faces. Made of quartzite.
  Priv. col., excellent quality, valued $300-400.

- Angostura from Randolf co., MO. Blade 6 3/32 in. long, 1 1/2 in. wide, 3/16 in. thick, Thin, narrow, symmetrical blade with straight base. Oblique parallel flaked; deep, wide serrations. Made of quartzite.
  Priv. col., museum quality, valued $500-650.

- Angostura from Effingham co., IL. Blade 5 1/4 in. long, 1 1/2 in. wide, 1/4 in. thick. Symmetrical, good quality workmanship. Thin base, deeply concave and notched. Sharp, fine serrations, oblique parallel flaking on both blade faces. Made of tan to brown pebble chert.
  Priv. col., museum quality, valued $475-650.

- Angostura from Effingham co., IL. Blade 6 1/3 in. long, 1 1/32 in. wide, 3/16 in. thick, Extremely thin and symmetrical, oblique parallel flaking, sharp serrations. Made of tan to brown pebble chert.
  Priv. col., excellent quality, valued $350-500.

- Angostura from Davis co., IA. Blade 4 1/2 in. long, 1 3/4 in. wide, 1/4 in. thick. Symmetrical, thin blade, oblique parallel flaked, serrated edges. Thinned straight base. Made of white pebble chert.
  Priv. col., excellent quality, valued $300-350.

- Angostura from Davis co., IA. Blade 5 2/3 in. long, 1 3/32 in. wide, 1/4 in. thick. Straight base, good workmanship, oblique parallel flaked, sharply serrated edges. Made of white pebble chert.
  Priv. col., excellent quality, valued $450-600.

- Angostura from Davis co., IA. Blade 4 1/2 in. long, 1 1/4 in. wide, 3/16 in. thick. Thin, angular convex edges, base concave and notched. Oblique parallel flaking on both blade faces. Made of white pebble chert.
  Priv. col., excellent quality, valued $400-500.

- Angostura from Antrim co., MI. Blade 6 1/8 in. long, 1 2/3 in. wide,

1/4 in. thick. Long, thin, symmetrical, concave edges. Oblique parallel flaking, finely serrated. Made of a green to gray chert.
Priv. col., excellent quality, valued $450-600.

• Angostura from Antrim co., MI. Blade 5 in. long, 2 2/3 in. wide, 5/8 in. thick. Thick, wide, convex edges, highly serrated. Blade is random flaked on one face, parallel on the other, straight base. Made of a green chert.
Priv. col., average quality, valued $200-300.

• Angostura from Atchison co., MO. Blade 3 7/8 in. long, 1 1/2 in. wide, 1/4 in. thick, Straight base, oblique parallel flaking, sharply serrated. Short, wide convex edges, pointed tip. Made of quartzite.
Priv. col., average quality, valued $150-200.

• Angostura blade from Atchison co., MO. Blade 4 1/2 in. long, 1 1/2 in. wide, 1/4 in. thick. Thinned base, deeply concave and notched. Oblique parallel flaking, sharp convex edges. Made of quartzite.
Priv. col., average quality, valued $100-200.

• Angostura from Atchison co., MO. Blade 5 in. long, 1 3/4 in. wide, 3/8 in. thick. Symmetrical, wide, convex and sharp edges. Heat-treated, multiple internal fractions, oblique parallel flaking, straight base. Made of quartzite.
Priv. col., average quality, valued $150-300.

Ashtabala: 4,000-1,500 B.P. Late Archaic

Ashtabala point or blade, medium to large in size, particularly found in Ohio and Pennsylvania. The points spread far into Arkansas. It is a thick, wide point (although I found many examples to be quite narrow), or a blade with an expanded stem and tapered shoulders.

◆ Ashtabala point from Columbus, OH. Point 1 7/8 in. long, 3/4 in. wide, 3/8 in. thick. Classic style, excellent symmetry. Made of white gray marbled chert.

Priv. col., museum quality, valued $650-800.

• Ashtabala Blade from Coles co., IL. Blade 4 1/2 in. long, 2 7/8 in. wide, 5/8 in. thick. Good symmetry, 3/4 in. long base. Made of Kaolin chert.
Priv. col., museum quality, valued $400-700.

• Ashtabala blade from Kentucky Lake area, northwestern KY. Blade 3 3/4 in. long, 1 1/4 in. wide, 1/4 in. thick. Made of a dark red chert.
Priv. col., excellent quality, valued $70-100.

• Ashtabala from Bulitt co., KY. Point 2 1/3 in. long, 1 7/8 in. wide, 1/4 in. thick. Wide point, thin expanded stem, tapered shoulders, concave. Made of yellow tan pebble chert.
Priv. col., museum quality , valued $200-275.

• Ashtabala from Bulitt co., KY. Blade 3 7/8 in. long, 3/4 in. wide, 3/8 in. thick. Thin, narrow, sharply serrated edgeds. Classic style piece of excellent symmetry. Made of yellow tan pebble chert.
Priv. col., excellent quality, valued $150-200.

• Ashtabala from Bulitt co., KY. Blade 4 3/8 in. long, 2 7/8 in. wide, 5/8 in. thick. Thick, wide, good symmetry, fine convex serrated edges. Made of yellow to tan pebble chert.
Priv. col., museum quality, valued $400-700.

• Ashtabala from Bullit co., KY. Blade 3 13/16 in. long, 1 1/8 in. wide, 1/4 in. thick. Narrow, symmetrical, sharp tip, sharp serrated edges. Made of yellow tan pebble chert.
Priv. col., excellent quality, valued $150-200.

• Ashtabala from Warren co., IN. Point 2 1/2 in. long, 1 1/8 in. wide, 3/16 in. thick. Wide point, expanded stem and tapered shoulders. Serrated edges with several nicks. Made of gray chert.
Priv. col., average quality, valued $50-65.

• Ashtabala from Holmes co., OH. 1 5/8 in. long, 1 in. wide, 3/8 in. thick. Wide, thick, sharply serrated, good symmetry, classic design. Made of gray marbled chert.
Priv. col., excellent quality, valued $250-300.

• Ashtabala from Holmes co., OH. Blade 4 1/3 in. long, 3 in. wide, 5/8 in. thick. Thick, wide, good symmetry, long base, sharp serrated

edges and point. Made of gray marbled chert.
Priv. col., museum quality, valued $350-500.

• Ashtabala from Warren co., IN. Blade 4 3/4 in. long, 1 1/2 in. wide,
1/4 in. thick. Thick, narrow, tapered shoulders. Made of gray chert.
Priv. col., average quality, valued $100-125.

• Ashtabala from Warren co., IN. Blade 4 1/4 in. long, 1 1/4 in. wide,
1/4 in. thick. Thick, narrow, tapered shoulders. Expanded stem and
concave base. Made of gray chert.
Priv. col., average quality, valued $125-175.

• Ashtabala from Darke co., OH. Point 1 7/8 in. long, 1 1/16 in. wide,
3/8 in. thick. Classic style, of excellent symmetry. Thick, wide, highly
serrated, with tapered shoulders. Made of white gray pebble chert.
Priv. col., museum quality, valued $350-400.

• Ashtabala from Darke co., OH. Blade 4 2/3 in. long, 3 in. wide,
5/8 in. thick. Good symmetry to the piece, long stem, concave base.
Fits the classic description of an Ashtabala. Made of white gray pebble
chert.
Priv. col., museum quality, valued $450-600.

• Ashtabala from Elliott co., KY. Blade 4 1/4 in. long, 2 1/4 in. wide,
1/4 in. thick. Classic design, wide, thick, sharply serrated. Made of
beige chert.
Priv. col., excellent quality, valued $200-300.

• Ashtabala from Elliott co., KY. Blade 4 1/4 in. long, 2 1/4 in. wide,
1/4 in. thick. Wide blade, expanded stem, tapered shoulders. Convex,
sharp edges, straight base. Made of beige chert.
Priv. col., excellent quality, valued $350-450.

• Ashtabala point from Columbus, OH. Point 1 5/8 in. long, 3/4 in.
wide, 1/4 in. thick. Made of white gray marbled chert.
Priv. col., museum quality, valued $650-800.

• Ashtabala from Cooper co., MO. Blade 5 1/2 in. long, 3 1/8 in.
wide, 5/8 in. thick. Good symmetry, long base. Classic, thick, widely
and sharply serrated. Made of lightweight white chert.
Priv. col., excellent quality, valued $400-500.

• Ashtabala from Cooper co., MO. Blade 5 3/4 in. long, 2 3/4 in. wide,

1/4 in. thick. Heat-treated, symmetrical, wide, thick, wide-spaced sharp
serrations. Made of lightweight white chert.
Priv. col., excellent quality, valued $700-1,000.

• Ashtabala from Cooper co., MO. Blade 5 1/16 in. long, 2 2/3 in.
wide, 1/2 in. thick. Heat-treated, thick, serrated edges. Wide blade with
an expanded stem and tapered shoulders. Made of lightweight white
chert.
Priv. col., museum quality, valued $650-800.

• Ashtabala from Fleming co., KY. Blade 5 7/8 in. long, 3 1/2 in.
wide, 3/8 in. thick. Classic style, wide, thick, sharply serrated edges and
tip. Heat-treated, excellent symmetry. Made of dull gray chert.
Priv. col., museum quality, valued $700-850.

• Ashtabala from Fleming co., KY. Blade 4 1/16 in. long, 2 5/8 in.
wide, 5/8 in. thick. Wide, thick, sharp edges though lacking serrations,
heat-treated. Symmetrical, square shoulders, long base. Made of dull
gray chert.
Priv. col., museum quality, valued $600-700.

• Ashtabala from Worth co., IA. Blade 5 3/4 in. long, 1 1/2 in. wide,
1/4 in. thick. Narrow, thick, symmetrical, long stem, concave base.
Tapered shoulders, finely serrated edges, long, pointed tip. Made of red
to brown marbled chert.
Priv. col., excellent quality, valued $700-1,000.

• Ashtabala from Worth co., IA. Point 2 3/8 in. long, 1 3/4 in. wide,
3/8 in. thick. Classic style, excellent symmetry. Made of red to brown
marbled chert.
Priv. col., museum quality, valued $500-750.

• Ashtabala from Coles co., IL. Blade 3 11/16 in. long, 2 7/8 in. wide,
5/8 in. thick. Wide, thick, convex edges, symmetrical, long stem,
convex base. Made of local tan chert.
Priv. col., excellent quality, valued $300-400.

• Ashtabala from Coles co., IL. Blade 4 1/4 in. long, 2 1/4 in. wide,
1/4 in. thick. Symmetrical, classically designed piece, straight base.
Made of local tan chert.
Priv. col., excellent quality, valued $350-500.

• Ashtabala point from Franklin co., OH. Point 3 in. long, 1 5/8 in.

wide, 1/4 in. thick. Wide-based point. Made of pinkish quartzit*
Priv. col., average quality, valued $45-65.

Augustin: 7,000-5,000 B.P. Mid-Archaic

Found predominantly in the southwestern states. Small to medium sized with contracting base, weak shoulders, generally triangular.

◆ Augustin from Yuma co., AZ. Point 2 in. long, 3/4 in. wide, 3/16 in. thick. Thin, symmetrical point with very sharp serrated edges, thin, sharp tip. Made of a black flint.

Grover Bohannon col., excellent quality, valued $10-20.

• Augustin from Yuma co., AZ. Point 1 5/8 in. long, 3/4 in. wide, 1/8 in. thick. Thin, symmetrical point with very sharp, deeply serrated edges. Made of a black flint.
Grover Bohannon col., excellent quality, valued $10-20.

• Augustin from Yuma co., AZ. Point 2 1/8 in. long, 7/8 in. wide, 1/8 in. thick. Thin symmetrical point with very sharp, serrated edges. Made of a black flint.
Grover Bohannon col., excellent quality, valued $10-20.

• Augustin from Yuma co., AZ. Point 1 7/8 in. long, 2/3 in. wide, 1/8 in. thick. Thin point with very sharp, deeply serrated edges. Made of yellow quartzite.
Juan Samudio col., average quality, valued $8-12.

• Augustin from Lubbock, TX. Point 2 1/8 in. long, 5/8 in. wide, 1/8 in. thick. Thin narrow point with very sharp, serrated edges. Made of gray pebble chert.
Juan Samudio col., excellent quality, valued $10-20.

Autauga: 9,000-7,000 B.P. Early Archaic

Autauga is a small point found predominantly in the southeastern United States. The style also appears abundantly throughout Tennessee. The base is straight. The edges are serrated and often beveled on one side of each face.

♦ Autauga point from northwestern TN. Point 1 1/4 in. long, 1 in. wide, 3/8 in. thick. Made of jasper.

Priv. col., museum quality, valued $50-75.

• Autauga point from VA. Point 1 5/8 in. long, 1 1/16 in. wide, 3/8 in. thick. Made of translucent quartz.
Priv. col., museum quality, valued $40-60.

• Autauga point from Dalton co., GA. Point 1 7/8 in. long, 1 3/16 in. wide, 5/8 in. thick. A very thick point despite exhibiting very fine serrating. Made of white quartz.
Priv. col., museum quality, valued $35-55.

• Autauga point from Hamilton co., TN. Point 1 1/2 in. long, 1 1/4 in. wide, 5/8 in. thick. The tangs are unusual and irregular. Made of Dover chert.
Priv. col., average quality, valued $15-20.

• Autauga from Hamilton co., TN. Point 1 5/8 in. long, 1 5/16 in. wide, 5/8 in. thick. A very thick, wide point, very fine serrated edges. Made of white pebble chert.
Priv. col., excellent quality, valued $25-35.

• Autauga from Hamilton co., TN. Point 2 1/2 in. long, 1 1/4 in. wide, 3/8 in. thick. Long and wide, thin point, fine sharp serrations. Made of Dover chert.
Priv. col., museum quality, valued $45-60.

• Autauga from Pickett co., TN. Point 2 1/4 in. long, 1 3/8 in. wide,

3/8 in. thick. Random flaked, wide and thick, roughly, but sharply
serrated. Made of brown to white marbled chert.
Grover Bohannon col., average quality, valued $15-25.

• Autauga from Pickett co., TN. Point 1 1/2 in. long, 1 3/16 in. wide,
3/8 in. thick. Classic, wide, thick, symmetrical. Serrated edges, beveled
on one edge of each face. The base is wide and straight. Made of brown
to white marbled chert.
Grover Bohannon col., excellent quality, valued $30-40.

• Autauga from Irwin co., GA. Point 1 11/16 in. long, 1 3/16 in. wide,
5/8 in. thick. Thick point, exhibiting very fine serrating. Wide,
straight, base. Made of pink quartz.
Priv. col., museum quality, valued $45-55.

• Autauga from Irwin co., GA. Point 1 5/8 in. long, 1 1/4 in. wide,
1/2 in. thick. Classic design, wide, thick, finely serrated. Base is wide
and straight. Made of pink quartz.
Priv. col., excellent quality, valued $35-50.

• Autauga from Irwin co., GA. Point 1 1/4 in. long, 1 1/32 in. wide,
1/2 in. thick. Nearly as wide as long, sharply serrated. Good
workmanship, wide straight base. Made of pink quartz.
Priv. col., museum quality, valued $65-85.

• Autauga from Graham co., NC. Point 2 1/8 in. long, 1 1/16 in. wide,
3/8 in. thick. Narrow, thick, good workmanship, finely serrated edges.
Made of milky quartz.
Priv. col., museum quality, valued $40-60.

• Autauga from Graham co., NC. Point 2 in. long, 1 7/16 in. wide,
5/8 in. thick. Thick point, nearly as wide as long. High quality
workmanship, sharp, fine serrating. Point long stemmed, as wide at
straight base as point. Made of milky quartz.
Priv. col., museum quality, valued $65-75.

• Autauga from Hamilton co., TN. Point 1 13/16 in. long, 1 1/4 in.
wide, 5/8 in. thick. Wide, thick, sharply serrated. Straight base, tangs
are irregular. Made of Dover chert.
Grover Bohannon col., excellent quality, valued $40-50.

• Autauga from Lewis co., TN. Point 1 1/2 in. long, 1 1/16 in. wide,
3/4 in. thick. Extremely thick, symmetrically wide, serrations are long
and random, appears beveled. Made of black chert.

Priv. col., average quality, valued $25-35.

• Autauga from Lewis co., TN. Point 1 3/8 in. long, 1 1/16 in. wide, 3/8 in. thick. Thick, wide, sharply serrated. Beveled on one side of each face, wide straight base. Point is symmetrical and heat-treated. Made of a black chert.
Priv. col., museum quality, valued $45-60.

• Autauga from Lewis co., TN. Point 2 7/8 in. long, 2 1/16 in. wide, 5/8 in. thick. Very thick point, long and nearly as wide as it long. Very fine serrating on edges. Heat-treated, beveled on one side of each face. Made of black chert.
Priv. col., museum quality, valued $55-75.

• Autauga from Dyer co., TN. Point 1 2/3 in. long, 1 1/4 in. wide, 1/8 in. thick. Thin, wide, symmetrical, good workmanship. Finely serrated, beveled on one side of each face, long tangs, convex base. Made of multi-toned brown chert.
Jim Smith col., museum quality, rare, valued $125-150.

• Autauga from Dyer co., TN. Point 1 3/4 in. long, 7/8 in. wide, 3/8 in. thick. Symmetrical, good workmanship, narrow point, good field patina. Beveled on one side of each face, highly serrated, concave base. Made of multi-toned brown chert.
Priv. col., museum quality, valued $80-95.

• Autauga from Dyer co., TN. Point 1 5/8 in. long, 3/4 in. wide, 3/8 in. thick. Symmetrical, good workmanship exhibited throughout this site. Good field patina, beveled on one side of each face, finely serrated, concave base. Made of multi-toned brown chert.
Priv. col., museum quality, valued $65-80.

• Autauga from Echois co., GA. Point 1 3/16 in. long, 1 1/16 in. wide, 5/16 in. thick. Thick point, as wide as it is long, fine serrations. Beveled on one side of each face, straight base. Made of quartzite.
Grover Bohannon col., average quality, valued $25-35.

• Autauga from Echois co., GA. Point 1 1/2 in. long, 1 1/16 in. wide, 1/2 in. thick. Thick, classically wide and symmetrical piece. Excellent workmanship for quality of the material. Tangs are wide, uneven, straight wide base. Made of quartzite.
Grover Bohannon col., museum quality, valued $45-65.

• Autauga from Echois co., GA Point 1 in. long, 1 in. wide, 3/8 in.

thick. Seemingly typical of points from this site is their near equal width and length. Beveled on one side of each face, finely serrated for material. Made of quartzite.
Grover Bohannon col., museum quality, valued $50-65.

• Autauga from Echois co., GA. Point 1 5/8 in. long, 1 1/2 in. wide, 1/8 in. thick. Typically wide and symmetrical, very thin, finely worked point. Uneven tangs, narrow straight base, sharply serrated and beveled on one side of each face. Made of quartzite.
Grover Bohannon col., museum quality, valued $45-60.

• Autauga from Echois co., GA. Point 1 7/8 in. long, 1 9/16 in. wide, 1/4 in. thick. Exhibits steep beveling on one side of each face, sharp, wide, serrating. Narrow straight base, parallel sweeping tangs. Made of quartzite.
Grover Bohannon col., excellent quality, valued $35-45.

• Autauga from Abieville co., SC. Point 1 1/8 in. long, 1 1/4 in. wide, 5/8 in thick. Thick, wider than it is long, tangs are snapped and parallel. Base is straight and as wide as the point. Made of brownish quartz.
Priv. col., excellent quality, valued $40-50.

• Autauga from Abieville co., SC. Point 1 1/4 in. long, 5/8 in. wide, 1/8 in. thick. Unusually thin and narrow, well worn, yet possibly reworked. Edges are concave, short tangs, convex base. Made of brownish quartz.
Priv. col., museum quality, valued $60-75.

• Autauga from Floyd co., VA. Point 1 7/8 in. long, 1 1/16 in. wide, 3/8 in. thick. Symmetrical, beveled on one side of each face, finely and sharply serrated. Made of amber.
Priv. col., museum quality, rare, valued $60-80.

• Autauga from Floyd co., VA. Point 1 5/8 in. long, 1 3/16 in. wide, 7/8 in. thick. A very thick point, yet symmetrical and well worked. Flaking long and thin, steeply beveled on one side of each face. Made of amber.
Priv. col., museum quality, rare, valued $55-75.

• Autauga from Floyd co., VA. Point 1 1/2 in. long, 1 3/8 in. wide, 5/8 in. thick. Thick, symmetrical, wide point. Beveled on one side each face, sharply serrated. The tangs are long and parallel, straight base. Made of amber.

Priv. col, museum quality, rare, valued $70-80.

• Autauga from Heard co., GA. Point 2 2/3 in. long, 1 3/32 in. wide, 3/8 in. thick. Long, narrow, symmetrical, finely and sharply serrated. Short pointed tangs, beveled on all four sides, straight wide base. Made of jasper.
Priv. col., museum quality, rare, valued $70-85.

• Autauga point from Heard co., GA. Point 5/8 in. long, 1 1/16 in. wide, 3/8 in. thick. Made of translucent quartz.
Priv. col., museum quality, valued $40-60.

• Autauga from Dalton co., GA. Point 1 7/16 in. long, 1 3/16 in. wide, 3/8 in. thick. Wide, symmetrical, finely serrated, long tanged. Beveled on one side of each face, straight base. Made of speckled quartzite.
Priv. col., average quality, valued $15-25.

• Autauga from Hamilton co., IN. Point 1 2/3 in. long, 1 1/4 in. wide, 1/4 in. thick. Thin, wide, symmetrical, beveled on one side of each face. Point is sharply beveled, convex base, tangs long and thin. Made of light gray chert.
Tim Rubbles col., excellent quality, valued $45-55.

CHAPTER 2 BAKER-BULVERDE

Baker: 8,000-6,000 B.P. Early Archaic

Baker is a medium sized midwestern point. The point is narrow with a long stem; the stem is always bifurcated. This point is slightly barbed typically with barbed shoulders.

◆ Baker point from Lubbock, TX. Point 2 1/2 in. long, 1 1/8 in. wide, 1/4 in. thick. Long stem with deep bifurcation. Point of a creamy brown chert.

Priv. col, museum quality, valued $65-85.

• Baker blade from Lubbock, TX. Blade 3 5/8 in. long, 1 3/8 in. wide, 1/4 in thick. Very symmetrical point, short stem, deep bifurcation. Made of a translucent chert.
Priv. col., museum quality, valued $100-150.

• Baker blade from Pope co., IL. Blade 4 1/16 in. long, 1 5/16 in. wide, 1/4 in. thick. Very symmetrical blade, deeply bifurcated short stem. Sharply barbed shoulders, serrated blade. Made of Cobden Hornstone chert.
Priv. col., museum quality, valued $135-200.

• Baker from Hardin co., IL. Blade 3 7/8 in. long, 1 7/8 in. wide,
1/4 in thick. Very symmetrical point, short stem, deeply bifurcated,
barbed shoulders. Made of a pink pebble chert.
Priv. col., average quality, valued $60-85.

• Baker from Pope co., IL. Blade 4 3/16 in. long, 1 1/2 in. wide,
1/4 in. thick. Thin symmetrical blade, deeply bifurcated short stem.
Sharply barbed shoulders, finely serrated edges. Made of Cobden chert.
Priv. col., museum quality, valued $100-160.

• Baker from Hartley co., TX. Point 2 2/3 in. long, 1 in. wide, 1/4 in.
thick. Thick, narrow, symmetrical, barbed shoulders. Long stem, base
deeply bifurcated. Made of cream chert.
Priv. col, excellent quality, valued $45-65.

• Baker from Hartley co., TX. Blade 4 3/8 in. long, 1 3/32 in. wide,
1/8 in thick. Thin, very narrow, symmetrical, heat-treated point. Short
stem, deep base bifurcation. Made of cream chert.
Priv. col., excellent quality, valued $60-75.

• Baker from Hartley co., TX. Blade 4 1/16 in. long, 1 7/16 in. wide,
1/4 in. thick. Thick, narrow, symmetrical, heat-treated blade. Long
barbed shoulders, classic deeply bifurcated short stem, serrated edges.
Made of cream chert.
Priv. col., museum quality, valued $125-150.

• Baker from Hartley co., TX. Point 3 1/8 in. long, 7/8 in. wide,
1/8 in. thick. Another thin and narrow point from this site. Heat-
treated, several nicks on one side, sharply serrated tip and edges. Made
of cream chert.
Priv. col, average quality, valued $35-55.

• Baker from Dallam co., TX. Blade 4 5/8 in. long, 1 3/8 in. wide,
3/8 in. thick. Symmetrical, narrow point, short stem, deeply bifurcated,
barbed shoulders. Made of dull gray chert.
Priv. col., museum quality, valued $100-125.

• Baker from Dallam co., TX. Blade 4 7/16 in. long, 1 1/16 in. wide,
1/4 in. thick. Narrow, symmetrical blade, sharp barbed shoulders.
Deeply bifurcated base, short stem, finely serrated blade. Made of dull
gray chert.
Priv. col., excellent quality, valued $85-100.

• Baker from Hall co., TX. Blade 4 1/2 in. long, 2 7/8 in. wide, 1/4 in. thick. Wide yet symmetrical, finely serrated edges, barbed tip and shoulders. Long stem with deep base bifurcation. Made of brown chert.
Priv. col, museum quality, valued $85-115.

• Baker from Hall co., TX. Point 2 3/8 in. long, 1 3/8 in. wide, 1/4 in thick. Wide, thick, symmetrical point, sharpened barbed shoulders, slight tip break. Short stem, deep bifurcated base. Made of brown chert.
Priv. col., average quality, valued $25-35.

• Baker from Pope co., IL. Blade 5 in. long, 1 11/32 in. wide, 1/4 in. thick. Large symmetrical blade, sharply serrated, deeply bifurcated base, short stem, barbed shoulders. Made of Cobden Hornstone chert.
Tim Rubbles col., museum quality, valued $175-250.

• Baker from Pope co., IL. Point 2 1/4 in. long, 1 1/32 in. wide, 1/4 in. thick. Long stem classical bifurcation. Wide asymmetrical point, short barbed shoulders. Made of Cobden Hornstone chert.
Tim Rubbles col, museum quality, valued $100-125.

• Baker from Pope co., IL. Blade 4 5/8 in. long, 2 1/8 in. wide, 1/4 in. thick. Wide, symmetrical point, short stem, deeply bifurcated base. Sort barbed shoulders, serrated edges with barbed tip. Made of Cobden Hornstone chert.
Tim Rubbles col., museum quality, valued $100-150.

• Baker from Pope co., IL. Blade 4 9/16 in. long, 1 5/32 in. wide, 1/4 in. thick. Very symmetrical narrow blade, sharp, fine edge serrations, finely serrated sharp tip. Deeply bifurcated short stem, sharply barbed shoulders. Made of Cobden Hornstone chert.
Tim Rubbles col., museum quality, valued $165-200.

• Baker from Anderson co., KS. Point 2 1/3 in. long, 1 1/8 in. wide, 3/16 in. thick. Symmetrical, heat-treated, angular, thin point, sharply serrated. Short stem with deep base bifurcation. Made of a creamy tan chert.
Priv. col, excellent quality, valued $65-85.

• Baker from Anderson co., KS. Blade 3 7/8 in. long, 1 3/16 in. wide, 1/4 in. thick. Heat-treated, symmetrical point, wide, crude serrated edges. Short stem, drooping shoulders, deep base bifurcation. Made of

creamy tan chert.
Priv. col., excellent quality, valued $70-85.

• Baker from Jasper co., IL. Blade 4 11/16 in long, 1 5/16 in. wide,
1/8 in. thick. Uniquely thin, symmetrical blade, long, sharp tipped
barbed shoulders, finely serrated edges. Deeply bifurcated short stem,
thinned base. Made of green white speckled pebble chert.
Priv. col., excellent quality, valued $85-100.

• Baker from Jasper co., IL. Point 2 1/2 in. long, 1 5/8 in. wide,
3/32 in. thick. Very thin, excellent workmanship, symmetrical, yet wide
for a Baker. Heat-treated, layered, serrated edges and tip. Long stem
with deep bifurcation. Made of green white speckled chert.
Priv. col, museum quality, rare, valued $165-235.

• Baker from Jasper co., IL. Blade 3 3/4 in. long, 1 1/4 in. wide,
1/4 in thick. Classic design, symmetrical point, short stem, deep
bifurcation. Heat-treated, sharply serrated edges. Made of green white
speckled chert.
Priv. col., museum quality, valued $90-120.

• Baker from Jasper co., IL. Blade 5 1/16 in. long, 1 5/16 in. wide,
3/16 in. thick. Thin, narrow blade, excellent workmanship, heat-treated.
Long, thinned and pointed shoulder barbs. Classic deeply bifurcated
short stem, highly serrated edges. Made of green white speckled chert.
Priv. col., museum quality, rare, valued $185-250.

Beaver Lake: 12,000-8,000 B.P. Paleo-transitional

Beaver Lake points and blades are found from Arkansas throughout the Southeast. Beaver Lake is a medium to large point or blade with flaring ears. The bases are ground and the blade recurved. Can be mistaken for a Cumberland, but Beaver Lake points and blades are much thinner.

♦ Beaver Lake point from Brown co., IL. Point 3 1/16 in. long,
1 1/2 in. wide, 5/8 in. thick. Base is 1 in. thick, blade unusually thick.
Made of pebble chert.

Priv. col., excellent quality, valued $55-85.

♦ Beaver Lake point from Giles co., TN. Point 2 3/8 in. long,
1 1/8 in. wide, 1/4 in. thick. Blade edges serrated and point distinctly
recurved. Made of a tan rose chert.

Priv. col., excellent quality, valued $50-75.

♦ Beaver Lake from Hardin co., IL. Point 1 5/8 in. long, 3/4 in. wide,
3/8 in. thick. Base fluted, with heavy patina. Made of Hardin gray
chert.

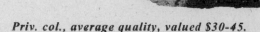

Priv. col., average quality, valued $30-45.

• Beaver Lake blade from Hamilton Co, TN. Point 2 3/4 in. long,
1 in. wide, 1/4 in. thick. Base fluted, symmetrical flaring ears, wide and
finely sharp serrations. Made of Dover chert.
Priv. col., museum quality, valued $75-100.

• Beaver Lake from Hardin co., IL. Blade 4 5/8 in. long, 1 1/4 in.
wide, 1/4 in. thick. Base fluted, classical collateral flaking. Upper two
thirds of blade is sharply serrated. The blade is slightly recurved. Made
of Fort Payne chert.
Priv. col., museum quality, rare, valued $450-600.

• Beaver Lake from Giles co., TN. Blade 4 3/8 in. long, 1 1/8 in.
wide, 1/4 in. thick. Blade thin and narrow, edges serrated with sharp
point tip. Made of Dover chert.
Grover Bohannon col., excellent quality, valued $90-135.

• Beaver Lake from Hardin co., IL. Point 2 5/8 in. long, 1 1/4 in.
wide, 3/8 in. thick. Base fluted, symmetrical point, finely serrated.

Made of Hardin gray chert.
Priv. col., excellent quality, valued $70-85.

• Beaver Lake from Hamilton co., TN. Point 2 1/4 in. long, 1 1/8 in.
wide, 1/4 in. thick. Base fluted, symmetrical flaring ears, rather thick
point. Wide-spaced and sharp serrations. Made of Dover chert.
Priv. col., museum quality, valued $85-110.

• Beaver Lake from St. Francis co., AR. Blade 4 5/8 in. long,
1 3/4 in. wide, 1/4 in. thick. Symmetrical, sharply serrated recurved
edges. Flaring rounded ears, ground concave base. Made of gray black
flint.
Grover Bohannon col., excellent quality, valued $250-300.

• Beaver Lake from St. Francis co., AR. Blade 5 1/2 in. long, 1 1/2 in.
wide, 1/4 in. thick. Symmetrical, sharp pointed tip, deeply serrated
recurved edges. Thinly fluted, long ears, particularly fine serrated blade
edges. Made of gray black flint.
Grover Bohannon col., museum quality, valued $275-350.

• Beaver Lake from Lee co., AR. Point 2 1/2 in. long, 1 5/8 in. wide,
3/8 in. thick. Wide, random flaked, edges serrated and point distinctly
recurved. Wide, yet symmetrical, convex ground base. Made of tan to
brown pebble chert.
Priv. col., excellent quality, valued $45-65.

• Beaver Lake from Hardin co., AR. Point 2 5/8 in. long, 3/4 in. wide,
1/2 in. thick. Narrow, reworked point, rounded tip, with prominate
recurved point edges. Base fluted, flaring pointed shoulder tangs. Made
of tan yellow pebble chert.
Priv. col., museum quality, valued $120-145.

• Beaver Lake from Calhoun co., AR. Point 2 1/4 in. long, 1 1/16 in.
wide, 1/4 in. thick. Random flaked, symmetrical flaring ears, sharp
serrations, parrallel point edges. Concave, ground, fluted base. Made of
black to yellow chert.
Priv. col., excellent quality, valued $85-110.

• Beaver Lake from Calhoun co., AR. Point 2 1/2 in. long, 1 1/3 in.
wide, 1/4 in. thick. Random flaked, symmetrical, parallel flaring ears.
Straight edges, wide, sharp, serrations. Made of black to yellow chert.
Priv. col., museum quality, valued $100-130.

• Beaver Lake from Calhoun co., AR. Point 3 1/8 in. long, 1 1/4 in.
wide, 1/4 in. thick. Random flaked, symmetrical, flaring ears. Widely
serrated classic recurved edges. Fluted, ground base. Made of black to
yellow chert.
Priv. col., excellent quality, valued $70-85.

• Beaver Lake from Bibb co., AL. Point 2 1/3 in. long, 1 in. wide,
1/8 in. thick. Extremely thin, angular with highly serrated recurved
edges, slight tip break. Base fluted and ground, flaring ears also ground.
Made of rose quartz.
Grover Bohannon col., average quality, rare, valued $75-100.

• Beaver Lake from Bibb co., AL. Blade 3 7/8 in. long, 1 1/2 in. wide,
1/8 in. thick. As thin as its smaller site mate, symmetrical, highly
serrated recurved edges. Base fluted, flaring ground tangs and base.
Made of rose quartz.
Grover Bohannon col., museum quality, rare, valued $150-200.

• Beaver Lake from Bibb co., AL. Point 2 1/4 in. long, 7/8 in. wide,
1/8 in. thick. Base fluted, symmetrical, long, flaring ears, good
workmanship. Recurved edges, wide spaced, sharp serrations. Made of
rose quartz.
Grover Bohannon col., museum quality, rare, valued $125-150.

• Beaver Lake from Bibb co., AL. Blade 5 in. long, 1 3/4 in. wide,
1/4 in. thick. Base fluted, classical design, symmetrically ground.
Good workmanship, recurved sides, widely serrated edges, long point
flaring to upward sweeping ears. Made of rose quartz.
Grover Bohannon col., museum quality, rare, valued $450-600.

Bella Coola: Historical

*The Bella Coola is a northwest coast culture. Their points
were of stone and medium to large in size. The Atlal was their primary
weapon, or hunting tool.*

◆ Bella coola from the northwest Pacific coast. Point 2 1/2 in. long,
1 3/8 in. wide, 5/32 in. thick. Two views. Point is beveled on the right
side. Made of light gray chert.

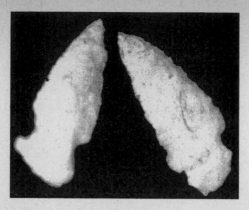

Southern IL Univ. Museum, Carbondale, IL. Average quality, valued $35-50.

♦ Bella Coola from the northwest Pacific coast. Point 2 1/2 in. long, 1 3/8 in. wide, 5/32 in. thick. Very delicate flaking on the edges of a very thin point. Made of nearly translucent gray chert.

Southern IL Univ. Museum, Carbondale, IL. Museum quality, valued $175-250.

Benton: 6,000-4,000 B.P. Mid-Archaic

Found throughout the Midwest and Southeast. Medium to large size point or blade with convex sides, May be corner notched, side notched or double notched. Stem expanded or bifurcated, concave to straight base. Exceptional workmanship is found in Benton points and blades. Most are parallel oblique flaked and beveled on all four sides.

♦ Benton from Monroe co., TN. Point 1 1/8 in. long, 3/4 in. wide, 1/8 in. thick. Very sharp points, parallel flaked. Made of brown pebble chert.

Grover Bohannon col., poor quality, valued $5-10.

• Benton from Monroe co., TN. Blade 3 1/2 in. long, 1 3/4 in. wide, 1/2 in. thick. Very thick crude blade, good field patina, parrel flaked, slight tip break. Made of gray chert.
Grover Bohannon col., excellent quality, valued $15-30.

• Benton from Monroe co., TN. Blade 4 1/2 in. long, 2 1/4 in. wide, 1/2 in. thick. Blade heat-treated, good field patina, parallel oblique flaked, sharp tip, sharply serrated. Made of gray chert.
Grover Bohannon col., museum quality, valued $25-40.

• Benton from Lexington co., KY. Point 1 7/8 in. long, 1 1/4 in. wide, 1/8 in. thick. Sharply serrated point, beveled on one side of each face, parallel oblique flaked. Good quality workmanship, side notched, concave base. Made of pinkish pebble chert.
Grover Bohannon col., excellent quality, valued $25-35.

• Benton from Hamilton co., TN. Point 2 1/2 in. long, 1 3/5 in. wide, 1/4 in. thick. Thin parallel flaked, finely serrated, good field Patina, several edge nicks on one side. Made of gray to black chert.
Jim Smith col., average quality, valued $15-20.

• Benton from Jackson co., IL. Blade 3 1/2 in. long, 2 1/4 in. wide, 1/2 in. thick. Blade heat-treated, good field patina, parallel oblique flaked, sharp tip, sharply serrated. Very wide, although symmetrical. Made of Mill Creek chert.
Tim Rubbles col., museum quality, valued $35-50.

• Benton from Geneva co., AL. Point 2 3/16 in. long, 1 2/3 in. wide, 1/4 in. thick. Sharply serrated edges, concave sides. Corner notched, stem expanded, concave base. Parallel oblique flaked and beveled on all four sides. Made of quartzite.
Priv. col., average quality, valued $15-25.

• Benton from Geneva co., AL. Point 2 1/8 in. long, 1 3/4 in. wide, 1/8 in. thick. Sharp tip point, parallel flaked. Beveled on one side of each face. Double side notched, bifurcated ground base. Made of

quartzite.
Priv. col., excellent quality, valued $25-40.

- Benton from Geneva co., AL. Blade 4 1/4 in. long, 1 1/3 in. wide, 1/2 in. thick. Thick, narrow, random flaked, crude blade. Slight tip break, side notched with uneven straight base. Made of quartzite.
Priv. col., poor quality, valued $8-12.

- Benton from Lowndes co., AL. Blade 5 1/3 in. long, 2 in. wide, 5/8 in. thick. Large blade with convex sides, corner notched, stem expanded, straight base. Exceptional workmanship, parallel oblique flaked, beveled on all four sides. Made of pink quartz.
Priv. col., museum quality, rare, valued $65-85.

- Benton from Lowndes co., AL. Blade 4 1/8 in. long, 1 2/3 in. wide, 1/8 in. thick. Sharp, parallel flaked, gradually and finely beveled on all four sides. Made of brown pebble chert.
Priv. col., excellent quality, valued $25-40.

- Benton from Lowndes co., AL. Blade 3 7/16 in. long, 1 3/4 in. wide, 1/3 in. thick. Parallel flaked, beveled on one side of each face. Made of brown pebble chert.
Priv. col., excellent quality, valued $30-45.

- Benton from Lowndes co., AL. Blade 5 in. long, 2 1/16 in. wide, 3/16 in. thick. Large, narrow, symmetrical, oblique parallel flaked. Narrow side notches, stem expanded, concave base. Exceptional workmanship, beveled on all four sides. Made of pink quartz.
Priv. col., museum quality, rare, valued $250-300.

- Benton from Jefferson co., TN. Point 1 in. long, 1/4 in. wide, 1/16 in. thick. Thin, narrow, excellent workmanship, parallel oblique flaked. Bifurcated stem, convex base. Made of brown to tan grainy pebble chert.
Tim Rubbles col., excellent quality, valued $35-50.

- Benton from Montgomery co., TN. Blade 3 7/8 in. long, 1 1/2 in. wide, 1/3 in. thick. Thick flaked, slight tip break. All four edges beveled, expanded stem, straight base. Made of gray pebble chert.
Priv. col., average quality, valued $15-20.

- Benton from Greene co., TN. Blade 5 1/2 in. long, 2 1/4 in. wide, 1/2 in. thick. Narrow, thick, heat-treated, parallel oblique flaked, sharp tip, sharply serrated edges. Bifurcated stem with concave base. Made of

white chert.
Priv. col., excellent quality, valued $25-40.

• Benton from Greene co., TN. Blade 4 7/8 in. long, 1 23/32 in. wide,
1/8 in. thick. Parallel oblique flaked, deeply side notched, beveled on
all four edges, finely serrated. Bifurcated stem, concave base. Made of
white chert.
Priv. col., excellent quality, valued $25-35.

• Benton from Hancock co., TN. Point 2 1/16 in. long, 1 1/2 in. wide,
1/4 in. thick. Thin parallel flaked, finely serrated, good workmanship.
Beveled on one side of each face. Expanded stem, straight base. Made of
black flint.
Priv. col., excellent quality, valued $25-30.

• Benton from Jackson co., IL. Blade 5 1/32 in. long, 2 1/8 in. wide,
1/2 in. thick. Parallel oblique flaked, sharp tip, sharply serrated, steeply
beveled on all four sides. Long bifurcated stem, concave base. Made of
Mill Creek chert.
Priv. col., excellent quality, valued $30-45.

• Benton from Jackson co., IL. Blade 4 1/16 in. long, 2 1/4 in. wide,
1/2 in. thick. Wide, parallel oblique flaked, sharp tip, sharply serrated,
steeply beveled. Bifurcated stem, concave base. Made of Mill Creek
chert.
Priv. col., excellent quality, valued $25-35.

• Benton from Schuyler co., IL. Blade 3 7/8 in. long, 2 in. wide,
1/8 in. thick. Sharp tip point, parallel oblique flaked, double side
notched. Thin, symmetrical, good workmanship, heat-treated. Expanded
stem, convex base. Made of tan pebble chert.
Priv. col., excellent quality, valued $35-45.

• Benton from Henderson co., IL. Point 2 1/2 in. long, 1 1/3 in. wide,
1/4 in. thick. Thin, fine, long, parallel flaking, finely serrated. Beveled
on one side of each face, parallel stem, straight base. Made of jasper.
Jim Smith col., museum quality, rare, valued $50-60.

• Benton from St. Clair co., IL. Blade 3 7/8 in. long, 2 in. wide,
5/8 in. thick. Symmetrical, heat-treated, thick, steeply beveled on all
four sides. Parallel oblique flaked, sharp tip, sharply serrated. Expanded
stem, convex base. Made of white chert with gold line through center.
Jim Smith col., museum quality, rare, valued $45-70.

• Benton from Monroe co., TN. Blade 4 1/2 in. long, 2 1/2 in. wide, 1/2 in. thick. Heat-treated, thick, steeply beveled on all four sides. Parallel oblique flaked, sharp tip, sharply serrated. Made of Dover chert.
Grover Bohannon col., museum quality, valued $25-40.

• Benton from Lexington co., KY. Blade 4 7/8 in. long, 2 1/4 in. wide, 1/8 in. thick. Thin, parallel oblique flaked, double side notched. Stem bifurcated, concave base. Made of pinkish pebble chert.
Priv. col., excellent quality, valued $25-35.

• Benton from Hamilton co., IL. Point 2 1/8 in. long, 1 3/8 in. wide, 1/4 in. thick. Thin, heat-treated, parallel flaked, finely serrated, beveled on one side of each face. Expanded stem, straight base. Made of Mill Creek chert.
Jim Smith col., average quality, valued $15-20.

• Benton from Jackson co., IL. Blade 3 1/2 in. long, 1 3/4 in. wide, 1/3 in. thick. Heat-treated, narrow, thin, parallel oblique flaked, steeply beveled on one side of each face. Finely serrated, expanded stem, straight base. Made of Mill Creek chert.
Jim Smith col., museum quality, valued $35-45.

Big Sandy: 10,000-2,500 B.P. Paleo-transitional to Late Archaic

Big Sandy points and blades are found mostly in the Southeast. Still it is not unusual to find them in the Midwest or along the Mississippi. Big Sandy is small to medium in size and side notched. Paleo forms demonstrate more striking basal grinding of stems, deep serrations, and horizontal flaking. Can look very close to a Pine Tree point or blade.

♦ Big Sandy from Williamson co., IL. Blade 2 3/4 in. long, 3/4 in. wide, 3/32 in. thick. Blade shows good field patina. Unique base and notching, very decorative blade, one of a kind. Made of high quality Mill Creek chert.

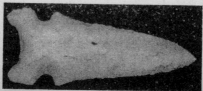

Priv. col., museum quality, rare, valued $120-175.

◆ Big Sandy broad base from Alexander co., IL. Point 2 1/2 in. long, 1 in. wide, 3/32 in. thick. Very-fine made point with a horizontally flaked base. The point and notching is very symmetrical. Made of an oily light brown chert with green streaks.

Priv. col., museum quality, valued $40-65.

◆ Big Sandy mouse ear from Blunt co., TN. Point 2 1/2 in. long, 1 1/4 in. wide, 3/16 in. thick. Made of high quality Mill Creek chert.

Les Grubbe col., average quality, valued $20-25.

◆ Big Sandy mouse ear from Blunt co., TN. Point 2 1/4 in. long, 1 3/8 in. wide, 1/4 in. thick. Made of white pebble chert.

Les Grubbe col., average quality, valued $25-35.

◆ Big Sandy point from Crenshaw co., AL. Point 1 3/4 in. long, 3/4 in. wide, 5/32 in. thick. Deeply serrated point, fairly symmetrical. Made of a mauve pebble chert.

Priv. col., excellent quality, value $25-35.

• Big Sandy from Wilcox co., AL. Point 1 2/3 in. long, 1 1/32 in. wide, 1/4 in. thick. Nearly as wide as long, quality workmanship, Side notches, deep wide, sharp, serrations. Horizontal flaking, basal ground stem, straight base. Made of gray chert.
Priv. col., excellent quality, valued $55-70.

• Big Sandy from Cooper co., TN. Point 1 5/8 in. long, 1 3/16 in. wide, 1/4 in. thick. Highly serrated, beveled base. Horizontal flaked, concave base. Made of pinkish chert.
Priv. col., excellent quality, valued $30-40.

• Big Sandy from Autauga co., AL. Point 1 1/4 in. long, 7/8 in. wide, 3/16 in. thick. Horizontal flaked, finely serrated. Finely fluted ground base. Fine symmetrical serrations on side notches. Made of oily black flint.
Priv. col., museum quality, valued $50-65.

• Big Sandy from Coosa co., AL. Point 2 1/8 in. long, 1 7/32 in. wide, 1/4 in. thick. Symmetrical point, sharply serrated. Thinly fluted ground base. Made of grainy pinkish quartzite.
Priv. col., excellent quality, valued $20-30.

• Big Sandy from Stewart co., TN. Point 1 3/8 in. long, 5/8 in. wide, 1/4 in. thick. Thick, serrated, beveled straight base. Symmetrical, horizontal flaked. Made of Dover chert.
Priv. col., excellent quality, valued $35-50.

• Big Sandy from Autauga co., AL. Point 1 1/2 in. long, 1/2 in. wide, 3/16 in. thick. Fine workmanship, thin, horizontal flaked. Fluted, straight ground base. Fine symmetrical serrations on blade, parallel side notches. Made of quartzite.
Priv. col., museum quality, valued $50-65.

• Big Sandy from Ashley co., AR. Point 1 3/16 in. long, 3/4 in. wide, 1/8 in. thick. Horizontal flaked, deep, wide serrations. Striking basal grinding of stems, fluted concave base. Made of oily black flint.
Priv. col., excellent quality, valued $30-40.

• Big Sandy from Williamson co., IL. Blade 2 2/3 in. long, 3/4 in. wide, 5/32 in. thick. Horizontal flaked, long and thin serrations. Edges are widely serrated, sharp, straight base. Made of Mill Creek chert.
Priv. col., museum quality, valued $60-75.

- Big Sandy broad base from Massac co., IL. Point 2 1/8 in. long, 1 3/32 in. wide, 1/8 in. thick. Finely made point, horizontal flaked with a horizontally flaked base. Narrow, symmetrical, wide, deep, sharp edge serrations. Made of muave chert.
Priv. col., museum quality, valued $45-60.

- Big Sandy mouse ear from Bledsoe co., TN. Point 1 1/2 in. long, 1 1/4 in. wide, 3/16 in. thick. Nearly as wide as long, symmetrical, wide, deep edge serrations. Made of Dover chert.
Priv. col., excellent quality, valued $40-55.

- Big Sandy mouse ear from Bledsoe co., TN. Point 2 in. long, 1 1/8 in. wide, 1/4 in. thick. Symmetrical, thick, wide edge serrations. Ground straight base. Made of gray pebble chert.
Tim Rubbles col., excellent quality, valued $30-35.

- Big Sandy from Williamson co., IL. Blade 2 3/8 in. long, 3/4 in. wide 5/32 in. thick. Good field patina, heat-treated, wide sharp serrations. Deeply side notched, concave edges and base. Made of Mill Creek chert.
Tim Rubbles col., museum quality, valued $80-100.

- Big Sandy broad base from Lake co., TN. Point 3 1/32 in. long, 1 in. wide, 3/32 in. thick. Narrow, concave edges, fine-made point horizontally flaked. The point is symmetrical, deep, wide side notches, concave base. Made of oily brown chert.
Priv. col., museum quality, valued $45-60.

- Big Sandy mouse ear from Henry co., TN. Point 2 2/3 in. long, 1 1/2 in. wide, 1/4 in. thick. Symmetrical, horizontal flaked, deep serrations. Wide side notches, ground concave base. Made of brown chert.
Priv. col., average quality, valued $25-35.

- Big Sandy mouse ear from Henry co., TN. Point 2 1/2 in. long, 1 1/2 in. wide, 1/4 in. thick. Deep, wide, serrations, horizontal flaked. Wide, shallow side notches, ground straight base. Made of gray pebble chert.
Priv. col., excellent quality, valued $30-35.

- Big Sandy from Saline co., IL. Blade 3 3/4 in. long, 1 3/4 in. wide, 1/8 in. thick. Blade is symmetrical, horizontal flaked, high quality workmanship. Deep, parallel side notching, ground concave base. Made

of high quality Mill Creek chert.
Priv. col., museum quality, valued $80-125.

• Big Sandy broad base from Saline co., IL. Point 2 1/8 in. long,
1 1/4 in. wide, 5/32 in. thick. Point horizontally flaked, deep parallel
side notches, symmetrical, ground concave base. Made of Mill Creek
chert.
Priv. col., excellent quality, valued $40-50.

• Big Sandy mouse ear from Fentress co., TN. Point 2 1/2 in. long,
1 1/4 in. wide, 3/16 in. thick. Symmetrical, sharply serrated point, thin,
horizontal flaking. Tip has slight break, base is rounded on ends and
ground. Made of dull gray chert.
Grover Bohannon col., average quality, valued $25-35.

• Big Sandy mouse ear from Fentress co., TN. Point 3 1/4 in. long,
1 1/8 in. wide, 1/4 in. thick. Horizontal flaked, sharp edge serrations.
Deep side notches, thinned straight base. Made of tan pebble chert.
Grover Bohannon col., excellent quality, valued $40-45.

• Big Sandy from Boone co., TN. Blade 4 in. long, 1 2/3 in. wide,
3/8 in. thick. Basal ground stem, deep serrations and horizontal flaking.
Made of tan pebble chert.
Priv. col., excellent quality, valued $45-50.

• Big Sandy from Hamilton co., IL. Point 2 1/4 in. long, 1 1/2 in.
wide, 1/2 in. thick. Horizontal flaked piece, sharply serrated edges and
tip. Deep and wide side notches, concave base. Made of Mill Creek
chert.
Priv. col., museum quality, valued $80-100.

• Big Sandy from Hamilton co., IL. Point 2 13/32 in. long, 1 in. wide,
5/32 in. thick. Fine workmanshp, horizontally flaked, thinned concave
base. The point and side notching is very symmetrical. Made of brown
pebble chert.
Priv. col., museum quality, valued $50-65.

• Big Sandy mouse ear from Lewis co., TN. Point 3 1/4 in. long,
1 1/2 in. wide, 1/4 in. thick. Serrated edges, beveled on one side of each
face. Horizontal, thin flaked piece, straight base, parallel side notches.
Made of tan to brown chert.
Priv. col., excellent quality, valued $30-45.

• Big Sandy mouse ear from Lewis co., TN. Blade 4 1/4 in. long,

1 3/4 in. wide, 1/4 in. thick. Serrated edges, beveled on one side of each
face, concave sides with wide concave base. Horizontal flaked, on blade
and base. Made of tan to brown chert.
Priv. col., excellent quality, value $50-65.

Blunt: 12,500-1,000 B.P. Paleo to Woodland

*Blunts are found throughout North America. Most blunts are
obviously made from broken points of all point types. Blunts are
believed to be hafted scrapers. Although there is some controversy;
there is reasonable evidence to suggest that blunts were also used for
hunting.*

◆ Blunt from Union co., IL. Point 1 1/8 in. long, 7/8 in. wide, 1/4 in.
thick. Very sharp, front edge beveled on one side. Straight base, Big
Sandy style base and stem. Made of a banded Cobden chert.

Grover Bohannon col., museum quality, rare, valued $25-35.

• Blunt from Hamilton co., IL. Blade 5 1/4 in. long, 2 in. wide, 1/2 in.
thick. Long, thin, sharp hafted blade. Stem is 1/3 the length, base
convex. Made of Mill Creek chert.
Priv. col., excellent quality, valued $45-60.

• Blunt from Hamilton co., IL. Point 3 1/8 in. long, 1 5/8 in. wide,
1/4 in. thick. Thin horizontal flakes, front edge beveled on both sides.
Straight base and stem. Made of Mill Creek chert.
Priv. col., excellent quality, valued $35-40.

• Blunt fom Alexander co., IL. Point 3 in. long, 1 1/3 in. wide, 1/2 in.
thick. Symmetrical, serrated, rounded tip, thinly serrated edges. Side
notched, concave Thebes type base. Evidence of hafting on point. Made
of white pebble chert.
Tim Rubbles col., excellent quality, valued $30-40.

• Blunt from Union co., IL. Point 2 1/8 in long, 1 7/8 in. wide, 1/4 in.

thick. Very round, wide, front edge beveled on one side. Straight base, Stillwell style base and stem. Made of a banded Cobden chert.
Tim Rubbles col., excellent quality, valued $25-30.

• Blunt from Humphreys co., TN. Point 2 7/8 in. long, 1 1/2 in. wide, 5/8 in. thick. Big Sandy type base, hafting marks. Typical rounded pony with stem, serrated on both sides.
Priv. col., average quality, valued $15-25.

• Blunt from Sevier co., TN. Point 3 1/8 in. long, 1 7/8 in. wide, 1/4 in. thick. Symmetrical, thin, sharp, front edge beveled and finely serrated on one side. Straight base and stem, hafting evidence. Made of a banded tan chert.
Priv. col., museum quality, valued $50-60.

• Blunt from Marion co., TN. Popint 2 1/2 in. long, 1 1/3 in. wide, 5/8 in. thick. Horizontally flaked, Big Sandy type base, deep side notches. Short stem with hafting marks. Made of Dover chert.
Grover Bohannon col., museum quality, valued $35-45.

• Blunt from Union co., IL. Point 3 1/8 in. long, 7/8 in. wide, 1/2 in. thick. Very sharp, front edge beveled on one side. Narrow, thick, though finely horizontally flaked. Straight base, Big Sandy style base and stem. Made of a banded Cobden chert.
Priv. col., excellent quality, rare, valued $55-75.

Bolen Beveled: 10,000-7,000 B.P. Early Archaic

Bolen Beveled are found east of the Mississippi. The point is small to medium in size, serrated on one side of each face. Some classify this point type generally as an E notch. The E-notch was very prominent in earlier Bolen Beveled pieces, and refers to a particular style of side notching. The base is generally uniform on the sides and can be concave, convex, or straight.

◆ Bolen Beveled from central GA. Point 2 1/4 in. long, 7/8 in. wide, 3/8 in. thick. Beveling tends to be concave. Made of brown quartzite.

Priv. col., excellent quality, valued $85-140.

• Bolen Beveled from northern GA. Point 2 29/32 in. long, 1 1/8 in. wide, 3/8 in. thick. Made of milky quartz, few flaws. *Priv. col., museum quality, valued $175-250.*

♦ Bolen Beveled from Ohio co., IN. Point 2 3/8 in. long, 3/4 in. wide, 3/16 in. thick. Heat-treated tip, right hand beveled. Made of a glossy yellow chert.

Priv. col., excellent quality, valued $65-85.

• Bolen Beveled from FL. Point 2 5/8 in. long, 7/8 in. wide, 5/32 in. thick. Made of coral. *Priv. col., average quality, valued $50-75.*

• Bolen Beveled from Onslow co., NC. Point 3 1/16 in. long, 2 in. wide, 1/4 in. thick. Finely beveled and serrated on one side of each face, heat-treated. Deep side notches, parallel stem sides, convex base. Made of highly fractured yellow quartz. *Priv. col., excellent quality, valued $85-125.*

• Bolen Beveled from Onslow co., NC. Point 2 3/4 in. long, 2 in. wide, 3/8 in thick. Beveled on one side of each face, sharp, wide, serrations. Wide side notches, finely flaked concave base with parallel straight sides. Made of brownish quartzite. *Priv. col., excellent quality, valued $85-100.*

• Bolen Beveled from Onslow co., NC. Point 2 2/3 in. long, 1 1/32 in. wide, 3/8 in. thick. Thin, narrow, beveled on all four sides, shallow E notched on side. Base is wide and straight. Made of yellow quartz. *Priv. col., museum quality, valued $150-225.*

• Bolen Beveled from Newberry co., SC. Point 2 5/8 in. long, 1 in. wide, 3/16 in. thick. Heat-treated, narrow, right hand beveled, sharply serrated tip. Wide side notches, parallel sides, concave base. Made of gray yellow chert. *Grover Bohannon col., museum quality, valued $225-275.*

• Bolen Beveled from Newberry co., SC. Point 2 9/16 in. long,
1 5/8 in. wide, 1/4 in. thick. Heat-treated, highly serrated on one side of
each face, right hand beveled. Deep, narrow side notches, concave sides
and base. Made of tan yellow chert.
Grover Bohannon col., excellent quality, valued $150-200.

• Bolen Beveled from Wilcox co., AL. Point 3 1/4 in. long, 7/8 in.
wide, 1/2 in. thick. Thick, wide, steeply beveled concave sides.
Symmetrical though very narrow point, wide notches, concave base.
Made of brown pebble chert.
Priv. col., excellent quality, valued $65-85

• Bolen Beveled from Lamar co., AL. Point 2 7/8 in. long, 1 3/16 in.
wide, 3/8 in. thick. Triangular, symmetrical, weak shoulders over
shallow notches. Edges finely serrated and concave with very sharp tip.
Base is convex with upward reaching base tangs. Made of milky quartz.
Priv. col., museum quality, valued $225-285.

• Bolen Beveled from Dillon co., SC. Point 2 1/2 in. long, 1 1/4 in.
wide, 1/8 in. thick. Heat-treated, right hand beveled, thin, narrow,
symmetrically angular. Wide notches, thin straight base. Made of white
yellow chert.
Priv. col., excellent quality, valued $80-100.

• Bolen Beveled from Dillon co., SC. Point 3 1/32 in. long, 1 7/8 in.
wide, 1/4 in. thick. Good workmanship, beveled and serrated on one
side of each face. Rounded prominent shoulders, deep, wide notches,
thin convex base. Made of white yellow chert.
Priv. col., museum quality, valued $150-185.

• Bolen Beveled from Dillon co., SC. Point 2 1/2 in. long, 1 3/8 in.
wide, 3/8 in. thick. Beveled, concave edges, finely serrated. Wide side
notches, straight base. Made of white yellow chert.
Priv. col., excellent quality, valued $85-100.

• Bolen Beveled from Dawson, GA. Point 2 2/3 in. long, 1 in. wide,
3/8 in. thick. Steeply beveled on one side of each face. Wide side
notches and parallel sided concave base. Made of gray chert.
Priv. col., museum quality, valued $125-150.

• Bolen Beveled from Adams co., IN. Point 2 1/8 in. long, 1 in.
wide, 3/16 in. thick. Heat-treated, beveled on all four sides, sharply
serrated concave edges. Shallow, wide side notches, straight base.

Made of white green speckled chert.
Priv. col., excellent quality, valued $70-85.

• Bolen Beveled from Adams co., IN. Point 3 in. long, 1 1/4 in. wide,
1/8 in. thick. Heat-treated, beveled and serrated on one side of each
face. Deep, narrow side notches, parallel straight sided concave base.
Made of white green speckled chert.
Priv. col, museum quality, valued $150-200.

• Bolen Beveled from Adams co., IN. Point 2 1/16 in. long, 7/8 in.
wide, 3/16 in. thick. Steep beveling, thin edge serrations, concave sides.
Good quality workmanship, horizontal flaked, pointed tip, wide, deep
side notches, concave base. Made of white green speckled chert.
Priv. col., museum quality, valued $85-100.

• Bolen Beveled from Ben Hill co., GA. Point 2 1/32 in. long,
1 1/8 in. wide, 1/4 in. thick. Crude workmanship, beveled on one side
of each face. Shallow side notches, thin, straight base. Made of grainy
quartzite.
Priv. col., average quality, valued $45-50.

• Bolen Beveled from Ben Hill co., GA. Point 2 5/8 in. long, 1 1/3 in.
wide, 3/16 in. thick. Sharp pointed tip, beveled on one side of each face.
Thinly flaked convex base. Made of grainy quartzite.
Priv. col, average quality, valued $50-60.

Bradley Spike: 4,000-1,500 B.P. Woodland

*Bradley Spikes are found in the geographical region where
the Ohio meets the Mississippi, and throughout the Southeast. It is a
narrowed, tapered point, small to medium in size. The shoulders are
tapered and the stem is contracting. Base can be, straight, concave,
fluted, snapped, or convex.*

◆ Bradley Spike from western TN. Point 2 5/8 in. long, 5/8 in. wide,
3/32 in. thick. Made of Dover chert.

Priv. col., museum quality, valued $25-35.

- Bradley Spike from Hamilton co., TN. Point 2 1/8 in. long, 5/8 in. wide, 5/32 in. thick. Thin tapered point. Made of Dover chert.
Priv. col., museum quality, valued $25-35.

- Bradley Spike from Alexander co., IL. Point 1 5/8 in. long, 3/8 in. wide, 3/32 in. thick. Narrow, thin, serrated edge, deeply contracting stem. Made of unidentified black flint.
Priv. col., museum quality, valued $25-35.

- Bradley Spike from Maury, TN. Point 3 3/8 in. long, 1 1/4 in. wide, 1/4 in. thick. Long, thin, beveled, random flaked. Thinned, snapped base, parallel straight shoulder. Made of brown multi-toned chert.
Grover Bohannon col., museum quality, valued $35-40.

- Bradley Spike from Hamilton co., TN. Point 2 5/8 in. long, 7/8 in. wide, 5/32 in. thick. Long angular, slightly left hand beveled point. Unusually finely serrated with sharp pointed tip. Made of Dover chert.
Priv. col., museum quality, valued $25-35.

- Bradley Spike from Oldham co., KY. Point 2 1/3 in. long, 5/8 in. wide, 3/32 in. thick. Thin finely flaked piece, sharp serrated edges. Made of tan pebble chert.
Priv. col., excellent quality, valued $20-30.

- Bradley Spike from Cole co., TN. Point 1 1/8 in. long, 7/8 in. wide, 1/4 in. thick. Thick wide point, still sharply serrated. Fine long, thin flaked, beveled on all four sides. Made of dark heavy flint.
Priv. col., average quality, valued $5-15.

- Bradley Spike from Sevier co., TN. Point 2 5/8 in. long, 1/2 in. wide, 3/32 in. thick. Thin, narrow, elongated point finely and sharply serrated. Extremely sharp, pointed tip. Made of dark gray slate.
Grover Bohannon col., excellent quality, valued $10-15.

- Bradley Spike from Sevier co., TN. Point 2 5/8 in. long, 1/2 in. wide, 3/16 in. thick. Narrow, thin, steeply beveled on all four sides, serrated edges. Very thin, sharply pointed tip. Virtually no shoulders, random flaked, unique rounded base. Made of dark gray slate.
Priv. col., museum quality, valued $25-35.

- Bradley Spike from Sevier co., TN. Point 2 7/16 in. long, 1 1/8 in. wide, 1/4 in. thick. Angular, horizontal flaked, weak uneven shoulders, shaply serrated edges and pointed tip. Point beveled on all four sides, long, narrow stem, snap base. Made of gray slate.

Priv. col., museum quality, valued $30-35.

• Bradley Spike from Pickett co., TN. Point 2 7/8 in. long, 1 in. wide, 3/8 in. thick. Long angular, thick, left hand beveled point. Finely serrated, random with sharp pointed tip. Shoulders weak, stem 1/3 length of point, concave base. Made of oily gray chert. *Jim Smith col., museum quality, valued $35-45.*

• Bradley Spike from Pickett co., TN. Point 3 1/8 in. long, 1 3/16 in. wide, 3/16 in. thick. Thin finely serrated, right hand beveled. Horizontal flaked piece, sharply serrated thin tip. Weak shoulders with expanding convex base. Made of oily gray chert. *Jim Smith col., museum quality, valued $40-55.*

• Bradley Spike from Pickett co., TN. Point 1 7/8 in. long, 1/2 in. wide, 7/32 in. thick. Symmetrically, narrow, thin, serrated edges. Random flaked, beveled on one side of each face. Symmetrically tapered shoulders, contracting snap base. Made of oily gray chert. *Jim Smith col., museum quality, valued $25-35.*

• Bradley Spike from Cole co., TN. Point 2 3/32 in. long, 1 1/8 in. wide, 5/32 in. thick. Symmetrically triangular point, horizontal flaked, beveled on one side of each face. Sharp tip, minute sharp edge serrations. Heat-treated, weak shoulders with ground straight base. Made of white pebble chert. *Priv. col., museum quality, valued $30-40.*

• Bradley Spike from Cole co., TN. Point 2 1/8 in. long, 1 3/8 in. wide, 3/8 in. thick. Triangular, steeply left hand beveled, heat-treated. Rounded shoulders, finely serrated with sharp pointed tip, straight base. Made of white pebble chert. *Priv. col., museum quality, valued $35-45.*

• Bradley Spike from Owen co., KY. Point 2 1/2 in. long, 13/16 in. wide, 1/8 in. thick. Thin, good workmanship, finely random flaked piece, sharp serrated edges and tip. Tapered shoulders, rounded base. Made of creamy light brown chert. *Priv. col., museum quality, valued $45-55.*

• Bradley Spike from Owen co., KY. Point 1 1/8 in. long, 1/4 in. wide, 3/32 in. thick. Beveled on one side of each face. Narrow, thin. serrated edges, rounded thinned base. Made of creamy light brown chert. *Priv. col., museum quality, valued $25-35.*

• Bradley Spike from Graves co., KY. Point 2 5/8 in. long, 1 1/4 in.
wide, 1/8 in. thick. Symmetrical, good workmanship, thin, left hand
beveled. Flaking is thin and layered, weak shoulders, straight base.
Made of a local brick red chert.
Priv. col., museum quality, valued $35-40.

• Bradley Spike from Graves co., KY. Point 2 5/8 in. long, 1 in. wide,
1/4 in. thick. Long, symmetrically angular, beveled point, needle sharp
tip. Finely serrated edges, random flaked, tapered shoulders, convex
base. Made of local brick red chert.
Priv. col., museum quality, valued $45-55.

• Bradley Spike from Graves co., KY. Point 2 3/4 in. long, 1/2 in.
wide, 3/32 in. thick. Thin, long, and very narrow; finely horizontal
flaked, sharp serrated edges. Needle sharp tip, symmetrically tapered
shoulders, round base. Made of local brick red chert.
Priv. col., museum quality, valued $50-65.

• Bradley Spike from Iberville co., LA. Point 1 5/8 in. long, 5/8 in.
wide, 1/4 in. thick. Narrow, thick, serrated edge, symmetrical, point
lancelate. Random flaked, thinned concave base. Made of dull gray flint.
Priv. col., excellent quality, valued $30-35.

• Bradley Spike from Iberville co., LA. Point 3 1/8 in. long, 1 1/8 in.
wide, 3/16 in. thick. Long, thin, steeply beveled on one side of each
face. Tapered shoulders, short snapped base. Made of dull gray flint.
Priv. col., museum quality, valued $45-50.

• Bradley Spike from Hamilton co., TN. Point 2 3/8 in. long,
1 1/16 in. wide, 1/2 in. thick. Thick, triangular, beveled on one side of
each face. Horizontal flaked, finely serrated with sharp, thin tip. Made
of multi-toned brown chert.
Grover Bohannon col., excellent quality, valued $25-35.

• Bradley Spike from Hamilton co., TN. Point 3 1/3 in. long, 7/8 in.
wide, 3/16 in. thick. Heat-treated, thin, narrow symmetrically angular
going from needle sharp tip to round, elogated base. Horizontal flaked,
sharp serrated edges, beveled on one side of each face. Made of a
multi-toned brown chert.
Priv. col., museum quality, valued $65-75.

• Bradley Spike from Grayson co., VA. Point 1 1/8 in. long, 1/4 in.
wide, 3/16 in. thick. Narrow, thin, serrated edges, slight tip break.

Random flaked with thinned convex base. Made of jasper.
Priv. col., average quality, rare, valued $25-35.

• Bradley Spike from Ohio co., WV. Point 2 in. long, 1 1/8 in. wide,
1/2 in. thick. Wide, thick, random flaked, rounded tip. Short parallel
barbs, straight base. Made of pinkish gray grained chert.
Priv. col., museum quality, valued $45-65.

• Bradley Spike from Ohio co., WV. Point 2 7/8 in. long, 7/8 in. wide,
1/8 in. thick. Long, narrow, thin, good workmanship, gradually beveled
on one side of each face. Heat-treated, sharp edges and tip point. Weak
yet horizontally parallel shoulders, straight base. Made of pinkish gray
grained chert.
Priv. col., museum quality, valued $65-75.

• Bradley Spike from Swain co., AL. Point 2 1/8 in. long, 3/4 in.
wide, 3/32 in. thick. Thin, narrow, beveled on all four sides, finely
random flaked, sharp serrated edges. Made of amber.
Priv. col., museum quality, rare, valued $85-100.

• Bradley Spike from Swain co., AL. Blade 3 5/8 in. long, 1 1/8 in.
wide, 1/16 in. thick. Narrow, paper thin, serrated edges, two worn holes
in point parallel to short barbed shoulders. Good workmanship, random
flaked, beveled on all four edges. Expanding stem with wide convex
basde. Made of amber.
Priv. col., museum quality, rare, valued $115-135.

• Bradley Spike from Catawba co., NC. Point 2 2/3 in. long, 1 1/8 in.
wide, 1/4 in. thick. Symmetrical, weak shouldered point. Beveled on
one side of each face, sharp point, minute edge serrating. The base and
stem are convex and flaked. Made of tan to golden brown streaked chert.
Priv. col., museum quality, valued $45-50.

• Bradley Spike from Catawba co., NC. Point 2 5/8 in. long,
1 1/16 in. wide, 3/16 in. thick. Symmetrical, weak shouldered, beveled
on one side of each face. Finely serrated, sharp, pointed and thinned tip.
The stem is straight and parallel, snapped base. Made of a local tan to
golden brown streaked chert.
Priv. col., museum quality, valued $50-65.

• Bradley Spike from Bracken co., KY. Point 1 1/3 in. long, 7/8 in.
wide, 3/16 in. thick. Thick, triangular, asymmetrical squared shoulders.
Good workmanship, horizontally flaked, sharp serrated edges. The point
tip and base are narrow, long, and rounded, the base much more than the

tip. Made of yellow to gray chert.
Priv. col., excellent quality, valued $30-35.

• Bradley Spike from Hart co., KY. Point 1 1/2 in. long, 7/16 in. wide,
3/32 in. thick. Narrow, thin, symmetrical, serrated edges, left hand
beveled. Wide, short stem, snapped base. Made of dark gray flint.
Priv. col., excellent quality, valued $20-30.

• Bradley Spike from Chester co., TN. Point 1 3/8 in. long, 1 1/8 in.
wide, 1/3 in. thick. Triangular, poor workmanship, random flaked,
several manufaturing gaps on edges. The stem is straight to an
expanding convex base. Made of gray blue chert.
Grover Bohannon col., average quality, valued $10-15.

• Bradley Spike from Chester co., TN. Point 3 1/16 in. long, 7/8 in.
wide, 1/2 in. thick. Long, narrow, quite thick, steeply beveled on one
side of each face. Finely serrated edges, sharp thinned tip. Expanding
stem, convex base. Made of gray blue chert.
Grover Bohannon col., museum quality, valued $40-45.

• Bradley Spike from Avery co., NC. Point 2 2/3 in. long, 3/4 in.
wide, 5/16 in. thick. Symmetrical, fine horizontal flaked, sharp serrated
edges. Weak rounded shoulders, concave base. Made of pink black-
spotted chert.
Priv. col., excellent quality, valued $35-40.

Buck Creek: 6,000-3,000 B.P. Mid to Late Archaic

Buck Creek is a large, broad stemmed, thin point or blade.
High quality flaking, many are needle sharp. Found throughout the
Midwest.

◆ Buck Creek from northern TN. Point 2 3/4 in. long, 1 1/4 in. wide,
3/8 in. thick. Made of a pinkish pebble chert.

Priv. col., museum quality, valued $50-75.

• Buck Creek blade from Paducah, KY. Blade 3 3/4 in. long, 1 3/4 in. wide, 1/4 in. thick. Blade is needle sharp. Made of a light to dark brown banded chert.
Priv. col., museum quality, valued $150-225.

• Buck Creek from Humphreys co., TN. Point 3 in. long, 1 3/4 in. wide, 3/8 in. thick. Made of Dover chert.
Priv. col., excellent quality, valued $75-100.

• Buck Creek from Sandusky co., IN. Blade 4 3/4 in. long, 2 1/4 in. wide, 1/4 in. thick. Symmetrical, good quality workmanship, long thin flaking. Edges minutely serrated and concave, deep corner notches, sharp tangs, convex base. Made of grainy lightweight pinkish white chert.
Priv. col., excellent quality, valued $160-185.

• Buck Creek from Mercer co., KY. Blade 4 1/8 in. long, 1 7/8 in. wide, 1/4 in. thick. Blade is needle sharp, edges uniformly serrated. Deep corner notches, short narrow stem, concave base. Made of tan white banded chert.
Priv. col., museum quality, valued $185-250.

• Buck Creek from Sandusky co., IN. Point 3 in. long, 1 3/16 in. wide, 1/4 in. thick. The tip is long and neddle sharp, edges sharply serrated. Deep corner notches, pointed tangs, short stem, wider convex base. Made of white pebble chert.
Priv. col., excellent quality, valued $80-110.

• Buck Creek from Bath co., KY. Point 2 3/16 in. long, 1 1/2 in. wide, 3/8 in. thick. Rounded, sharply serrated tip, convex serrated side. Wide, symmetrical, deep corner notched, long snapped tangs, concave base. Made of pinkish pebble chert.
Priv. col., museum quality, valued $65-85.

• Buck Creek from Bath co., KY. Blade 3 7/8 in. long, 1 3/4 in. wide, 1/8 in. thick. Blade is needle sharp, 1/2 in. long tip, entire blade very thin. High quality workmanship, long and thinly flaked from center to edges. Wide corner notches, uniform tangs, convex base. Made of light brown, near translucent quartz.
Priv. col., museum quality, rare, valued $650-775.

• Buck Creek from Greenbriar co., WV. Point 2 5/8 in. long, 1 3/4 in. wide, 1/4 in. thick. Point is uniform, triangular with sharp edges and tip. Corner notches are wide, tangs extend to a convex base. Made of oily

brown chert.
Priv. col., excellent quality, valued $125-150.

• Buck Creek from Osage co., MO. Blade 4 3/4 in. long, 1 1/2 in.
wide, 3/8 in. thick. Narrow, symmetrical, thin, and uniform. Excellent
workmanship, minute flaking throughout the blade. Deep narrow corner
notches, tangs long and ground, base convex. Made of pinkish white
chert.
Priv. col., museum quality, valued $750-875.

• Buck Creek blade from Osage co., MO. Blade 4 3/4 in. long,
1 3/4 in. wide, 1/4 in. thick. Good workmanship, quality thin flaking,
concave edges, tip is needle sharp. Shallow, sharply serrated on edges,
heat-treated. Deep, narrow, uniform corner notches, short tangs, straight
base. Made of pinkish white chert.
Priv. col., museum quality, valued $850-925.

• Buck Creek from Humphreys co., TN. Point 2 13/16 in. long,
1 2/3 in. wide, 1/4 in. thick. Heat-treated, good workmanship, serrated
by long thin flakes. Deep corner notches, long tangs to convex base.
Made of Dover chert.
Priv. col., excellent quality, valued $175-250.

• Buck Creek from Humphreys co., TN. Point 2 1/4 in. long, 1 1/16 in.
wide, 3/8 in. thick. Good workmanship, serrated by long, thin flakes.
Long tangs to base, grounded, straight base. Made of Dover chert.
Priv. col., excellent quality, valued $150-175.

• Buck Creek from Harrison co., MO. Blade 3 13/16 in. long,
1 1/2 in. wide, 1/4 in. thick. Tip 1/3 in. long, needle sharp, sharply
serrated concave side. Uneven tangs, angular corner notches, thinned
concave base. Made of light brown chert.
Priv. col., excellent quality, valued $150-200.

• Buck Creek from Humphreys co., TN. Blade 5 in. long, 2 1/16 in.
wide, 1/4 in. thick. Good workmanship, high quality flaking, minute
razor sharp serrated edges. Triangular blade, concave sides and base.
One of the largest Buck Creeks I have ever seen, although there are
numerous larger on record. Made of Dover chert.
Priv. col., museum quality, valued $1,250-1,500.

• Buck Creek from Henderson co., TN. Blade 4 1/2 in. long, 1 2/3 in.
wide, 3/8 in. thick. High quality workmanship throughout, concave
edges with 1/3 in. long, needle sharp, thin tip. Edges are finely serrated

and concave. Tangs are pointed and serrated reaching to the convex base. Made of pink pebble chert.
Priv. col., excellent quality, valued $500-675.

• Buck Creek blade from Henderson co., TN. Blade 3 23/32 in. long, 1 3/4 in. wide, 3/16 in. thick. Blade is symmetrical, well flaked, convex edges sharply serrated, tip is needle sharp. The tangs are long and ground, deep narrow corner notches, convex base. Made of pink pebble chert.
Priv. col., museum quality, valued $750-825.

• Buck Creek from Humphreys co., TN. Point 3 3/16 in. long, 1 3/4 in. wide, 3/16 in. thick. Thin, symmetrical, serrated convex edges. Ground short tangs, wide shallow corner notches, convex base. Made of Dover chert.
Priv. col., excellent quality, valued $85-100.

• Buck Creek from Humphreys co.,TN. Point 2 5/8 in. long, 1 1/2 in. wide, 1/8 in. thick. Extremely thin, symmetrical 1/8 in. long needle sharp tip. Deep corner notches, uneven tangs, concave base Made of lightweight white chert.
Priv. col., excellent quality, valued $75-125.

• Buck Creek from McCraken co., KY. Blade 4 1/3 in. long, 1 2/3 in. wide, 1/4 in. thick. Tip is 1/4 in. long, finely serrated, and needle sharp. The edges are highly serrated and concave. Long pointed tangs, deep corner notches, straight base Made of oily gray banded chert.
Priv. col., museum quality, valued $500-625.

• Buck Creek from McCraken co., KY. Point 3 1/32 in. long, 1 1/4 in. wide, 3/8 in. thick. Triangular, convex sides, highly serrated, sharp tip. Deep corner notches, short tangs, straight base. Made of oily gray banded chert.
Priv. col., excellent quality, valued $175-230.

• Buck Creek from Bracken co., KY. Point 2 1/8 in. long, 1 in. wide, 3/8 in. thick. Narrow, symmetrical point, concave edges, sharply serrated. Sharp, broad tip, deep corner notches, straight base. Made of pinkish pebble chert.
Priv. col., museum quality, valued $85-125.

• Buck Creek blade from Bracken co., KY. Blade 3 23/32 in. long, 1 1/4 in. wide, 1/4 in. thick. Thick, narrow, finely serrated edges and tip. Blade tip is needle sharp, deep corner notches, short tangs, convex

base. Made of brown pebble chert.
Priv. col., museum quality, valued $150-225.

• Buck Creek from Fulton co., KY. Point 3 1/8 in. long, 1 9/16 in. wide, 3/8 in. thick. Symmetrical, yet crudely worked, random flaked, deep corner notches, straight base. Made of quartzite.
Priv. col., average quality, valued $55-70.

• Buck Creek from Powell co., KY. Point 2 3/8 in. long, 7/8 in. wide, 3/8 in. thick. Symmetrical, narrow, finely serrated concave edges. Sharp, 1/8 in. long tip, deep corner notches, long tangs, short stem, convex base. Made of gray pebble chert.
Priv. col., excellent quality, valued $65-85.

• Buck Creek from Powell co., KY. Blade 4 3/32 in. long, 1 1/3 in. wide, 1/4 in. thick. Symmetrical, narrow, finely serrated concave edges. The tip is needle sharp, deep, wide, corner notches, short tangs, long expanding stem, convex base. Made of gray pebble chert.
Priv. col., excellent quality, valued $185-250.

• Buck Creek from Powell co., KY. Blade 4 1/8 in. long, 1 3/16 in. wide, 3/8 in. thick. Symmetrical, thin, narrow concave edges, sharply serrated. Random flaked, deep corner notches, straight base. Made of tan to gray chert.
Priv. col., excellent quality, valued $255-300.

• Buck Creek from Boyle co., KY. Point 2 7/8 in. long, 1 1/16 in. wide, 1/4 in. thick. Narrow, symmetrical, minutely serrated concave edges. Sharp, thin tip, deep corner notches, convex base. Made of silver gray flint.
Priv. col., excellent quality, valued $85-125.

• Buck Creek from Boyle co., KY. Blade 3 3/4 in. long, 1 1/32 in. wide, 1/4 in. thick. Thick, symmetrical, triangular, finely serrated edges and tip. Sharp tip, deep corner notches, long pointed tangs, concave base. Made of silver gray flint.
Priv. col., excellent quality, valued $150-200.

• Buck Creek from Meade co., KY. Point 2 1/8 in. long, 11/16 in. wide, 1/4 in. thick. Symmetrical, good workmanship, random flaked, sharp serrated concave edges. Deep corner notches, concave base. Made of tan yellow chert.
Priv. col., excellent quality, valued $65-80.

Bulverde: 5,000-800 B.P. Mid-Archaic to Woodland

A medium sized point with barbed shoulders and a long rectangular stem. Predominantly a medium sized midwestern point. Edges may be serrated, beveled on one side of each face. The stem may be fluted. The base can be straight, concave, or convex.

◆ Bulverde from southeastern MO. 2 7/16 in. long, 1 1/4 in. wide, 3/8 in. thick. Made of Dover chert.

Priv. col., excellent quality, valued $15-25.

• Bulverde from Davies co., KY. Point 2 1/4 in. long, 1 in. wide, 7/32 in. thick. Random flaked, beveled on one side of each edge, poor workmanship. Made of quartzite.
Priv. col., average quality, valued $8-15.

• Bulverde from Jackson co., KY. Point 3 in. long, 1 in. wide, 5/32 in. thick. Wide rectangular stem, beveled on one side of each face. Made of translucent quartz.
Priv. col., museum quality, valued $25-40.

• Bulverde from northern KY. Point 3 in. long, 1 in. wide, 5/32 in. thick. Made of translucent quartz.
Priv. col., museum quality, valued $25-40.

• Bulverde from Davies co., KY. Point 1 9/16 in. long, 1 1/3 in. wide, 7/32 in. thick. Barbed shoulders, wide straight base. Made of quartzite.
Priv. col., excellent quality, valued $20-30.

• Bulverde from Harrison co., KY. Point 3 1/16 in. long, 1 1/2 in. wide, 1/4 in. thick. Triangular, parallel barbed shoulders, beveled on one side of each face. Sharp tip, straight base and stem. Made of tan pebble chert.

Priv. col., museum quality, valued $25-40.

• Bulverde from Harrison co., KY. Point 2 3/8 in. long, 1 1/2 in. wide, 1/3 in. thick. Wide, thick, weak shoulders, long stem. One side of each face beveled, several edge nicks. Corner notched, sloping tangs, concave base. Made of dull gray chert.
Priv. col., average quality, valued $15-20.

• Bulverde from Dickins co., TX. Point 2 in. long, 1 in. wide, 1/3 in. thick. Stem as long as point, thick, crudely beveled on one side of each face. Short parallel tangs, straight parallel stem, concave base. Made of grainy pink chert.
Priv. col., museum quality, valued $25-40.

• Bulverde from Dickins co., TX. Point 2 5/8 in. long, 1 in. wide, 1/4 in. thick. Narrow, barbed point, long serrated stem, even barbed shoulders. Beveled on one side of each face, concave base. Made of gray chert.
Priv. col., museum quality, valued $35-50.

• Bulverde from Reagan co., TX. Point 2 1/2 in. long, 1 7/8 in. wide, 1/2 in. thick. Very triangular thick point, beveled on one side of each face. Angular side notches, serrated straight stem, concave base. Made of milky quartz.
Priv. col., museum quality, valued $50-60.

• Bulverde from Lubbock co., TX. Point 2 7/16 in. long, 1 3/16 in. wide, 1/2 in. thick. Serrated tip and edges, left hand beveled. Weak, tapered shoulders, serrated stem, convex base. Made of gray flint.
Juan Samudio col., museum quality, valued $35-45.

• Bulverde from Lubbock co., TX. Point 3 in. long, 2 in. wide, 11/32 in. thick. Long, wide, thick, triangular point, sharp unserrated edges. Wide stem, straight base. Made of gray flint.
Juan Samudio col., museum quality, valued $35-40.

• Bulverde from Kimble co., TX. Point 2 3/4 in. long, 1 2/3 in. wide, 1/4 in. thick. Triangular, beveled on one side of each face. Straight wide stem, straight base. Made of quartzite.
Priv. col., excellent quality, valued $20-25.

• Bulverde from Kimble co., TX. Point 2 1/8 in. long, 1 1/2 in. wide, 11/32 in. thick. Triangular, beveled on one side of each face. Slight tip

break, straight wide stem, convex base. Made of quartzite.
Priv. col., average quality, valued $15-20.

• Bulverde from Adair co., KY. Point 3 1/32 in. long, 2 1/16 in. wide,
5/8 in. thick. Sharp tip, parallel barbed shoulders, beveled on one side
of each face, sharply serrated. Heat-treated point, straight stem, concave
base. Made of white pebble chert.
Priv. col., museum quality, valued $45-50.

• Bulverde from Kimble co., TX. Point 2 3/4 in. long, 2 in. wide,
1/3 in. thick. Beveled on one side of each face, symmetrical, finely
serrated edges. Straight wide stem, convex base. Made of tan to brown
chert.
Priv. col., excellent quality, valued $20-25.

• Bulverde from Dyer co., TN. Point 2 in. long, 1 2/3 in. wide,
13/32 in. thick. Triangular, thick, tip break, straight wide stem, convex
base. Made of gray chert.

• Bulverde from Henry co., KY. Point 2 11/32 in. long, 1 5/8 in. wide,
1/4 in. thick. Sharp serrated tip, long barbed shoulders, beveled on one
side of each face, sharply serrated. Heat-treated point, straight stem,
concave base. Made of white-tan pebble chert.
Priv. col., excellent quality, valued $35-45.

• Bulverde from Kimble co., TX. Point 2 3/4 in. long, 1 2/3 in. wide,
1/4 in. thick. Triangular, beveled on one side of each face. Straight wide
stem, straight base. Made of quartzite.
Priv. col., excellent quality, valued $20-25.

• Bulverde from Kimble co., TX. Point 2 1/8 in. long, 1 1/2 in. wide,
11/32 in. thick. Triangular, beveled on one side of each face. Slight tip
break, straight wide stem, convex base. Made of quartzite.
Priv. col., average quality, valued $15-20.

• Bulverde from Adair co., KY. Point 3 1/32 in. long, 2 1/16 in. wide,
5/8 in. thick. Sharp tip, parallel barbed shoulders, beveled on one side
of each face, sharply serrated. Heat-treated point, straight stem, concave
base. Made of white pebble chert.
Priv. col., museum quality, valued $45-50.

• Bulverde from Madison co., TX. Point 2 1/2 in. long, 1 3/4 in. wide, 1/4 in. thick. Triangular, symmetrical, beveled on one side of each face, sharply serrated. Straight wide stem, concave base. Made of dull gray chert.
Priv. col., excellent quality, valued $20-25.

• Bulverde from Kimble co., TX. Point 2 1/8 in. long, 1 1/2 in. wide, 1/2 in. thick. Triangular, beveled on one side of each face. Straight wide stem, convex base. Made of quartzite.
Priv. col., average quality, valued $15-20.

• Bulverde from Madison co., TX. Point 2 17/32 in. long, 2 1/4 in. wide, 1/2 in. thick. Sharp tip, parallel tanged shoulders, beveled on one side of each face, sharply serrated. Heat-treated point, straight stem, concave base. Made of gray chert.
Priv. col., museum quality, valued $35-40.

• Bulverde from Madison co., TX. Point 2 1/4 in. long, 1 1/2 in. wide, 1/4 in. thick. Thin, symmetrical, beveled on one side of each face. Straight narrow stem, concave base. Made of gray chert.
Priv. col., excellent quality, valued $30-35.

CHAPTER 3
CACHE RIVER-CYPRESS CREEK

Cache River: 8,000-5,000 B.P. Mid to Early Archaic

Small to medium point, slightly concave base. Points are fairly thin, triangular, and side notched. Edges are generally convex and serrated, some are beveled on one side of each face. Base sides parallel, base concave or straight.

◆ Cache River point from Cache River, AR. Point 2 3/4 in. long, 1 3/8 in. wide, 3/8 in. thick. Made of brown pebble chert.

Priv. col., excellent quality, valued $35-50.

◆ Cache River point from Union co., IL. Point 3 in. long, 1 7/16 in. wide, 3/32 in. thick. Very thin serrated blade. Made of Cobden chert.

Les Grubbe col., museum quality, valued $100-125.

• Cache River point from Cache River, AR. Point 2 1/4 in. long, 1in.wide, 3/16 in. thick. Made of fine oily tan chert.
Priv. col., excellent quality, valued $55-80.

• Cache River from southeastern MO. Point 2 5/16 in. long, 7/8 in. wide, 3/16 in. thick. Made of pebble chert.
Priv. col., average quality, valued $15-20.

• Cache River from Cache River, AR. Point 2 1/4 in. long, 1 1/8 in. wide, 3/8 in. thick. Sharply and finely serrated point. Made of tan pebble chert.
Priv. col., excellent quality, valued $30-45.

• Cache River from Union co., IL. Blade 3 3/8 in. long, 1 9/16 in. wide, 1/8 in. thick. Very thin, finely serrated blade, unique workmanship. Made of Cobden chert.
Priv. col., museum quality, valued $100-125.

• Cache River from Cache River, AR. Point 2 3/4 in. long, 1 2/3 in. wide, 5/16 in. thick. Finely serrated point, distinct concave base, with deep side notches. Made of tan pebble chert.
Priv. col., museum quality, valued $75-90.

• Cache River from Sikeston, MO. Point 2 3/16 in. long, 3/4 in. wide, 3/8 in. thick. Symmetrical serrated point with uniform side notches, slightly concave base. Made of pink pebble chert.
Priv. col., excellent quality, valued $55-70.

• Cache River from Jackson co., IL. Point 1 3/4 in. long, 7/8 in. wide, 3/8 in. thick. Finely serrated, concave base, shallow side notches. Made of marbled brown to tan pebble chert.
Priv. col., excellent quality, valued $45-60.

• Cache River from Union co., IL. Blade 3 5/16 in. long, 1 11/16 in. wide, 1/4 in. thick. Very thin serrated blade, concave base, flowing base tangs, deeply side notched. Made of Kaolin chert.
Tim Rubbles col., museum quality, rare, valued $180-225.

• Cache River from Jackson co., IL. Point 2 1/8 in. long, 1 in. wide, 1/4 in. thick. Classical design. Made of Mill Creek chert.
Priv. col., excellent quality, valued $45-70.

• Cache River from St. Louis co., MO. Blade 3 5/16 in. long, 1 5/8 in.

wide, 5/16 in. thick. Thin deeply concave base with deep side notches.
Sharply serrated and heat treated. Made of Mill Creek chert.
Priv. col., excellent quality, valued $45-60.

• Cache River point from Cache River, AR. Point 2 3/8 in. long,
1 1/8 in. wide, 1/4 in. thick. Deeply side notched, finely serrated,
concave base. Slight tip break. Made of brown pebble chert.
Jim Smith col., excellent quality, valued $25-30.

• Cache River from Caldwell co., MO. Point 2 1/2 in. long, 1 1/8 in.
wide, 1/4 in. thick. Sharply serrated edges, side corner notches. Sharp
tip, parallel base sides, concave base. Made of white pebble chert.
Priv. col., excellent quality, valued $35-40.

• Cache River from New Madrid co., MO. Point 3 1/8 in. long,
1 3/8 in. wide, 1/4 in. thick. Sharply and finely serrated tip and edges.
Deep side notches, uniform straight-sided lower stem, concave base.
Made of tan streaked pebble chert.
Priv. col., excellent quality, valued $30-45.

• Cache River from New Madrid co., MO. Blade 3 in. long, 1 1/2 in.
wide, 1/3 in. thick. Thick, finely and sharply serrated edges, good
workmanship. Deep side notches, uniform straight base. Made of tan
streaked pebble chert.
Priv. col., museum quality, valued $60-75.

• Cache River from New Madrid co., MO. Point 2 13/16 in. long,
1 1/8 in. wide, 3/8 in. thick. Thin, symmetrical, fine serrated edges.
Deep, narrow side notches, uniform straight base. Made of white pebble
chert.
Priv. col., excellent quality, valued $45-50.

• Cache River from Howell co., MO. Point 3 1/4 in. long, 2 1/8 in.
wide, 3/8 in. thick. Thin, sharply and finely serrated point. Deep side
notches, parallel base sides, concave base. Made of tan to brown pebble
chert.
Priv. col., excellent quality, valued $40-45.

• Cache River from Johnson co., IL. Point 3 1/4 in. long, 1 1/2 in.
wide, 1/8 in. thick. Thin finely serrated edges, good workmanship.
Uniform straight base. Made of Mill Creek chert.
Priv. col., museum quality, valued $45-65.

Cahokia: 1,000-400 B.P. Mississippian

The Cahokia mounds are located in west central Illinois just east of the Mississippi. The complex has more than 140 mounds. Some associate Cahokia with the Caddo culture. Points are small to medium in size, very thin, triangular, and may have more than one notch per side. Many of these points are very finely serrated and sharp.

◆ Cahokia point from Johnson co., IL. Point 1 3/4 in. long, 3/4 in. wide, 5/32 in. thick. Exhibits both side notches and center base notch. Made of Mill Creek chert.

Les Grubbe col., average quality, valued $10-15.

◆ Cahokia prestige bird point from Cahokia, IL. Point 29/32 in. long, 21/32 in. wide below notching, 1/2 in. above notching, 3/32 in. thick. Exhibits both side notches and a center base notch. Such fine work with Mill Creek chert is extremely rare.

les Grubbe col., museum quality, rare, valued $150-200.

• Cahokia war point from Union co., IL. Point 1 1/2 in. long, 21/32 in. wide, 3/32 in. thick. Typical of Cahokia war points. Point is long, thin, sharply serrated on both edges. Made of Mill Creek chert. *Les Grubbe col., excellent quality, valued $45-65.*

◆ Cahokia from Alexander co., IL. Point 1/2 in. long, 1/4 in. wide, 1/8 in. thick. Made of quartzite.

Grover Bohannon col., average quality, valued $15-20.

◆ Cahokia from Cooper co., MO. Point 1 1/4 in. long, 7/16 in. wide, 3/16 in. thick. Very symmetrical point, even parallel side notches, base also notched. Finely serrated with sharp edges and tip. Made of white pebble chert.

Grover Bohannon col., museum quality, valued $50-80.

◆ Cahokia from Jackson co., IL. Point 1 1/4 in. long, 7/16 in. wide, 1/8 in. thick. Exceptional workmanship, very sharp, finely serrated, symmetrical point. Unique material part of an early 1900 burial find. Made of unflawed garnet.

Grover Bohannon col., museum quality, rare, valued $150-180.

• Cahokia from Brown co., IL. Point 2/3 in. long, 1/2 in. wide, 1/8 in. thick. Thin, symmetrical, wide deep serrations, deep side notches. Base wide, straight, and notched. Made of Mill Creek chert.
Priv. col., excellent quality, valued $35-40.

• Cahokia from Brown co., MO. Point 1 in. long, 1 1/16 in. wide, 3/16 in. thick. Thin, symmetrical point, even parallel side notches, base also notched. Heat treated, finely serrated, with sharp edges and tip. Made of white pebble chert.
Priv. col., museum quality, valued $50-60.

• Cahokia from Saline co., IL. Point 1 1/8 in. long, 1 5/16 in. wide, 1/8 in. thick. Thin, good workmanship, sharp, finely serrated, symmetrical point. Wide notched, straight parallel sided base. Made of

gray chert.
Priv. col., excellent quality, valued $40-50.

Calf Creek: 8,000-5,000 B.P. Early to Mid-Archaic

Calf Creek is medium to large in size point or blade. Thin with deep parallel notches. Good to excellent workmanship throughout this type. Edges are finely or sharply serrated. Very unique style.

• Calf Creek from Alexander co., IL. Point 2 1/8 in. long, 1 1/2 in. wide, 1/4 in. thick. Made of quartzite.
Priv. col., excellent quality, valued $850-1,000.

♦ Calf Creek from southwestern AR. Point 2 5/8 in. long, 1 27/32 in. wide, 5/32 in. thick. Made of pink quartz.

Priv. col., museum quality, valued $2,000-3,500.

• Calf Creek from Jackson co., IL. Blabe 4 1/8 in. long, 2 5/8 in. wide, 1/8 in. thick. Thin, symmetrical, sharply serrated tip and edges. Deep basal notches 1/3 length of blade, narrow stem, concave base. Made of Cobden Hornstone chert.
Grover Bohannon col., museum quality, rare, valued $2,600-3,000.

• Calf Creek from Jackson co., IL. Blade 5 in. long, 3 1/8 in. wide, 3/16 in. thick. Thin, high quality workmanship, random flaked, sharp edges. Deep symmetrical basal notches, stem narrow, base concave. Made of pinkish chert.
Priv. col., museum quality, valued $1,850-2,000.

• Calf Creek from Coshocton co., OH. Blabe 4 5/8 in. long, 2 7/8 in. wide, 3/16 in. thick. Thin, symmetrical, sharply serrated edges. Deep

basal notches, narrow stem, concave base. Made of Coshocton chert.
Priv. col., museum quality, rare, valued $2,000-2,500.

• Calf Creek from Schuyler co., IL. Blade 4 1/2 in. long, 3 in. wide,
1/4 in. thick. Thin, good workmanship, thinly flaked, sharply serrated
edges. Deep basal notches, narrow stem, concave base. Made of oily
gray chert.
Priv. col., museum quality, valued $1,500-2,000.

Catan: 4,000-300 B.P. Archaic to Mississippian to Historic

*Found throughout the Midwest. Small to medium sized point,
lanceolate (tear drop) shaped. Generally random flaked with rounded
base.*

◆ Catan from Stewart co., TN. Point 2 1/4 in. long, 1 5/8 in. wide,
1/4 in. thick. Heat treated, random flaked, fairly sharp with prominent
shoulder tangs. Made of light gray chert.

Grover Bohannon col., excellent quality, valued $8-15.

• Catan from Stewart co., TN. Point 1 3/4 in. long, 1 1/8 in. wide,
1/4 in. thick. Random flaked, sharp though unserrated with flaring
shoulder tangs. Made of tan pebble chert.
Grover Bohannon col., excellent quality, valued $8-15.

• Catan from Hamilton co., TN. Point 2 3/16 in. long, 1 3/8 in. wide,
1/4 in. thick. Random flaked, sharp edges with parallel shoulder tangs.
Made of Dover chert.
Priv. col., museum quality, valued $18-25.

• Catan from St. Clair co., IL. Point 2 in. long, 1 5/8 in. wide, 1/3 in.
thick. Heat treated, thick point, random flaked, crude workmanship with

prominent, uneven shoulder tangs. Made of Mill Creek chert.
Tim Rubbles col., average quality, valued $4-10.

• Catan from Cumberland co., TN. Point 2 5/8 in. long, 1 1/2 in. wide,
1/2 in. thick. Random flaked, sharp edges, wide round base. Made of
dark gray chert.
Priv. col., excellent quality, valued $10-15.

• Catan from St. Clair co., MO. Point 2 7/16 in. long, 1 3/8 in. wide,
1/2 in. thick. Angular, thick point, random flaked, good workmanship,
symmetrical round base. Made of lightweight pebble chert.
Priv. col., excellent quality, valued $15-20.

• Catan from Holt co., MO. Point 2 5/16 in. long, 1 5/8 in. wide,
1/3 in. thick. Triangular, random flaked, sharp, convex edges, straight
base. Made of white to tan chert.
Priv. col., museum quality, valued $20-25.

• Catan from Sangamon co., IL. Point 1 1/2 in. long, 1 3/8 in. wide,
1/2 in. thick. Heat treated, thick point, random flaked, good
workmanship, triangular, rounded base. Made of white pebble chert.
Priv. col., excellent quality, valued $10-15.

Citrus: 3,500-2,000 B.P. Late Archaic to Woodland

*A medium to large southeastern point or blade. Point or
blade is wide stemmed and basal notched. Very few intact Citrus
pieces are less than average-excellent quality.*

◆ Citrus from southeastern FL. Point 1 29/32 in. long, 1 3/8 in. wide,
5/32 in. thick. Made of coral.

Priv. col., excellent quality, valued $120-175.

• Citrus from south central GA. Point 3 in. long, 1 3/4 in. wide, 1/4 in. thick. Made of pebble chert.
Priv. col., average quality, valued $45-70.

• Citrus point from northeastern AL. Point 2 5/8 in. long, 1 3/4 in. wide, 1/4 in. thick. Very deep basal notches. Made of agate.
Priv. col., museum quality, rare, valued $300-450.

• Citrus from Baldwin co., GA. Blade 3 2/3 in. long, 1 3/4 in. wide, 1/4 in. thick. Thin, angular symmetrical blade, snapped base, very sharp edges. Made of white to pink grainy quartzite.
Grover Bohannon col., museum quality, valued $145-190.

• Citrus point from Hamilton co., KY. Point 2 7/8 in. long, 1 3/5 in. wide, 1/4 in. thick. Deep basal notches, sharply and finely serrated edges. Made of black flint.
Priv. col., museum quality, valued $200-250.

• Citrus from Elmore co., ID. Blade 4 1/2 in. long, 2 in. wide, 3/16 in. thick. Sharp, thin, convex edges, wide stemmed, tangs parallel with straight base. Deep basal notched, good workmanship. Made of greenish gray chert.
Priv. col, museum quality, valued $200-250.

• Citrus from Citrus co., FL. Blade 4 7/32 in. long, 1 7/8 in. wide, 1/8 in. thick. Very thin, high quality workmanship, sharp, minutely serrated edges. Shallow, uniform basal notches, snapped tangs, convex base. Made of pink white coral.
Priv. col., museum quality, rare, valued $250-325.

• Citrus from Butts co., GA. Point 3 1/4 in. long, 1 5/8 in. wide, 3/16 in. thick. Sharp edges, beveled on one side of each face. Deep basal notches, ground, straight parallel tangs and base. Made of yellow quartz.
Priv. col., excellent quality, valued $75-100.

• Citrus from Citrus co., FL. Blade 4 5/8 in. long, 2 1/4 in. wide, 1/4 in. thick. Triangular, sharp edges, good workmanship, very deep basal notches. Tangs are parallel to base and rounded, base straight. Made of quartzite.
Priv. col., average quality, valued $65-85.

• Citrus from Dixie co., FL. Blade 5 1/32 in. long, 2 7/8 in. wide,

3/16 in. thick. Blade is triangular, sharp convex edges, thinned pointed tip. Wide stem, deep basal notches, rounded tangs, convex base. Made of dense white chert.
Priv. col., excellent quality, valued $225-275.

• Citrus from Dixie co., FL. Point 2 19/32 in. long, 1 3/8 in. wide, 1/4 in. thick. Triangular, wide, serrated convex edges, slight tip break, several edge nicks. Wide stem, deep basal notches, rounded tangs, straight base. Made of dense white chert.
Priv. col., average quality, valued $60-75.

• Citrus from Lanier co., GA. Point 3 in. long, 2 in. wide, 1/4 in. thick. Symmetrical, wide, convex serrated edges, thin serrated, sharp tip. Deep basal notches, snapped tangs and parallel convex base. Made of grainy amber pebble chert.
Priv. col., excellent quality, valued $150-200.

• Citrus from Grayson co., VA. Point 2 7/8 in. long, 1 1/4 in. wide, 1/4 in. thick. Triangular, symmetrical, excellent workmanship, minutely serrated edges. Very deep basal notches, short snapped tangs, convex base. Made of highly fractured light brown quartz.
Priv. col., excellent quality, valued $200-250.

• Citrus from Grayson co., VA. Blade 5 1/4 in. long, 2 7/8 in. wide, 3/16 in. thick. Blade is wide, serrated convex edges, very thin. Thinly flaked and sharp tip. Wide stemmed, narrow tangs and basal notched, straight base. Made of brownish quartz.
Priv. col., museum quality, valued $375-450.

• Citrus from Levy co., FL. Point 1 3/4 in. long, 1 3/8 in. wide, 3/16 in. thick. Nearly as wide as long, wide serrated edges. Shallow basal notched, rounded tangs, parallel to a convex base. Made of pink to white chert.
Priv. col., excellent quality, valued $150-185.

• Citrus from Brooks co., GA. Blade 3 13/16 in. long, 1 5/8 in. wide, 1/4 in. thick. Symmetrical, sharp serrated edges and tip. Convex edges, shallow basal notches, beveled on one edge of each face. Short rounded ground tangs, straight base. Made of grainy white pebble chert.
Priv. col., average quality, valued $65-80.

• Citrus from Brooks co., GA. Point 2 3/8 in. long, 1 1/2 in. wide, 1/8 in. thick. Heat treated, sharp straight edges, good workmanship. Very deep basal notches, narrow stem, convex base. Made of gray chert.

Priv. col., excellent quality, valued $125-150.

• Citrus from Nart co., KY. Blade 4 3/4 in. long, 2 1/16 in. wide, 3/16 in. thick. Blade is wide, edges minutely serrated, convex edges, sharp tip. Wide stemmed and deeply basal notched, straight base. Made of brown chert.
Priv. col., excellent quality, valued $325-375.

• Citrus from Nart co., KY. Point 2 1/2 in. long, 1 3/16 in. wide, 5/16 in. thick. Thick, symmetrical, finely serrated edges. Deep basal notches, long rounded tangs parallel to convex base. Made of gray tan chert.
Priv. col., excellent quality, valued $140-185.

• Citrus from Wheeler co., GA. Point 3 1/32 in. long, 1 7/8 in. wide, 1/4 in. thick. Good workmanship, convex serrated edges, sharp, thin tip. Deep basal notches, narrow stem, straight base. Made of white pebble chert.
Priv. col., excellent quality, valued $85-120.

• Citrus from Wheeler co., GA. Blade 4 5/8 in. long, 2 3/4 in. wide, 1/4 in. thick. Serrated convex edges, long pointed tangs. Very deep basal notches, straight base. Made of white pebble chert.
Priv. col., excellent quality, valued $100-140.

• Citrus from Harris co., GA. Point 2 9/32 in. long, 1 2/3 in. wide, 1/4 in. thick. Symmetrical, heat treated, sharply serrated edges. Deep basal notches, long tangs parallel to straight base. Made of quartzite.
Priv. col., average quality, valued $60-75.

• Citrus from Laurens co., GA. Blade 4 1/3 in. long, 2 in. wide, 1/2 in. thick. Symmetrical, thick, beveled on one side of each face. Deep basal notches, narrow stem, short tangs, convex base. Made of gray pebble chert.
Priv. col., excellent quality, valued $350-450.

• Citrus point from Laurens co., GA. Point 2 7/8 in. long, 1 3/16 in. wide, 1/4 in. thick. Narrow, thick, good workmanship, sharp unserrated edges and tip. Very deep basal notches, wide stem, straight base. Made of gray pebble chert.
Priv. col., excellent quality, valued $175-200.

• Citrus from Echols co., GA. Blade 3 25/32 in. long, 1 2/3 in. wide,

1/4 in. thick. Symmetrical, heat treated, sharp serrated edges. Shallow basal notches, snapped tangs, straight base. Made of pink coral.
Priv. col., museum quality, rare, valued $300-375.

• Citrus from Echols co., GA. Point 3 3/16 in. long, 2 in. wide, 1/4 in. thick. Heat treated, sharp serrated convex edges, thinned tip. Shallow basal notches, long ground tangs, convex base. Made of brown pebble chert.
Priv. col., excellent quality, valued $250-300.

• Citrus from Lawrence co., KY. Blade 4 13/16 in. long, 2 1/8 in. wide, 5/32 in. thick. Symmetrical, serrated edges, beveled on one side of each face. Thin, narrow stem, long narrow basal notches. Piece from a local cache find. Tangs are thin and pointed, convex base. Made of tan chert.
Priv. col., museum quality, valued $420-475.

• Citrus from Lawrence co., KY. Blade 5 1/2 in. long, 2 1/4 in. wide, 1/4 in. thick. Part of a local cache find. Narrow, symmetrical, thin, narrow stem. Beveled on one side of each face, deep basal notches. Thin, long, deep basal notches, convex base. Made of Dover chert.
Priv. col., musem quality, valued $450-500.

• Citrus from Coosa co., AL. Point 2 3/8 in. long, 1 3/4 in. wide, 3/8 in. thick. Thick, slight tip break, deep basal notches. Stem is wide, short, parallel to straight base. Made of quartzite.
Priv. col., average quality, valued $35-50.

Clovis: 20,000-8,000 B.P. Early Paleo

The Clovis point is found throughout North America. It is concave based, fluted many times on both sides. Clovis points and blades may date back as far as 30,000 B.P. There is a great deal of variety in the point or blade shape as well as in the material used.

◆ Clovis blade from Hancock co., IL. Blade 3 3/4 in. long, 1 5/8 in. wide, 3/8 in. thick. Made of Mill Creek chert.

Tim Crawford col., excellent quality, valued $300-350.

• Clovis blade from Hardin co., IL. Blade 3 3/5 in. long, 1 7/8 in. wide, 5/8 in. thick. Deep yet fine fluting on both faces, very sharply serrated upper third. Made of Mill Creek chert.
Tim Rubbles col., excellent quality, valued $200-250.

♦ Clovis blade from Calhoun co., IL. Blade 4 3/8 in. long, 1 1/2 in. wide, 3/8 in. thick. Fluting goes 1/2 in. up the blade. If not for the nicks on the blade it would be exceptional. Made of unknown flint.

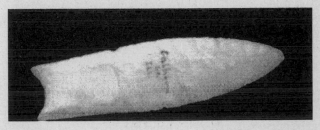

Tim Crawford col., excellent quality, valued $300-350.

♦ Clovis point from Schulyer co., IL. Point 2 1/8 in. long, 3/4 in. wide, 3/16 in. thick. Point is unfluted. Made of fire treated light gray chert.

Priv. col., museum quality, valued $100-175.

♦ Clovis from Union co., IL. Point 2 5/8 in. long, 1 7/8 in. wide, 5/8 in. thick. Fluted, good field patina. Made of Cobden chert.

Les Grubbe col., excellent quality, valued $200-250.

• Clovis from Calhoun co., IL. Blade 4 1/8 in. long, 1 7/16 in. wide, 5/16 in. thick. Heat treated, fluting fine, wide and shallow up 2/3 of the blade. Made of tan pebble chert.
Priv. col., excellent quality, valued $300-350.

• Clovis from St. Clair co., IL. Point 2 1/8 in. long, 7/8 in. wide, 3/16 in. thick. Point fluted, wide, sharp, and heat treated. Made of Mill Creek chert.
Priv. col., average quality, valued $80-125.

• Clovis from Union co., IL. Blade 4 5/8 in. long, 2 1/8 in. wide, 1/4 in. thick. Double fluted, heat treated, a few small blade nicks on one edge, very light in weight. Made of unidentified white chert.
Jim Smith col., average quality, valued $75-150.

• Clovis point from Johnson co., IL. Point 2 in. long, 7/8 in. wide, 1/4 in. thick. Heat treated, double fluted, deeply concave based. Made of Cobden chert.
Priv. col., museum quality, valued $250-300.

• Clovis from Johnson co., IL. Point 2 1/3 in. long, 1 1/8 in. wide, 1/4 in. thick. Double fluted, deep and high on point. Made of Kaolin chert.
Priv. col., museum quality, rare, valued $420-475.

• Clovis from Cooper co., TN. Blade 3 3/4 in. long, 1 5/8 in. wide, 5/8 in. thick. Thick, finely fluted on both faces, sharply serrated edges. Round serrated tip, beveled on all four edges. Concave base, sharp pointed base tangs. Made of brown banded chert.
Priv. col., excellent quality, valued $250-300.

• Clovis from Bledsoe co., TN. Blade 4 1/2 in. long, 1 15/16 in. wide, 1/4 in. thick. Thin, symmetrical, beveled and serrated on all four sides. Fine, wide, shallow fluting up entire blade. Widely serrated edges, shallow concave base. Made of marbled tan pebble chert.

Priv. col., excellent quality, valued $350-375.

• Clovis from Sevier co., TN. Point 3 1/8 in. long, 1 1/4 in. wide, 1/4 in. thick. Point symmetrical, fluted, narrow, beveled on one side of each face. Minutely serrated edges, concave base. Made of Dover chert. *Priv. col., museum quality, valued $300-400.*

• Clovis from Hardin co., TN. Blade 3 7/8 in. long, 1 1/2 in. wide, 3/8 in. thick. Deep concave base, fluted on both faces, very sharply serrated edges. Made of tan yellow chert. *Priv. col., excellent quality, valued $200-250.*

• Clovis from Grainger co., TN. Blade 4 7/8 in. long, 2 3/4 in. wide, 5/8 in. thick. Heat treated, thick, wide fluting on both sides, fine serrations, concave base. Made of tan to white pebble chert. *Priv. col., excellent quality, valued $300-350.*

• Clovis from Carroll co., IL. Point 2 3/8 in. long, 1 in. wide, 3/16 in. thick. Point fluted, symmetrical, sharply serrated, heat treated. Base is concave, tangs ground. Made of Mill Creek chert. *Jim Smith Col., excellent quality, valued $150-175.*

• Clovis from Carrol co., IL. Blade 3 27/32 in. long, 1 1/2 in. wide, 3/8 in. thick. Deep fine fluting on both faces, sharply serrated tip and edges. Symmetrical, shallow concave base. Made of Mill Creek chert. *Jim Smith col., excellent quality, valued $200-250.*

• Clovis from Ford co., IL. Blade 4 7/8 in. long, 1 7/8 in. wide, 1/2 in. thick. Heat treated, deep fluting on both sides, concave base, beveled on one side of each face. Made of multi-toned tan pebble chert. *Priv. col., excellent quality, valued $300-350.*

• Clovis from Hancock co., IL. Blade 4 1/8 in. long, 1 3/8 in. wide, 3/16 in. thick. Narrow fluted on one side, sharply serrated edges, heat treated. Round serrated tip, deep concave base, pointed tangs. Made of white pebble chert. *Priv. col., excellent quality, $180-240.*

• Clovis from Massac co., IL. Blade 3 13/16 in. long, 2 1/32 in. wide, 5/8 in. thick. Thick, wide, deeply fluted on both faces, sharply serrated. Concave base, rounded tangs. Made of gray chert. *Priv. col., excellent quality, valued $150-200.*

♦ Clovis from Union co., IL. Point 2 1/8 in. long, 3/4 in. wide, 3/8 in. thick. Concave base, fluted on both faces, heat treated. Made of brown chert.

Les Grubbe col., excellent quality, valued $150-200.

• Clovis from Massac co., IL. Blade 4 1/4 in. long, 1 7/8 in. wide, 7/16 in. thick. Wide, thick, deeply fluted on one face, finely serrated. Rounded tangs, deep concave base. Made of gray chert.
Priv. col., excellent quality, valued $250-300.

• Clovis from White co., IL. Point 2 5/8 in. long, 2 in. wide, 3/16 in. thick. Point shallow fluted on both faces, wide, sharply serrated pointed tip. Concave base, pointed tangs. Made of pinkish pebble chert.
Priv. col., excellent quality, valued $150-175.

• Clovis from White co., IL. Blade 4 3/4 in. long, 2 3/8 in. wide, 1/2 in. thick. Wide, thick, symmetrical, deep fine fluting on both faces, very sharply serrated edges and rounded tip. Concave base, long, rounded tangs. Made of Mill Creek chert.
Priv. col., excellent quality, valued $200-250.

♦ Clovis from Johnson co., IL. Point 2 3/8 in. long, 1 in. wide, 3/16 in. thick. Double fluted, symmetrical, sharply serrated, heat treated. Concave base, tangs ground. Made of brown chert.

Les Grubbe col., excellent quality, valued $150-175.

• Clovis from Brule co., SD. Blade 5 1/8 in. long, 1 11/16 in. wide, 1/4 in. thick. Narrow, symmetrical lengthwise, heat treated, fluted on

one face, finely serrated edges and tip. Rounded tangs, shallow concave base. Made of white speckled gray chert.
Priv. col., museum quality, valued $400-450.

• Clovis from Brule co., SD. Point 2 1/2 in. long, 1 1/8 in. wide, 5/16 in. thick. Point fluted on both sides, symmetrical, sharply serrated tip and edges. Point beveled on one side of each face. Serrated, long, pointed tangs, deeply concave. Made of oily gray chert.
Priv. col., excellent quality, valued $125-150.

Cobbs Triangular: 8,000-5,000 B.P. Early Archaic

Large blade, thin, with rounded and squared base. Found throughout the southeastern United States. One side of each face is generally beveled.

◆ Cobbs Triangular from GA. Blade 4 5/8 in. long, 1 11/16 in. wide, 5/32 in. thick. Made of a Georgia pebble chert.

Priv. col., average quality, valued $50-75.

• Cobbs Triangular from north TN. Blade 5 1/8 in. long, 1 3/4 in. wide, 3/8 in. thick. Concave beveled sides. Made of Dover chert.
Priv. col., museum quality, valued $275-400.

• Cobbs Triangular from Hamilton co., TN. Blade 4 3/8 in. long, 1 3/4 in. wide, 3/8 in. thick. Beveled edges, crudely serrated. Made of Dover chert.
Priv. col., museum quality, valued $325-400.

• Cobbs Triangular from Monroe co., TN. Blade 5 3/8 in. long, 1 3/4 in. wide, 5/8 in. thick. Thick blade, concave beveled edges, serrated round base. Made of Dover chert.
Grover Bohannon col., museum quality, valued $375-400.

• Cobbs Triangular from Hamilton co., TN. Blade 6 1/8 in. long,
2 1/16 in. wide, 3/8 in. thick. Long, angular, with beveled sides. Made
of Dover chert.
Priv. col., museum quality, valued $375-450.

• Cobbs Triangular from Atlanta, GA. Blade 4 1/8 in. long,
1 13/16 in. wide, 1/2 in. thick. Classic Cobbs design, steeply beveled,
with unusually sharp tip. Made of grainy pinkish pebble chert.
Priv. col., average quality, valued $60-85.

• Cobbs Triangular from Stewart co., TN. Blade 5 3/8 in. long,
1 1/4 in. wide, 3/8 in. thick. Concave beveled edges. Made of tan to
dark brown marbled chert.
Priv. col., excellent quality, valued $175-280.

• Cobbs Triangular from Hamilton co., TN. Blade 5 1/8 in. long,
1 1/4 in. wide, 3/8 in. thick. Beveled on one side of each face, thin,
narrow with ground classical base. Made of Dover chert.
Priv. col., museum quality, valued $325-440.

• Cobbs Triangular from Abberville co., SC. Blade 5 1/8 in. long,
2 1/2 in. wide, 1/2 in. thick. Symmetrical, steeply beveled on one side
of each face, serrated sharp tip. Widest point 1/3 up from the round base
of the blade. Made of oily gray chert.
Priv. col., excellent quality, valued $150-185.

• Cobbs Triangular from Horry co., SC. Blade 4 5/8 in. long, 2 1/4 in.
wide, 3/8 in. thick. Thin, beveled on one side of each face, serrated
edges. Tapered base edges, straight base. Made of oily gray chert.
Priv. col., excellent quality, valued $125-180.

• Cobbs Triangular from Grady co., GA. Blade 5 1/4 in. long,
2 1/4 in. wide, 5/8 in. thick. Thick, beveled on one side of each face,
sharply serrated to ground round base. Made of pink to white chert.
Priv. col., museum quality, valued $350-400.

• Cobbs Triangular from Grady co., GA. Blade 4 7/8 in. long,
1 7/8 in. wide, 1/4 in. thick. Thin, narrow, symmetrical, beveled on all
four edges. One-third of an inch long needle sharp tip. Straight ground
base. Made of local pink to white chert.
Priv. col., excellent quality, valued $160-185.

• Cobbs Triangular from Grady co., GA. Blade 5 in. long, 1 3/4 in.

wide, 5/8 in. thick. Narrow, thick, steeply beveled and serrated concave edges. Bottom 1/3 of blade ground rather than serrated, round base. Made of pink to white chert.
Priv. col., excellent quality, valued $225-300.

• Cobbs Triangular from Rabum co., GA. Blade 5 1/8 in. long, 1 1/2 in. wide, 1/4 in. thick. Thin, narrow, symmetrical, beveled on one side of each face. Serrated edges, thinned tip, ground straight base. Made of gray white speckled chert.
Priv. col., museum quality, valued $275-350.

Conejo: 4,000-3,000 B.P. Late Archaic

Found throughout the Midwest. Medium sized point, corner notched. Usually exhibits an expanding concave base, with tangs flaring in the base's direction.

♦ Conejo from Knox co., KY. Point 3/4 in long, 1 in. wide, 3/16 in. thick. Very detailed quality workmanship. Concave base with long pointed tangs, deep side notches. Made of a translucent light gray chert.

Grover Bohannon col., museum quality, rare, valued $50-75.

• Conejo from Saline co., IL. Point 1 1/4 in. long, 1 in. wide, 1/4 in. thick. Concave base with falling rounded tangs, deeply side notched, very sharp edges with prominent tip. Made of gray pebble chert.
Priv. col., museum quality, valued $35-45.

• Conejo from Wabash co., IN. Point 3/4 in. long, 1 1/32 in. wide, 1/8 in. thick. High quality workmanship, heat treated. Concave base with symmetrical rounded tangs, deep side notches. Made of brown pebble chert.
Priv. col., museum quality, valued $45-55.

• Conejo from Knox co., KY. Point 1 1/4 in. long, 1 in. wide, 3/16 in.

thick. Thin for a Conejo as well as narrow, very finely serrated edges.
Concave base with short rounded tangs, several small edge nicks, deep
side angle notches. Made of Dover chert.
Grover Bohannon col., excellent quality, rare, valued $50-65.

• Conejo from Lauden co., TN. Point 3/8 in. long, 1/2 in. wide,
3/32 in. thick. Detailed quality workmanship, deeper than usual
serrations. Concave base with long downward angling tangs, deep
symmetrical side notches. Made of brown Bullseye chert.
Grover Bohannon col., museum quality, rare, valued $70-95.

• Conejo from Knox co., KY. Point 1 1/8 in. long, 1 in. wide, 3/16 in.
thick. Concave base with long, pointed tangs, narrow side notches.
Made of tan pebble chert.
Priv. col., excellent quality, valued $35-55.

• Conejo from Humphreys co., TN. Point 1 1/4 in. long, 1 in. wide,
3/16 in. thick. Thin, beveled on one side of each face, very finely
serrated edges. Corner notched, concave base with rounded tangs. Made
of Dover chert.
Priv. col., excellent quality, valued $35-45.

• Conejo from Jackson co., IL. Point 1 3/8 in. long, 1 1/2 in. wide,
3/16 in. thick. Heat treated, thin, good workmanship, crudely beveled on
one side of each face, sharp edge serrations. Concave base, downward
angling tangs, deep corner notches. Made of Mill Creek chert.
Tim Rubbles col., museum quality, valued $50-65.

• Conejo from Hamilton co., IL. Point 1 1/4 in. long, 1 1/8 in. wide,
3/16 in. thick. Triangular, thin, beveled on one side of each face.
Concave base with parallel pointed tangs, corner notched. Made of Mill
Creek chert.
Tim Rubbles col., excellent quality, valued $45-55.

Coosa: 2,000-1,500 B.P. Woodland

     *Predominantly a southeastern point extending into the
Midwest. Small to medium point, usually serrated with short snapped
base. Rounded to horizontal shoulders, shallow side notched.*

◆ Coosa from Stewart co., TN. Point 1 3/8 in. long, 3/4 in. wide,
3/16 in. thick. Sharp serrated edges, snap base, finely sharpened tip.

Made of light gray chert.

Grover Bohannon col., excellent quality, valued $15-25.

• Coosa from Fort Lauderdale, FL. Point 1 7/8 in. long, 3/5 in. wide,
3/16 in. thick. Deep and sharply serrated edges, typical snap base.
Made of pinkish quartzite.
Priv. col., average quality, valued $8-15.

• Coosa from Ballard co., KY. Point 2 1/2 in. long, 7/8 in. wide,
1/8 in. thick. Snap base, shallow side notched. Made of tan chert.
Priv. col., excellent quality, valued $20-30.

• Coosa from Ballard co., KY. Point 1 7/8 in. long, 3/4 in. wide,
1/8 in. thick. Sharply serrated edges, snap base. Made of tan chert.
Priv. col., excellent quality, valued $15-25.

• Coosa from Fort Lauderdale, FL. Point 1 7/8 in. long, 31/32 in.
wide, 3/16 in. thick. Deep and sharply serrated edges, typical snap
base. Made of pinkish quartzite.
Priv. col., average quality, valued $8-15.

• Coosa from Wilkes co., GA. Point 1 5/32 in. long, 3/4 in. wide,
1/4 in. thick. Deep and widely serrated edges. Convex base, short
parallel shoulders. Made of quartzite.
Priv. col., excellent quality, valued $12-20.

• Coosa from Wilkes co., GA. Point 1 7/8 in. long, 1 1/4 in. wide,
3/16 in. thick. Sharp serrated edges, weak shouldes, snap base, thinly
sharpened point tip. Made of quartzite.
Priv. col., average quality, valued $10-15.

• Coosa from Wilkes co., GA. Point 1 5/8 in. long, 3/4 in. wide,
3/16 in. thick. Deep, wide, sharply serrated edges, heat treated. Weak
shoulders, short snap base. Made of pinkish chert.
Priv. col., excellent quality, valued $15-20.

• Coosa from Wilkes co., GA. Point 7/8 in. long, 11/16 in. wide,
3/16 in. thick. Good quality wokmanship, thin horizontal flaked,
sharply serrated edges. Heat treated, serrated needle tip with short

snapped base. Rounded shoulders, shallow side notched. Made of pinkish chert.
Priv. col., museum quality, rare, valued $45-60.

• Coosa from Levy co., FL. Point 1 1/8 in. long, 3/4 in. wide, 1/4 in. thick. Symmetrical, rounded shoulders, sharp serrated edges, snap base, finely sharpened point tip. Made of marbled gray chert.
Priv. col., excellent quality, valued $15-25.

• Coosa from Levy co., FL. Point 1 5/8 in. long, 11/16 in. wide, 5/16 in. thick. Thick, right hand beveled, deep, sharply serrated edges. Shallow side notches, parallel shoulders, snap base. Made of pinkish gray chert.
Priv. col., excellent quality, valued $12-18.

• Coosa from Caldwell co., LA. Point 2 in. long, 1 1/32 in. wide, 1/8 in. thick. Deep, wide, serrated edges, rounded tip. Shallow side notched, weak shoulder with short snapped base. Made of yellow white pebble chert.
Tim Rubbles col., excellent quality, valued $20-25.

• Coosa from Caldwell co., LA. Point 1 1/8 in. long, 3/4 in. wide, 3/16 in. thick. Sharp serrated edges, finely and thinly sharpened tip. Made of yellow white pebble chert.
Tim Rubbles col., excellent quality, valued $15-25.

• Coosa from Livingston co., LA. Point 1 7/8 in. long, 13/16 in. wide, 3/16 in. thick. Symmetrical, thin, deep, wide edge serrations. Side notches, horizontal barbed shoulders, thined base. Made of quartzite.
Priv. col., average quality, valued $8-15.

• Coosa from Calhoun co., WV. Point 1 3/32 in. long, 1 in. wide, 1/4 in. thick. Heat treated tip, serrated edges, left hand beveled. Rounded shoulder with short snapped base. Made of dense black flint.
Priv. col., excellent quality, valued $12-18.

• Coosa from Page co., VA. Point 1 3/8 in. long, 1 1/4 in. wide, 3/16 in. thick. Sharp serrated convex edges, fine, sharp tip. Rounded shoulders, thinned snap base. Made of light gray chert.
Priv. col., excellent quality, valued $15-20.

• Coosa from Page co., VA. Point 1 3/8 in. long, 2/3 in. wide, 1/8 in. thick. Thin, narrow, symmetrical, deep, sharp, edge serrations.

Shallow side notches, uneven shoulders, snap base. Made of light gray chert.
Priv. col., excellent quality, valued $15-20.

• Coosa from Union co., SC. Point 1 in. long, 13/16 in. wide, 3/8 in. thick. Thick, edges serrated, crude workmanship. Rounded uneven shoulders with short snapped base. Made of grainy amber chert.
Priv. col., average quality, valued $8-12.

• Coosa from Stewart co., TN. Point 1 1/8 in. long, 3/4 in. wide, 1/4 in. thick. Sharply serrated edges, symmetrical, finely sharpened tip. Shallow side notches, parallel barbs, convex base. Made of light gray chert.
Priv. col., excellent quality, valued $15-25.

• Coosa from Stokes co., NC. Point 1 5/8 in. long, 1 3/16 in. wide, 3/16 in. thick. Wide, symmetrical, deep and sharply serrated edges. Rounded shoulders, snap base. Made of quartzite.
Priv. col., average quality, valued $8-15.

• Coosa from Stokes co., NC. Point 1 1/3 in. long, 1 in. wide, 1/4 in. thick. Symmetrical, serrated edges and tip. Rounded shoulders with short snapped base. Made of quartzite.
Priv. col., average quality, valued $10-15.

• Coosa from Stokes co., NC. Point 2 3/8 in. long, 1 1/2 in. wide, 3/16 in. thick. Long, thin, sharply serrated edges, beveled on one side of each. Finely sharpened tip, weak shoulders, straight base. Made of lightweight, marbled gray white chert.
Priv. col., museum quality, valued $25-35.

• Coosa from Stokes co., NC. Point 1 7/8 in. long, 1 5/16 in. wide, 3/16 in. thick. Fine sharply serrated edges, good workmanship, right hand beveled. Shallow side notches, pointed horizontal shoulders, snap base. Made of lightweight marbled gray white chert.
Priv. col., museum quality, valued $25-30.

• Coosa from Stokes co., NC. Point 2 1/8 in. long, 1 1/4 in. wide, 1/4 in. thick. Long, symmetrical, finely serrated edges and tip. Horizontal shoulders, shallow side notched, straight base. Made of lightweight gray white marbled chert.
Priv. col., museum quality, valued $30-40.

• Coosa from Lamar co., AL. Point 2 3/8 in. long, 1 2/3 in. wide,

3/16 in. thick. Heat treated, long, thin and symmetrical. Sharp serrated edges, finely sharpened tip. Horizontal barbed shoulders, deep side notches, snap base. Made of white pebble chert.
Priv. col., excellent quality, valued $25-30.

• Coosa from Lamar co., AL. Point 1 7/8 in. long, 3/4 in. wide, 3/16 in. thick. Thin, narrow, symmetrical, deep and sharply serrated edges. Heat treated, horizontal barbed shoulder, typical shallow side notches, snap base. Made of white pebble chert.
Priv. col., excellent quality, valued $20-25.

Copena: 5,000-1,200 B.P. Mid-Archaic to Woodland

Copena is a medium to large point or blade. Copena types (there are several) are found throughout the Southeast and Midwest. Copena styles are identified by their recurved blade edges, random flaking, and concave bases. The Classic Clovis is generally found in burials. Many are thin with high quality primary and secondary flaking with only a slight concave base.

♦ Copena Classic blade from Livingston, KY. Blade 4 5/8 in. long, 1 5/8 in. wide, 3/16 in. thick. The blade was a recent field find at a mound base after a rain. The blade is very thin with symmetrical serrated edges. Made of an unidentified oily black chert with gray and brown streaks.

Tony Clinton col., museum quality, valued $1,850-2,300.

• Copena Classic from TN. Blade 3 5/8 in. long, 1 1/2 in. wide, 5/16 in. thick. Made of Dover chert.
Priv. col., average quality, valued $25-40.

◆ Copena point from Union co., IL. Point 3 1/4 in. long, 1 1/4 in. wide, 5/8 in. thick. Made of Mill Creek chert.

Les Grubbe col., excellent quality, valued $75-125.

◆ Copena Corner Tang from Lubbock, TX. Blade 3 7/8 in. long, 1 7/32 in. wide, 1/4 in. thick. Made of pink and white pebble chert.

Priv. col., excellent quality, valued $100-150.

◆ Copena Corner Tang from Stewart co., TN. Point 1 5/8 in. long, 3/4 in. wide, 1/8 in. thick. Exceptionally fine workmanship, long, thin flaking. Symmetrical and very sharp point. Made of beige pebble chert.

Grover Bohannon col., museum quality, rare, $175-250.

• Copena Triangular from Hardin co., TN. Point 2 3/4 in. long, 3/4 in. wide, 3/16 in. thick. Made of Dover chert.
Priv. col., excellent quality, valued $50-65.

• Copena Triangular from Pulaski co., KY. Point 1 7/8 in. long, 7/8 in. wide, 5/32 in. thick. Made of quartzite.
Priv. col., poor quality, valued $8-15.

• Copena Auriculate from Trousdale co., TN. Point 2 7/8 in. long,
1 1/4 in. wide, 1/8 in. thick. Good workmanship, long, thin, angular,
finely serrated concave edges. Symmetrical, sharp tip, concave base.
Made of grainy pink pebble chert.
Priv. col., excellent quality, $75-100.

• Copena Triangular from Trousdale co., TN. Blade 3 3/4 in. long,
1 1/2 in. wide, 3/16 in. thick. Good workmanship, thinly flaked, minute
edge serrations. Symmetrical blade, sharp tip, straight base. Made of
dense gray chert.
Priv. col., excellent quality, valued $60-75.

• Copena Auriculate from Pulaski co., KY. Point 3 7/8 in. long,
1 5/8 in. wide, 1/4 in. thick. Upper third of blade finely and sharply
serrated, wider serrations on bottom 2/3 of blade. Pointed base tangs,
deep auriculate base. Made of tan pebble chert.
Priv. col., excellent quality, valued $75-95.

• Copena Round Base from Sevier co., TN. Blade 3 7/8 in. long,
1 3/4 in. wide, 1/8 in. thick. Thin, symmetrical, good workmanship,
long, thin flaking. Wide, irregular serrated edges, very sharp pointed
tip. Thinned round base. Made of white pebble chert.
Priv. col., museum quality, $125-150.

• Copena Triangular from Sevier co., TN. Point 2 5/8 in. long,
1 1/32 in. wide, 3/16 in. thick. Minute, sharply serrated edges, slight tip
break. Parallel edges near symmetrically rounded base. Made of white
pebble chert.
Priv. col., museum quality, valued $75-95.

• Copena Triangular from Cape Giradeau co., MO. Blade 4 7/8 in.
long, 2 5/8 in. wide, 1/4 in. thick. Good workmanship, thin parallel
oblique flaked, sharp edges, tip, and base. Symmetrical in form,
slightly concave base. Made of black speckled white chert.
Priv. col., museum quality, valued $125-150.

• Copena Corner Tang from St. Charles co., MO. Blade 4 1/8 in. long,
2 3/4 in. wide, 1/8 in. thick. Fine workmanship, long, wide, thin, wide
flaking. Symmetrical, sharp edges, beveled tip. Made of beige brown
marbled chert.
Priv. col., museum quality, $165-225.

• Copena Triangular from St. Charles co., MO. Point 2 13/16 in. long,
1 1/4 in. wide, 3/16 in. thick. Symmetrical, sharply serrated edges and

tip. Random flaked, straight flaked base. Made of pinkish white pebble chert.
Priv. col., excellent quality, valued $60-75.

• Copena Triangular from Bibb co., AL. Point 3 7/8 in. long, 1 7/8 in. wide, 5/32 in. thick. Thinly flaked, sharp deep edge serrations, triangular tip. Wide straight base. Made of yellow white chert.
Priv. col., excellent quality, valued $80-125.

• Copena Triangular from Stewart co., TN. Blade 4 3/8 in. long, 2 1/2 in. wide, 3/16 in. thick. Exceptional workmanship, long, thin flaking, deep, narrow edge serrations. Symmetrical and very sharp tip, straight base. Made of Dover chert.
Priv. col., museum quality, $125-150.

• Copena Triangular from Hardin co., IL. Point 4 3/4 in. long, 2 3/4 in. wide, 5/16 in. thick. Good workmanship, symmetrical piece, fine edge serrations. Thinned straight, wide base. Made of Mill Creek chert.
Tim Rubbles col., excellent quality, valued $145-165.

• Copena Triangular from Johnson co., KY. Point 2 7/8 in. long, 1 3/8 in. wide, 5/32 in. thick. Crude workmanship, erratically random flaked, edges sporadically serrated. Slightly thinned concave base. Made of quartzite.
Priv. col., poor quality, valued $15-25.

Culbreath: 5,00-3,000 B.P. Late Archaic to Woodland

The Culbreath is endemic to the Gulf states. It is a medium to large point or blade. Tangs are rounded, blade is broad and basal notched. Edges convex, bases sometimes snapped.

• Culbreath from Sutton co., TX. Blade 4 3/8 in. long, 2 1/16 in. wide, tangs are rounded, blade is broad, convex side. Wide basal notches, wide stem, snap base. Made of gray chert.
Priv. col., average quality, valued $75-85.

♦ Culbreath point from FL. Point 2 1/8 in. long, 1 5/8 in. wide, 1/4 in. thick. Made of coral.

Priv. col., average quality, valued $45-60.

◆ Culbreath from Monroe co., TN. Point 7/16 in. long, 7/16 in. wide, 3/32 in. thick. Very symmetrical, heat treated, finely serrated. Made of quartz.

Grover Bohannon col., museum quality, valued $75-100.

• Culbreath from Crenshaw co., AL. Blade 4 1/2 in. long, 3 1/32 in. wide, 1/4 in. thick. Thin, wide, tangs are rounded, shorter than base, blade is broad and basal notched. Edges convex, base snapped. Made of sugar quartz.
Priv. col., excellent quality, valued $145-180.

• Culbreath point from Crenshaw co., AL. Point 2 7/8 in. long, 2 in. wide, 1/4 in. thick. Symmetrical, convex edges, triangular sharp tip. Basal notched, rounded tangs, straight base. Made of quartzite.
Priv. col., excellent quality, valued $45-60.

• Culbreath from Geneva co., AL. Point 3 7/16 in. long, 2 9/16 in. wide, 7/32 in. thick. Finely serrated convex edges, symmetrical. Deep, wide basal notches, snapped base, parallel tangs. Made of rose quartz.
Tim Rubbles col., museum quality, valued $85-100.

• Culbreath from Geneva co., AL. Blade 4 3/8 in. long, 3 in. wide, 3/8 in. thick. Good workmanship, sharply serrated, tangs are rounded, blade is broad, edges convex. Tangs reach to straight base. Made of near

translucent amber chert.
Tim Rubbles col., excellent quality, valued $75-100.

• Culbreath from Hillsborough co., FL. Point 3 1/8 in. long, 2 in.
wide, 1/4 in. thick. Sharp, unserrated convex edges, symmetrical, heat
treated. Short tangs, wide basal notches, snapped base. Made of grainy
white chert.
Priv. col., excellent quality, valued $65-80.

• Culbreath from Coosa co., AL. Point 2 7/16 in. long, 1 15/32 in.
wide, 3/32 in. thick. Thin, very symmetrical, heat treated, finely
serrated, convex edges, rounded tip. Deep basal notches, narrow stem,
straight base. Made of yellow tan chert.
Priv. col., excellent quality, valued $65-80.

• Culbreath from Sutton co., TX. Point 2 1/2 in. long, 1 7/8 in. wide,
1/4 in. thick. Symmetrical, convex edges, sharp tip and edges. Shallow,
wide basal notches, narrow stem, straight base. Made of gray chert.
Priv. col., excellent quality, valued $65-80.

• Culbreath from Cottle co., TX. Blade 4 7/16 in. long, 2 1/8 in. wide,
3/32 in. thick. Very thin, symmetrical, heat treated, finely serrated
convex edges, rounded tip. Narrow, deep basal notches, snap base.
Made of gray banded chert.
Juan Samudio col., museum quality, valued $175-200.

• Culbreath from Wilcox co., AL. Blade 5 in. long, 3 1/2 in. wide,
1/3 in. thick. Sharp edges, rounded tip, convex edges. Tangs are
rounded, blade is broad and basal notched, base snapped. Made of pink
white chert.
Priv. col., excellent quality, valued $250-350.

• Culbreath point from Levy, FL. Point 2 1/8 in. long, 1 5/8 in. wide,
1/4 in. thick. Convex serrated edges, serrated thinned tip. Snapped tang,
shallow, narrow basal notches, snapped base. Made of pink to
white coral.
Priv. col., excellent quality, valued $55-65.

• Culbreath from Somerville co., TX. Blade 5 1/16 in. long, 3 7/16 in.
wide, 5/32 in. thick. Very symmetrical, heat treated, finely serrated,
wide convex edges. Deep basal notches, long tangs parallel with straight
base. Made of tan to brown marbled chert.
Priv. col., museum quality, valued $275-300.

• Culbreath from Somerville co., TX. Blade 4 1/4 in. long, 2 1/3 in. wide, 1/4 in. thick. Blade is broad, edges convex, sharp edges and tip. Long tangs, deep basal notches, snapped base. Made of tan to brown marbled chert.
Priv. col., excellent quality, valued $150-200.

• Culbreath from Levy co., FL. Point 2 3/8 in. long, 1 5/8 in. wide, 3/16 in. thick. Symmetrical, good workmanship, convex edges, pointed tip. Shallow, wide basal notches, straight base. Made of coral.
Priv. col., excellent quality, valued $75-90.

• Culbreath from Monroe co., TN. Point 2 5/16 in. long, 1 11/16 in. wide, 5/32 in. thick. Symmetrical, heat treated, finely serrated convex edges. Triangular, deep basal notches, snapped tangs and base. Made of Dover chert.
Priv. col., museum quality, valued $75-100.

• Culbreath from Harrison co., TN. Blade 3 7/8 in. long, 2 1/3 in. wide, 1/4 in. thick. Tangs are rounded, blade is broad and basal notched, snapped base. Edges convex and finely serrated. Made of Dover chert.
Priv. col., excellent quality, valued $85-100.

• Culbreath from Livingston co., LA. Point 2 1/4 in. long, 1 11/16 in. wide, 1/4 in. thick. Broad, convex edges, rounded tip. Shallow basal notches, snapped tangs and base. Made of rose quartz.
Priv. col., museum quality, valued $145-160.

• Culbreath from Livingston co., LA. Point 1 9/16 in. long, 1 1/2 in. wide, 7/32 in. thick. Symmetrical, finely and sharply serrated, convex edges. Shallow basal notches, snapped parallel base and tangs. Made of rose quartz.
Priv. col., museum quality, valued $75-100.

• Culbreath from Caddo co., AL. Point 2 11/16 in. long, 1 7/16 in. wide, 3/16 in. thick. Very symmetrical, classic basal notches, finely serrated. Made of yellow quartz.
Priv. col., museum quality, valued $75-100.

• Culbreath point from Red River, LA. Point 2 5/8 in. long, 1 7/8 in. wide, 1/4 in. thick. Symmetrical, classic design. Made of quartzite.
Priv. col., average quality, valued $45-60.

• Culbreath from Red River co., LA. Point 3 1/16 in. long, 2 5/16 in.

wide, 1/8 in. thick. Very symmetrical, convex edges, finely serrated edges and tip. Deep symmetrical, rounded basal notches, short snapped tangs. Made of quartz.
Jim Smith col., museum quality, valued $75-100.

Cumberland: 15,000-8,000 B.P. Paleo

The Cumberland is a medium to large blade with faces fluted. The fluting travels nearly the entire length of the piece. Cumberland pieces demonstrate advanced flaking techniques. Be cautious: this is an infrequently found type, and there are numerous reproductions out there. However, when you find an authentic Cumberland you will have a very unique and quality piece.

♦ Cumberland from Hamilton co., TN. Point 2 1/8 in. long, 3/4 in. wide, 3/16 in. thick. Rare serrated form with smooth fluting. Made of Dover chert.

Tim Crawford col., museum quality, valued $450-600.

♦ Cumberland unfluted from Fulton co., IL. Point 3 5/16 in. long, 1 1/4 in. wide, 3/8 in. thick. Point is fire treated. Made of a fine pink chert.

Priv. col., museum quality, rare, valued $650-850.

• Cumberland from Smith co., TN. Blade 3 1/2 in. long, 3/4 in. wide, 3/16 in. thick. Classic design, upper half serrated. Made of Dover chert. *Priv. col., museum quality, rare, valued $800-1,000.*

◆ Cumberland from Smith co., TN. Point 2 1/2 in. long, 7/8 in. wide, 3/16 in. thick. Made of Dover chert.

Priv. col., excellent quality, valued $250-300.

• Cumberland from Smith co., TN. Blade 4 3/32 in. long, 2 in. wide, 1/2 in. thick. Fluting travels nearly the entire length of the piece. Demonstrates high quality flaking, beveled on one side of each face. Concave fish tail base. Made of dense brown chert. *Priv. col., museum quality, valued $750-900.*

• Cumberland from Greer co., OK. Point is 3 5/16 in. long, 1 1/4 in. wide, 7/16 in. thick. Heat treated, 3/4 length fluted on both sides. Beveled on one side of each face, finely serrated. Made of a fine pink chert. *Tim Rubbles col., museum quality, valued $550-700.*

• Cumberland from Hyde co., NC. Blade 4 1/8 in. long, 2 3/4 in. wide, 5/16 in. thick. Serrated, beveled on one side of each face, smooth full blade fluting. Concave base with fish tail type base tangs. Made of white grained chert. *Priv. col., museum quality, valued $650-850.*

• Cumberland from Hyde co., NC. Blade 3 3/4 in. long, 1 7/8 in. wide, 3/16 in. thick. Thin, long beveling on all four sides, 3/4 of blade serrated. Deep concave base, serrated tangs. Made of white grained chert. *Priv. col., museum quality, valued $500-600.*

• Cumberland from Warren co., OH. Point 2 27/32 in. long, 1 7/8 in. wide, 1/2 in. thick. Steeply beveled on all four sides, thick, convex edges. Concave base, fully fluted. Made of greenish chert.

Priv. col., excellent quality, valued $350-400.

• Cumberland from Warren co., OH. Blade 4 3/4 in. long, 2 2/3 in. wide, 3/16 in. thick. Symmetrical, fully fluted, finely serrated edges and point. Concave base, pointed base tangs. Made of greenish chert. *Priv. col., museum quality, valued $300-400.*

• Cumberland from Warren co., OH. Blade 5 in. long, 1 15/16 in. wide, 1/2 in. thick. Fluting nearly the entire length of the blade. Good workmanship, wide thin flaking, concave base. Made of greenish chert. *Priv. col., museum quality, valued $500-650.*

• Cumberland unfluted from Johnson co., IL. Point is 3 1/8 in. long, 1 3/16 in. wide, 3/8 in. thick. Thick, heat treated, long sharp serrations, finely beveled tip. Fluting up the entire point on both faces, concave base. Made of a fine pink chert. *Priv. col., museum quality, valued $450-550.*

• Cumberland from Cardin co., PA. Point 2 1/2 in. long, 3/4 in. wide, 3/16 in. thick. Narrow, thin, serrated, with smooth fluting on both faces. Heat treated, concave base, rounded tangs. Made of glossy muti-toned tan chert. *Priv. col., museum quality, valued $350-450.*

• Cumberland from Cardin co., PA. Blade 3 11/16 in. long, 1 1/4 in. wide, 3/16 in. thick. Narrow, thin, beveled and serrated on all four edges. Fully thin fluting, both sides, heat treated, concave base. Made of glossy multi-toned tan chert. *Priv. col., museum quality, valued $600-800.*

• Cumberland from Alleghany co., NC. Point 2 1/4 in. long, 1 5/8 in. wide, 3/16 in. thick. Symmetrical, thin, beveled on one side of each face. Triangular tip, concave base. Made of pink to white banded chert. *Priv. col., excellent quality, valued $350-400.*

• Cumberland from Alleghany co., NC. Blade 3 3/4 in. long, 1 1/2 in. wide, 3/16 in. thick. Narrow, symmetrical, beveled on one side of each face. Good workmanship, finely serrated edges. Thin tanged concave base. Made of local pink to white banded chert. *Priv. col., museum quality, valued $600-750.*

• Cumberland from Alleghany co., NC. Blade 4 7/16 in. long, 2 1/4 in. wide, 1/4 in. thick. Heat treated, narrow, symmetrical, beveled

on one side of each face. Quality workmanship, sharp serrated edges. Long ground base tangs, concave base. Made of a local pink to white banded chert.
Priv. col., museum quality, valued $750-900.

• Cumberland from Hamilton co., TN. Point 2 3/8 in. long, 1 1/2 in. wide, 7/16 in. thick. Symmetrical, beveled on all four sides, serrated edges. Fluted on both sides, rounded base tangs, concave base. Made of Dover chert.
Priv. col., museum quality, rare, valued $600-800.

• Cumberland from Smith co., TN. Blade 5 1/2 in. long, 2 3/4 in. wide, 7/16 in. thick. Long, symmetrical, beveled on one side of each face, upper half serrated. Full fluting on both faces, concave base. Made of Dover chert.
Priv. col., museum quality, rare, valued $1,000-1,250.

• Cumberland from Smith co., TN. Point 3 1/8 in. long, 1 13/16 in. wide, 1/4 in. thick. Symmetrical, one edge of each face beveled, serrated. Fluting on both sides, full length, concave base. Made of Dover chert.
Priv. col., museum quality, rare, valued $650-850.

• Cumberland from Smith co., TN. Blade 4 1/2 in. long, 2 1/4 in. wide, 5/16 in. thick. Symmetrical, beveled on one side of each face. Serrated, thin fluting up length of both sides, concave base. Made of Dover chert.
Priv. col., museum quality, rare, valued $800-1,000.

• Cumberland from Fayette co., OH. Point 3 1/2 in. long, 1 7/8 in. wide, 1/4 in. thick. Beveled on all four sides, finely serrated upper third. Heat treated, fluted on both sides, concave base. Made of creamy white chert.
Priv. col., excellent quality, valued $250-300.

• Cumberland from Fayette co., OH. Blade 4 3/4 in. long, 1 2/3 in. wide, 1/2 in. thick. Narrow, thick, steeply beveled on all four sides, finely serrated edges. Heat treated, fluted on both faces, concave base. Made of creamy white chert.
Priv. col., museum quality, valued $400-600.

Cuney: 400-200 B.P. Historic

Found predominantly in the midwestern states. The Cuney is a small point with high quality workmanship. The base is bifurcated, the point is barbed and triangular.

♦ Cuney from Hamilton co., TN. Point 7/8 in. long, 1/4 in. wide, 3/32 in. thick. Sharp and deeply serrated. Made of a black pebble chert.

Grover Bohannon col., excellent quality, valued $20-25.

♦ Cuney from Stewart co., AR. Point 5/8 in. long, 3/16 in. wide, 1/16 in. thick. Sharp, thin, narrow, symmetrical, classical base, small tip break. Made of mauve pebble chert.

Grover Bohannon col., average quality, valued $10-15.

• Cuney from Hamilton co., TN. Point 1 1/8 in. long, 1/4 in. wide, 1/8 in. thick. Sharp and deeply serrated, narrow and triangularly symmetrical. Made of tan pebble chert.
Grover Bohannon col., excellent quality, valued $25-35.

• Cuney from Stewart co., TN. Point 13/16 in. long, 3/16 in. wide, 1/18 in. thick. High quality workmanship, sharp, thin, narrow, symmetrical. Made of dark brown pebble chert.
Grover Bohannon col., museum quality, valued $30-45.

• Cuney from Hamilton co., TN. Point 1 1/16 in. long, 1/4 in. wide, 1/8 in. thick. Sharp, deep, wide serrations, long, narrow and triangularly symmetrical. Made of Dover chert.
Grover Bohannon col., museum quality, rare, valued $45-65.

- Cuney from Union co., IL. Point 1 in. long, 1/3 in. wide, 1/8 in. thick. Heat treated, narrow, triagular, high quality workmanship. Corner notched, long pointed barbs, finely serrated. The stem and base are bifurcated. Made of dense white chert.
Tim Rubbles col., excellent quality, valued $30-40.

- Cuney from Union co., IL. Point 27/32 in. long, 1/4 in. wide, 1/16 in. thick. Extremely thin, heat treated, sharp, wide serrations. Angular corner notches, long pointed barbs, bifurcated stem. Made of dense white chert.
Tim Rubbles col., excellent quality, valued $20-25.

- Cuney from Sangamon co., IL. Point 1 1/8 in. long, 9/16 in. wide, 1/16 in. thick. Sharp, thin, triangularly symmetrical, classic stem and base. Made of gray pebble chert.
Priv. col., excellent quality, valued $20-25.

- Cuney from Hamilton co., TN. Point 1 1/8 in. long, 5/16 in. wide, 1/8 in. thick. Sharp, wide serrations, narrow, triangularly symmetrical. Classic bifurcated stem and base. Made of tan pebble chert.
Grover Bohannon col., excellent quality, valued $30-35.

- Cuney from Houston co., TN. Point 1 in. long, 1/2 in. wide, 1/8 in. thick. Triangularly symmetrical, finely serrated, high quality workmanship. The base is bifurcated, the point is barbed. Made of a black flint.
Grover Bohannon col., excellent quality, valued $30-35.

- Cuney from Houston co., TN. Point 7/8 in. long, 1/3 in. wide, 1/6 in. thick. Sharply and finely serrated, triangular, corner notched rounded barbs. Classic bifurcated stem and base. Made of black flint.
Grover Bohannon col., excellent quality, valued $20-25.

- Cuney from Hempstead co., AR. Point 1 3/8 in. long, 13/16 in. wide, 1/16 in. thick. Sharp, thin, narrow, symmetrical, pointed barbs, finely serrated edges. Classic bifurcated stem and base. Made of brown pebble chert.
Priv. col., excellent quality, valued $30-35.

- Cuney from Hempstead co., AR. Point 1 1/8 in. long, 1/2 in. wide, 1/8 in. thick. Thin, sharp, deep, wide serrations, narrow and triangular. Classic bifurcated stem and base. Made of brown pebble chert.

Priv. col., excellent quality, valued $30-35.

• Cuney from Drew co., AR. Point 1 5/16 in. long, 1/3 in. wide, 1/8 in. thick. Good workmanship, narrow, triangular, finely serrated. Corner notched, sharp barbs, concave base. Made of white chert.
Priv. col., museum quality, valued $40-50.

• Cuney from Harrison co., MO. Point 1 3/8 in. long, 1/2 in. wide, 3/32 in. thick. Thin, narrow, corner notched, short, rounded barbs. Sharp and deeply serrated edges and tip. Base is concave. Made of pink pebble chert.
Priv. col., museum quality, valued $40-45.

• Cuney from Harrison co., MO. Point 1 5/8 in. long, 9/16 in. wide, 1/16 in. thick. Heat treated, thin, narrow, triangularly symmetrical, finely serrated. Deep corner notches, straight stem, concave base. Made of milky quartz.
Priv. col., museum quality, rare, valued $50-65.

• Cuney from Izard co., AR. Point 1 1/4 in. long, 1/2 in. wide, 1/8 in. thick. Thin, narrow, triangularly symmetrical, sharp. Classic bifurcated stem and base. Made of yellow tan pebble chert.
Priv. col., excellent quality, valued $20-25.

• Cuney from Izard co., AR. Point 1 7/16 in. long, 1/3 in. wide, 1/8 in. thick. Thin, narrow, triangular, sharp, deep edge serrations. Classic bifurcated stem and base. Made of a brown pebble chert.
Priv. col., excellent quality, valued $20-25.

• Cuney from Stewart co., AR. Point 1 3/32 in. long, 1/2 in. wide, 1/8 in. thick. Sharp, thin, narrow, symmetrical, classical base. Made of quartzite.
Grover Bohannon col., average quality, valued $10-15.

• Cuney from Humphreys co., TN. Point 1 1/8 in. long, 1/2 in. wide, 1/4 in. thick. Sharp and deeply serrated, thick, triangularly symmetrical. Classical bifurcated stem and base. Made of quartzite.
Priv. col., average quality, valued $10-15.

Cypress Creek: 7,000-3,000 B.P. Mid-Archaic

Southern point or blade of medium to large size. Asymmetrical short shoulder barbs. One barb may be tapered. Rounded base, often bulbous. The larger Cypress Creek blades are broad stemmed with an expanded base. These larger blades are beveled on all four sides.

• Cypress Creek from Union co., IL. Point 2 1/4 in. long, 1 1/4 in. wide, 3/8 in. thick. Deep side notches and long tangs. Shallow serrations, slight tip break. Made of false jasper.
Priv. col., average quality, valued $25-35.

♦ Cypress Creek from southern IL. Point 2 23/32 in. long, 1 3/32 in. wide, 5/32 in. thick. Made of pink false jasper.

Les Grubbe col., excellent quality, valued $10-15.

• Cypress Creek from Union co., IL. Point 2 3/4 in. long, 3 1/32 in. wide, 1/4 in. thick. Made of a uniform gray chert.
Priv. col., average quality, valued $6-10.

♦ Cypress Creek from Union co., IL. Point 3 in. long, 1 1/4 in. wide, 3/8 in. thick. Corner notched with prominent tangs. Made of a local gray brown flint.

Les Grubbe col., museum quality, rare, valued $65-80.

• Cypress Creek from Dekalb co., IL. Blade 3 3/4 in. long, 1 3/8 in. wide, 1/4 in. thick. Deeply corner notched with flaring snapped tangs. Thin, finely serrated and sharp. Made of tan pebble chert.
Priv. col., museum quality, valued $185-280.

◆ Cypress Creek from Union co., IL. Point 2 3/4 in. long, 1 1/4 in. wide, 3/8 in. thick. Exceptional notches and tangs, fire treated. Made of red rose jasper.

Les Grubbe col., museum quality, rare, valued $125-175.

◆ Cypress Creek from Union co., IL. Point 2 3/4 in long, 1 1/2 in. wide, 5/8 in. thick. Perfect condition, beveled on one edge of each face. Extremely rare made of Kaolin chert.

Les Grubbe col., museum quality, rare, valued $300-450.

• Cypress Creek from Union co., IL. Blade 3 2/3 in. long, 1 1/4 in. wide, 1/4 in. thick. Corner notched with prominent tangs. Thin, finely serrated and sharp. Made of Mill Creek chert.
Tim Rubbles col., museum quality, valued $225-260.

• Cypress Creek from Sangamon co., IL. Point 2 3/4 in. long, 1 3/4 in. wide, 3/8 in. thick. Deep side notches and long tangs. Shallow serrations, symmetrical and quite sharp tip and edges. Made of white to yellow chert.
Priv. col., excellent quality, valued $85-135.

• Cypress Creek from Ashley co., AR. Blade 4 in. long, 1 1/2 in. wide, 1/4 in. thick. Corner notched with short rounded tangs. Thin, beveled on one side of each face, finely serrated and sharp. Blade edges

concave, base convex. Made of dark gray chert.
Priv. col., museum quality, valued $185-260.

- Cypress Creek from Ashley co., AR. Blade 4 1/4 in. long, 2 1/4 in. wide, 3/8 in. thick. Deep side notches and long tangs. Shallow edge serrations even on stem, beveled on all four sides. Narrow rounded tangs parallel side notches. Concave, thinned base. Made of dark gray chert.
Priv. col., excellent quality, valued $125-165.

- Cypress Creek from Dekalb co., IL. Blade 3 3/4 in. long, 1 1/2 in. wide, 1/4 in. thick. Deeply corner notched with flaring uneven snapped tangs. Thin, finely serrated, beveled on all four sides. Made of tan pebble chert.
Priv. col., museum quality, valued $225-280.

- Cypress Creek from Adams co., IL. Blade 4 1/3 in. long, 2 1/8 in. wide, 1/4 in. thick. Beveled on all four sides, corner notched with short rounded tangs. Thin, finely serrated, base is concave. Made of yellow tan chert.
Priv. col., excellent quality, valued $185-260.

- Cypress Creek from Adams co., IL. Blade 4 1/4 in. long, 2 3/8 in. wide, 3/8 in. thick. Beveled on all four sides, deep side notches, long parallel tangs. Sharp serrations, thinned convex base. Made of multi-toned white to gold chert.
Priv. col., museum quality, valued $250-350.

- Cypress Creek from Adams co., IL. Blade 3 13/16 in. long, 1 1/2 in. wide, 1/4 in. thick. Thin, symmetrical, concave edges, finely serrated, beveled on all four sides. Deep corner notches with flaring pointed tangs. Notches and base serrated and convex. Made of tan to white pebble chert.
Priv. col., excellent quality, valued $145-180.

- Cypress Creek from Adams co., IL. Point 2 1/3 in. long, 1 3/4 in. wide, 1/4 in. thick. Wide, symmetrical, corner notched, asymmetrical barbs, one snapped the other pointed. Thin, sharp, convex edges. Base narrowing and rounded. Made of Mill Creek chert.
Priv. col., average quality, valued $45-60.

- Cypress Creek from Henderson co., IL. Point 2 1/4 in. long, 1 7/8 in. wide, 3/8 in. thick. Wide, symmetrical, deep corner notches, barbed asymmetrical. Made of white pebble chert.

Priv. col., average quality, valued $25-35.

• Cypress Creek from Henderson co., IL. Blade 4 1/3 in. long, 2 3/8 in. wide, 1/4 in. thick. Symmetrical, beveled on one side of each face. Thin, finely serrated and sharp. Shallow side notches, base thinned and concave. Made of tan pebble chert.
Priv. col., excellent quality, valued $150-200.

• Cypress Creek from Henderson co., IL. Blade 3 5/8 in. long, 1 1/2 in. wide, 1/4 in. thick. Symmetrical, beveled on all four sides, sharp thin serrations. Corner notched with uniform barbs. Stem sides serrated, concave base. Made of gray white chert.
Priv. col., excellent quality, valued $145-160.

• Cypress Creek from Henderson co., IL. Point 2 1/2 in. long, 1 1/4 in. wide, 3/8 in. thick. Symmetrical, convex edges, sharp edges crudely serrated. Deep side notches and long asymmetrical barbs, one tapered. Made of quartzite.
Priv. col., average quality, valued $25-35.

• Cypress Creek from Larmar co., AL. Point 2 1/3 in. long, 1 3/8 in. wide, 1/4 in. thick. Crude workmanship, thin, sharp edges, rounded tip. Corner notched, asymmetrical barbs, one snapped. Made of quartzite.
Priv. col., poor quality, valued $15-20.

• Cypress Creek from Larmar co., AL. Point 3 in. long, 1 3/4 in. wide, 1/4 in. thick. Side notched with asymmetrical barbs, longer of the two tapered. Thin, sharp, uneven base. Made of quartzite.
Priv. col., average quality, valued $35-40.

• Cypress Creek from Craig Head co., AR. Point 2 1/4 in. long, 1 7/8 in. wide, 3/8 in. thick. Symmetrical, convex sides, deep side notches and long asymmetrical barbs. Shallow, fine serrations, sharp tip. Base tapered and rounded. Made of brown Arkansas chert.
Priv. col., excellent quality, valued $100-135.

• Cypress Creek from Craig Head co., AR. Blade 4 1/4 in. long, 1 5/8 in. wide, 1/4 in. thick. Deeply corner notched, horizontal short snapped barbs. Thin, finely serrated and sharp. Beveled on all four sides, concave edges and base. Made of brown Arkansas chert.
Priv. col., museum quality, valued $250-300.

• Cypress Creek from Union co., SC. Blade 3 2/3 in. long, 2 1/4 in. wide, 1/ in. thick. Thick, finely serrated and sharp, asymmetrical barbs, longer of the two tapered. Stem narrowing, base rounded. Made of lightweight white chert.
Priv. col., museum quality, valued $100-150.

• Cypress Creek from Union co., SC. Point 2 3/4 in. long, 2 1/4 in. wide, 3/8 in. thick. Thin, wide, convex beveled and serrated edges. Shallow, thin serrations, side notched, wide straight base. Made of jasper.
Priv. col., museum quality, valued $125-165.

• Cypress Creek from Dillon co., SC. Blade 3 7/8 in. long, 1 5/8 in. wide, 1/4 in. thick. Thin, finely serrated and sharp. Beveled on all four sides, small pointed tip. Deep corner notches, long stem, convex base. Made of marbled tan chert.
Priv. col., museum quality, valued $250-300.

CHAPTER 4
DALLAS-DOVETAIL

<u>Dallas: 4,000-1,500 B.P. Late Archaic to Woodland</u>

Predominantly a midwestern point. Small to medium in size, long stemmed, short point or blade, weak shoulders. Stem base usually ground but may be snapped.

♦ Dallas from Hamilton co., TN. Point 5/16 in. long, 1/4 in. wide, 1/8 in. thick. Unique workmanship for a Dallas. Sharp, lightly serrated, with sharp tip. Slightly convex ground base. Made of a high grade quartzite.

Grover Bohannon col., museum quality, valued $30-45.

• Dallas from Jackson co., IL. Point 11/16 in. long, 3/8 in. wide, 1/8 in. thick. Sharp, lightly serrated with sharp tip. Slightly convex ground base with long stem. Made of Mill Creek chert.
Tim Rubbles col., excellent quality, valued $20-35.

• Dallas from Cumberland co., IL. Point 1 1/16 in. long, 5/8 in. wide, 3/16 in. thick. Point narrow, long stemmed, long point, weak shoulders. Stem base snapped. Made of dark gray slate.
Tim Rubbles col., average quality, valued $10-15.

• Dallas from Hamilton co., TN. Point 7/16 in. long, 1/4 in. wide, 1/8 in. thick. Fine workmanship, crude material. Sharp, lightly serrated with small tip break. Slightly convex ground base. Made of low grade quartzite.
Priv. col., average quality, valued $7-12.

• Dallas from Hamilton co., TN. Point 1 5/16 in. long, 1/4 in. wide, 1/8 in. thick. Sharp, lightly serrated, very narrow and angular, lacking in symmetry. Snap convex ground base. Made of Dover chert.
Grover Bohannon col., museum quality, rare, valued $50-65.

• Dallas from Mercer co., KY. Point 13/32 in. long, 1/4 in. wide, 1/4 in. thick. Thick point even for a Dallas. Sharp, serrated to near beveled with sharp tip. Convex to bulbous ground base. Made of a green pebble chert.
Priv. col., average quality, valued $10-20.

• Dallas from Hamilton co., TN. Point 1 5/16 in. long, 5/8 in. wide, 1/8 in. thick. High quality workmanship for a Dallas. Sharp, finely serrated with rounded tip. Slightly convex ground base. Made of high grade pinkish quartzite.
Grover Bohannon col., excellent quality, valued $25-40.

• Dallas from Union co., IL. Point 1/2 in. long, 3/8 in. wide, 3/16 in. thick. Thin, narrow, deeply serrated long-stemmed point, weak shouldered. Stem short, base snapped. Made of Kaolin chert.
Priv. col., museum quality, rare, valued $70-85.

• Dallas from Stewart co., TN. Point 5/16 in. long, 3/8 in. wide, 1/8 in. thick. Good workmanship, several edge nicks, sharp, lightly serrated with long pointed tip. Convex ground base. Made of tan to brown pebble chert.
Jim Smith col., average quality, valued $10-25.

• Dallas from Hamilton co., TN. Point 1 13/16 in. long, 1/2 in. wide, 1/8 in. thick. Long and angular for a Dallas. Sharp, deeply serrated with finely serrated sharp tip. Slightly convex ground base. Made of tan to dark brown unidentified chert.
Priv. col., museum quality, valued $20-40.

• Dallas from Kearney co., NE. Point 1 1/4 in. long, 3/4 in. wide, 1/4 in. thick. Narrow, long, parallel sided, stemmed, weak shoulders. Beveled on one side of each face, convex ground base. Made of dull gray chert.
Priv. col., museum quality, valued $30-35.

• Dallas from Kearney co., NE. Point 11/16 in. long, 1/3 in. wide, 1/8 in. thick. Good workmanship, sharp, lightly serrated, point smaller than stem. Slightly convex ground base. Made of tan banded chert.
Priv. col., excellent quality, valued $20-25.

• Dallas from Kearney co., NE. Point 1 9/16 in. long, 1 1/4 in. wide, 1/8 in. thick. Sharply serrated, very narrow, thin, long thin pointed barbs. Wide stem, snapped convex ground base. Made of banded tan chert.
Priv. col., excellent quality, valued $30-45.

• Dallas from New Madrid co., MO. Point 1 in. long, 1/2 in. wide, 1/4 in. thick. Thick, symmetrical, weak shoulders, sharply serrated edge and wide stem, thinned tip. Convex ground base. Made of white pebble chert.
Priv. col., excellent quality, valued $30-40.

• Dallas from New Madrid co., MO. Point 1 1/3 in. long, 2/3 in. wide, 1/4 in. thick. Thick, symmetrical, finely serrated, sharp barbs. Straight ground base. Made of white pebble chert.
Priv. col., excellent quality, valued $25-30.

Dalton: 12,000-4,000 B.P. Paleo to Mid-Archaic

Dalton points and blades are found throughout the midwestern and southeastern United States. Daltons are medium to quite large in size. They are distinguished by their basal grinding and usually concave base. Some Dalton's are finely serrated with high quality parallel flaking. Side beveling is frequent and the points are thin with quality flaking.

◆ Dalton Classic from Livingston co., KY. Point 2 1/2 in. long, 1 1/8 in. wide, 3/16 in. thick. Right hand beveled, found 10/6/91. Made of Dover chert.

Tony Clinton col., museum quality, valued $80-120.

• Dalton Classic from Martin co., IN. Blade 4 1/2 in. long, 1 1/8 in. wide, 3/16 in. thick. Thin, narrow, oblique flaked, right hand beveled, sharply serrated edges. Fluted, concave base, ground basal tangs. Made of glossy brown chert.
Priv. col., museum quality, valued $850-1,200.

♦ Dalton Classic from Mills co., IA. Blade 4 7/8 in. long,
1 7/8 in. wide, 5/32 in. thick. Edge serrations are fine and sharp, very
symmetrical with distinctive parallel flaking. Made of a dark brown
oily chert.

Fred Suite col., museum quality, rare, valued $1,000-1,250.

♦ Dalton Classic from southeastern MO. Blade 4 1/2 in. long, 1 1/2 in.
wide, 1/4 in. thick. Blade is beveled and fluted. Made of brown pebble
chert.

Fred Suite col., excellent quality, valued $350-400.

♦ Dalton Classic from central IL. Point 2 1/4 in. long, 1 in. wide,
3/8 in. thick. Half moon blood line through the point, very fine
serrations. Made of translucent brown chert.

Les Grubbe col., museum quality, rare, valued $200-250.

♦ Dalton Classic from Stoddard co., MO. Point 3 in. long, 1 5/16 in.
wide, 5/32 in. thick. Both edges are beveled on one face. Made of
brown Missouri pebble chert.

Fred Suite col., average quality, valued $90-125.

◆ Dalton Classic from Union co., IL. Point 2 1/8 in. long, 1/2 in. wide, 5/8 in. thick. Point has been reworked over time, good field patina. Made of Mill Creek chert.

Les Grubbe col., excellent quality, valued $75-100.

◆ Dalton Classic from Union co., IL. Blade 4 in. long, 1 1/4 in. wide, 5/32 in. thick. Deep, fine side grooves. Made of a local pinkish brown pebble chert.

Les Grubbe col., museum quality, valued $800-1,000.

◆ Dalton Classic from Union co., IL. Blade 3 1/2 in. long, 1 5/8 in. wide, 1/4 in. thick. Heavy patina, deep blood groove. Made of local brown speckled pebble chert.

Les Grubbe col., museum quality, valued $850-1,100.

◆ Dalton Classic from TN. Point 2 5/8 in. long, 1 in. wide, 1/4 in. thick. Fluted with double center notch. Made of Dover chert.

Les Grubbe col., excellent quality, valued $85-140.

♦ Dalton Classic from Johnson co., IL. Point 2 3/4 in. long, 1 1/4 in. wide, 1/4 in. thick. Heavy patina, fluted with exceptionally long tails, finely serrated. Made of local brown pebble chert.

Les Grubbe col., museum quality, valued $225-300.

• Dalton Classic from Martin co., IN. Blade 4 1/4 in. long, 1 1/3 in. wide, 1/3 in. thick. Thin, finely serrated, high quality workmanship, parallel flaked. Beveled on all four sides, shallow concave base. Made of greenish chert.
Priv. col., museum quality, valued $700-850.

• Dalton Classic from Midland co., TX. Blade 4 7/8 in. long, 1 1/2 in. wide, 1/4 in. thick. Thin, narrow, parallel oblique flaked. Edges serrated, fine, sharp, symmetrical, base concave. Made of dull gray chert.
Priv. col., museum quality, valued $850-1,000.

• Dalton Classic from Wabash co., IN. Blade 3 3/4 in. long, 1 3/8 in. wide, 1/4 in. thick. Heat treated, distinct blood groove. Made of brown pebble chert.
Priv. col., museum quality, valued $750-1,000.

• Dalton Classic from Midland co., TX. Blade 4 11/32 in. long, 1 1/2 in. wide, 1/4 in. thick. Blade is beveled on all four side, thin, serrated, narrow and symmetrical. Base is concave, ground, and fluted. Made of dull gray chert.
Priv. col., excellent quality, valued $500-600.

Dalton Colbert: 10,000-5,000 B.P. Late Paleo to Early Archaic

Predominantly a midwestern into the Southeast point or

blade, medium to large in size. Squared base unique to the Dalton
Colbert. Auriculate point or blade, weak, ground hafting area. High
quality workmanship, often parallel flaked and serrated.

◆ Dalton Colbert from central MO. Point 3 1/8 in. long, 3/4 in. wide,
1/8 in. thick. Point is beveled on opposing faces with fine, sharp
serrated sides. Ground hafting area evident. Light, almost delicate,
parallel flaking. The point base is uniquely not squared. Made of light
green chert.

Tim Crawford col., museum quality, rare, valued $150-225.

• Dalton Colbert from Childress co., TX. Point 2 3/8 in. long, 1 in.
wide, 1/8 in. thick. Very thin, narrow, beveled on opposing faces with
fine, sharp, serrated edges. Thin, fine, parallel flaking, shallow side
notches, concave base. Made of light gray chert.
Priv. col., museum quality, valued $100-150.

• Dalton Colbert from Humphreys co., TN. Point 3 in. long, 1 2/3 in.
wide, 1/8 in. thick. Thin, wide, symmetrical, beveled on one side of
each face, wide, sharp, serrated edges. Good field patina, hafting area
evident, parallel flaked. Wide concave base, ground tangs. Made of
Dover chert.
Priv. col., museum quality, rare, valued $150-200.

• Dalton Colbert from Hamilton co., TN. Point 2 1/8 in. long, 3/4 in.
wide, 1/4 in. thick. Thick, narrowing from tip to base, beveled on one
side of each face, shallow sharp serrations. Random flaked, side
notched, concave base. Made of porous pink chert.
Priv. col., average quality, valued $50-75.

• Dalton Colbert from Johnson co., IL. Point 2 1/4 in. long, 1 in. wide,
1/4 in. thick. Heavy patina, heat treated, deeply fluted with long tails,
finely serrated edges and tip. Made of brown pebble chert.
Jim Smith col., museum quality, valued $200-250.

• Dalton Colbert from Jackson co., IL. Point 3 1/16 in. long, 1 1/4 in.
wide, 1/4 in. thick. Symmetrical, beveled on opposing faces, fine sharp
serrated edges. Ground concave base, snapped tangs. Made of Mill

Creek chert.
Tim Rubbles col., excellent quality, valued $125-150.

Dalton Greenbriar: 10,000-6,000 B.P. Late Paleo to Early Archaic

Found throughout the midwestern, eastern, and southeastern United States. Point or blade medium to large in size. Auriculate with concave base. Often fluted on both sides, serrated, always basal ground. Can be beveled on either or both sides. Usually thin, with high quality workmanship.

• Dalton Greenbriar from Jefferson co., TN. Point 2 7/8 in. long,
1 3/16 in. wide, 1/4 in. thick. Point minutely serrated, poor
workmanship, thin sharp tip. Thin, triangularly narrow, shallow side
notches, straight base. Made of gray pebble chert.
Priv. col., average quality, valued $45-50.

• Dalton Greenbriar from Shoshone co., ID. Point 3 1/8 in. long,
3/4 in. wide, 3/16 in. thick. Thin, narrow, finely serrated, beveled on
one side of each face. Thinned concave base, ground base tangs. Made
of pink chert.
Priv. col., museum quality, valued $100-130.

♦ Dalton Greenbriar from Pettis co., MO. Point 3 1/4 in. long,
1 5/8 in. wide, 1/4 thick. Very symmetrical point, sharp, with uniform
serrations. Made of Cobden Hornstone chert.

Fred Suite col., museum quality, valued $500-650.

♦ Dalton Greenbriar from central TN. Point 2 5/8 in. long, 3/4 in.
wide, 5/32 in. thick. Nearly square base, upper half of point serrated,
poorly defined hafting area. Made of tan pebble chert.

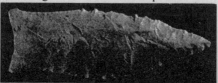

Priv. col., average quality, valued $35-50.

♦ Dalton Greenbriar from Union co., IL. Point 2 1/8 in. long, 3/4 in. wide, 1/4 in. thick. Blood groove spans 2/3 of point, finely serrated. Made of high quality Mill Creek chert.

Les Grubbe col., excellent quality, valued $120-160.

♦ Dalton Greenbriar from Johnson co., IL. Point 2 1/2 in. long, 1 in. wide, 5/8 in. thick. Fire treated, highly serrated with distinct hafting marks. Made of local pinkish pebble chert.

Les Grubbe col., excellent quality, valued $60-85.

• Dalton Greenbriar from Elmore co., ID. Point 2 11/32 in. long, 1 1/2 in. wide, 5/8 in. thick. Symmetrical, thick, heat treated, highly serrated, steeply beveled on opposing edges. Shallow side notched, flaring ground basal tangs, concave base. Made of pinkish tan chert. *Priv. col., museum quality, valued $150-200.*

• Dalton Greenbriar from Cass co., IA. Point 2 3/8 in. long, 1 3/4 in. wide, 7/32 in. thick. Wide, thick, symmetrical, beveled on one edge of each face. Shallow side notches, tapered shoulders, ground tangs, concave base. Made of yellow tan pebble chert. *Priv. col., museum quality, valued $125-150.*

• Dalton Greenbriar from Osceola co., IA. Point 3 1/8 in. long, 1 1/4 in. wide, 1/4 in. thick. Symmetrical, finely serrated and gradually beveled edges. Parallel flaked, good workmanship, tapered shoulders. Shallow side notches, long thin basal tangs, concave base. Made of high quality pink chert. *Priv. col., museum quality, valued $160-200.*

• Dalton Greenbriar from Sauk co., WI. Point 2 1/3 in. long, 7/8 in.

wide, 3/8 in. thick. Narrow, thin, symmetrical, heat treated, highly serrated, parallel flaked. Sharp tip, shallow side notches, thinned concave base. Made of local green chert.
Priv. col., museum quality, valued $200-250.

• Dalton Greenbriar from Wood co., WI. Point 3 1/8 in. long, 1 1/4 in. wide, 3/16 in. thick. Thin, triangularly symmetrical, thin parallel flaked, sharply and minutely serrated edges. Convex edges, near square base. Made of tan banded chert.
Priv. col., excellent quality, valued $125-150.

• Dalton Greenbriar from Otsego co., MI. Point 2 1/2 in. long, 1 1/8 in. wide, 1/4 in. thick. Symmetrical, finely serrated edges, beveled on one side of each face. Straight sides, concave base. Made of green white speckled chert.
Priv. col., excellent quality, valued $100-120.

• Dalton Greenbriar from Huron co., MI. Point 2 15/16 in. long, 1 in. wide, 1/4 in. thick. Symmetrical, thin, beveled on one side of each face, sharply serrated. Sharp thin tip, straight sides, concave base. Made of pinkish pebble chert.
Priv. col., excellent quality, valued $120-150.

• Dalton Greenbriar from Tripp co., SD. Point 2 7/8 in. long, 1 1/16 in. wide, 1/2 in. thick. Symmetrical, thick, beveled on all four edges, wide, rounded serrations. Rounded tip, shallow side notches, long thin basal tangs, concave base. Made of tan chert.
Priv. col., excellent quality, valued $85-100.

• Dalton Greenbriar from Miner co., SD. Point 2 1/8 in. long, 1 1/4 in. wide, 1/4 in. thick. Thick, triangularly symmetrical, finely serrated edges. Shallow side notches, ground concave base. Made of grainy white chert.
Priv. col., average quality, valued $40-60.

• Dalton Greenbriar from Hartley co., TX. Point 2 1/32 in. long, 1 in. wide, 5/8 in. thick. Thick, narrow, beveled on one side of each face, highly serrated edges. Thinned concave base. Made of pinkish pebble chert.
Priv. col., excellent quality, valued $80-100.

Dalton Hemphill: 12,000-5,000 B.P. Mid-Paleo to Early Archaic

Predominantly a midwestern point or blade extending into the East. Point or blade medium to large in size. Tapered to weak shoulders, edges serrated, ground base.

• Dalton Hemphill from Alexander co., IL. Blade 3 23/32 in. long, 1 1/16 in. wide, 1/8 in. thick. Heat treated, thin, narrow, concave, serrated edges. Tapered shoulders, shallow side notches, concave ground base. Made of Mill Creek chert.
Priv. col., excellent quality, valued $250-350.

♦ Point from Fulton co., IL. Point 1 3/4 in. long, 13/16 in. wide, 1/8 in. thick. Heavy field patina. Made of Cobden Hornstone chert.

Priv. col., museum quality, rare, valued $250-325.

• Dalton Hemphill from Union co., IL. Point 3 1/8 in. long, 1 5/16 in. wide, 1/8 in. thick. Thin, symmetrical, sharp, minutely serrated edges, thin parallel flaked. Side notched, concave, tanged ground base. Made of Cobden Hornstone chert.
Priv. col., museum quality, rare, valued $450-600.

• Dalton Hemphill from Johnson co., IL. Point 2 3/16 in. long, 11/16 in. wide, 1/8 in. thick. Thin, narrow, wide, deep, thin edge serrations on upper half of point. Lower half parallel flaked. Base fish tailed, ground, and concave. Made of Cobden Hornstone chert.
Priv. col., museum quality, rare, valued $275-350.

• Dalton Hemphill from Union co., IL. Blade 4 1/3 in. long, 1 13/16 in. wide, 1/8 in. thick. Thin, symmetrical, quality workmanship, finely serrated edges, right hand beveled. Side notched, tapered shoulders, ground concave base. Made of Kaolin chert.
Priv. col., museum quality, rare, valued $650-725.

• Dalton Hemphill from Fulton co., IL. Blade 3 7/8 in. long, 1 1/8 in. wide, 1/8 in. thick. Thin, narrow, good workmanship, finely serrated, sharp thin tip. Shallow, wide side notches, tapered shoulders, ground

concave base. Made of dense white chert.
Priv. col., museum quality, valued $250-325.

• Dalton Hemphill from Alexander co., IL. Blade 4 3/4 in. long,
1 3/16 in. wide, 1/8 in. thick. Thin, narrow, concave edges, sharply
serrated, thinned tip. Deep side notches, horizontal barbed shoulders,
concave base. Made of Mill Creek chert.
Priv. col., excellent quality, valued $300-375.

•Dalton Hemphill from Hamilton, TN. Blade 3 5/8 in. long, 1 1/4 in.
wide, 1/4 in. thick. Fluted blade with deeply concave base and flaring
tails. Made of Dover chert.
Grover Bohannon col., museum quality, valued $185-240.

Dalton Nuckolls: 10,000-5,000 B.P. Late Paleo

*A midwestern to southeastern point or blade. Medium to large
in size. Base is lobbed to square, and concave.*

♦ Point from Johnson co., IL. Point 2 1/2 in. long, 3/4 in. wide,
1/4 in. thick. Both faces of point are beveled. Highly polished Kaolin
chert.

Les Grubbe col., average quality, valued $45-60.

• Dalton Nuckolls from Kiowa co., OK. Point 2 1/2 in. long, 7/8 in.
wide, 1/4 in. thick. Narrow, thick, finely serrated, shallow fluted with
blood groove. Shallow asymmetrical side notches, concave base. Made
of white pebble chert.
Priv. col., excellent quality, valued $120-165.

• Dalton Nuckolls from Stoddard co., MO. Point 2 in. long, 5/8 in.
wide, 1/4 in. thick. Finely serrated, shallow fluted with blood groove.
Several small blade nicks. Made of white pebble chert.
Priv. col., average quality, valued $80-125.

• Dalton Nuckolls from Morrow co., OH. Blade 4 1/16 in. long,
1 1/8 in. wide, 1/4 in. thick. Narrow, beveled concave edges, finely
serrated, shallow fluted with blood groove. Parallel flaked, uniform

straight sides, concave base. Made of grainy white pebble chert.
Priv. col., average quality, valued $80-100.

• Dalton Nuckolls from St. Clair co., MO. Point 2 3/8 in. long, 1 in.
wide, 1/4 in. thick. Symmetrical, finely serrated, shallow fluted with
blood groove. Beveled on one side of each face. Ground concave base.
Made of white pebble chert.
Priv. col., excellent quality, valued $80-100.

• Dalton Nuckolls from Stoddard co., MO. Point 2 in. long, 5/8 in.
wide, 1/4 in. thick. Finely serrated, shallow fluted, with blood groove.
Several small blade nicks. Made of white pebble chert.
Priv. col., average quality, valued $80-125.

Dalton Tallahassee: 10,000-8,000 B.P. Late Paleo

*Predominantly a southeastern point or blade. Medium to large
in size, thin, triangular. Serrated edges, expanded shoulders, with
concave base.*

• Dalton Tallahassee from central FL. Point 1 1/4 in. long, 7/8 in.
wide, 1/4 in. thick. Thick, deeply fluted, short tails, rounded tip. Made
of low grade quartzite.
Priv. col., average quality, valued $30-45.

• Dalton Tallahassee from Amelia co., VA. Point 1 1/8 in. long,
7/8 in. wide, 1/4 in. thick. Thick, wide, convex serrated edges, right
hand beveled. Thin sharp minutely serrated tip. Shallow thinned
concave base. Made of banded gray chert.
Priv. col., excellent quality, valued $40-65.

◆ Dalton Tallahassee from Amelia co., VA. Point 1 3/4 in. long,
7/8 in. wide, 3/16 in. thick. Thin, deep narrow, sharp edge serrations,
fluted, left hand beveled, rounded tip. Thin concave base. Made of
banded gray chert.

Priv. col., excellent quality, valued $50-65.

• Dalton Tallahassee from Levy co., FL. Point 3 1/4 in. long, 7/8 in. wide, 1/8 in. thick. Thin, deep serrated edges, long thin tip. Auriculate, symmetrical, concave base. Made of quartzite.
Priv. col., average quality, valued $35-45.

Darl: 2,500-1,000 B.P. Woodland

The Darl is a midwestern triangular Woodland point or blade. Ranges from small to large in size. Darls have slightly concave bases, shoulders are tapered to barbed. Many have very distinct beveling on one side of each face. Darls are not very common, a unique flaking type, and exhibit good workmanship. In this guide the Darl shows a significant increase in value. I regret I could not acquire more photos or listings.

♦ Darl from Lubbock, TX. Point 2 1/2 in. long, 1/4 in. wide, 1/8 in. thick. This is a very fine point, thin, narrow, and extremely sharp. Made of a glossy mauve chert.

Priv. col., museum quality, valued $100-150.

• Darl from Lubbock, TX. Blade 3 11/16 in. long, 1/2 in. wide, 1/4 in. thick. Classic narrow Darl design, sharp edges with slight tip break. Made of flat gray chert.
Priv. col., average quality, valued $45-65.

♦ Darl from central TX. Point 2 1/4 in. long, 1/2 in. wide, 1/8 in. thick. Beveled on one side of each face. Made of black flint.

Priv. col., museum quality, valued $80-120.

♦ Darl from northeastern AR. Point 1 5/8 in. long, 5/16 in. wide, 1/8 in. thick. Heat treated, sharp edges, rounded shoulders, beveled on one side of each face. Made of very oily gray to white chert.

Grover Bohannon col., excellent quality, valued $60-80.

• Darl from Lubbock, TX. Blade 4 1/2 in. long, 1 5/8 in. wide, 3/16 in. thick. Long, thin, sharp. Made of flat gray chert. *Priv. col., museum quality, valued $125-185.*

• Darl point from Lubbock, TX. Point 1 2/3 in. long, 1/4 in. wide, 1/8 in. thick. Thin, finely worked and serrated point, extremely sharp tip with rounded base. Made of a light gray chert. *Priv. col., excellent quality, valued $40-55.*

Darmon: 8,000-4,000 B.P. Early to Mid-Archaic

Darmon points are generally found in the Southeast. The points are small to medium size. They are side notched, triangular, with a wide convex to straight base.

♦ Darmon from TN. Point 1 1/2 in. long, 1 1/6 in. wide, 1/8 in. thick. Made of Buffalo river chert.

Priv. col., average quality, valued $10-15.

• Darmon from Hamilton co., TN. Point 1 in. long, 7/16 in. wide, 1/8 in. thick. Point is small, side notched, triangular, with a wide convex base. Made of Dover chert.
Priv. col., museum quality, valued $35-50.

• Darmon from Hamilton co., TN. Point 1 1/8 in. long, 1 3/16 in. wide, 5/16 in. thick. Point is classic in form, unusually thick. Made of light tan pebble chert.
Priv. col., average quality, valued $10-15.

• Darmon from Stewart co., TN. Point 1 3/8 in. long, 13/16 in. wide, 1/8 in. thick. Side notched, triangular, straight base. Made of greenish pebble chert.
Priv. col., average quality, valued $15-25.

• Darmon from Hamilton co., TN. Point 1 5/16 in. long, 11/16 in. wide, 1/8 in. thick. Point is thin, finely flaked, side notched, triangular, with a wide straight base. Made of Dover chert.
Grover Bohannon col., museum quality, valued $45-70.

• Darmon from southeastern AR. Point 1 in. long, 7/16 in. wide, 3/16 in. thick. Deep side notches, triangular, with a wide convex base. Made of tan pebble chert.
Priv. col., excellent quality, valued $35-55.

• Darmon from Memphis, TN. Point 1 3/8 in. long, 11/16 in. wide, 1/8 in. thick. Thin, side notched, sharp serrated edges. Made of Dover chert.
Priv. col., excellent quality, valued $30-45.

• Darmon from Franklin co., IL. Point 1 3/8 in. long, 7/16 in. wide, 1/8 in. thick. Point thin, triangular, side notched, with a wide convex base. Made of unidentified yellow chert.
Tim Rubbles col., museum quality, valued $45-55.

• Darmon from Hamilton co., TN. Point 1 5/8 in. long, 1 7/16 in. wide, 3/16 in. thick. Point is classic, unusually thin, wide straight base, large for a Darmon. Made of light gray pebble chert.
Priv. col., excellent quality, valued $30-45.

• Darmon from Hamilton co., TN. Point 2 1/4 in. long, 1 7/16 in. wide, 3/16 in. thick. Symmetrical, thin edge serrations, deep parallel side notched. Wide convex base. Made of Dover chert.

Priv. col., museum quality, valued $35-50.

• Darmon from Hamilton co., IN. Point 1 11/32 in. long, 13/16 in. wide, 5/16 in. thick. Triangular, thick, crudely serrated edges, rounded tip. Side notched, uneven barbs, base straight and as wide as point. Made of grainy white pebble chert.
Priv. col., average quality, valued $10-15.

• Darmon from Wabash co., IN. Point 2 3/8 in. long, 1 1/32 in. wide, 1/8 in. thick. Triangular, thin parallel flaked, minutely serrated edges, sharp thin tip. Deep side notches, expanding straight base. Made of greenish chert.
Priv. col., museum quality, valued $45-65.

• Darmon from Lucas co., OH. Point 2 3/16 in. long, 1 1/8 in. wide, 1/8 in. thick. Thin, narrow, good workmanship, finely parallel flaked, triangular, thin, wide edge serrations. Side notched, wide straight base. Made of grainy white chert.
Priv. col., excellent quality, valued $30-40.

• Darmon from Lucas co., OH. Point 1 3/8 in. long, 7/16 in. wide, 1/8 in. thick. Poor workmanship, side notched, triangular, with a wide convex base. Made of grainy white chert.
Priv. col., average quality, valued $15-20.

• Darmon from Graham co., NC. Point 1 1/8 in. long, 1 1/16 in. wide, 5/16 in. thick. Wide, thick, poor quality workmanship, one edge serrated. Uneven side notches, asymmetrical shoulders, one barbed one tapered. Expanding, short, convex base. Made of black slate.
Priv. col., poor quality, valued $5-10.

• Darmon from Boone co., WV. Point 1 3/8 in. long, 1 1/16 in. wide, 1/2 in. thick. Wide, very thick, poor workmanship, rounded tip, choppily serrated edges. Side notched, triangular, chipped straight base. Made of quartzite.
Priv. col., poor quality, valued $5-10.

• Darmon from Tyler co., WV. Point 1 11/16 in. long, 1 in. wide, 1/8 in. thick. Narrow, thin, finely flaked, sharply serrated. Side notched, triangular, one side broken off, wide straight base. Made of oily gray chert.
Priv. col., average quality, valued $8-12.

Decatur: 9,000-3,000 B.P. Early Archaic

Decatur is a small to medium point, corner notched, usually beveled on one side of each face. The bases, stems, and tang ends are usually fractured. High quality flaking. Many bases also ground.

♦ Decatur from Crenshaw co., AL. Point 1 3/4 in. long, 1 1/2 in. wide, 3/16 in. thick. Made of Charter Cave Flint.

Priv. col., museum quality, valued $100-150.

• Decatur blade from Overton co., TN. Blade 3 7/8 in. long, 1 1/8 in. wide, 3/16 in. thick. Thin, narrow, highly serrated, concave edges, flaring tangs. Deep corner notches, straight base. Made of Dover chert. *Priv. col., museum quality, valued $150-250.*

• Decatur point from Overton co., TN. Point 1 1/2 in. long, 1 1/8 in. wide, 1/4 in. thick. Triangular, wide, deep serrated edges, horizontal shoulder barbs. Beveled on one side of each face. Side notched with convex base. Made of Dover chert. *Priv. col., excellent quality, valued $65-80.*

• Decatur from Humphreys co., TN. Blade 3 1/2 in. long, 1 3/16 in. wide, 1/4 in. thick. Small corner notches, straight base. Serrated edges, right side beveled. Made of milky quartz. *Priv. col., excellent quality, valued $85-100.*

• Decatur from Humphreys co., TN. Point 1 1/2 in. long, 1 1/16 in. wide, 1/8 in. thick. Heat treated, chert type predominantly found in southern Illinois. Parallel flaked, thin, serrated edges, sharp tip. Narrow side notches, thin straight base. Made of Mill Creek chert. *Priv. col., excellent quality, valued $65-80.*

• Decatur from Humphreys co., TN. Point 2 1/8 in. long, 1 1/8 in. wide, 3/16 in. thick. Sharply right side beveled, very sharp edges. Side

notched, convex base. Made of Dover chert.
Grover Bohannon col., museum quality, valued $175-260.

* Decatur from Hamilton co., TN. Point 1 7/8 in. long, 1 1/8 in. wide,
1/4 in. thick. Narrow, beveled point, uniquely sharp, pointed tip. Made
of Dover chert.
Priv. col., excellent quality, valued $85-100.

* Decatur blade from Memphis, TN. Blade 3 5/8 in. long, 1 7/16 in.
wide, 1/4 in. thick. Small corner notches, narrow blade, right side
beveled, slight tip break. Made of gray pebble chert.
Grover Bohannon col., average quality, valued $65-80.

* Decatur point from Memphis, TN. Point 2 1/8 in. long, 1 3/16 in.
wide, 1/8 in. thick. Point beveled on one side of each face, deeply
serrated and heat treated. Made of white to light gray pebble chert.
Grover Bohannon col., average quality, valued $55-70.

* Decatur from Hamilton co., IL. Blade 4 1/2 in. long, 2 1/2 in. wide,
1/4 in. thick. Serrated edges, triangular, convex edges, beveled on one
edge of each face. Narrow, deep corner notches, straight base. Made of
rose quartz.
Priv. col., museum quality, rare, valued $165-250.

* Decatur from Champaign co., IL. Blade 4 1/8 in. long, 2 3/16 in.
wide, 1/8 in. thick. Thin, convex, serrated edges, heat treated, parallel
flaked, thin tip. Snapped barbs, narrow side notches, straight base. Made
of oily gray pink chert.
Priv. col., excellent quality, valued $145-180.

* Decatur from Dade co., MO. Point 3 1/32 in. long, 1 in. wide,
3/16 in. thick. Thin, narrow, concave, sharply serrated edges, right side
beveled. Side notched, thinned convex base. Made of white chert.
Jim Smith col., excellent quality, valued $150-200.

* Decatur from Pettis co., MO. Point 1 7/8 in. long, 1 1/8 in. wide,
1/4 in. thick. Convex edges, beveled on one side of each face, sharp
serrated edges, pointed tip. Pointed barbed shoulders, corner notched,
concave base. Made of banded white to golden brown chert.
Priv. col., museum quality, rare, valued $165-225.

* Decatur from Pettis co., TN. Blade 3 5/8 in. long, 1 1/8 in. wide,
1/4 in. thick. Narrow, parallel flaked, sharply serrated edges and tip.

Snapped horizontal, uniform barbs, left hand beveled, serrated stem.
Small corner notches, straight base. Made of banded white to golden
brown chert.
Priv. col., museum quality, rare, valued $185-250.

• Decatur from Caldwell co., MO. Point 2 1/2 in. long, 1 1/16 in.
wide, 1/8 in. thick. Heat treated. Chert of type found commonly in
southern Illinois. Parallel flaked, thin, serrated edges, sharp tip. Narrow,
deep, side notches, straight base. Made of Mill Creek chert.
Priv. col., excellent quality, valued $85-100.

• Decatur from Humphreys co., TN. Blade 3 5/8 in. long, 1 1/16 in.
wide, 3/16 in. thick. Narrow, concave edges, finely serrated, parallel
flaked. Sharply right side beveled, very sharp serrated tip. Side notched,
short, horizontal pointed barbs, convex base. Made of Dover chert.
Priv. col., museum quality, valued $275-225.

• Decatur from Logan co., NE. Point 2 1/8 in. long, 1 1/8 in. wide,
1/8 in. thick. Narrow, thin, concave edges, right hand beveled point,
finely serrated, sharp, pointed tip. Made of dull gray flint.
Priv. col., excellent quality, valued $80-100.

Dovetail: 10,000-5,000 B.P. Early Archaic

*Dovetails are predominantly found in the Southeast and
Midwest. Points and blades are medium to large in size, with the
distinctive Dovetail base. They are generally left side beveled on one
edge of each face. The base is always convex and grooved, but may be
fractured on both sides of base or center notched.*

◆ Dovetail blade from Livingston, KY. Blade 4 in. long, 1 5/8 in.
wide, 5/8 in. thick. Blade symmetrically beveled and finely serrated.
Blade found by Tony Clinton 10/6/91 on the Tennessee River. Made of
dark, oily, high quality Dover chert.

Tony Clinton Col., museum quality, rare, valued $1,200-1,500.

♦ Dovetail contemporary reproduction, originally from the George Bellamy collection. Blade is heat treated and poorly figured. Blade 9 in. long, 1 5/16 in. wide, 5/16 in. thick.

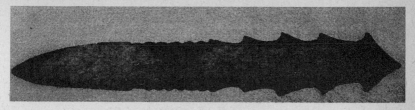

Tony Clinton col., reproduction, valued $15-20.

♦ Dovetail from southern IL. Point 2 1/8 in. long, 1 1/16 in. wide, 3/16 in. thick. Very symmetrical left hand beveled point, even, wide percussion flaking. Point is glossy brown with a distinct light tan skin mark on tail. Made of brown pebble chert.

Priv. col., museum quality, valued $475-650.

• Dovetail blade from Jackson co., IL. Blade 4 1/2 in. long, 1 3/4 in. wide, 1/4 in. thick. Heat treated, exceptional tail formation. Blade exhibits fine sharp serrations and left hand beveling. Made of pebble chert.
Priv. col., museum quality, valued $700-850.

♦ Dovetail from Stewart co., TN. Blade 8 3/4 in. long, 2 1/2 in. wide, 1/2 in. thick. Not enough can be said about this blade; it is as symmetrical as any blade I have ever seen. The coloring is high quality classic Dover. It is finely serrated, left hand beveled, and extremely sharp. Made of Dover chert.

David Zinkie col., museum quality, rare, valued $1,500-2,000.

♦ Dovetail from Delaware co., OH. Blade 4 in. long, 1 1/2 in. wide,
1/4 in. thick. Two dark bands spiral this finely serrated blade. One
band is on the tail, the other 1/3 of the way down from the tip of the
blade. Made of highly polished Flint Ridge chert.

Charles McCorkle col., museum quality, rare, valued $1,600-2,100.

• Dovetail from Union co., IL. Point 3 1/4 in. long, 1 31/32 in. wide,
7/8 in. thick. Wide, thick point exhibiting a very distinctly wide tail.
Made of Mill Creek chert.
Les Grubbe col., average quality, valued $90-130.

• Dovetail from Jackson co., IL. Blade 4 5/8 in. long, 1 3/4 in. wide,
1/4 in. thick. Heat treated, very narrow large, wide tail. Made of Mill
Creek chert.
Tim Rubbles col., excellent quality, valued $300-450.

• Dovetail from Stewart co., MO. Blade 5 3/4 in. long, 2 1/2 in. wide,
1/2 in. thick. Symmetrical blade, finely serrated, left hand beveled,
extremely sharp, deeply notched with classic small tail. Made of white
pebble chert.
Priv. col., museum quality, valued $500-700.

• Dovetail from Booneville, MO. Blade 4 7/16 in. long, 1 7/8 in. wide,
1/4 in. thick. Finely serrated, thick and wide blade of classic design.
Made of tan pebble chert.
Priv. col., museum quality, valued $650-800.

• Dovetail from Union co., IL. Point 2 1/4 in. long, 15/16 in. wide,
1/8 in. thick. Angular thin point, very fine workmanship, extremely
sharp tip. Made of Mill Creek chert.
Priv. col., excellent quality, valued $300-400.

• Dovetail from Pike co., IL. Point 2 1/2 in. long, 1 1/16 in. wide,

3/16 in. thick. Thin, symmetrical, convex edges, left hand beveled, percussion flaked, sharply serrated edges. Deep, narrow side notches, wide fanning dovetail. Made of brown to tan pebble chert. *Priv. col., museum quality, valued $450-500.*

• Dovetail from Pike co., IL. Blade 4 7/8 in. long, 3 in. wide, 1/4 in. thick. Symmetrical, convex, highly serrated edges, heat treated, beveling on all four sides. Deep, narrow corner notches, classical fanning dovetail base. Made of pink black speckled pebble chert. *Priv. col., museum quality, valued $600-750.*

• Dovetail from Hardin co., IL. Blade 6 3/4 in. long, 3 1/2 in. wide, 1/2 in. thick. Symmetrical, concave edges, beveled on one side of each face. Blade exhibits fine thin parallel flaking, sharp minute edge serrations. The base is wide and fanning, and deep symmetrical corner notches. Made of Kaolin chert. *Priv. col., museum quality, rare, valued $1,200-1,600.*

• Dovetail from Cumberland co., IL. Blade 5 in. long, 1 2/3 in. wide, 1/4 in. thick. Thin, concave, reworked edges, finely serrated blade. Parallel flaked, left hand beveled, thinned sharp tip. Side notched base wider than the blade. Made of local glossy tan chert from Clark co., Illinois. *Priv. col., excellent quality, valued $350-450.*

• Dovetail from Cumberland co., IL. Point 3 1/8 in. long, 1 5/16 in. wide, 3/16 in. thick. Symmetrical, thin, left hand beveled point, thin, wide, percussion flaking, edges distinctly and sharply serrated. Deep corner notches, thinned fanning dovetail base. Made of a local Clark co. glossy tan chert. *Priv. col., excellent quality, valued $275-350.*

• Dovetail from Clark co., IL. Blade 7 1/2 in. long, 2 7/8 in. wide, 1/4 in. thick. Long, thin, straight, highly serrated edges, beveled on one side of each face. Heat treated, turning much of the blade red. Exceptional percussion flaking. Deep, narrow, side notches, short, symmetrical dovetail thinned base. Made of glossy tan chert. *Priv. col., museum quality, valued $750-950.*

• Dovetail from Shelby co., MO. Blade 7 3/4 in. long, 2 2/3 in. wide, 1/4 in. thick. Thin, symmetrical, narrow straight edges, beveled on opposing sides. High quality workmanship, long thin percussion flaking, sharply serrated edges, serrations facing the tip. The tip is long, pointed, and finely serrated. Thinned base, classic dovetail. Made of white chert. *Priv. col., museum quality, valued $1,000-1,500.*

• Dovetail from Wayne co., MO. Blade 5 in. long, 1 3/4 in. wide,
1/4 in. thick. Thin, symmetrical, narrow, good workmanship, parallel
percussion flaked. Fine, sharply serrated edges, side notched, thin,
symmetrical dovetail base. Made of grainy white chert.
Priv. col., excellent quality, valued $400-500.

• Dovetail from Wayne co., MO. Blade 4 1/8 in. long, 1 7/16 in. wide,
3/16 in. thick. Thin, symmetrical, left hand beveled, wide percussion
flaking. Side notched, serrated edges, wide tail. Made of brown pebble
chert.
Priv. col., museum quality, valued $525-650.

• Dovetail from Jackson co., IL. Blade 5 1/2 in. long, 2 1/4 in. wide,
1/4 in. thick. Heat treated, parallel, sharply serrated, beveled on all four
edges. Deep, narrow corner notches, exceptional tail formation. Made of
Mill Creek chert.
Priv. col., museum quality, valued $700-850.

• Dovetail from Jackson co., IL. Blade 6 1/4 in. long, 2 1/2 in. wide,
1/2 in. thick. Symmetrical, heat treated, finely serrated, left hand
beveled, extremely sharp. Deep side notches, thinned dovetail base.
Made of Milk Creek chert.
Priv. col., museum quality, valued $600-700.

• Dovetail from Delaware co., OH. Blade 4 3/4 in. long, 2 1/3 in.
wide, 1/4 in. thick. Thin, symmetrical, finely serrated edges, percussion
flaked, thinned tip. Tail symmetrical, wider than the blade, classic
design. Made of Flint Ridge chert.
Priv. col., excellent quality, valued $350-450.

• Dovetail from Delaware co., OH. Blade 5 1/4 in. long, 1 7/8 in. wide,
1/4 in. thick. Thin, symmetrical, finely serrated blade edges, parallel.
Deep, narrow, uniform side notches, classical dovetail base, thin. Made
of Flint Ridge chert.
Priv. col., museum quality, rare, valued $1,000-1,250.

• Dovetail from Delaware co., OH. Blade 6 in. long, 2 1/4 in. wide,
1/4 in. thick. Thin, finely, minutely serrated blade edges. Percussion
flaked, deep, narrow, uniform side notches. Classic shaped base,
ground. Made of Flint Ridge chert.
Priv. col., museum quality, rare, valued $1,500-2,000.

CHAPTER 5 ECUSTA-EVA

Ecusta: 8,000-1,000 B.P. Early Archaic

Predominantly found in the outheast, particularly Tennessee. Ecusta is a small point with one edge of each face sharply beveled. They are serrated and side notched, with ground bases and notches. Because of the high quality workmanship and variety exhibited in Ecusta points, their value has raised in the last several years.

◆ Ecusta from Hamilton co., TN. Point 1 5/8 in. long, 1 in. wide, 1/8 in. thick. Exceptional point, very sharp tip, sharply beveled and finely serrated. High polish to the piece. Made of a deep glossy black chert.

Priv. col., museum quality, rare, valued $125-200.

• Ecusta from Perry co., TN. Point 1 1/8 in. long, 5/8 in. wide, 1/8 in. thick. Classic Ecusta. Made of Dover chert.
Priv. col., museum quality, valued $85-145.

• Ecusta from northwestern TN. Point 2 in. long, 1 5/8 in. wide, 3/16 in. thick. Fluted point with all four sides steeply beveled. Made of pebble chert.
Priv. col., excellent quality, valued $45-70.

• Ecusta from Perry co., TN. Point 2 1/8 in. long, 1 5/8 in. wide, 3/16 in. thick.

Steeply beveled, wide spaced serrations, random flaking. Made of low grade quartzite.
Priv. col., average quality, valued $15-25.

• Ecusta from central KY. Point 2 1/16 in. long, 1 11/16 in. wide, 1/4 in. thick. Beveled on one edge of each face. Random flaked point with fine, sharp serrations. Made of gray pebble chert.
Priv. col., museum quality, valued $120-165.

• Ecusta from Alexander co., KY. Point 1 3/16 in. long, 3/4 in. wide, 3/16 in. thick. Classical Ecusta markings, small tip break. Made of low grade quartzite.
Priv. col., average quality, valued $10-20.

• Ecusta from Hamilton co., TN. Point 1 3/8 in. long, 1 1/32 in. wide, 1/8 in. thick. Classically designed point, very sharp tip, edges beveled and finely serrated. Made of dull black chert.
Grover Bohannon col., museum quality, valued $105-140.

• Ecusta from Perry co., IL. Point 1 5/8 in. long, 5/8 in. wide, 1/8 in. thick. Thin, finely serrated, deeply beveled on one edge of each face. Made of Cobden chert.
Jim Smith col., museum quality, valued $95-165.

• Ecusta from Memphis, TN. Point 2 3/16 in. long, 1 7/8 in. wide, 3/16 in. thick. Fluted point with all four sides steeply beveled. Heat treated, wide yet symmetrical. Made of pinkish pebble chert.
Grover Bohannon col., excellent quality, valued $55-75.

• Ecusta from Perry co., TN. Point 2 5/8 in. long, 1 7/8 in. wide, 5/16 in. thick. Steeply beveled on one edge of each side, wide serrations, sharp, random flaked. Made of Dover chert.
Priv. col., excellent quality, valued $25-35.

• Ecusta from Union co., IL. Point 2 3/8 in. long, 1 1/2 in. wide, 7/16 in. thick. Steeply beveled on all four sides, very fine, widely spaced and sharp serrations. Made of Kaolin chert.
Priv. col., museum quality, rare, valued $150-225.

• Ecusta from Wabash co., IN. Point 1 31/32 in. long, 1 1/16 in. wide, 1/4 in. thick. Classic piece, with very sharp serrations and tip. Made of red jasper.
Priv. col., museum quality, rare, valued $165-210.

• Ecusta from Adair co., KY. Point 2 1/8 in. long, 1 in. wide, 3/16 in. thick.

Point beveled on all four sides, pointed, wide spaced edge serrations. Tip is very pointed and sharp, deep side notches, pointed barbs, wide convex base. Made of dark brown chert.
Priv. col., museum quality, valued $40-60.

• Ecusta from Adair co., KY. Point 2 3/8 in. long, 1 1/3 in. wide, 1/8 in. thick. Edges beveled and finely serrated, sharp pointed. Concave base. Made of dull gray chert.
Priv. col., museum quality, valued $85-100.

• Ecusta from Perry co., KY. Point 2 1/8 in. long, 7/8 in. wide, 1/8 in. thick. Thin, finely serrated, deeply beveled on one edge of each face. Wide corner notches, sharp tanged, convex base. Made of tan yellow chert.
Priv. col., excellent quality, valued $65-80.

• Ecusta from Perry co., KY. Point 3 1/16 in. long, 1 1/4 in. wide, 1/8 in. thick. Fine, thin, serrated edges, very long, thinned tip. Random flaked, shallow, uniform side notches, wide, parallel sided straight base. Made of yellow tan chert.
Priv. col., excellent quality, valued $100-150.

• Ecusta from Bullitt co., KY. Point 1 1/2 in. long, 1 1/16 in. wide, 1/8 in. thick. Thin, triangularly symmetrical, very sharp tip, edges beveled on all four sides and finely serrated. Barbed shoulders, narrow uniform side notches, thinned concave base. Made of glossy black chert.
Priv. col., museum quality, valued $85-120.

• Ecusta from Page co., VA. Point 1 7/8 in. long, 3/4 in. wide, 1/8 in. thick. Thin, narrow, finely serrated, beveled on one edge of each face. Side notched, barbed shoulders, convex thinned base. Made of white to pink chert.
Priv. col., museum quality, valued $75-100.

• Ecusta from Page co., VA. Point 1 5/16 in. long, 3/4 in. wide, 3/16 in. thick. Narrow, thin, symmetrical, heat treated, long deep random flaked. Beveled on one side of each face, edges serrated. Side notched, barbed shoulders and base tangs, convex base. Made of white to pink chert.
Priv. col., excellent quality, valued $50-80.

• Ecusta from Page co., VA. Point 1 7/8 in. long, 1 9/32 in. wide, 1/8 in. thick. Thin sharp tip, heat treated, beveled on all four sides, edges finely serrated. Side notched, barbed shoulders, thinned concave base. Made of white to pink chert.
Priv. col., museum quality, valued $100-120.

• Ecusta from Perry co., IL. Point 2 in. long, 1 1/8 in. wide, 1/8 in. thick. Thin, finely serrated, beveled on all four sides, minute sharp serrations. Side notched, tapered shoulders, concave thinned base. Made of Mill Creek chert.
Jim Smith col., excellent quality, valued $65-85.

• Ecusta from Alexander co., IL. Point 2 5/16 in. long, 1 1/3 in. wide, 3/16 in. thick. Symmetrical, beveled on all four sides, sharp serrated edges. Shallow side notches, tapered shoulders, ground base. Made of rose quartz.
Jim Smith col., museum quality, valued $100-120.

• Ecusta from Alexander co., IL. Point 3 1/4 in. long, 1 3/32 in. wide, 1/8 in. thick. Very sharp tip, edges beveled on one side of each face and finely serrated. Shallow side notches, tapered shoulders, convex base. Made of Mill Creek chert.
Grover Bohannon col., museum quality, valued $100-120.

• Ecusta from Perry co., IL. Point 2 5/8 in. long, 1 3/8 in. wide, 1/8 in. thick. Thin, finely serrated, deeply beveled on one edge of each face. Narrow side notches, tapered shoulders. convex base. Made of dense tan chert.
Priv. col., museum quality, valued $125-165.

• Ecusta from Perry co., IL. Point 1 7/16 in. long, 7/8 in. wide, 1/3 in. thick. Narrow, thick, steeply beveled on all four sides, serrated edges. Heat treated tapered shoulders, concave base. Made of dense tan chert.
Priv. col., excellent quality, valued $80-120.

• Ecusta from Davidson co., TN. Point 1 3/8 in. long, 1 5/32 in. wide, 1/8 in. thick. Nearly as wide as long, triangular, all four edges beveled and finely serrated. Tapered shoulders, convex, thinned base. Made of multi-toned brown chert.
Grover Bohannon col., museum quality, valued $100-140.

• Ecusta from Davidson co., TN. Point 2 3/8 in. long, 1 in. wide, 1/8 in. thick. Thin, triangularly narrow, finely serrated, deeply beveled on one edge of each face. Barbed shoulders, convex base. Made of Dover chert.
Priv. col., museum quality, valued $125-185.

• Ecusta from Chester co., TN. Point 1 11/16 in. long, 1 1/4 in. wide, 5/8 in. thick. Wide, thick, steeply beveled on all four sides, poor quality workmanship. Tapered shoulders, convex base. Made of quartzite.
Priv. col., average quality, valued $30-40.

• Ecusta from Chester co., TN. Point 1 7/8 in. long, 1 7/32 in. wide, 1/8 in. thick. Thin, triangular, evenly beveled on all four sides, very sharp tip, edges,

poor workmanship. Tapered shoulders, thinned concave base. Made of dull gray chert.
Priv. col., average quality, valued $45-50.

• Ecusta from Lake co., TN. Point 2 5/8 in. long, 1 5/8 in. wide, 1/8 in. thick. Thin, finely serrated, steeply beveled on one edge of each face, sharply serrated. Pecussion flaked, deep side notches, barbed shoulders, convex base. Made of near translucent brown chert.
Priv. col., museum quality, rare, valued $165-185.

Edwards: 2,000-1,000 B.P. Woodland to Mississippian

Edwards are found throughout the Midwest. Edwards is a small barbed point, very sharp and quite thin. Edwards exhibits long flaring base ears. Some examples are minutely serrated and very thin and sharp. These points are small enough and designed in such a way as to be truly arrowheads as well as atlatl points.

♦ Edwards from central TX. Point 2 in. long, 5/8 in. wide, 1/8 in. thick. Tan to brown pebble chert.

Priv. col., excellent quality, valued $65-100.

• Edwards from Madison co., IL. Point 1 15/16 in. long, 1/2 in. wide, 1/8 in. thick. Very finely serrated and sharp point. Unusual when using this type of material. Made of Mill Creek chert.
Priv. col., museum quality, rare, valued $200-275.

• Edwards from Coles co., IL. Point 1 3/16 in. long, 3/8 in. wide, 1/16 in. thick. Made of a brown grained quartzite.
Priv. col., average quality, valued $25-40.

• Edwards from northeastern TX. Point 1 1/8 in. long, 7/16 in. wide, 1/8 in. thick. Very symmetrical for an Edwards, polished with thick, wide tail. Made of marblized blue on pink chert.
Priv. col., museum quality, rare, valued $350-500.

• Edwards from Hardin co., IL. Point 2 1/4 in. long, 5/8 in. wide, 1/8 in. thick. Like most museum to average quality Edwards, the point is finely serrated and quite sharp. Made of Cobden Hornstone chert.
Priv. col., excellent quality, valued $85-125.

• Edwards from Jasper co., IL. Point 1 7/8 in. long, 3/8 in. wide, 3/16 in. thick. Small nick in point base. Made of unidentified white chert.
Priv. col., excellent quality, valued $65-100.

• Edwards from Lucas co., OH. Point 1 1/2 in. long, 1/2 in. wide, 1/4 in. thick. Thick, yet very sharp point, finely serrated with distinct upward flaring ears. Made of gray on pink pebble chert.
Priv. col., excellent quality, valued $85-125.

• Edwards from Gallatin co., IL. Point 2 5/8 in. long, 1/2 in. wide, 1/8 in. thick. Point large for an Edwards, 1/4 in. long base ears with a sweeping flare. Made of jasper.
Priv. col., museum quality, rare, valued $275-350.

• Edwards from Gallatin co., IL. Point 2 3/4 in. long, 7/8 in. wide, 1/8 in. thick. Point finely serrated, sharp, upward flaring ears. Made of Cobden chert.
Priv. col., excellent quality, valued $85-115.

• Edwards from Calhoun co., IL. Point 1 3/8 in. long, 3/8 in. wide, 3/16 in. thick. Small, narrow, symmetrical point. Made of white pebble chert.
Priv. col., excellent quality, valued $65-90.

• Edwards from Columbus, OH. Point 2 1/3 in. long, 5/8 in. wide, 1/4 in. thick. Very sharp point, finely serrated with outward flaring ears. Made of pink pebble chert.
Priv. col., excellent quality, valued $85-115.

• Edwards from Greene co., IL. Point 1 1/16 in. long, 1/3 in. wide, 5/32 in. thick. Symmetrical, minute, wide serrations, sharp, thin tip. Deep, wide corner notches; wide, thin, round tanged, concave base. Made of greenish chert.
Priv. col., excellent quality, valued $100-175.

• Edwards from Greene co., IL. Point 2 1/8 in. long, 3/4 in. wide, 1/16 in. thick. Thin, angularly narrow, good workmanship, finely serrated, rounded side notches, fish tail base. Made of light creamy brown chert.
Priv. col., excellent quality, valued $75-100.

• Edwards from Greene co., Il. Point 1 1/2 in. long, 13/16 in. wide, 1/8 in.

thick. Symmetrical, wide, base wider than point. Highly serrated edges, slight tip
break. Made of pinkish white chert.
Priv. col., average quality, valued $150-200.

- Edwards from Franklin co., IL. Point 2 1/2 in. long, 7/8 in. wide, 1/8 in. thick.
Thin, narrow, finely serrated, tip needle sharp. Narrow, concave blade, deep
uniform side notches. Made of white pebble chert.
Tim Rubbles col., excellent quality, valued $200-250.

- Edwards from Franklin co., IL. Point 2 1/16 in. long, 1/2 in. wide, 3/16 in.
thick. Narrow, thin, distinct serrations, needle sharp tip, good field patina.
Narrow stem, base uniform with sides, concave base. Made of tan gray chert.
Priv. col., excellent quality, valued $250-300.

- Edwards from Coles co., IL. Point 1 5/8 in. long, 5/16 in. wide, 1/16 in. thick.
High quality workmanship, extremely thin and narrow, minute sharp serrations,
paper thin needle sharp point. Uniform corner notches, flaring, rounded base ears,
base concave. Made of a local green gray chert.
Priv. col., museum quality, rare, valued $450-500.

- Edwards from Greer co., OK. Point 1 1/2 in. long, 11/16 in. wide, 1/8 in.
thick. Symmetrical, long, deep serrations. Side notched. Flaring base tangs of
concave base from the widest portion of point. Made of grainy pink chert.
Priv. col., excellent quality, valued $100-150.

- Edwards from Greer co., OK. Point 2 1/3 in. long, 7/8 in. wide, 1/8 in. thick.
Angular, finely serrated, edges very sharp. Corner notched with round base tangs,
base just slightly concave. Made of white pebble chert.
Priv. col., excellent quality, valued $200-275.

- Edwards from Payne co., OK. Point 2 1/16 in. long, 5/8 in. wide, 1/8 in. thick.
Long, narrow, thin, finely serrated, needle sharp tip. Good field patina, quality
workmanship, atypical pointed shoulder barbs. Corner notched, narrow stem,
flaring concave base. Made of dense white chert.
Priv. col., museum quality, valued $250-325.

- Edwards from Pickaway co., OH. Point 1 13/16 in. long, 7/16 in. wide,
1/8 in. thick. Symmetrical, thin, serrations from center to edge of point. Good
workmanship, heat treated, some field patina. Corner notched, barbed shoulders,
serrated flaring concave base. Made of false jasper.
Priv. col., excellent quality, valued $175-240.

- Edwards from Crocket co., TX. Point 1 3/8 in. long, 1/2 in. wide, 1/8 in.

thick. Symmetrical, thin, finely serrated, barbed shoulders. Side notched, one side of flaring concave base broken. Made of pink chert.
Priv. col., average quality, valued $65-80.

• Edwards from Elk co., KS. Point 2 1/16 in. long, 17/32 in. wide, 1/8 in. thick. Thin, narrow, finely serrated edges, good field patina. Narrow stem, shallow side notches, tapered shoulders. Rounded flaring base tangs, serrated concave base. Made of black silver flint.
Priv. col., excellent quality, valued $145-180.

Ellis: 4,000-2,000 B.P. Late Archaic

A midwestern point small to medium in size. Corner notched, tapered or barbed shoulders, with an expanded stem. Base is generally convex or straight.

◆ Ellis from Monroe co., TN. Point 1 in. long, 1/2 in. wide, 5/32 in. thick. Very finely and sharply serrated. Shallow corner notched, classic tapered shoulders. Prestige point from burial site, early 1900s. Made of translucent white chert.

Grover Bohannon col., museum quality, valued $35-45.

• Ellis from Gallatin co., KY. Point 7/8 in. long, 1/4 in. wide, 1/8 in. thick. Deeply corner notched, barbed shoulders, with an expanded stem. Base is straight. Made of white pebble chert.
Grover Bohannon col., excellent quality, valued $25-35.

• Ellis from Hamilton co., TN. Point 1 1/8 in. long, 1/2 in. wide, 1/4 in. thick. Finely and sharply serrated, thick. Symmetrically corner notched, barbed shoulders, convex base. Made of Dover chert.
Priv. col., museum quality, valued $35-55.

• Ellis from Alexander co., IL. Point 23/32 in. long, 1/4 in. wide, 1/8 in. thick. Symmetrical point, corner notched, tapered, with expanded stem. Base straight. Made of Mill Creek chert.
Priv. col., excellent quality, valued $25-35.

- Ellis from Monroe co., TN. Point 1 3/16 in. long, 5/8 in. wide, 7/32 in. thick.
Finely and sharply serrated. Shallow corner notches, tapered shoulders. Made
of Dover chert.
Grover Bohannon col., museum quality, valued $45-65.

- Ellis from Stewart co., MO. Point 7/8 in. long, 1/4 in. wide, 1/8 in. thick.
Corner notched, sharp barbed shoulders, wide serrations with an expanded stem.
Base is convex. Made of tan pebble chert.
Priv. col., excellent quality, valued $25-35.

- Ellis from Humphreys co., TN. Point 1 1/32 in. long, 1/2 in. wide, 7/32 in.
thick. Very thick, heat treated, sharply serrated. Shallow corner notched, short
tapered shoulders. Made of white pebble chert.
Priv. col., average quality, valued $15-25.

- Ellis from Stewart co., MO. Point 5/8 in. long, 1/4 in. wide, 3/16 in. thick.
Corner notched, barbed shoulders. Base is straight and expanded. Made of dark
brown chert.
Priv. col., excellent quality, valued $25-35.

- Ellis from Monroe co., IL. Point 1 3/32 in. long, 1/2 in. wide, 5/32 in. thick.
High quality workmanship, finely and sharply serrated, with sharp pointed tip.
Symmetrically corner notched, classic tapered shoulders. Made of a local
translucent green gray chert.
Tim Rubbles col., museum quality, valued $35-45.

- Ellis from Stewart co., TN. Point 1 3/8 in. long, 1/2 in. wide, 1/8 in. thick.
Corner notched, tapered shoulders, expanded stem. Base is convex with nick in
center. Made of quartzite.
Priv. col., average quality, valued $10-20.

- Ellis from Monroe co., TN. Point 1 5/32 in. long, 2/3 in. wide, 7/32 in. thick.
Very finely sharp serrated edges. Symmetrical deep corner notches, unusually
wide for an Ellis, somewhat long tapered shoulders, convex. Prestige point from
burial site, early 1900s. Made of translucent tan chert.
Grover Bohannon col., museum quality, valued $45-65.

- Ellis from Stewart co., TN. Point 1 3/8 in. long, 1/2 in. wide, 1/8 in. thick.
Corner notched, tapered and ground shoulders, atypical stem. Base convex and
serrated. Made of high grade quartzite.
Priv. col., excellent quality, valued $25-35.

- Ellis from Jasper co., IL. Point 1 1/3 in. long, 1/2 in. wide, 1/8 in. thick. Thin,

finely and sharply serrated, long and angular. Shallow corner notches, tapered shoulders. Made of heavy, dull black flint.
Priv. col., excellent quality, valued $25-35.

- Ellis from Cooper co., MO. Point 1 1/8 in. long, 2/3 in. wide, 1/8 in. thick. Long, thin, corner notched, tapered, expanded stem. Base is straight. Made of grainy white chert.
Priv. col., average quality, valued $15-25.

- Ellis from Monroe co., TN. Point 1 1/32 in. long, 1/2 in. wide, 3/16 in. thick. Very finely and sharply serrated, shallow corner notches, classic tapered shoulders. Made of Dover chert.
Priv. col., museum quality, valued $45-55.

- Ellis from Adair co., KY. Point 1 1/8 in. long, 7/8 in. wide, 1/8 in. thick. Symmetrically triangular point, heat treated, corner notched, tapered, with expanded stem. Base is straight. Made of tan chert.
Priv. col., excellent quality, valued $25-35.

- Ellis from Adair co., KY. Point 1 5/16 in. long, 7/8 in. wide, 1/4 in. thick. Sharply serrated, heat treated, triangular, rounded tip. Shallow corner notches, tapered shoulders, convex base. Made of tan chert.
Priv. col., excellent quality, valued $25-40.

- Ellis from Shelby co., KY. Point 1 in. long, 3/4 in. wide, 1/8 in. thick. Thin, sharp barbed shoulders, one broken, wide serrations. Expanded stem, convex base. Made of gray pebble chert.
Priv. col., average quality, valued $5-10.

- Ellis from Nart co., KY. Point 2 1/32 in. long, 1 1/4 in. wide, 1/4 in. thick. One of the largest Ellises I've personally seen. Symmetrical, serrated edges. Point corner notched, tapered shoulders. Expanded stem, straight base. Made of gray chert.
Ben Hill col., excellent quality, valued $25-35.

- Ellis from Nart co., KY. Point 1 5/16 in. long, 1 in. wide, 3/16 in. thick. Thin, finely and sharply serrated. Shallow corner notches, tapered shoulders, straight base. Made of gray chert.
Ben Hill col., museum quality, valued $40-50.

- Ellis from Nart co., KY. Point 1 3/8 in. long, 1 1/8 in. wide, 3/16 in. thick. Poor workmanship, asymmetrical, one side of point wider and offset from stem. Corner notched, sharp barbed shoulders, expanded stem. Base is convex, one tang

higher than the other. Made of tan pebble chert.
Ben Hill col., average quality, valued $8-15.

- Ellis from Emmet co., IA. Point 1 3/32 in. long, 13/16 in. wide, 1/8 in. thick.
Thin, symmetrical, serrated edges, corner notched, tapered shoulders. Expanded
stem, convex base. Made of pink black speckled chert.
Priv. col., excellent quality, valued $25-35.

- Ellis from Emmet co., IA. Point 1 7/16 in. long, 1 1/8 in. wide, 5/16 in. thick.
Beveled on one side of each face, thick, triangular, finely and sharply serrated.
Deep parallel corner notches, tapered shoulders, thinned convex base. Made of
translucent gray chert.
Priv. col., museum quality, rare, valued $65-85.

- Ellis from Emmet co., IA. Point 1 1/8 in. long, 1/2 in. wide, 1/8 in. thick. Thin,
narrow, serrated on one side of each face. Corner notched, sharp barbed
shoulders, expanded stem, convex base. Made of tan pebble chert.
Priv. col., excellent quality, valued $25-35.

Ensor: 4,500-1,200 B.P. Late Archaic to Woodland

*Ensors are predominantly a midwestern point or blade. The Ensor is
corner notched, symmetrical, narrow, and thin. The base varies from straight
to convex to concave. They are often barbed and serrated.*

◆ Ensor split-base from central AR. Blade 3 5/8 in. long, 1 3/8 in. wide,
3/16 in. thick. Made of an oily brown chert.

Priv. col., museum quality, valued $150-250.

- Ensor from Beaumont, TX. Point 2 1/2 in. long, 5/8 in. wide, 3/16 in. thick.
Point heat treated, serrated and barbed. Base concave, uneven corner notches.
Made of an unidentified white chert.
Priv. col., museum quality, valued $85-125.

- Ensor from Beaumont, TX. Point 2 1/16 in. long, 3/4 in. wide, 1/8 in. thick. Sharp point without serrations, convex base with small nick. Made of Leon River chert.
Priv. col., average quality, valued $40-65.

- Ensor from Hardin co., TN. Point 2 3/8 in. long, 1/2 in. wide, 1/8 in. thick. Point has been reworked, very fine yet distinct serrations. Straight base with deep corner notches. Made of Dover chert.
Priv. col., excellent quality, valued $65-90.

- Ensor from northeastern TX. Point 2 1/8 in. long, 1/2 in. wide, 1/8 in. thick. Point long, thin, yet very symmetrical, heat treated. Finely serrated and barbed. Base concave, symmetrical corner notches. Made of black flint.
Priv. col., museum quality, valued $65-100.

- Ensor from Midland co., TX. Point 2 5/16 in. long, 7/8 in. wide, 1/8 in. thick. Sharp point, thin, fine serrations, convex base. Made of milky gray chert.
Priv. col., excellent quality, valued $90-125.

- Ensor from Hardin co., IN. Point 1 7/8 in. long, 1/2 in. wide, 1/8 in. thick. Point heat treated, very sharp distinct serrations. Straight base with deep corner notches. Made of green chert.
Priv. col., excellent quality, valued $85-120.

- Ensor from Butler co., MO. Blade 3 1/2 in. long, 1 7/16 in. wide, 3/16 in. thick. Heat treated, parallel flaked, finely serrated. Deep side notches, wide, thin, straight base. Made of white chert.
Priv. col., excellent quality, valued $75-100.

- Ensor from Butler co., MO. Point 2 13/16 in. long, 1 1/4 in. wide, 1/8 in. thick. Wide, convex sides, sharp serrations, pointed and barbed shoulders. Side notched, convex base. Made of lightweight, porous white chert.
Priv. col., average quality, valued $45-50.

- Ensor from Harrison co., MO. Point 2 7/8 in. long, 2/3 in. wide, 1/8 in. thick. Very finely serrated edges, long needle tip. Corner notched, long rounded shoulder tangs, straight base. Made of Cobden chert.
Priv. col., museum quality, valued $135-160.

- Ensor from Jay co., IN. Point 2 1/3 in. long, 9/16 in. wide, 3/16 in. thick. Heat treated, thin, narrow concave edges minutely serrated. Uniform deep corner notches, sharp shoulder barbs, concave base. Made of greenish black speckled chert.

Priv. col., museum quality, valued $85-115.

- Ensor from Jay co., IN. Point 2 3/16 in. long, 3/4 in. wide, 1/8 in. thick. Sharply serrated, symmetrical, narrow, thin, parallel flaked. Side notched, horizontal pointed barbs, convex base. Made of light gray chert. *Priv. col., excellent quality, valued $60-85.*

- Ensor from Wabash co., IN. Point 3 1/8 in. long, 3/4 in. wide, 1/8 in. thick. Extremely symmetrical, minute edge serrations, concave sides, base parallel to sides. Good field patina, random flaked, serrated shoulder barbs. Side notched, concave base. Made of greenish chert. *Priv. col., museum quality, valued $125-180.*

- Ensor from Wabash co., IN. Point 2 1/2 in. long, 1 1/16 in. wide, 3/16 in. thick. Thin, wide convex sides, heat treated, edges finely serrated. Barbed shoulders, base concave, corner notched. Made of greenish chert. *Priv. col., museum quality, valued $85-125.*

- Ensor from Pope co., IL. Point 2 3/16 in. long, 3/4 in. wide, 1/8 in. thick. Sharp serrated edges, thin, short horizontal shoulder barbs. Side notched, thin convex base. Made of yellow white local chert. *Tim Rubbles col., excellent quality, valued $70-85.*

- Ensor from Pope co., IL. Point 2 7/8 in. long, 2/3 in. wide, 1/8 in. thick. Sharply serrated concave edges, very sharp tip, thin large random flaking. Corner notched, distinct barbs, concave base. Made of local yellow white chert. *Tim Rubbles col., excellent quality, valued $100-150.*

- Ensor from Pope co., IL. Point 2 1/2 in. long, 5/8 in. wide, 3/32 in. thick. Very thin, quality random flaking, heat treated, finely serrated and barbed. Base concave, deep corner notches. Made of a local yellow white chert. *Priv. col., excellent quality, valued $85-125.*

- Ensor from Hamilton co., IL. Point 3 1/16 in. long, 3/4 in. wide, 1/8 in. thick. Thin, concave sides, sharp edge serrations, slight tip break. Corner notched, horizontal pointed barbs, convex base. Made of Mill Creek chert. *Priv. col., average quality, valued $40-50.*

- Ensor from Hardin co., IL. Point 2 in. long, 7/16 in. wide, 1/8 in. thick. Thin, parallel flaked, very fine distinct edge serrations. Barbed shoulders, corner notched, straight base. Made of gray chert. *Priv. col., excellent quality, valued $75-85.*

• Ensor from Champaign co., IL. Point 2 5/8 in. long, 5/8 in. wide, 1/8 in. thick. Thin, narrow, highly serrated concave edges, heat treated. Base concave, corner notched, barbed shoulders. Made of white chert.
Priv. col., excellent quality, valued $85-100.

• Ensor from Lipscomb co., TX. Point 2 7/16 in. long, 3/4 in. wide, 3/16 in. thick. Sharp, thin tip, wide serrations, concave sides. Convex base, tapered shoulders, side notched. Made of Leon River chert.
Priv. col., excellent quality, valued $120-165.

• Ensor from Lipscomb co., TX. Point 3 3/8 in. long, 11/16 in. wide, 1/8 in. thick. Thin, parallel flaked, extremely sharp concave edges, heat treated. Side notched, tapered shoulders, convex base. Made of Leon River chert.
Priv. col., museum quality, valued $150-200.

Etley: 4,000-2,500 B.P. Late Archaic

Etley is a large midwestern blade. The blade is straight based with an expanded stem. Etley blades are narrow, recurved, with an angular tip. The Etley is a very aesthetically appealing blade and much sought after.

♦ Etley from Henry co., OH. Point 2 in. long, 1 5/16 in. wide, 1/4 in. thick. Unusually short Etley, tip has been reworked. Due to the material used the base is uneven rather than straight. Heavy field patina. Made of Mill Creek chert.

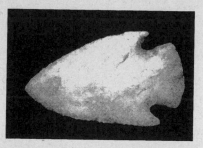

Priv. col., excellent quality, rare, valued $65-100.

♦ Etley from Johnson co., IL. Blade 4 1/8 in. long, 1 1/2 in. wide, 1/4 in. thick. Blade is heat treated, with tip break and several blade nicks. Classic design. Made of Mill Creek chert.

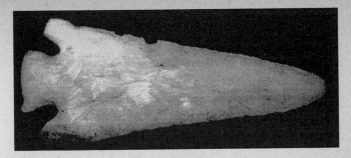

Priv. col., average quality, valued $85-125.

- Etley from Lucas co., OH. Blade 6 1/8 in. long, 2 in. wide, 1/4 in. thick. Blade has a 1/4 in. long angular tip. Deep side notches with snapped base. Made of an unidentified white chert.
Priv. col., museum quality, valued $200-250.

- Etley from Lucas co., OH. Blade 6 3/8 in. long, 2 1/4 in. wide, 1/4 in. thick. Quality workmanship, thin, narrow, deeply recurved, with an angular tip. Made of a local white chert.
Priv. col., excellent quality, valued $45-80.

- Etley from Wabash co., IN. Point 2 1/4 in. long, 1 7/16 in. wide, 1/4 in. thick. Unusually wide Etley, needle sharp tip, deeply side notched and symmetrical. Base is unevenly snapped. Made of tan to yellow pebble chert.
Priv. col., excellent quality, valued $65-80.

- Etley from Johnson co., IL. Blade 4 1/8 in. long, 1 1/2 in. wide, 1/4 in. thick. Blade is heat treated, with very sharply serrated tip. Made of Mill Creek chert.
Priv. col., excellent quality, valued $85-125.

- Etley from Lucas co., KY. Blade 5 3/8 in. long, 2 1/32 in. wide, 1/4 in. thick. Blade has straight base, angular tip. Deep, wide side notches. Made of white pebble chert.
Tim Rubbles col., museum quality, valued $185-275.

- Etley from Allegan co., MI. Blade 5 in. long, 2 1/16 in. wide, 1/4 in. thick. Thin, symmetrical, finely serrated, needle sharp tip. Wide stem, corner notched, thinned straight base. Made of pink to white marbled chert.
Priv. col., excellent quality, rare, valued $225-280.

- Etley from Hillsdale co., MI. Blade 5 1/8 in. long, 1 2/3 in. wide, 1/4 in. thick. Blade is heat treated, finely serrated edges. Needle sharp tip, straight sides, triangular blade. Made of glossy, dense gray chert.

Priv. col., museum quality, valued $185-225.

• Etley from Montcalm co., MI. Blade 5 7/8 in. long, 2 5/16 in. wide, 1/4 in. thick. Blade thinnly serrated, triangular tip. Deep corner notches, rounded tangs, straight snapped base. Made of white black speckled chert.
Priv. col., excellent quality, valued $180-200.

• Etley from Montcalm co., MI. Blade 6 1/32 in. long, 1 15/16 in. wide, 3/8 in. thick. Symmetrical, serrated edges, tip has been reworked. Deep side notches, horizontal shoulders, expanding stem, straight base. Made of gray banded chert.
Priv. col., excellent quality, valued $165-200.

• Etley from Menominee co., WI. Blade 4 1/2 in. long, 1 7/8 in. wide, 1/4 in. thick. Heat treated, finely serrated edges, needle sharp tip, shoulder tangs extending beyond base. Deep corner notched, expanded stem, straight base. Made of white brown banded chert.
Priv. col., excellent quality, valued $185-225.

• Etley from Menominee co., WI. Blade 6 1/8 in. long, 3 in. wide, 1/4 in. thick. Wide, highly serrated convex edges, heat treated, thinned, sharp distinct tip. Short horizontal barbs, corner notched, snapped, straight base. Made of white and brown banded chert.
Priv. col., museum quality, valued $200-250.

• Etley from Menominee co., WI. Blade 3 7/8 in. long, 1 1/4 in. wide, 3/16 in. thick. Blade edges are finely serrated and have been reworked. Blade from the same site as previous Menominee co., pieces. Good field patina, heat treated tip. Corner notched, rounded tangs extending beyond snapped straight base. Made of brown and white banded chert.
Priv. col., excellent quality, valued $165-200.

• Etley from Buffalo co., WI. Blade 5 1/8 in. long, 1 13/16 in. wide, 1/4 in. thick. Blade is heat treated, with minutely serrated edges, several blade nicks. Corner notched, rounded tangs, staight base. Made of pink chert.
Priv. col., average quality, valued $65-85.

• Etley from Clark co., IL. Blade 6 in. long, 2 3/4 in. wide, 1/4 in. thick. Finely serrated edges, symmetrical, parallel flaked, long, thinned, angular tip. Deep side notches, short rounded tangs, straight snapped base. Made of white pebble chert.
Priv. col., museum quality, valued $180-200.

• Etley from Greenbriar co., WV. Blade 5 in. long, 1 11/16 in. wide, 1/4 in. thick. Good field patina, thin parallel flaked from center to edges, triangular

needle sharp tip. Wide corner notches, short rounded tangs, wide convex base.
Made of grainy beige chert.
Priv. col., excellent quality, valued $95-130.

• Etley from Johnson co., IL. Blade 5 1/8 in. long, 1 19/32 in. wide, 1/4 in.
thick. Heat treated, serrated edges. Shallow, wide corner notches, short rounded
tangs. Long stem, convex base. Made of Mill Creek chert.
Priv. col., excellent quality, valued $85-125.

• Etley from Johnson co., IL. Blade 6 1/8 in. long, 2 3/8 in. wide, 1/4 in. thick.
Blade is finely serrated, heat treated, wide rounded tangs. Deep corner notches
with snapped base. Made of Mill Creek chert.
Priv. col., excellent quality, valued $100-150.

• Etley from Effingham co., IL. Point 3 1/16 in. long, 1 3/8 in. wide, 1/4 in.
thick. Sharp edge unserrated, heat treated, rounded tangs. Corner notched,
expanded stem, convex base. Made of gray chert.
Priv. col., excellent quality, valued $95-120.

• Etley from Effingham co., IL. Blade 4 1/3 in. long, 1 5/8 in. wide, 1/4 in.
thick. Blade heat treated, sharp edges and tip, barbed shoulders. Corner notched,
straight base. Made of gray white banded chert.
Priv. col., excellent quality, valued $85-125.

• Etley from Jefferson co., IA. Blade 6 5/8 in. long, 2 3/4 in. wide, 1/4 in. thick.
Thin, symmetrical, parallel flaked, wide shallow edge serrations. Deep side
notches, pointed horizontal barbs with snapped base. Made of white and pink
banded chert.
Amir Naktari col., museum quality, valued $200-250.

• Etley from Jefferson co., IA. Point 2 27/32 in. long, 1 7/16 in. wide, 1/4 in.
thick. Good workmanship, some field patina, thin parallel flaked, edge serrations
minute and close though distinct. Shallow side notches, rounded tangs, convex
base. Made of tan pebble chert.
Amir Naktari col., excellent quality, valued $165-200.

• Etley from Mills co., IA. Blade 4 1/16 in. long, 1 1/2 in. wide, 1/2 in. thick.
Symmetrical yet thick, heat treated, finely serrated, triangular tip, several blade
nicks. Side notched, barbed shoulders, straight base. Made of grainy white
chert.
Priv. col., average quality, valued $55-85.

• Etley from Osceola co., IA. Blade 6 in. long, 3 1/16 in. wide, 1/4 in. thick.

Finely serrated convex edges, long needle sharp tip. Deep side notches with snapped base. Made of white pebble chert.
Priv. col., excellent quality, valued $150-200.

• Etley from Henry co., OH. Point 2 3/4 in. long, 1 3/16 in. wide, 1/4 in. thick. Sharp, minute edge serrations, good workmanship, parallel flaked, rounded tip. Vertical corner notches, base tangs parallel to straight base. Made of pink white chert.
Priv. col., excellent quality, valued $125-140.

• Etley from Henry co., OH. Blade 5 1/8 in. long, 1 3/4 in. wide, 1/4 in. thick. Symmetrical, fine minute edge serration, heat treated, slight tip break, 3 blade nicks on one side. Corner notched, sharp barbs, convex base. Made of tan pebble chert.
Priv. col., average quality, valued $75-85.

• Etley from Henry co., OH. Blade 6 3/8 in. long, 2 1/2 in. wide, 1/4 in. thick. Sharp unserrated edges, good workmanship, random flaked, rounded tip. Deep side notches, horizontal barbs, snapped base. Made of white pebble chert.
Priv. col., excellent quality, valued $300-350.

Eva: 10,000-5,000 B.P. Early to Mid-Archaic

Eva is predominantly found throughout Tennessee and southwestern Kentucky. The Eva is also prevalent in the area surrounding the joining of the Mississippi and Ohio rivers. Evas are triangular, medium to large in size. The point or blade is shallow basal notched, tangs occasionally flared, with parallel flaking and recurved sides.

◆ Eva from Memphis, TN. Blade 4 in. long, 1 3/4 in. wide, 1/2 in. thick. Snapped base. Made of Dover chert.

Tony Clinton col., excellent quality, valued $65-80.

◆ Eva from Cape Giradeau co., MO. Point 2 3/8 in. long, 1 1/32 in. wide,

1/4 in. thick. Very sharp tip and edges, random flaking, shallow snapped base. Glossy black chert with silver streaks in the upper half.

Priv. col., museum quality, rare, valued $150-200.

• Eva from Franklin co., IL. Blade 3 5/8 in. long, 1 2/3 in. wide, 3/8 in. thick. Blade is triangular, with shallow basal notches, flaring tangs, parallel flaked, recurved sides. Made of Mill Creek chert.
Priv. col., excellent quality, valued $95-140.

• Eva from Memphis, TN. Blade 4 in. long, 1 3/4 in. wide, 1/2 in. thick. Snapped base. Made of Dover chert.
Priv. col., excellent quality, valued $75-90.

• Eva from Gallatin co., TN. Point 2 1/8 in. long, 1 3/32 in. wide, 1/4 in. thick. Very sharp edges, parallel flaked, shallow snapped base, long flaring tangs. Made of streaked brown chert.
Priv. col., museum quality, valued $100-150.

• Eva from Giles co., TN. Point 2 11/16 in. long, 1 5/8 in. wide, 1/4 in. thick. Highly defined and sharp serrated point. Made of Dover chert.
Priv. col., average quality, valued $45-65.

• Eva from Paducah, KY. Blade 3 3/4 in. long, 1 1/2 in. wide, 3/8 in. thick. Blade exhibits parallel pressure flaking, edges are finely serrated, stem is snapped base, tip extremely sharp and pointed. Made of Mill Creek chert.
Priv. col., museum quality, valued $150-200.

• Eva from Hamilton co., TN. Point 2 5/8 in. long, 1 3/4 in. wide, 1/4 in. thick. Very wide point, long fine edge flaking, snapped base, with long tangs. Made of Dover chert.
Priv. col., museum quality, valued $125-150.

• Eva from Alexander co., IL. Blade 4 in. long, 1 1/3 in. wide, 3/16 in. thick. Heat treated, sharply serrated recurved edges, parallel flaked, sharp thinned tip. Shallow basal notches, tangs flared, short convex base. Made of Mill Creek

chert.
Tim Rubbles col., excellent quality, valued $50-60.

• Eva from Alexander co., IL. Blade 3 3/4 in. long, 1 1/4 in. wide, 1/4 in. thick.
High quality workmanship, thin parallel flaking, sharp serrated edges, recurved
side. Basal notched, snap base. Made of Mill Creek chert.
Tim Rubbles col., excellent quality, valued $65-80.

• Eva from Lafayette co., KY. Point 2 5/8 in. long, 1 in. wide, 1/4 in. thick.
Triangular, sharply serrated tip and edges, random flaking. Shallow basal
notches, snapped base. Made of gray silver flint.
Priv. col., museum quality, valued $125-160.

• Eva from Lafayette co., KY. Blade 3 7/8 in. long, 1 1/2 in. wide, 1/4 in. thick.
Triangular, parallel flaked, highly serrated edges. Shallow basal notches, snapped
base and tangs. Made of yellow pebble chert.
Priv. col., excellent quality, valued $45-70.

• Eva from Lafayette co., KY. Blade 4 1/32 in. long, 1 1/3 in. wide, 3/16 in.
thick. Triangular, with parallel flaking and sharply serrated recurved sides.
Shallow basal notches, tangs flaring, narrowing convex base. Made of gray flint.
Priv. col., excellent quality, valued $100-125.

• Eva from Hamilton co., IL. Blade 4 1/2 in. long, 1 3/4 in. wide, 1/4 in. thick.
Thin, widely serrated recurved edges, parallel flaked. Snap base, deep basal
notches, flaring tangs. Made of Kaolin chert.
Priv. col., museum quality, rare, valued $365-380.

• Eva from Trousdale co., TN. Point 2 5/8 in. long, 1 5/32 in. wide, 1/4 in.
thick. Sharply serrated tip and edges, random flaked. Shallow basal notches, snap
tangs and base. Made of translucent glossy black chert.
Priv. col., museum quality, valued $100-150.

• Eva from Trousdale co., TN. Blade 3 29/32 in. long, 1 1/3 in. wide, 1/8 in.
thick. Delicately thin, parallel flaked, triangular, sharply serrated recurved edges.
Shallow basal notches, barbed shoulders, narrowing convex base. Made of black
flint.
Priv. col., excellent quality, valued $100-130.

• Eva from Jefferson co., TN. Point 3 in. long, 1 1/8 in. wide, 1/8 in. thick.
Triangular, parallel flaked, highly serrated recurved sides. Basal notched, short
rounded tangs, convex base. Made of pink chert.
Priv. col., excellent quality, valued $75-100.

- Eva from Jefferson co., TN. Blade 4 3/32 in. long, 1 1/2 in. wide, 1/4 in. thick. Good workmanship, parallel flaked, minute sharp edge serrations. Snap base, deep basal notches, flaring tangs. Made of Dover chert. *Priv., col., excellent quality, valued $100-180.*

- Eva from Knox co., TN. Point 2 1/2 in. long, 1 in. wide, 1/4 in. thick. Sharply serrated tip and edges, random flaking. Shallow basal notches, snap base. Made of black flint. *Priv. col., museum quality, valued $100-120.*

- Eva from Franklin co., TN. Blade 3 11/16 in. long, 1 1/3 in. wide, 3/8 in. thick. Blade is triangular, edges are recurved and deeply serrated, random flaked. Shallow basal notches, short snapped tangs, convex base. Made of beige and brown banded chert. *Priv. col., museum quality, valued $120-160.*

- Eva from Franklin co., TN. Point 2 5/8 in. long, 1 13/16 in. wide, 3/16 in. thick. Thin, finely serrated edges, triangular thinned tip, random flaked. Shallow basal notches, tangs flared, convex base. Made of gray chert. *Priv. col., excellent quality, valued $75-95.*

- Eva from Monroe co., TN. Blade 4 2/3 in. long, 1 7/8 in. wide, 1/4 in. thick. Thin, symmetrical highly serrated recurved edges. Snapped base and tangs, deep basal notches. Made of Dover chert. *Grover Bohannon col., excellent quality, valued $85-100.*

- Eva from Pulaski co., IL. Point 2 1/8 in. long, 1 3/32 in. wide, 1/4 in. thick. Very sharp serrated recurved edges, needle sharp tip, random flaked. Shallow basal notched, snapped base and tangs. Made of Cobden Hornstone chert. *Priv. col., museum quality, rare, valued $175-200.*

- Eva from Pike co., IL. Blade 3 5/8 in. long, 1 1/2 in. wide, 3/16 in. thick. Thin, triangular, parallel flaked, minutely fine serrations, recurved sides. Shallow basal notches, short ground tangs, convex base. Made of glossy gray chert. *Priv. col., excellent quality, valued $100-140.*

- Eva from Pike co., IL. Point 2 21/32 in. long, 1 1/2 in. wide, 1/4 in. thick. Triangular, sharply serrated recurved edges, rounded tip, random flaked. Shallow basal notches, tangs flared, snapped base. Made of grainy tan chert. *Priv. col., average quality, valued $55-70.*

- Eva from Cocke co., TN. Blade 4 in. long, 1 5/8 in. wide, 1/3 in. thick. Parallel flaked, wide serrations, recurved sides, slight tip break. Snap base, deep

basal notches, barbed shoulders. Made of Dover chert.
Priv. col., average quality, valued $45-60.

• Eva from Cocke co., TN. Point 2 2/3 in. long, 1 3/32 in. wide, 1/4 in. thick.
Sharp serrated tip and edges, recurved sides, random flaked, shallow basal
notches, short tangs, snapped base. Made of glossy black chert.
Priv. col., museum quality, valued $150-200.

• Eva from Fentress co., TN. Blade 3 7/8 in. long, 1 2/3 in. wide, 3/8 in. thick.
Triangular, symmetrical, sharply serrated recurved edges. Shallow basal notches,
snapped base and tangs. Made of marbled tan chert.
Priv. col., excellent quality, valued $100-125.

• Eva from Fentress co., TN. Point 2 1/8 in. long, 7/8 in. wide, 1/8 in. thick.
Symmetrically triangular, finely serrated concave sides, sharp tip. Shallow basal
notches, tangs flared, with convex base. Made of white pebble chert.
Priv. col., excellent quality, valued $50-65.

• Eva from Maury co., TN. Blade 4 in. long, 2 1/4 in. wide, 1/2 in. thick.
Symmetrically triangular, finely serrated recurved edges, parallel flaked. Snap
base, deep basal notches, flaring tangs. Made of Dover chert.
Priv. col., excellent quality, valued $125-150.

• Eva from Maury co., TN. Point 2 7/16 in. long, 1 3/32 in. wide, 1/4 in. thick.
Sharply serrated tip and edges, random flaking, recurved edges. Shallow basal
notches, snap tangs and base. Made of gray chert.
Priv. col., excellent quality, valued $75-100.

• Eva from Franklin co., IL. Blade 3 7/8 in. long, 1 1/3 in. wide, 1/4 in. thick.
Symmetrically triangular, finely serrated recurved blade, rounded tip. Shallow
basal notches, snapped base and tangs.
Priv. col., excellent quality, valued $125-150.

• Eva from Lewis co., TN. Blade 4 1/3 in. long, 1 1/4 in. wide, 1/4 in. thick.
Triangular, parallel flaking, sharply serrated recurved sides. Shallow basal
notches, concave base, tangs flared. Made of light gray chert.
Priv. col., excellent quality, valued $150-175.

• Eva from Clay co., TN. Blade 4 1/16 in. long, 1 1/2 in. wide, 1/3 in. thick.
Finely serrated, recurved edges, slight tip break. Snapped base, deep basal
notches, flaring tangs. Made of Dover chert.
Priv. col., average quality, valued $45-60.

- Eva from New Madrid co., MO. Point 2 5/8 in. long, 1 1/16 in. wide, 1/4 in. thick. Minutely serrated edges, needle sharp tip, recurved edges, random flaking. Shallow basal notches, rounded tangs, snapped base. Made of white pebble chert. *Priv. col., excellent quality, valued $135-180.*

- Eva from Franklin co., IL. Point 2 7/8 in. long, 1 in. wide, 1/2 in. thick. Point has finely serrated edges, sides concave, rounded tip. Base is shallow basal notched, tangs flared. Made of Mill Creek chert. *Priv, col., excellent quality, valued $50-70.*

- Eva from Humphreys co., TN. Blade 3 3/4 in. long, 1 3/4 in. wide, 1/2 in. thick. Finely serrated recurved edges, several nicks on both sides of the blade. Snapped base and tangs, deep basal notches. Made of Dover chert. *Grover Bohannon col., average quality, valued $45-60.*

- Eva from Randolph co., MO. Point 2 3/4 in. long, 1 3/32 in. wide, 1/4 in. thick. Needle sharp tip, serrated recurved edges, random flaking, shallow notched snapped base. Made of white pebble chert. *Priv. col., excellent quality, valued $100-125*

CHAPTER 6
FAIRLAND-FRIO

Fairland: 3,000-1,000 B.P. Woodland

Fairland points are small to medium sized points. Fairlands are expanded stemmed usually with a thinned concave base. Point or blade shoulders are rounded or tapered.

♦ Fairland Classic from northern TX. Point 1 29/32 in. long, 1 1/4 in. wide, 3/16 in. thick. Made of a dull Rose quartz.

Priv. col., museum quality, valued $85-125.

• Fairland from central TN. Point 2 3/16 in. long, 1 5/16 in. wide, 1/8 in. thick. Made of Missouri pebble chert.
Priv. col., excellent quality, valued $45-90.

• Fairland from Alexander co., IL. Point 2 1/4 in. long, 1 3/4 in. wide, 1/8 in. thick. Narrow, flat notches, slightly concave base, reworked top. Made of Mill Creek chert.
Priv. col., average quality, valued $25-60.

• Fairland blade from central TX. Blade 4 in. long, 1 13/16 in. wide, 3/16 in.

thick. Thin blade with long smooth flaking. Possibly a ceremonial Fairland.
Made of a red brown veined jasper.
Priv. col., museum quality, rare, valued $175-250.

• Fairland from Williamson co., IL. Blade 4 1/3 in. long, 2 in. wide, 1/4 in.
thick. Expanded stem with a thinned concave base. Blade shoulders are rounded.
Made of local gray chert.
Priv. col., average quality, valued $25-60.

• Fairland from Hamilton co., TN. Point 2 9/32 in. long, 1 1/4 in. wide, 3/16 in.
thick. Thin, narrow, displays fine workmanship. Made of Dover chert.
Priv. col., museum quality, valued $125-175.

• Fairland from Hamilton co., TN. Point 2 in. long, 1 7/16 in. wide, 1/8 in.
thick. Wide, thin blade finely flaked, thinned concave base. Made of white
pebble chert.
Priv. col., excellent quality, valued $55-80.

• Fairland from Alexander co., IL. Blade 5 1/4 in. long, 2 1/3 in. wide, 1/8 in.
thick. Narrow, very thin, thin parallel flaked, minutely serrated edges. Deep side
notches, slightly concave base. Made of Mill Creek chert.
Priv. col., excellent quality, valued $100-140.

• Fairland from Cape Giradeau co., MO. Blade 5 1/8 in. long, 2 in. wide,
1/4 in. thick. Thin, symmetrical, good workmanship, parallel flaking, highly
serrated edges. Deep side notches, sharp barbed shoulders, thinned concave base.
Made of dark brown chert.
Priv. col., museum quality, valued $145-200.

• Fairland from Hamilton co., TN. Point 3 in. long, 1 1/2 in. wide, 1/8 in. thick.
Wide, thin, finely serrated and random flaked. Thinned concave base, shallow
side notches. Made of white pebble chert.
Priv. col., excellent quality, valued $65-80.

• Fairland from Union co., IL. Blade 5 1/4 in. long, 2 1/4 in. wide, 1/8 in. thick.
Narrow, thin, symmetrically serrated edges. Deep side notches, slightly concave
base. Made of Mill Creek chert.
Priv. col., excellent quality, valued $125-150.

• Fairland from Butler co., MO. Blade 5 3/8 in. long, 1 1/16 in. wide, 1/4 in.
thick. Thin, parallel flaked, finely serrated. Side notched, sharp shoulder barbs,
thinned concave base. Made of light brown chert.
Priv. col., excellent quality, valued $185-250.

• Fairland from Hamilton co., TN. Point 2 1/3 in. long, 1 3/16 in. wide, 1/8 in. thick. Wide, thin blade, finely flaked, thinned concave base. Made of tan brown pebble chert.
Priv. col., excellent quality, valued $65-80.

• Fairland from Adams co., IN. Blade 5 1/2 in. long, 2 1/4 in. wide, 1/8 in. thick. Narrow, thin, sharply serrated edges, serrated rounded tip, deep notches, slightly concave base. Made of Mill Creek chert.
Priv. col., excellent quality, valued $185-200.

• Fairland from Adams co., IN. Blade 4 7/8 in. long, 1 11/16 in. wide, 1/4 in. thick. Thin, long smooth parallel flaking, highly serrated edges, thinned concave base. Made of greenish chert.
Priv. col., museum quality, valued $145-200.

Flint Creek: 3,500-1,000 B.P. Woodland

Found throughout the Southeast into the Midwest. Point or blade medium to large in size. Thick, narrow, sharply serrated. Expanded stem, straight, convex, or concave. Side notched, tapered to barbed shoulders.

◆ Flint Creek from Hamilton co., TN. Point 2 in. long, 5/8 in. wide, 3/16 in. thick. Deep, long, sharp serrations, slight tip break. Deep side notches, tapered shoulders, fractured straight base. Made of black flint.

Grover Bohannon col., average quality, valued $3-8.

• Flint Creek from Atlanta, GA. Point 2 1/8 in. long, 7/8 in. wide, 1/3 in. thick. Thick, sharply serrated, symmetrical. Expanded stem, concave base, side notches, barbed shoulders. Made of quartzite.
Priv. col., average quality, valued $5-10.

• Flint Creek from Booneville co., NC. Point 1 1/2 in. long, 3/8 in. wide, 3/16 in. thick. Fine, shallow, sharp serrations. Deep side notches, barbed shoulders, straight base. Made of light gray flint.
Grover Bohannon col., excellent quality, valued $15-25.

- Flint Creek from Booneville co., NC. Point 1 7/8 in. long, 5/8 in. wide, 1/4 in. thick. Thick, symmetrically narrow, sharply serrated. Expanded stem, straight base. Side notched, weak tapered shoulders. Made of pink quartzite. *Grover Bohannon col., excellent quality, valued $15-25.*

- Flint Creek from Hamilton co., TN. Point 2 1/3 in. long, 7/8 in. wide, 1/4 in. thick. Deep, shallow, sharp serrations, very sharp tip. Side notched, tapered shoulders, concave base. Made of gray pebble chert. *Grover Bohannon col., excellent quality, valued $15-20.*

- Flint Creek from southern NC. Point 1 3/8 in. long, 9/16 in. wide, 1/4 in. thick. Heat treated, thick, narrow, sharply serrated, symmetrical. Stem concave, shallow side notches, weak barbed shoulders. Made of tan pebble chert. *Priv. col., museum quality, valued $25-35.*

- Flint Creek from Hamilton co., TN. Point 2 1/3 in. long, 3/4 in. wide, 5/16 in. thick. Thick point, deeply serrated. Deep side notches, tapered shoulders, straight base. Made of Dover chert. *Priv. col., museum quality, rare, valued $45-80.*

- Flint Creek from Hamilton co., TN. Point 1 9/16 in. long, 5/8 in. wide, 5/16 in. thick. Narrow, with deep, long, sharp serrations, very sharp pointed tip. Side notched, several edge nicks, tapered shoulders, straight base. Made of Dover chert. *Grover Bohannon col., average quality, valued $10-15.*

- Flint Creek from Fort Lauderdale, FL. Point 1 3/8 in. long, 7/8 in. wide, 5/32 in. thick. Thick, broad, sharply serrated. Expanded stem, convex base. Side notched, tapered shoulders. Made of grainy quartzite. *Priv. col., poor quality, valued $5-10.*

- Flint Creek from Hamilton co., TN. Point 2 3/32 in. long, 3/4 in. wide, 7/16 in. thick. Very thick, deep, long serrations, finely serrated tip. Side notched, barbed shoulders, straight base. Made of Dover chert. *Grover Bohannon col., museum quality, rare, valued $55-80.*

- Flint Creek from southern NC. Point 1 3/8 in. long, 11/32 in. wide, 1/4 in. thick. Heat treated, thick, symmetrically narrow, sharply serrated. Expanded stem, straight base. Side notched, barbed shoulders. Made of pink to gray pebble chert. *Priv. col., excellent quality, valued $20-30.*

- Flint Creek from Hamilton co., TN. Point 2 5/8 in. long, 5/8 in. wide,

5/16 in. thick. Thick, very angular, deep, long, sharp serrations. Side notched, tapered shoulders, concave base. Made of mauve pebble chert.
Grover Bohannon col., excellent quality, valued $30-45.

* Flint Creek from southern NC. Point 1 7/8 in. long, 17/32 in. wide, 5/8 in. thick. Thick, symmetrically narrow, sharply serrated edges and tip. Expanded stem, straight base. Side notched, weak tapered shoulders. Made of quartzite.
Priv. col., average quality, valued $8-15.

* Flint Creek from Monroe co., TN. Point 3 in. long, 7/8 in. wide, 7/16 in. thick. Long, symmetrical, sharp serrations, slight tip break. Deep, uneven side notches, tapered shoulders, straight base. Made of gray chert.
Grover Bohannon col., excellent quality, valued $10-20.

* Flint Creek from Wilcox co., AL. Point 3 1/16 in. long, 7/8 in. wide, 1/2 in. thick. Thick, sharply serrated, symmetrical, beveled on one side of each face. Expanded stem, concave base, side notched, barbed shoulders. Made of quartzite.
Priv. col., excellent quality, valued $25-40.

* Flint Creek from Boone co., MO. Blade 4 1/2 in. long, 1 in. wide, 3/16 in. thick. Fine workmanship, shallow, wide, sharp serrations, right hand beveled. Deep side notches, barbed shoulders, straight base. Made of light gray flint.
Priv. col., excellent quality, valued $35-45.

* Flint Creek from Boone co., MO. Blade 4 7/8 in. long, 5/8 in. wide, 5/16 in. thick. Thick, symmetrically narrow, right hand beveled, sharply serrated. Expanded stem, shallow corner notched, convex base, weak tapered shoulders. Made of white pebble chert.
Priv. col., museum quality, valued $75-85.

Folsom: 15,000-9,000 B.P. Paleo

Folsom points and blades are found predominantly in the Midwest, but nearly extend to both the East and West Coasts. They are small to medium points for the most, with concave bases, side notches, and pointed tangs. Folsoms are thin, fluted, with high quality workmanship and thin quality flaking. Note: Many fakes have been made—use caution. There are still plentiful original examples. Do a patina test and check for full blade fluting, ground hafting areas, and extremely fine although uniform flaking.

◆ Folsom from Union co., IL. Point 3 1/8 in. long, 1 1/4 in. wide, 3/16 in. thick.

Very symmetrical and finely crafted point, one of a kind. Made of a black, silver, and brown pebble chert.

Priv. col., museum quality, rare, valued $1,200-1,500.

◆ Folsom from Coffer co., KS. Point 2 1/2 in. long, 1/2 in. wide, 5/16 in. thick. Notice small nicks along the blade and one nicked tang. Very fine and symmetrical fluting. Made of Mill Creek chert.

Priv. col., excellent quality, valued $550-650.

• Folsom from southeastern TN. Point 1 1/7 in. long, 3/4 in. wide, 3/16 in. thick. Full but shallow fluting, very thin point. Symmetry is remarkable, as well as the material. Made of translucent amber.
Priv. col., museum quality, rare, valued $3,800-4,500.

• Folsom from Union co., IL. Point 2 1/8 in. long, 1 in. wide, 3/16 in. thick. Point fully deeply fluted, quality serration work on edges, one tang noticeably longer than the other. Made of Cobden chert.
Priv. col., average quality, valued $225-300.

• Folsom from NC. Point 2 3/16 in. long, 1 1/32 in. wide, 1/4 in. thick. Deeply fluted with symmetrical parallel flaking. Made of gray flint.
Priv. col., excellent quality, valued $450-550.

• Folsom from Cumberland co., KY. Point 2 1/8 in. long, 5/8 in. wide, 5/16 in. thick. Wide point, fully fluted. Made of a high grade pink pebble chert.
Priv. col., museum quality, valued $1,800-2,200.

• Folsom from Cumberland co., KY. Point 2 5/16 in. long, 1 5/32 in. wide, 1/4 in. thick. Concave base, deep side notches, and pointed tangs. Thin, fluted, with high quality workmanship, thin flaking. Made of fine pink pebble chert.
Tim Rubbles col., museum quality, valued $1,200-1,500.

• Folsom from Jasper co., IL. Blade 3 7/8 in. long, 2 1/4 in. wide, 3/16 in. thick. Very symmetrical and finely serrated blade. Fluted, concave base, symmetrical side notches. Made of brown pebble chert.
Priv. col., museum quality, valued $1,00-1,200.

• Folsom from Franklin co., IL. Point 2 5/8 in. long, 1/2 in. wide, 1/4 in. thick. Extremely narrow point with long pointed tip, one snapped tang. Very fine and symmetrical fluting, concave base. Made of yellow tan pebble chert.
Priv. col., excellent quality, valued $500-600.

• Folsom from Hamilton co., TN. Point 1 7/8 in. long, 7/8 in. wide, 3/16 in. thick. Full, but shallow fluting, narrow, very thin point. Symmetry is remarkable, as is the material. Made of jasper.
Priv. col., museum quality, rare, valued $2,600-3,400.

• Folsom from Union co., IL. Blade 4 1/8 in. long, 1 31/32 in. wide, 3/16 in. thick. Deep fluting, sharply serrated edges, symmetrical tangs, noticeably long. Made of Cobden Hornstone chert.
Priv. col., excellent quality, rare, valued $3,000-4,200.

• Folsom point from Nashville, TN. Point 2 7/16 in. long, 1 5/32 in. wide, 1/4 in. thick. Deeply fluted with symmetrical parallel flaking. Made of pink to gray flint.
Priv. col., excellent quality, valued $1,350-1,800.

• Folsom from Wabash co., IN. Point 2 1/4 in. long, 11/16 in. wide, 3/16 in. thick. Narrow fluted on one side of the point. Long, prominent, upward angling pressure flaked edges, very sharp. Made of Dover chert.
Priv. col., museum quality, valued $1,500-2,000.

• Folsom from Richmond co., NC. Point 3 1/16 in. long, 1 3/32 in. wide, 1/4 in. thick. Deeply fluted, symmetrical parallel flaking, thin sharp serrations. Classic concave base, pointed, serrated base tangs. Made of Rose quartz.
Priv. col., museum quality, valued $1,450-1,750.

• Folsom from Richmond co., NC. Point 2 7/8 in. long, 1 1/8 in. wide, 5/16 in. thick. Wide, fully fluted, minutely serrated edges, very sharp pointed tip. Classic concave base, sharp tangs. Made of pink chert.
Priv. col., museum quality, valued $1,500-2,000.

• Folsom from Richmond co., NC. Point 1 5/16 in. long, 1 3/32 in. wide, 1/4 in. thick. Thick, wide fluted, high quality workmanship, thin edges beyond flutes finely serrated. Concave base and pointed tangs. Made of fine pink chert.

Priv. col., museum quality, valued $1,800-2,200.

• Folsom from Swain co., NC. Blade 2 1/8 in. long, 2 in. wide, 3/16 in. thick. Very symmetrical, thin wide fluting, finely serrated edges, tip, and tangs. Concave base. Made of cream to gold brown marbled chert.
Priv. col., museum quality, valued $3,500-4,000.

• Folsom from Swain co., NC. Point 2 1/16 in. long, 1 5/32 in. wide, 1/2 in. thick. Thick, deeply fluted, symmetrical, parallel flaked, deeply serrated edges. Concave base, ground tangs. Made of translucent amber quartz.
Priv. col., excellent quality, rare, valued $2,450-2,750.

• Folsom from Morrow co., OH. Point 2 1/4 in. long, 7/8 in. wide, 5/16 in. thick. Symmetrical, thick, thin full fluting, randomly serrated edges. Concave base, ground basal notches. Made of quartzite.
Priv. col., average quality, valued $400-600.

• Folsom from Morrow co., OH. Point 2 5/16 in. long, 1 1/8 in. wide, 1/4 in. thick. Thin, fluted, high quality workmanship, thin parallel flaking. Beveled on one side of each face, serrated on opposing edges. Concave base, pointed tangs. Made of white pebble chert.
Priv. col., excellent quality, valued $800-950.

• Folsom from Morrow co., OH. Blade 3 3/4 in. long, 2 in. wide, 3/16 in. thick. Thin, wide fluting, symmetrical and finely serrated blade. Concave base, symmetrical ground basal tangs. Made of brown tan pebble chert.
Priv. col., excellent quality, valued $750-900.

• Folsom from Morrow co., OH. Point 2 3/32 in. long, 1 1/16 in. wide, 1/4 in. thick. Deeply fluted with symmetrical parallel flaking, finely serrated edges. Pointed basal tangs, concave base. Made of gray to white pebble chert.
Priv. col., excellent quality, valued $550-650.

• Folsom from Morrow co., OH. Point 2 1/4 in. long, 1 in. wide, 7/16 in. thick. Thick, wide flutes, steeply serrated edges, random flaked. Sharp serrated tangs, concave base. Made of pinkish pebble chert.
Priv. col., excellent quality, valued $800-1,000.

• Folsom from Lore co., OK. Point 2 5/32 in. long, 1 3/16 in. wide, 1/4 in. thick. Thin, fluted, with high quality workmanship, thin, fine parallel flaking, minute edge serrations. Concave base, and pointed tangs. Made of translucent pink chert.
Priv. col., museum quality, valued $1,000-1,500.

- Folsom from Lore co., OK. Blade 3 7/8 in. long, 2 1/4 in. wide, 3/16 in. thick. Thin, narrow, thin fluting, symmetrical and finely serrated blade. Concave base, sharp pointed basal tangs. Made of brown tan pebble chert. *Priv. col., excellent quality, valued $1,200-1,700.*

- Folsom from Lore co., OK. Point 2 5/16 in. long, 1 3/32 in. wide, 1/4 in. thick. Thinly and deeply fluted with symmetrical parallel flaking, wide, thin edge serrations. Concave base, rounded tangs. Made of oily black flint. *Priv. col., excellent quality, valued $650-750.*

- Folsom from Cumberland co., KY. Point 2 3/8 in. long, 1 1/3 in. wide, 5/16 in. thick. Wide, thick, deep fluted, finely serrated edges. Ground tangs, concave base. Made of tan pebble chert. *Priv. col., excellent quality, valued $800-1,200.*

- Folsom from Cumberland co., KY. Point 2 5/16 in. long, 1 1/4 in. wide, 1/4 in. thick. Thin, fluted, good workmanship, thin parallel flaking. Concave base, pointed tangs. Made of gray pebble chert. *Priv. col., museum quality, valued $800-1,000.*

- Folsom from Kimble co., TX. Point 2 1/16 in. long, 1 5/8 in. wide, 5/16 in. thick. Wide, point fully fluted, thin, fine edge serrations, heat treated. Rounded tangs, concave base. Made of dull gray chert. *Priv. col., museum quality, valued $1,500-1,800.*

- Folsom from Kimble co., TX. Point 2 7/16 in. long, 1 1/3 in. wide, 1/4 in. thick. Thin, fluted, with high quality workmanship, thin flaking. Concave base, and pointed tangs. Made of dull gray chert. *Priv. col., museum quality, valued $1,200-1,500.*

Fox Valley: 9,000-4,000 B.P. Early to Mid-Archaic

Fox Valley points are found throughout the East and southeastern Midwest. The stem of this small, triangular point is short and bifurcated. Point is generally serrated with flaring shoulders. Wings are sometimes clipped.

◆ Fox Valley from Clark co., IL. Point 1 5/8 in. long, 1 1/8 in. wide, 3/16 in. thick. Fine serrations, very symmetrical point blade. Made of a dark black chert.

Priv. col., museum quality, rare, valued $85-100.

• Fox Valley point from Hamilton co., TN. Point 1 1/4 in. long, 7/8 in. wide, 5/16 in. thick. Classical style with wide serrations, flaring shoulders, symmetrically bifurcated stem. Made of Dover chert.
Priv. col., average quality, valued $15-20.

• Fox Valley from northwestern KY. Point 1 3/4 in. long, 1 1/8 in. wide, 5/16 in. thick. Classic style with wide serrations, flaring shoulders, symmetrically bifurcated stem. Made of Dover chert.
Priv. col., excellent quality, valued $35-50.

• Fox Valley from Cumberland co., IL. Point 1 11/16 in. long, 1 1/8 in. wide, 1/4 in. thick. Very symmetrical, uniform throughout point. Made of gray Cobden chert.
Priv. col., excellent quality, valued $45-75.

• Fox Valley point from Hamilton co., TN. Point 1 3/4 in. long, 1 1/8 in. wide, 1/4 in. thick. Stem small, triangular, and bifurcated. Point is serrated, flaring shoulders, wings clipped. Made of Dover chert.
Grover Bohannon col., excellent quality, valued $65-85.

• Fox Valley from Lawrence co., IL. Point 2 1/8 in. long, 1 3/8 in. wide, 1/8 in. thick. Finely serrated, symmetrical point. Made of a dark gray chert.
Priv. col., museum quality, valued $65-85.

• Fox Valley from Hamilton co., TN. Point 1 3/4 in. long, 7/8 in. wide, 1/8 in. thick. Wide edge serrations, flaring shoulders, one with small break, symmetrically bifurcated stem. Made of Dover chert.
Priv. col., excellent quality, valued $35-40.

• Fox Valley from Cumberland co., KY. Point 2 3/4 in. long, 1 3/8 in. wide, 7/32 in. thick. Fine serrations, flaring shoulders, symmetrically notched, bifurcated stem. Made of pinkish grained pebble chert.
Priv. col., excellent quality, valued $35-50.

• Fox Valley from Cumberland co., IL. Point 11/16 in. long, 7/8 in. wide,
1/8 in. thick. Very symmetrical, short and thin point. Made of Cobden chert.
Priv. col., excellent quality, valued $45-75.

• Fox Valley from Hardin co., TN. Point 1 2/3 in. long, 1 in. wide, 1/4 in. thick.
Small, triangular, and bifurcated stem. Point is serrated, flaring shoulders, wings
clipped. Made of dark brown chert.
Priv. col., excellent quality, valued $55-65.

• Fox Valley from Lawrence co., IL. Point 2 1/32 in. long, 1 1/8 in. wide, 1/8 in.
thick. Finely serrated edges, symmetrical point, very thin. Made of a gray to pink
pebble chert.
Priv. col., excellent quality, valued $45-65.

• Fox Valley from Hamilton co., TN. Point 1 3/8 in. long, 5/8 in. wide, 1/8 in.
thick. Fine sharp edge serrations, flaring shoulders, very narrow elongated point,
symmetrically bifurcated stem. Made of Dover chert.
Jim Smith col., excellent quality, valued $65-80.

• Fox Valley from Seneca co., NY. Point 1 13/16 in. long, 1 1/8 in. wide, 1/4 in.
thick. Symmetrical, uniform, triangular, sharply serrated flaring shoulders. Corner
notched. bifurcated stem. Made of gray chert.
Priv. col., excellent quality, valued $65-75.

• Fox Valley from Seneca co., NY. Point 1 2/3 in. long, 1 1/3 in. wide, 1/4 in.
thick. Point is serrated, bent tip, flaring clipped tangs. Stem small, triangular, and
bifurcated. Made of milky quartz.
Priv. col., museum quality, valued $65-85.

• Fox Valley from Cortland co., NY. Point 2 in. long, 1 1/8 in. wide, 1/8 in.
thick. Thin, narrow, finely serrated, horizontal, pointed tangs, triangularly
symmetrical point. Narrow stem, bifurcated base. Made of translucent gray chert.
Priv. col., museum quality, valued $65-85.

• Fox Valley from Brazos co., TX. Point 1 3/4 in. long, 7/8 in. wide, 1/8 in.
thick. Thin, narrow, wide edge serrations, upward flaring serrated tangs. Narrow
stem bifurcated base. Made of gray chert.
Priv. col., excellent quality, valued $40-50.

• Fox Valley from Lubbock co., TX. Point 1 7/16 in. long, 1 1/8 in. wide,
1/3 in. thick. Symmetrical, triangular, uniform, thin flaking and serrating
throughout. Highly serrated edges, sharp serrated tip. Made of gray chert.

Priv. col., excellent quality, valued $45-75.

- Fox Valley from Cottle co., TX. Point 1 3/4 in. long, 1 1/8 in. wide, 1/8 in. thick. Thin, finely serrated, upward flaring tangs. Stem short, triangular, and bifurcated. Clipped wings, bifurcated base. Made of Dover chert.
Priv. col., excellent quality, valued $65-85.

- Fox Valley from Titus co., TX. Point 2 1/32 in. long, 1 7/8 in. wide, 1/8 in. thick. Finely serrated, symmetrical, serrated edges and serrated clipped wings. Made of dull gray chert.
Priv. col., excellent quality, valued $45-55.

- Fox Valley from Fentress co., TN. Point 1 1/4 in. long, 7/8 in. wide, 1/8 in. thick. Thin, triangular, side edge serrations, flaring shoulders. Wide stem bifurcated base. Made of white pebble chert.
Priv. col., excellent quality, valued $35-45.

Fresno: 1,200 to Historical 200 B.P. and Mississippian

Located in the Midwest into Southeast. A small point, very thin, triangular, straight to convex sides, straight to concave base. Numerous examples are deeply serrated and side notched.

◆ Fresno from Lubbock co., TX. Point 1 3/16 in. long, 1/4 in. wide, 1/8 in. thick. Lower two-thirds of point deeply serrated, upper third fine and extremely sharp, concave base. Made of a mauve pebble chert.

Priv. col., excellent quality, valued $35-50.

- Fresno from Memphis, TN. Point 1 3/8 in. long, 3/16 in. wide, 5/32 in. thick. Point deeply serrated one side. Made of jasper.
Priv. col., excellent quality, valued $45-60.

- Fresno from Jackson co., IL. Point 1 7/8 in. long, 5/16 in. wide, 1/8 in. thick. Point shows only shallow serration, straight base. Made of quartz.
Priv. col., museum quality, valued $50-80.

• Fresno from Effingham co., IL. Point 1 1/4 in. long, 1/4 in. wide, 1/16 in. thick. Paper thin, translucent, deeply serrated, side notched with concave base. Made of Rose quartz.
Priv. col., museum quality, rare, valued $75-100.

• Fresno from Coles co., IL. Point 1 1/4 in. long, 1/4 in. wide, 1/16 in. thick. Thin, triangular, straight sides, concave base. Deeply serrated and symmetrically side notched. Made of dark gray slate.
Priv. col., average quality, valued $15-25.

• Fresno from Lauden co., TN. Point 1 9/16 in. long, 1/2 in. wide, 1/8 in. thick. Point deeply serrated, shallow side notched, edges extremely sharp, concave base. Made of a tan pebble chert.
Priv. col., excellent quality, valued $35-50.

• Fresno from Memphis, TN. Point 1 5/8 in. long, 5/16 in. wide, 3/32 in. thick. Point deeply serrated on one side of each edge. Thin, symmetrical point with pointed tip and straight base. Made of banded brown chert.
Grover Bohannon col., excellent quality, valued $45-60.

• Fresno from Jackson co., IL. Point 1 1/8 in. long, 7/16 in. wide, 1/8 in. thick. Point shows long thin serration, deep side notches. Heat treated with straight base. Made of Kaolin chert.
Priv. col., museum quality, rare, valued $100-160.

• Fresno from Effingham co., IL. Point 1 2/3 in. long, 1/4 in. wide, 1/16 in. thick. Very thin, narrow and symmetrically angular, deeply serrated, side notched with concave base. Made of Rose quartz.
Priv. col., museum quality, valued $85-110.

• Fresno from Halifax co., VA. Point 1 5/8 in. long, 7/16 in. wide, 1/8 in. thick. Shallow, widely spaced serrations, triangular tip. Deep side notches, straight base. Made of quartzite.
Priv. col., average quality, valued $15-20.

• Fresno from Clarke co., VA. Point 1 1/3 in. long, 1/4 in. wide, 3/16 in. thick. Thin, deep, irregular serrations, neddle-sharp tip. Side notched with concave base. Made of milky quartz.
Priv. col., museum quality, valued $80-90.

• Fresno from Clarke co., VA. Point 1 1/4 in. long, 1/2 in. wide, 1/16 in. thick. Thin, triangular, deep, wide, serrations, symmetrical straight sides. Side notched, concave base. Made of dark gray chert.

Priv. col., excellent quality, valued $35-45.

• Fresno from Iberville Parish, LA. Point 1 3/8 in. long, 7/16 in. wide, 1/8 in. thick. Good workmanship, fine, shallow serrated edges. Side notched, straight base. Made of Rose quartz.
Priv. col., museum quality, valued $50-80.

• Fresno from Lubbock co., TX. Point 1 1/2 in. long, 1/4 in. wide, 1/16 in. thick. Paper thin, translucent, wide serrations, neddle-sharp tip. Side notched with concave base. Made of quartzite.
Juan Samudio col., average quality, valued $15-30.

• Fresno from Lubbock co., TX. Point 1 1/3 in. long, 3/8 in. wide, 1/16 in. thick. Thin, triangular, straight sides, deeply serrated, uniform side notched. Good field patina, convex base. Made of dull gray chert.
Juan Samudio col., excellent quality, valued $25-35.

• Fresno from Dillon co., SC. Point 1 1/8 in. long, 5/16 in. wide, 1/8 in. thick. Sharp unserrated edges, angular, symmetrically triangular, straight base. Made of white pebble chert.
Grover Bohannon col., excellent quality, valued $35-50.

• Fresno from Dillon co., SC. Point 1 1/8 in. long, 5/32 in. wide, 1/16 in. thick. Thin, sharply serrated, triangular neddle-sharp tip. Deeply side notched with concave base. Made of Rose quartz.
Grover Bohannon col., excellent quality, valued $45-60.

• Fresno from Dillon co., SC. Point 1 1/16 in. long, 1/4 in. wide, 1/8 in. thick. Thin, narrow, deep, wide, serrated, triangular, straight sides. Side notched, straight base. Made of quartzite.
Private col., average quality, valued $15-20.

• Fresno from Dillon co., SC. Point 1 1/4 in. long, 1/4 in. wide, 1/16 in. thick. Translucently thin, deeply serrated, triangular neddle-sharp tip. Side notched with concave base. Made of Rose quartz.
Grover Bohannon col., excellent quality, valued $45-60.

• Fresno from Dillon co., SC. Point 1 5/16 in. long, 1/2 in. wide, 1/8 in. thick. Thin, deep, wide, serrations, triangular, straight sides. Side notched, convex base. Made of white chert.
Grover Bohannon col., excellent quality, valued $35-45.

• Fresno from Dillon co., SC. Point 1 in. long, 1/4 in. wide, 1/8 in. thick. Thin,

deep, sharp, serrations, thinned neddle-sharp tip. Side notched, convex base. Made of white chert.
Grover Bohannon col., excellent quality, valued $40-50.

• Fresno from Newberry co., SC. Point 1 11/16 in. long, 1/4 in. wide, 1/8 in. thick. Long, thin, narrow, deep, wide, serrated edges, excellent workmanship. Side notched, straight base widest part of point. Made of jasper.
Grover Bohannon col., museum quality, rare, valued $85-125.

• Fresno from Newberry co., SC. Point 1 1/8 in. long, 1/3 in. wide, 1/8 in. thick. Thin, deep, narrow serrations, triangular neddle-sharp tip. Side notched, concave base. Made of Rose quartz.
Grover Bohannon col., museum quality, valued $65-80.

• Fresno from Hopkins co., TX. Point 1 3/16 in. long, 1/4 in. wide, 1/8 in. thick. Thin, long, narrow, deep, wide, serrations, concave sides. Side notched, concave base. Made of translucent amber chert.
Priv. col., museum quality, valued $45-65.

• Fresno from Zapata co., TX. Point 1 7/16 in. long, 13/16 in. wide, 1/8 in. thick. Thin, deep, narrow, edge serrations, straight sides. Side notched, convex base. Made of tan pebble chert.
Priv. col., excellent quality, valued $45-50.

• Fresno from Zapata co., TX. Point 1 1/4 in. long, 1/3 in. wide, 1/8 in. thick. Thin, deep, sharp, serrations, neddle-sharp tip. Side notched, concave base. Made of tan pebble chert.
Priv. col., excellent quality, valued $40-50.

• Fresno from Reagan co., TX. Point 1 1/16 in. long, 1/2 in. wide, 1/8 in. thick. Thin, narrow, deep triangular serrations. Side notched, straight base. Made of tan to brown chert.
Priv. col., museum quality, valued $65-85.

• Fresno from Sutton co., TX. Point 1 1/3 in. long, 1/4 in. wide, 1/8 in. thick. Thin, deep, wide serrations, neddle-sharp tip. Side notched, concave base. Made of quartzite.
Priv. col., average quality, valued $15-20.

• Fresno from Dallas co., TX. Point 1 1/16 in. long, 5/16 in. wide, 1/8 in. thick. Thin, deep, wide, serrations, triangular, straight sides. Side notched, concave base. Made of white pebble chert.
Priv. col., excellent quality, valued $35-45.

- Fresno from Dallas co., TX. Point 1 1/2 in. long, 1/2 in. wide, 1/4 in. thick. Heat treated, thick, deep, sharp, serrated edges, thinned tip. Side notched, convex base. Made of tan white chert.
Priv. col., excellent quality, valued $45-65.

- Fresno from Dallas co., TX. Point 1 11/16 in. long, 1/3 in. wide, 1/8 in. thick. Thin, narrow, deep, wide, serrated edges, quality workmanship. Side notched, straight base. Made of tan white chert.
Priv. col., museum quality, valued $85-100.

- Fresno from Jeff Davis co., TX. Point 1 1/3 in. long, 7/16 in. wide, 1/8 in. thick. Thin, deep, narrow serrations, triangular neddle-sharp tip. Side notched, concave base. Made of quartzite.
Priv. col., average quality, valued $20-25.

- Fresno from Union co., SC. Point 1 3/16 in. long, 9/32 in. wide, 1/8 in. thick. Thin, deep, pointed, edge serrations, triangular, slightly convex sides. Side notched, convex base. Made of gray chert.
Priv. col., excellent quality, valued $40-45.

- Fresno from Union co., SC. Point 1 1/3 in. long, 7/16 in. wide, 1/8 in. thick. Thin, deep, sharp, serrations, thinned sharp tip. Side notched, convex base. Made of gray marbled chert.
Priv. col., museum quality, valued $40-50.

- Fresno from Caroll co., MO. Point 1 9/16 in. long, 5/16 in. wide, 1/8 in. thick. Thin, narrow, deep, wide, serrated edges. Side notched, straight base. Made of false jasper.
Priv. col., average quality, valued $25-30.

- Fresno from Caroll co., MO. Point 1 1/4 in. long, 5/16 in. wide, 1/8 in. thick. Thin, deep, narrow edge serrations, neddle-sharp tip. Side notched, concave base. Made of quartzite.
Priv. col., average quality, valued $15-20.

- Fresno from Union co., IL. Point 1 2/3 in. long, 9/16 in. wide, 1/8 in. thick. Symmetrical, sharp, narrow serrations, thinned sharp tip. Side notched, parallel sided convex base. Made of Mill Creek chert.
Priv. col., museum quality, valued $40-50.

- Fresno from Bibb co., AL. Point 1 11/16 in. long, 1/4 in. wide, 1/8 in. thick. Thin, narrow, shallow, wide, serrated edges. Side notched, convex base. Made of milky quartz.

Priv. col., excellent quality, valued $55-70.

• Fresno from Bibb co., AL. Point 1 1/32 in. long, 7/16 in. wide, 1/8 in. thick. Symmetrical point, deep, narrow edge serrations, neddle-sharp tip. Side notched, straight base. Made of light gray chert.
Priv. col., excellent quality, valued $35-40.

Friley: 5,000-800 B.P. Late Woodland

Midwestern point, small, triangular and thin. Shoulders flare outward and toward tip. The bases are rounded or eared. Usually a rough looking point.

♦ Friley from Hardin co., IL. Point 1 1/4 in. long, 1/2 in wide, 1/8 in. thick. Made of quartzite.

Priv. col., museum quality, valued $80-120.

• Friley from Johnson co., IL. Point 1 1/4 in. long, 1/4 in. wide, 1/8 in. thick. Narrow point with widely spaced serrations. Upward flaring tangs with a snapped base. Made of creamy white quartz.
Priv. col., museum quality, valued $100-150.

• Friley from Lafayette co., KY. Point 1 1/16 in. long, 1/2 in. wide, 3/32 in. thick. Point slim and uniquely angular, heat treated, slight tang break. Made of a lightweight white chert.
Priv. col., excellent quality, valued $35-50.

• Friley from Lafayette co., KY. Point 1 1/4 in. long, 1/4 in. wide, 1/8 in. thick. Point triangular and thin. Shoulders flare outward and toward tip. The base is rounded. Made of lightweight white local chert.
Priv. col., excellent quality, valued $45-60.

• Friley from Hardin co., IL. Point 1 1/2 in. long, 1/2 in. wide, 1/8 in. thick. Ears flare upward, wide spaced and sharp serrations, base is snapped. Made of Cobden chert.
Priv. col., museum quality, valued $70-100.

• Friley from Williamson co., IL. Point 1 1/4 in. long, 3/8 in. wide, 1/8 in. thick. Narrow point, heat treated with widely spaced serrations. Upward flaring tangs with a snap base. Made of creamy white pebble chert.
Jim Smith col., museum quality, valued $120-150.

• Friley from Lafayette co., IN. Point 2 1/16 in. long, 1/2 in. wide, 5/32 in. thick. Point is narrow, angularly symmetrical, upward flaring tangs, small tip break. Made of tan pebble chert.
Priv. col., average quality, valued $15-30.

• Friley from Randolph co., MO. Point 1 1/2 in. long, 1/2 in. wide, 1/8 in. thick. Pointed thin ears flaring upward, heat treated. Fine sharp serrations, snapped base. Made of tan white pebble chert.
Priv. col., excellent quality, valued $50-80.

• Friley from St. Francis co., AR. Point 1 in. long, 3/8 in. wide, 1/8 in. thick. Symmetrical, heat treated, widely spaced serrations. Upward flaring tangs, convex base. Made of lightweight white chert.
Priv. col., excellent quality, valued $80-100.

• Friley from St. Francis co., AR. Point 2 in. long, 1/2 in. wide, 5/16 in. thick. Narrow, angularly symmetrical, horizontal flaring tangs. Bifurcated base. Made of tan yellow chert.
Priv. col., excellent quality, valued $45-50.

• Friley from Harrison co., AR. Point 1 1/3 in. long, 1/2 in. wide, 1/8 in. thick. Ears flare upward moving symmetrically into convex base, random serrations. Made of Arkansas brown chert.
Priv. col., excellent quality, valued $60-80.

• Friley from Harrison co., AR. Point 1 7/8 in. long, 1/4 in. wide, 1/8 in. thick. Narrow point, fine, minute, serrations. Upward flaring tangs, concave base. Made of Arkansas brown chert.
Priv. col., museum quality, valued $100-115.

• Friley from Craig Head co., AR. Point 2 3/16 in. long, 7/16 in. wide, 7/32 in. thick. Point is narrow, angular, horizontal tangs, rounded base. Made of pink pebble chert.
Priv. col., excellent quality, valued $75-80.

• Friley from Craig Head co., AR. Point 1 3/4 in. long, 5/16 in. wide, 1/8 in. thick. Ears flare upward, minute sharply serrated edges. Horizontal tangs, base is snapped. Made of gray flint.

Priv. col., excellent quality, valued $70-80.

• Friley from Wayne co., MO. Point 1 1/2 in. long, 7/16 in. wide, 1/8 in. thick. Narrow, heat treated, fine minute serrations. Pointed upward flaring tangs, rounded base. Made of grainy white black speckled chert.
Priv. col., average quality, valued $40-50.

• Friley from Wayne co., MO. Point 1 13/16 in. long, 1/2 in. wide, 7/32 in. thick. Point is narrow, symmetrical, finely serrated edges. Notched above upward flaring tangs, rounded base. Made of tan brown chert.
Priv. col., excellent quality, valued $65-80.

• Friley from Harrison co., MO. Point 1 11/32 in. long, 1/2 in. wide, 3/16 in. thick. Ears wide, flaring upward, wide-spaced sharp serrations, convex base. Made of grainy white chert.
Priv. col., average quality, valued $20-30.

• Friley from Harrison co., MO. Point 1 1/3 in. long, 3/8 in. wide, 1/8 in. thick. Symmetrical point, heat treated, widely spaced serrations. Horizontal, serrated horizontal flaring tangs, rounded base. Made of creamy tan chert.
Priv. col., excellent quality, valued $80-100.

• Friley from Adams co., IN. Point 2 3/16 in. long, 1/2 in. wide, 5/32 in. thick. Point is narrow, angular, upward flaring pointed tangs. Short narrow stem, bifurcated base. Made of banded tan chert.
Priv. col., museum quality, valued $85-100.

• Friley from Adams co., IN. Point 1 1/8 in. long, 1 1/2 in. wide, 1/8 in. thick. Ears flaring upward, wider than long, fine serrations. Narrowing, convex base. Made of greenish chert.
Priv. col., museum quality, valued $75-90.

• Friley from Wabash co., IN. Point 1 1/16 in. long, 1/2 in. wide, 1/8 in. thick. Narrow point, random serrated edges, heat treated. Upward flaring tangs with rounded base. Made of local greenish chert.
Priv. col., museum quality, valued $100-125.

• Friley from Adams co., OH. Point 2 3/16 in. long, 9/16 in. wide, 11/32 in. thick. Point is angularly symmetrical, thick, finely serrated. Ground upward flaring tangs, bifurcated. Made of banded tan chert.
Priv. col., excellent quality, valued $45-60.

- Friley from Adams co., OH. Point 1 3/4 in. long, 1/3 in. wide, 1/8 in. thick. Ears flare upward, wide-spaced and sharp serrations, base is thinned, and rounded. Made of greenish chert.
Priv. col., museum quality, valued $70-80.

- Friley from Wyandot co., OH. Point 1 1/2 in. long, 3/8 in. wide, 1/8 in. thick. Narrow point, heat treated, rounded serrations. Serrated upward flaring tangs with a snap base. Made of beige pebble chert.
Priv. col., excellent quality, valued $100-120.

- Friley from Holmes co., OH. Point 2 3/16 in. long, 1/2 in. wide, 7/32 in. thick. Point is narrow, angularly symmetrical, upward flaring tangs, bifurcated base. Made of tan pebble chert.
Priv. col., excellent quality, valued $45-60.

- Friley from Holmes co., OH. Point 1 5/8 in. long, 7/16 in. wide, 1/8 in. thick. Sharply serrated edges, thinned tip, ears flare upward, tips are pointed. Wide rounded base. Made of white pebble chert.
Priv. col., excellent quality, valued $60-85.

- Friley from Williamson co., IL. Point 1 3/4 in. long, 1/2 in. wide, 1/8 in. thick. Narrow point, heat treated, wide deep serrations. Upward flaring tangs, rounded base. Made of creamy tan pebble chert.
Priv. col., excellent quality, valued $90-100.

- Friley from Lafayette co., IN. Point 2 3/16 in. long, 2/3 in. wide, 5/32 in. thick. Point is narrow, symmetrical, upward flaring tangs, short narrow stem, bifurcated. Made of tan chert.
Priv. col., excellent quality, valued $65-80.

- Friley from Gallatin co., IL. Point 1 2/3 in. long, 1/2 in. wide, 1/8 in. thick. Sharp tipped, ears flare upward, sharply serrated, base is snapped. Made of gray pebble chert.
Priv. col., excellent quality, valued $70-80.

- Friley from Gallatin co., IL. Point 1 7/8 in. long, 5/16 in. wide, 1/8 in. thick. Narrow, heat treated, deep widely spaced serrations. Serrated upward flaring tangs, straight base. Made of white pebble chert.
Priv. col., excellent quality, valued $60-80.

- Friley from Davie co., NC. Point 2 1/8 in. long, 1/2 in. wide, 5/32 in. thick. Narrow, angularly symmetrical, horizontal flaring tangs. Finely and minutely serrated edges, bifurcated base. Made of grainy tan pebble chert.

Priv. col., excellent quality, valued $75-90.

• Friley from Davie co., NC. Point 1 5/8 in. long, 5/8 in. wide, 1/8 in. thick. Finely serrated sharp edges, ears flare upward and are serrated. Base is bifurcated. Made of white pebble chert.
Priv. col., excellent quality, valued $50-70.

• Friley from Williamson co., IL. Point 2 1/4 in. long, 5/8 in. wide, 1/8 in. thick. Narrow, randomly serrated edges, widely spaced, heat treated. Thin horizontal tangs with concave base. Made of white pebble chert.
Priv. col., excellent quality, valued $100-130.

• Friley from Huron co., MI. Point 2 1/16 in. long, 1/2 in. wide, 5/32 in. thick. Point is narrow, deep distinct random serrations, symmetrical, upward flaring tangs. The base is concave and irregular. Made of pink gray chert.
Priv. col., average quality, valued $15-30.

• Friley from Huron co., MI. Point 1 11/16 in. long, 7/16 in. wide, 1/8 in. thick. One side of point exhibits long thin serration, the other, sharp distinct serrations. Side notched, concave base. Made of pink chert.
Priv. col., museum quality, rare, valued $150-180.

• Friley from Allegan co., MI. Point 1 3/4 in. long, 3/8 in. wide, 1/8 in. thick. Narrow, heat treated, widely spaced edge serrations. Side nothced, concave base. Made of mauve chert.
Priv. col., museum quality, rare, valued $175-200.

• Friley from Allegan co., MI. Point 1 1/16 in. long, 1/2 in. wide, 7/32 in. thick. Point is wide, symmetrical, finely serrated edges. Shallow side notches, concave base. Made of marbled tan chert.
Priv. col., museum quality, valued $150-180.

• Friley from Buffalo co., WI. Point 2 1/2 in. long, 1/2 in. wide, 1/8 in. thick. Wide spaced and sharp serrations, very sharp tip. Horizontal barbs, bifurcated base. Made of gold brown to white banded chert.
Priv. col., museum quality, valued $80-100.

• Friley from Buffalo co., WI. Point 1 3/4 in. long, 7/8 in. wide, 1/8 in. thick. Wide, heat treated, edges exhibit widely spaced serrations. Upward flaring tangs with a convex base. Made of white pebble chert.
Priv. col., excellent quality, valued $70-90.

• Friley from Pike co., IL. Point 2 in. long, 1 in. wide, 3/16 in. thick. Point

triangularly symmetrical, rounded horizontal tangs. Corner notched, concave base. Made of gray pebble chert.
Priv. col., excellent quality, valued $75-80.

- Friley from Pike co., IL. Point 1 3/8 in. long, 1/2 in. wide, 1/8 in. thick. Ears flare upward, wide-spaced and sharp serrations along edges and tangs. Narrow stem bifurcated base. Made of Cobden chert.
Tim Rubbles col., museum quality, valued $80-100.

- Friley from Pike co., IL. Point 1 3/4 in. long, 5/8 in. wide, 1/8 in. thick. Symmetrical, heat treated, edge serrations widely spaced and rounded. Upward flaring tangs, ground rounded base. Made of gray white pebble chert.
Tim Rubbles col., museum quality, valued $120-150.

Frio: 5,000-1,500 B.P. Late Woodland

Midwestern point, small, triangular, and thin. Shoulders enlarged, distinct, flaring outward and toward the tip. The base is rounded or eared. Rough to extremely fine workmanship.

◆ Frio from Southwest KY. Point 1 3/4 in. long, 1 1/2 in. wide, 3/16 in. thick. Deep side notches with long flaring ears, notch in straight base. Made of Dover chert.

Priv. col., museum quality, valued $75-100.

- Frio from Gallatin co., IL. Point 2 1/4 in. long, 1 1/8 in. wide, 3/16 in. thick. Serrated with wide corner notches and notched concave base.
Priv. col., excellent quality, valued $35-55.

- Frio from Williamson co., IL. Point 2 3/16 in. long, 1 3/8 in. wide, 1/4 in. thick. Narrow, notched, fish tail like base, deep side notches. Made of vein quartz.
Priv. col., average quality, valued $15-25.

• Frio from central TN. Point 2 5/8 in. long, 1 1/2 in. wide, 1/4 in. thick. Short, wide fish tail base, shallow side notches, deep serrations. Made of vein quartz.
Priv. col., museum quality, valued $50-85.

• Frio from Gallatin co., IL. Point 1 3/4 in. long, 1 1/3 in. wide, 7/16 in. thick. Thick, triangular, deeply side notched. Shoulders flare outward and toward the tip. The base exhibits distinct flaring ears. Made of greenish pebble chert found along Saline River.
Priv. col., average quality, valued $20-35.

• Frio from Hardin co., KY. Point 1 1/4 in. long, 1 5/32 in. wide, 3/16 in. thick. Wide symmetrical point, deeply side notched, flaring ears, straight base. Made of white gold banded chert.
Priv. col., museum quality, valued $95-130.

• Frio from Gallatin co., IL. Point 2 in. long, 1 3/8 in. wide, 1/4 in. thick. Serrated, heat treated deep corner notches, thick point, concave base. Made of Mill Creek chert.
Priv. col., excellent quality, valued $45-65.

• Frio from Gallatin co., IL. Point 2 5/16 in. long, 1 5/8 in. wide, 1/4 in. thick. Narrow, deeply side notched, fish tail like base, deep concave base, slight tip break. Made of Mill Creek chert.
Priv. col., average quality, valued $15-25.

• Frio from Jackson co., IL. Point 2 7/16 in. long, 1 5/8 in. wide, 1/4 in. thick. Deeply side notched, fish tail like base. Made of Cobden chert.
Priv. col., museum quality, valued $75-95.

• Frio from Hamilton, TN. Point 2 1/16 in. long, 1 1/4 in. wide, 1/4 in. thick. Short, thick, wide fish tail base, shallow side notches, deep, sharp edges serrations. Made of low grade quartzite.
Priv. col., average quality, valued $25-35.

• Frio from Massac co., IL. Blade 4 3/16 in. long, 1 1/2 in. wide, 1/4 in. thick. Narrow, symmetrical, fine workmanship, beveled on one side of each face. Edges finely serrated, deep side notches. Flaring concave base. Made of vein quartz.
Priv. col., excellent quality, valued $65-75.

• Frio from Cooper co., TN. Blade 3 5/8 in. long, 1 2/3 in. wide, 1/4 in. thick. Symmetrical, concave sides, deep sharp serrated edges. Shallow corner notches,

wide fish tail base, Made of glossy gray chert.
Priv. col., museum quality, valued $65-85.

• Frio from Grainger co., TN. Blade 3 3/4 in. long, 1 2/3 in. wide, 7/16 in. thick. Thick, triangular, deep side notches. Beveled and serrated on one side of each face. Deep, uniform corner notches, flaring ears. Base is wide and basal notched. Made of Dover chert.
Priv. col., museum quality, valued $80-95.

• Frio from Grainger co., TN. Blade 3 13/16 in. long, 1 3/4 in. wide, 1/4 in. thick. Symmetrical, beveled and serrated on one side of each face. Corner notched, fish tail bifurcated base. Made of Dover chert.
Priv. col., museum quality, valued $75-85.

• Frio from Grainger co., TN. Blade 3 5/8 in. long, 1 1/2 in. wide, 1/4 in. thick. Narow, concave sides, beveled on one side of each face, deeply serrated edges. Corner notched, pointed barbed shoulders, short, wide fish tail base. Made of Dover chert.
Priv. col., museum quality, valued $70-85.

• Frio from Gallatin co., IL. Blade 3 3/4 in. long, 2 1/3 in. wide, 7/16 in. thick. Thick, triangular, deep side notches. Minutely serrated edges, thinned pointed tip. Shoulders flare outward and toward the tip. Base has distinct flaring ears, basal notched. Made of greenish pebble chert found along Saline River.
Priv. col., museum quality, rare, valued $100-135.

• Frio from Williamson co., IL. Blade 4 1/16 in. long, 1 5/8 in. wide, 1/4 in. thick. Symmetrical, good workmanship, beveled on one side of each face, sharply serrated. Basal notched, deep side notches, barbed shoulders. Made of green chert from Iron Montain, Union co., Illinois.
Priv. col., museum quality, rare, valued $180-250.

• Frio from Greene co., TN. Point 2 5/8 in. long, 1 1/4 in. wide, 1/4 in. thick. Symmetrical, deep side notches, finely serrated edges. Shoulders flare outward and toward the tip. Wide concave base. Made of gray chert.
Priv. col., excellent quality, valued $50-65.

• Frio from Bledsoe co., TN. Point 2 3/4 in. long, 1 1/2 in. wide, 7/16 in. thick. Thick, triangular, deeply side notched. Beveled on one side of each face. Barbed shoulders, concave base, flaring ears. Made of tan pebble chert.
Priv. col., excellent quality, valued $50-65.

CHAPTER 7
GARTH SLOUGH-GUNTHER

<u>Garth Slough: 10,000-3,500 B.P. Early Archaic</u>

Small southeastern point with expanded barbs and a short straight base. Blade edges are finely serrated and concave. Occasionally pieces have clipped tangs.

♦ Garth Slough from northwestern. TN. Point 1 5/32 in. long, 1 in. wide, 1/8 in. thick. Finely serrated with clipped tangs. Made of a mauve pebble chert.

Priv. col., museum quality, valued $45-80.

• Garth Slough from Hamilton co., TN. Point 1 5/8 in. long, 1 1/4 in. wide, 3/16 in. thick. Point is finely serrated exhibiting long clipped tangs extending below a short straight base. Made of Dover chert.
Priv. col., museum quality, valued $35-50.

• Garth Slough from northwestern KY. Point 1 7/8 in. long, 1 3/16 in. wide, 1/8 in. thick. Long, thin pressure flaking toward base. Base extends slightly bellow parallel tangs. Made of milky white quartz.
Priv. col., excellent quality, valued $15-25.

• Garth Slough from Alexander co., IL. Point 1 1/2 in. long, 1 in. wide,

3/16 in. thick. One side of each face beveled, very fine serrations, one broken tang. Made of Cobden Hornstone chert.
Priv. col., average quality, valued $10-15.

- Garth Slough from Alexander co., IL. Point 1 2/3 in. long, 1 3/32 in. wide, 3/16 in. thick. Expanded barbs with short straight base. Point edges finely serrated and concave, clipped tangs. Made of Mill Creek chert.
Grover Bohannon col., excellent quality, valued $20-30.

- Garth Slough from Humphreys co., TN. Point 1 15/32 in. long, 7/8 in. wide, 1/8 in. thick. Finely serrated, good workmanship, clipped tangs. Made of white pebble chert.
Priv. col., excellent quality, valued $45-60.

- Garth Slough from Hamilton co., TN. Point 1 5/8 in. long, 1 1/4 in. wide, 3/16 in. thick. Point is finely serrated exhibiting long clipped tangs extending below a short straight base. Made of Dover chert.
Priv. col., museum quality, valued $35-50.

- Garth Slough from northwestern KY. Point 1 7/8 in. long, 1 3/16 in. wide, 1/8 in. thick. Point exhibits long thin pressure flaking toward base. Base extends slightly bellow parallel tangs. Made of milky white quartz.
Priv. col., excellent quality, valued $15-25.

- Garth Slough from Alexander co., IL. Point 1 1/2 in. long, 1 in. wide, 3/16 in. thick. One side of each face beveled, very fine serrations, one broken tang. Made of Cobden Hornstone chert.
Priv. col., average quality, valued $10-15.

- Garth Slough from Henry co., TN. Point 1 5/16 in. long, 1 1/2 in. wide, 3/16 in. thick. Finely serrated edges and tangs, beveled on one side of each face. Long clipped tangs extending below a short straight base. Made of white pebble chert.
Priv. col., museum quality, valued $35-40.

- Garth Slough from Ballard co., KY. Point 1 5/8 in. long, 1 1/16 in. wide, 1/8 in. thick. Fine, long, thin pressure flaking, beveled on one side of each face, finely serrated edges. Base extends slightly below parallel pointed tangs. Made of yellow quartz.
Priv. col., museum quality, valued $35-55.

- Garth Slough from Oldham co., KY. Point 1 2/3 in. long, 1 1/8 in. wide, 3/16 in. thick. One side of each face beveled, finely serrated edge and tangs. Narrow stem convex base. Made of tan pebble chert.

Priv. col., excellent quality, valued $15-25.

- Garth Slough from Henderson co., TN. Point 1 3/8 in. long, 1 in. wide, 3/16 in. thick. Finely serrated edges, beveled on one side of each face. Long clipped tangs extending below a short straight base. Made of Dover chert.
Priv. col., museum quality, valued $35-45.

- Garth Slough from Nart co., KY. Point 1 in. long, 7/16 in. wide, 1/8 in. thick. Long thin pressure flaking angled toward base. Minute edge serrations. Base extends slightly bellow parallel tangs. Made of quartzite.
Priv. col., average quality, valued $15-20.

- Garth Slough from Bullitt co., KY. Point 1 1/3 in. long, 1 1/2 in. wide, 3/16 in. thick. One side of each face beveled, very fine serrations, wider than long. Expanded stem convex base. Made of tan pebble chert.
Priv. col., excellent quality, valued $20-25.

- Garth Slough from Boone co., WV. Point 1 5/8 in. long, 1 1/8 in. wide, 3/16 in. thick. Symmetrical, finely serrated edges, clipped tangs, short straight base. Made of gray marbled chert.
Priv. col., museum quality, valued $35-45.

- Garth Slough from Boone co., WV. Point 2 1/8 in. long, 1 7/16 in. wide, 1/8 in. thick. Beveled on one side of each face, sharply serrated edges, long thin pressure flaking toward base. Convex base extends slightly below parallel tangs. Made of gray marbled chert.
Priv. col., museum quality, valued $30-45.

- Garth Slough from Boone co., WV. Point 1 2/3 in. long, 1 in. wide, 3/16 in. thick. One side of each face beveled, very fine serrated concave sides. Stem is long and expanding, straight base. Made of dark brown chert.
Priv. col., excellent quality, valued $20-25.

- Garth Slough from Halifax co., VA. Point 2 3/8 in. long, 1 3/4 in. wide, 3/16 in. thick. Point is finely serrated, needle sharp tip. Long clipped tangs extending below a short straight base. Made of gray flint.
Priv. col., excellent quality, valued $30-40.

- Garth Slough from Halifax co., VA. Point 1 5/8 in. long, 1 3/8 in. wide, 1/8 in. thick. Thin pressure flaking, edges finely serrated. Convex base extends slightly below pointed parallel tangs. Made of quartzite.
Priv. col., excellent quality, valued $35-45.

- Garth Slough from Halifax co., VA. Point 1 1/4 in. long, 1 in. wide, 3/16 in. thick. One side of each face beveled, fine edge and tang serrations, one broken tang. Short snapped base. Made of white pebble chert.
Priv. col., average quality, valued $10-15.

- Garth Slough from Russell co., VA. Point 1 7/8 in. long, 1 1/4 in. wide, 3/16 in. thick. Thin, narrow, finely serrated edges and tip. Long clipped tangs extending below a short straight base. Made of dark gray chert.
Priv. col., excellent quality, valued $35-50.

- Garth Slough from Russell co., VA. Point 2 1/8 in. long, 1 5/16 in. wide, 1/8 in. thick. Thin, symmetrical, pressure flaked. Base extends below thin parallel serrated tangs. Made of white to tan chert.
Priv. col., excellent quality, valued $35-45.

- Garth Slough from Alexander co., IL. Point 1 7/8 in. long, 1 1/2 in. wide, 3/16 in. thick. Symmetrical, good workmanship, one side of each face beveled, fine edge serrations. Thinned concave base. Made of Cobden Hornstone chert.
Priv. col., museum quality, valued $50-55.

- Garth Slough from Caddo co., LA. Point 2 in. long, 1 1/3 in. wide, 3/16 in. thick. Finely serrated edges, slight tip break. Long clipped tangs extending below a short snap base. Made of translucent yellow chert.
Priv. col., average quality, valued $25-30.

- Garth Slough from Caddo co., LA. Point 1 3/8 in. long, 1 3/32 in. wide, 1/8 in. thick. Thin pressure flaking toward base. Base is short, long parallel tangs. Made of milky quartz.
Priv. col., excellent quality, valued $25-30.

- Garth Slough from Caddo co., LA. Point 1 7/8 in. long, 1 in. wide, 1/8 in. thick. One side of each face beveled, finely serrated edges. Short horizontal barbed shoulders. Made of milky quartz.
Priv. col., museum quality, valued $40-45.

Godar: 4,500-3,500 B.P. Late Archaic

Found in the Midwest, medium to large point or blade. Varies widely in width and symmetry, side notched with full base, convex, concave, straight, etc. Some pieces are parallel flaked and finely serrated.

♦ Godar from Humphreys co., TN. Blade 3 3/4 in. long, 7/8 in. wide, 1/4 in. thick. Heavy field patina, parallel flaked and finely serrated. Made of white pebble chert.

Priv. col., museum quality, valued $120-160.

• Godar from Johnson co., IL. Blade 4 3/8 in. long, 1 3/8 in. wide, 1/4 in. thick. Deeply side notched, concave base, parallel flaked and sharply serrated. Made of Mill Creek chert.
Priv. col., museum quality, valued $100-130.

• Godar from Humphreys co., TN. Point 2 1/4 in. long, 7/8 in. wide, 1/4 in. thick. Heat treated, parallel flaked and finely serrated. Made of pink on gray pebble chert.
Priv. col., museum quality, valued $70-100.

• Godar from Jackson co., IL. Blade 3 5/8 in. long, 1 7/8 in. wide, 3/8 in. thick. Wide blade, thick, shallow side notches with convex base, finely serrated, one side of each face slightly beveled. Made of Mill Creek chert.
Priv. col., excellent quality, valued $80-100.

• Godar from Humphreys co., TN. Blade 5 1/4 in. long, 1 7/8 in. wide, 1/4 in. thick. Heat treated, unusually long and symmetrical, parallel flaked and finely serrated. Made of tan pebble chert.
Priv. col., museum quality, valued $120-160.

• Godar from Humphreys co., TN. Point 2 3/8 in. long, 5/8 in. wide, 1/4 in. thick. Thick, yet narrow point, side notched, straight based. Indistinct parallel flaking and finely serrated. Made of Dover chert.
Priv. col., average quality, valued $60-80.

• Godar from Hamilton co., TN. Blade 3 2/3 in. long, 7/8 in. wide, 3/16 in. thick. Heavy field patina, heat treated, distinct parallel flaking, sharply serrated. Made of white to yellow chert.
Priv. col., museum quality, valued $140-180.

• Godar from Jackson co., IL. Blade 4 in. long, 1 1/2 in. wide, 1/3 in. thick. Symmetrical, beveled on one side of each face, finely serrated edges, rounded tip. Side notched with concave base. Made of Mill Creek chert.

Tim Rubbles col., excellent quality, valued $70-85.

- Godar from Union co., IL. Blade 3 13/16 in. long, 1 1/8 in. wide, 1/4 in. thick. Beveled on all four sides, parallel flaked and finely serrated. Shallow side notches, concave base. Made of white pebble chert.
Priv. col., excellent quality, valued $80-100.

- Godar from Johnson co., IL. Blade 3 7/8 in. long, 1 1/2 in. wide, 1/4 in. thick. Poor workmanship, uneven side notches, concave base. Made of Mill Creek chert.
Priv. col., average quality, valued $40-50.

- Godar from Johnson co., IL. Point 2 in. long, 1 3/8 in. wide, 1/2 in. thick. Beveled on one side of each face, poor workmanship, rounded tip. Uneven deep side notches, straight base. Made of Mill Creek chert.
Priv. col., average quality, valued $20-30.

- Godar from Johnson co., IL. Blade 3 7/8 in. long, 1 7/8 in. wide, 1/2 in. thick. Thick blade, beveled one one side of each face, sharply serrated, shallow side notched with convex base. Made of Mill Creek chert.
Priv. col., excellent quality, valued $65-85.

- Godar from Martin co., IN. Point 2 3/8 in. long, 1 1/2 in. wide, 1/3 in. thick. Beveled on one side of one face, finely serrated. Side notched, convex base. Made of light gray chert.
Priv. col., excellent quality, valued $60-80.

- Godar from Martin co., IN. Blade 3 7/8 in. long, 1 7/8 in. wide, 1/4 in. thick. Beveled on one side of each face, parallel flaked and finely serrated. Deep side notches, concave base. Made of white tan pebble chert.
Priv. col., museum quality, valued $100-120.

- Godar from Jay co., IN. Blade 4 1/8 in. long, 1 5/8 in. wide, 1/4 in. thick. Thin, symmetrical, parallel flaked and sharply serrated. Shallow side notches, straight base. Made of false jasper.
Priv. col., museum quality, valued $80-100.

- Godar from Calhoun co., AR. Point 2 1/2 in. long, 1 1/8 in. wide, 1/4 in. thick. Heat treated, parallel flaked, finely serrated edges. Deep side notches, parallel sided concave base. Made of gray pebble chert.
Priv. col., museum quality, valued $60-80.

- Godar from Lee co., AR. Blade 3 5/8 in. long, 1 9/16 in. wide, 5/8 in. thick.

Thick, finely serrated edges, one side of each face. Shallow side notched, convex base. Made of high grade quartzite.
Priv. coll., excellent quality, valued $85-100.

• Godar form Lee co., AR. Blade 4 1/16 in. long, 1 1/2 in. wide, 1/3 in. thick. Highly serrated edges, sharp pointed tip. Side notched, parallel sided straight base. Made of grainy tan chert.
Priv. col., average quality, valued $75-80.

• Godar from Lee co., AR. Blade 3 13/16 in. long, 7/8 in. wide, 1/4 in. thick. Thin, narrow, beveled concave sides, parallel flaked and finely serrated. Deep symmetrical side notches, concave base. Made of white tan pebble chert.
Priv. col., excellent quality, valued $100-120.

• Godar from Izard co., AR. Blade 4 3/4 in. long, 2 1/8 in. wide, 1/4 in. thick. Thin, heat treated, parallel flaked and sharply serrated. Deep side notches, concave base. Made of pink chert.
Priv. col., museum quality, valued $120-150.

• Godar from Izard co., AR. Point 2 1/2 in. long, 1 3/8 in. wide, 1/4 in. thick. Heat treated, parallel flaked, finely serrated edges. Deep side notches, concave base. Made of pink chert.
Priv. col., museum quality, valued $70-100.

• Godar from Izard co., AR. Blade 3 7/8 in. long, 1 3/8 in. wide, 3/8 in. thick. Thin blade, finely serrated, one side of each face beveled. Shallow side notched, convex base. Made of pink chert.
Priv. col., excellent quality, valued $80-100.

• Godar from Little River co., AR. Blade 3 3/4 in. long, 1 1/4 in. wide, 1/4 in. thick. Concave side, finely serrated, parallel flaked. Deep side notches, parallel sided concave base. Made of white pebble chert.
Priv. col., excellent quality, valued $100-120.

• Godar from Hamilton co., IL. Blade 4 1/2 in. long, 2 1/8 in. wide, 1/4 in. thick. Thin, parallel flaked and sharply serrated. Deeply side notched, concave base. Made of Mill Creek chert.
Priv. col., museum quality, valued $85-100.

• Godar from Humphreys co., TN. Blade 4 1/4 in. long, 1 7/8 in. wide, 1/4 in. thick. Thin, symmetrical, heat treated, parallel flaked and finely serrated. Side notched, convex base. Made of gray pebble chert.
Priv. col., excellent quality, valued $70-85.

- Godar from Jackson co., IL. Blade 3 5/8 in. long, 2 1/8 in. wide, 3/8 in. thick. Wide, finely serrated on one side of each face. Shallow side notches, convex base. Mabe of Cobden chert.
Priv. col., museum quality, valued $120-150.

- Godar from Jackson co., IL. Blade 4 1/16 in. long, 1 7/8 in. wide, 1/4 in. thick. Heat treated, parallel flaked and finely serrated. Deep side notches, concave base. Made of white pebble chert.
Priv. col., excellent quality, valued $85-100.

- Godar from Johnson co., IL. Blade 3 27/32 in. long, 1 1/2 in. wide, 1/4 in. thick. Symmetrical, parallel flaked and sharply serrated. Deep side notches, straight base. Made of Mill Creek chert.
Priv. col., excellent quality, valued $80-90.

- Godar from Humphreys co., TN. Point 2 1/4 in. long, 1 1/8 in. wide, 1/4 in. thick. Heat treated, parallel flaked and finely serrated. Shallow side notches, concave base. Made of pink on gray pebble chert.
Priv. col., museum quality, valued $90-100.

Golondrina: 9,000-6,500 B.P. Paleo-Transitional

Medium to large point or blade found mainly in the Midwest. Golondrinas are characterized by their rounded ears and deeply concave bases.

◆ Golondrina from northeastern AR. Point 2 1/8 in. long, 1 in. wide, 1/4 in. thick. Fire treated. Made of tan pebble chert.

Priv. col., excellent quality, valued $80-120.

- Golondrina from Alexander co., IL. Blade 4 1/4 in. long, 1 1/2 in. wide, 5/16 in. thick. One ear turned inward, uneven concave base, very symmetrical point. Made of Dover chert.
Priv. col., museum quality, valued $300-400.

• Golondrina from Warren co., TN. Blade 3 7/8 in. long, 1 3/16 in. wide,
1/4 in. thick. Thin with distinct horizontal transverse flaking, deep concave base.
Made of Dover chert.
Priv. col., museum quality, valued $250-325.

• Golondrina from southwestern KY. Blade 4 in. long, 1 3/4 in. wide, 5/16 in.
thick. Random flaking, concave base, one ear broken off halfway up. Made of
pink pebble chert.
Priv. col., average quality, valued $80-125.

• Golondrina from Williamson co., IL. Point 2 1/4 in. long, 1 1/8 in. wide,
1/4 in. thick. Point parallel flaked on one side of each face. Opposing sides
random flaked, point very sharp, rough concave base, disproportionate tangs.
Made of Mill Creek chert.
Priv. col., poor quality, valued $35-50.

• Golondrina from Hardin co., TN. Blade 4 1/8 in. long, 1 5/16 in. wide,
1/4 in. thick. Thin, symmetrical, horizontal transverse flaked, deep concave base.
Made of Dover chert.
Grover Bohannon col., museum quality, valued $250-325.

• Golondrina from Hamilton co., KY. Blade 4 3/16 in. long, 1 3/4 in. wide,
1/4 in. thick. Thin, symmetrical, random flaked, concave base. Made of tan
pebble chert.
Priv. col., excellent quality, valued $70-100.

• Golondrina from Williamson co., IL. Blade 4 1/4 in. long, 1 5/8 in. wide,
1/4 in. thick. Blade horizontal transverse flaked, beveled on one side of each
face, sharply serrated, concave base, symmetrical tangs. Made of Cobden chert.
Tim Rubbles col., museum quality, valued $335-400.

• Golondrina from Alexander co., IL. Blade 4 1/2 in. long, 1 2/3 in. wide,
1/4 in. thick. Classical design, very symmetrical point. Made of Mill Creek chert.
Priv. col., excellent quality, valued $200-280.

• Golondrina from Alexander co., IL. Blade 4 in. long, 1 1/4 in. wide, 1/4 in.
thick. Thin, horizontal transverse flaking, deep concave base. Made of Mill
Creek chert.
Priv. col., excellent quality, valued $220-225.

• Golondrina from Alexander co., IL. Blade 4 in. long, 1 3/4 in. wide, 5/16 in.
thick. Random flaked, concave base. Made of white pebble chert.
Priv. col., average quality, valued $80-100.

• Golondrina from Union co., IL. Point 2 1/2 in. long, 1 1/4 in. wide, 1/4 in. thick. Parallel flaked, point very sharp, rough concave base. Made of Mill Creek chert.
Priv. col., average quality, valued $65-80.

• Golondrina from Union co., IL. Blade 4 5/16 in. long, 1 3/4 in. wide, 5/16 in. thick. Concave base, very symmetrical point. Made of Mill Creek chert.
Priv. col., excellent quality, valued $200-300.

• Golondrina from Union co., IL. Blade 3 7/8 in. long, 1 5/16 in. wide, 1/4 in. thick. Distinct horizontal transverse flaking, deep concave base. Made of Cobden chert.
Priv. col., museum quality, valued $350-375.

• Golondrina from Dade co., MO. Blade 5 in. long, 2 in. wide, 5/16 in. thick. Horizontal flaking, concave base. Made of pink chert.
Priv. col., average quality, valued $80-100.

• Golondrina from Dade co., MO. Point 2 1/3 in. long, 1 1/8 in. wide, 3/16 in. thick. Parallel flaked, very sharp, concave base. Made of pinkish chert.
Priv. col., average quality, valued $55-70.

• Golondrina from Dade co., MO. Blade 4 1/16 in. long, 1 1/2 in. wide, 7/16 in. thick. Concave base, thick, symmetrical point. Made of white pebble chert.
Priv. col., excellent quality, valued $180-240.

• Golondrina from Warren co., TN. Blade 3 5/8 in. long, 1 1/2 in. wide, 1/4 in. thick. Horizontal transverse flaking, deep concave base. Made of Dover chert.
Priv. col., museum quality, valued $250-325.

• Golondrina from Masac co., IL. Blade 4 1/32 in. long, 1 2/3 in. wide, 5/16 in. thick. Horizontal flaking, concave base. Made of tan pebble chert.
Priv. col., average quality, valued $80-125.

• Golondrina from Masac co., IL. Blade 4 1/4 in. long, 1 5/8 in. wide, 1/4 in. thick. Parallel flaked, heat treated, sharp tip, concave base. Made of Mill Creek chert.
Priv. col., excellent quality, valued $135-150.

• Golondrina from Coles co., IL. Blade 4 1/8 in. long, 1 1/4 in. wide, 3/16 in. thick. Thin, concave base, very symmetrical point. Made of Cobden Hornstone chert.
Priv. col., museum quality, valued $300-400.

- Golondrina from Coles co., IL. Blade 3 13/16 in. long, 1 1/4 in. wide, 1/4 in. thick. Thin, horizontal transverse flaking, deep concave base. Made of greenish tan chert.
Priv. col., museum quality, valued $250-325.

- Golondrina from Coles co., IL. Blade 4 in. long, 2 in. wide, 3/16 in. thick. Wide, thin, random flaking, concave base. Made of pinkish pebble chert.
Priv. col., excellent quality, valued $180-225.

- Golondrina from Clark co., IL. Point 2 1/3 in. long, 1 3/8 in. wide, 1/4 in. thick. Parallel flaked, sharp, rough concave base. Made of gray chert.
Priv. col., average quality, valued $55-70.

- Golondrina from Clark co., IL. Point 2 1/4 in. long, 1 1/8 in. wide, 5/16 in. thick. Concave base, symmetrical point. Made of gray chert.
Priv. col., museum quality, valued $150-200.

- Golondrina from Warren co., TN. Blade 4 1/8 in. long, 1 5/16 in. wide, 1/4 in. thick. Thin horizontal transverse flaking, deep concave base. Made of Dover chert.
Priv. col., museum quality, valued $350-425.

- Golondrina from Warren co., TN. Blade 4 3/4 in. long, 1 1/3 in. wide, 5/16 in. thick. Random flaking, concave base. Made of pinkish pebble chert.
Priv. col., excellent quality, valued $180-225.

- Golondrina from Warren co., IL. Point 4 1/4 in. long, 1 3/8 in. wide, 1/4 in. thick. Parallel flaked, sharp tip, concave base. Made of white pebble chert.
Priv. col., excellent quality, valued $235-250.

Gram Cave: 9,000-5,000 B.P. Paleo-Transitional to Mid-Archaic

Midwestern medium to large, point or blade. Narrow, recurved sides, pointed ears, side notched with concave base.

◆ Gram Cave from Andrew co., MO. Blade 4 3/4 in. long, 1 3/8 in. wide, 3/8 in. thick. Perfectly symmetrical blade. Made of a light green chert.

Priv. col., museum quality, rare, valued $200-250.

◆ Gram Cave from Union co., IL. Point 2 1/4 in. long, 1 1/4 in. wide, 5/8 in. thick. Symmetrical, wide, thick, well beveled. Made of Mill Creek chert.

Les Grubbe col., excellent quality, valued $125-150.

◆ Gram Cave from Union co., IL. Point 2 1/4 in. long, 3/4 in. wide, 3/32 in. thick. Fire treated E-notch beveled point. Made of Mill Creek chert.

Les Grubbe col., average quality, valued $50-65.

◆ Gram Cave blades. *Right*: from Andrew co., MO. Made of a light green chert. *Left*: from Union co., IL. Made of Mill Creek chert.

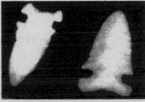

Les Grubbe col. Right: museum quality, valued $200-250. Left: average quality, valued $50-65.

◆ Gram Cave from Union co., IL. Point 2 21/32 in. long, 1 in. wide, 1/4 in. thick. Deep E-notched beveled point. Made of Mill Creek chert.

Les Grubbe col., average quality, valued $50-65.

• Gram Cave from Union co., IL. Point 2 23/32 in. long, 1 3/32 in. wide, 5/32 in. thick. Very symmetrical, finely serrated, deep even E-notched point. Made of local pink false jasper.
Les Grubbe col., museum quality, valued $175-250.

◆ Gram Cave from central TN. Blade 4 5/8 in. long, 1 1/4 in. wide, 1/4 in.

thick. Very symmetrical, finely serrated with rare fluting. Made of Dover chert.

Les Grubbe col., museum quality, rare, valued $250-350.

♦ Gram Cave from Union co., IL. Blade 3 1/2 in. long, 1 3/8 in. wide, 1/4 in. thick. Heavy field patina, symmetrical and beveled. Made of high quality Mill Creek chert.

Les Grubbe col., excellent quality, valued $125-175.

♦ Gram Cave from Union co., IL. Point 3 in. long, 1 1/4 in. wide, 5/8 in. thick. Symmetrical classic design point. Made of tan chert.

Les Grubbe col., museum quality, valued $175-250.

• Gram Cave from Saline co., IL. Point 3 1/8 in. long, 1 1/4 in. wide, 1/3 in. thick. Symmetrical, well beveled, concave base. Made of tan to white chert.
Priv. col., excellent quality, valued $125-150.

• Gram Cave from Saline co., IL. Blade 3 3/4 in. long, 1 3/4 in. wide, 3/16 in. thick. Heat treated, beveled, classic concave base. Made of gray chert.
Priv. col., excellent quality, valued $150-165.

• Gram Cave from Adams co., MO. Point 2 1/2 in. long, 1 1/8 in. wide, 1/4 in. thick. Heat treated, classic design. Made of white pebble chert.
Priv. col., museum quality, valued $200-250.

• Gram Cave from Union co., IL. Point 2 7/16 in. long, 1 1/8 in. wide, 1/4 in.

thick. Deep E-notched, beveled edges, classical base. Made of Kaolin chert.
Priv. col., museum quality, rare, valued $350-465.

- Gram Cave from Union co., IL. Point 2 2/3 in. long, 1 7/32 in. wide, 3/16 in.
thick. Classic design. Made of Cobden chert.
Priv. col., museum quality, valued $250-350.

- Gram Cave from Union co., IL. Point 2 1/4 in. long, 1 1/4 in. wide, 1/3 in.
thick. Symmetrical, wide, thick, well beveled. Made of Mill Creek chert.
Jim Smith col., excellent quality, valued $125-150.

- Gram Cave from Union co., IL. Point 2 1/4 in. long, 1 1/16 in. wide, 5/32 in.
thick. Heat treated, classical design. Made of Mill Creek chert.
Jim Smith col., average quality, valued $50-65.

- Gram Cave from Pike co., IL. Point 2 3/4 in. long, 1 5/16 in. wide, 1/4 in.
thick. Classic Gram Cave. Made of Mill Creek chert.
Priv. col., excellent quality, valued $150-175.

- Gram Cave from Pike co., IL. Blade 4 3/4 in. long, 1 23/32 in. wide, 1/3 in.
thick. Made of mauve pebble chert.
Priv. col., excellent quality, valued $300-350.

- Gram Cave from Pike co., IL. Blade 4 1/4 in. long, 2 1/16 in. wide, 5/8 in.
thick. Heat treated, symmetrical, wide, thick, steeply beveled, concave base.
Made of pinkish pebble chert.
Priv. col., excellent quality, valued $225-275.

- Gram Cave from Massac co., IL. Point 2 1/2 in. long, 1 1/4 in. wide, 1/4 in.
thick. Classic Gram Cave. Made of multi-toned gray chert.
Priv. col., average quality, valued $50-65.

- Gram Cave from Union co., IL. Point 2 1/32 in. long, 1 1/8 in. wide, 1/4 in.
thick. Steeply beveled. Made of Mill Creek chert.
Priv. col., average quality, valued $50-65.

- Gram Cave from Jefferson co., MO. Point 2 1/4 in. long, 1 1/4 in. wide,

1/8 in. thick. Symmetrical, wide, thin, well beveled. Made of yellow white chert.
Priv. col., excellent quality, valued $125-150.

- Gram Cave from Jefferson co., MO. Point 2 1/2 in. long, 1 1/4 in. wide,
5/32 in. thick. Heat treated, symmetrical, beveled point. Made of tan chert.

Priv. col., average quality, valued $50-65.

• Gram Cave from Clark co., IL. Point 2 1/3 in. long, 1 in. wide, 1/2 in. thick. Thick, steeply beveled point. Made of false jasper.
Priv. col., average quality, valued $50-65.

• Gram Cave from Union co., IL. Point 2 2/3 in. long, 1 1/3 in. wide, 1/4 in. thick. Classic design. Made of Cobden chert.
Priv. col., museum quality, valued $200-275.

• Gram Cave from Jackson co., IL. Point 2 3/4 in. long, 1 5/8 in. wide, 5/8 in. thick. Symmetrical, wide, thick, beveled, concave base. Made of Mill Creek chert.
Tim Rubbles col., excellent quality, valued $125-150.

• Gram Cave from Alexander co., IL. Point 2 1/2 in. long, 7/8 in. wide, 3/16 in. thick. Heat treated E-notch, beveled on one side of each face. Made of Mill Creek chert.
Priv. col., average quality, valued $50-65.

• Gram Cave from Andrew co., MO. Blade 4 1/16 in. long, 2 in. wide, 3/16 in. thick. Symmetrical, heat treated, concave base. Made of white pebble chert.
Les Grubbe col., museum quality, valued $200-250.

• Gram Cave from Johnson co., IL. Point 2 1/2 in. long, 1 1/8 in. wide, 1/4 in. thick. Steeply beveled, poor workmanship. Made of gray chert.
Priv. col., average quality, valued $50-65.

• Gram Cave from Union co., IL. Point 2 2/3 in. long, 1 9/32 in. wide, 1/3 in. thick. Heat treated, classic design. Made of tan pebble chert.
Priv. col., excellent quality, valued $125-175.

• Gram Cave from Union co., IL. Point 2 1/4 in. long, 1 1/2 in. wide, 5/8 in. thick. Heat treated, symmetrical, wide, thick, well beveled. Made of Mill Creek chert.
Priv. col., excellent quality, valued $125-150.

• Gram Cave from Union co., IL. Point 2 1/2 in. long, 1 1/4 in. wide, 5/32 in. thick. Heat treated, E-notch beveled, concave base. Made of Mill Creek chert.
Priv. col., average quality, valued $50-65.

• Gram Cave from Andrew co., MO. Point 2 2/3 in. long, 1 1/4 in. wide,

3/16 in. thick. Classic design. Made of light green chert.
Priv. col., right museum quality, valued $200-250.

• Gram Cave from Howell co., MO. Point 2 1/3 in. long, 1 1/32 in. wide,
1/4 in. thick. Deep E-notched beveled point. Made of mauve chert.
Priv col., average quality, valued $50-65.

• Gram Cave from Union co., IL: Point 2 3/4 in. long, 1 3/8 in. wide, 1/4 in.
thick. Classic design, slight tip break.
Priv. col., poor quality, valued $20-30.

Greenbriar: 10,000-6,000 B.P. Paleo-Transitional

*Southeast to Midwest point or blade, medium to large size. Edges
generally finely serrated, wide side notches, broad tapered shoulders. The base
is ground, convex, straight, lobbed, eared, or bifurcated. Fluting may occur in
earlier points or blades.*

♦ Greenbriar from central KY. Blade 3 1/2 in. long, 1 1/4 in. wide, 1/4 in.
thick. Right side beveled blade, finely serrated. Straight base with hafting marks.
Made of glossy tan brown chert.

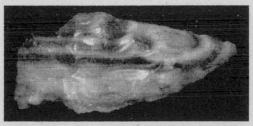

Priv. col., excellent quality, rare, valued $140-165.

♦ Greenbriar from central KY. Blade 4 in. long, 1 3/8 in. wide, 3/16 in. thick.
Very light in weight, finely serrated. Made of a tan brown marbled chert.

Priv. col., average quality, valued $35-50.

• Greenbriar from Pope co., IL. Point 2 1/2 in. long, 7/8 in. wide, 1/4 in. thick. Finely serrated, shallow notches, concave fluted base. Made of Dover chert. *Priv. col., museum quality, valued $125-175.*

• Greenbriar from Perry co., TN. Blade 3 5/8 in. long, 1 3/4 in. wide, 5/16 in. thick. Finely serrated, deep side notches, flaring tangs, unfluted concave base. Made of Dover chert. *Priv. col., museum quality, valued $250-300.*

• Greenbriar from northwestern. TN. Blade 4 1/16 in. long, 1 1/32 in. wide, 1/4 in. thick. Finely serrated, needle sharp tip, virtually no notches, flaring tangs, shallow concave base. Made of Kent chert. *Priv. col., museum quality, rare, valued $350-450.*

• Greenbriar from Jackson co., IL. Point 2 3/8 in. long, 1 5/8 in. wide, 3/16 in. thick. Point very sharp, finely serrated, long pointed tip. Deep side notches, straight and fluted base. Made of Cobden Hornstone chert. *Priv. col., museum quality, rare, valued $400-500.*

• Greenbriar from Bullitt co., KY. Blade 5 in. long, 1 7/8 in. wide, 3/16 in. thick. Finely serrated, classic design. Made of brown marbled chert. *Priv. col., excellent quality, valued $135-180.*

• Greenbriar from Powell co., KY. Point 2 1/2 in. long, 1 1/8 in. wide, 1/4 in. thick. Finely serrated, concave fluted base. Made of tan pebble chert. *Priv. col., excellent quality, valued $100-125.*

• Greenbriar from Perry co., TN. Blade 3 5/8 in. long, 2 1/4 in. wide, 5/16 in. thick. Finely serrated, wide, thick, concave base. Made of marbled tan chert. *Priv. col., museum quality, valued $225-250.*

• Greenbriar from Powell co., TN. Blade 4 3/16 in. long, 1 7/32 in. wide, 1/4 in. thick. Finely serrated, needle sharp tip, shallow concave base. Made of white pebble chert. *Priv. col., museum quality, valued $300-350.*

• Greenbriar from Jackson co., IL. Point 2 5/8 in. long, 1 1/8 in. wide, 1/4 in. thick. Classic design, concave edges. Made of Cobden Hornstone chert. *Priv. col., museum quality, rare, valued $300-375.*

• Greenbriar from Owen co., KY. Blade 4 2/3 in. long, 1 3/4 in. wide, 5/16 in. thick. symmetrical, finely serrated, concave sides and base. Made of brown chert. *Priv. col., excellent quality, valued $55-70.*

- Greenbriar from Pope co., IL. Point 2 1/3 in. long, 1 in. wide, 1/4 in. thick. Finely serrated, fluted, classical concave base. Made of pink black speckled chert.
Priv. col., museum quality, valued $125-175.

- Greenbriar from Perry co., TN. Blade 4 5/8 in. long, 2 1/4 in. wide, 5/16 in. thick. Finely serrated, flaring tangs, unfluted, concave base. Made of Dover chert.
Priv. col., museum quality, valued $350-400.

- Greenbriar from Franklin co., TN. Blade 4 1/32 in. long, 1 1/2 in. wide, 1/4 in. thick. Finely serrated, needle sharp tip, concave base. Made of mauve pebble chert.
Priv. col., museum quality, rare, valued $350-450.

- Greenbriar from Jackson co., TN. Blade 4 3/8 in. long, 1 5/8 in. wide, 3/16 in. thick. Finely serrated, long pointed tip, fluted, classic concave base. Made of white tan pebble chert.
Priv. col., excellent quality, valued $100-125.

- Greenbriar from Clinton co., KY. Point 2 in. long, 1 3/32 in. wide, 3/16 in. thick. Classic concave side style. Made of tan brown chert.
Priv. col., average quality, valued $35-50.

- Greenbriar from Pike co., IL. Point 2 1/3 in. long, 1 3/8 in. wide, 1/4 in. thick. Finely serrated, convex edges, concave fluted base. Made of gray chert.
Priv. col., excellent quality, valued $75-100.

- Greenbriar from Pickett co., TN. Blade 3 5/8 in. long, 1 3/4 in. wide, 5/16 in. thick. Finely serrated, shallow side notches, flaring tangs, fluted concave base. Made of greenish chert.
Priv. col., museum quality, valued $250-300.

- Greenbriar from Pickett co., TN. Blade 4 3/32 in. long, 1 1/2 in. wide, 1/4 in. thick. Heat treated, finely serrated, flaring tangs, shallow concave base. Made of greenish chert.
Priv. col., museum quality, valued $300-350.

- Greenbriar from Jackson co., KY. Point 2 7/8 in. long, 1 1/8 in. wide, 3/16 in. thick. Concave edges, finely serrated, long thin tip, concave fluted base. Made of purple chert.
Priv. col., museum quality, valued $120-150.

• Greenbriar from Hopkins co., KY. Blade 3 7/8 in. long, 1 1/3 in. wide, 3/16 in. thick. Classic design, fluted, concave base. Made of a tan yellow marbled chert.
Priv. col., excellent quality, valued $85-100.

• Greenbriar from Hopkins co., KY. Point 2 7/16 in. long, 1 in. wide, 1/4 in. thick. Finely serrated, concave edges, concave fluted base. Made of brown pebble chert.
Priv. col., excellent quality, valued $75-85.

• Greenbriar from Perry co., TN. Blade 4 1/8 in. long, 1 3/4 in. wide, 1/4 in. thick. Finely serrated, flaring tangs, unfluted concave base. Made of white pebble chert.
Priv. col., excellent quality, valued $150-200.

• Greenbriar from Perry co., TN. Blade 4 in. long, 1 5/32 in. wide, 1/4 in. thick. Finely serrated, needle sharp tip, concave base. Made of white pebble chert.
Priv. col., excellent quality, valued $250-350.

• Greenbriar from Jackson co., KY. Point 2 3/8 in. long, 1 1/8 in. wide, 1/4 in. thick. Concave sides, finely serrated, long pointed tip, fluted base. Made of banded tan chert.
Priv. col., excellent quality, valued $85-125.

• Greenbriar from Jackson co., KY. Blade 5 1/32 in. long, 2 3/8 in. wide, 5/16 in. thick. Made of banded tan chert.
Priv. col., museum quality, valued $350-450.

• Greenbriar from White co., IL. Point 2 1/8 in. long, 7/8 in. wide, 1/4 in. thick. Finely serrated, concave edges, concave fluted base. Made of gray pebble chert.
Priv. col., excellent quality, valued $125-150.

• Greenbriar from Perry co., TN. Blade 4 5/8 in. long, 1 7/8 in. wide, 1/8 in. thick. Thin, finely serrated, concave base. Made of Dover chert.
Priv. col., museum quality, valued $250-300.

• Greenbriar from Sevier co., TN. Blade 4 5/16 in. long, 1 1/8 in. wide, 1/4 in. thick. Finely serrated, needle sharp tip, flaring tangs, concave base. Made of Kent chert.
Priv. col., museum quality, rare, valued $275-350.

• Greenbriar from Jackson co., IL. Point 2 5/8 in. long, 1 1/2 in. wide, 3/16 in. thick. Finely serrated, long needle sharp tip. Deep side notches, fluted base.

Made of Cobden chert.
Priv. col., museum quality, valued $175-225.

Guilford: 6,500-5,000 B.P. Archaic

Gulifords are thick points or blades, medium to large in size. Round base variant has a convex stem. Yuma variant straight to concave base. Usually made of quartzite or pebble chert material. Found predominantly in the Carolinas.

◆ Guilford round base variant from Stokes co., NC. Point 2 3/4 in. long, 1 1/32 in. wide, 5/8 in. thick. Crudely chipped. Made of pebble chert.

Priv. col., average quality, valued $5-10.

• Guilford straight base from Boone co., SC. Point 3 in. long, 1 5/8 in. wide, 5/8 in. thick. Unusually fine workmanship, slightly concave base. Made of vein quartz.
Priv. col., excellent quality, valued $15-25.

• Guilford straight base from Boone co., SC. Point 3 3/16 in. long, 1 3/8 in. wide, 1/2 in. thick. Classic concave base. Made of quartzite.
Priv. col., excellent quality, valued $15-25.

• Guilford straight base from Boone co., SC. Point 3 1/16 in. long, 1 1/8 in. wide, 1/4 in. thick. Classic design. Made of vein quartz.
Priv. col., excellent quality, valued $15-25.

• Guilford straight base from Boone co., SC. Point 2 in. long, 7/8 in. wide, 1/4 in. thick. Classic design. Made of vein quartz.
Priv. col., excellent quality, valued $15-25.

• Guilford straight base from Boone co., SC. Point 2 2/3 in. long, 1 1/2 in. wide, 1/2 in. thick. Classic design, concave base. Made of vein quartz.
Priv. col., excellent quality, valued $15-25.

- Guilford straight base from Boone co., SC. Point 2 1/3 in. long, 1 1/8 in. wide, 3/8 in. thick. Good workmanship, slightly concave base. Made of rose quartz.
Priv. col., excellent quality, valued $15-25.

- Guilford straight base from Horry co., SC. Point 3 1/4 in. long, 1 7/8 in. wide, 5/8 in. thick. Good workmanship, concave base. Made of white pebble chert.
Priv. col., excellent quality, valued $15-25.

- Guilford straight base from Horry co., SC. Point 3 in. long, 1 7/8 in. wide, 3/8 in. thick. Made of grainy quartzite.
Priv. col., average quality, valued $5-15.

- Guilford straight base from Horry co., SC. Point 2 1/3 in. long, 1 1/8 in. wide, 3/8 in. thick. Made of vein quartz.
Priv. col., excellent quality, valued $15-25.

- Guilford round base variant from Boone co., SC. Point 2 1/8 in. long, 3/4 in. wide, 1/4 in. thick. Typical lanceolate style. Made of quartzite.
Priv. col., museum quality, valued $25-35.

- Guilford round base variant from Boone co., SC. Point 2 7/8 in. long, 7/8 in. wide, 1/8 in. thick. Made of quartzite.
Priv. col., average quality, valued $5-15.

- Guilford round base variant from Boone co., SC. Point 2 3/8 in. long, 3/4 in. wide, 3/16 in. thick. Made of quartzite.
Priv. col., excellent quality, valued $10-15.

- Guilford round base variant from Boone co., SC. Point 3 1/32 in. long, 1 in. wide, 1/4 in. thick. Made of translucent yellow vein quartz.
Priv. col., museum quality, rare, valued $45-65.

- Guilford round base variant from Boone co., SC. Point 3 in. long, 1 1/16 in. wide, 1/4 in. thick. Made of vein quartz.
Priv. col., museum quality, valued $25-35.

- Guilford round base variant from Boone co., SC. Point 3 1/8 in. long, 1 1/4 in. wide, 1/4 in. thick. Made of grainy white pebble chert.
Priv. col., excellent quality, valued $15-25.

- Guilford round base variant from Horry co., SC. Point 2 5/8 in. long, 3/4 in.

wide, 1/8 in. thick. Made of banded slate.
Priv. col., excellent quality, valued $25-30.

- Guilford round base from Dillon co., SC. Point 2 7/8 in. long, 1 1/16 in. wide, 1/4 in. thick. Made of vein quartz.
Priv. col., museum quality, valued $25-35.

- Guilford round base from Dillon co., SC. Point 2 3/4 in. long, 13/16 in. wide, 1/4 in. thick. Made of quartzite.
Priv. col., average quality, valued $5-15.

- Guilford Yuma variant from Union co., SC. Point 2 3/8 in. long, 11/16 in. wide, 1/4 in. thick. Symmetrical, concave fluting on stem, virtually no shoulders. Made of crystal.
Priv. col., average quality, valued $8-15.

- Guilford Yuma variant from Union co., SC. Point 2 5/8 in. long, 15/16 in. wide, 1/4 in. thick. Made of quartzite.
Priv. col., average quality, valued $8-15.

- Guilford Yuma variant from Abberville co., SC. Point 3 3/8 in. long, 1 1/16 in. wide, 1/4 in. thick. Good workmanship. Made of gray shale.
Priv. col., excellent quality, valued $10-20.

- Guilford Yuma variant from Abberville co., SC. Point 3 1/32 in. long, 1 1/3 in. wide, 1/4 in. thick. Good workmanship, symmetrical, concave fluting on stem. Made of gray shale.
Priv. col., excellent quality, valued $15-25.

- Guilford Yuma variant from Abberville co., SC. Point 2 5/8 in. long, 1 1/16 in. wide, 3/16 in. thick. Made of gray shale.
Priv. col., excellent quality, valued $15-20.

- Guilford Yuma variant from Newberry co., SC. Point 2 3/8 in. long, 1 in. wide, 1/8 in. thick. Symmetrical, thin, good workmanship. Made of banded slate.
Priv. col., museum quality, valued $25-35.

- Guilford Yuma variant from Newberry co., SC. Point 3 1/8 in. long, 1 3/16 in. wide, 1/4 in. thick. Made of quartzite.
Priv. col., average quality, valued $10-15.

- Guilford Yuma variant from Horry co., SC. Point 2 5/8 in. long, 1 1/8 in. wide, 1/4 in. thick. Made of quartzite.

...ge quality, valued $10-15.

)-200 B.P. Woodland to Historic

Western and midwestern point. Triangular, thin long barbs on base. High quality flaked points with straight to concave sides. Stem parallel to slightly expanded at base.

◆ Gunther from Boone co., IA. Point 1 1/2 in. long, 7/8 in. wide, 1/8 in. thick. Very thin, sharply serrated with unusually long stem. Made of pink pebble chert.

Priv. col., museum quality, valued $200-300.

• Gunther from Union co., IL. Point 1 3/4 in. long, 3/4 in. wide, 1/8 in. thick. More concave than triangular, tangs flaring parallel to a short straight base. Point was reworked at one time, very fine serrations. Made of Buffalo River chert. *Priv. col., excellent quality, valued $85-125.*

• Gunther from Lubbock co., TX. Point 2 in. long, 1 in. wide, 3/16 in. thick. Prominent fine serrations, snapped base. Made of gray flint. *Priv. col., average quality, valued $25-40.*

• Gunther from Spokane, WA. Point 1 1/2 in. long, 1/2 in. wide, 1/8 in. thick. Point sides concave, long sweeping tangs, snapped base. Made of agate. *Priv. col., museum quality, rare, valued $175-250.*

• Gunther from Union co., IL. Point 1 3/4 in. long, 3/4 in. wide, 1/8 in. thick. More concave than triangular, tangs flaring parallel to a short straight base. Point was reworked at one time, very fine serrations. Made of Buffalo River chert. *Priv. col., excellent quality, valued $85-125.*

• Gunther from Lubbock co., TX. Point 2 1/8 in. long, 1 in. wide, 3/16 in. thick. Classic snapped base, side notched design. Made of dull gray flint. *Juan Samudio col., excellent quality, valued $35-50.*

• Gunther from Lubbock co., TX. Point 1 2/3 in. long, 3/4 in. wide, 1/8 in. thick. Classic snapped base, concave edge design. Made of dull gray flint. *Juan Samudio col., excellent quality, valued $45-50.*

• Gunther from Brule co., SD. Point 1 7/8 in. long, 1 in. wide, 1/8 in. thick. Tangs parallel to a short straight base. Made of local red banded chert. *Priv. col., museum quality, rare, valued $100-125.*

• Gunther from Brule co., SD. Point 2 1/16 in. long, 1 in. wide, 3/16 in. thick. Straight base design. Made of red banded chert. *Priv. col., museum quality, rare, valued $125-140.*

• Gunther from Russell co., VA. Point 1 1/3 in. long, 5/8 in. wide, 1/8 in. thick. Sides concave, long sweeping tangs, snapped base. Made of vein quartz. *Priv. col., museum quality, valued $75-125.*

• Gunther from McPherson co., SD. Point 2 1/3 in. long, 1 1/8 in. wide, 1/8 in. thick. Made of golden brown chert. *Priv. col., excellent quality, valued $65-75.*

• Gunther from McPherson co., SD. Point 2 in. long, 1 1/32 in. wide, 1/8 in. thick. Made of local golden brown chert. *Priv. col., excellent quality, valued $45-60.*

• Gunther from Archer co., TX. Point 1 7/8 in. long, 13/16 in. wide, 1/8 in. thick. Sides concave, long sweeping tangs, snapped base. Seemingly an import from Brule co., SD. Made of red banded chert. *Priv. col., museum quality, rare, valued $75-125.*

• Gunther from Union co., IL. Point 1 7/8 in. long, 3/4 in. wide, 1/8 in. thick. Made of Kaolin chert. *Priv. col., museum quality, rare, valued $125-175.*

• Gunther from Union co., IL. Point 2 3/8 in. long, 1 1/4 in. wide, 3/16 in. thick. Made of Cobden chert. *Priv. col., excellent quality, valued $65-80.*

• Gunther from Union co., IL. Point 2 1/2 in. long, 1 1/8 in. wide, 1/8 in. thick. Made of Mill Creek chert. *Priv. col., excellent quality, valued $45-50.*

• Gunther from Union co., IL. Point 1 2/3 in. long, 3/4 in. wide, 1/8 in. thick.

Made of Cobden chert.
Priv. col., excellent quality, valued $65-75.

• Gunther from Union co., IL. Point 3 in. long, 1 1/3 in. wide, 1/8 in. thick.
Made of gray chert.
Priv. col., excellent quality, valued $45-60.

• Gunther from Horry co., SC. Point 2 1/4 in. long, 1 1/32 in. wide, 1/8 in. thick.
Made of speckled agate.
Priv. col., museum quality, rare, valued $100-125.

• Gunther from Horry co., SC. Point 1 3/4 in. long, 1 1/32 in. wide, 1/8 in. thick.
Made of milky quartz.
Priv. col., excellent quality, valued $85-100.

• Gunther from Lawrence co., KY. Point 3 1/16 in. long, 1 2/3 in. wide, 3/16 in.
thick. Made of dark gray flint.
Priv. col., average quality, valued $25-40.

• Gunther from Spokane, WA. Point 1 1/2 in. long, 1/2 in. wide, 1/8 in. thick.
Point sides concave, long sweeping tangs, snap base. Made of agate.
Priv. col., museum quality, rare, valued $175-250.

• Gunther from Union co., IL. Point 1 3/4 in. long, 3/4 in. wide, 1/8 in. thick.
More concave than triangular, tangs flaring parallel to a short straight base. Point
was reworked at one time, very fine serrations. Made of Buffalo River chert.
Priv. col., excellent quality, valued $85-125.

• Gunther from Lubbock, TX. Point 2 in. long, 1 in. wide, 3/16 in. thick.
Prominent fine serrations, snapped base. Made of gray flint.
Priv. col., average quality, valued $25-40.

• Gunther from Spokane, WA. Point 1 1/2 in. long, 1/2 in. wide, 1/8 in. thick.
Point sides concave, long sweeping tangs, snapped base. Made of agate.
Priv. col., museum quality, rare, valued $175-250.

• Gunther from Union co., IL. Point 1 3/4 in. long, 3/4 in. wide, 1/8 in. thick.
Made of gray flint.
Priv. col., excellent quality, valued $85-125.

• Gunther from Coffey co., KS. Point 3 in. long, 1 1/3 in. wide, 3/16 in. thick.
Made of glossy black flint.

Priv col., average quality, valued $25-40.

- Gunther from Coffey co., KS. Point 2 1/2 in. long, 1 3/32 in. wide, 1/8 in. thick. Made of vein quartz.
Priv. col., museum quality, valued $75-85.

CHAPTER 8
HAMILTON-HOLLAND

Hamilton: 2,000-800 B.P. Woodland to Mississippian

Southeastern point small to medium in size. Triangular point, very thin, concave sides and base, high quality serrations.

♦ Hamilton from central KY. Point 1 3/8 in. long, 5/8 in. wide at base, 1/16 in. thick. Made of a grainy pebble chert.

Priv. collection, excellent quality, valued $35-50.

• Hamilton from Hamilton co., TN. Point 1 1/2 in. long, 3/4 in. wide, 3/32 in. thick. Point very sharp, finely serrated, extremely sharp tip. Piece is a very symmetrical triangle. Made of Dover chert.
Priv. collection, museum quality, valued $55-100.

• Hamilton from Alexander co., IL. Point 1 3/8 in. long, 3/4 in. wide, 3/32 in. thick. Tip and point very sharp, very thin, finely serrated, with concave base. Made of Cobden chert.
Priv. collection, excellent quality, valued $55-70.

• Hamilton from northwestern KY. Point 1 3/4 in. long, 7/8 in. wide, 1/8 in. thick. Point finely serrated, very symmetrical, concave sides and base. Made of jasper.
Priv. collection, museum quality, valued $85-120.

• Hamilton from Pope co., IL. Point 1 5/8 in. long, 3/4 in. wide, 5/32 in. thick. Tip and point very sharp, very thin, finely serrated, very symmetrical with concave base. Made of Cobden Hornstone chert.
Priv. collection, excellent quality, valued $85-120.

• Hamilton from Alexander co., IL. Point 2 1/8 in. long, 7/8 in. wide, 5/16 in. thick. Point very symmetrical, sharp, thin, finely serrated, with concave sides and base. Made of Cobden chert.
Priv. collection, museum quality, valued $155-190.

• Hamilton from southeastern MO. Point 2 1/4 in. long, 1 1/8 in. wide, 3/16 in. thick. Point finely serrated, concave base. Made of unidentified white pebble chert.
Priv. collection, museum quality, valued $75-100.

• Hamilton from southern Pope co., IL. Point 2 1/8 in. long, 7/8 in. wide, 7/32 in. thick. Tip and point very sharp, finely serrated, very symmetrical with concave sides and base. Made of Cobden Hornstone chert.
Priv. col., museum quality, valued $185-220.

• Hamilton from Alexander co., IL. Point 2 1/8 in. long, 7/8 in. wide, 5/16 in. thick. Point very symmetrical, sharp, thin, finely serrated, with concave sides and base. Made of Cobden chert.
Priv. col., museum quality, valued $155-190.

• Hamilton from Adair co., KY. Point 1 1/8 in. long, 5/8 in. wide at base, 1/16 in. thick. Heat treated, concave base. Made of tan pebble chert.
Priv. col., excellent quality, valued $35-50.

• Hamilton from Adair co., KY. Point 1 1/4 in. long, 11/16 in. wide at base, 1/16 in. thick. Concave base. Made of tan pebble chert.
Priv. col., excellent quality, valued $35-50.

• Hamilton from Graves co., KY. Point 1 3/4 in. long, 7/8 in. wide at base, 1/16 in. thick. Made of gray white pebble chert.
Priv. col., excellent quality, valued $35-50.

• Hamilton from Graves co., KY. Point 1 3/8 in. long, 7/8 in. wide at base, 1/16 in. thick. Made of grainy white pebble chert.
Priv. col., excellent quality, valued $35-50.

• Hamilton from Graves co., KY. Point 1 5/8 in. long, 1 in. wide at base, 1/8 in.

thick. Made of porous pink pebble chert.
Priv. col., excellent quality, valued $35-50.

• Hamilton from Graves co., KY. Point 1 3/16 in. long, 5/8 in. wide at base, 1/16 in. thick. Made of gray pebble chert.
Priv. col., excellent quality, valued $35-50.

• Hamilton from Harrison co., KY. Point 1 3/4 in. long, 1 1/32 in. wide at base, 1/16 in. thick. Made of a green gray pebble chert.
Priv. col., excellent quality, valued $35-50.

• Hamilton from Harrison co., KY. Point 1 3/32 in. long, 5/8 in. wide at base, 1/8 in. thick. Made of a green gray pebble chert.
Priv. col., excellent quality, valued $35-50.

• Hamilton from central KY. Point 1 3/8 in. long, 5/8 in. wide at base, 1/16 in. thick. Made of a grainy pebble chert.
Priv. collection, excellent quality, valued $35-50.

• Hamilton from Lewis co., WV. Point 1 5/8 in. long, 13/16 in. wide at base, 1/16 in. thick. Made of a grainy tan pebble chert.
Priv. col., excellent quality, valued $35-50.

• Hamilton from Lewis co., WV. Point 1 13/32 in. long, 1 in. wide at base, 1/16 in. thick. Made of a gray pebble chert.
Priv. col., excellent quality, valued $35-50.

• Hamilton from Lewis co., WV. Point 1 3/8 in. long, 5/8 in. wide at base, 1/16 in. thick. Made of a gray chert.
Priv. col., excellent quality, valued $35-50.

• Hamilton from Ohio co., WV. Point 1 1/2 in. long, 13/16 in. wide at base, 1/16 in. thick. Made of milky quartz.
Priv. col., museum quality, valued $135-150.

• Hamilton from Ohio co., WV. Point 1 5/8 in. long, 15/16 in. wide at base, 1/16 in. thick. Made of gray quartz.
Priv. col., excellent quality, valued $100-125.

• Hamilton from Ohio co., WV. Point 1 3/8 in. long, 1 in. wide at base, 1/16 in. thick. Made of garnet.
Priv. col., museum quality, rare, valued $175-225.

Hamilton Stemmed: 3,500-1,000 B.P. Woodland to Mississippian

Southeastern point or blade, medium to large in size. Edges are recurved, points and blades needle sharp, barbed expanded stem. Hamilton stemmed points or blades are barbed, corner notched with sharp tips.

◆ Hamilton stemmed from Williamson co., IL. Blade 3 5/8 in. long, 1 1/4 in. wide, 1/4 in. thick. Very symmetrical blade, sharply serrated. Unusually fine horizontal flaking with parallel stem. Made of Dover chert.

Priv. col., museum quality, rare, valued $150-250.

◆ Hamilton stemmed from Hardin co., TN. Point 3 1/2 in. long, 1 1/4 in. wide, 3/32 in. thick. Uneven uniquely sharp notches, slightly convex base, very sharp. Made of tan pink chert.

Priv. col., average quality, valued $65-85.

• Hamilton stemmed from Gallatin co., IL. Blade 4 1/16 in. long, 1 1/2 in. wide, 1/4 in. thick. Blade horizontally flaked and finely serrated. Extremely wide stem with convex base. Made of Cobden Hornstone chert.
Tim Rubbles col., museum quality, valued $125-200.

• Hamilton stemmed from southeast MO. Point 2 7/8 in. long, 1 5/8 in. wide, 1/8 in. thick. Edges are recurved, point needle sharp, barbed expanded stem. Made of brown pebble chert.
Priv. col., excellent quality, valued $100-165.

• Hamilton stemmed from southwestern IL. Point 2 5/8 in. long, 1 3/8 in. wide, 1/4 in. thick. Edges are recurved, point needle sharp, horizontally flaked, barbed expanded stem. Made of Mill Creek chert.
Priv. col., excellent quality, valued $90-145.

• Hamilton stemmed from Jackson co., IL. Blade 3 9/16 in. long, 1 1/3 in. wide, 1/4 in. thick. Blade horizontally flaked and finely serrated, wide stem with convex base. Made of Kaolin chert.
Tim Rubbles col., museum quality, rare, valued $185- 250.

• Hamilton stemmed from southeastern MO. Point 1 7/8 in. long, 13/16 in. wide, 1/8 in. thick. Sides are recurved, sharp, barbed expanded stem. Made of pink brown pebble chert.
Priv. col., excellent quality, valued $100-165.

• Hamilton stemmed from Coles co., IL. Point 2 1/8 in. long, 1 1/8 in. wide, 1/4 in. thick. Edges are recurved, point needle sharp, horizontally flaked, barbed expanded stem. Made of white gray speckled pebble chert.
Priv. col., excellent quality, valued $120-175.

• Hamilton stemmed from Humphreys co., TN. Blade 4 3/16 in. long, 1 1/3 in. wide, 1/4 in. thick. Horizontally flaked. Made of Dover chert.
Grover Bohannon col., museum quality, valued $125-200.

• Hamilton stemmed from Humphreys co., TN. Point 2 1/8 in. long, 1 7/16 in. wide, 1/8 in. thick. Edges are recurved. Made of brown pebble chert.
Grover Bohannon col., excellent quality, valued $100-165.

• Hamilton stemmed from Hamilton co., TN. Point 3 1/8 in. long, 1 7/8 in. wide, 1/4 in. thick. Edges are recurved, horizontally flaked. Made of white pebble chert.
Priv. col., excellent quality, valued $90-145.

• Hamilton stemmed from Giles co., TN. Blade 5 1/16 in. long, 2 1/3 in. wide, 1/4 in. thick. Blade horizontally flaked. Made of Dover chert.
Grover Bohannon col., museum quality, valued $125-200.

• Hamilton stemmed from Marion co., MO. Point 3 in. long, 1 11/16 in. wide, 1/8 in. thick. Made of brown pebble chert.
Priv. col., average quality, valued $60-75.

• Hamilton stemmed from Marion co., MO. Point 2 7/8 in. long, 1 1/2 in. wide, 1/4 in. thick. Made of white pebble chert.
Priv. col., excellent quality, valued $70-95.

- Hamilton stemmed from Howell co., IL. Blade 4 5/16 in. long, 1 3/4 in. wide, 1/4 in. thick. Blade horizontally flaked. Made of Cobden Hornstone chert. *Jim Smith col., museum quality, valued $125-200.*

- Hamilton stemmed from Howell co., MO. Point 2 5/8 in. long, 1 3/8 in. wide, 1/8 in. thick. Made of porous white pebble chert. *Priv. col., average quality, valued $50-65.*

- Hamilton stemmed from Howell co., MO. Point 2 5/8 in. long, 1 3/8 in. wide, 1/4 in. thick. Made of Mill Creek chert. *Priv. col., excellent quality, valued $90-125.*

- Hamilton stemmed from Howell co., MO. Blade 5 1/16 in. long, 2 1/8 in. wide, 1/4 in. thick. Made of white pebble chert. *Priv. col., excellent quality, valued $100-120.*

- Hamilton stemmed from Coosa co., AL. Point 3 1/32 in. long, 1 7/8 in. wide, 1/8 in. thick. Made of translucent brown quartz. *Priv. col., excellent quality, valued $100-125.*

- Hamilton stemmed from Coosa co., AL. Point 2 13/16 in. long, 1 1/2 in. wide, 1/4 in. thick. Made of banded red slate. *Priv. col., excellent quality, valued $90-125.*

- Hamilton stemmed from Coosa co., AL. Blade 4 5/16 in. long, 1 2/3 in. wide, 1/4 in. thick. Made of gray chert. *Priv. col., excellent quality, valued $85-100.*

- Hamilton stemmed from southeastern AL. Blade 3 7/8 in. long, 1 7/8 in. wide, 1/8 in. thick. Made of brown tan pebble chert. *Priv. col., excellent quality, valued $100-115.*

- Hamilton stemmed from southwestern AL. Point 2 1/8 in. long, 1 1/4 in. wide, 1/4 in. thick. Made of quartzite. *Priv. col., average quality, valued $50-65.*

- Hamilton stemmed from Gallatin co., IL. Blade 4 7/16 in. long, 2 1/3 in. wide, 1/4 in. thick. Made of Cobden chert. *Priv. col., museum quality, valued $150-200.*

- Hamilton stemmed from Clay co., MO. Point 3 1/8 in. long, 1 11/16 in. wide, 1/8 in. thick. Made of grainy brown pebble chert.

Priv. col., average quality, valued $80-100.

• Hamilton stemmed from Clay co., MO. Point 2 5/8 in. long, 1 1/2 in. wide, 1/4 in. thick. Made of white chert.
Priv. col., excellent quality, valued $90-125.

• Hamilton stemmed from Clay co., MO. Blade 4 11/16 in. long, 1 1/2 in. wide, 1/4 in. thick. Made of white pebble chert.
Priv. col., museum quality, valued $100-125.

• Hamilton stemmed from Lowndes co., AL. Point 1 7/8 in. long, 1 1/16 in. wide, 1/8 in. thick. Made of glossy tan chert.
Priv. col., excellent quality, valued $80-100.

• Hamilton stemmed from Lowndes co., AL. Point 2 3/8 in. long, 1 1/8 in. wide, 1/4 in. thick. Edges are recurved, point needle sharp, horizontally flaked, barbed expanded stem. Made of banded tan chert.
Priv. col., excellent quality, valued $90-125.

Hardaway: 12,000-8,000 B.P. Paleo

Southeastern point, small to medium in size, expanded tangs, concave base, shallow side notches. Hardaways with ground ears and bases which are fluted are called Hardaway Dalton.

♦ Hardaway from central MO. Point 2 1/2 in. long, 1 in. wide, 3/16 in. thick. Unique point, fine serrations, sharp tip with ground ears.

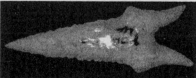

Priv. col., museum quality, rare, valued $350-450.

♦ Hardaway Dalton from southern IL. Point 1 5/8 in. long, 1/2 in. wide, 3/16 in. thick. Fluted, ground ears. Made of Cobden Hornstone chert.

Priv. col., museum quality, rare, valued $250-350.

- Hardaway from Moore co., NC. Point 1 1/2 in. long, 3/4 in. wide, 3/16 in. thick. Medium serrations toward blade tip. Virtually no shoulders, fluted concave base. Made of banded slate.
Priv. col., excellent quality, valued $50-65.

- Hardaway from Moore co., NC. Point 1 5/8 in. long, 5/8 in. wide, 1/8 in. thick. Shallow side notches, flaring tangs, slightly concave base. Made of crystal.
Priv. col., excellent quality, rare, valued $85-100.

- Hardaway from Moore co., NC. Point 1 3/8 in. long, 1 in. wide, 1/4 in. thick. Deep side notches, near fish tail concave base. Made of milky quartz.
Priv. col., average quality, valued $20-35.

- Hardaway from Moore co., NC. Point 1 3/16 in. long, 1 in. wide, 1/4 in. thick. Deep side notches, concave base. Made of gray slate.
Priv. col., average quality, valued $15-25.

- Hardaway from Moore co., NC. Point 1 7/8 in. long, 11/16 in. wide, 1/4 in. thick. Deep side notches, flaring tangs, slightly concave base. Made of rose crystal.
Priv. col., excellent quality, rare, valued $95-120.

- Hardaway from central NC. Point 1 1/8 in. long, 7/8 in. wide, 3/16 in. thick. Deep side notches, concave base. Made of brown slate.
Priv. col., average quality, valued $20-35.

- Hardaway from Moore co., NC. Point 1 5/16 in. long, 1 in. wide, 1/4 in. thick. Fine workmanship, deep side notches, flaring tangs, one with small break, concave base. Made of green pebble chert.
Priv. col., excellent quality, valued $45-65.

- Hardaway from Moore co., NC. Point 1 3/8 in. long, 9/16 in. wide, 3/16 in. thick. Deep side notches, very fine and thin, flaring tangs, slightly concave base. Made of white crystal.
Priv. col., excellent quality, rare, valued $95-135.

- Hardaway from Yarkin co., NC. Point 1 7/8 in. long, 1 1/32 in. wide, 1/4 in. thick. Made of milky quartz.
Priv. col., excellent quality, valued $40-45.

- Hardaway from Yarkin co., NC. Point 2 1/16 in. long, 1 5/32 in. wide, 1/4 in. thick. Deep side notches, concave base. Made of quartzite.

Priv. col., average quality, valued $15-25.

• Hardaway from Yarkin co., NC. Point 2 in. long, 13/16 in. wide, 1/4 in. thick. Made of quartzite.
Priv. col., average quality, valued $15-20.

• Hardaway from Yarkin co., NC. Point 2 3/8 in. long, 1 1/16 in. wide, 3/16 in. thick. Deep side notches, concave base. Made of brownish quartzite.
Priv. col., average quality, valued $20-25.

• Hardaway from Yarkin co., NC. Point 2 1/3 in. long, 1 3/32 in. wide, 1/4 in. thick. Made of milky quartz.
Priv. col., average quality, valued $20-35.

• Hardaway from Yarkin co., NC. Point 2 3/16 in. long, 1 7/8 in. wide, 1/4 in. thick. Made of gray chert.
Priv. col., excellent quality, valued $35-45.

• Hardaway from Wataga co., NC. Point 2 7/16 in. long, 1 1/16 in. wide, 1/4 in. thick. Made of quartzite.
Priv. col., excellent quality, valued $15-20.

• Hardaway from Wataga co., NC. Point 1 5/8 in. long, 3/4 in. wide, 3/16 in. thick. Made of porous white chert.
Priv. col., average quality, valued $25-30.

• Hardaway from Wataga co., NC. Point 1 7/8 in. long, 1 1/3 in. wide, 1/4 in. thick. Made of quartzite.
Priv. col., average quality, valued $20-35.

• Hardaway from Gates co., NC. Point 1 9/16 in. long, 1 1/8 in. wide, 1/4 in. thick. Made of gray chert.
Priv. col., excellent quality, valued $45-65.

• Hardaway from Gates co., NC. Point 2 1/8 in. long, 1 5/16 in. wide, 1/4 in. thick. Made of quartzite.
Priv. col., average quality, valued $15-30.

• Hardaway from Gates co., NC. Point 2 1/32 in. long, 1 7/8 in. wide, 3/16 in. thick. Made of brown pebble chert.
Priv. col., excellent quality, valued $60-70.

- Hardaway from Gates co., NC. Point 1 1/8 in. long, 1 in. wide, 3/16 in. thick. Deep side notches, near fish tail concave base. Made of quartzite. *Priv. col., average quality, valued $20-35.*

- Hardaway from Swain co., NC. Point 2 3/16 in. long, 1 1/2 in. wide, 1/4 in. thick. Made of banded red slate. *Priv. col., average quality, valued $15-25.*

- Hardaway from Swain co., NC. Point 2 1/8 in. long, 1 3/16 in. wide, 1/4 in. thick. Made of quartzite. *Priv. col., average quality, valued $25-30.*

- Hardaway from Swain co., NC. Point 1 5/8 in. long, 7/8 in. wide, 3/16 in. thick. Made of brown chert. *Priv. col., excellent quality, valued $45-60.*

- Hardaway from Swain co., NC. Point 2 3/8 in. long, 1 2/3 in. wide, 1/4 in. thick. Made of milky quartz. *Priv. col., excellent quality, valued $70-85.*

- Hardaway from Swain co., NC. Point 2 3/16 in. long, 2 in. wide, 1/4 in. thick. Made of dark gray chert. *Priv. col., excellent quality, valued $55-75.*

- Hardaway from Page co., SC. Point 2 1/3 in. long, 1 1/2 in. wide, 1/4 in. thick. Made of rose quartz. *Priv. col., museum quality, rare, valued $100-120.*

- Hardaway from Page co., SC. Point 2 1/8 in. long, 1 3/8 in. wide, 1/8 in. thick. Made of gray shale. *Priv. col., excellent quality, valued $45-60.*

- Hardaway from Page co., SC. Point 1 7/8 in. long, 1 1/4 in. wide, 3/16 in. thick. Made of milky quartz. *Priv. col., excellent quality, valued $60-75.*

- Hardaway from Page co., SC. Point 2 1/16 in. long, 1 1/3 in. wide, 1/4 in. thick. Made of gray shale. *Priv. col., excellent quality, valued $45-65.*

- Hardaway from Grayson co., VA. Point 2 5/32 in. long, 1 5/16 in. wide, 1/4 in. thick. This piece is shown at several shows in the southeast each year—it's

worth seeing. Made of garnet.
Priv. col., museum quality, rare, valued $625-750.

• Hardaway from Grayson co., VA. Point 2 1/8 in. long, 1 7/8 in. wide, 3/16 in. thick. Made of translucent brown chert.
Priv. col., museum quality, valued $200-250.

• Hardaway from Grayson co., VA. Point 1 5/8 in. long, 1 1/8 in. wide, 1/4 in. thick. Deep side notches, near fish tail concave base. Made of translucent amber chert.
Priv. col., museum quality, valued $250-325.

• Hardaway from Calhoun co., WV. Point 1 13/16 in. long, 1 1/4 in. wide, 1/4 in. thick. Made of quartzite.
Priv. col., average quality, valued $15-25.

• Hardaway from Calhoun co., WV. Point 2 7/8 in. long, 1 11/16 in. wide, 5/32 in. thick. Made of yellow quartz.
Priv. col., museum quality, rare, valued $250-320.

• Hardaway from Calhoun co., WV. Point 2 1/8 in. long, 1 1/8 in. wide, 3/16 in. thick. Although wide, piece is very symmetrical. Good workmanship. Deep side notches, flaring basal tangs, concave base. Made of multi-toned shale.
Priv. col., museum quality, valued $200-300.

• Hardaway from Halifax co., VA. Point 2 2/3 in. long, 1 13/16 in. wide, 1/3 in. thick. Made of vein quartz.
Priv. col., excellent quality, valued $120-175.

• Hardaway from Halifax co., VA. Point 1 13/16 in. long, 1 1/3 in. wide, 3/16 in. thick. Made of banded gray black shale.
Priv. col., excellent quality, valued $175-250.

• Hardaway from Halifax co., VA. Point 1 7/8 in. long, 1 3/16 in. wide, 1/8 in. thick. Made of shale.
Priv. col., excellent quality, valued $125-160.

• Hardaway from Green Brier co., WV. Point 2 1/8 in. long, 1 17/32 in. wide, 3/16 in. thick. Made of brown shale.
Priv. col., excellent quality, valued $175-250.

• Hardaway from Green Brier co., WV. Point 2 3/8 in. long, 1 1/2 in. wide, 1/4 in. thick. Made of milky quartz.

Priv. col., excellent quality, valued $70-115.

• Hardaway from Moore co., NC. Point 2 3/16 in. long, 1 3/8 in. wide, 1/4 in. thick. Made of quartzite.
Priv. col., average quality, valued $25-35.

• Hardaway from Moore co., NC. Point 2 1/8 in. long, 1 7/16 in. wide, 1/2 in. thick. Made of quartzite.
Priv. col., average quality, valued $45-50.

• Hardaway from Baldwin co., GA. Point 2 1/8 in. long, 1 5/8 in. wide, 3/16 in. thick. Made of quartzite.
Priv. col., average quality, valued $25-40.

• Hardaway from Baldwin co., GA. Point 1 23/32 in. long, 1 1/16 in. wide, 1/8 in. thick. Made of rose quartz.
Priv. col., excellent quality, valued $120-185.

• Hardaway from Baldwin co., GA. Point 1 9/16 in. long, 1 3/32 in. wide, 1/4 in. thick. Made of quartzite.
Priv. col., average quality, valued $15-25.

• Hardaway from Butts co., GA. Point 1 7/16 in. long, 1 1/16 in. wide, 1/8 in. thick. Made of quartzite.
Priv. col., average quality, valued $15-20.

• Hardaway from Cedar co., GA. Point 2 1/8 in. long, 1 5/8 in. wide, 3/16 in. thick. Made of banded deep brown shale.
Priv. col., excellent quality, valued $200-250.

Hardin: 9,000-6,000 B.P. Early Archaic

Found throughout the Midwest and eastern states. Large point or blade, triangular, barbed with an expanded stem.

• Hardin from Owen co., IN. Blade 4 1/16 in. long, 1 1/2 in. wide, 3/8 in. thick. Deep, fine serrations, symmetrical sharp blade edges, slight tip break. Made of light gray chert.
Priv. col., average quality, valued $275-325.

• Hardin from Owen co., IN. Blade 3 5/8 in. long, 1 11/16 in. wide, 3/8 in. thick. Hardin, finely serrated, symmetrical sharp blade. Made of light tan chert. *Priv. col., excellent quality, valued $325-375.*

♦ Hardin from Owen co., IN. Blade 3 3/8 in. long, 1 9/16 in. wide, 3/8 in. thick. Unique colored Hardin, fine serrations, symmetrical sharp blade. Made of green lined, light tan chert.

Randall Kimbell col., museum quality, valued $650-900.

♦ Hardin from Shelby co., IL. Blade 4 in. long, 1 5/8 in. wide, 3/8 in. thick. Heavy field patina, left hand beveled. Made of Mill Creek chert.

Priv. col., museum quality, valued $175-225.

♦ Hardin from Shelby co., IL. Point 2 5/8 in. long, 1 1/4 in. wide, 5/8 in. thick. Long tangs, deep notches, rounded ground point. Made of Dover chert.

Priv. col., average quality, valued $75-100.

♦ Hardin from Johnson co., IL. Blade 3 1/2 in. long, 1 1/4 in. wide, 5/32 in. thick. Very thin blade, left hand beveled. Made of Mill Creek chert.

Priv. col., excellent quality, valued $100-125.

♦ Hardin from Hardin co., IL. Point 1 27/32 in. long, 1 1/16 in. wide, 1/8 in. thick. Very wide, barbed prestige point, sharp tip, finely serrated. Made of tan pebble chert.

Priv. col., museum quality, valued $120-175.

♦ Hardin from Gallatin co., IL. Point 1 3/4 in. long, 1 1/8 in. wide, 1/8 in. thick. Wide based, deep serrations, rounded ground tip. Prestige point. Made of pebble chert.

Les Grubbe col., average quality, valued $75-100.

♦ Hardin from Union co., IL. Point 2 1/16 in. long, 1 1/4 in. wide, 3/16 in. thick. Apparent field patina, minute tip break, slightly concave base, left hand beveled. Made of a local tan chert.

Les Grubbe col., average quality, valued $75-100.

• Hardin from Union co., IL. Point 2 1/8 in. long, 1 5/8 in. wide, 5/16 in. thick.
Some field patina, concave base, deep notched. Made of Mill Creek chert.
Les Grubbe col., average quality, valued $60-80.

♦ Hardin from Union co., IL. Blade 4 in. long, 1 3/8 in. wide, 5/8 in. thick.
Very fine symmetrical blade, barbed stem, point quite sharp. Made of Cobden
chert.

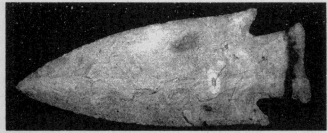

Les Grubbe col., museum quality, valued $275-350.

♦ Hardin from Pike co., IL. Blade 3 3/8 in. long. 1 1/2 in. wide, 5/16 in. thick.
Symmetrical blade, wide stem, slightly concave. Made of Mill Creek chert.

Priv. col., excellent quality, valued $150-200.

• Hardin from Williamson co., IL. Point 2 3/8 in. long, 1 3/8 in. wide, 7/16 in.
thick. Wide stemmed, concave base, deep notched. Made of Mill Creek chert.
Priv. col., average quality, valued $50-70.

• Hardin from Union co., IL. Point 1 7/8 in. long, 1 1/8 in. wide, 3/16 in. thick.
Very symmetrical, thin, concave base, weekly notched. Made of Mill Creek
chert.
Grover Bohannon col., excellent quality, valued $80-100.

• Hardin from southeastern MO. Point 1 7/16 in. long, 1 in. wide, 3/32 in.
thick. Some field patina, very symmetrical and thin, uniquely wide stem, concave
base, deep notched. Made of pebble chert.
Priv. col., excellent quality, valued $100-130.

• Hardin from Union co., IL. Point 2 3/8 in. long, 1 1/8 in. wide, 5/16 in. thick.

Finely worked, possibly a prestige point, concave base, deep notched with slight tangs. Made of Kaolin chert.
Jim Smith col., museum quality, rare, valued $160-200.

* Hardin from Union co., IL. Point 1 1/8 in. long, 5/8 in. wide, 3/16 in. thick. Random flaked, concave base, shallow notched. Made of gray green pebble chert.
Priv. col., excellent quality, valued $70-90.

* Hardin from Union co., IL. Point 2 7/8 in. long, 1 5/8 in. wide, 1/4 in. thick. Thin wide point, finely serrated and sharp, concave base, deep notched. Made of Mill Creek chert.
Tim Rubbles col., excellent quality, valued $90-120.

* Hardin from Union co., IL. Point 2 3/32 in. long, 1 1/8 in. wide, 3/16 in. thick. Some field patina, thin, slight tip break, concave base, very uneven notches. Made of Mill Creek chert.
Priv. col., average quality, valued $50-70.

* Hardin from Union co., IL. Point 1 7/8 in. long, 1 1/16 in. wide, 5/16 in. thick. Thick point, seems reworked from larger piece, some field patina, concave base, deep notched. Made of Mill Creek chert.
Jim Smith col., average quality, valued $60-80.

* Hardin from Shelby co., IL. Blade 4 1/4 in. long, 1 5/8 in. wide, 3/8 in. thick. Left hand beveled, sharp finely serrated. Made of green black grained chert.
Priv. col., museum quality, valued $155-205.

* Hardin from Cumberland co., IL. Point 2 3/8 in. long, 1 1/8 in. wide, 3/8 in. thick. Long tangs, one broken, deep notches, concave base. Made of Kaskaskia chert.
Priv. col., average quality, valued $75-100.

* Hardin from Johnson co., IL. Blade 5 1/2 in. long, 1 3/4 in. wide, 5/16 in. thick. Very thin blade, left hand beveled, long, symmetrical and narrow. Made of Mill Creek chert.
Les Grubbe col., excellent quality, valued $130-170.

* Hardin from Jackson co., IL. Point 2 1/8 in. long, 1 11/32 in. wide, 3/16 in thick. Point finely serrated, concave base, with left hand beveling. Made of Johnson co. Bullseye chert.
Tim Rubbles., excellent quality, valued $160-240.

• Hardin from Gallatin co., IL. Point 2 3/32 in. long, 1 in. wide, 3/16 in. thick. Prestige point, extremely deep and sharp serrations. Made of unidentified gray banded chert.
J. Hastings col., museum quality, valued $190-250.

• Hardin from Emmet co., IA. Blade 5 1/16 in. long, 2 1/4 in. wide, 5/16 in. thick. Made of banded orange tan chert.
Amir Naktari col., museum quality, rare, valued $375-500.

• Hardin from Cass co., IA. Blade 4 3/8 in. long, 1 7/8 in. wide, 5/16 in. thick. Made of green pink speckled chert.
Priv. col., excellent quality, valued $160-200.

• Hardin from Cass co., IA. Blade 4 3/4 in. long, 2 3/8 in. wide, 1/2 in. thick. Made of white pebble chert.
Priv. col., excellent quality, valued $175-225.

• Hardin from Coshocton co., OH. Blade 3 7/8 in. long. 1 1/2 in. wide, 5/32 in. thick. Made of Coshocton chert.
Priv. col., museum quality, valued $350-375.

• Hardin from Coshocton co., OH. Point 4 1/16 in. long, 1 3/4 in. wide, 3/16 in. thick. Made of Coshocton chert.
Priv. col., museum quality, valued $375-400.

• Hardin from Coshocton co., OH. Point 2 5/8 in. long, 1 7/8 in. wide, 3/16 in. thick. Made of Coshocton chert.
Priv. col., museum quality, valued $260-300.

• Hardin from Coshocton co., OH. Blade 4 3/32 in. long, 2 3/8 in. wide, 1/2 in. thick. Made of Coshocton chert.
Priv. col., museum quality, valued $275-350.

• Hardin from Clay co., MO. Blade 3 5/8 in. long. 1 2/3 in. wide, 5/16 in. thick. Made of white pebble chert.
Priv. col., excellent quality, valued $125-175.

• Hardin from Clay co., MO. Point 2 5/16 in. long, 1 1/2 in. wide, 3/16 in. thick. Made of tan chert.
Priv. col., average quality, valued $45-60.

• Hardin from Shelby co., MO. Point 2 1/2 in. long, 1 9/16 in. wide, 5/16 in.

thick. Made of white chert.
Priv col., average quality, valued $40-60.

• Hardin from Shelby co., MO. Blade 4 1/3 in. long, 2 in. wide, 3/8 in. thick. Made of yellow tan chert.
Priv. col., excellent quality, valued $175-250.

• Hardin from Shelby co., MO. Blade 3 13/16 in. long, 1 2/3 in. wide, 5/16 in. thick. Made of false jasper.
Priv. col., average quality, valued $50-60.

Harpeth River: 10,000-8,000 B.P. Paleo-Transitional

Found in the southeastern states, particularly Kentucky. Points or blades are medium to large in size. They are beveled and serrated on all four sides. Thick points or blades, narrow, shallow side notched or expanded stem. The base is usually ground.

♦ Harpeth River from Williamson co., IL. Blade 3 1/8 in. long, 7/8 in. wide, 1/4 in. thick. Deep notches, fairly sharp, steep beveling. Made of Dover chert.

Priv. col., museum quality, valued $150-200.

• Harpeth River from Jackson co., IL. Blade 3 1/2 in. long, 1 1/32 in. wide, 5/16 in. thick. Notching barely visible, yet blade is steeply beveled and excellently serrated. Made of Buffalo Creek chert.
Priv. col., museum quality, valued $120-170.

• Harpeth River from Humphreys co., TN. Blade 3 3/4 in. long, 1 1/4 in. wide, 1/4 in. thick. Soft, thin, sharply serrated, with long sharp tip. Expanded stem, beveled on all four sides, opposing faces very steep. Made of Dover chert.
Priv. col., excellent quality, valued $150-230.

• Harpeth River from western TN. Blade 3 5/8 in. long, 1 in. wide, 3/16 in. thick. Very symmetrical, finely serrated, and sharp. Deeply side notched above a straight base. Made of Dover chert.

Priv. col., excellent quality, valued $100-150.

• Harpeth River from Humphreys co., TN. Point 2 7/8 in. long, 1 3/16 in. wide, 1/4 in. thick. Steeply beveled, sharply serrated, very thin, long horizontal flaking tip broken. Made of Dover chert.
Priv. col., average quality, valued $65-85.

• Harpeth River from Johnson co., IL. Blade 3 7/8 in. long, 1 3/32 in. wide, 3/16 in. thick. Notching very fine and distinct, blade is steeply beveled and excellently serrated. Made of Mill Creek chert.
Priv. col., museum quality, valued $125-180.

• Harpeth River from southern Pope co., IL. Blade 4 in. long, 1 1/2 in. wide, 1/4 in. thick. Steeply beveled, finely serrated, deep side notches.
Priv. col., excellent quality, valued $100-145.

• Harpeth River from Humphreys co., TN. Point 3 1/8 in. long, 1 5/16 in. wide, 1/4 in. thick. Steeply beveled, sharply serrated, very thin, long fine layered horizontal flaking. Made of Dover chert.
Priv. col., museum quality, valued $195-245.

• Harpeth River from Johnson co., IL. Blade 4 7/8 in. long, 1 11/32 in. wide, 7/16 in. thick. Notching very fine and distinct, thin, symmetrical, blade is steeply beveled and excellently serrated. Made of Mill Creek chert.
Priv. col., museum quality, valued $135-180.

• Harpeth River from Cumberland co., IL. Blade 4 5/16 in. long, 1 1/3 in. wide, 1/4 in. thick. Steeply beveled, finely serrated, thin, deep side notches. Made of green gray pebble chert.
Priv. col., excellent quality, valued $100-145.

• Harpeth River from Humphreys co., TN. Point 2 1/8 in. long, 1 in. wide, 1/4 in. thick. Steeply beveled, sharply serrated, somewhat thick, tip broken, several edge nicks. Made of Dover chert.
Priv. col., average quality, valued $45-65.

• Harpeth River from Johnson co., IL. Blade 5 7/8 in. long, 1 27/32 in. wide, 3/16 in. thick. One of the longest Harpeth River blades I have ever seen, notching very fine and distinct, horizontal flaked. Blade is steeply beveled, sharp and excellently serrated. Made of Kaolin chert.
Priv. col., museum quality, rare, valued $325-430.

• Harpeth River from southern Pope co., IL. Blade 4 3/32 in. long, 1 1/8 in.

wide, 1/4 in. thick. Rather thick for a long, narrow blade, steeply beveled, one concave side, finely serrated, deep side notches. Made of a dark oily pebble chert.
Priv. col., excellent quality, valued $100-145.

• Harpeth River from northeastern TN. Blade 4 3/4 in. long, 1 3/4 in. wide, 1/4 in. thick. Oily dense chert, blade thin, finely serrated, long sharp tip. Steeply beveled on one side of each blade edge. Made of Black Creek chert.
Priv. col., museum quality, valued $200-275.

• Harpeth River from western TN. Blade 4 5/8 in. long, 1 in. wide, 1/2 in. thick. Very symmetrical, finely serrated, and sharp, thick and narrow, left hand beveled. Deep side notches, straight, short base. Made of Dover chert.
Priv. col., museum quality, valued $200-250.

• Harpeth River from Humphreys co., TN. Point 1 7/8 in. long, 11/16 in. wide, 1/8 in. thick. Steeply beveled, small, thin, horizontal flaked. Made of Dover chert.
Priv. col., museum quality, valued $150-175.

• Harpeth River from Humphreys co., TN. Point 2 1/16 in. long, 1 1/4 in. wide, 3/8 in. thick. Sharply serrated, very thin, fine, long horizontal flaking. Made of Dover chert.
Priv. col., museum quality, valued $165-235.

• Harpeth River from Williamson co., IL. Blade 3 1/8 in. long, 7/8 in. wide, 1/4 in. thick. Deep notches, fairly sharp, steep beveling. Made of Dover chert.
Priv. col., museum quality, valued $150-200.

• Harpeth River from Jackson co., IL. Blade 3 1/2 in. long, 1 1/32 in. wide, 5/16 in. thick. Notching barely visible, yet blade is steeply beveled and excellently serrated. Made of Buffalo Creek chert.
Priv. col., museum quality, valued $120-170.

• Harpeth River from Humphreys co., TN. Blade 3 3/4 in. long, 1 1/4 in. wide, 1/4 in. thick. Soft, thin, sharply serrated, with long sharp tip. Expanded stem, beveled on all four sides, opposing faces very steep. Made of Dover chert.
Priv. col., excellent quality, valued $150-230.

• Harpeth River from western TN. Blade 3 5/8 in. long, 1 in. wide, 3/16 in. thick. Very symmetrical, finely serrated, and sharp. Deep side notches above a straight base. Made of Dover chert.
Priv. col., excellent quality, valued $100-150.

• Harpeth River from Humphreys co., TN. Point 2 7/8 in. long, 1 3/16 in. wide, 1/4 in. thick. Steeply beveled, sharply serrated, very thin, long horizontal flaking, tip broken. Made of Dover chert.
Priv. col., average quality, valued $65-85.

• Harpeth River from Humphreys co., TN. Point 5 7/8 in. long, 2 3/16 in. wide, 1/4 in. thick. Made of Dover chert.
Priv. col., museum quality, valued $850-1,000.

• Harpeth River from Humphreys co., TN. Blade 3 27/32 in. long, 1 3/8 in. wide, 3/16 in. thick. Made of Dover chert.
Priv. col., museum quality, valued $150-200.

• Harpeth River from Oldham co., KY. Blade 4 1/2 in. long, 1 2/3 in. wide, 1/4 in. thick. Made of banded tan chert.
Priv. col., excellent quality, valued $300-450.

• Harpeth River from Oldham co., KY. Point 3 in. long, 1 3/16 in. wide, 1/4 in. thick. Made of white tan chert.
Priv. col., excellent quality, valued $395-450.

• Harpeth River from Oldham co., KY. Blade 4 7/8 in. long, 2 in. wide, 5/16 in. thick. Made of yellow white chert.
Priv. col., excellent quality, valued $235-285.

• Harpeth River from Meade co., KY. Point 2 1/8 in. long, 1 5/16 in. wide, 1/4 in. thick. Made of green white speckled pebble chert.
Priv. col., museum quality, rare, valued $450-550.

• Harpeth River from Meade co., KY. Blade 3 7/8 in. long, 1 11/32 in. wide, 3/16 in. thick. Good workmanship. Made of pinkish pebble chert.
Priv. col., museum quality, valued $325-380.

• Harpeth River from Meade co., KY. Blade 4 1/3 in. long, 2 1/16 in. wide, 1/4 in. thick. Made of dense white chert.
Priv. col., excellent quality, valued $200-245.

• Harpeth River from Meade co., KY. Point 2 7/8 in. long, 1 5/16 in. wide; 3/18 in. thick. Made of quartzite.
Priv. col., average quality, valued $150-200.

• Harpeth River from Webster co., KY. Blade 5 1/8 in. long, 2 1/3 in. wide,

5/16 in. thick. Excellent workmanship, even for a Harpeth River. Made of brown chert.
Priv. col., museum quality, rare, valued $1,000-1,200.

Hayes: 1,500-600 B.P. Mississippian

Found in the Midwest, small to medium sized point. Base resembles that of the Turkeytail, edges are generally finely and deeply serrated. Points are recurved with pointed tangs.

◆ Hayes from southwestern TN. Point 1 1/2 in. long, 3/4 in. wide, 1/8 in. thick. Displays classic Hayes features, except unimpressive edge serrations, sharp pointed tip. Made of pink pebble chert.

Grover Bohannon col., average quality, valued $25-40.

• Hayes from Hamilton co., TN. Point 1 1/3 in. long, 5/8 in. wide, 1/8 in. thick. Thin, base similar to a true Turkeytail, edges are fine, widely and deeply serrated. Point is recurved with pointed medium flaring tangs. Made of Dover chert.
Priv. col., museum quality, valued $65-80.

• Hayes from Stewart co., TN. Point 1 11/32 in. long, 3/4 in. wide, 1/8 in. thick. Narrow for a Hayes, thin, classic Hayes features, sharp, deep edges serrations. Heat treated, sharp pointed tip. Made of white pebble chert.
Grover Bohannon col., excellent quality, valued $45-60.

• Hayes from Stewart co., TN. Point 1 5/8 in. long, 2/3 in. wide, 3/16 in. thick. Symmetrical point, edges, finely and deeply serrated. Point recurved with pointed upward flaring tangs. Made of local brown banded chert.
Priv. col., museum quality, valued $60-75.

• Hayes from Jackson co., IL. Point 1 7/8 in. long, 1 1/4 in. wide, 1/8 in. thick. Very thin and symmetrical point, impressive serrated edges. Made of Mill Creek chert.
Priv. col., excellent quality, valued $35-50.

• Hayes from Johnson co., IL. Point 1 3/8 in. long, 1 1/4 in. wide, 1/8 in. thick. Classic base, edges are finely and deeply serrated. Point is recurved with pointed tangs. Made of Mill Creek chert.
Priv. col., excellent quality, valued $45-60.

• Hayes from Cooper co., MO. Point 1 13/32 in. long, 5/8 in. wide, 1/8 in. thick. Very symmetrical, classic Hayes features, deep, yet close edge serrations, sharp finely serrated tip. Made of pink to gray pebble chert.
Tim Rubbles col., excellent quality, valued $55-70.

• Hayes from Stewart co., TN. Point 1 9/32 in. long, 1 3/4 in. wide, 1/8 in. thick. Bell shaped. Made of white pebble chert.
Grover Bohannon col., excellent quality, valued $40-50.

• Hayes from Stewart co., TN. Point 1 5/8 in. long, 1 2/3 in. wide, 3/16 in. thick. Bell shaped. Made of banded brown chert.
Priv. col., museum quality, valued $60-75.

• Hayes from Jackson co., KY. Point 1 7/8 in. long, 1 1/4 in. wide, 1/8 in. thick. Made of yellow tan chert.
Priv. col., excellent quality, valued $35-50.

• Hayes from Johnson co., KY. Point 1 3/4 in. long, 1 1/8 in. wide, 1/8 in. thick. Edges sharply and deeply serrated, triangular stem. Made of translucent light brown chert.
Priv. col., museum quality, rare, valued $145-160.

• Hayes from Johnson co., KY. Point 1 23/32 in. long, 1 1/8 in. wide, 1/8 in. thick. Made of pink white chert.
Priv. col., excellent quality, valued $55-70.

• Hayes from Johnson co., KY. Point 1 11/32 in. long, 1 1/4 in. wide, 1/8 in. thick. Made of white pebble chert.
Priv. col., excellent quality, valued $45-60.

• Hayes from Metcalfe co., KY. Point 1 7/8 in. long, 1 1/3 in. wide, 3/18 in. thick. Made of heat treated white chert. Made of local brown banded chert.
Priv. col., excellent quality, valued $60-75.

• Hayes from White co., IL. Point 1 1/8 in. long, 7/8 in. wide, 1/8 in. thick. Made of yellow chert.
Priv. col., excellent quality, valued $45-50.

- Hayes from White co., IL. Point 1 5/8 in. long, 1 1/16 in. wide, 1/8 in. thick. Made of tan pebble chert.
Priv. col., excellent quality, valued $45-60.

- Hayes from Cape Giradeau co., MO. Point 1 29/32 in. long, 7/8 in. wide, 1/8 in. thick. Made of pinkish chert.
Priv. col., excellent quality, valued $55-70.

- Hayes from Cape Giradeau co., MO. Point 1 13/16 in. long, 7/8 in. wide, 1/8 in. thick. Made of white pebble chert.
Priv. col., excellent quality, valued $45-60.

- Hayes from Searcy co., AR. Point 1 5/8 in. long, 1 1/3 in. wide, 1/8 in. thick. Made of Arkansas brown chert.
Priv. col., museum quality, valued $60-75.

- Hayes from Searcy co., AR. Point 1 7/8 in. long, 1 1/4 in. wide, 1/8 in. thick. Made of white chert.
Priv. col., excellent quality, valued $35-50.

- Hayes from Johnson co., IL. Point 1 3/8 in. long, 1 1/4 in. wide, 1/8 in. thick. Made of Mill Creek chert.
Priv. col., excellent quality, valued $45-60.

- Hayes from Searcy co., AR. Point 2 in. long, 1 3/8 in. wide, 1/8 in. thick. Made of gray pebble chert.
Priv. col., excellent quality, valued $55-70.

- Hayes from Searcy co., AR. Point 1 5/8 in. long, 3/4 in. wide, 1/8 in. thick. Heat treated, long needle sharp tip. Made of Arkansas brown chert.
Priv. col., museum quality, valued $65-80.

- Hayes from Caldwell Parish, LA. Point 1 7/8 in. long, 1 in. wide, 3/16 in. thick. Made of high grade quartzite.
Priv. col., average quality, valued $20-25.

- Hayes from Caldwell Parish, LA. Point 1 2/3 in. long, 1 1/4 in. wide, 1/8 in. thick. Made of banded white red chert.
Priv. col., excellent quality, valued $45-55.

- Hayes from Caldwell Parish, LA. Point 1 1/3 in. long, 1 in. wide, 1/8 in. thick. Made of translucent gray chert.

Priv. col., museum quality, valued $85-100.

• Hayes from Cooper co., MO. Point 1 22/32 in. long, 7/8 in. wide, 1/8 in. thick. Made of pink to gray pebble chert.
Priv. col., excellent quality, valued $55-70.

Heavy Duty: 7,000-5,000 B.P. Early to Mid-Archaic

Predominantly an eastern point or blade, medium to large in size. Point or blade generally serrated, concave base, stem usually parallel.

♦ Heavy Duty from Cooper co., MO. Blade 4 5/8 in. long, 1 3/4 in. wide, 5/8 in. thick. Random flaked with unique concave flaring tail, uneven side notches. Serrations deep and irregular. Made of a dark pebble chert.

Priv. col., excellent quality, valued $75-100.

• Heavy Duty from Jasper co., IL. Blade 5 1/4 in. long, 1 1/4 in. wide, 1/4 in. thick. Blade classic, horizontally flaked, weak shoulders, concave base. Made of yellow white pebble chert.
Priv. col., museum quality, valued $140-225.

• Heavy Duty from Ohio co., OH. Point 2 3/4 in. long, 7/8 in. wide, 3/16 in. thick. Point sharp and deep, finely serrated, distinct shoulders above long parallel stem with concave base.
Jim Radder col., museum quality, valued $125-175.

• Heavy Duty from Stewart co., TN. Blade 3 7/8 in. long, 3/4 in. wide, 1/4 in. thick. Wide distinct serrations, fluted along one side of the blade to just into the stem. Even protruding shoulders above a concave base, wide parallel stem. Made of Dover chert.
J. Hastings col., museum quality, rare, valued $350-500.

• Heavy Duty from southern TN. Blade 6 3/8 in. long, 1 5/8 in. wide, 1/4 in. thick. Exceptional piece, deeply side notched, finely serrated, flared concave base. Randomly flaked, very narrow, sides slightly beveled, very sharp. Made of Dover chert.
Grover Bohannon col., museum quality, valued $245-500.

• Heavy Duty from northwestern KY. Blade 5 11/16 in. long, 1 in. wide, 3/16 in. thick. Transverse flaked, edges ground, deep corner notches, snapped tangs, short stem, deeply concave base. Made of porous pebble chert.
Grover Bohannon col., average quality, valued $45-55.

• Heavy Duty from Sangamon co., IL. Blade 6 5/8 in. long, 1 7/8 in. wide, 1/4 in. thick. Thin very angular narrow blade, deep, wide, edge flaking, wide serrations. Stem wide, with concave base. Made of green black grained pebble chert.
Priv. col., museum quality, valued $250-365.

• Heavy Duty from Cumberland co., IL. Blade 5 3/8 in. long, 1 5/8 in. wide, 1/4 in. thick. Thin blade, deep, blunt tipped, rounded shoulders, stem concave and only 3/16 in. thicker than the blade. Deep dull serrations. Stem straight based, very light material. Made of an unidentified cream white chert.
Priv. col., average quality, valued $95-135.

• Heavy Duty from Boone co., MO. Blade 6 3/8 in. long, 2 1/8 in. wide, 1/4 in. thick. Thin blade, poorly serrated. Stem extremely wide and concave based. Made of quartzite.
Priv. col., poor quality, valued $15-25.

• Heavy Duty from Alexander co., IL. Blade 4 5/8 in. long, 2 3/8 in. wide, 1/4 in. thick. Thin blade, deep, wide, blunt tip, with ground edges. Heat treated, poorly serrated, with concave base. Made of quartzite.
Priv. col., average quality, valued $45-65.

• Heavy Duty from Wabash co., IN. Blade 5 3/32 in. long, 2 1/8 in. wide, 1/4 in. thick. Thin blade, slight tip break, deep serrations. Classic design, very sharp. Stem straight based. Made of unidentified black chert.
Priv. col., average quality, valued $50-65.

• Heavy Duty from Alexander co., IL. Blade 5 13/32 in. long, 1 1/2 in. wide, 3/16 in. thick. Thin blade, narrow, fine layered serrations, extremely sharp and pointed tip. Stem wide and straight based. Made of quartzite.
Priv. col., excellent quality, valued $85-135.

• Heavy Duty from Alexander co., IL. Blade 4 5/16 in. long, 1 5/8 in. wide, 1/4 in. thick. Thin blade, deep, wide serrations. Stem wide and straight based. Made of Mill Creek chert.
Priv. col., excellent quality, valued $75-95.

• Heavy Duty from Jackson co., IL. Blade 6 3/8 in. long, 2 5/16 in. wide, 11/32 in. thick. Thin blade, finely serrated, blunt tip, random flaking. Stem extremely wide and concave based. Made of poor quality (grainy) quartzite.
Priv. col., average quality, valued $40-55.

• Heavy Duty from Clark co., IL. Blade 4 5/8 in. long, 2 3/8 in. wide, 1/4 in. thick. Made of quartzite.
Priv. col., average quality, valued $45-65.

• Heavy Duty from Clark co., IL. Blade 5 1/3 in. long, 2 1/4 in. wide, 1/4 in. thick. Made of pink chert.
Priv. col., excellent quality, valued $80-125.

• Heavy Duty from Clark co., IL. Blade 5 13/16 in. long, 1 3/4 in. wide, 3/16 in. thick. Heat treated. Made of white chert.
Priv. col., excellent quality, valued $105-145.

• Heavy Duty from Jackson co., IL. Blade 4 3/16 in. long, 1 7/8 in. wide, 1/4 in. thick. Made of Mill Creek chert.
Priv. col., excellent quality, valued $85-115.

• Heavy Duty from Jackson co., IL. Blade 6 1/4 in. long, 2 1/16 in. wide, 1/4 in. thick. Made of gray pebble chert.
Priv. col., average quality, valued $575-650.

• Heavy Duty from Hardin co., IL. Blade 5 1/8 in. long, 2 in. wide, 1/4 in. thick. Made of tan white chert.
Priv. col., excellent quality, valued $350-450.

• Heavy Duty from Wabash co., IN. Blade 5 1/3 in. long, 2 1/3 in. wide, 1/4 in. thick. Made of unidentified local black chert.
Priv. col., museum quality, valued $500-650.

• Heavy Duty from Jasper co., IL. Blade 5 1/2 in. long, 1 2/3 in. wide, 3/16 in. thick. Heat treated. Made of tan yellow chert.
Priv. col., museum quality, valued $850-950.

• Heavy Duty from Cumberland co., IL. Blade 4 3/16 in. long, 1 7/8 in. wide, 1/4 in. thick. Made of dense white chert.
Priv. col., excellent quality, valued $275-325.

• Heavy Duty from Cumberland co., IL. Blade 6 1/8 in. long, 2 1/16 in. wide, 1/3 in. thick. Made of dense white chert.
Priv. col., excellent quality, valued $240-285.

• Heavy Duty from Cumberland co., IL. Blade 4 7/8 in. long, 2 in. wide, 1/4 in. thick. Left hand beveled. Made of greenish chert.
Priv. col., excellent quality, valued $350-400.

• Heavy Duty from Adams co., IN. Blade 4 5/32 in. long, 2 1/8 in. wide, 1/4 in. thick. Classic design, very sharp. Made of silver black chert.
Priv. col., museum quality, valued $550-650.

• Heavy Duty from Adams co., IN. Blade 5 1/32 in. long, 1 13/16 in. wide, 3/16 in. thick. Made of greenish chert.
Priv. col., museum quality, valued $385-435.

• Heavy Duty from White co., IL. Blade 4 1/16 in. long, 2 in.wide, 1/4 in. thick. Made of Mill Creek chert.
Priv. col., excellent quality, valued $175-250.

• Heavy Duty from White co., IL. Blade 6 1/32 in. long, 2 3/16 in. wide, 7/32 in. thick. Made of white pebble chert.
Priv. col., excellent quality, valued $180-225.

• Heavy Duty from Adams co., IL. Blade 4 1/8 in. long, 2 1/8 in. wide, 1/4 in. thick. Made of quartzite.
Priv. col., average quality, valued $45-65.

• Heavy Duty from Adams co., IL. Blade 5 1/32 in. long, 2 1/32 in. wide, 1/4 in. thick. Made of gray chert.
Priv. col., excellent quality, valued $250-350.

• Heavy Duty from Fulton co., IL. Blade 5 13/16 in. long, 2 1/4 in. wide, 3/16 in. thick. Made of brown white marbled chert.
Priv. col., museum quality, valued $850-1,000.

• Heavy Duty from Fulton co., IL. Blade 4 7/16 in. long, 2 5/8 in. wide, 1/4 in. thick. Made of porous white pink chert.

Priv. col., poor quality, valued $55-65.

• Heavy Duty from St. Clair co., IL. Blade 6 in. long, 2 7/16 in. wide, 1/2 in. thick. Made of white pebble chert.
Priv. col., average quality, valued $150-200.

• Heavy Duty from St. Clair co., IL. Blade 4 1/8 in. long, 2 1/32 in. wide, 1/4 in. thick. Made of quartzite.
Priv. col., average quality, valued $45-65.

• Heavy Duty from St. Clair co., IL. Blade 5 1/32 in. long, 2 3/16 in. wide, 1/4 in. thick. Made of Mill Creek chert.
Priv. col., excellent quality, valued $250-350.

• Heavy Duty from Greene co., IL. Blade 5 1/2 in. long, 1 29/32 in. wide, 3/16 in. thick. Heat treated. Made of white chert.
Priv. col., excellent quality, valued $385-435.

• Heavy Duty from Greene co., IL. Blade 4 13/16 in. long, 1 5/8 in. wide, 1/4 in. thick. Made of Mill Creek chert.
Priv. col., excellent quality, valued $275-350.

• Heavy Duty from Greene co., IL. Blade 6 1/8 in. long, 2 7/16 in. wide, 1/3 in. thick. Made of white chert.
Priv. col., average quality, valued $40-55.

• Heavy Duty from DeWitt co., IL. Blade 4 7/8 in. long, 2 1/8 in. wide, 1/4 in. thick. Made of quartzite.
Priv. col., average quality, valued $45-65.

• Heavy Duty from Wabash co., IN. Blade 5 7/32 in. long, 2 1/8 in. wide, 1/4 in. thick. Made of unidentified local black chert.
Priv. col., museum quality, valued $500-650.

• Heavy Duty from Wabash co., IN. Blade 5 13/32 in. long, 2 1/4 in. wide, 3/16 in. thick. Made of local black chert.
Priv. col., museum quality, valued $685-735.

• Heavy Duty from Wabash co., IN. Blade 4 15/16 in. long, 1 5/8 in. wide, 3/16 in. thick. Made of greenish chert.
Priv. col., excellent quality, valued $575-650.

- Heavy Duty from Sangamon co., IL. Blade 6 in. long, 2 1/16 in. wide, 1/3 in. thick. Made of white tan chert.
Priv. col., excellent quality, valued $400-550.

Hemphill: 8,000-3,000 B.P. Early to Mid-Archaic

Located throughout the Midwest into the Northeast. Medium to large sized point or blade, side notched, convex to parallel sides. Thin points and blades of high quality work.

◆ Hemphill from Union co., IL. Point 3 in. long, 1 in. wide, 3/16 in. thick. Concave base, deeply side notched and very symmetrical. Made of Mill Creek chert.

Les Grubbe col., excellent quality, valued $125-200.

◆ Hemphill from Union co., IL. Blade 3 1/2 in. long, 1 1/4 in. wide, 3/16 in. thick. Concave base, deep side notches, near parallel sides. Made of Mill Creek chert.

Les Grubbe col., excellent quality, valued $125-200.

◆ Hemphill from central TN. Blade 4 5/16 in. long, 1 1/4 in. wide, 5/16 in. thick. Concave base, left hand beveled, with long thin flaking. Made of unidentified white to light tan chert.

Les Grubbe col., excellent quality, valued $150-225.

- Hemphill from Johnson co., IL. Blade 3 7/8 in. long, 1 3/4 in. wide, 5/16 in. thick. Concave base, deep side notches, very symmetrical, thin flaking. Made of Mill Creek chert.
Priv. col., excellent quality, valued $125-200.

- Hemphill from Union co., IL. Point 2 1/2 in. long, 1 1/16 in. wide, 1/8 in. thick. Concave base, deep side notches, near parallel sides, heavily left hand beveled. Made of Mill Creek chert.
Priv. col., excellent quality, valued $115-180.

- Hemphill from Williamson co., IL. Blade 3 3/4 in. long, 1 3/16 in. wide, 1/4 in. thick. Concave base, parallel sides and base, left hand beveled, several blade nicks. Made of Dover chert.
Priv. col., average quality, valued $75-100.

- Hemphill from Johnson co., IL. Point 2 7/8 in. long, 1 1/16 in. wide, 3/16 in. thick. Concave base, deeply side notched, left hand beveled, random flaked. Made of Kaolin chert.
Priv. col., museum quality, rare, valued $300-375.

- Hemphill from Williamson co., IL. Blade 3 7/8 in. long, 1 5/16 in. wide, 1/4 in. thick. Concave base, parallel base, left hand beveled, very symmetrical. Made of Cobden chert.
Priv. col., museum quality, valued $275-300.

- Hemphill from Clark co., IL. Blade 4 in. long, 1 3/4 in. wide, 1/4 in. thick. Concave base, concave blade sides, steeply left hand beveled, deep side notches, very symmetrical. Made of a green gray streaked unidentified chert.
Priv. col., museum quality, valued $300-375.

- Hemphill from Johnson co., IL. Blade 4 7/8 in. long, 1 3/4 in. wide, 5/16 in. thick. Concave base, deep side notches, very symmetrical, random flaking. Made of Mill Creek chert.
Priv. col., excellent quality, valued $175-220.

- Hemphill from Clark co., IL. Blade 4 1/2 in. long, 1 5/8 in. wide, 1/4 in. thick. Concave base, concave blade sides, left hand beveled, deep side notches, small tip break. Made of unidentified gray chert.
Priv. col., average quality, valued $75-100.

- Hemphill from Coles co., IL. Blade 4 1/8 in. long, 1 3/4 in. wide, 1/4 in. thick. Concave base, concave blade sides, left hand beveled, deep side notches, very symmetrical layered flaking. Made of a local pebble chert.
Priv. col., museum quality, valued $275-300.

- Hemphill from Johnson co., IL. Blade 5 3/8 in. long, 1 13/16 in. wide, 7/16 in. thick. Concave base, unusually long and thin Hemphill, deep side notches, very symmetrical, random flaking. Made of Cobden Hornstone chert.

Priv. col., museum quality, rare, valued $375-420.

• Hemphill from Clark co., IL. Blade 4 in. long, 1 5/8 in. wide, 1/4 in. thick. Concave base, concave blade sides, left hand beveled, deep side notches, small tip break. Made of unidentified gray chert.
Priv. col., average quality, valued $75-100.

• Hemphill from Seneca co., NY. Point 2 1/3 in. long, 1 3/16 in. wide, 1/8 in. thick. Made of mauve chert.
Priv. col., excellent quality, valued $125-180.

• Hemphill from Seneca co., NY. Blade 3 7/8 in. long, 1 3/16 in. wide, 1/4 in. thick. Edges reworked and steeply beveled. Made of mauve chert.
Priv. col., excellent quality, valued $175-200.

• Hemphill from Seneca co., NY. Blade 3 7/8 in. long, 1 1/16 in. wide, 3/16 in. thick. Made of white tan chert.
Priv. col., excellent quality, valued $100-175.

• Hemphill from Otsego co., NY. Blade 3 5/8 in. long, 1 3/16 in. wide, 1/4 in. thick. Made of pink chert.
Priv. col., excellent quality, valued $150-200.

• Hemphill from Otsego co., NY. Point 2 3/4 in. long, 1 in. wide, 1/8 in. thick. Left hand beveled. Made of white tan chert.
Priv. col., excellent quality, valued $135-180.

• Hemphill from Otesgo co., NY. Blade 3 3/4 in. long, 1 3/8 in. wide, 1/4 in. thick. Made of gray black speckled chert.
Priv. col., excellent quality, valued $175-200.

• Hemphill from Lewis co., NY. Point 2 1/8 in. long, 1 in. wide, 3/16 in. thick. Made of gray chert.
Priv. col., museum quality, valued $280-350.

• Hemphill from Lewis co., NY. Blade 3 3/4 in. long, 1 1/3 in. wide, 1/4 in. thick. Made of gray chert.
Priv. col., excellent quality, valued $300-350.

• Hemphill from Snyder co., PA. Point 2 1/3 in. long, 1 1/8 in. wide, 1/8 in. thick. Made of multi-tone gray blue chert.
Priv. col., museum quality, valued $150-180.

• Hemphill from Synder co., PA. Blade 3 7/8 in. long, 1 5/16 in. wide, 1/4 in. thick. Made of multi-toned gray blue chert.
Priv. col., museum quality, valued $175-250.

• Hemphill from Forest co., PA. Blade 3 7/8 in. long, 1 1/16 in. wide, 3/16 in. thick. Made of greenish chert.
Priv. col., excellent quality, valued $200-275.

• Hemphill from Forest co., PA. Blade 3 3/4 in. long, 1 1/4 in. wide, 1/4 in. thick. Made of gray pebble chert.
Priv. col., excellent quality, valued $175-225.

• Hemphill from Lucas co., OH. Point 2 1/32 in. long, 1 1/16 in. wide, 1/8 in. thick. Made of white chert.
Priv. col., excellent quality, valued $225-280.

• Hemphill from Lucas co., OH. Blade 3 13/16 in. long, 1 3/32 in. wide, 1/4 in. thick. Made of white yellow chert.
Priv. col., excellent quality, valued $275-300.

• Hemphill from Coshocton co., OH. Point 2 3/8 in. long, 1 5/16 in. wide, 3/16 in. thick. Made of Coshocton chert.
Priv. col., museum quality, rare, valued $275-375.

• Hemphill from Morgan co., OH. Blade 3 5/8 in, long, 1 1/16 in. wide, 1/4 in. thick. Has been resharpened, left hand beveled. Made of gray white chert.
Priv. col., excellent quality, valued $175-200.

Hernando: 4,500-2,000 B.P. Late Archaic

Hernando points and blades are found predominantly in the Gulf states. Hernando pieces are of good to excellent workmanship, seemingly regardless of the material used. Medium to large sized triangular point or blade. Short based with deep corner notches and flaring tangs, edges may be straight to concave. Base is snapped.

◆ Hernando from Fort Lauderdale FL. Point 2 3/8 in. long, 1 1/4 in. wide, 1/8 in. thick. Classic design, finely serrated. Made of vein quartz.

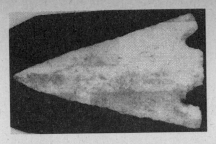

Priv. col., excellent quality, valued $125-160.

◆ Hernando from Fort Lauderdale, FL. Point 2 1/4 in. long, 1 1/4 in. wide, 3/16 in. thick. Classic concave design, very fine and sharp serrations, thick squared tangs, pointed tip. Made of jasper.

Priv. col., museum quality, rare, valued $400-520.

• Hernando from Fort Lauderdale, FL. Point 2 1/8 in. long, 1 1/4 in. wide, 3/16 in. thick. Point thin, base broken, tangs snapped straight below stem. Very sharp distinct serrations, point toward blade tip. Tip pointed and sharp. Made of a flaky quartzite.
Priv. col., average quality, valued $25-35.

• Hernando from Red River Parish, LA. Point 2 7/8 in. long, 1 1/3 in. wide, 1/8 in. thick. Made of quartzite.
Priv. col., excellent quality, valued $125-160.

• Hernando from Red River Parish, LA. Point 2 3/4 in. long, 1 1/2 in. wide, 3/16 in. thick. Made of rose quartz.
Priv. col., museum quality, rare, valued $300-350.

• Hernando from Caddo Parish, LA. Point 2 7/8 in. long, 1 1/2 in. wide, 3/16 in. thick. Made of quartzite.
Priv. col., excellent quality, valued $75-85.

• Hernando from Caddo Parish, LA. Point 2 3/16 in. long, 1 1/4 in. wide,

1/8 in. thick. Made of multi-toned brown to white chert.
Priv. col., museum quality, valued $275-360.

• Hernando from Sumpter co., FL. Point 2 3/4 in. long, 1 1/3 in. wide, 3/16 in. thick. Made of milky quartz.
Priv. col., museum quality, valued $350-420.

• Hernando from Sumpter co., FL. Point 2 3/8 in. long, 1 1/4 in. wide, 3/16 in. thick. Made of banded golden chert.
Priv. col., museum quality, valued $450-550.

• Hernando from Sumpter co., FL. Point 2 1/2 in. long, 1 1/16 in. wide, 1/8 in. thick. Made of quartzite.
Priv. col., excellent quality, valued $125-160.

• Hernando from Levy co., FL. Point 3 1/16 in. long, 1 1/3 in. wide, 3/16 in. thick. Made of jasper.
Priv. col., museum quality, rare, valued $600-750.

• Hernando from Gates co., FL. Point 2 3/8 in. long, 1 1/4 in. wide, 3/16 in. thick. Made of quatzite.
Priv. col., excellent quality, valued $150-200.

• Hernando from Gates co., FL. Point 3 1/8 in. long, 1 5/16 in. wide, 1/8 in. thick. Made of translucent brown chert.
Priv. col., excellent quality, valued $225-250.

• Hernando from Bibb co., AL. Point 2 1/2 in. long, 1 1/16 in. wide, 3/16 in. thick. Made of red chert.
Priv. col., museum quality, rare, valued $450-500.

• Hernando from Lamar co., AL. Point 2 1/8 in. long, 1 1/2 in. wide, 3/16 in. thick. Made of quartzite.
Priv. col., average quality, valued $60-70.

• Hernando from Lamar co., AL. Point 2 5/8 in. long, 1 1/3 in. wide, 1/8 in. thick. Made of banded white red chert.
Priv. col., excellent quality, valued $175-220.

• Hernando from Coosa co., AL. Point 2 1/3 in. long, 1 1/4 in. wide, 3/16 in. thick. Made of false jasper.
Priv. col., excellent quality, valued $100-200.

- Hernando from Geneva co., AL. Point 2 1/8 in. long, 1 1/4 in. wide, 3/16 in. thick. Made of quartzite.
Priv. col., average quality, valued $65-80.

- Hernando from Geneva co., AL. Point 2 3/16 in. long, 1 3/4 in. wide, 1/8 in. thick. Made of high grade multi-colored quartzite.
Priv. col., excellent quality, valued $185-200.

- Hernando from Geneva co., AL. Point 2 5/16 in. long, 1 1/3 in. wide, 3/16 in. thick. Made of gray pebble chert.
Priv. col., museum quality, valued $200-250.

- Hernando from Crenshaw co., AL. Point 2 7/8 in. long, 1 1/4 in. wide, 1/4 in. thick. Made of high grade gray to white quartzite.
Priv. col., excellent quality, valued $270-300.

- Hernando from Crenshaw co., AL. Point 2 3/32 in. long, 1 5/32 in. wide, 1/4 in. thick. Made of quartzite.
Priv. col., excellent quality, valued $125-150.

- Hernando from Tunica co., MS. Point 3 1/32 in. long, 1 1/3 in. wide, 1/8 in. thick. Made of milky quartz.
Priv. col., museum quality, valued $400-500.

- Hernando from Tunica co., MS. Point 2 3/8 in. long, 1 1/2 in. wide, 3/16 in. thick. Made of quartzite.
Priv. col., average quality, valued $45-60.

- Hernando from Benton co., MS. Point 2 13/32 in. long, 1 1/8 in. wide, 1/4 in. thick. Made of quartzite.
Priv. col., excellent quality, valued $125-180.

- Hernando from Benton co., MS. Point 2 1/2 in. long, 1 1/3 in. wide, 3/16 in. thick. Made of false jasper.
Priv. col., excellent quality, valued $100-120.

- Hernando from Benton co., MS. Point 2 3/8 in. long, 1 1/2 in. wide, 5/16 in. thick. Made of quartzite.
Priv. col., excellent quality, valued $140-180.

Hillsborough: 7,000-5,000 B. P. Mid-Archaic

Southern point or blade, medium to large in size. Broad, barbed shoulders extending below base. Base triangular shaped, small and contracting.

♦ Hillsborough from Little Rock, AR. Point 3 1/2 in. long, 1 3/4 in. wide, 1/8 in. thick. Thin for a Hillsborough, finely serrated, sharp, yet rounded tip. Made of brown flint.

Luke Sims col., excellent quality, valued $400-550.

• Hillsborough from southeastern GA. Blade 5 3/4 in. long, 3 3/8 in. wide, 1/4 in. thick. Long, thin, horizontal flaking. Finely serrated, blunt tip, parallel shoulders above rather than below base. Made of high quality quartzite.
Priv. col., excellent quality, valued $850-1,100.

• Hillsborough from Hamilton co., TN. Blade 5 1/16 in long, 2 5/8 in. wide, 1/4 in. thick. Finely serrated with long sharp tip. Symmetrical, typical triangular contracting base, barbs extending below base. Made of Dover chert.
Priv. col., museum quality, valued $950-1,200.

• Hillsborough from Hardin co., KY. Blade 4 3/8 in. long, 1 7/8 in. wide, 3/16 in. thick. Thin, heat treated, sharp fine serrations, barbed shoulders parallel to base. Made of oily white chert.
Priv. col., excellent quality, valued $650-850.

• Hillsborough from Madison co., IL. Blade 6 1/8 in. long, 2 7/16 in. wide, 3/16 in. thick. Found in an Adena burial site in Madison co., IL. Long, thin, symmetrical, horizontal parallel flaking. Deep sharp edge serrations, straight base. Made of grainy quartzite.
Priv. col., average quality, valued $350-500.

• Hillsborough from Issaquena co., MS. Blade 4 7/16 in. long, 2 7/8 in. wide,

1/4 in. thick. Made of white pebble chert.
Priv. col., excellent quality, valued $150-200.

• Hillsborough from Issaquena co., MS. Blade 5 3/8 in. long, 2 in. wide,
3/16 in. thick. Made of gray white chert.
Priv. col., excellent quality, valued $450-650.

• Hillsborough from Madison co., FL. Blade 6 1/32 in. long, 2 7/16 in. wide,
3/16 in. thick. Made of gray brown quartzite.
Priv. col., average quality, valued $150-200.

• Hillsborough from Madison co., FL. Blade 5 7/16 in. long, 2 7/8 in. wide,
1/4 in. thick. Made of mikly quartz.
Priv. col., museum quality, valued $850-1,000.

• Hillsborough from Holmes co., FL. Blade 4 3/32 in. long, 1 7/8 in. wide,
1/4 in. thick. Made of oily brown chert.
Priv. col., excellent quality, valued $750-950.

• Hillsborough from Madison co., FL. Blade 6 1/16 in. long, 2 5/16 in. wide,
3/16 in. thick. Made of white to tan chert.
Priv. col., museum quality, valued $850-1,000.

• Hillsborough from Holmes co., FL. Blade 5 1/32 in. long, 2 7/8 in. wide,
1/4 in. thick. Heat treated. Made of high grade quartzite.
Priv. col., museum quality, valued $950-1,200.

• Hillsborough from Wakulla co., FL. Blade 5 3/8 in. long, 2 1/8 in. wide,
1/8 in. thick. Heat treated. Made of translucent white chert.
Priv. col., museum quality, rare, valued $1,500-1,650.

• Hillsborough from Wakulla co., FL. Blade 6 in. long, 2 9/16 in. wide, 1/8 in.
thick. Heat treated. Made of green gray chert.
Priv. col., excellent quality, valued $650-800.

• Hillsborough from Wakulla co., FL. Blade 5 5/16 in. long, 2 3/8 in. wide,
1/4 in. thick. Heat treated. Made of high grade milky quartz.
Priv. col., museum quality, rare, valued $1,250-1,500.

• Hillsborough from Gulf co., FL. Blade 4 7/8 in. long, 1 1/32 in. wide, 3/16 in.
thick. Made of glossy white chert.
Priv. col., museum quality, valued $750-850.

- Hillsborough from Gulf co., FL. Blade 6 in. long, 2 5/16 in. wide, 5/16 in. thick. Made of grainy quartzite.
Priv. col., average quality, valued $250-300.

- Hillsborough from Gulf co., FL. Blade 5 7/16 in. long, 2 5/8 in. wide, 1/4 in. thick. Made of quartzite.
Priv. col., average quality, valued $150-200.

- Hillsborough from Baker co., FL. Point 2 3/8 in. long, 1 7/32 in. wide, 3/16 in. thick. Made of white tan pebble chert.
Priv. col., excellent quality, valued $350-450.

- Hillsborough from Baker co., FL. Point 3 1/32 in. long, 1 9/16 in. wide, 3/16 in. thick. Made of grainy quartzite.
Priv. col., average quality, valued $150-175.

- Hillsborough from Baker co., FL. Point 3 1/16 in. long, 1 5/8 in. wide, 1/4 in. thick. Made of high quality quartzite.
Priv. col., excellent quality, valued $500-600.

- Hillsborough from Baker co., FL. Blade 2 7/8 in. long, 1 1/8 in. wide, 3/16 in. thick. Made of quartzite.
Priv. col., excellent quality, valued $150-250.

- Hillsborough from Issaquena co., MS. Point 2 1/8 in. long, 13/16 in. wide, 3/16 in. thick. Made of quartzite.
Priv. col., average quality, valued $200-300.

- Hillsborough from Issaquena co., MS. Blade 5 7/16 in. long, 2 1/8 in. wide, 1/4 in. thick. Heat treated. Made of translucent gray white chert.
Priv. col., museum quality, valued $850-1,000.

- Hillsborough from Lanier co., GA. Blade 4 1/8 in. long, 1 5/8 in. wide, 3/16 in. thick. Made of lightweight white chert.
Priv. col., excellent quality, valued $450-550.

- Hillsborough from Grady co., GA. Blade 5 1/8 in. long, 2 1/16 in. wide, 3/16 in. thick. Made of quartzite.
Priv. col., average quality, valued $150-200.

Holland: 10,000-8,000 B.P. Paleo-Transitional

Found throughout the Midwest and East. Point or blade generally medium to large in size. High quality workmanship, finely made points and blades with weak shoulders, knobbed bases, weak ears, and ground bases. May be horizontally or obliquely flaked.

◆ Holland from Brown co., TN. Point 3 1/2 in. long, 2 1/2 in. wide, 1/4 in. thick. Classic design for a Holland point, symmetrically wide and thin. Parallel oblique flaked with small nick in base. Made of Cobden Hornstone chert.

Priv. col., museum quality, valued $650-900.

• Holland from St. Louis co., MO. Blade 6 1/4 in. long, 1 3/16 in. wide, 1/4 in. thick. Symmetrical, narrow blade, slightly concave base, well ground.
Priv. col., excellent quality, valued $300-425.

• Holland from Brown co., IL. Blade 5 7/8 in. long, 1 1/2 in. wide, 1/4 in. thick. Symmetrical, thin, with ground concave base. Made of Mill Creek chert.
Priv. col., excellent quality, valued $375-500.

• Holland from Brown co., TN. Point 2 7/8 in. long, 1 1/2 in. wide, 1/4 in. thick. Symmetrical, wide and thin. Parallel oblique flaked, ground concave base. Made of Bullseye chert.
Priv. col., museum quality, valued $650-800.

• Holland from Brown co., TN. Point 3 in. long, 2 1/4 in. wide, 1/4 in. thick. Classic design, point, symmetrically wide and thin. Parallel oblique flaked, concave ground base. Made of Dover chert.
Tim Rubbles col., excellent quality, valued $525-650.

• Holland from Franklin co., IL. Blade 4 1/3 in. long, 1 1/16 in. wide, 3/16 in. thick. Very thin and sharp blade with parallel oblique flaking. Made of Cobden chert.
Priv. col., museum quality, valued $600-725.

• Holland from St. Louis co., MO. Blade 5 1/8 in. long, 1 5/16 in. wide, 1/4 in. thick. Symmetrical, wide blade, slightly concave base, heavily ground. Made of Mill Creek chert.
Priv. col., excellent quality, valued $350-450.

• Holland from Brown co., IL. Blade 5 1/8 in. long, 1 1/2 in. wide, 1/4 in. thick. Symmetrical, thin, narrow with ground concave base. Made of Mill Creek chert.
Priv. col., excellent quality, valued $375-500.

• Holland from Humphreys co., TN. Point 3 1/16 in. long, 2 3/4 in. wide, 1/4 in. thick. Classic design, point, symmetrical, wide and thin. Parallel oblique flaked, concave ground base. Made of Dover chert.
Tim Rubbles col., excellent quality, valued $525-650.

• Holland from Franklin co., IL. Blade 5 2/3 in. long, 1 5/16 in. wide, 5/8 in. thick. Very thin, unusually narrow and sharp blade with parallel oblique flaking. Made of tan, dense, oily pebble chert.
Priv. col., museum quality, valued $600-725.

• Holland from St. Louis co., MO. Blade 5 1/4 in. long, 1 3/16 in. wide, 1/4 in. thick. Symmetrical, re-worked blade, slightly concave base, well ground.
Priv. col., excellent quality, valued $325-400.

• Holland from Brown co., IL. Blade 5 1/8 in. long, 1 1/8 in. wide, 1/4 in. thick. Symmetrical, thin, narrow with ground concave base. Made of white pebble chert.
Priv. col., average quality, valued $275-350.

• Holland from Brown co., IL. Point 2 5/8 in. long, 1 3/4 in. wide, 5/16 in. thick. Classic design, point, symmetrically wide and unusually thick. Parallel oblique flaked, concave ground base. Made of Cobden chert.
Tim Rubbles col., excellent quality, valued $585-750.

• Holland from Franklin co., IL. Blade 5 1/3 in. long, 1 7/16 in. wide, 3/16 in. thick. Very thin, narrow, reworked or beveled, and sharp blade with parallel oblique flaking. Made of Kaolin chert.
Priv. col., museum quality, rare, valued $800-925.

• Holland from Franklin co., IL. Blade 3 5/8 in. long, 1 3/16 in. wide, 5/16 in. thick. Thick, yet sharp blade with parallel oblique flaking, slight tip break. Made of Mill Creek chert.
Priv. col., average quality, valued $100-225.

- Holland from St. Louis co., MO. Blade 6 3/4 in. long, 1 3/16 in. wide, 1/4 in. thick. Symmetrical, very narrow blade, slightly concave base, well ground, excellent workmanship. Made of jasper.
Priv. col., museum quality, rare, valued $800-925.

- Holland from Brown co., IL. Blade 5 7/8 in. long, 1 1/2 in. wide, 1/4 in. thick. Symmetrical, thin, with ground concave base. Made of Mill Creek chert.
Priv. col., excellent quality, valued $375-500.

- Holland from Ben Hill co., GA. Blade 5 1/32 in. long, 1 3/8 in. wide, 1/4 in. thick. Made of white pebble chert.
Priv. col., average quality, valued $250-350.

- Holland from Brown co., IL. Point 5 5/8 in. long, 1 1/4 in. wide, 5/16 in. thick. Made of white black speckled chert.
Tim Rubbles col., excellent quality, valued $250-350.

- Holland from Brown co., IL. Blade 5 1/8 in. long, 1 3/16 in. wide, 3/16 in. thick. Made of Mill Creek chert.
Priv. col., museum quality, valued $800-925.

- Holland from Brown co., IL. Blade 6 5/8 in. long, 1 7/16 in. wide, 1/4 in. thick. Excellent workmanship, superb parallel oblique flaking. Made of Kaolin chert.
Priv. col., museum quality, rare, valued $2,000-2,250.

- Holland from St. Louis co., MO. Blade 6 3/4 in. long, 2 in. wide, 1/4 in. thick. Excellent workmanship, heat treated. Made of glossy white chert.
Priv. col., museum quality, valued $1,000-1,250.

- Holland from Brown co., IL. Blade 5 1/8 in. long, 1 1/2 in. wide, 1/4 in. thick. Made of Mill Creek chert.
Priv. col., excellent quality, valued $650-800.

- Holland from Brown co., IL. Blade 5 in. long, 1 1/8 in. wide, 1/4 in. thick. Made of white pebble chert.
Priv. col., excellent quality, valued $375-450.

- Holland from Brown co., IL. Point 3 1/8 in. long, 1 1/4 in. wide, 1/4 in. thick. Made of dense white chert.
Priv. col., excellent quality, valued $385-450.

- Holland from Brown co., IL. Blade 5 1/8 in. long, 1 3/16 in. wide, 3/16 in.

thick. Made of Kaolin chert.
Priv. col., museum quality, rare, valued $1,000-1,250.

• Holland from Franklin co., IA. Blade 4 5/8 in. long, 1 3/8 in. wide, 1/4 in. thick. Made of banded chert.
Priv. col., excellent quality, valued $400-525.

• Holland from Franklin co., IA. Blade 6 in. long, 1 3/8 in. wide, 1/4 in. thick. Made of jasper.
Priv. col., museum quality, rare, valued $1,200-1,350.

• Holland from Franklin co., IA. Blade 5 3/8 in. long, 1 1/4 in. wide, 3/16 in. thick. Made of banded chert.
Priv. col., excellent quality, valued $675-850.

• Holland from Franklin co., IA. Blade 4 5/8 in. long, 1 1/8 in. wide, 1/4 in. thick. Made of white tan pebble chert.
Priv. col., excellent quality, valued $675-850.

• Holland from Mills co., IA. Point 2 7/8 in. long, 1 1/2 in. wide, 3/16 in. thick. Made of copper chert.
Priv. col., museum quality, rare, valued $850-1,150.

• Holland from Mills co., IA. Blade 4 2/3 in. long, 1 3/16 in. wide, 3/16 in. thick. Made of copper chert.
Priv. col., museum quality, rare, valued $900-1,000.

• Holland from Mills co., IA. Blade 4 5/8 in. long, 1 3/16 in. wide, 3/16 in. thick. Made of porous white chert.
Priv. col., average quality, valued $200-250.

• Holland from Massac co., IL. Blade 6 in. long, 1 3/16 in. wide, 1/3 in. thick. Excellent workmanship. Made of gray chert.
Priv. col., museum quality, valued $800-950.

• Holland from Massac co., IL. Blade 5 5/8 in. long, 1 1/2 in. wide, 1/3 in. thick. Made of grainy white chert.
Priv. col., excellent quality, valued $500-600.

• Holland from Massac co., IL. Blade 5 1/4 in. long, 1 1/8 in. wide, 1/4 in. thick. Made of white pebble chert.
Priv. col., excellent quality, valued $750-950.

- Holland from Greene co., IL. Point 2 1/8 in. long, 1 1/16 in. wide, 1/8 in. thick. Made of dense white chert.
Priv. col., excellent quality, valued $650-750.

- Holland from Greene co., IL. Blade 5 1/2 in. long, 1 5/16 in. wide, 3/16 in. thick. Made of dense glossy white chert.
Priv. col., excellent quality, valued $800-925.

- Holland from Franklin co., IL. Blade 4 3/8 in. long, 1 3/16 in. wide, 3/16 in. thick. Made of Mill Creek chert.
Priv. col., excellent quality, valued $400-525.

- Holland from Osage co., MO. Blade 6. in long, 1 3/16 in. wide, 1/4 in. thick. Made of jasper.
Priv. col., museum quality, rare, valued $1,200-1,500.

- Holland from Osage co., MO. Blade 5 3/8 in. long, 1 1/2 in. wide, 1/8 in. thick. Made of white pebble chert.
Priv. col., excellent quality, valued $650-800.

CHAPTER 9
JACK'S REEF-KNIGHT ISLAND

Jack's Reef: 1,500-800 B.P. Late Woodland to Mississippian

Jack's Reef points and blades are from the Midwest. They are small to large in size. Thin points and blades, corner notched, base convex to straight, unique and triangular. For too long Jack's Reef points and blades have not been given adequate consideration by collectors.

◆ Jack's Reef from Perry co., TN. Point 7/8 in. long, 3/8 in. wide, 3/16 in. thick. Extremely symmetrical point with nodule skin visible on stem base. Fine point for the quality of material used. Made of gray flint.

Grover Bohannon col., museum quality, valued $95-140.

◆ Jack's Reef from Lauden co., TN. Point 3/4 in. long, 3/4 in. wide, 1/8 in. thick. Wide, random flaked, converse rounded tip, slight break of straight base stem. Made of unidentified rose gray chert.

Grover Bohannon col., excellent quality, valued $65-90.

- Jack's Reef from Murphysboro co., TN. Point 1 3/16 in. long, 5/8 in. wide, 1/4 in. thick. Symmetrical, random flaked point, straight base. Several small nicks across both edges. Made of gray flint.
Grover Bohannon col., average quality, valued $35-40.

♦ Jack's Reef corner notched from southeastern AL. Point 1 1/2 in. long, 3/4 in. wide, 1/8 in. thick. Corner notched, finely worked, random flaked. Made of mauve on tan chert.

Priv. col., museum quality, valued $85-100.

- Jack's Reef corner notched from Hardin co., TN. Point 2 5/8 in. long, 5/8 in. wide, 3/16 in. thick. Symmetrical, narrow, thin point, straight base on long stem. Point displays fine serrations on both edges. Corner notches are deep and uniform. Made of gray pebble chert.
Priv. col., museum quality, valued $250-350.

- Jack's Reef corner notched from Columbus, OH. Point 1 3/8 in. long, 5/8 in. wide, 1/8 in. thick. Deep uniform corner notches, thin, fine horizontal flaked, edges sharply serrated. Upper 1/3 of point triangular and very sharp. Long point, star shaped stem and base. Made of milky white quartzite.
Priv. col., average quality, valued $25-50.

♦ Jack's Reef Pentagonal from Hamilton co., TN. Point 1 5/8 in. long, 3/4 in. wide, 1/8 in. thick. Typical of pentagonal style, symmetrical, finely serrated edges and point. Made of pink pebble chert.

Priv. col., excellent quality, valued $65-90.

- Jack's Reef Pentagonal from Columbus, OH. Point 1 1/2 in. long, 1 in. wide, 3/32 in. thick. Very symmetrical, finely serrated edges, triangular sharp upper 1/3. Made of quartzite.
Priv. col., average quality, valued $25-40.

- Jack's Reef Pentagonal from Pope co., IL. Point 3/4 in. long, 5/8 in. wide, 1/8 in. thick. Concave base with very small sides, triangular upper 2/3 quite sharp. Made of clear quartz.
Priv. col., excellent quality, valued $65-80.

- Jack's Reef from Murphysboro co., TN. Point 1 7/8 in. long, 1 in. wide, 3/16 in. thick. Thick point, very symmetrical and finely worked point. Made of Dover chert.
Grover Bohannon col., museum quality, rare, valued $285-350.

- Jack's Reef from Murphysboro co., TN. Point 1 3/4 in. long, 1 in. wide, 1/4 in. thick. Thick point, symmetrical and finely serrated, several small edge nicks. Made of Dover chert.
Grover Bohannon col., excellent quality, valued $145-185.

- Jack's Reef from Hamilton co., TN. Point 2 1/8 in. long, 1 2/3 in. wide, 1/4 in. thick. Heat treated, symmetrical, yet roughly worked point, convex base. Made of Mill Creek chert.
Grover Bohannon col., average quality, valued $55-70.

- Jack's Reef from Clark co., IL. Point 2 5/8 in. long, 1 5/16 in. wide, 3/16 in. thick. Thin, symmetrical, finely worked, sharp pointed tip, concave. Made of white pebble chert.
Priv. Col., excellent quality, valued $165-200.

- Jack's Reef from Johnson co., IL. Point 2 1/4 in. long, 1 5/16 in. wide, 1/4 in. thick. Made of gray chert.
Priv. col., excellent quality, valued $85-100.

- Jack's Reef corner notched from Johnson co., IL. Point 2 in. long, 1 in. wide, 1/4 in. thick. Made of gray chert.
Priv. col., excellent quality, valued $75-110.

- Jack's Reef corner notched from Union co., IL. Point 1 3/8 in. long, 9/16 in. wide, 3/16 in. thick. Made of Cobden chert.
Priv. col., museum quality, valued $135-200.

- Jack' Reef corner notched from Johnson co., IL. Point 2 1/4 in. long, 1 in. wide, 1/4 in. thick. Made of white pebble chert.
Priv. col., excellent quality, valued $65-80.

- Jack's Reef from Johnson co., IL. Point 2 1/2 in. long, 1 1/2 in. wide, 1/4 in. thick. Made of Mill Creek chert.

Priv. col., excellent quality, valued $75-90.

- Jack's Reef from Union co., IL. Point 1 7/8 in. long, 1 1/16 in. wide, 3/16 in. thick. Made of Cobden chert.
Priv. col., museum quality, valued $150-250.

- Jack' Reef from Johnson co., IL. Point 1 3/4 in. long, 1 5/16 in. wide, 1/4 in. thick. Made of gray chert.
Priv. col., excellent quality, valued $85-100.

- Jack's Reef from Sandusky co., OH. Point 2 1/16 in. long, 1 1/3 in. wide, 1/4 in. thick. Made of white tan chert.
Priv. col., excellent quality, valued $75-80.

- Jack's Reef from Union co., IL. Point 1 5/8 in. long, 1 1/8 in. wide, 3/16 in. thick. Made of Cobden chert.
Priv. col., museum quality, valued $200-225.

- Jack' Reef from Sandusky co., OH. Point 2 in. long, 1 7/16 in. wide, 1/4 in. thick. Made of white tan chert.
Priv. col., excellent quality, valued $85-100.

- Jack's Reef from Sandusky co., OH. Point 2 1/8 in. long, 1 2/3 in. wide, 1/4 in. thick. Made of gray chert
Priv. col., excellent quality, valued $75-110.

- Jack's Reef from Morgan co., OH. Point 1 5/8 in. long, 1 1/8 in. wide, 3/16 in. thick. Made of tan chert.
Priv. col., excellent quality, valued $200-250.

- Jack's Reef from Morgan co., OH. Point 1 3/4 in. long, 1 5/16 in. wide, 1/8 in. thick. Made of white chert.
Priv. col., excellent quality, valued $85-100.

- Jack's Reef from Morgan co., OH. Point 2 in. long, 1 13/16 in. wide, 3/16 in. thick. Made of white tan chert.
Priv. col., excellent quality, valued $75-100.

- Jack's Reef from Warren co., OH. Point 1 3/8 in. long, 1 3/16 in. wide, 3/16 in. thick. Made of gray green chert.
Priv. col., museum quality, valued $225-250.

• Jack' Reef from Warren co., OH. Point 1 3/4 in. long, 1 7/16 in. wide, 1/4 in.
thick. Made of gray green chert.
Priv. col., museum quality, valued $250-300.

• Jack's Reef from Warren co., OH. Point 2 1/3 in. long, 1 1/2 in. wide, 1/4 in.
thick. Made of porous white chert.
Priv. col., average quality, valued $25-30.

• Jack's Reef from Union co., IL. Point 2 1/8 in. long, 1 7/16 in. wide, 3/16 in.
thick. Made of quartzite.
Priv. col., poor quality, valued $10-15.

Johnson: 9,000-5,000 B.P. Early to Mid-Archaic

*Johnson points and blades are found throughout the Midwest and
Southeast. Johnsons are thick expanded stemmed points or blades,
predominantly with a concave base. Excellent workmanship is exhibited
throughout this type. Shoulders vary and may be tapered, barbed, or straight.
The usually concave bases are ground and thin.*

♦ Johnson from Cooper co., MO. Point 3/4 in. long, 5/16 in. wide, 1/8 in. thick.
Random flaked with unique convex base. Weak shoulders. Point was part of a
burial find in the early 1900s. Made of jasper.

Grover Bohannon col., excellent quality, valued $25-35.

• Johnson from Hamilton co., TN. Point 2 1/4 in. long, 1 3/8 in. wide, 5/16 in.
thick. Random flaked, unusually sharp tip for a Johnson, classical form. Made of
black flint.
Priv. col., excellent quality, valued $50-75.

• Johnson from Wabash co., IN. Blade 3 7/8 in. long, 2 1/4 in. wide, 1/4 in.
thick. Deeply concave base, classical straight shoulders. Symmetrical blade
exhibiting fine workmanship. Made of greenish white pebble chert.
Priv. col., excellent quality, valued $50-65.

• Johnson from Washington co., IN. Blade 4 3/8 in. long, 2 3/4 in. wide, 1/4 in. thick. Thin, random flaked deeply concave base, barbed shoulders. Symmetrical blade exhibiting fine workmanship. Made of white pebble chert.
Priv. col., excellent quality, valued $45-60.

• Johnson from Williamson co., IL. Blade 3 3/4 in. long, 2 in. wide, 1/4 in. thick. Random flaked, thin, concave base, straight shoulders. One edge has several nicks, long stem. Made of tan pebble chert.
Priv. col., average quality, valued $25-35.

• Johnson from Williams co., KY. Point 1 7/8 in. long, 3/4 in. wide, 1/8 in. thick. Thin, deeply concave base, classical straight shoulders, serrated edges, random flaked. Symmetrical blade, fine workmanship. Made of tan to white pebble chert.
Priv. col., excellent quality, valued $45-55.

• Johnson from Wabash co., IN. Blade 4 5/8 in. long, 2 1/2 in. wide, 1/4 in. thick. Thin, narrow, symmetrical, concave base, tapered shoulders. Made of greenish white pebble chert.
Priv. col., museum quality, valued $55-80.

• Johnson from Jackson co., IL. Point 2 1/8 in. long, 1 1/4 in. wide, 1/8 in. thick. Thin, random flaked, concave base, classical straight shoulders. Symmetrical blade exhibiting fine workmanship, slight tip break. Made of Mill Creek chert.
Tim Rubbles col., average quality, valued $20-25.

• Johnson from Bullitt co., KY. Point 2 1/3 in. long, 3/4 in. wide, 1/8 in. thick. Made of tan to white pebble chert.
Priv. col., excellent quality, valued $45-55.

• Johnson from Bullitt co., KY. Point 3 1/8 in. long, 2 in. wide, 1/4 in. thick. Made of tan white pebble chert.
Priv. col., excellent quality, valued $45-60.

• Johnson from Bullitt co., KY. Point 2 5/8 in. long, 1 1/2 in. wide, 1/8 in. thick. Made of gray chert.
Priv. col., excellent quality, valued $40-55.

• Johnson from Bullitt co., KY. Point 2 7/8 in. long, 1 2/3 in. wide, 1/8 in. thick. Made of tan to white pebble chert.
Priv. col., excellent quality, valued $45-55.

- Johnson from Adams co., IN. Blade 4 1/32 in. long, 2 1/4 in. wide, 1/4 in. thick. Made of greenish white pebble chert.
Priv. col., excellent quality, valued $50-60.

- Johnson from Jackson co., IN. Point 2 3/8 in. long, 1 1/4 in. wide, 1/8 in. thick. Made of white gray chert.
Priv. col., excellent quality, valued $40-45.

- Johnson from Miami co., IN. Point 2 7/8 in. long, 1 7/16 in. wide, 1/8 in. thick. Made of tan to mauve chert.
Priv. col., museum quality, valued $65-75.

- Johnson from Miami co., IN. Blade 4 5/8 in. long, 2 1/2 in. wide, 1/4 in. thick. Made of greenish white chert.
Priv. col., museum quality, valued $70-80.

- Johnson from Miami co., IN. Point 2 1/3 in. long, 1 5/16 in. wide, 1/8 in. thick. Made of mauve chert.
Priv. col., museum quality, valued $80-85.

- Johnson from Miami co., IN. Point 3 1/16 in. long, 2 in. wide, 1/8 in. thick. Made of tan to white pebble chert.
Priv. col., excellent quality, valued $45-55.

- Johnson from Steuben co., IN. Blade 3 7/8 in. long, 1 2/3 in. wide, 1/4 in. thick. Made of white pebble chert.
Priv. col., excellent quality, valued $55-60.

- Johnson from Steuben co., IN. Point 2 1/3 in. long, 1 1/2 in. wide, 1/8 in. thick. Made of gray chert.
Priv. col., average quality, valued $20-25.

- Johnson from Orange co., IN. Point 2 7/16 in. long, 1 3/4 in. wide, 1/8 in. thick. Made of tan to white pebble chert.
Priv. col., excellent quality, valued $45-55.

- Johnson from Orange co., IN. Point 3 1/8 in. long, 2 1/16 in. wide, 1/4 in. thick. Made of banded tan chert.
Priv. col., museum quality, valued $65-80.

- Johnson from Orange co., IN. Point 2 1/8 in. long, 1 1/3 in. wide, 1/8 in. thick. Heat treated. Made of banded tan chert.

Priv. col., museum quality, valued $70-85.

• Johnson from Orange co., IN. Point 2 7/32 in. long, 1 13/16 in. wide, 1/8 in. thick. Made of white pebble chert.
Priv. col., excellent quality, valued $45-55.

• Johnson from Posey co., IN. Blade 2 7/8 in. long, 2 1/32 in. wide, 1/4 in. thick. Made of greenish gray chert.
Priv. col., museum quality, valued $65-80.

• Johnson from Posey co., IN. Point 2 11/32 in. long, 1 1/4 in. wide, 1/8 in. thick. Made of gray white pebble chert.
Priv. col., average quality, valued $20-25.

• Johnson from Martin co., IN. Point 2 7/8 in. long, 3/4 in. wide, 1/8 in. thick. Point has been reworked, left hand beveled. Made of tan to white pebble chert.
Priv. col., excellent quality, valued $45-55.

• Johnson from Wabash co., IN. Point 2 5/8 in. long, 1 3/16 in. wide, 1/4 in. thick. Made of greenish white pebble chert.
Priv. col., museum quality, valued $55-65.

• Johnson from Jackson co., IL. Point 3 1/8 in. long, 1 1/3 in. wide, 1/8 in. thick. Slight tip break. Made of Mill Creek chert.
Priv col., average quality, valued $20-25.

• Johnson from Wabash co., IN. Point 2 7/8 in. long, 1 3/4 in. wide, 1/8 in. thick. Made of tan to white pebble chert.
Priv. col., excellent quality, valued $45-55.

• Johnson from Wabash co., IN. Point 2 5/8 in. long, 1 1/2 in. wide, 1/4 in. thick. Made of green gray chert.
Priv. col., museum quality, valued $55-70.

• Johnson from Jackson co., IN. Point 2 1/3 in. long, 1 1/2 in. wide, 1/8 in. thick. Made of yellow tan pebble chert.
Priv. col., average quality, valued $20-25.

Jude: 9,000-6,000 B.P. Early Arachic

Predominantly a southeastern point. Small, convex to straight edges, barbed, expanded, to parallel stem. The stem is generally as large or

larger than the point. Bases are concave, straight, bifurcated, or convex.
Shoulders are tapered, barbed, or square. Some points may have beveled edges
on one side of each face.

♦ Jude from central KY. Point 1 1/4 in. long, 1 1/8 in. wide, 3/16 in. thick.
Wide yet symmetrical point, heat treated, beveled on one edge of each face.
Believed made of Charter Cave flint.

Priv. col, museum quality, valued $40-60.

• Jude from Pulaski co., KY. Point 1 1/2 in. long, 1/3/8 in. wide, 1/4 in. thick.
Wide, thick point, concave base with long parallel tangs. Right side beveled,
very sharp. Made of tan pebble chert.
Priv. col., museum quality, valued $55-80.

• Jude from Hamilton co., TN. Point 1 1/8 in. long, 1 3/16 in. wide, 3/16 in.
thick. Point wider than long, beveled on one side of each face. Serrated point
with rounded tip and concave bifurcated stem. Made of Dover chert.
Priv. col., museum quality, valued $80-100.

• Jude from Murphysboro co., TN. Point 1 2/3 in. long, 1 1/2 in. wide, 3/16 in.
thick. Typically wide Jude, beveled and serrated on one side of each face. Very
sharp tip with thin, bifurcated stem. Made of pinkish pebble chert.
Priv. col., excellent quality, valued $35-50.

• Jude from Jasper co., IL. Point 2 in. long, 1 5/8 in. wide, 1/4 in. thick.
Symmetrical thick point, beveled on one side of each face. Concave base with
uniquely short stem. Made of pinkish chert.
Priv. col., excellent quality, valued $35-50.

• Jude from Cooper co., MO. Point 1 7/8 in. long, 1 5/8 in. wide, 1/8 in. thick.
Thin, heat treated symmetrical point, beveled on one side of each face, concave
base. Made of unidentified local white chert.
Priv. col., excellent quality, valued $40-60.

• Jude from Jackson co., IL. Point 2 3/32 in. long, 1 3/8 in. wide, 1/4 in. thick.

Symmetrical, very narrow, yet thick point, beveled on one side of each face, concave base. Made of Cobden chert.
Priv. col., excellent quality, valued $50-65.

- Jude from Jasper co., IL. Point 1 1/2 in. long, 1 1/8 in. wide, 1/4 in. thick. Thick point, beveled on one side of each face. Concave base with typical long stem. Made of greenish pebble chert.
Priv. col., excellent quality, valued $45-60.

- Jude from Alexander co., IL. Point 2 1/32 in. long, 1 2/3 in. wide, 1/4 in. thick. Symmetrical point, random flaked, beveled on one side of each face. Concave base, bordering on crude workmanship, with short stem. Made of Mill Creek chert.
Priv. col., average quality, valued $20-30.

- Jude from Alexander co., IL. Point 1 1/2 in. long, 1 1/8 in. wide, 1/4 in. thick. Made of Mill Creek chert.
Priv. col., excellent quality, valued $35-50.

- Jude from Cape Giradeau co., MO. Point 1 5/8 in. long, 1 1/32 in. wide, 1/8 in. thick. Made of local white chert.
Priv. col., excellent quality, valued $40-60.

- Jude from Cape Giradeau co., MO. Point 2 13/32 in. long, 1 1/8 in. wide, 1/8 in. thick. Made of local white chert.
Priv. col., excellent quality, valued $50-65.

- Jude from Cape Giradeau co., MO. Point 1 1/3 in. long, 1 in. wide, 1/4 in. thick. Made of white chert.
Priv. col., excellent quality, valued $45-60.

- Jude from Randoulph co., MO. Point 2 7/32 in. long, 1 3/8 in. wide, 3/16 in. thick. Made of pinkish chert.
Priv. col., excellent quality, valued $50-60.

- Jude from Johnson co., IL. Point 1 1/2 in. long, 1 5/8 in. wide, 1/4 in. thick. Symmetrical thick point, wider than it is long. Beveled on one side of each face. Concave base with typically long stem. Made of Mill Creek chert.
Priv. col., average quality, valued $25-30.

- Jude from Jasper co., IL. Point 2 in. long, 1 1/8 in. wide, 1/8 in. thick. Symmetrical, thin and narrow point, beveled on one side of each face. Concave base with bifurcated short stem. Made of local greenish pebble chert.

Priv. col., museum quality, valued $40-50.

- Jude from Jasper co., IL. Point 1 7/8 in. long, 1 3/8 in. wide, 1/4 in. thick. Made of tan white chert.
Priv. col., excellent quality, valued $35-50.

- Jude from Stoddard co., MO. Point 1 7/8 in. long, 1 5/16 in. wide, 1/8 in. thick. Made of pink white speckled chert.
Priv. col., excellent quality, valued $40-60.

- Jude from Stoddard co., MO. Point 1 31/32 in. long, 1 3/8 in. wide, 3/8 in. thick. Heat treated. Made of quartzite.
Priv. col., average quality, valued $15-25.

- Jude from Stoddard co., MO. Point 1 1/2 in. long, 7/8 in. wide, 3/16 in. thick. Made of greenish gray chert.
Priv. col., excellent quality, valued $45-60.

- Jude from Stoddard co., MO. Point 1 3/32 in. long, 3/4 in. wide, 1/4 in. thick. Made of porous pinkish chert.
Priv. col., average quality, valued $20-30.

- Jude from Clay co., MO. Point 1 1/3 in. long, 7/8 in. wide, 1/4 in. thick. Made of quartzite.
Priv. col., average quality, valued $25-30.

- Jude from Clay co., MO. Point 1 2/3 in. long, 1 1/8 in. wide, 1/8 in. thick. Made of gray pebble chert.
Priv. col., excellent quality, valued $35-45.

- Jude from Hamilton co., IL. Point 2 in. long, 1 1/32 in. wide, 1/4 in. thick. Made of gray chert.
Priv. col., excellent quality, valued $35-40.

- Jude from Hamilton co., IL. Point 1 5/8 in. long, 1 in. wide, 1/8 in. thick. Made of white chert.
Priv. col., excellent quality, valued $40-45.

- Jude from Hamilton co., IL. Point 1 17/32 in. long, 1 1/8 in. wide, 1/4 in. thick. Made of Cobden chert.
Priv. col., excellent quality, valued $50-65.

Priv. col., excellent quality, valued $30-40.

- Jude from White co., IL. Point 1 1/2 in. long, 1 3/8 in. wide, 1/4 in. thick. Small repaired tip break. Made of tan pebble chert. *Priv. col., average quality, valued $25-30.*

- Jude from Gallatin co., IL. Point 1 2/3 in. long, 1 1/8 in. wide, 1/8 in. thick. Made of gray chert. *Priv. col., excellent quality, valued $45-50.*

- Jude from Gallatin co., IL. Point 2 in. long, 1 1/8 in. wide, 1/4 in. thick. Made of gray chert. *Priv. col., excellent quality, valued $35-50.*

- Jude from Gallatin co., IL. Point 1 3/8 in. long, 1 5/8 in. wide, 1/8 in. thick. Made of local gray chert. *Priv. col., excellent quality, valued $40-60.*

- Jude from Gallatin co., IL. Point 2 in. long, 1 3/8 in. wide, 1/4 in. thick. Made of gray chert. *Priv. col., excellent quality, valued $50-55.*

- Jude from Hardin co., IL. Point 1 3/8 in. long, 1 1/8 in. wide, 1/4 in. thick. Made of gray chert. *Priv. col., excellent quality, valued $45-60.*

- Jude from Hardin co., IL. Point 2 1/32 in. long, 1 1/3 in. wide, 1/4 in. thick. Made of gray chert. *Priv. col., excellent quality, valued $40-50.*

- Jude from Hardin co., IL. Point 1 1/2 in. long, 1 7/8 in. wide, 1/4 in. thick. Heat treated. Made of Mill Creek chert. *Priv. col., excellent quality, valued $35-40.*

- Jude from Hardin co., IL. Point 1 1/2 in. long, 1 1/16 in. wide, 1/8 in. thick. Made of white chert. *Priv. col., average quality, valued $12-20.*

- Jude from Hardin co., IL. Point 2 1/8 in. long, 1 5/8 in. wide, 1/4 in. thick. Made of gray chert. *Priv. col., excellent quality, valued $35-50.*

- Jude from Jackson co., IL. Point 1 2/3 in. long, 1 1/8 in. wide, 1/4 in. thick.
Made of Cobden chert.
Priv. col., excellent quality, valued $45-60.

- Jude from Jackson co., IL. Point 1 21/32 in. long, 1 1/3 in. wide, 1/4 in. thick.
Made of Mill Creek chert.
Priv. col., average quality, valued $20-30.

- Jude from Johnson co., IL. Point 1 1/2 in. long, 1 5/8 in. wide, 1/4 in. thick.
Made of Mill Creek chert.
Priv. col., average quality, valued $25-30.

- Jude from Jasper co., IL. Point 1 2/3 in. long, 1 1/8 in. wide, 1/8 in. thick.
Made of greenish white chert.
Priv. col., excellent quality, valued $35-40.

Kays: 5,000-2,000 B.P. Mid-Archaic to Woodland

*Kays are southeastern points or blades medium to large in size.
Narrow point or blade, stem sides parallel. The shoulders are tapered to square.*

◆ Kays from Hamilton co., TN. Point 2 7/16 in. long, 1 1/32 in. wide, 3/16 in.
thick. Square shoulders, straight base, narrow, symmetrical and finely serrated.
Made of quartzite.

Grover Bohannon col., excellent quality, valued $10-15.

- Kays from Murphysboro co., TN. Point 2 in. long, 1 5/32 in. wide, 3/16 in.
thick. Square shoulders, straight base, wide yet symmetrical, finely serrated
edges. Made of Dover chert.
Priv. col., museum quality, valued $30-40.

- Kays from Hamilton co., TN. Point 2 3/16 in. long, 1 3/32 in. wide, 5/16 in. thick. Square shoulders, straight base, thick, random flaked, narrow, finely serrated. Made of Dover chert.
Priv. col., museum quality, valued, $35-50.

- Kays from Hamilton co., TN. Point 1 11/16 in. long, 1 5/32 in. wide, 1/8 in. thick. Thin point, square shoulders, straight base, symmetrical and finely serrated. Made of Dover chert.
Grover Bohannon col., excellent quality, valued $25-35.

- Kays from Stewart co., TN. Point 1 7/16 in. long, 11/32 in. wide, 3/16 in. thick. Fine workmanship, heat treated, square shoulders, straight base, narrow, symmetrical, finely serrated. Made of gray pebble chert.
Priv. col., excellent quality, valued $35-45.

◆ Kays from Hamilton co., TN. Blade 3 7/8 in. long, 1 3/16 in. wide, 1/4 in. thick. Symmetrical, thin, finely serrated edges, typically narrow. Square shoulders with straight base. Made of Dover chert.

Grover Bohannon col., museum quality, valued $65-80.

- Kays from Hamilton co., TN. Blade 4 5/8 in. long, 1 13/16 in. wide, 1/4 in. thick. Thin, symmetrical, excellent workmanship, quite large, finely and sharply serrated edges, narrow. Square shoulders, straight base. Made of Dover chert.
Priv. col., museum quality, rare, valued $85-100.

- Kays from southeastern TN. Blade 3 5/8 in. long, 1 7/16 in. wide, 3/16 in. thick. Thin, narrow, finely serrated edges, sharp point tip. Square shoulders with wide, parallel straight base. Made of dark gray pebble chert.
Priv. col., excellent quality, valued $35-45.

- Kays from Hamilton co., TN. Blade 4 1/8 in. long, 1 5/16 in. wide, 1/4 in. thick. Symmetrical, narrow, thin, heat treated, finely serrated, slight tip break. Tapered shoulders with straight base. Made of Dover chert.
Priv. col., average quality, valued $15-25.

• Kays from Murphysboro co., TN. Blade 4 7/8 in. long, 2 3/16 in. wide, 1/4 in. thick. Symmetrical, very thin, sharply and finely serrated edges, typically narrow. Tapered shoulders, straight base. Made of tan pebble chert. *Priv. col., excellent quality, valued $35-45.*

• Kays from Hamilton co., TN. Blade 3 3/4 in. long, 1 3/16 in. wide, 3/8 in. thick. Symmetrical, heat treated, finely serrated edges, narrow, very sharp tip. Square shoulders with straight base. Made of white pebble chert. *Grover Bohannon col., excellent quality, valued $30-45.*

• Kays from Murphysboro co., TN. Point 2 in. long, 1 5/32 in. wide, 3/16 in. thick. Square shoulders, straight base, wide yet symmetrical, finely serrated edges. Made of Dover chert. *Priv. col., museum quality, valued $30-40.*

• Kays from Hamilton co., TN. Point 2 3/16 in. long, 1 3/32 in. wide, 5/16 in. thick. Square shoulders, straight base, thick, random flaked, narrow, finely serrated. Made of Dover chert. *Priv. col., museum quality, valued, $35-50.*

• Kays from Hamilton co., TN. Blade 4 1/16 in. long, 1 2/3 in. wide, 1/8 in. thick. Made of Dover chert. *Priv. col., museum quality, valued $55-65.*

• Kays from Hamilton co., TN. Point 2 11/16 in. long, 1 1/32 in. wide, 3/16 in. thick. Made of Dover chert. *Priv. col., museum quality, valued $45-55.*

• Kays from Hamilton co., TN. Blade 4 3/8 in. long, 1 5/16 in. wide, 1/4 in. thick. Made of Dover chert. *Priv. col., museum quality, valued $65-80.*

• Kays from Calhoun co., AR. Blade 4 in. long, 1 15/32 in. wide, 3/16 in. thick. Made of Arkansas brown chert. *Priv. col., museum quality, valued $30-40.*

• Kays from Drew co., AR. Blade 3 13/16 in. long, 1 in. wide, 5/16 in. thick. Made of gray flint. *Priv. col., average quality, valued, $15-20.*

• Kays from Drew co., AR. Point 2 1/16 in. long, 1 5/8 in. wide, 1/8 in. thick. Made of gray flint. *Priv. col., excellent quality, valued $25-35.*

- Kays from Drew co., AR. Point 3 5/16 in. long, 1 1/3 in. wide, 3/16 in. thick. Made of gray pebble chert.
Priv. col., excellent quality, valued $35-45.

- Kays from Drew co., AR. Blade 4 1/8 in. long, 1 7/16 in. wide, 1/4 in. thick. Made of white tan chert.
Priv. col., excellent quality, valued $35-45.

- Kays from Murphysboro co., TN. Point 2 9/16 in. long, 1 1/2 in. wide, 3/16 in. thick. Made of gray chert.
Priv. col., excellent quality, valued $30-40.

- Kays from Murphysboro co., TN. Point 2 3/16 in. long, 1 in. wide, 5/16 in. thick. Made of tan chert.
Priv. col., average quality, valued $15-20.

- Kays from Murphysboro co., TN. Point 3 1/32 in. long, 1 7/32 in. wide, 1/8 in. thick. Made of gray black speckled chert.
Priv. col., excellent quality, valued $35-45.

- Kays from Stewart co., TN. Blade 3 7/16 in. long, 1 5/32 in. wide, 3/16 in. thick. Made of gray pink pebble chert.
Priv. col., excellent quality, valued $35-45.

- Kays from Stewart co., TN. Blade 3 7/8 in. long, 1 9/16 in. wide, 1/4 in. thick. Made of pinkish chert.
Priv. col., excellent quality, valued $40-45.

- Kays from Stewart co., TN. Point 2 3/8 in. long, 1 5/16 in. wide, 3/16 in. thick. Made of Dover chert.
Priv. col., museum quality, valued $30-40.

- Kays from Howell co., MO. Point 2 13/16 in. long, 1 1/32 in. wide, 3/16 in. thick. Made of white chert.
Priv. col., excellent quality, valued $35-50.

- Kays from Howell co., MO. Point 2 11/16 in. long, 1 1/8 in. wide, 1/8 in. thick. Made of white chert.
Priv. col., excellent quality, valued $25-35.

- Kays from Howell co., MO. Point 2 1/2 in. long, 1 1/32 in. wide, 3/16 in. thick. Made of gray tan pebble chert.

Priv. col., excellent quality, valued $35-45.

• Kays from Hamilton co., KY. Blade 3 7/8 in. long, 1 1/2 in. wide, 1/4 in. thick. Made of tan to white chert.
Priv. col., excellent quality, valued $40-45.

Kent: 4,000-1,000 B.P. Mid-Archaic to Woodland

Found in the midwestern United States. A medium to large sized point or blade. Somewhat narrow points or blades, stems parallel sided. Shoulders are distinct and tapered to squared. The base is generally straight.

◆ Kent from Knoxville co., TN. Point is 1/2 in. long, 1/4 in. wide, 3/16 in. thick. Beveled prestige or burial point atypical size. Square shoulders and straight base. Made of dark gray, pink speckled pebble chert.

Grover Bohannon col., excellent quality, rare, valued $45-65.

• Kent from Knoxville co., TN. Point 2 1/2 in. long, 1 1/4 in. wide, 3/16 in. thick. Beveled, thin, symmetrical, sharp. Tapered shoulders and straight base. Made of gray pebble chert.
Priv. col., excellent quality, valued $40-50.

• Kent from Hamilton co., TN. Point 1 7/8 in. long, 1 3/16 in. wide, 3/8 in. thick. Beveled, thick, square shoulders and straight base. Made of pink on tan pebble chert.
Priv. col., excellent quality, valued $35-45.

• Kent from Ohio co., IN. Point 2 7/8 in. long, 1 3/8 in. wide, 1/4 in. thick. Symmetrical point with fine parallel flaking, concave base. Made of tan pebble chert.
Priv. col., museum quality, valued $60-90.

• Kent from northeastern Arkansas. Blade 3 1/4 in. long, 1 1/4 in. wide, 1/4 in. thick. Parallel flaked blade, long tangs, deep concave base. Made of banded

gray chert.
Grover Bohannon col., museum quality., valued $55-85.

• Kent from Lauden co., TN. Blade 3 5/8 in. long, 1 5/8 in. wide, 5/16 in. thick.
Symmetrical blade, sharp rounded tip, parallel flaked with sharp serrated edges.
Base is thinned and concave. Made of Dover chert.
Priv. col., museum quality, valued $50-85.

• Kent from Jasper co., IL. Blade 3 7/8 in. long, 1 7/8 in. wide, 1/4 in. thick.
Symmetrical blade, thin, parallel flaking, concave base. Made of greenish pebble
chert.
Priv. col., excellent quality, valued $45-65.

• Kent from Ohio co., IN. Blade 4 1/4 in. long, 2 3/8 in. wide, 5/16 in. thick.
Symmetrical blade, very sharp edges, fine parallel flaking, concave base. Made
of tan pebble chert.
Priv. col., excellent quality, valued $50-70.

• Kent from Wabash co., IN. Blade 4 1/8 in. long, 2 1/8 in. wide, 1/4 in. thick.
Symmetrical, thin, fine parallel flaking. Heat treated, long tanged blade, concave
base. Made of greenish pebble chert.
Priv. col., excellent quality, valued $45-60.

• Kent from Ohio co., IN. Blade 3 5/8 in. long, 1 7/8 in. wide, 11/32 in. thick.
Symmetrical, edges serrated, random flaking, concave base. Made of tan pebble
chert.
Priv. col., average quality, valued $30-40.

• Kent from Hardin co., IN. Point 3 7/8 in. long, 1 5/8 in. wide, 1/4 in. thick.
Symmetrical blade, heat treated, with fine parallel flaking, concave base. Made
of Mill Creek chert.
Priv. col., excellent quality, valued $45-60.

• Kent from Graves co., KY. Point 2 2/3 in. long, 1 1/4 in. wide, 3/16 in. thick.
Made of gray green pebble chert.
Priv. col., excellent quality, valued $40-50.

• Kent from Graves co., KY. Point 2 7/8 in. long, 1 3/4 in. wide, 3/8 in. thick.
Made of tan pebble chert.
Priv. col., average quality, valued $15-25.

• Kent from Graves co., KY. Point 2 5/8 in. long, 1 1/4 in. wide, 1/4 in. thick.
Made of tan pebble chert.

Priv. col., excellent quality, valued $30-35.

• Kent from Graves co., KY. Blade 3 3/4 in. long, 1 3/4 in. wide, 1/4 in. thick. Made of quartzite.
Priv. col., average quality, valued $5-15.

• Kent from Graves co., KY. Blade 3 5/8 in. long, 2 in. wide, 7/16 in. thick. Made of quartzite.
Priv. col., average quality, valued $10-15.

• Kent from Graves co., KY. Point 2 1/3 in. long, 1 1/2 in. wide, 3/16 in. thick. Made of quartzite.
Priv. col., average quality, valued $10-15.

• Kent from Lawrence co., KY. Blade 3 1/2 in. long, 1 1/4 in. wide, 1/4 in. thick. Made of white pebble chert.
Priv. col., excellent quality, valued $15-25.

• Kent from Lawrence co., KY. Blade 3 7/8 in. long, 1 2/3 in. wide, 5/16 in. thick. Made of gray pebble chert.
Priv. col., excellent quality, valued $20-30.

Kinney: 5,000-2,000 B.P. Mid-Archaic

Kinney is predominantly a midwestern point or blade medium to large in size. They are thin, triangular, with concave to straight edges. The base is usually concave.

◆ Kinney from Hamilton co., TN. Point 2 1/2 in. long, 1 1/2 in. wide, 1/4 in. thick. Upper two-thirds of point finely and sharply serrated, concave base. Made of quartzite.

Grover Bohannon col., average quality, valued $25-40.

• Kinney from Alexander co., IL. Point 2 3/8 in. long, 1 3/4 in. wide, 1/4 in.

thick. Entire point edges finely serrated. Symmetrically triangular though wide, straight edges with concave base. Made of Mill Creek chert.
Priv. col., museum quality, valued $65-80.

- Kinney from Alexander co., IL. Point 2 5/8 in. long, 1 1/2 in. wide, 1/4 in. thick. Heat treated, finely serrated. Symmetrically triangular, straight edges with concave base. Made of Mill Creek chert.
Tim Rublles col., excellent quality, $50-65.

- Kinney from Alexander co., IL. Blade 3 7/8 in. long, 2 1/4 in. wide, 1/4 in. thick. Thin, triangular, edges sharply serrated. Symmetrical, only slightly concave base, near straight. Made of Mill Creek chert.
Priv. col., excellent quality, valued $45-60.

- Kinney from Gallatin co., IL. Point 2 1/8 in. long, 1 5/16 in. wide, 1/4 in. thick. Point edges finely and sharply serrated. Symmetrical, straight edges with concave base. Made of Kaolin chert.
Priv. col., museum quality, rare, valued $85-110.

- Kinney from Johnson co., IL. Point 1 5/8 in. long, 1 1/4 in. wide, 7/16 in. thick. Thick point, edges roughly and crudely serrated. Straight edges, tip heat treated, with concave base. Made of gray pebble chert.
Priv. col., average quality, valued $20-30.

- Kinney from Alexander co., IL. Blade 4 3/8 in. long, 3 3/4 in. wide, 1/4 in. thick. Very thin, convex edges, finely serrated. Symmetrical though wide, heat treated, concave base. Made of Mill Creek chert.
Priv. col., excellent quality, valued $65-85.

- Kinney from Alexander co., IL. Blade 5 1/8 in. long, 3 1/32 in. wide, 1/4 in. thick. Made of Mill Creek chert.
Priv. col., excellent quality, valued $250-350.

- Kinney from Carlise co., KY. Point 2 7/8 in. long, 1 1/2 in. wide, 1/4 in. thick. Made of tan chert.
Priv. col., excellent quality, valued $85-100.

- Kinney from Carlise co., KY. Point 3 5/8 in. long, 1 3/4 in. wide, 7/16 in. thick. Made of yellow gray chert.
Priv. col., average quality, valued $20-30.

- Kinney from Carlise co., KY. Blade 4 7/8 in. long, 2 1/4 in. wide, 1/4 in.

thick. Made of tan chert.
Priv. col., excellent quality, valued $145-180.

- Kinney from Carlise co., KY. Point 2 5/8 in. long, 1 3/16 in. wide, 1/4 in. thick. Made of tan white chert.
Priv. col., excellent quality, valued $85-120.

- Kinney from Carlise co., KY. Point 3 1/8 in. long, 1 1/3 in. wide, 3/16 in. thick. Made of gray pebble chert.
Priv. col., excellent quality, valued $100-130.

- Kinney from Carlise co., KY. Blade 4 1/8 in. long, 2 in. wide, 1/4 in. thick. Made of porous white chert.
Priv. col., average quality, valued $15-30.

- Kinney from Harrison co., KY. Point 3 in. long, 1 9/16 in. wide, 1/4 in. thick. Made of Kaolin chert.
Priv. col., museum quality, rare, valued $185-200.

- Kinney from Harrison co., KY. Point 2 5/32 in. long, 1 1/4 in. wide, 3/16 in. thick. Made of banded gray pebble chert.
Priv. col., museum quality, valued $120-180.

- Kinney from Harrison co., KY. Blade 5 7/8 in. long, 2 1/4 in. wide, 1/4 in. thick. Made of banded golden brown white chert.
Priv. col., museum quality, valued $450-600.

- Kinney from Texas co., OK. Point 2 1/8 in. long, 1 1/16 in. wide, 3/16 in. thick. Made of dull gray flint.
Priv. col., excellent quality, valued $85-120.

- Kinney from Texas co., OK. Point 1 7/8 in. long, 1 in. wide, 3/16 in. thick. Made of silver gray flint.
Priv. col., average quality, valued $20-30.

- Kinney from Texas co., OK. Blade 4 1/8 in. long, 2 1/16 in. wide, 1/4 in. thick. Made of gray chert.
Priv. col., excellent quality, valued $45-60.

- Kinney from Texas co., OK. Point 2 7/8 in. long, 1 5/16 in. wide, 3/16 in. thick. Made of black flint.
Priv. col., museum quality, valued $65-80.

- Kinney from Lore co., OK. Point 1 7/8 in. long, 1 1/4 in. wide, 7/16 in. thick. Made of gray pebble chert.
Priv. col., average quality, valued $20-30.

- Kinney from Lore co., OK. Blade 5 in. long, 2 1/3 in. wide, 1/4 in. thick. Made of dull gray flint.
Priv. col., excellent quality, valued $85-120.

- Kinney from Sabine co., TX. Point 2 1/2 in. long, 1 1/3 in. wide, 1/4 in. thick. Made of banded pink chert.
Priv. col., museum quality, rare, valued $100-120.

- Kinney from Sabine co., TX. Point 3 1/32 in. long, 1 1/4 in. wide, 3/16 in. thick. Made of gray pebble chert.
Priv. col., average quality, valued $30-40.

- Kinney from Sabine co., TX. Blade 4 3/8 in. long, 2 1/4 in. wide, 1/4 in. thick. Made of yellow gray chert.
Priv. col., excellent quality, valued $125-160.

- Kinney from Sabine co., TX. Point 2 5/8 in. long, 1 1/2 in. wide, 1/4 in. thick. Made of glossy gray chert.
Priv. col., excellent quality, valued $75-80.

- Kinney from Sabine co., TX. Point 2 1/3 in. long, 1 1/4 in. wide, 5/16 in. thick. Made of gray pebble chert.
Juan Samudio col., excellent quality, valued $65-80.

- Kinney from Hartley co., TX. Blade 4 1/2 in. long, 2 1/16 in. wide, 1/4 in. thick. Made of muti-toned tan chert.
Priv. col., excellent quality, valued $50-70.

- Kinney from Hartley co., TX. Point 2 7/8 in. long, 1 9/16 in. wide, 1/4 in. thick. Excellent workmanship. Made of agate.
Priv. col., museum quality, rare, valued $150-180.

- Kinney from Hartley co., TX. Point 2 5/8 in. long, 1 1/3 in. wide, 3/16 in. thick. Made of gray pebble chert.
Priv. col., average quality, valued $20-25.

- Kinney from Elmore co., ID. Blade 4 3/8 in. long, 2 1/32 in. wide, 1/4 in. thick. Made of banded brown white chert.

Priv. col., excellent quality, valued $125-160.

• Kinney from Elmore co., ID. Blade 5 1/8 in. long, 1 1/3 in. wide, 1/4 in. thick. Excellent workmanship, edges finely and sharply serrated, needle sharp tip. Symmetrical, straight edges with concave base. Made of obsidian. *Priv. col., museum quality, rare, valued $600-850.*

• Kinney from Madison co., ID. Point 1 7/8 in. long, 1 1/2 in. wide, 7/16 in. thick. Rounded convex sides. Made of translucent gray chert. *Priv. col., museum quality, valued $80-120.*

• Kinney from Madison co., ID. Blade 4 3/8 in. long, 2 1/3 in. wide, 1/4 in. thick. Made of white pink chert. *Priv. col., excellent quality, valued $65-80.*

• Kinney from Madison co., ID. Point 2 1/3 in. long, 1 1/2 in. wide, 1/4 in. thick. Made of quartzite. *Priv. col., average quality, valued $15-20.*

• Kinney from Pratt co., KS. Point 2 5/8 in. long, 1 1/2 in. wide, 5/16 in. thick. Made of gray pebble chert. *Priv. col., excellent quality, valued $60-70.*

• Kinney from Pratt co., KS. Blade 3 7/8 in. long, 2 1/2 in. wide, 1/4 in. thick. Made of oily dense white chert. *Priv. col., excellent quality, valued $100-125.*

• Kinney from Pratt co., KS. Point 2 7/32 in. long, 1 7/16 in. wide, 1/4 in. thick. Made of translucent tan chert. *Priv. col., museum quality, rare, valued $95-130.*

• Kinney from Pratt co., KS. Point 1 5/8 in. long, 1 1/4 in. wide, 3/16 in. thick. Fine workmanship, heat treated tip. Made of gray pebble chert. *Priv. col., excellent quality, valued $45-65.*

• Kinney from Pratt co., KS. Blade 3 7/8 in. long, 3 in. wide, 1/4 in. thick. Made of tan white chert. *Priv. col., excellent quality, valued $55-60.*

• Kinney from Pratt co., KS. Point 3 1/8 in. long, 1 15/16 in. wide, 5/32 in. thick. Heat treated tip. Made of golden white marbled chert. *Priv. col., museum quality, rare, valued $100-140.*

- Kinney from Barber co., KS. Point 2 5/16 in. long, 1 1/4 in. wide, 3/16 in. thick. Made of gray pebble chert.
Priv. col., museum quality, valued $65-75.

- Kinney from Barber co., KS. Blade 4 7/8 in. long, 2 1/2 in. wide, 1/4 in. thick. Made of tan chert.
Priv. col., excellent quality, valued $60-70.

- Kinney from Elk co., KS. Point 2 1/3 in. long, 1 1/4 in. wide, 1/4 in. thick. Made of porous white pink chert.
Priv. col., average quality, valued $25-30.

- Kinney from Comanche co., TX. Point 3 1/8 in. long, 1 1/4 in. wide, 7/16 in. thick. Poor workmanship. Made of quartzite.
Priv. col, average quality, valued $20-25.

Kirk: 9,500-5,500 B.P. Early to Mid-Archaic

Kirk is a medium to large point or blade found in the East and Southeast. The two recognized categories are Kirk Corner-notched and Kirk Serrated.

Kirk Corner-notched displays convex or recurved edges, many examples are highly and sharply serrated. They are beveled on one side of each edge of each face, the point or blade is deeply corner notched. The base is straight, auriculate, convex, and concave.

Kirk Serrated are recognized by their barbs, stem, deep notches, and fine, wide, thin serrations. The stem is parallel to expanding, beveled on opposing faces. The base is convex, straight, or concave.

◆ Kirk Corner-notched from Calloway co., KY. Blade 4 1/4 in. long, 2 in. wide, 1/4 in. thick. Very symmetrical blade with classic corner-notch designs, corner notch 1/2 in. deep. Made of Dover chert.

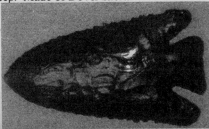

David Zinkie col., museum quality, valued $700-800.

- Kirk Corner-notched from Alexander co., IL. Blade 3 3/4 in. long, 1 5/8 in. wide, 1/4 in. thick. Deeply notched, short convex based stem, finely serrated, tip very sharp. Made of Kaolin chert.
Priv. col., museum quality, rare, valued $1,650-2,100.

- Kirk Corner-notched from Alexander co., IL. Blade 4 1/4 in. long, 1 7/8 in. wide, 1/4 in. thick. Deeply notched, thin, sharply serrated, heat treated. Convex base, pointed tip, very sharp. Made of Mill Creek chert.
Priv. col., excellent quality, valued $200-300.

- Kirk Corner-notched from Jackson co., IL. Blade 3 13/16 in. long, 1 3/8 in. wide, 7/16 in. thick. Thick though finely worked, very deep corner-notched, short stem. Finely serrated, one edge on each face beveled. Made of Cobden chert.
Tim Rubbles col., excellent quality, valued $450-600.

- Kirk Corner-notched from Sangamon co., IL. Blade 4 3/4 in. long, 2 3/8 in. wide, 1/4 in. thick. Deeply notched, thin, fine workmanship, beveled on one edge of each face. Finely and sharply serrated, tip rounded, but very sharp. Made of white to gray chert.
Priv. col., museum quality, valued $1,200-1,500.

- Kirk Corner-notched from Union co., IL. Blade 4 5/8 in. long, 2 in. wide, 1/4 in. thick. Blade is steeply beveled on one side of each face, edges are finely serrated. Stem is long and straight based. Made of Cobden Hornstone chert.
Priv. col., museum quality, rare, valued $950-1,250.

- Kirk Corner-notched from central TN. Blade 4 1/16 in. long, 1 7/8 in. wide, 3/16 in. thick. Blade beveled on one edge of each face, deeply notched, fine sharp serrations. Long serrated, sharp, pointed tangs, convex base. Made of Dover chert.
Priv. col., excellent quality, valued $300-450.

- Kirk Corner-notched from Williamson co., IL. Point 2 3/8 in. long, 1 in. wide, 3/16 in. thick. Point finely serrated and beveled on one edge of each face. Short stem with straight base. Made of Cobden chert.
Priv. col., museum quality, valued $200-250.

- Kirk Corner-notched from Marion co., IL. Point 2 5/8 in. long, 1 1/16 in. wide, 7/16 in. thick. Beveled on all four sides, serrations are long and wide. Thick point, narrow with concave base. Made of Mill Creek chert.
Priv. col., excellent quality, valued $125-160.

- Kirk Corner-notched from Marion co., IL. Point 2 7/8 in. long, 1 3/16 in. wide, 11/16 in. thick. Beveled on one face of each edge. Thick point, narrow, serrated crudely. Heat treated with concave base. Made of Mill Creek chert. *Priv. col., average quality, valued $80-100.*

- Kirk Corner-notched from Marion co., IL. Point 2 1/2 in. long, 1 1/4 in. wide, 3/16 in. thick. Beveled on all four sides, serrations are long and thin. Thin point, symmetrical and sharp. Heat treated with concave base. Despite the material this is an example of very fine workmanship. Made of Mill Creek chert. *Priv. col, museum quality, rare, valued $750-1,000.*

- Kirk Corner-notched from Madison co., IL. Point 2 5/8 in. long, 1 5/16 in. wide, 3/16 in. thick. Beveled on all four sides, serrations are long and wide. Thin point, symmetrical, finely flaked. Short stem with convex base. Made of gray chert. *Priv. col., excellent quality, valued $150-225.*

- Kirk Corner-notched from Williamson co., IL. Point 1 5/8 in. long, 1 1/16 in. wide, 7/16 in. thick. Very thick and wide point, beveled on all four sides, wide serrations. Long pointed tangs parallel to a concave base. Made of white pink speckled chert. *Priv. col., excellent quality, valued $100-150.*

- Kirk Corner-notched from Williamson co., IL. Blade 4 13/32 in. long, 2 in. wide, 1/4 in. thick. Made of Kaolin chert. *Priv. col., museum quality, rare, valued $1,250-1,600.*

- Kirk Corner-notched from Williamson co., IL. Blade 4 3/4 in. long, 2 1/8 in. wide, 1/4 in. thick. Made of Mill Creek chert. *Priv. col., excellent quality, valued $300-400.*

- Kirk Corner-notched from Williamson co., IL. Blade 5 1/16 in. long, 2 5/8 in. wide, 1/4 in. thick. Made of Mill Creek chert. *Priv. col., excellent quality, valued $550-650.*

- Kirk Corner-notched from Williamson co., IL. Blade 3 5/8 in. long, 1 7/8 in. wide, 1/4 in. thick. Good workmanship, heat treated. Made of gray chert. *Priv. col., museum quality, valued $650-800.*

- Kirk Corner-notched from Jackson co., IL. Blade 5 1/4 in. long, 2 7/8 in. wide, 1/4 in. thick. Made of Cobden Hornstone chert. *Priv. col., museum quality, rare, valued $1,200-1,400.*

• Kirk Corner-notched from Jackson co., IL. Blade 4 11/16 in. long, 1 7/8 in. wide, 5/32 in. thick. Made of Cobden chert.
Priv. col., museum quality, valued $450-600.

• Kirk Corner-notched from White co., IL. Blade 3 3/4 in. long, 2 in. wide, 1/4 in. thick. Made of local white chert.
Priv. col., museum quality, valued $650-800.

• Kirk Corner-notched from White co., IL. Blade 4 1/2 in. long, 1 7/8 in. wide, 1/4 in. thick. Made of porous beige chert.
Priv. col., average quality, $40-50.

• Kirk Corner-notched from White co., IL. Blade 3 31/32 in. long, 2 1/8 in. wide, 7/16 in. thick. Good workmanship considering the material. Made of quartzite.
Priv. col., average quality, valued $50-60.

• Kirk Corner-notched from Hamilton co., IL. Blade 3 7/8 in. long, 1 5/8 in. wide, 1/4 in. thick. Made of porous pink chert.
Priv. col., average quality, valued $65-70.

• Kirk Corner-notched from Hamilton co., IL. Blade 4 1/2 in. long, 1 7/8 in. wide, 3/16 in. thick. Made of white black speckled chert.
Priv. col., excellent quality, $200-300.

• Kirk Corner-notched from Jackson co., IL. Blade 3 15/16 in. long, 1 3/4 in. wide, 1/2 in. thick. Made of Cobden chert.
Priv. col., excellent quality, valued $450-600.

• Kirk Corner-notched from Jackson co., IL. Blade 5 3/4 in. long, 2 7/8 in. wide, 1/4 in. thick. Heat treated upper 1/2. Made of high grade Mill Creek chert.
Priv. col., museum quality, valued $1,000-1,200.

• Kirk Corner-notched from Jackson co., IL. Blade 4 1/3 in. long, 1 7/8 in. wide, 1/4 in. thick. Made of Mill Creek chert.
Priv. col., excellent quality, $200-300.

• Kirk Corner-notched from Jackson co., IL. Point 2 13/16 in. long, 1 3/8 in. wide, 3/16 in. thick. Made of Cobden chert.
Priv. col., excellent quality, valued $550-600.

♦ Kirk Serrated from Davidson co., TN. Blade 3 1/2 in. long, 1 3/8 in. wide,

1/4 in. thick. Straight parallel stem, straight base. Widely spaced deep edge serrations, upper 1/3 of blade beveled on one edge of each face. Made of Dover chert.

Priv. col., excellent quality, valued $150-200.

• Kirk Serrated from Davidson co., TN. Blade 4 1/3 in. long, 1 3/8 in. wide, 1/4 in. thick. Thin, narrow, very sharply serrated edges. Blade beveled on one edge of each face, heat treated. Expanded stem below barbed shoulders, concave base. Made of Dover chert.
Priv. col., museum quality, valued $1,000-1,300.

• Kirk Serrated from Calloway co., KY. Point 2 1/8 in. long, 1 in. wide, 3/16 in. thick. Narrow symmetrical point, beveled on one edge of each face. Wide and deep serrations, sharp edges, convex base. Deeply notched, with barbed shoulders. Made of white tan pebble chert.
Priv. col., excellent quality, valued $265-385.

• Kirk Serrated from Calloway co., KY. Point 2 1/16 in. long, 1 1/8 in. wide, 1/4 in. thick. Symmetrical point, beveled on one edge of each face. Wide and deep, fine serrations, sharp edges, with concave base. Shallow notched, heat treated, with barbed shoulders. Made of white tan pebble chert.
Priv. col., excellent quality, valued $250-325.

• Kirk Serrated from Calloway co., KY. Point 2 5/8 in. long, 1 1/2 in. wide, 3/16 in. thick. Narrow, thin, symmetrical point, beveled on one edge of each face. Fine and deep serrations, sharp edges, convex base. Deeply notched, short stemmed with barbed shoulders. Made of white tan pebble chert.
Priv. col., excellent quality, valued $450-575.

• Kirk Serrated from Gallatin co., KY. Point 2 3/8 in. long, 1 3/32 in. wide, 3/16 in. thick. Narrow, thin, symmetrical point, beveled on one edge of each face. Close, very pointed, and deep serrations, sharp edges, straight base. Deeply notched, heat treated, with flaring barbed shoulders. Made of white pebble chert.
Priv. col., excellent quality, valued $350-425.

• Kirk Serrated from Gallatin co., KY. Point 2 1/8 in. long, 1 7/32 in. wide,

5/16 in. thick. Wide, thick point, crudely beveled on one edge of each face. Wide, triangular, very pointed, and deep serrations, straight base. Shallow, notched, heat treated, slight tip break, with barbed shoulders. Made of white pebble chert.
Priv. col., average quality, valued $55-80.

• Kirk Serrated from Hardin co., IL. Blade 3 7/8 in. long, 1 7/8 in. wide, 3/16 in. thick. Thick, wide, symmetrical blade finely serrated and sharp. Widely spaced pointed serrations, straight barbed shoulders, concave base. Made of oily gray chert.
Priv. col., excellent quality, valued $65-75.

• Kirk Serrated from Pope co., IL. Blade 3 5/8 in. long, 1 1/2 in. wide, 3/16 in. thick. Upper 1/3 of the blade finely serrated and sharp. Lower 2/3 of blade displays widely spaced rounded serrations, blade is fluted to above straight barbed shoulders. Made of Cobden Hornstone chert.
Priv. col., museum quality, rare, valued $375-450.

• Kirk Serrated from Davidson co., TN. Blade 4 1/3 in. long, 1 3/8 in. wide, 1/4 in. thick. Made of Dover chert.
Priv. col., museum quality, valued $100-130.

• Kirk Serrated from Davidson co., TN. Point 2 3/8 in. long, 1 1/32 in. wide, 3/16 in. thick. Made of white chert.
Priv. col., excellent quality, valued $65-85.

• Kirk Serrated from Davidson co., TN. Point 2 7/16 in. long, 1 3/8 in. wide, 1/4 in. thick. Made of banded white brown chert.
Priv. col., excellent quality, valued $150-175.

• Kirk Serrated from Calloway co., KY. Point 2 5/8 in. long, 1 1/2 in. wide. 3/16 in. thick. Made of marbled white red slate.
Priv. col., excellent quality, valued $50-75.

• Kirk Serrated from Marion co., KY. Point 3 1/8 in. long, 1 3/8 in. wide, 3/16 in. thick. Made of bright white pebble chert.
Priv. col., excellent quality, valued $75-125.

• Kirk Serrated from Marion co., KY. Point 2 5/8 in. long, 1 13/32 in. wide, 3/16 in. thick. Made of white pebble chert.
Priv. col., excellent quality, valued $65-75.

• Kirk Serrated from Cumberland co., TN. Point 3 1/3 in. long, 1 3/8 in. wide,

1/4 in. thick. Made of Dover chert.
Priv. col., museum quality, valued $180-300.

• Kirk Serrated from Cumberland co., TN. Point 2 7/8 in. long, 1 1/4 in. wide, 3/16 in. thick. Made of banded white tan chert.
Priv. col., excellent quality, valued $65-85.

• Kirk Serrated from Carroll co., TN. Point 2 5/16 in. long, 1 1/8 in. wide, 1/4 in. thick. Made of white tan chert.
Priv. col., excellent quality, valued $50-75.

• Kirk Serrated from Carroll co., TN. Point 2 5/8 in. long, 1 1/2 in. wide, 3/16 in. thick. Made of dense chert.
Priv. col., excellent quality, valued $50-75.

• Kirk Serrated from Gallatin co., KY. Point 2 3/8 in. long, 1 3/32 in. wide, 3/16 in. thick. Made of white gray chert.
Priv. col., excellent quality, valued $50-75.

• Kirk Serrated from Gallatin co., KY. Point 3 1/32 in. long, 1 23/32 in. wide, 5/16 in. thick. Made of white brown pebble chert.
Priv. col., excellent quality, valued $75-85.

• Kirk Serrated from Dyer co., TN. Blade 4 1/8 in. long, 2 1/8 in. wide, 1/4 in. thick. Made of Dover chert.
Priv. col., museum quality, valued $200-325.

• Kirk Serrated from Dyer co., TN. Point 2 5/8 in. long, 1 2/3 in. wide, 3/16 in. thick. Made of tan pebble chert.
Priv. col., excellent quality, valued $165-185.

• Kirk Serrated from Dyer co., TN. Point 2 5/16 in. long, 1 1/8 in. wide, 1/4 in. thick. Made of white tan banded chert.
Priv. col., museum quality, valued $125-150.

• Kirk Serrated from Jefferson co., TN. Point 2 7/8 in. long, 1 1/3 in. wide, 3/16 in. thick. Heat treated. Made of white tan pebble chert.
Priv. col., excellent quality, valued $85-125.

• Kirk Serrated from Jefferson co., TN. Point 3 1/8 in. long, 1 13/32 in. wide, 3/16 in. thick. Made of porous pink chert.
Priv. col., average quality, valued $35-45.

• Kirk Serrated from Jefferson co., TN. Point 2 7/8 in. long, 2 1/32 in. wide, 3/16 in. thick. Reworked concave edges. Made of oily white chert.
Priv. col., excellent quality, valued $85-120.

• Kirk Serrated from Davidson co., TN. Blade 4 1/3 in. long, 1 7/8 in. wide, 1/4 in. thick. Made of Dover chert.
Priv. col., museum quality, valued $175-300.

• Kirk Serrated from Boyle co., KY. Point 2 7/8 in. long, 1 1/2 in. wide, 3/16 in. thick. Made of yellow tan pebble chert.
Priv. col., excellent quality, valued $125-135.

• Kirk Serrated from Boyle co., KY. Point 3 1/16 in. long, 2 in. wide, 1/4 in. thick. Good workmanship. Made of beige chert.
Priv. col., excellent quality, valued $150-250.

• Kirk Serrated from Chester co., KY. Point 2 5/8 in. long, 1 1/4 in. wide, 3/16 in. thick. Made of gray chert.
Priv. col., excellent quality, valued $150-175.

• Kirk Serrated from Chester co., KY. Point 2 7/8 in. long, 1 1/2 in. wide, 3/16 in. thick. Made of gray chert.
Priv. col., excellent quality, valued $100-125.

• Kirk Serrated from Chester co., KY. Point 2 3/4 in. long, 1 1/3 in. wide, 5/16 in. thick. Made of gray chert.
Priv. col., excellent quality, valued $45-65.

• Kirk Serrated from Newberry co., SC. Point 2 1/8 in. long, 1 1/3 in. wide, 3/16 in. thick. Made of marble gray slate.
Priv. col., excellent quality, valued $65-85.

• Kirk Serrated from Newberry co., SC. Point 2 5/16 in. long, 1 1/8 in. wide, 1/4 in. thick. Made of tan gray slate.
Priv. col., average quality, valued $25-35.

• Kirk Serrated from Calloway co., KY. Point 2 5/16 in. long, 1 1/2 in. wide, 3/16 in. thick. Made of yellow white chert.
Priv. col., excellent quality, valued $55-75.

• Kirk Serrated from Hopkins co., KY. Point 2 17/32 in. long, 1 1/8 in. wide, 3/16 in. thick. Made of white to brown chert.

Priv. col., excellent quality, valued $100-125.

• Kirk Serrated from Gallatin co., KY. Point 2 1/8 in. long, 1 9/32 in. wide, 5/16 in. thick. Made of porous white chert.
Priv. col., average quality, valued $25-35.

• Kirk Serrated from Davidson co., TN. Blade 4 1/32 in. long, 1 7/8 in. wide, 1/4 in. thick. Excellent workmanship. Made of Dover chert.
Priv. col., museum quality, valued $650-800.

• Kirk Serrated from Grundy co., KY. Point 2 7/8 in. long, 1 1/3 in. wide, 3/16 in. thick. Heat treated. Made of marbled gray mauve chert.
Priv. col., museum quality, valued $250-325.

• Kirk Serrated from Grundy co., KY. Point 2 3/16 in. long, 1 1/8 in. wide, 3/16 in. thick. Made of translucent tan chert.
Priv. col., museum quality, valued $250-300.

• Kirk Serrated from Gallatin co., KY. Point 3 1/32 in. long, 1 1/2 in. wide, 3/16 in. thick. Made of white pink chert.
Priv. col., excellent quality, valued $50-75.

• Kirk Serrated from Gallatin co., KY. Point 2 5/8 in. long, 1 3/32 in. wide, 3/16 in. thick. Made of gray pebble chert.
Priv. col., excellent quality, valued $80-100.

• Kirk Serrated from Gallatin co., KY. Point 2 3/8 in. long, 1 11/32 in. wide, 5/16 in. thick. Made of white pebble chert.
Priv. col., average quality, valued $45-55.

Knight Island: 1,500-800 B.P. Late Woodland

Predominantly from the Southeast. A small to medium sized point. Points are very narrow, thin, straight based and side notched.

◆ Knight Island from Littlerock, AR. Point 2 3/8 in. long, 5/8 in. wide, 1/8 in. thick. Deeply notched, straight uniform base, very angular point. Narrow and symmetrical. Made of a pink pebble chert.

Priv. col., excellent quality, valued $35-50.

• Knight Island from Littlerock, AR. Point 2 1/8 in. long, 5/16 in. wide, 1/8 in. thick. Deeply notched, straight uniform base, very angular point. Narrow, thin, finely worked and symmetrical. Made of a pink pebble chert.
Priv. col., excellent quality, valued $30-40.

• Knight Island from Hamilton co., TN. Point 1 7/8 in. long, 5/8 in. wide, 1/8 in. thick. Deeply notched parallel stemmed. Point thinly fluted, straight based, edges very sharp. Made of Dover chert.
Priv. col., museum quality, valued $65-80.

• Knight Island from Littlerock, AR. Point 2 3/8 in. long, 5/16 in. wide, 1/8 in. thick. Deeply notched, straight uniform base, very angular point. Narrow and symmetrical. Made of a pink pebble chert.
Priv. col., average quality, valued $30-40.

• Knight Island from central TN. Point 2 1/16 in. long, 5/8 in. wide, 1/8 in. thick. Deeply notched, straight uniform base, very angular point. Narrow, thin, sharp, and symmetrical. Made of a tan pebble chert.
Priv. col., excellent quality, valued $45-60.

• Knight Island from Atlanta, GA. Point 2 1/2 in. long, 5/8 in. wide, 1/8 in. thick. Shallow notched, straight base, very angular point. Narrow, thin, and symmetrical. Made of a pink grained quartzite.
Priv. col., average quality, valued $25-35.

• Knight Island from Calloway co., KY. Point 2 1/8 in. long, 5/16 in. wide, 1/8 in. thick. Deeply notched, straight base, very angular point, slight tip break. Narrow, exceptionally thin and symmetrical. Made of a pink white pebble chert.
Priv. col., average quality, valued $30-40.

• Knight Island from Littlerock, AR. Point 2 3/8 in. long, 1 in. wide, 1/8 in. thick. Deeply notched, straight base, point finely worked, heat treated with several edge nicks on one side. Thick, somewhat wide and symmetrical. Made of a pink pebble chert.
Priv. col., average quality, valued $20-30.

- Knight Island from Hamilton co., TN. Point 1 1/8 in. long, 5/8 in. wide, 1/8 in. thick. Very sharp tip, finely serrated, sharp edges. Deep side notches, straight uniform base. Made of Dover chert.
Grover Bohannon col., museum quality, rare, valued $85-125.

- Knight Island from Morgan co., AL. Point 1 31/32 in. long, 1 1/4 in. wide, 1/8 in. thick. Made of high grade pink chert.
Priv. col., museum quality, valued $50-60.

- Knight Island from Morgan co., AL. Point 2 1/8 in. long, 11/16 in. wide, 1/8 in. thick. Heat treated. Made of pink chert.
Priv. col., excellent quality, valued $35-40.

- Knight Island from Morgan co., AL. Point 2 in. long, 7/8 in. wide, 1/8 in. thick. Made of quartzite.
Priv. col., average quality, valued $15-20.

- Knight Island from Little River co., AR. Point 2 1/3 in. long, 9/16 in. wide, 1/8 in. thick. Made of gray flint.
Priv. col., average quality, valued $30-40.

- Knight Island from Little River co., AR. Point 2 5/16 in. long, 7/8 in. wide, 1/8 in. thick. Made of Arkansas brown chert.
Priv. col., excellent quality, valued $45-60.

- Knight Island from Barrow co., GA. Point 2 1/4 in. long, 1 1/8 in. wide, 1/8 in. thick. Made of banded shale.
Priv. col., average quality, valued $25-35.

- Knight Island from Barrow co., GA. Point 2 3/8 in. long, 1 3/16 in. wide, 1/8 in. thick. Made of porous pink chert.
Priv. col., average quality, valued $25-30.

- Knight Island from Barrow co., GA. Point 2 1/8 in. long, 13/16 in. wide, 1/8 in. thick. Made of white pebble chert.
Priv. col., excellent quality, valued $30-40.

- Knight Island from Humphreys co., TN. Point 1 7/8 in. long, 1 in. wide, 1/8 in. thick. Made of Dover chert.
Priv. col., museum quality, valued $65-80.

- Knight Island from Humphreys co., TN. Point 2 5/8 in. long, 1 5/16 in. wide,

1/8 in. thick. Made of Dover chert.
Priv. col., museum quality, valued $70-90.

• Knight Island from Humphreys co., TN. Point 2 7/16 in. long, 1 3/32 in. wide, 1/8 in. thick. Made of Dover chert.
Priv. col., excellent quality, valued $45-60.

• Knight Island from Stewart co., TN. Point 3 1/32 in. long, 1 5/8 in. wide, 1/8 in. thick. Made of Dover chert.
Priv. col., museum quality, valued $85-100.

• Knight Island from Stewart co., TN. Point 2 1/8 in. long, 1 1/16 in. wide, 1/8 in. thick. Made of gray chert.
Priv. col., excellent quality, valued $35-50.

• Knight Island from Hamilton co., TN. Point 2 5/8 in. long, 1 3/16 in. wide, 1/8 in. thick. Made of shale.
Priv. col., average quality, valued $20-30.

• Knight Island from Hamilton co., TN. Point 2 7/8 in. long, 1 5/8 in. wide, 1/8 in. thick. Made of Dover chert.
Priv. col., museum quality, valued $65-80.

• Knight Island from Grainger co., TN. Point 2 3/8 in. long, 1 3/16 in. wide, 1/8 in. thick. Heat treated. Made of tan pebble chert.
Priv. col., excellent quality, valued $40-60.

• Knight Island from Grainger co., TN. Point 2 11/16 in. long, 1 3/8 in. wide, 1/8 in. thick. Made of tan pebble chert.
Priv. col., excellent quality, valued $45-60.

• Knight Island from Webster co., KY. Point 2 1/2 in. long, 1 1/32 in. wide, 1/8 in. thick. Made of quartzite.
Priv. col., average quality, valued $25-35.

• Knight Island from Calloway co., KY. Point 2 1/8 in. long, 1 1/16 in. wide, 1/8 in. thick. Made of gray pebble chert.
Priv. col., excellent quality, valued $35-50.

• Knight Island from Henry co., KY. Point 2 3/8 in. long, 1 in. wide, 1/8 in. thick. Good workmanship. Made of tan pebble chert.
Priv. col., excellent quality, valued $40-50.

- Knight Island from Henderson co., KY. Point 1 7/8 in. long, 7/8 in. wide, 1/8 in. thick. Made of yellow tan chert.
Priv. col., excellent quality, valued $45-60.

- Knight Island from Henderson co., KY. Point 2 3/8 in. long, 1 3/16 in. wide, 1/8 in. thick. Made of gray pink pebble chert.
Priv. col., average quality, valued $30-40.

- Knight Island from Cooper co., TN. Point 2 5/16 in. long, 1 1/8 in. wide, 1/8 in. thick. Made of tan pebble chert.
Priv. col., excellent quality, valued $45-60.

- Knight Island from Oldam co., KY. Point 2 1/3 in. long, 1 in. wide, 1/8 in. thick. Made of quartzite.
Priv. col., average quality, valued $25-35.

- Knight Island from Calloway co., KY. Point 2 1/8 in. long, 5/16 in. wide, 1/8 in. thick. Made of banded chert.
Priv. col., excellent quality, valued $40-50.

- Knight Island from Calloway co., KY. Point 2 7/8 in. long, 1 3/32 in. wide, 3/16 in. thick. Made of a pink pebble chert.
Priv. col., excellent quality, valued $35-45.

- Knight Island from Bath co., KY. Point 2 3/8 in. long, 1 3/16 in. wide, 1/8 in. thick. Made of pebble chert.
Priv. col., excellent quality, valued $30-40.

- Knight Island from Union co., SC. Point 1 5/8 in. long, 13/16 in. wide, 1/8 in. thick. Made of quartzite.
Priv. col., average quality, valued $25-30.

- Knight Island from Union co., SC. Point 2 7/8 in. long, 1 3/16 in. wide, 1/8 in. thick. Made of gray slate.
Priv. col., average quality, valued $30-35.

- Knight Island from Union co., SC. Point 2 1/16 in. long, 7/8 in. wide, 1/8 in. thick. Made of gray tan pebble chert.
Priv. col., excellent quality, valued $45-60.

- Knight Island from Calloway co., KY. Point 2 1/16 in. long, 1 1/8 in. wide,

1/8 in. thick. Made of grained quartzite.
Priv. col., average quality, valued $25-35.

- Knight Island from Calloway co., KY. Point 2 1/8 in. long, 5/16 in. wide, 1/8 in. thick. Made of pebble chert.
Priv. col., average quality, valued $20-25.

CHAPTER 10
LAMPASOS-LOST LAKE

Lampasos: 9,000-6,000 B.P. Early Archaic

Found throughout the Midwest, a medium to large sized point or blade. Square to tapered shoulders, edges finely serrated. Good workmanship, beveled one side of each face. Bases are usually concave. Stems are both straight and concave, or deeply concave with flaring base tangs.

◆ Lampasos from Marion co., TN. Point 1 13/32 in. long, 3/4 in. wide, 1/8 in. thick. Beveled on one side of each face, sharp tip, concave base, tapered shoulders. Made of white pebble chert.

Grover Bohannon col., excellent quality, valued $45-70.

• Lampasos from Union co., IL. Blade 3 7/8 in. long, 1 5/8 in. wide, 1/4 in. thick. Symmetrical, tapered shoulders, edges finely serrated. Good workmanship, beveled on one side of each face. Base is concave. Stem straight based with short tangs. Made of Cobden chert.
Priv. col., museum quality, valued $80-100.

• Lampasos from Williamson co., IL. Point 2 3/8 in. long, 1 1/8 in. wide, 1/4 in. thick. Square shoulders, thick point, edges sharply serrated. High quality workmanship, steeply beveled on one side of each face. Base is concave, stems straight with flaring base tangs. Made of Mill Creek chert.

Priv. col., average quality, valued $20-30.

• Lampasos from Union co., IL. Point 1 7/8 in. long, 1 3/8 in. wide, 1/4 in. thick. Thick, wide point, yet finely serrated. Tapered shoulders, heat treated, two small nicks on one edge. Beveled on one side of each face. Base is straight. Stem concave, flaring base tangs. Made of oily, dense, gray chert.
Priv. col., excellent quality, valued $35-45.

• Lampasos from Marion co., TN. Point 1 9/16 in. long, 5/8 in. wide, 1/8 in. thick. Thin point, finely serrated, beveled on one side of each face, sharp rounded tip. Heat treated, concave base, short square base tangs, tapered shoulders. Made of white pebble chert.
Grover Bohannon col., excellent quality, valued $45-70.

᾽ Lampasos from Union co., IL. Blade 3 5/8 in. long, 1 1/2 in. wide, 1/4 in. thick. Made of Mill Creek chert.
Priv. col., excellent quality, valued $50-60.

• Lampasos from Union co., IL. Point 2 7/8 in. long, 1 3/8 in. wide, 1/4 in. thick. Heat treated. Made of Mill Creek chert.
Priv. col., excellent quality, valued $30-40.

• Lampasos from Union co., IL. Point 3 7/8 in. long, 1 1/2 in. wide, 1/4 in. thick. Made of gray chert.
Priv. col., excellent quality, valued $35-45.

• Lampasos from Marion co., TN. Point 1 13/16 in. long, 7/8 in. wide, 1/8 in. thick. Made of Dover chert.
Priv. col., museum quality, valued $80-100.

• Lampasos from Union co., IL. Blade 3 11/16 in. long, 1 5/8 in. wide, 1/4 in. thick. Made of Cobden chert.
Priv. col., museum quality, valued $80-100.

• Lampasos from Johnson co., IL. Point 2 1/2 in. long, 1 1/8 in. wide, 1/4 in. thick. Made of gray green pebble chert.
Priv. col., excellent quality, valued $40-50.

• Lampasos from Johnson co., IL. Point 2 7/8 in. long, 1 3/8 in. wide, 1/4 in. thick. Made of oily gray chert.
Priv. col., excellent quality, valued $35-45.

• Lampasos from Johnson co., IL. Point 1 19/32 in. long, 13/16 in. wide, 1/8 in. thick. Made of gray chert.
Priv. col., excellent quality, valued $40-50.

• Lampasos from Johnson co., IL. Point 2 7/8 in. long, 1 5/8 in. wide, 1/4 in. thick. Made of Cobden chert.
Priv. col., museum quality, valued $80-100.

• Lampasos from Sutton co., TX. Point 2 1/8 in. long, 1 3/8 in. wide, 1/4 in. thick. Made of glossy pink chert.
Priv. col., excellent quality, valued $40-50.

• Lampasos from Sutton co., TX. Point 2 7/8 in. long, 1 5/8 in. wide, 1/4 in. thick. Made of dull gray chert.
Priv. col., excellent quality, valued $35-45.

• Lampasos from Sutton co., TX. Point 2 11/16 in. long, 1 1/16 in. wide, 1/8 in. thick. Made of dull gray chert.
Priv. col., museum quality, valued $55-65.

• Lampasos from Motley co., TX. Point 3 1/8 in. long, 1 5/8 in. wide, 1/4 in. thick. Made of dull gray flint.
Priv. col., museum quality, valued $80-100.

• Lampasos from Motley co., TX. Point 2 3/8 in. long, 1 1/2 in. wide, 1/4 in. thick. Made of dull gray flint.
Priv. col., excellent quality, valued $40-50.

• Lampasos from Motley co., TX. Point 2 5/8 in. long, 1 5/8 in. wide, 1/4 in. thick. Made of dull gray flint.
Priv. col., excellent quality, valued $45-55.

• Lampasos from Motley co., TX. Point 2 1/16 in. long, 1 7/16 in. wide, 1/8 in. thick. Made of dull gray flint.
Priv. col., excellent quality, valued $45-55.

• Lampasos from Kimble co., TX. Point 2 1/2 in. long, 1 5/8 in. wide, 1/4 in. thick. Made of quartzite.
Priv. col., average quality, valued $20-30.

• Lampasos from Kimble co., TX. Point 2 1/3 in. long, 1 3/8 in. wide, 1/4 in.

thick. Made of glossy gray chert.
Priv. col., excellent quality, valued $40-50.

• Lampasos from Kimble co., TX. Point 2 1/8 in. long, 1 5/8 in. wide, 1/4 in.
thick. Made of dull gray chert.
Priv. col., excellent quality, valued $35-45.

• Lampasos from Kimble co., TX. Point 2 1/16 in. long, 1 7/16 in. wide, 1/8 in.
thick. Made of dull gray chert.
Priv. col., museum quality, valued $55-65.

• Lampasos from Midland co., TX. Point 2 5/8 in. long, 1 1/2 in. wide, 1/4 in.
thick. Made of dense white chert.
Priv. col., museum quality, valued $60-70.

• Lampasos from Midland co., TX. Point 2 3/8 in. long, 1 3/8 in. wide, 1/4 in.
thick. Made of glossy white chert.
Priv. col., excellent quality, valued $45-50.

• Lampasos from Midland co., TX. Point 2 5/8 in. long, 1 1/4 in. wide, 1/4 in.
thick. Made of dull gray chert.
Priv. col., excellent quality, valued $45-50.

• Lampasos from Sutton co., TX. Point 2 7/16 in. long, 1 11/16 in. wide, 1/8 in.
thick. Made of dull gray chert.
Priv. col., museum quality, valued $55-60.

• Lampasos from Union co., IL. Point 2 3/8 in. long, 1 1/2 in. wide, 1/4 in.
thick. Made of Cobden chert.
Priv. col., museum quality, valued $80-100.

• Lampasos from Union co., IL. Point 2 7/8 in. long, 1 7/16 in. wide, 1/4 in.
thick. Made of glossy pink chert.
Priv. col., excellent quality, valued $70-80.

• Lampasos from Alexander co., IL. Point 2 1/2 in. long, 1 7/8 in. wide, 1/4 in.
thick. Made of Mill Creek chert.
Priv. col., excellent quality, valued $45-50.

• Lampasos from Alexander co., IL. Point 2 9/16 in. long, 1 3/16 in. wide,
1/8 in. thick. Made of dull gray chert.

Priv. col., excellent quality, valued $55-65.

• Lampasos from Alexander co., IL. Point 2 5/8 in. long, 1 11/16 in. wide, 1/4 in. thick. Made of glossy gray chert.
Priv. col., excellent quality, valued $60-70.

• Lampasos from Alexander co., IL. Point 2 1/3 in. long, 1 3/8 in. wide, 1/4 in. thick. Made of Mill Creek chert.
Priv. col., excellent quality, valued $45-50.

• Lampasos from Alexander co., IL. Point 2 11/16 in. long, 1 5/16 in. wide, 1/8 in. thick. Made of Mill Creek chert.
Priv. col., excellent quality, valued $55-65.

Lange: 6,000-1,000 B.P. Mid-Archaic to Woodland

Lange is a midwestern point or blade medium to large in size. Langes exhibit expanded stems, convex to straight bases, and tapered shoulders.

♦ Lange from central TX. Point 3 in. long, 1 in. wide, 3/16 in. thick. Narrow, steeply beveled, parallel stemmed, soft shoulders. Made of gray pink speckled pebble chert.

Priv. col., excellent quality, valued $25-45.

• Lange from Lubbock co., TX. Point 2 1/8 in. long, 1 1/16 in. wide, 3/16 in. thick. Narrow, beveled on all four sides, parallel stemmed, soft shoulders, slight tip break. Made of gray flint.
Juan Samudio col., average quality, valued $10-15.

• Lange from south central OK. Point 2 3/8 in. long, 1 1/2 in. wide, 5/8 in. thick. Symmetrical, steeply beveled, sharply serrated, parallel stemmed, classic tapered shoulders. Made of pinkish pebble chert.
Priv. col., museum quality, valued $65-80.

• Lange from Louden co., TN. Blade 3 5/8 in. long, 1 3/16 in. wide, 1/4 in. thick. Deeply corner notched, thin concave base, finely flaked, sharp serrations. Very sharp, right hand beveled. Made of Dover chert.
Priv. col., museum quality, valued $40-60.

• Lange from Hamilton co., TN. Blade 4 3/8 in. long, 1 3/16 in. wide, 1/4 in. thick. Deeply corner notched, thin, narrow, concave base, fine serrations. Very sharp, right hand beveled. Made of gray pebble chert.
Priv. col., excellent quality, valued $25-35.

• Lange from Wabash co., IN. Blade 3 3/8 in. long, 1 5/16 in. wide, 1/4 in. thick. Deep corner notches, thin, wide with concave base, sharp thin serrations, right hand beveled. Made of greenish pebble chert.
Priv. col., excellent quality, valued $30-40.

• Lange from Louden co., TN. Blade 4 3/8 in. long, 1 5/32 in. wide, 1/4 in. thick. Shallow corner notched, thin concave base, crudely flaked, wide spaced sharp serrations, right hand beveled. Made of Dover chert.
Priv. col., average quality, valued $15-25.

• Lange from Marion co., TN. Point 2 1/2 in. long, 7/8 in. wide, 1/4 in. thick. Thin concave base, soft shoulders, finely serrated edges. Very thin and sharp tip, right hand beveled. Made of low quality quartzite.
Priv. col., average quality, valued $10-15.

• Lange from Parker co., TX. Point 2 5/8 in. long, 1 7/16 in. wide, 1/4 in. thick. Made of tan yellow chert.
Priv. col., excellent quality, valued $40-60.

• Lange from Parker co., TX. Blade 4 in. long, 2 1/16 in. wide, 1/4 in. thick. Made of gray flint.
Priv. col., excellent quality, valued $25-35.

• Lange from Parker co., TX. Blade 3 7/8 in. long, 1 11/16 in. wide, 1/4 in. thick. Made of tan to brown pebble chert.
Priv. col., excellent quality, valued $30-40.

• Lange from Parker co., TX. Blade 4 1/32 in. long, 1 5/32 in. wide, 1/4 in. thick. Made of black flint.
Priv. col., average quality, valued $15-25.

- Lange from Parker co., TX. Point 2 1/2 in. long, 1 3/8 in. wide, 1/4 in. thick. Made of quartzite.
Priv. col., average quality, valued $10-15.

- Lange from Parker co., TX. Point 2 5/16 in. long, 1 1/3 in. wide, 1/3 in. thick. Made of gray pebble chert.
Priv. col., excellent quality, valued $55-60.

- Lange from Somerville co., TX. Point 3 1/8 in. long, 1 7/16 in. wide, 1/4 in. thick. Made of quartzite.
Priv. col., average quality, valued $20-30.

- Lange from Somerville co., TX. Point 3 in. long, 1 1/3 in. wide, 1/4 in. thick. Made of gray pebble chert.
Priv. col., excellent quality, valued $25-35.

- Lange from Parker co., TX. Blade 4 in. long, 2 1/16 in. wide, 1/4 in. thick. Made of gray flint.
Priv. col., excellent quality, valued $25-35.

- Lange from Titus co., TX. Blade 3 5/8 in. long, 2 in. wide, 1/4 in. thick. Made of brown chert.
Priv. col., excellent quality, valued $30-40.

- Lange from Titus co., TX. Blade 3 19/32 in. long, 1 7/32 in. wide, 1/4 in. thick. Made of silver black flint.
Priv. col., excellent quality, valued $35-45.

- Lange from Titus co., TX. Point 2 2/3 in. long, 1 1/2 in. wide, 1/4 in. thick. Made of silver black flint.
Priv. col., excellent quality, valued $40-45.

- Lange from Lipscomb co., TX. Point 2 11/16 in. long, 1 1/2 in. wide, 1/3 in. thick. Good field patina. Made of gray chert.
Priv. col., excellent quality, valued $55-60.

- Lange from Lipscomb co., TX. Point 2 1/2 in. long, 1 7/16 in. wide, 1/4 in. thick. Made of tan chert.
Priv. col., excellent quality, valued $40-50.

• Lange from Lampasos co., TX. Point 3 in. long, 2 1/32 in. wide, 1/4 in. thick.
Made of dull gray flint.
Priv. col., excellent quality, valued $35-45.

• Lange from Lampasos co., TX. Blade 3 7/8 in. long, 2 in. wide, 1/4 in. thick.
Made of dull gray chert.
Priv. col., excellent quality, valued $30-40.

• Lange from Lampasos co., TX. Blade 3 1/32 in. long, 1 11/32 in. wide, 1/4 in.
thick. Made of dull black flint.
Priv. col., excellent quality, valued $45-50.

• Lange from Lampasos co., TX. Point 2 1/3 in. long, 1 5/8 in. wide, 1/4 in.
thick. Made of dull black flint.
Priv. col., excellent quality, valued $40-45.

• Lange from Andrews co., TX. Blade 4 1/4 in. long, 2 1/32 in. wide, 1/4 in.
thick. Made of gray flint.
Priv. col., excellent quality, valued $35-40.

• Lange from Andrews co., TX. Point 3 1/8 in. long, 2 1/4 in. wide, 1/4 in. thick.
Made of banded tan chert.
Priv. col., excellent quality, valued $50-60.

• Lange from Andrews co., TX. Point 2 21/32 in. long, 1 9/32 in. wide, 1/4 in.
thick. Made of black flint.
Priv. col., excellent quality, valued $45-50.

• Lange from Andrews co., TX. Point 2 1/2 in. long, 1 1/3 in. wide, 1/4 in. thick.
Made of black flint.
Priv. col., excellent quality, valued $40-45.

Langtry: 5,000-2,000 B.P. Mid-Archaic to Woodland

*Langtry are found predominantly in the Midwest. They are medium
sized, triangular points with square, tapered, or barbed shoulders. The stem
base is generally concave and thin. The base may be straight or convex and
fluted.*

◆ Langtry from Marshall co., TN. Point 2 1/2 in. long, 1 1/2 in. wide, 3/16 in.
thick. Long tanged, straight base, fluted stem. Symmetrical, finely flaked, sharp
tip and edges. Made of glossy brown chert.

Grover Bohannon col., excellent quality, valued $55-80.

• Langtry from Hamilton co., TN. Point 2 3/8 in. long, 7/8 in. wide, 3/16 in.
thick. Square shoulders, concave base, fluted base. Symmetrical and narrow
point. Made of Dover chert.
Priv. col., museum quality, valued $80-110.

• Langtry from Stewart co., TN. Point 2 1/8 in. long, 1 3/8 in. wide, 3/16 in.
thick. Square shoulders, concave base, fluted base. Symmetrical, wide, finely
flaked sharp edges. Made of tan pebble chert.
Priv. col., excellent quality, valued $75-85.

• Langtry from Hamilton co., TN. Point 2 5/8 in. long, 1 3/8 in. wide, 1/4 in.
thick. Square shoulders, straight base, thinly fluted base. Symmetrical, high
quality workmanship. Made of Dover chert.
Grover Bohannon col., excellent quality, valued $65-80.

• Langtry from Marshall co., TN. Point 2 3/16 in. long, 1 3/8 in. wide, 3/16 in.
thick. Square shoulders, concave base, fluted base. Symmetrical, thin, heat treated
point. Made of white chert.
Priv. col, museum quality, valued $80-110.

• Langtry from southern AK. Point 1 1/2 in. long, 1 1/8 in. wide, 1/4 in. thick.
Long tanged, deep notched, rounded tip, long thin flaking. Unusually convex
base caused by the material skin. Made of the same glossy brown chert of the
Langtry found in Marshall co., TN.
Priv. col., excellent quality, valued $30-40.

• Langtry from Childress co., TX. Point 2 2/3 in. long, 1 1/3 in. wide, 1/4 in.
thick. Made of banded tan brown chert.

Priv. col., excellent quality, valued $40-55.

• Langtry from Childress co., TX. Point 2 7/8 in. long, 1 1/2 in. wide, 3/16 in. thick. Made of marbled white tan chert
Priv. col., excellent quality, valued $50-60.

• Langtry from Crockett co., TX. Point 2 7/16 in. long, 1 1/2 in. wide, 1/4 in. thick. Made of Arkansas brown chert.
Priv. col., museum quality, valued $85-100.

• Langtry from Crockett co., TX. Point 2 7/16 in. long, 1 1/4 in. wide, 1/4 in. thick. Made of brown chert.
Priv. col., excellent quality, valued $55-60.

• Langtry from Crockett co., TX. Point 2 3/8 in. long, 1 1/3 in. wide, 1/4 in. thick. Made of white chert.
Priv. col., excellent quality, valued $55-60.

• Langtry from Floyd co., TX. Point 3 1/8 in. long, 1 5/8 in. wide, 1/4 in. thick. Made of banded tan brown chert.
Priv. col., excellent quality, valued $40-55.

• Langtry from Floyd co., TX. Point 2 7/8 in. long, 1 1/4 in. wide, 3/16 in. thick. Made of white tan chert.
Priv. col., excellent quality, valued $50-60.

• Langtry from Floyd co., TX. Point 2 13/16 in. long, 1 1/2 in. wide, 1/4 in. thick. Made of gray flint.
Priv. col., average quality, valued $15-20.

• Langtry from Floyd co., TX. Point 2 7/16 in. long, 1 1/4 in. wide, 1/4 in. thick. Made of gray flint.
Priv. col., average quality, valued $20-25.

• Langtry from Cochran co., TX. Point 3 in. long, 1 11/16 in. wide, 1/4 in. thick. Made of gray white chert.
Priv. col., excellent quality, valued $40-55.

• Langtry from Cochran co., TX. Point 2 7/8 in. long, 1 1/4 in. wide, 3/16 in. thick. Made of gray white chert.
Priv. col., excellent quality, valued $50-60.

- Langtry from Cochran co., TX. Point 3 in. long, 1 5/8 in. wide, 1/4 in. thick. Made of gray white chert.
Priv. col., excellent quality, valued $50-60.

- Langtry from Cochran co., TX. Point 2 17/32 in. long, 1 1/2 in. wide, 1/4 in. thick. Made of gray flint.
Priv. col., average quality, valued $20-25.

- Langtry from Cottle co., TX. Point 2 1/2 in. long, 1 5/8 in. wide, 1/4 in. thick. Made of banded tan chert.
Priv. col., excellent quality, valued $40-55.

- Langtry from Cottle co., TX. Point 2 5/8 in. long, 1 1/3 in. wide, 3/16 in. thick. Made of white chert.
Priv. col., excellent quality, valued $50-60.

- Langtry from Cottle co., TX. Point 2 3/16 in. long, 1 1/2 in. wide, 1/4 in. thick. Made of gray chert.
Priv. col., excellent quality, valued $45-50.

- Langtry from Cottle co., TX. Point 2 9/16 in. long, 1 1/4 in. wide, 1/4 in. thick. Made of dull gray flint.
Priv. col., average quality, valued $20-25.

- Langtry from Kiowa co., NC. Point 3 1/8 in. long, 1 5/8 in. wide, 1/4 in. thick. Made of banded tan brown chert.
Priv. col., excellent quality, valued $40-55.

- Langtry from Kiowa co., NC. Point 2 5/8 in. long, 1 1/3 in. wide, 3/16 in. thick. Made of tan chert.
Priv. col., excellent quality, valued $50-60.

- Langtry from Kiowa co., NC. Point 2 15/16 in. long, 1 1/2 in. wide, 1/4 in. thick. Made of dull gray flint.
Priv. col., average quality, valued $15-20.

- Langtry from Kiowa co., NC. Point 2 11/16 in. long, 1 1/3 in. wide, 1/4 in. thick. Made of gray slate.
Priv. col., average quality, valued $20-25.

• Langtry from Woods co., OK. Point 3 in. long, 1 7/8 in. wide, 1/4 in. thick.
Made of quartzite.
Priv. col., average quality, valued $20-25.

• Langtry from Woods co., OK. Point 2 5/8 in. long, 1 1/2 in. wide, 3/16 in.
thick. Made of high quality quartzite.
Priv. col., average quality, valued $15-20.

• Langtry from Wood co., OK. Point 2 1/16 in. long, 1 1/2 in. wide, 1/4 in.
thick. Made of silver gray flint.
Priv. col., average quality, valued $15-20.

• Langtry from Wood co., OK. Point 2 5/16 in. long, 1 1/3 in. wide, 1/4 in.
thick. Made of silver gray flint.
Priv. col., average quality, valued $20-25.

• Langtry from Payne co., OK. Point 2 1/3 in. long, 1 5/8 in. wide, 1/4 in. thick.
Made of marbled tan chert.
Priv. col., excellent quality, valued $40-55.

• Langtry from Wood co., OK. Point 2 3/8 in. long, 1 1/2 in. wide, 3/16 in.
thick. Made of gray shale.
Priv. col., average quality, valued $25-30.

• Langtry from Wood co., OK. Point 2 11/16 in. long, 1 1/2 in. wide, 1/4 in.
thick. Made of gray shale.
Priv. col., average quality, valued $15-20.

• Langtry from Wood co., OK. Point 2 1/2 in. long, 1 1/2 in. wide, 1/4 in. thick.
Made of gray shale.
Priv. col., average quality, valued $20-25.

Leaf Point: 2,500-1,500 B.P. Woodland

*Found throughout the Midwest and Southeast. Medium to large sized
point or blade. Points and blades exhibit high quality workmanship, they are
thin and broad. More often than not these thin points and blades are part of a
cache find. Leaf Point is also called the North Point.*

• Leaf Point from Knoxville co., TN. Point 2 in. long, 7/8 in. wide, 3/16 in. thick. Thinly flaked, prestige burial point. Made of light gray chert. *Grover Bohannon col., excellent quality, valued $45-65.*

◆ Leaf Point from Johnson co., IL. Point 2 1/4 in. long, 1 1/2 in. wide, 1/4 in. thick in center. Very fine example, symmetrical, sharp, thin fine flaking. Made of Bullseye chert.

Les Grubbe col., museum quality, valued $115-135.

• Leaf Point from Giles co., TN. Blade 3 7/8 in. long, 2 1/4 in. wide, 3/16 in. thick. Wide, very thin and sharp edges. Made of tan pebble chert. *Priv. col., museum quality, valued $135-165.*

• Leaf Point from Green co., IL. Blade 5 in. long, 2 1/2 in. wide, 1/4 in. thick. Thin, narrow blade for this type, excellent workmanship. Made of Bullseye chert. *Tim Crawford col., museum quality, valued $145-200.*

◆ Leaf Point from Stewart co., TN. Blade 5 3/4 in. long, 3 in. wide, 1/4 in. thick. Symmetrically rounded blade. Random flaked, several edge nicks. Made of dense black chert.

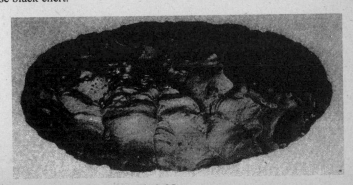

Priv. col., average quality, valued $60-85.

◆ Leaf Point from Humphreys co., TN. Blade 3 1/2 in. long, 1 7/8 in. wide, 3/16 in. thick. Unique material, symmetrical, very thin and sharp. Cache find blade, high quality flaking. Made of cream white pebble chert with large gold spots in the chert.

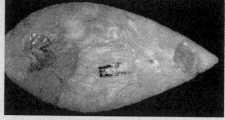

Priv. col., museum quality, valued $150-185.

• Leaf Point from Grainger co., TN. Blade 3 1/8 in. long, 2 1/4 in. wide, 3/16 in. thick. Made of tan pebble chert.
Priv. col., museum quality, valued $165-185.

• Leaf Point from Green co., IL. Blade 5 1/8 in. long, 2 1/3 in. wide, 1/4 in. thick. Made of tan Bullseye chert.
Priv. col., museum quality, valued $200-225.

• Leaf Point from Grainger co., TN. Blade 5 3/4 in. long, 3 in. wide, 1/4 in. thick. Made of dense black flint.
Priv. col., average quality, valued $60-85.

• Leaf Point from Grainger co., TN. Blade 3 7/8 in. long, 1 5/8 in. wide, 3/16 in. thick. Made of cream white pebble chert.
Priv. col., museum quality, valued $150-175.

• Leaf Point from Grainger co., TN. Blade 4 3/4 in. long, 2 1/3 in. wide, 1/4 in. thick. Made of dense black chert.
Priv. col., average quality, valued $50-65.

• Leaf Point from Grainger co., TN. Blade 4 1/8 in. long, 1 7/8 in. wide, 3/16 in. thick. Made of dense black chert.
Priv. col., average quality, valued $50-75.

• Leaf Point from Grainger co., TN. Blade 5 3/4 in. long, 3 in. wide, 1/4 in. thick. Made of dense black flint.
Priv. col., average quality, valued $60-85.

- Leaf point from Grainger co., TN. Blade 4 3/8 in. long, 2 in. wide, 3/16 in. thick. Heat treated. Made of white pebble chert.
Priv. col., museum quality, valued $125-150.

- Leaf Point from Meigs co., TN. Blade 4 1/4 in. long, 1 7/8 in. wide, 1/4 in. thick. Made of dense glossy black chert.
Priv. col., museum quality, valued $160-185.

- Leaf Point from Meigs co., TN. Blade 4 in. long, 1 15/16 in. wide, 3/16 in. thick. Made of dense glossy black chert.
Priv. col., museum quality, valued $150-175.

- Leaf Point from Meigs co., TN. Point 3 1/4 in. long, 1 5/8 in. wide, 1/4 in. thick. Made of dense glossy black chert.
Priv. col., museum quality, valued $160-185.

- Leaf Point from Meigs co., TN. Blade 3 3/4 in. long, 1 11/16 in. wide, 3/16 in. thick. Made of dense glossy black chert.
Priv. col., museum quality, valued $150-175.

- Leaf Point from Grainger co., TN. Blade 4 3/4 in. long, 2 1/3 in. wide, 1/4 in. thick. Made of dense black chert.
Priv. col., average quality, valued $50-65.

- Leaf Point from Grainger co., TN. Blade 4 1/8 in. long, 1 7/8 in. wide, 3/16 in. thick. Made of dense black chert.
Priv. col., average quality, valued $50-75.

- Leaf Point from Grainger co., TN. Blade 5 3/4 in. long, 3 in. wide, 1/4 in. thick. Made of dense black flint.
Priv. col., average quality, valued $60-85.

- Leaf Point from Grainger co., TN. Blade 4 3/8 in. long, 2 in. wide, 3/16 in. thick. Heat treated. Made of white pebble chert.
Priv. col., museum quality, valued $125-150.

- Leaf Point from Coles co., TN. Blade 4 1/8 in. long, 1 7/8 in. wide, 3/16 in. thick. Made of glossy tan chert.
Priv. col., excellent quality, valued $100-115.

- Leaf Point from Coles co., TN. Blade 4 7/8 in. long, 2 1/16 in. wide, 1/3 in. thick. Made of glossy tan chert.
Priv. col., excellent quality, valued $100-125.

- Leaf Point from Coles co., TN. Point 6 1/4 in. long, 2 3/8 in. wide, 1/4 in. thick. Made of dense black chert.
Priv. col., museum quality, valued $165-185.

- Leaf Point from Coles co., TN. Blade 5 3/4 in. long, 2 1/16 in. wide, 3/16 in. thick. Made of dense black chert.
Priv. col., museum quality, valued $175-225.

- Leaf Point from Grainger co., TN. Blade 4 3/4 in. long, 2 1/3 in. wide, 1/4 in. thick. Made of dense black chert.
Priv. col., average quality, valued $50-65.

- Leaf Point from Grainger co., TN. Blade 4 1/8 in. long, 1 7/8 in. wide, 3/16 in. thick. Made of dense black chert.
Priv. col., average quality, valued $50-75.

- Leaf Point from Grainger co., TN. Blade 5 3/4 in. long, 3 in. wide, 1/4 in. thick. Made of dense black flint.
Priv. col., average quality, valued $60-85.

- Leaf point from Grainger co., TN. Blade 4 3/8 in. long, 2 in. wide, 3/16 in. thick. Heat treated. Made of white pebble chert.
Priv. col., museum quality, valued $125-150.

- Leaf Point from Meigs co., TN. Blade 4 1/4 in. long, 1 7/8 in. wide, 1/4 in. thick. Made of dense glossy black chert.
Priv. col., museum quality, valued $160-185.

- Leaf Point from Meigs co., TN. Blade 4 in. long, 1 15/16 in. wide, 3/16 in. thick. Made of dense glossy black chert.
Priv. col., museum quality, valued $150-175.

- Leaf Point from Jefferson co., TN. Blade 5 1/4 in. long, 2 5/8 in. wide, 1/4 in. thick. Made of Dover chert.
Priv. col., museum quality, valued $185-225.

• Leaf Point from Jefferson co., TN. Blade 5 3/4 in. long, 1 11/16 in. wide, 3/16 in. thick. Made of marbled gray chert.
Priv. col., museum quality, valued $250-275.

• Leaf Point from Davidson co., TN. Blade 5 1/3 in. long, 3 3/8 in. wide, 1/4 in. thick. Made of banded tan chert.
Priv. col., museum quality, valued $360-385.

• Leaf Point from Davidson co., TN. Blade 4 5/32 in. long, 2 1/16 in. wide, 3/16 in. thick. Made of banded white black chert.
Priv. col., museum quality, valued $300-375.

• Leaf Point from Davidson co., TN. Blade 5 1/16 in. long, 2 1/8 in. wide, 1/4 in. thick. Made of Dover chert.
Priv. col., museum quality, valued $285-325.

• Leaf Point from Henderson co., TN. Blade 5 1/3 in. long, 2 13/16 in. wide, 1/4 in. thick. Made of marbled gray white chert.
Priv. col., museum quality, valued $350-425.

• Leaf Point from Maury co., TN. Blade 5 1/4 in. long, 2 7/8 in. wide, 1/4 in. thick. Made of dense glossy brown chert.
Priv. col., excellent quality, valued $460-525.

• Leaf Point from Maury co., TN. Blade 4 3/8 in. long, 2 1/16 in. wide, 3/16 in. thick. Made of dense glossy brown chert.
Priv. col., museum quality, valued $250-275.

• Leaf Point from Maury co., TN. Blade 5 1/3 in. long, 2 3/8 in. wide, 1/4 in. thick. Made of marbled tan shale.
Priv. col., excellent quality, valued $65-75.

• Leaf Point from Blunt co., TN. Blade 5 1/32 in. long, 3 in. wide, 3/16 in. thick. Made of marbled gray shale.
Priv. col., excellent quality, valued $60-75.

Lecroy: 9,000-5,000 B.P. Early to Mid-Archaic

Predominantly a southeastern small to medium sized point.

Considerable variety exhibited throughout point edges, serrated, usually wide, drooping or expanded base tangs. Wide concave based stems usually ground.

♦ Lecroy from Louden co., TN. Point 1 1/4 in. long, 1/2 in. wide, 3/8 in. thick. Snapped base, shallow notches, finely serrated edges. Deep base notches with small thin flute up point. Made of white pebble chert.

Grover Bohannon col., excellent quality, valued $15-20.

• Lecroy from Knoxville co., TN. Point 1 5/8 in. long, 1/2 in. wide, 3/8 in. thick. Concave base, drooping tangs, shallow notches, finely serrated edges, deep base notches. Made of tan white ringed pebble chert.
Priv. col., excellent quality, valued $15-20.

♦ Lecroy from western VA. Point 1 1/4 in. long, 3/4 in. wide, 1/4 in. thick. Soft shoulders, deeply basal notched, sharply serrated tip. Made of shale.

Priv. col., excellent quality, valued $15-25.

• Lecroy from Louden co., TN. Point 1 1/2 in. long, 5/8 in. wide, 3/16 in. thick. Sharp tip, base concave and ground, shallow notches, finely serrated edges. Deep base notches with wide drooping tangs, wide, thin point. Made of tan chert.
Priv. col., museum quality, valued $30-40.

• Lecroy from Humphreys co., TN. Point 1 3/4 in. long, 1/2 in. wide, 3/8 in. thick. Shallow notches, finely serrated sharp edges. Deep base notches with classical drooping basal tangs. Made of Dover chert.
Priv. col., museum quality, valued $5-10.

• Lecroy from Hamilton co., TN. Point 2 in. long, 1 1/4 in. wide, 1/4 in. thick. Deep wide serrations, ground concave, rounded base. Made of milky quartz.

Priv. col., average quality, valued $5-10.

• Lecroy from Bibb co., AL. Point 2 1/3 in. long, 1 5/8 in. wide, 1/2 in. thick. Made of high grade quartzite.
Priv. col., average quality, valued $10-15.

• Lecroy from Bibb co., AL. Point 1 7/8 in. long, 1 1/2 in. wide, 3/8 in. thick. Made of quartzite.
Priv. col., average quality, valued $5-10.

• Lecroy from Bibb co., AL. Point 2 1/3 in. long, 1 5/8 in. wide, 1/2 in. thick. Made of high grade quartzite.
Priv. col., average quality, valued $10-15.

• Lecroy from Bibb co., AL. Point 1 7/8 in. long, 1 1/2 in. wide, 3/8 in. thick. Made of quartzite.
Priv. col., average quality, valued $5-10.

• Lecroy from Geneva co., AL. Point 2 in. long, 1 1/3 in. wide, 1/4 in. thick. Made of milky quartz.
Priv. col., museum quality, valued $35-40.

• Lecroy from Geneva co., AL. Point 2 1/32 in. long, 1 3/8 in. wide, 1/2 in. thick. Made of rose quartz.
Priv. col., museum quality, valued $50-65.

• Lecroy from Lee co., AR. Point 1 5/8 in. long, 1 1/3 in. wide, 1/4 in. thick. Made of pink quartzite.
Priv. col., average quality, valued $15-20.

• Lecroy from Lee co., AR. Point 2 1/8 in. long, 1 2/3 in. wide, 1/4 in. thick. Made of milky quartz.
Priv. col., museum quality, valued $55-60.

• Lecroy from Lee co., AR. Point 2 1/32 in. long, 1 7/8 in. wide, 5/16 in. thick. Made of Arkansas brown chert.
Priv. col., excellent quality, valued $50-65.

• Lecroy from Lee co., AR. Point 2 1/4 in. long, 1 11/32 in. wide, 3/8 in. thick. Made of gray chert.
Priv. col., excellent quality, valued $35-40.

- Lecroy from Lamar co., AL. Point 2 in. long, 1 1/3 in. wide, 1/4 in. thick. Made of milky quartz.
Priv. col., museum quality, valued $45-50.

- Lecroy from Lamar co., AL. Point 2 1/8 in. long, 1 3/8 in. wide, 1/2 in. thick. Made of brown banded slate.
Priv. col., average quality, valued $10-15.

- Lecroy from Lamar co., AL. Point 2 1/16 in. long, 1 1/2 in. wide, 3/8 in. thick. Made of quartzite.
Priv. col., average quality, valued $5-10.

- Lecroy from Lamar co., AL. Point 2 1/4 in. long, 1 2/3 in. wide, 1/4 in. thick. Made of rose quartz.
Priv. col., museum quality, valued $65-70.

- Lecroy from Lowndes co., AL. Point 2 1/3 in. long, 1 7/8 in. wide, 1/2 in. thick. Made of high grade pink quartzite.
Priv. col., exellent quality, valued $20-35.

- Lecroy from Lowndes co., AL. Point 1 7/8 in. long, 1 5/8 in. wide, 3/8 in. thick. Made of high grade pink quartzite.
Priv. col., excellent quality, valued $25-40.

- Lecroy from Lowndes co., AL. Point 2 1/3 in. long, 1 2/3 in. wide, 1/4 in. thick. Made of milky quartz.
Priv. col., museum quality, valued $55-60.

- Lecroy from Lowndes co., AL. Point 2 1/8 in. long, 1 7/8 in. wide, 1/2 in. thick. Made of quartzite.
Priv. col., average quality, valued $10-15.

- Lecroy from Bullock co., AL. Point 1 7/8 in. long, 1 5/8 in. wide, 3/8 in. thick. Made of quartzite.
Priv. col., average quality, valued $5-10.

- Lecroy from Bullock co., AL. Point 1 1/2 in. long, 1 1/3 in. wide, 1/4 in. thick. Made of quartzite.
Priv. col., average quality, valued $5-10.

- Lecroy from Bullock co., AL. Point 2 1/3 in. long, 1 2/3 in. wide, 1/4 in. thick. Made of quartzite.
Priv. col., average quality, valued $15-20.

- Lecroy from Bullock co., AL. Point 1 5/8 in. long, 1 1/3 in. wide, 3/8 in. thick. Made of quartzite.
Priv. col., average quality, valued $5-10.

- Lecroy from Colbert co., AL. Point 2 1/32 in. long, 1 2/3 in. wide, 1/4 in. thick. Made of gray shale.
Priv. col., excellent quality, valued $25-30.

- Lecroy from Colbert co., AL. Point 2 1/8 in. long, 1 5/8 in. wide, 1/2 in. thick. Made of gray shale.
Priv. col., excellent quality, valued $25-35.

- Lecroy from Colbert co., AL. Point 1 3/8 in. long, 1 1/4 in. wide, 1/4 in. thick. Made of high grade pink quartzite.
Priv. col., average quality, valued $15-20.

- Lecroy from Colbert co., AL. Point 2 1/2 in. long, 1 13/16 in. wide, 1/4 in. thick. Made of quartzite.
Priv. col., average quality, valued $15-20.

- Lecroy from Cleburne co., AL. Point 2 1/4 in. long, 1 7/8 in. wide, 1/2 in. thick. Made of quartzite.
Priv. col., average quality, valued $10-15.

- Lecroy from Cleburne co., AL. Point 2 3/8 in. long, 1 1/2 in. wide, 3/8 in. thick. Made of quartzite.
Priv. col., average quality, valued $5-10.

- Lecroy from Cleburne co., AL. Point 2 1/16 in. long, 1 2/3 in. wide, 1/4 in. thick. Made of quartzite.
Priv. col., average quality, valued $15-20.

- Lecroy from Cleburne co., AL. Point 2 in. long, 1 5/8 in. wide, 1/2 in. thick. Made of rose quartz.
Priv. col., museum quality, valued $65-85.

• Lecroy from Ashley co., AR. Point 1 5/8 in. long, 1 1/4 in. wide, 1/4 in. thick.
Made of Arkansas brown chert.
Priv. col., museum quality, valued $55-70.

• Lecroy from Ashley co., AR. Point 2 1/8 in. long, 1 29/32 in. wide, 1/4 in.
thick. Made of Arkansas brown chert.
Priv. col., museum quality, valued $55-60.

• Lecroy from Ashley co., AR. Point 2 1/32 in. long, 1 7/8 in. wide, 1/2 in.
thick. Made of quartzite.
Priv. col., average quality, valued $10-15.

• Lecroy from Onslow co., NC. Point 1 7/8 in. long, 1 5/8 in. wide, 1/4 in. thick.
Made of banded gray slate.
Priv. col., excellent quality, valued $25-30.

• Lecroy from Perry co., AL. Point 2 1/2 in. long, 1 1/2 in. wide, 1/4 in. thick.
Made of gray chert.
Priv. col., excellent quality, valued $35-40.

• Lecroy from Perry co., AL. Point 1 23/32 in. long, 1 3/8 in. wide, 1/2 in. thick.
Made of quartzite.
Priv. col., average quality, valued $10-15.

• Lecroy from Perry co., AL. Point 1 5/8 in. long, 1 1/2 in. wide, 1/4 in. thick.
Made of quartzite.
Priv. col., average quality, valued $10-15.

• Lecroy from Izard co., AR. Point 2 1/8 in. long, 1 5/8 in. wide, 1/4 in. thick.
Made of gray chert.
Priv. col., excellent quality, valued $35-50.

• Lecroy from Arery co., NC. Point 2 1/32 in. long, 1 5/8 in. wide, 1/2 in. thick.
Made of high grade marbled slate.
Priv. col., excellent quality, valued $40-45.

• Lecroy from Arery co., NC. Point 1 7/8 in. long, 1 1/3 in. wide, 3/8 in. thick.
Made of tan banded slate.
Priv. col., average quality, valued $5-10.

• Lecroy from Arery co., NC. Point 2 in. long, 1 1/3 in. wide, 1/4 in. thick. Made of quartzite.
Priv. col., average quality, valued $5-10.

• Lecroy from Catawba co., NC. Point 2 11/32 in. long, 1 5/8 in. wide, 1/2 in. thick. Made of quartzite.
Priv. col., average quality, valued $15-25.

• Lecroy from Catawba co., NC. Point 1 3/8 in. long, 1 1/16 in. wide, 1/4 in. thick. Made of pink chert.
Priv. col., excellent quality, valued $35-40.

• Lecroy from Stokes co., NC. Point 2 1/8 in. long, 1 29/32 in. wide, 1/4 in. thick. Made of pink gray chert.
Priv. col., museum quality, valued $55-60.

• Lecroy from Swain co., NC. Point 2 1/32 in. long, 1 7/8 in. wide, 1/3 in. thick. Made of red slate.
Priv. col., average quality, rare, valued $30-35.

Lerma: 12,000-8,000 B.P. Paleo to Early Archaic

Lerma are found from Siberia through North, Central, and South America. Large, narrow, lanceolate blades with pointed or rounded base. Usually thick blades, beveled on one side of each face.

◆ Lerma pointed base from Stewart co., TN. Blade 3 3/4 in. long, 3/4 in. wide, 1/4 in. thick. Highly serrated with sharp tip and classic Lerma design, rounded base. Made of Dover chert.

Priv. col., excellent quality, valued $120-160.

• Lerma pointed base from Stewart co., TN. Blade 5 3/4 in. long, 1 3/4 in. wide, 1/4 in. thick. Made of Dover chert.
Priv. col., museum quality, valued $200-260.

- Lerma pointed base from Bledsoe co., TN. Blade 5 1/4 in. long, 1 1/3 in. wide, 1/4 in. thick. Highly serrated with sharp tip and classic Lerma design, rounded base. Made of white pebble chert.
Priv. col., excellent quality, valued $120-160.

- Lerma pointed base from Bledsoe co., TN. Blade 5 3/4 in. long, 2 1/16 in. wide, 3/16 in. thick. Made of gray chert.
Priv. col., museum quality, valued $180-230.

- Lerma pointed base from Bledsoe co., TN. Blade 5 1/4 in. long, 1 1/3 in. wide, 1/4 in. thick. Made of white tan chert.
Priv. col., excellent quality, valued $120-160.

- Lerma pointed base from Clay co., TN. Blade 5 3/4 in. long, 1 3/4 in. wide, 1/4 in. thick. Made of Dover chert.
Priv. col., museum quality, valued $200-250.

- Lerma pointed base from Bledsoe co., TN. Blade 5 in. long, 1 1/3 in. wide, 1/4 in. thick. Made of marbled gray white chert.
Priv. col., excellent quality, valued $150-180.

- Lerma pointed base from Cumberland co., TN. Blade 5 1/2 in. long, 2 3/16 in. wide, 1/4 in. thick. Made of gray chert.
Priv. col., museum quality, valued $200-250.

- Lerma pointed base from Cumberland co., TN. Blade 4 3/4 in. long, 1 1/3 in. wide, 1/4 in. thick. Made of gray tan chert.
Priv. col., excellent quality, valued $150-200.

- Lerma pointed base from Franklin co., TN. Blade 6 3/4 in. long, 1 7/8 in. wide, 1/4 in. thick. Made of gray chert.
Priv. col., excellent quality, valued $100-160.

- Lerma pointed base from Franklin co., TN. Blade 6 1/8 in. long, 2 1/3 in. wide, 1/4 in. thick. Made of white gray Bullseye chert.
Priv. col., museum quality, valued $230-260.

- Lerma pointed base from Franklin co., TN. Blade 4 5/8 in. long, 2 in. wide, 3/16 in. thick. Concave, reworked sides. Made of gray chert.
Priv. col., excellent quality, valued $150-200.

• Lerma pointed base from Pickett co., TN. Blade 5 1/16 in. long, 1 2/3 in. wide, 1/4 in. thick. Made of gray tan chert.
Priv. col., excellent quality, valued $140-180.

• Lerma pointed base from Pickett co., TN. Blade 7 3/4 in. long, 2 1/3 in. wide, 1/4 in. thick. Made of high grade pink chert.
Priv. col., museum quality, valued $500-600.

• Lerma pointed base from Pickett co., TN. Blade 6 1/3 in. long, 1 2/3 in. wide, 1/4 in. thick. Made of greenish pebble chert.
Priv. col., excellent quality, valued $220-260.

• Lerma pointed base from Pickett co., TN. Blade 4 1/4 in. long, 2 in. wide, 3/16 in. thick. Made of gray chert.
Priv. col., excellent quality, valued $150-200.

• Lerma pointed base from Humphreys co., TN. Blade 5 1/2 in. long, 2 1/3 in. wide, 1/4 in. thick. Made of glossy white chert.
Priv. col., excellent quality, valued $150-180.

• Lerma pointed base from Stewart co., TN. Blade 6 1/4 in. long, 2 1/4 in. wide, 1/4 in. thick. Made of Dover chert.
Priv. col., museum quality, valued $280-360.

• Lerma pointed base from Sevier co., TN. Blade 5 1/3 in. long, 1 1/8 in. wide, 1/4 in. thick. Concave edges. Made of white pebble chert.
Priv. col., excellent quality, valued $140-190.

• Lerma pointed base from Sevier co., TN. Blade 5 1/8 in. long, 2 1/32 in. wide, 3/16 in. thick. Made of gray chert.
Priv. col., excellent quality, valued $180-250.

• Lerma pointed base from Sevier co., TN. Blade 6 1/32 in. long, 1 2/3 in. wide, 1/4 in. thick. Made of glossy white tan chert.
Priv. col., museum quality, valued $320-460.

• Lerma pointed base from Sevier co., TN. Blade 5 1/3 in. long, 1 3/4 in. wide, 1/4 in. thick. Made of Dover chert.
Priv. col., museum quality, valued $300-360.

• Lerma pointed base from Blunt co., TN. Blade 5 1/3 in. long, 1 2/3 in. wide, 1/4 in. thick. Excellent workmanship. Made of white Bullseye chert. *Priv. col., museum quality, rare, valued $400-600.*

• Lerma pointed base from Blunt co., TN. Blade 6 1/3 in. long, 2 1/16 in. wide, 5/16 in. thick. Made of gray chert. *Priv. col., museum quality, valued $480-550.*

• Lerma pointed base from Clay co., TN. Blade 4 5/8 in. long, 1 2/3 in. wide, 1/4 in. thick. Heat treated. Made of yellow tan chert. *Priv. col., excellent quality, valued $100-140.*

• Lerma pointed base from Cocke co., TN. Blade 5 1/3 in. long, 1 7/8 in. wide, 1/4 in. thick. Made of Dover chert. *Priv. col., museum quality, valued $200-260.*

• Lerma pointed base from Cocke co., TN. Blade 6 1/8 in. long, 2 1/3 in. wide, 1/4 in. thick. Made of white pebble chert. *Priv. col., excellent quality, valued $220-260.*

• Lerma pointed base from Chester co., TN. Blade 5 1/4 in. long, 2 1/16 in. wide, 5/16 in. thick. Made of gray chert. *Priv. col., museum quality, valued $200-250.*

• Lerma pointed base from Chester co., TN. Blade 5 17/32 in. long, 2 1/16 in. wide, 1/4 in. thick. Made of high grade pink chert. *Priv. col., museum quality, valued $260-300.*

◆ Lerma from Stewart co., TN. Point 1 1/2 in. long, 3/4 in. wide, 3/32 in. thick. Unusually thin, small prestige point. Made of light gray chert.

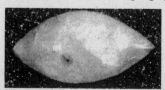

Grover Bohannon col., museum quality, rare, valued $1,000-1,200.

• Lerma pointed base from Stewart co., TN. Point 2 3/4 in. long, 3/4 in. wide, 1/4 in. thick. Made of Dover chert. *Priv. col., museum quality, valued $200-250.*

- Lerma pointed base from Stewart co., TN. Blade 2 1/4 in. long, 1 in. wide, 1/4 in. thick. Made of gray pebble chert.
Priv. col., excellent quality, valued $100-150.

- Lerma pointed base from Hardin co., IL. Blade 7 3/4 in. long, 2 11/16 in. wide, 7/16 in. thick. Made of gray chert.
Priv. col., museum quality, valued $350-400.

- Lerma pointed base from Hardin co., IL. Point 3 1/4 in. long, 1 1/8 in. wide, 1/4 in. thick. Made of gray chert.
Priv. col., excellent quality, valued $200-250.

♦ Lerma round base from northwestern KY. Blade 4 1/2 in. long, 1 1/16 in. wide, 1/4 in. thick. Hafting marks near rounded base, classic design. Made of brown crystalline chert.

Priv. col., average quality, valued $65-90.

- Lerma round base from Marshall co., TN. Blade 5 7/8 in. long, 1 1/2 in. wide, 1/4 in. thick. Exceptional piece, heat treated at base, good field patina. Made of a very lightweight tan brown marbled chert.
Grover Bohannon col., museum quality, rare, valued $350-425.

- Lerma from Humphreys co., TN. Blade 4 7/8 in. long, 1 2/3 in. wide, 1/4 in. thick. Symmetrical piece, uniquely steeply beveled on all four sides. Rounded base, good field patina. Made of tan chert.
Grover Bohannon col., excellent quality, valued $250-325.

- Lerma round base from Marshall co., TN. Blade 5 1/8 in. long, 1 1/2 in. wide, 1/4 in. thick. Narrow, thin, heat treated, rounded base. Made of Dover chert.
Priv. col., museum quality, valued $300-375.

- Lerma round base from Henderson co., TN. Blade 6 in. long, 2 1/8 in. wide, 1/4 in. thick. Heat treated, rounded base, wide, yet symmetrical, very sharp tip. Made of Dover chert.
Priv. col., museum quality, rare, valued $325-400.

◆ Lerma round base from Griffin co., IL. Blade 6 1/8 in. long, 2 3/8 in. wide, 3/16 in. thick. Symmetrical blade, finely serrated and flaked. very sharp edges and tip. Hafting marks near flaked base. Made of Mill Creek chert.

Priv. col., museum quality, valued $350-500.

• Lerma round base from Union co., IL. Blade 6 in. long, 2 in. wide, 1/4 in. thick. Made of Kaolin chert.
Les Grubbe col., museum quality, rare, valued $350-425.

• Lerma round base from Madison co., IL. Blade 5 3/8 in. long, 1 3/4 in. wide, 1/4 in. thick. Made of gray chert.
Priv. col., museum quality, valued $300-350.

• Lerma round base from Madison co., IL. Blade 4 7/8 in. long, 1 1/3 in. wide, 1/4 in. thick. Made of tan brown chert.
Priv. col., museum quality, valued $300-350.

• Lerma round base from Humphreys co., TN. Blade 6 7/8 in. long, 2 2/3 in. wide, 1/4 in. thick. Made of grainy white chert.
Priv. col., average quality, valued $100-125.

• Lerma round base from Johnson co., IL. Blade 5 3/8 in. long, 1 1/2 in. wide, 1/4 in. thick. Made of Mill Creek chert.
Priv. col., excellent quality, valued $200-250.

• Lerma round base from Union co., IL. Blade 5 1/32 in. long, 1 11/16 in. wide, 1/4 in. thick. Made of Cobden Hornstone chert.
Priv. col., museum quality, rare, valued $450-500.

• Lerma round base from Jackson co., IL. Blade 5 1/2 in. long, 1 1/2 in. wide, 1/4 in. thick. Made of Cobden Hornstone chert.
Priv. col., museum quality, rare, valued $450-500.

• Lerma round base from Humphreys co., TN. Blade 3 7/8 in. long, 1 1/3 in. wide, 1/4 in. thick. Made of gray chert.
Priv. col., excellent quality, valued $250-300.

• Lerma round base from Marshall co., TN. Blade 5 1/8 in. long, 1 1/2 in. wide, 1/4 in. thick.
Priv. col, museum quality, valued $300-375.

• Lerma round base from Johnson co., IL. Blade 6 7/8 in. long, 3 1/3 in. wide, 1/4 in. thick. Concave edges widening drastically at base. Made of Mill Creek chert.
Priv. col., average quality, valued $100-150.

• Lerma round base from Hamilton co., IL. Blade 6 7/8 in. long, 2 2/3 in. wide, 1/4 in. thick. Made of Cobden Hornstone chert.
Priv. col., excellent quality, rare, valued $500-525.

• Lerma round base from Johnson co., IL. Blade 4 3/8 in. long, 1 1/2 in. wide, 1/4 in. thick. Made of Mill Creek chert.
Priv. col., excellent quality, valued $200-250.

• Lerma round base from Johnson co., IL. Blade 5 7/32 in. long, 1 11/16 in. wide, 1/4 in. thick. Made of Cobden chert.
Priv. col., museum quality, valued $450-500.

• Lerma round base from Jackson co., IL. Blade 4 7/8 in. long, 1 1/3 in. wide, 1/4 in. thick. Made of gray chert.
Tim Rubbles col., excellent quality, valued $300-400.

• Lerma round base from Madison co., IL. Blade 4 7/8 in. long, 1 1/3 in. wide, 1/4 in. thick. Made of tan brown chert.
Priv. col., museum quality, valued $300-350.

• Lerma round base from Madison co., IL. Blade 5 1/8 in. long, 2 1/8 in. wide, 1/4 in. thick. Made of white tan pebble chert.
Priv. col., excellent quality, valued $200-225.

• Lerma round base from Johnson co., IL. Blade 5 5/8 in. long, 1 1/2 in. wide, 1/4 in. thick. Made of Mill Creek chert.
Priv. col., excellent quality, valued $200-250.

• Lerma round base from Johnson co., IL. Blade 5 15/32 in. long, 1 13/16 in. wide, 1/4 in. thick. Made of Cobden chert.
Priv. col., museum quality, valued $350-400.

• Lerma round base from Alexander co., IL. Blade 4 3/8 in. long, 1 1/3 in. wide, 1/4 in. thick. Made of gray chert.
Priv col., excellent quality, valued $175-225.

• Lerma round base from Alexander co., IL. Blade 5 5/8 in. long, 1 1/3 in. wide, 1/4 in. thick. Good workmanship, heat treated. Made of Mill Creek chert.
Priv. col., museum quality, valued $300-350.

• Lerma round base from Pickett co., TN. Blade 6 1/8 in. long, 2 1/3 in. wide, 1/4 in. thick. Made of glossy gray pink chert.
Priv. col., museum quality, valued $400-425.

• Lerma round base from Johnson co., IL. Blade 5 1/3 in. long, 1 1/2 in. wide, 1/4 in. thick. Made of Mill Creek chert.
Priv. col., excellent quality, valued $200-250.

• Lerma round base from Union co., IL. Blade 5 9/32 in. long, 1 3/4 in. wide, 1/4 in. thick. Made of Cobden chert.
Tim Rubbles col., museum quality, valued $450-500.

• Lerma round base from Humphreys co., TN. Blade 4 3/8 in. long, 1 1/2 in. wide, 1/4 in. thick. Made of gray chert.
Priv. col., poor quality, valued $65-85.

• Lerma round base from Madison co., KY. Blade 4 1/2 in. long, 1 2/3 in. wide, 1/4 in. thick. Made of tan pebble chert.
Priv. col., poor quality, valued $60-85.

• Lerma round base from Humphreys co., TN. Blade 3 7/8 in. long, 1 2/3 in. wide, 1/4 in. thick. Made of porous white pebble chert.
Priv. col., poor quality, valued $50-75.

• Lerma round base from Johnson co., IL. Blade 5 1/2 in. long, 1 1/4 in. wide, 1/4 in. thick. Made of Mill Creek chert.
Priv. col., poor quality, valued $50-75.

- Lerma round base from Johnson co., IL. Blade 5 11/32 in. long, 1 1/16 in.
wide, 1/4 in. thick. Made of green gray chert from Clear Creek.
Priv. col., museum quality, rare, valued $450-500.

- Lerma round base from Alexander co., IL. Blade 6 1/2 in. long, 2 1/8 in. wide,
1/4 in. thick. Made of gray chert.
Priv. col., museum quality, valued $600-700.

- Lerma round base from Madison co., IL. Blade 5 1/32 in. long, 1 1/2 in. wide,
1/4 in. thick. Heat treated, good workmanship. Made of tan brown chert.
Priv. col., museum quality, valued $400-450.

- Lerma round base from Cape Girardeau co., MO. Blade 6 3/8 in. long,
2 3/32 in. wide, 1/4 in. thick. Made of white chert.
Priv. col., museum quality, valued $500-525.

- Lerma round base from Cape Giradeau co., MO. Blade 5 3/8 in. long,
1 5/8 in. wide, 1/4 in. thick. Part of same find as previous piece. Made of high
grade pink chert.
Priv. col., excellent quality, valued $300-350.

- Lerma round base from Randolph co., MO. Blade 5 7/32 in. long, 1 1/16 in.
wide, 1/4 in. thick. Excellent workmanship. Made of Cobden Hornstone chert
from Union co., IL.
Priv. col., museum quality, rare, valued $650-700.

- Lerma round base from Holt co., MO. Blade 5 1/8 in. long, 1 1/3 in. wide,
1/4 in. thick. Made of white chert.
Jim Smith Col., excellent quality, valued $250-350.

- Lerma round base from Marion co., MO. Blade 6 1/3 in. long, 1 7/8 in. wide,
1/4 in. thick. Excellent workmanship, good field patina. Made of tan brown chert.
Priv. col., museum quality, valued $500-650.

- Lerma round base from Marion co., MO. Blade 6 1/8 in. long, 2 1/2 in. wide,
1/4 in. thick. Made of dense white chert.
Priv. col., excellent quality, valued $350-425.

- Lerma round base from Lafayett co., MO. Blade 5 3/8 in. long, 1 5/8 in. wide,
1/4 in. thick. Made of mauve chert.
Priv. col., excellent quality, valued $300-350.

• Lerma round base from Osage co., MO. Blade 5 1/2 in. long, 1 13/16 in. wide, 1/4 in. thick. Made of Arkansas brown chert.
Priv. col., museum quality, rare, valued $450-500.

• Lerma round base from Holt co., MO. Blade 3 5/8 in. long, 1 2/3 in. wide, 1/4 in. thick. Made of gray chert.
Priv. col., poor quality, valued $40-50.

• Lerma round base from Marion co., MO. Blade 4 3/8 in. long, 1 1/3 in. wide, 1/4 in. thick. Made of tan brown chert.
Priv. col., poor quality, valued $30-50.

• Lerma round base from Holt co., MO. Blade 6 5/8 in. long, 2 2/3 in. wide, 1/4 in. thick. Made of grainy white chert.
Priv. col., average quality, valued $100-125.

• Lerma round base from Johnson co., IL. Blade 5 5/8 in. long, 1 3/4 in. wide, 1/4 in. thick. Made of Mill Creek chert.
Priv. col., excellent quality, valued $200-250.

• Lerma round base from Union co., IL. Blade 5 1/3 in. long, 1 11/16 in. wide, 1/4 in. thick. Numerous blade nicks. Made of brown marbled chert.
Priv. col., poor quality, valued $45-50.

• Lerma round base from Humphreys co., TN. Blade 4 1/8 in. long, 1 1/3 in. wide, 1/4 in. thick. Made of gray chert.
Priv. col., poor quality, valued $45-60.

Levanna: 1,300-500 B.P. Late Woodland to Mississippian

Eastern and southeastern small to medium sized point. Triangular, thin, wide, with concave to straight base.

♦ Levanna from Humphreys co., TN. Point 5/8 in. long, 1/4 in. wide, 1/8 in. thick. Symmetrical, thin, finely serrated, triangular point. Made of light gray chert.

Grover Bohannon col., museum quality, valued $10-15.

• Levanna from Hamilton co., TN. Point 1 3/8 in. long, 3/4 in. wide, 1/8 in. thick. Symmetrical, thin, finely serrated, heat treated, triangular point. Made of light gray chert.
Grover Bohannon col., museum quality, valued $20-25.

• Levanna from Humphreys co., TN. Point 1 5/8 in. long, 2/3 in. wide, 1/8 in. thick. Symmetrical, thin, finely serrated, classic triangular point. Made of light gray chert.
Grover Bohannon col., museum quality, valued $10-15.

• Levanna from Knoxville co., TN. Point 1 3/8 in. long, 5/8 in. wide, 3/16 in. thick. Symmetrical, thin, wide, finely serrated, sharp triangular point. Made of Dover chert.
Priv. col., excellent quality, valued $5-10.

◆ Levanna from central VA. Point 3/4 in. long, 1 in. wide, 1/8 in. thick. Irregular shaped point, concave base and sides. Made of purple chert.

Priv. col., average quality, valued $3-5.

• Levanna from Stewart co., TN. Point 3/4 in. long, 7/16 in. wide, 1/8 in. thick. Finely serrated, sharp, symmetrically triangular point. Made of shale.
Grover Bohannon col., museum quality, valued $5-10.

• Levanna from Essex co., VA. Point 1 1/8 in. long, 3/4 in. wide, 1/8 in. thick. Made of translucent light gray chert.
Priv. col., museum quality, valued $20-25.

• Levanna from Essex co., VA. Point 1 3/8 in. long, 3/4 in. wide, 1/8 in. thick. Made of light gray chert.
Priv. col., excellent quality, valued $10-15.

• Levanna from Essex co., VA. Point 1 1/16 in. long, 7/8 in. wide, 3/16 in. thick. Made of coal black chert.
Priv. col., excellent quality, valued $10-15.

● Levanna from Essex co., VA. Point 1 1/2 in. long, 1 in. wide, 1/8 in. thick. Made of quartzite.
Priv. col., average quality, valued $2-5.

●Levanna from Highland co., VA. Point 1 1/3 in. long, 1 1/3 in. wide, 1/8 in. thick. Made of brown chert.
Priv. col., excellent quality, valued $10-15.

● Levanna from Highland co., VA. Point 1 1/8 in. long, 7/8 in. wide, 3/16 in. thick. Made of brown chert.
Priv. col., excellent quality, valued $5-10.

● Levanna from Highland co., VA. Point 1 1/2 in. long, 1 1/3 in. wide, 1/8 in. thick. Made of brown chert.
Priv. col., excellent quality, valued $10-15.

● Levanna from Highland co., VA. Point 1 3/8 in. long, 1 1/2 in. wide, 1/8 in. thick. Made of light gray pebble chert.
Priv. col., excellent quality, valued $10-15.

● Levanna from Patrick co., VA. Point 1 1/3 in. long, 1 1/8 in. wide, 3/16 in. thick. Made of quartzite.
Priv. col., average quality, valued $5-10.

● Levanna from Patrick co., VA. Point 1 1/8 in. long, 7/8 in. wide, 1/8 in. thick. Made of light gray chert.
Priv. col., excellent quality, valued $10-15.

● Levanna from Patrick co., VA. Point 1 1/8 in. long, 1 in. wide, 1/8 in. thick. Made of gray chert.
Priv. col., excellent quality, valued $10-15.

●Levanna from Mathews co., VA. Point 1 3/4 in. long, 1 1/8 in. wide, 3/16 in. thick. Made of rose quartz.
Priv. col., museum quality, valued $25-30.

● Levanna from Mathews co., VA. Point 1 3/8 in. long, 1 1/8 in. wide, 1/8 in. thick. Made of light gray chert.
Priv. col., excellent quality, valued $10-15.

- Levanna from Mathews co., VA. Point 1 1/8 in. long, 1 1/3 in. wide, 1/8 in. thick. Made of light gray chert.
Priv. col., excellent quality, valued $10-15.

- Levanna from Mathews co., VA. Point 1 3/8 in. long, 1 1/8 in. wide, 3/16 in. thick. Made of quartzite.
Priv. col., excellent quality, valued $5-10.

- Levanna from Grayson co., VA. Point 1 3/8 in. long, 1 in. wide, 1/8 in. thick. Made of gray chert.
Priv. col., excellent quality, valued $15-20.

- Levanna from Grayson co., VA. Point 1 5/8 in. long, 1 3/8 in. wide, 1/8 in. thick. Made of light gray chert.
Priv. col., excellent quality, valued $10-15.

- Levanna from Grayson co., VA. Point 1 3/8 in. long, 1 1/8 in. wide, 3/16 in. thick. Made of quartzite.
Priv. col., excellent quality, valued $5-10.

- Levanna from Clarke co., VA. Point 1 3/8 in. long, 1 1/4 in. wide, 1/8 in. thick. Made of light gray chert.
Priv. col., average quality, valued $10-15.

- Levanna from Clarke co., VA. Point 1 1/2 in. long, 1 1/3 in. wide, 1/8 in. thick. Made of quartzite.
Priv. col., average quality, valued $5-10.

- Levanna from central WV. Point 1 3/8 in. long, 1 in. wide, 3/16 in. thick. Made of grainy brown chert.
Priv. col., average quality, valued $5-10.

Levey: 7,000-3,000 B.P. Mid-Archaic

Located in the southeastern U.S. Medium sized point, wide tapered or barbed shoulders. Short stemmed snapped base.

◆ Levey from Marshall co., TN. Point 1 1/4 in. long, 7/8 in. wide, 1/4 in. thick.

Very rough point, crudely flaked, one edge nick, good field patina. Made of quartzite.

Grover Bohannon col., poor quality, valued $4-6.

♦ Levey from Marshall co., TN. Point 1 in. long, 5/8 in. wide, 1/8 in. thick. Well-made point for a Levey, heavy patina, rounded tip. Point beveled on one side of each face. Made of Mill Creek chert.

Grover Bohannon col., excellent quality, valued $15-25.

• Levey from Perry co., TN. Point 1 5/8 in. long, 2/3 in. wide, 1/4 in. thick. Highly serrated, fine workmanship, sharp tip, beveled on one side of each face. Made of tan pebble chert.
Priv. col., excellent quality, valued $15-20.

• Levey from Davidson co., TN. Point 1 1/8 in. long, 3/4 in. wide, 1/4 in. thick. Heat treated, highly serrated, rounded tip. Several small nicks in point edges. Made of white pebble chert.
Priv. col., poor quality, valued $5-10.

• Levey from Humphreys co., TN. Point 2 5/8 in. long, 1 3/4 in. wide, 3/16 in. thick. Long and wide for a Levey, point highly serrated, sharp tip. Concave base, unusual for this type. Made of pinkish pebble chert.
Priv. col., museum quality, valued $20-30.

• Levey from Davidson co., TN. Point 1 3/4 in. long, 1/3 in. wide, 3/16 in. thick. Long and narrow point, beveled on one side each face. Well-made point highly serrated, sharp tip. Made of amber colored quartz.
Priv. col., museum quality, valued $35-45.

• Levey from Caddo Parish, LA. Point 2 5/8 in. long, 1 2/3 in. wide, 1/4 in. thick. Made of high grade quartzite.
Priv. col., excellent quality, valued $15-20.

• Levey from Caddo Parish, LA. Point 2 1/8 in. long, 1 3/4 in. wide, 1/4 in. thick. Made of white pink pebble chert.
Priv. col., excellent quality, valued $25-30.

• Levey from Barrow co., GA. Point 2 1/8 in. long, 1 3/4 in. wide, 3/16 in. thick. Made of white chert.
Priv. col., excellent quality, valued $20-30.

• Levey from Barrow co., GA. Point 2 3/4 in. long, 2 1/3 in. wide, 3/16 in. thick. Made of amber colored quartz.
Priv. col., museum quality, valued $35-45.

• Levey from Barrow co., GA. Point 1 7/8 in. long, 1 2/3 in. wide, 1/4 in. thick. Made of marbled tan chert.
Priv. col., museum quality, valued $25-30.

• Levey from Dawson co., GA. Point 3 1/8 in. long, 2 1/2 in. wide, 1/4 in. thick. Made of quartzite.
Priv. col., poor quality, valued $5-10.

• Levey from Dawson co., GA. Point 2 5/8 in. long, 2 1/16 in. wide, 3/16 in. thick. Made of dense glossy white chert.
Priv. col., museum quality, valued $40-50.

• Levey from Dawson co., GA. Point 1 7/8 in. long, 1 1/3 in. wide, 3/16 in. thick. Made of beige chert.
Priv. col., museum quality, valued $35-45.

• Levey from Rabun co., GA. Point 2 5/8 in. long, 1 2/3 in. wide, 1/4 in. thick. Fine workmanship. Made of marble brown tan slate.
Priv. col., excellent quality, valued $25-30.

• Levey from Rabun co., GA. Point 1 3/8 in. long, 2/3 in. wide, 1/4 in. thick. Heat treated. Made of white pebble chert.
Priv. col., average quality, valued $10-15.

- Levey from Rabun co., GA. Point 2 3/8 in. long, 1 3/4 in. wide, 1/4 in. thick. Made of greenish pebble chert.
Priv. col., excellent quality, valued $20-30.

- Levey from Harris co., GA. Point 2 1/4 in. long, 1 2/3 in. wide, 3/16 in. thick. Made of quartzite.
Priv. col., average quality, valued $15-20.

- Levey from Harris co., GA. Point 1 5/8 in. long, 1 1/3 in. wide, 1/4 in. thick. Made of tan to yellow chert.
Priv. col., excellent quality, valued $15-20.

- Levey from Harris co., GA. Point 1 7/8 in. long, 1 1/4 in. wide, 1/4 in. thick. Made of white pebble chert.
Priv. col., excellent quality, valued $25-30.

- Levey from Laurens co., GA. Point 2 7/8 in. long, 1 3/4 in. wide, 3/16 in. thick. Good workmanship. Made of high grade pink chert.
Priv. col., museum quality, valued $50-60.

- Levey from Laurens co., GA. Point 2 3/4 in. long, 1 3/4 in. wide, 3/16 in. thick. Made of quartzite.
Priv. col., average quality, valued $15-20.

- Levey from Dixie co., FL. Point 2 3/8 in. long, 1 2/3 in. wide, 1/4 in. thick. Made of tan pebble chert.
Priv. col., excellent quality, valued $15-20.

- Levey from Dixie co., FL. Point 1 1/8 in. long, 3/4 in. wide, 1/4 in. thick. Made of white pebble chert.
Priv. col., poor quality, valued $5-10.

- Levey from Dixie co., FL. Point 2 5/8 in. long, 1 7/8 in. wide, 3/16 in. thick. Made of pinkish gray pebble chert.
Priv. col., museum quality, valued $40-45.

- Levey from Dixie co., FL. Point 1 3/4 in. long, 1 1/8 in. wide, 3/16 in. thick. Made of amber quartzite.
Priv. col., poor quality, valued $5-10.

• Levey from Gilchrist co., FL. Point 1 3/8 in. long, 2/3 in. wide, 1/4 in. thick. Made of quartzite.
Priv. col., average quality, valued $15-20.

• Levey from Gilchrist co., FL. Point 1 1/8 in. long, 1 in. wide, 1/4 in. thick. Made of quartzite.
Priv. col., poor quality, valued $5-10.

• Levey from Gilchrist co., FL. Point 2 1/2 in. long, 1 3/4 in. wide, 1/4 in. thick. Heat treated. Made of pinkish quartzite.
Priv. col., average quality, valued $10-20.

• Levey from Gilchrist co., FL. Point 2 1/4 in. long, 1 1/3 in. wide, 3/16 in. thick. Made of quartzite.
Priv. col., average quality, valued $10-15.

Little Bear Creek: 4,500-1,200 B.P. Late Archaic to Woodland

Found predominantly in the southeastern states. A medium to large sized point or blade. Usually narrow, long parallel stems, edges convex. Even average quality pieces are exceptionally crafted. Squared shoulders, slightly barbed. Base is fractured or snapped. Edges are usually beveled on one side of each face, finely and sharply serrated.

♦ Little Bear Creek found in the Cumberland River, Livingston co., KY. Blade 4 7/8 in. long, 1 3/8 in. wide, 5/16 in. thick. Stem 1/2 in. long, narrow, finely worked, sharply serrated with sharp tip. Made of Dover chert.

Tony Clinton col., museum quality, valued $250-350.

♦ Little Bear Creek from Humphreys co., TN. Blade 3 7/8 in. long, 1 3/4 in. wide, 1/4 in. thick. Finely serrated blade, tip very sharp, narrow blade. Parallel shoulders, slightly concave sided stem with straight base. Made of Dover chert.

Priv. col., museum quality, valued $350-500.

- Little Bear Creek from Hamilton co., TN. Blade 4 3/8 in. long, 1 2/3 in. wide, 1/4 in. thick. Finely serrated blade, tip very sharp, narrow blade. Parallel square shoulders, slightly concave stem with snapped base. Made of Dover chert. *Priv. col., museum quality, valued $380-520.*

- Little Bear Creek from Shelby co., IL. Blade 3 3/4 in. long, 2 1/4 in. wide, 1/4 in. thick. Finely serrated blade, beveled on one edge of each face, wide yet symmetrical blade. Square shoulders, concave stem with straight base. Made of greenish pebble chert. *Priv. col., excellent quality, valued $250-300.*

- Little Bear Creek from Pulaski co., KY. Blade 5 3/8 in. long, 1 2/3 in. wide, 1/4 in. thick. Finely serrated blade, tip sharp, thin, narrow blade. Parallel barbed shoulders, slightly concave stem, straight base. Made of tan pink speckled chert. *Priv. col., average quality, valued $150-200.*

- Little Bear Creek from Johnson co., IL. Blade 4 1/8 in. long, 2 in. wide, 1/4 in. thick. Deeply beveled on one side of each face, finely serrated and sharp. Made of Mill Creek chert. *Priv. col., excellent quality, valued $200-250.*

- Little Bear Creek from Tunice co., MS. Blade 4 3/4 in. long, 1 1/2 in. wide, 1/4 in. thick. Made of dark gray chert. *Priv. col., excellent quality, valued $250-300.*

- Little Bear Creek from Sharkey co., MS. Blade 5 1/4 in. long, 2 1/16 in. wide, 1/4 in. thick. Made of greenish pink chert. *Priv. col., excellent quality, valued $275-350.*

- Little Bear Creek from Sharkey co., MS. Blade 5 1/3 in. long, 1 3/4 in. wide, 1/4 in. thick. Made of gray pink chert. *Priv. col., excellent quality, valued $250-300.*

- Little Bear Creek from Sharkey co., MS. Blade 5 1/32 in. long, 2 in. wide,

1/4 in. thick. Made of yellow tan chert.
Priv. col., excellent quality, valued $250-350.

• Little Bear Creek from Sharkey co., MS. Blade 4 2/3 in. long, 2 1/4 in. wide, 1/4 in. thick. Made of gray chert.
Priv. col., excellent quality, valued $250-300.

• Little Bear Creek from Kemper co., MS. Point 3 1/2 in. long, 1 1/4 in. wide, 1/4 in. thick. Made of dull white chert.
Priv. col., excellent quality, valued $250-300.

• Little Bear Creek from Kemper co., MS. Point 3 1/3 in. long, 1 3/16 in. wide, 1/4 in. thick. Made of pink chert.
Priv. col., excellent quality, valued $250-300.

• Little Bear Creek from Jasper co., MS. Blade 4 3/4 in. long, 1 3/16 in. wide, 1/4 in. thick. Made of marbled white brown chert.
Priv. col., excellent quality, valued $275-350.

• Little Bear Creek from Jasper co., MS. Blade 5 1/32 in. long, 1 11/16 in. wide, 1/4 in. thick. Made of marbled white brown chert.
Priv. col., excellent quality, valued $300-350.

• Little Bear Creek from Jasper co., MS. Blade 5 1/2 in. long, 2 1/8 in. wide, 1/4 in. thick. Excellent workmanship. Made of white chert.
Priv. col., excellent quality, valued $375-450.

• Little Bear Creek from Jasper co., MS. Blade 5 1/3 in. long, 1 3/4 in. wide, 3/16 in. thick. Good workmanship. Made of marbled white brown chert.
Priv. col., excellent quality, valued $325-400.

• Little Bear Creek from Jasper co., MS. Point 3 1/4 in. long, 1 3/16 in. wide, 1/4 in. thick. Made of pinkish white chert.
Priv. col., excellent quality, valued $250-275.

• Little Bear Creek from Leake co., MS. Point 3 1/8 in. long, 1 1/3 in. wide, 1/4 in. thick. Made of white chert.
Priv. col., average quality, valued $50-80.

• Little Bear Creek from Leake co., MS. Blade 3 1/4 in. long, 1 5/16 in. wide, 1/4 in. thick. Made of white pebble chert.

Priv. col., average quality, valued $100-125.

• Little Bear Creek from Leake co., MS. Blade 5 1/3 in. long, 1 3/4 in. wide, 1/4 in. thick. Beveled on one side of each face. Made of gray pink chert. *Priv. col., excellent quality, valued $250-300.*

• Little Bear Creek from Butts co., GA. Blade 5 1/32 in. long, 2 in. wide, 1/4 in. thick. Excellent workmanship. Made of pink pebble chert. *Priv. col., excellent quality, valued $375-450.*

• Little Bear Creek from Butts co., GA. Blade 5 2/3 in. long, 1 1/3 in. wide, 1/4 in. thick. Excellent workmanship. Made of gray pink speckled chert. *Priv. col., museum quality, valued $550-700.*

• Little Bear Creek from Ben Hill co., GA. Blade 4 1/3 in. long, 2 1/32 in. wide, 1/4 in. thick. Made of translucent brown chert. *Priv. col., museum quality, valued $475-550.*

• Little Bear Creek from Ben Hill co., GA. Blade 5 1/2 in. long, 2 1/8 in. wide, 1/4 in. thick. Good workmanship. Made of high grade pink chert. *Priv. col., museum quality, valued $650-800.*

• Little Bear Creek from Ben Hill co., GA. Blade 5 in. long, 1 5/16 in. wide, 1/4 in. thick. Good workmanship. Made of greenish black speckled chert. *Priv. col., museum quality, valued $575-650.*

• Little Bear Creek from Livingston Parish, LA. Blade 5 1/3 in. long, 1 3/4 in. wide, 1/4 in. thick. Right hand beveled. Made of gray chert. *Priv. col., excellent quality, valued $350-400.*

• Little Bear Creek from Livingston Parish, LA. Point 2 1/2 in. long, 13/16 in. wide, 1/8 in. thick. Excellent workmanship, beveled on one side of each face. The serrating is minute and distinct. Made of pink chert. *Priv. col., museum quality, valued $575-650.*

• Little Bear Creek from Livingston Parish, LA. Blade 5 2/3 in. long, 2 in. wide, 3/16 in. thick. Excellent workmanship. Made of gray pink chert. *Priv. col., museum quality, valued $350-400.*

Livermore: 1,200-500 B.P. Mississippian

Found in the Midwest. Small to medium sized point. Very narrow,
widely serrated, with flaring barbs. Usually with sharp distinct tips.

◆ Livermore from Johnson co., IL. Point 1 5/8 in. long, 3/16 in. wide, 1/8 in.
thick. Deeply serrated round tip. Long wide tangs, rounded bulbous stem. Made
of pinkish pebble chert.

Priv. col., average quality, valued $5-10.

• Livermore from Johnson co., IL. Point 1 3/8 in. long, 1/4 in. wide, 1/8 in.
thick. Deeply serrated round tip, symmetrical, narrow. Long tangs, rounded
bulbous stem. Made of Mill Creek chert.
Priv. col., average quality, valued $5-10.

• Livermore from Union co., IL. Point 1 7/8 in. long, 3/16 in. wide, 1/8 in. thick.
Deep, wide serrations, very narrow point. Long tangs, long stem, straight base.
Made of Cobden chert.
Priv. col., excellent quality, valued $25-30.

• Livermore from Johnson co., IL. Point 2 1/8 in. long, 7/16 in. wide, 1/8 in.
thick. Deeply serrated, sharp round tip, parallel tangs, very sharp edges. Made of
pinkish pebble chert.
Priv. col., excellent quality, valued $15-20.

• Livermore from Marshall co., TN. Point 1 7/8 in. long, 3/16 in. wide, 3/16 in.
thick. Wide, deep serrations, flaring tangs. Sharp tip finely serrated.
Priv. col., museum quality, valued $60-90.

• Livermore from Atchison co., KS. Point 1 1/2 in. long, 1 1/4 in. wide, 1/8 in.
thick. Made of gray chert.
Priv. col., average quality, valued $5-10.

• Livermore from Ballard co., KY. Point 1 1/8 in. long, 7/16 in. wide, 1/8 in.
thick. Made of tan chert.
Priv. col., average quality, valued $5-10.

- Livermore from Barber co., KS. Point 1 1/8 in. long, 7/16 in. wide, 1/8 in. thick. Made of gray chert.
Priv. col., average quality, valued $5-10.

- Livermore from Cheyenne co., KS. Point 1 3/8 in. long, 1/4 in. wide, 1/8 in. thick. Crude workmanship, excellent material. Made of marbled gray chert.
Priv. col., average quality, valued $5-10.

- Livermore from Cheyenne co., KS. Point 1 3/8 in. long, 5/16 in. wide, 1/8 in. thick. Made of gray marbled chert.
Priv. col., excellent quality, valued $25-30.

- Livermore from Cheyenne co., KS. Point 1 1/2 in. long, 1 in. wide, 1/8 in. thick. Made of marbled gray chert.
Priv. col., excellent quality, valued $15-20.

- Livermore from Cheyenne co., KS. Point 2 1/8 in. long, 1 1/16 in. wide, 1/8 in. thick. Excellent workmanship and material. Made of marbled gray chert.
Priv. col., average quality, valued $5-10.

- Livermore from Cheyenne co., KS. Point 1 5/16 in. long, 1/2 in. wide, 1/8 in. thick. Made of marbled gray chert.
Priv. col., average quality, valued $5-10.

- Livermore from Cheyenne co., KS. Point 1 3/4 in. long, 1 1/32 in. wide, 1/8 in. thick. Made of gray marbled chert.
Priv. col., average quality, valued $5-10.

- Livermore from Pratt co., KS. Point 1 1/2 in. long, 1 1/4 in. wide, 1/8 in. thick. Made of dull gray chert.
Priv. col., average quality, valued $10-15.

- Livermore from Pratt co., KS. Point 2 1/8 in. long, 1 7/16 in. wide, 5/16 in. thick. Made of gray chert.
Priv. col., average quality, valued $5-10.

- Livermore from Pratt co., KS. Point 7/8 in. long, 1/8 in. wide, 1/8 in. thick. Good workmanship, very narrow Livermore. Made of gray chert.
Priv. col., excellent quality, valued $25-30.

- Livermore from Carlise co., KY. Point 1 1/8 in. long, 11/16 in. wide, 1/8 in. thick. Made of tan brown chert.
Priv. col., excellent quality, valued $25-30.

- Livermore from Carlise co., KY. Point 1 1/2 in. long, 1 1/32 in. wide, 1/8 in. thick. Made of gray chert.
Priv. col., excellent quality, valued $25-30.

- Livermore from Carlise co., KY. Point 2 1/32 in. long, 1 3/16 in. wide, 1/8 in. thick. Made of gray chert.
Priv. col., museum quality, valued $45-50.

- Livermore from Clinton co., KY. Point 1 3/8 in. long, 1 1/4 in. wide, 1/8 in. thick. Made of marbled pink gray chert.
Priv. col., excellent quality, valued $20-25.

- Livermore from Clinton co., KY. Point 1 3/8 in. long, 13/16 in. wide, 1/8 in. thick. Made of pink gray marbled chert.
Priv. col., excellent quality, valued $25-30.

- Livermore from Oldam co., KY. Point 1 1/3 in. long, 13/16 in. wide, 1/8 in. thick. Made of gray chert.
Priv. col., excellent quality, valued $15-20.

- Livermore from Bullitt co., KY. Point 1 5/8 in. long, 1 3/16 in. wide, 1/8 in. thick. Made of tan white chert.
Priv. col., excellent quality, valued $15-20.

- Livermore from Bullitt co., KY. Point 1 7/8 in. long, 1 1/4 in. wide, 1/8 in. thick. Heat treated. Made of tan white chert.
Priv. col., excellent quality, valued $25-30.

- Livermore from Bullitt co., KY. Point 1 5/8 in. long, 1 1/16 in. wide, 1/8 in. thick. Made of gray chert.
Priv. col., excellent quality, valued $25-30.

- Livermore from White co., IL. Point 2 1/2 in. long, 1 2/3 in. wide, 1/8 in. thick. Excellent workmanship. Made of white chert.
Priv. col., museum quality, valued $45-60.

Llano: 10,000-7,000 B.P. Late Paleo

Found predominantly in the Midwest. Medium to large sized point or blade. Triangular points and blades generally serrated. The base is fluted or long flaked and thin. Mostly parallel flaked.

* Llano from Humphreys co., TN. Point 2 1/4 in. long, 1 in. wide, 1/4 in. thick.

Heavily serrated, flaring tangs, highly fluted. Made of jasper.
Grover Bohannon col., museum quality, valued $80-120.

* Llano from Gallatin co., IL. Point 2 11/16 in. long, 1 1/8 in. wide, 3/16 in. thick. Point is triangular, serrated. The base is fluted and thin, parallel flaked. Made of tan chert.
Priv. col., excellent quality, valued $60-80.

* Llano from Perry co., TN. Point 2 3/4 in. long, 1 in. wide, 1/8 in. thick. Narrow, thin, symmetrical, with flaring tangs, parallel flaked. Made of white quartzite grained pebble chert.
Grover Bohannon col., average quality, valued $30-45.

* Llano from Owen co., MO. Blade 3 7/8 in. long, 2 in. wide, 1/4 in. thick. Blade, triangular, symmetrical, blade highly serrated. The base is fluted and flaked thin. Thin, angular, parallel flaked. Made of white chert.
Priv. col., excellent quality, valued $45-60.

* Llano from Perry co., TN. Point 2 3/4 in. long, 1 1/2 in. wide, 3/16 in. thick. Point sharply serrated, flaring tangs, fluted. Made of Dover chert.
Priv. col., museum quality, valued $70-100.

◆ Llano from Lubbock co., TX. point 1 1/4 in. long, 1 5/8 in. wide, 1/4 in. thick. Wide, finely serrated, flaring tangs, deep concave base. Made of pink quartzite.

Priv. col., excellent quality, valued $40-70.

- Llano from Lubbock co., TX. Point 2 1/8 in. long, 1 3/8 in. wide, 1/2 in. thick.
Thick, finely serrated, flaring tangs, several edge nicks, deep concave base. Made of white pebble chert.
Priv. col., average quality, valued $20-40.

- Llano from Craig co., OK. Point 2 1/32 in. long, 1 1/3 in. wide, 7/16 in. thick. Made of tan chert.
Priv. col., average quality, valued $10-20.

- Llano from Craig co., OK. Point 2 in. long, 1 3/32 in. wide, 5/16 in. thick. Made of quartzite.
Priv. col., average quality, valued $20-30.

- Llano from Craig co., OK. Point 2 1/2 in. long, 1 1/3 in. wide, 1/2 in. thick. Made of quartzite.
Priv. col., average quality, valued $10-15.

- Llano from Craig co., OK. Point 2 11/32 in. long, 1 1/2 in. wide, 1/2 in. thick. Made of quartzite.
Priv. col., average quality, valued $10-20.

- Llano from Craig co., OK. Point 2 1/2 in. long, 1 9/32 in. wide, 7/16 in. thick. Made of quartzite.
Priv. col., average quality, valued $20-30.

- Llano from Payne co., OK. Point 2 17/32 in. long, 1 1/3 in. wide, 1/2 in. thick. Made of tan chert.
Priv. col., average quality, valued $10-20.

- Llano from Payne co., OK. Point 2 1/3 in. long, 1 3/16 in. wide, 1/4 in. thick. Made of quartzite.
Priv. col., average quality, valued $20-30.

- Llano from Johnson co., IL. Point 2 1/3 in. long, 1 1/3 in. wide, 7/16 in. thick. Made of Cobden chert.
Priv. col., museum quality, valued $40-60.

- Llano from Johnson co., IL. Point 2 5/8 in. long, 1 11/32 in. wide, 5/16 in. thick. Beveled on one side of each face. Made of Cobden chert.
Priv. col., museum quality, valued $50-70.

• Llano from Johnson co., IL. Point 2 13/32 in. long, 1 1/3 in. wide, 7/16 in. thick. Made of gray chert.
Priv. col., excellent quality, valued $30-40.

• Llano from Johnson co., IL. Point 2 1/4 in. long, 1 3/16 in. wide, 1/4 in. thick. Made of Mill Creek chert.
Priv. col., excellent quality, valued $35-40.

• Llano from Hardin co., IL. Point 2 21/32 in. long, 1 2/3 in. wide, 1/2 in. thick. Made of grainy gray chert.
Priv. col., average quality, valued $10-20.

• Llano from Hardin co., IL. Point 2 1/16 in. long, 1 13/32 in. wide, 5/16 in. thick. Made of gray chert.
Priv. col., excellent quality, valued $25-35.

• Llano from Gallatin co., IL. Point 2 1/3 in. long, 1 1/2 in. wide, 7/16 in. thick. Made of gray chert.
Priv. col., excellent quality, valued $40-45.

• Llano from Gallatin co., IL. Point 2 1/4 in. long, 1 1/2 in. wide, 9/16 in. thick. Made of gray chert.
Priv. col., excellent quality, valued $40-50.

• Llano from Cumberland co., IL. Blade 4 1/2 in. long, 2 1/16 in. wide, 1/4 in. thick. Long blade, triangular, sharply serrated. The base is fluted, parallel flaked. Made of greenish pebble chert.
Priv. col, excellent quality, valued $60-75.

Lost Lake: 9,000-6,000 B.P. Early Archaic

Found predominantly throughout the Midwest and Southeast. Medium to large sized point or blade. Corner notched, symmetrical, beveled on one edge of each face. High quality flaking workmanship, finely to sharply serrated.

♦ Lost Lake from Humphreys co., IL. Blade 3 1/2 in. long, 1 1/4 in. wide, 1/8 in. thick. Very deeply corner notched, steeply beveled on all four sides, finely serrated and thin. Straight base, sharply serrated tip. Made of Dover chert.

Priv. col., museum quality, valued $125-175.

◆ Lost Lake from Stewart co., TN. Blade 3 1/8 in. long, 1 1/4 in. wide, 3/16 in. thick. Beveled, tapered blade, sharply serrated, parallel flaked. Deep corner notches with rounded tangs, concave base with rounded corners. Made of Dover chert.

Priv. col., excellent quality, valued $80-120.

◆ Lost Lake from Buffalo River, Wayne co., TN. Blade 3 1/2 in. long, 1 7/8 in. wide, 1/4 in. thick. Deep 3/4 in. notches, beautiful symmetrical parallel flaked piece, sharp and finely serrated. Made of Buffalo River chert.

Bob Maples col., museum quality, valued $300-450.

◆ Lost Lake from northwestern TN. Point 2 1/4 in. long, 1 1/2 in. wide, 3/16 in. thick. Straight based, deep notched with symmetrical rounded tangs. Heat treated with fine sharp serrations. Made of Dover chert.

Les Grubbe col., excellent quality, valued $80-130.

◆ Lost Lake from northwestern TN. Blade 4 in. long, 1 13/32 in. wide, 1/4 in. thick. Very deep corner notches, thin flaring tangs, slightly convex base. Very finely serrated beveled edges. Made of Dover chert.

Les Grubbe col., excellent quality, valued $120-160.

◆ Lost Lake from Marshall co., TN. Blade 7 7/8 in. long, 2 3/4 in. wide, 1/4 in. thick. Very large, truly a spectacular and very rare piece. Thin and finely parallel flaked, finely and sharply serrated. Smooth beveling on opposing sides, extremely symmetrical, with deep notches. Crystalline natural hole in blade. Made of Dover chert.

Grover Bohannon col., museum quality, rare, valued $2,750-3,500.

• Lost Lake from Delta co., MI. Blade 4 1/2 in. long, 1 1/2 in. wide, 1/8 in. thick. Thin, deeply corner notched, steeply beveled on one edge of each face, Sharply serrated, straight base. Made of unidentified green pink speckled chert. *Priv. col., excellent quality, $100-150.*

• Lost Lake from Champaign co., IL. Point 2 1/8 in. long, 1/3 in. wide, 1/4 in. thick. Beveled, thick, tapered blade, sharply serrated, parallel flaked. Typical deep corner notches with long ground tangs, concave base with rounded corners. Made of tan to gray chert. *Priv. col., excellent quality, valued $90-125.*

• Lost Lake from Wayne co., TN. Blade 3 5/8 in. long, 1 3/8 in. wide, 1/4 in. thick. Deep notches, symmetrical parallel flaked though thick, sharp and finely serrated. Made of Buffalo River chert
Priv. col., excellent quality, valued $200-250.

• Lost Lake from JoDavies co., IL. Point 2 in. long, 1 1/3 in. wide, 3/16 in. thick. Wide, parallel flaked, deep notched, symmetrical rounded tangs. Symmetrical point despite its width, finely and sharply serrated. Made of Cobden chert.
Priv. col., excellent quality, valued $120-180.

• Lost Lake from Maury co., TN. Blade 4 1/2 in. long, 1 17/32 in. wide, 1/8 in. thick. Deep corner notches, thin, snapped, flaring tangs, shallow concave base. Finely serrated, beveled on opposing edges. Made of local gray chert.
Priv. col., excellent quality, valued $250-360.

• Lost Lake from Hardin co., IL. Blade 3 5/8 in. long, 1/3 in. wide, 1/4 in. thick. Made of gray chert.
Priv. col., excellent quality, valued $180-200.

• Lost Lake from Wayne co., TN. Blade 3 5/8 in. long, 1 3/8 in. wide, 1/4 in. thick. Good workmanship, beveled on all four edges. Made of Buffalo River chert.
Priv. col., excellent quality, valued $200-250.

• Lost Lake from Metcalfe co., KY. Point 2 1/8 in. long, 1/3 in. wide, 1/4 in. thick. Made of tan gray chert.
Priv. col., excellent quality, valued $90-125.

• Lost Lake from Metcalfe co., KY. Blade 4 3/8 in. long, 2 1/2 in. wide, 1/4 in. thick. Made of glossy brown chert
Priv. col., excellent quality, valued $200-250.

• Lost Lake from Metcalfe co., KY. Blade 4 1/8 in. long, 1 1/2 in. wide, 1/4 in. thick. Made of tan chert.
Priv. col., excellent quality, valued $90-125.

• Lost Lake from Metcalfe co., KY. Blade 3 7/8 in. long, 2 in. wide, 1/4 in. thick. Made of glossy brown chert
Priv. col., museum quality, valued $400-450.

• Lost Lake from Massac co., IL. Point 2 5/8 in. long, 1 1/3 in. wide, 1/4 in. thick. Made of tan to gray chert.
Priv. col., excellent quality, valued $90-125.

• Lost Lake from Massac co., IL. Point 2 7/8 in. long, 1 1/2 in. wide, 1/4 in. thick. Made of Mill Creek chert
Priv. col., excellent quality, valued $100-150.

• Lost Lake from Massac co., IL. Point 2 3/4 in. long, 1 1/3 in. wide, 1/4 in. thick. Made of tan to gray chert.
Priv. col., excellent quality, valued $100-125.

• Lost Lake from Pope co., IL. Blade 4 5/8 in. long, 2 1/8 in. wide, 1/4 in. thick. Made of Kaolin chert
Priv. col., museum quality, rare, valued $700-850.

• Lost Lake from Pope co., IL. Point 4 1/8 in. long, 2 1/3 in. wide, 3/16 in. thick. Heat treated. Made of tan gray chert.
Priv. col., excellent quality, valued $150-175.

• Lost Lake from Pope co., IL. Blade 3 5/8 in. long, 1 1/4 in. wide, 1/4 in. thick. Made of Cobden chert
Priv. col., excellent quality, valued $200-250.

• Lost Lake from DeWitt co., IL. Point 2 1/2 in. long, 1 1/3 in. wide, 1/4 in. thick. Made of tan to gray chert.
Priv. col., excellent quality, valued $120-150.

• Lost Lake from DeWitt co., IL. Blade 3 7/8 in. long, 1 3/8 in. wide, 1/4 in. thick. Made of Cobden chert
Priv. col., excellent quality, valued $200-250.

CHAPTER 11
MADISON-NOOTKA

Madison: 1,100-150 B.P. Mississippian to Historical

Found in the Midwest and throughout the entire East. Symmetrically triangular point, small to medium in size. Maybe notched on two or three sides with straight base. Base is predominantly concave. Good workmanship exhibited throughout this piece type. Edges are finely serrated and sharp.

◆ Madisons from Hamilton co., TN. *Left*: point 1 3/4 in. long, 1/2 in. wide, 1/8 in. thick; *right*: point 1 2/3 in. long, 5/8 in. wide, 3/16 in. thick. Both points beveled and serrated with straight bases. Both made of a lightweight white pebble chert.

Priv. col., Left: average quality, valued $15-25; right: average quality, valued $12-20.

◆ Madison from Hamilton co., TN. Point 1 5/8 in. long, 2/3 in. wide, 1/8 in. thick. Finely and sharply serrated, thinned concave base. Made of purple chert.

Priv. col., museum quality, valued $30-40.

◆ Madison from Henderson co., TN. Point 1 1/2 in. long, 1/2 in. wide, 1/16 in. thick. Finely serrated, very thin, sharp symmetrically triangular point. Transverse flaking, with slightly concave base. Made of dark gray chert.

Grover Bohannon col., museum quality, valued $30-45.

• Madison from Hamilton co., TN. Point 2 3/4 in. long, 2 1/4 in. wide, 1/8 in. thick. Point beveled and serrated with straight, thinned bases. Made of white pebble chert.
Priv. col., excellent quality, valued $20-30.

• Madison from Henderson co., TN. Point 1 7/8 in. long, 1/2 in. wide, 1/8 in. thick. Finely, serrated, thinned, narrow, concave base. Made of purple chert.
Priv. col., museum quality, valued $25-40.

• Madison from Henderson co., TN. Point 1 1/2 in. long, 1/2 in. wide, 1/8 in. thick. Finely and sharply serrated, symmetrically triangular point. Transverse flaked, heat treated, concave base. Made of Dover chert.
Grover Bohannon col., museum quality, valued $30-40.

• Madison from Fayette co., TN. Point 2 1/4 in. long, 1 1/2 in. wide, 1/4 in. thick. Point beveled and serrated with straight bases. Made of light tan pebble chert.
Priv. col., average quality, valued $15-20.

• Madison from Dyer co., TN. Point 1 7/8 in. long, 1/2 in. wide, 1/8 in. thick. Finely and sharply serrated, thin and narrow. Symmetrical point with straight base, deep side notches. Made of Dover chert.
Priv. col., excellent quality, valued $20-30.

• Madison from Hamilton co., TN. Point 2 1/8 in. long, 2/3 in. wide, 3/16 in. thick. Sharply serrated, thick, narrow symmetrical point. Transverse flaked, with straight base. Made of Dover chert.
Priv. col., excellent quality, valued $20-35.

• Madison from Swain co., NC. Point 1 in. long, 1/2 in. wide, 1/8 in. thick. Made of milky quartz.
Grover Bohannon col., museum quality, valued $30-40.

• Madison from Swain co., NC. Point 1 1/4 in. long, 11/16 in. wide, 5/16 in. thick. Made of quartzite.
Priv. col., average quality, valued $5-10.

- Madison from Swain co., NC. Point 1 1/16 in. long, 5/8 in. wide, 1/8 in. thick. Made of white chert.
Priv. col., excellent quality, valued $20-30.

- Madison from Hamilton co., TN. Point 2 1/32 in. long, 3/4 in. wide, 3/16 in. thick. Made of Dover chert.
Priv. col., excellent quality, valued $20-35.

- Madison from Davie co., NC. Point 1 5/8 in. long, 1 1/8 in. wide, 1/8 in. thick. Made of white chert.
Priv. col., excellent quality, valued $30-40.

- Madison from Davie co., NC. Point 1 1/4 in. long, 13/16 in. wide, 3/16 in. thick. Made of quartzite.
Priv. col., average quality, valued $10-15.

- Madison from Davie co., NC. Point 1 3/16 in. long, 7/8 in. wide, 1/8 in. thick. Made of white chert.
Priv. col., excxellent quality, valued $25-35.

- Madison from Davie co., NC. Point 1 1/8 in. long, 7/8 in. wide, 1/8 in. thick. Made of milky quartz.
Priv. col., museum quality, valued $30-40.

- Madison from Davie co., NC. Point 1 3/4 in. long, 1 1/16 in. wide, 5/16 in. thick. Made of quartzite.
Priv. col., average quality, valued $5-10.

- Madison from Davie co., NC. Point 1 3/16 in. long, 1 1/8 in. wide, 1/8 in. thick. Made of white chert.
Priv. col., average quality, valued $10-15.

- Madison from Yarkin co., NC. Point 1 1/4 in. long, 1 in. wide, 1/8 in. thick. Made of banded slate.
Priv. col., average quality, valued $10-20.

- Madison from Yarkin co., NC. Point 1 1/3 in. long, 13/16 in. wide, 5/16 in. thick. Made of quartzite.
Priv. col., average quality, valued $5-10.

- Madison from Yarkin co., NC. Point 1 5/16 in. long, 1 1/32 in. wide, 1/8 in. thick. Made of banded white brown chert.

Priv. col., museum quality, valued $35-40.

• Madison from Humphreys co., TN. Point 2 1/16 in. long, 1 1/2 in. wide, 1/8 in. thick. Excellent workmanship. Made of Dover chert.
Priv. col., museum quality, valued $50-60.

• Madison from Humphreys co., TN. Point 2 1/4 in. long, 1 5/16 in. wide, 5/16 in. thick. Made of quartzite.
Priv. col., average quality, valued $15-20.

• Madison from Jefferson co., TN. Point 1 3/16 in. long, 7/8 in. wide, 1/8 in. thick. Made of gray white chert.
Priv. col., excellent quality, valued $20-25.

• Madison from Jefferson co., TN. Point 1 7/8 in. long, 5/8 in. wide, 1/8 in. thick. Made of vein quartz.
Priv. col., museum quality, valued $30-40.

• Madison from Knox co., TN. Point 1 1/4 in. long, 1 in. wide, 3/16 in. thick. Made of quartzite.
Grover Bohannon col., average quality, valued $5-10.

• Madison from Knox co., TN. Point 1 5/16 in. long, 5/8 in. wide, 1/8 in. thick. Made of marbled white brown chert.
Priv. col., excellent quality, valued $25-35.

Marshall: 6,000-2,000 B.P. Mid-Archaic to Woodland

A Midwest point or blade, medium to large in size. Marshalls can be crude to very high in quality of workmanship. They are either corner or basal notched with long barbs. The bases are concave and thin.

♦ Marshall from Derby co., OH. Blade 4 in. long, 2 in. wide, 1/4 in. thick. Heat treated, short stem, deep corner notches. Highly serrated blade with sharp tip and edges. Made of gray tan to white pebble chert.

Charles McCorkle col., museum quality, valued $150-200.

• Marshall from Adams co., IL. Blade 3 3/4 in. long, 2 in. wide, 1/4 in. thick. Heat treated, symmetrical, yet crudely worked. Straight base with deep corner notches. Made of Mill Creek chert.
Charles McCorkle col., average quality, valued $40-70.

• Marshall from Jasper co., IL. Blade 4 3/4 in. long, 2 1/8 in. wide, 1/4 in. thick. Heat treated, deep basal notches. Narrow, symmetrical, thin, high quality workmanship. Highly serrated blade with sharp tip and edges. Made of greenish pebble chert.
Priv. col., museum quality, valued $250-300.

• Marshall from Adams co., IL. Point 2 1/4 in. long, 2 in. wide, 1/2 in. thick. Heat treated, wide and thick, crudely worked. Straight base with shallow corner notches. Made of Mill Creek chert.
Tim Rubbles col., average quality, valued $30-50.

• Marshall from Derby co., OH. Point 2 5/16 in. long, 1 1/2 in. wide, 3/16 in. thick. Heat treated, short stem, deep corner notches. Very thin and symmetrical, high quality workmanship. Highly serrated blade, beveled on one edge of each face. Made of gray tan to white pebble chert.
Priv. col., excellent quality, valued $100-150.

• Marshall from Williamson co., IL. Blade 5 3/4 in. long, 2 7/8 in. wide, 1/4 in. thick. Thin, narrow, symmetrical, high quality workmanship. Straight base with deep parallel corner notches. High estimated value due to material and workmanship. Made of Mill Creek chert.
Priv. col., excellent quality, valued $200-270.

• Marshall from Lucas co., OH. Blade 4 2/3 in. long, 1 7/8 in. wide, 1/4 in. thick. Symmetrical, narrow, thin, high quality workmanship. Heat treated, short stem, deep corner notches. Highly serrated blade with sharp tip and edges. Made of white pebble chert.
Priv. col., museum quality, valued $250-300.

• Marshall from Ballard co., KY. Blade 4 3/4 in. long, 2 11/16 in. wide, 1/4 in. thick. Heat treated, symmetrical, wide, yet thin. Convex base with deep basal notches. Made of white pebble chert.
Priv. col., excellent quality, valued $140-200.

• Marshall from Hamilton co., IL. Blade 3 7/8 in. long, 2 in. wide, 3/16 in. thick. Narrow, thin, long stem, deep corner notches. Highly serrated blade, good workmanship, with sharp edges. Made of gray pebble chert.

Priv. col., excellent quality, valued $85-100.

• Marshall from Adams co., IL. Point 1 3/4 in. long, 1 in. wide, 1/4 in. thick. Heat treated, thick, symmetrical, yet crudely worked. Concave base with shallow corner notches. Made of Mill Creek chert.
Priv. col., average quality, valued $50-75.

• Marshall from Lucas co., OH. Blade 3 2/3 in. long, 2 in. wide, 3/8 in. thick. Thick, narrow, heat treated, deep corner notches. Highly serrated blade with sharp tip and edges. Made of tan pebble chert.
Priv. col., excellent quality, valued $115-140.

• Marshall from Johnson co., IL. Point 2 1/4 in. long, 1 1/16 in. wide, 1/4 in. thick. Heat treated, crudely worked, thick with poorly worked edges. Straight base with deep corner notches. Made of Mill Creek chert.
Priv. col., poor quality, valued $20-30.

• Marshall from Adair co., KS. Point 2 2/3 in. long, 1 5/8 in. wide, 1/8 in. thick. Good workmanship. Made of white chert.
Priv. col., excellent quality, valued $150-200.

• Marshall from Adair co., KS. Point 3 1/4 in. long, 1 2/3 in. wide, 1/4 in. thick. Made of dull gray chert.
Priv. col., excellent quality, valued $200-225.

• Marshall from Cass co., IA. Blade 3 15/16 in. long, 1 3/8 in. wide, 3/16 in. thick. Made of banded red white chert.
Priv. col., museum quality, valued $550-650.

• Marshall from Cass co., IA. Point 2 1/2 in. long, 1 1/2 in. wide, 1/4 in. thick. Several nicks on each blade side. Made of pinkish gray chert.
Priv. col., average quality, valued $35-40.

• Marshall from Cass co., IA. Blade 4 9/32 in. long, 1 5/8 in. wide, 3/8 in. thick. Made of tan pebble chert.
Priv. col., excellent quality, valued $200-300.

• Marshall from Franklin co., IA. Blade 3 13/16 in. long, 2 1/8 in. wide, 1/4 in. thick. Made of grainy white chert.
Priv. col., average quality, valued $80-125.

• Marshall from Miner co., SD. Point 3 in. long, 1 1/2 in. wide, 1/8 in. thick. Excellent workmanship. Made of jasper.

Priv. col., museum quality, rare, valued $500-650.

• Marshall from Lampasas co., TX. Blade 3 7/8 in. long, 1 1/3 in. wide, 3/16 in. thick. Made of dull gray chert.
Priv. col., excellent quality, valued $275-350.

• Marshall from Lampasas co., TX. Point 2 2/3 in. long, 1 1/8 in. wide, 1/4 in. thick. Unusually poor material for a Marshall, good workmanship. Made of quartzite.
Priv. col., average quality, valued $85-125.

• Marshall from Lampasas co., TX. Blade 4 5/32 in. long, 1 7/8 in. wide, 1/3 in. thick. Made of marbled brick red chert.
Priv. col., museum quality, rare, valued $550-650.

• Marshall from Sutton co., TX. Point 3 1/8 in. long, 1 3/8 in. wide, 1/4 in. thick. Made of gray pebble chert.
Priv. col., excellent quality, valued $200-250.

• Marshall from Sutton co., TX. Point 2 3/4 in. long, 7/8 in. wide, 1/4 in. thick. Narrow, layered serrated edges, right hand beveled. Made of glossy dense brown chert.
Priv. col., museum quality, rare, valued $450-600.

• Marshall from Sutton co., TX. Blade 4 1/8 in. long, 1 2/3 in. wide, 1/8 in. thick. Made of dull gray chert.
Priv. col., average quality, valued $100-150.

• Marshall from Briscoe co., TX. Point 2 1/2 in. long, 1 1/3 in. wide, 1/4 in. thick. Heat treated. Made of white chert.
Priv. col., average quality, valued $75-85.

• Marshall from Briscoe co., TX. Point 3 1/3 in. long, 1 7/8 in. wide, 1/8 in. thick. Made of dull gray flint.
Priv. col., excellent quality, valued $250-300.

• Marshall from Briscoe co., TX. Point 2 1/2 in. long, 1 5/16 in. wide, 1/4 in. thick. Heat treated. Made of white chert.
Priv. col., excellent quality, valued $250-325.

• Marshall from Briscoe co., TX. Point 3 in. long, 1 1/2 in. wide, 1/4 in. thick. Heat treated. Made of white chert.
Priv. col., excellent quality, valued $200-250.

• Marshall from Jeff Davis co., TX. Blade 3 7/8 in. long, 1 1/4 in. wide, 3/16 in. thick. Made of high grade pink chert.
Priv. col., museum quality, valued $450-550.

• Marshall from Jeff Davis co., TX. Point 2 7/8 in. long, 1 1/3 in. wide, 1/8 in. thick. Good workmanship. Made of bright white chert.
Priv. col., excellent quality, valued $125-150.

• Marshall from Jeff Davis co., TX. Blade 4 1/32 in. long, 1 7/8 in. wide, 1/4 in. thick. Made of gray chert.
Priv. col., museum quality, valued $350-400.

Matanzas: 4,500-2,500 B.P. Late Archaic to Mississippian

A midwestern piece, small to medium in size. Often a narrow point or blade, side notched. Base is straight or convex, more rarely concave. Edges are generally finely serrated.

♦ Matanzas from Marshall co., TN. Point 1 1/4 in. long, 1/4 in. wide, 1/8 in. thick. Straight base, very narrow point. Made of white pink speckled pebble chert.

Grover Bohannon col., average quality, valued $15-25.

• Matanzas from Dyer co., TN. Blade 3 1/2 in. long, 7/8 in. wide, 3/16 in. thick. Narrow blade, deeply side notched. Base is slightly concave. Edges are sharp and finely serrated. Made of gray chert.
Grover Bohannon col., excellent quality, valued $30-45.

• Matanzas from De Kalb co., TN. Point 1 3/4 in. long, 1/2 in. wide, 1/8 in. thick. Narrow, sharply serrated, deep side notches. Made of pinkish pebble chert.
Grover Bohannon col., excellent quality, valued $25-35.

• Matanzas from Henderson co., KY. Point 2 1/16 in. long, 1 in. wide, 1/8 in. thick. Point wide for the Matanzas, side notched. Base is straight, edges finely serrated. Made of yellow tan local chert.
Priv. col., excellent quality, valued $30-40.

• Matanzas from Henderson co., KY. Point 1 1/2 in. long, 1/3 in. wide, 1/8 in.

thick. Narrow, yet deeply side notched, heat treated. Convex base edges sharply serrated. Made of local yellow tan chert.
Priv. col., museum quality, valued $65-85.

• Matanzas from Williamson co., IL. Point 2 1/8 in. long, 13/16 in. wide, 1/8 in. thick. Symmetrical, thin, side notched, serrated edges. Unique concave base. Made of Cobden chert.
Priv. col., excellent quality, valued $35-45.

• Matanzas from Boone co., MO. Point 2 7/16 in. long, 1 1/32 in. wide, 1/8 in. thick. Made of brown chert.
Priv. col., excellent quality, valued $30-40.

• Matanzas from Boone co., MO. Point 1 2/3 in. long, 7/8 in. wide, 1/8 in. thick. Made of grainy tan chert.
Priv. col., average quality, valued $25-35.

• Matanzas from Boone co., MO. Point 3 1/2 in. long, 1 5/16 in. wide, 1/8 in. thick. Heat treated. Made of brown chert.
Priv. col., excellent quality, valued $55-65.

• Matanzas from Cape Giradeau co., MO. Point 2 13/16 in. long, 1 5/32 in. wide, 1/8 in. thick. Made of brown chert.
Priv. col., excellent quality, valued $35-45.

• Matanzas from Cape Giradeau co., MO. Point 1 3/4 in. long, 11/16 in. wide, 1/8 in. thick. Excellent workmanship. Made of agate.
Priv. col., museum quality, rare, valued $65-85.

• Matanzas from Randolph co., MO. Point 2 11/32 in. long, 13/16 in. wide, 1/4 in. thick. Made of white pebble chert.
Priv. col., excellent quality, valued $30-40.

• Matanzas from Randolph co., MO. Point 2 2/3 in. long, 1 1/2 in. wide, 1/8 in. thick. Made of brown pebble chert.
Priv. col., museum quality, valued $40-50.

• Matanzas from Atchison co., MO. Point 3 1/8 in. long, 1 1/32 in. wide, 3/16 in. thick. Heat treated. Made of yellow tan chert.
Priv. col., excellent quality, valued $40-45.

• Matanzas from Boone co., KY. Point 2 3/16 in. long, 1 in. wide, 1/8 in. thick. Made of brown tan chert.

Priv. col., excellent quality, valued $30-40.

• Matanzas from Henry co., KY. Point 3 in. long, 1 1/4 in. wide, 1/8 in. thick. Made of yellow chert.
Priv. col., average quality, valued $15-25.

• Matanzas from Boyle co., KY. Point 2 2/3 in. long, 7/8 in. wide, 1/8 in. thick. Heat treated, tip break. Made of tan chert.
Priv. col., average quality, valued $5-15.

• Matanzas from Boyle co., KY. Point 2 7/16 in. long, 1 5/32 in. wide, 1/8 in. thick. Made of translucent brown chert.
Priv. col., museum quality, valued $50-60.

• Matanzas from Henry co., KY. Point 1 11/16 in. long, 7/8 in. wide, 1/8 in. thick. Made of tan chert.
Priv. col., average quality, valued $15-25.

• Matanzas from Henry co., KY. Point 3 in. long, 1 1/4 in. wide, 1/8 in. thick. Made of yellow chert.
Priv. col., museum quality, valued $25-35.

McCorkle: 8,000-6,000 B.P. Early Archaic

Found throughout the Midwest into the Southeast. Medium to large sized points and blades. Thin pieces generally serrated, corner notched. Base deeply notched with large round ends.

◆ McCorkle from Adams co., IL. Point 2 1/8 in. long, 1 3/4 in. wide, 1/4 in. thick. Finely serrated, deep symmetrical base notches. Rounded base tangs, sharp tips, deep corner notches. Made of light gray chert.

Charles McCorkle col., museum quality, valued $350-500.

- McCorkle from Green co., IL. Point 2 1/2 in. long, 1 3/4 in. wide, 3/16 in. thick. Deeply serrated, finely flaked, very sharp tip, classic McCorkle. Made of Cobden chert.
Priv. col., museum quality, valued $280-375.

- McCorkle from Bedford co., TN. Point 2 1/2 in. long, 1 1/4 in. wide, 1/4 in. thick. Sharp edges, unusually soft shoulders, rounded tip. Made of gray chert.
Grover Bohannon col., average quality, valued $60-85.

- McCorkle from Dyer co., TN. Point 2 3/16 in. long, 1 5/8 in. wide, 1/4 in. thick. Finely serrated with classic McCorkle design. Made of gray to white chert.
Priv. col., excellent quality, valued $150-220.

- McCorkle from Hancock co., IL. Point 2 1/3 in. long, 1 3/4 in. wide, 1/4 in. thick. Wide, thick, deeply side notched, wide serrations, good workmanship in flaking, very finely serrated sharp tip. Heat treated, classic design. Made of cream pebble chert.
Priv. col., museum quality, valued $200-275.

- McCorkle from Hancock co., IL. Point 2 in. long, 1 1/16 in. wide, 1/8 in. thick. Sharp edges, thin, symmetrical, rounded base tangs. Made of cream pebble chert.
Priv. col., museum quality, valued $260-325.

- McCorkle from Fayette co., TN. Point 2 7/16 in. long, 1 5/8 in. wide, 3/16 in. thick. Finely serrated, deep side notches, classic McCorkle design. Made of gray chert.
Grover Bohannon col., excellent quality, valued $150-220.

- McCorkle from Hancock co., IL. Point 2 1/8 in. long, 1 1/4 in. wide, 3/16 in. thick. Deeply serrated, fine, thin, flaked, very sharp tip, uniformly symmetrical. Made of Mill Creek chert.
Priv. col., excellent quality, valued $180-275.

- McCorkle from Blount co., TN. Point 3 1/2 in. long, 1 1/2 in. wide, 1/4 in. thick. Sharp edges, unusually long and narrow piece, rounded tangs. Made of gray chert.
Grover Bohannon col., average quality, valued $60-85.

- McCorkle from Dyer co., TN. Point 2 5/16 in. long, 1 5/8 in. wide, 1/4 in. thick. Made of local gray to white chert.
Priv. col., excellent quality, valued $100-140.

- McCorkle from Dyer co., TN. Point 2 1/3 in. long, 1 7/8 in. wide, 1/4 in. thick. Finely serrated with classic McCorkle design. Made of gray white chert. *Priv. col., excellent quality, valued $150-220.*

- McCorkle from Dyer co., TN. Point 2 1/16 in. long, 1 1/3 in. wide, 1/4 in. thick. Good workmanship. Made of bright white chert. *Priv. col., museum quality, valued $200-275.*

- McCorkle from Henderson co., TN. Point 2 3/4 in. long, 1 3/16 in. wide, 1/8 in. thick. Made of glossy brown chert. *Priv. col., museum quality, valued $230-300.*

- McCorkle from Henderson co., TN. Point 2 11/16 in. long, 1 1/2 in. wide, 3/16 in. thick. Made of dull gray chert. *Priv. col., excellent quality, valued $150-200.*

- McCorkle from Henderson co., TN. Point 2 1/2 in. long, 1 1/3 in. wide, 3/16 in. thick. Made of Mill Creek chert. *Priv. col., excellent quality, valued $150-175.*

- McCorkle from Henderson co., TN. Point 2 5/16 in. long, 1 7/8 in. wide, 1/4 in. thick. Made of gray white chert. *Priv. col., excellent quality, valued $150-200.*

- McCorkle from Henderson co., TN. Point 2 1/3 in. long, 1 3/4 in. wide, 1/4 in. thick. Heat treated. Made of gray chert. *Priv. col., museum quality, valued $200-250.*

- McCorkle from Adams co., IL. Point 3 in. long, 1 7/16 in. wide, 1/8 in. thick. Made of cream chert, occasional brown lines through material. *Priv. col., excellent quality, valued $275-350.*

- McCorkle from Adams co., IL. Point 2 7/16 in. long, 1 1/2 in. wide, 3/16 in. thick. Made of gray chert. *Priv. col., excellent quality, valued $250-300.*

- McCorkle from Adams co., IL. Point 2 1/2 in. long, 1 1/3 in. wide, 3/16 in. thick. Made of high grade Mill Creek chert. *Priv. col., excellent quality, valued $180-250.*

- McCorkle from White co., IL. Point 3 /16 in. long, 1 7/8 in. wide, 1/4 in. thick. Good workmanship. Made of glossy gray chert.

Priv. col., museum quality, valued $450-500.

• McCorkle from White co., IL. Point 2 2/3 in. long, 1 3/4 in. wide, 1/8 in. thick. Good workmanship. Made of white pebble chert.
Priv. col., museum quality, valued $300-375.

• McCorkle from Clark co., IL. Point 2 in. long, 1 3/16 in. wide, 1/8 in. thick. Made of gray chert.
Priv. col., museum quality, valued $280-325.

• McCorkle from Clark co., IL. Point 2 13/16 in. long, 1 5/8 in. wide, 3/16 in. thick. Made of gray chert.
Priv. col., excellent quality, valued $150-200.

• McCorkle from St. Clair co., IL. Point 2 1/4 in. long, 1 1/2 in. wide, 3/16 in. thick. Made of Mill Creek chert.
Priv. col., excellent quality, valued $180-250.

• McCorkle from St. Clair co., IL. Point 2 3/16 in. long, 1 5/8 in. wide, 1/4 in. thick. Made of dense white chert.
Priv. col., excellent quality, valued $175-220.

• McCorkle from Hamilton co., IL. Point 2 2/3 in. long, 1 1/2 in. wide, 3/16 in. thick. Heat treated. Made of white pebble chert.
Priv. col., excellent quality, valued $225-275.

• McCorkle from Hamilton co., IL. Point 2 1/2 in. long, 1 5/16 in. wide, 1/8 in. thick. Made of white chert.
Priv. col., excellent quality, valued $220-300.

• McCorkle from Effingham co., IL. Point 2 9/16 in. long, 1 5/8 in. wide, 3/16 in. thick. Made of gray chert.
Priv. col., excellent quality, valued $150-225.

• McCorkle from Effingham co., IL. Point 2 1/2 in. long, 1 1/3 in. wide, 5/32 in. thick. Made of gray white pebble chert.
Priv. col., excellent quality, valued $180-225.

McIntire: 6,000-4,000 B.P. Mid to Late Archaic

Found predominantly in the southeast, medium to large in size point or blade. Broad parallel expanded stems. Shoulders barbed or squared.

Straight, convex, or concave bases.

◆ McIntire from Humphreys co., TN. Point 1 5/8 in. long, 1 1/4 in. wide, 5/16 in. thick. Straight base, broad stem, square shoulders. Made of gray pebble chert.

Grover Bohannon col., excellent quality, valued $25-40.

• McIntire from Hancock co., TN. Point 2 3/4 in. long, 2 in. wide, 1/4 in. thick. Broad parallel expanded stem, shoulders barbed. Straight, thinned base. Made of tan pebble chert.
Priv. col., excellent quality, valued $40-50.

• McIntire from Humphreys co., TN. Point 1 7/8 in. long, 1 1/2 in. wide, 1/8 in. thick. Wide, symmetrical, fine workmanship, thin for a McIntire. Convex base, broad stem, square shoulders. Made of Dover chert.
Grover Bohannon col., museum quality, valued $65-80.

• McIntire from Dyer co., TN. Blade 4 1/2 in. long, 2 1/4 in. wide, 1/4 in. thick. Thin, symmetrical, broad parallel expanded stem. Shoulders barbed, heat treated, concave base. Made of gray chert.
Grover Bohannon col., museum quality, valued $100-150.

• McIntire from Grundy co., TN. Blade 3 5/8 in. long, 1 1/4 in. wide, 3/16 in. thick. Symmetrical, narrow, thin, heat treated. Straight base, broad stem, square shoulders. Made of cream pebble chert.
Priv. col., excellent quality, valued $85-100.

• McIntire from Coffee co., TN. Point 2 7/8 in. long, 1 1/3 in. wide, 1/2 in. thick. Very thick, symmetrical, sharply serrated, broad parallel expanded stem, shoulders barbed, straight base. Made of brown to tan chert.
Priv. col., excellent quality, valued $30-40.

• McIntire from Coffee co., TN. Point 2 5/8 in. long, 1 1/4 in. wide, 5/16 in. thick. From same sight as above, straight base, broad stem, barbed shoulders. Made of brown to tan pebble chert.

Priv. col., excellent quality, valued $25-40.

- McIntire from Dyer co., TN. Blade 4 in. long, 2 3/4 in. side, 1/4 in. thick. Thin, wide, symmetrical, broad parallel expanded stem. Shoulders barbed, concave base. Made of gray chert.
Priv. col., excellent quality, valued $75-100.

- McIntire from Cleburne co., AL. Point 2 3/8 in. long, 1 1/4 in. wide, 1/2 in. thick. Made of brown to tan slate.
Priv. col., excellent quality, valued $30-40.

- McIntire from Cleburne co., AL. Point 2 7/8 in. long, 1 1/3 in. wide, 1/2 in. thick. Made of light brown chert.
Priv. col., excellent quality, valued $25-40.

- McIntire from Cleburne co., AL. Point 3 in. long, 1 3/4 in. side, 5/16 in. thick. Made of white gray chert.
Priv. col., excellent quality, valued $45-60.

- McIntire from Graves co., KY. Blade 3 5/8 in. long, 1 1/2 in. wide, 3/16 in. thick. Made of tan pebble chert.
Priv. col., average quality, valued $25-30.

- McIntire from Graves co., KY. Point 2 7/8 in. long, 1 1/2 in. wide, 1/2 in. thick. Made of brown chert.
Priv. col., excellent quality, valued $30-40.

- McIntire from Graves co., KY. Point 2 15/16 in. long, 1 1/8 in. wide, 7/16 in. thick. Made of brown white marbled chert.
Priv. col., excellent quality, valued $45-60.

- McIntire from Holmes co., FL. Point 2 1/8 in. long, 1 1/16 in. wide, 1/2 in. thick. Made of gray shale.
Priv. col., average quality, valued $10-20.

- McIntire from Holmes co., FL. Point 2 7/8 in. long, 1 1/4 in. wide, 1/2 in. thick. Made of quartzite.
Priv. col., average quality, valued $15-20.

- McIntire from Holmes co., FL. Point 3 3/32 in. long, 1 1/3 in. side, 1/2 in. thick. Made of gray shale.
Priv. col., average quality, valued $15-20.

• McIntire from Sharkey co., MS. Point 3 1/8 in. long, 1 1/2 in. wide, 1/4 in. thick. Made of quartzite.
Priv. col., average quality, valued $25-30.

• McIntire from Sharkey co., MS. Point 2 1/2 in. long, 1 1/32 in. wide, 1/2 in. thick. Made of high grade quartzite.
Priv. col., excellent quality, valued $30-40.

• McIntire from Graves co., MS. Point 2 3/8 in. long, 1 1/8 in. wide, 9/16 in. thick. Crude workmanship. Made of gray chert.
Priv. col., average quality, valued $5-10.

McKean: 9,000-4,000 B.P. Paleo-Transitional to Mid-Archaic

Found from the Midwest throughout the southeastern states. Small to medium sized point or blade. Basal notched, symmetrical and finely worked though generally narrow. Flaking in earlier forms is random, developing over time into parallel.

◆ McKean from Cooper co., MO. Point 1 1/4 in. long, 5/8 in. wide, 1/8 in. thick. Classic McKean form, finely chipped with repaired tip. Made of white chert.

Grover Bohannon col., average quality, valued $55-65.

◆ McKean from Lubbock co., TX. Blade 3 3/16 in. long, 3/4 in. wide, 3/16 in. thick. Classic form, narrow serrated blade. Heat treated tip. Made of tan chert.

Priv. col., museum quality, valued $200-300.

• McKean from Cleburne co., AL. Point 2 1/3 in. long, 7/8 in. wide, 1/4 in. thick. Basal notched, symmetrical and finely worked, narrow. Flaking is parallel.

Made of banded slate.
Priv. col., excellent quality, valued $65-85.

- McKean from Drew co., AR. Point 1 1/4 in. long, 1/2 in. wide, 1/8 in. thick. Classic McKean form, finely parallel flaked, needle sharp tip. Made of white chert.
Priv. col., excellent quality, valued $55-65.

- McKean from Lubbock co., TX. Point 1 13/16 in. long, 5/8 in. wide, 3/16 in. thick. Classic form, narrow, sharply serrated edges. Heat treated, thinned base. Made of gray white chert.
Priv. col., museum quality, valued $150-200.

- McKean from Jefferson co., MO. Point 2 1/8 in. long, 7/8 in. wide, 3/16 in. thick. Basal notched, symmetrical and finely worked, narrow. Flaking is random, ground base. Made of white chert.
Priv. col., excellent quality, valued $65-75.

- McKean from Sullivan co., MO. Point 1 1/2 in. long, 7/16 in. wide, 1/8 in. thick. Classic McKean form, parallel flaked, finely serrated edges. Shallow basal notched base. Made of white chert.
Priv. col, excellent quality, valued $85-125.

- McKean from Sullivan co., MO. Blade 3 1/2 in. long, 1 2/3 in. wide, 1/8 in. thick. Wide, thin, serrated blade. Heat treated, parallel flaked, basal notched base. Made of local white chert.
Priv. col., museum quality, valued $160-220.

- Mckean from Sullivan co., MO. Blade 3 7/16 in. long, 1 in. wide, 5/32 in. thick. Basal notched, symmetrical and finely worked though generally narrow. Flaking parallel, heat treated, very sharp tip and edges. Made of local white chert.
Priv. col., museum quality, valued $275-350.

- McKean from Elk co., PA. Point 2 1/4 in. long, 1 1/32 in. wide, 1/8 in. thick. Made of vein quartz.
Priv. col., museum quality, valued $200-265.

- McKean from Elk co., PA. Point 2 13/16 in. long, 7/8 in. wide, 1/4 in. thick. Made of brick red white streaked slate.
Priv. col., museum quality, valued $180-225.

- Mckean from Cardin co., PA. Point 2 9/16 in. long, 1 in. wide, 5/16 in. thick.

Made of dull green chert.
Priv. col., museum quality, valued $175-200.

• McKean from Cardin co., PA. Point 2 1/4 in. long, 1 1/8 in. wide, 1/8 in. thick. Made of white chert.
Priv. col., excellent quality, valued $100-165.

• McKean from Cardin co., PA. Blade 3 3/4 in. long, 7/8 in. wide, 1/4 in. thick. Heat treated, good field patina. Made of white chert.
Priv. col., museum quality, valued $150-200.

• McKean from Snyder co., PA. Point 1 3/4 in. long, 11/32 in. wide, 3/32 in. thick. Excellent workmanship. Made of gray green pebble chert.
Priv. col., museum quality, valued $200-250.

• McKean from Snyder co., PA. Point 2 3/16 in. long, 7/8 in. wide, 1/4 in. thick. Made of high grade quartzite.
Priv. col., excellent quality, valued $100-120.

• McKean from Synder co., PA. Point 2 1/16 in. long, 1 1/32 in. wide, 5/16 in. thick. Made of dull pink chert.
Priv. col., museum quality, valued $175-240.

• McKean from Synder co., PA. Point 2 1/2 in. long, 1 1/8 in. wide, 1/8 in. thick. Made of white to gray chert.
Priv. col., excellent quality, valued $100-125.

• McKean from Avery co., NC. Point 2 1/4 in. long, 1 1/2 in. wide, 1/8 in. thick. Made of quartzite.
Priv. col., average quality, valued $50-65.

• McKean from Avery co., NC. Point 2 3/16 in. long, 7/8 in. wide, 1/4 in. thick. Made of high grade pink chert.
Priv. col., museum quality, valued $180-200.

• Mckean from Avery co., NC. Point 2 7/16 in. long, 1 in. wide, 7/16 in. thick. Made of dull gray chert.
Priv. col., excellent quality, valued $125-150.

• McKean from Wataga co., NC. Point 2 1/4 in. long, 7/8 in. wide, 1/8 in. thick. Made of white chert.
Priv. col., excellent quality, valued $100-165.

Midland: 12,000-8,500 B.P. Paleo

Located in Canada, the Northeast, and the Midwest. Small to medium sized point. Widest part of point one-third down from the tip. Sharp edges throughout, concave thinned bases.

◆ Midland from Marshall co., TN. Point 2 1/2 in. long, 1 1/4 in. wide, 3/16 in. thick. Base is ground, point has several small edge nicks. The tip is sharp and rounded. Made of a grainy jasper.

Grover Bohannon col., excellent quality, valued $350-500.

• Midland from Marshall co., TN. Point 1 3/4 in. long, 5/8 in. wide, 1/8 in. thick. Narrow, finely serrated, sharp tip. Base is concave and thinly ground. Made of Dover chert.
Grover Bohannon col., museum quality, valued $500-650.

• Midland from Grundy co., TN. Point 2 in. long, 1 1/16 in. wide, 3/16 in. thick. Symmetrical, sharply serrated edges, slight tip break. Base is concave and heat treated, ground. Made of gray chert.
Grover Bohannon col., average quality, valued $75-100.

• Midland from Marshall co., TN. Point 1 7/8 in. long, 5/8 in. wide, 1/8 in. thick. Made of Dover chert.
Priv. col., museum quality, valued $500-650.

• Midland from Marshall co., TN. Point 2 1/16 in. long, 1 1/16 in. wide, 3/16 in. thick. Made of conglomerate stone.
Priv. col., museum quality, rare, valued $750-900.

• Midland from Beaverhead co., MT. Point 2 1/8 in. long, 1 in. wide, 3/16 in. thick. Made of tan brown chert.
Priv. col., average quality, valued $75-100.

• Midland from Beaverhead co., MT. Point 2 5/8 in. long, 7/8 in. wide, 1/8 in. thick. Made of tan brown chert.
Priv. col., museum quality, valued $300-350.

- Midland from Beaverhead co., MT. Point 2 7/16 in. long, 1 1/8 in. wide, 3/16 in. thick. Made of gray chert.
Priv. col., museum quality, valued $350-400.

- Midland from Marshall co., TN. Point 1 7/8 in. long, 5/8 in. wide, 1/8 in. thick. Made of Dover chert.
Priv. col., museum quality, valued $500-650.

- Midland from Marshall co., TN. Point 2 1/16 in. long, 1 1/16 in. wide, 3/16 in. thick. Made of conglomerate stone.
Priv. col., museum quality, rare, valued $750-900.

- Midland from Beaverhead co., MT. Point 2 1/8 in. long, 1 in. wide, 3/16 in. thick. Made of tan brown chert.
Priv. col., average quality, valued $75-100.

- Midland from Beaverhead co., MT. Point 2 5/8 in. long, 7/8 in. wide, 1/8 in. thick. Made of tan brown chert.
Priv. col., museum quality, valued $300-350.

- Midland from Beaverhead co., MT. Point 2 7/16 in. long, 1 1/8 in. wide, 3/16 in. thick. Made of gray chert.
Priv. col., museum quality, valued $350-400.

- Midland from Converse co., WY. Point 2 7/8 in. long, 1 in. wide, 1/8 in. thick. Made of marbled pink white chert.
Priv. col., museum quality, valued $500-550.

- Midland from Converse co., WY. Point 2 11/16 in. long, 1 1/8 in. wide, 3/16 in. thick. Made of gray chert.
Priv. col., museum quality, valued $350-400.

- Midland from Sublette co., WY. Point 3 1/32 in. long, 1 1/8 in. wide, 3/16 in. thick. Made of brown chert.
Priv. col., excellent quality, valued $75-100.

- Midland from Daniels co., MT. Point 2 2/3 in. long, 7/8 in. wide, 1/8 in. thick. Made of tan white chert.
Priv. col., museum quality, valued $300-350.

- Midland from Daniels co., MT. Point 2 5/8 in. long, 1 1/8 in. wide, 3/16 in. thick. Made of gray chert.

Priv. col., museum quality, valued $350-400.

• Midland from Daniels co., MT. Point 2 7/8 in. long, 1 1/4 in. wide, 1/8 in. thick. Made of pink black speckled chert.
Priv. col., museum quality, valued $250-350.

• Midland from Natrona co., WY. Point 3 1/16 in. long, 1 3/16 in. wide, 3/16 in. thick. Made of pink gray check.
Priv. col., museum quality, valued $400-500.

• Midland from Natrona co., WY. Point 2 5/8 in. long, 1 in. wide, 3/16 in. thick. Made of tan brown chert.
Priv. col., average quality, valued $75-100.

• Midland from Natrona co., WY. Point 2 5/8 in. long, 7/8 in. wide, 1/8 in. thick. Made of tan brown chert.
Priv. col., excellent quality, valued $100-150.

• Midland from Lake co., MT. Point 2 7/16 in. long, 1 1/8 in. wide, 3/16 in. thick. Made of gray chert.
Priv. col., museum quality, valued $350-400.

• Midland from Treasure co., MT. Point 2 7/8 in. long, 7/8 in. wide, 1/8 in. thick. Good field patina. Made of dull gray chert.
Priv. col., excellent quality, valued $200-250.

• Midland from Treasure co., MT. Point 2 9/16 in. long, 1 1/16 in. wide, 3/16 in. thick. Made of white chert.
Priv. col., excellent quality, valued $150-200.

• Midland from Treasure co., MT. Point 3 1/8 in. long, 1 1/4 in. wide, 3/16 in. thick. Made of tan chert.
Priv. col., average quality, valued $55-70.

• Midland from Philips co., MT. Point 2 7/8 in. long, 1 1/8 in. wide, 1/8 in. thick. Made of tan chert.
Priv. col., average quality, valued $60-75.

• Midland from Philips co., MT. Point 2 7/16 in. long, 1 1/4 in. wide, 3/16 in. thick. Made of gray chert.
Priv. col., average quality, valued $50-90.

Mississippian: 1,200-300 B.P. Mississippian to Historic

Found almost exclusively in the Mississippi Valley. Large size blade. The blades are heavily beveled on all four sides or one side of each face. Thick blades in the center thinning toward edges, fine high quality horizontal flaking throughout type. The tips are rounded and very sharp. The bases are snapped or round.

◆ Mississippian from Cooper co., MO. Blade 6 5/8 in. long, 2 1/4 in. wide, 1/2 in. thick. Thickness at center, high ridged center. Heavily right hand beveled with sharp edges. Sharp wide blade tip, snapped base. Made of gray chert.

Priv. col., excellent quality, valued $100-150.

◆ Mississippian from Johnson co., IL. Blade 5 3/4 in. long, 3 3/4 in. wide, 5/8 in. thick. Extremely thin Mississippian, very sharply serrated and steeply beveled. Snap base. Made of Kaolin chert.

Les Grubbe col., excellent quality, rare, valued $100-150.

• Mississippian from Randolph co., MO. Blade 6 3/8 in. long, 2 3/4 in. wide, 7/16 in. thick. Thin, heat treated, sharply and steeply beveled. Sharp rounded blade tip, snapped base. Made of tan pebble chert.
Priv. col., museum quality, valued $200-250.

• Mississippian from Johnson co., IL. Blade 5 1/8 in. long, 2 3/4 in. wide, 1/2 in. thick. Crudely worked, thick Mississippian, steeply beveled. Snap base, heat treated. Made of Mill Creek chert.
Priv. col., poor quality, valued $30-50.

- Mississippian from Hamilton co., MO. Blade 6 1/8 in. long, 3 1/2 in. wide, 5/8 in. thick. Thick, heat treated, high ridged center. Long thin horizontal flaking to edges, beveled with sharp edges. Sharp wide blade tip, snapped base. Made of Mill Creek chert.
Priv. col., average quality, valued $60-85.

- Mississippian from Jackson co., IL. Blade 5 3/16 in. long, 2 7/8 in. wide, 5/16 in. thick. Thin, symmetrical, sharply serrated and steeply beveled. Snap base, heat treated. Made of Mill Creek chert.
Tim Rubbles col., excellent quality, valued $60-100.

- Mississippian from Johnson co., IL. Blade 5 3/8 in. long, 2 3/4 in. wide, 1/3 in. thick. Good workmanship, heat treated. Made of Mill Creek chert.
Priv. col., excellent quality, valued $70-90.

- Mississippian from Johnson co., IL. Blade 5 1/8 in. long, 3 1/16 in. wide, 1/2 in. thick. Made of Mill Creek chert.
Priv. col., excellent quality, valued $70-95.

- Mississippian from Johnson co., IL. Blade 5 9/16 in. long, 2 7/8 in. wide, 5/16 in. thick. Made of Mill Creek chert.
Priv. col., excellent quality, valued $60-100.

Montell: 5,000-1,000 B.P. Mid-Archaic to Late Woodland

Found predominantly in the Midwest and into the Southeast. Small to medium sized points. Bifurcated base, barbed shoulders, ears usually squared. Often the point is beveled on one side of each face.

◆ Montell from Humphreys co., TN. Point 2 1/2 in. long, 1 1/2 in. wide, 1/4 in. thick. Bifurcated snapped base, snapped ears, edges finely serrated. Made of gray chert.

Grover Bohannon col., excellent quality, valued $15-25.

◆   Montell from southeastern AK. Point 1 2/3 in. long, 1 1/16 in. wide, 3/16 in. thick. Weak shouldered and uneven tangs, deeply bifurcated base. Made of pink pebble chert.

Priv. col., average quality, valued $10-15.

•   Montell from Giles co., TN. Point 1 1/2 in. long, 7/8 in. wide, 1/4 in. thick. Thick, symmetrical, beveled on one side of each face. Bifurcated snapped base, snapped ears, edges finely serrated. Made of brown chert.
Priv. col., museum quality, valued $35-45.

•   Montell from Giles co., TN. Point 1 3/4 in. long, 3/4 in. wide, 3/16 in. thick. Symmetrical, beveled on one side of each face. Parallel tangs, bifurcated base. Made of tan pebble chert.
Priv. col., excellent quality, valued $20-25.

•   Montell from Lampasas co., TX. Point 2 1/2 in. long, 1 1/8 in. wide, 1/4 in. thick. Made of quartzite.
Priv. col., average quality, valued $10-15.

•   Montell from Lampasas co., TX. Point 1 7/8 in. long, 3/4 in. wide, 5/16 in. thick. Made of quartzite.
Priv. col., average quality, valued $5-10.

•   Montell from Lampasas co., TX. Point 2 1/4 in. long, 1 1/4 in. wide, 5/16 in. thick. Made of quartzite.
Priv. col., average quality, valued $10-15.

•   Montell from Lampasas co., TX. Point 2 1/8 in. long, 7/8 in. wide, 5/16 in. thick. Made of quartzite.
Priv. col., average quality, valued $10-15.

•   Montell from Lubbock co., TX. Point 2 2/2 in. long, 1 1/4 in. wide, 1/4 in. thick. Long, needle sharp tip. Made of glossy brown chert.
Priv. col., museum quality, valued $40-65.

•   Montell from Lipscomb co., TX. Point 2 7/8 in. long, 1 1/2 in. wide, 5/16 in.

thick. Made of quartzite.
Priv. col., average quality, valued $10-15.

- Montell from Lipscomb co., TX. Point 2 1/2 in. long, 1 3/8 in. wide, 7/16 in. thick. Made of quartzite.
Priv. col., average quality, valued $10-15.

- Montell from Sutton co., TX. Point 1 7/8 in. long, 1 1/4 in. wide, 5/16 in. thick. Made of dull gray chert.
Priv. col., excellent quality, valued $30-35.

- Montell from Sutton co., TX. Point 2 1/3 in. long, 1 3/8 in. wide, 1/4 in. thick. Made of gray chert.
Priv. col., excellent quality, valued $20-25.

- Montell from Sutton co., TX. Point 1 7/8 in. long, 1 3/4 in. wide, 5/16 in. thick. Poor workmanship. Made of quartzite.
Priv. col., average quality, valued $5-10.

- Montell from Motley co., TX. Point 2 3/4 in. long, 1 3/8 in. wide, 1/4 in. thick. Good workmanship. Made of glossy tan chert.
Priv. col., excellent quality, valued $30-35.

- Montell from Motley co., TX. Point 2 7/8 in. long, 1 1/2 in. wide, 5/16 in. thick. Good workmanship. Made of quartzite.
Priv. col., average quality, valued $15-20.

- Montell from Motley co., TX. Point 2 1/2 in. long, 1 1/8 in. wide, 1/4 in. thick. Made of gray chert.
Priv. col., excellent quality, valued $20-25.

- Montell from Zapata co., TX. Point 1 7/8 in. long, 1 1/2 in. wide, 5/16 in. thick. Made of quartzite.
Priv. col., average quality, valued $10-15.

- Montell from Zapata co., TX. Point 2 1/3 in. long, 1 3/8 in. wide, 1/4 in. thick. Made of quartzite.
Priv. col., average quality, valued $10-15.

- Montell from Paul co., TX. Point 2 1/8 in. long, 1 3/8 in. wide, 5/16 in. thick. Made of white chert.
Priv. col., excellent quality, valued $25-30.

• Montell from Paul co., TX. Point 2 1/3 in. long, 1 5/8 in. wide, 1/4 in. thick. Made of white chert.
Priv. col., excellent quality, valued $20-25.

• Montell from Paul co., TX. Point 2 7/8 in. long, 2 3/4 in. wide, 7/16 in. thick. Poor workmanship. Made of quartzite.
Priv. col., average quality, valued $10-15.

• Montell from Dickins co., TX. Point 2 1/4 in. long, 1 5/8 in. wide, 1/4 in. thick. Made of quartzite.
Priv. col., average quality, valued $10-15.

• Montell from Dickins co., TX. Point 1 5/8 in. long, 3/4 in. wide, 7/16 in. thick. Made of quartzite.
Priv. col., average quality, valued $5-10.

• Montell from Dickins co., TX. Point 2 5/8 in. long, 1 5/8 in. wide, 1/4 in. thick. Made of quartzite.
Priv. col., average quality, valued $10-15.

• Montell from Floyd co., TX. Point 2 7/8 in. long, 1 3/4 in. wide, 5/16 in. thick. Made of quartzite.
Priv. col., average quality, valued $10-15.

Motley: 4,500-2,500 B.P. Late Archaic to Woodland

Found predominantly in the Southeast. Medium to large sized point or blade. Deep and wide side notches, prominently barbed. Base convex, occasionally straight.

♦ Motley from Hamilton co., TN. Point 2 1/2 in. long, 1 1/8 in. wide, 1/4 in. thick. Heat treated, deep notched, one side of each face beveled, highly serrated edges. Made of Dover chert.

Priv. col., museum quality, rare, valued $250-325.

◆ Motley from Hamilton co., TN. Point 1 in. long, 1/2 in. wide, 1/8 in. thick. Symmetrical, finely worked, burial point. Sharply serrated, uniform corner notches, convex base. Made of jasper.

Grover Bohannon col., museum quality, rare, valued $200-275.

• Motley from Hamilton co., TN. Blade 4 1/2 in. long, 2 1/3 in. wide, 1/4 in. thick. Heat treated, deep parallel notches, one side of each face beveled, highly serrated edges. Prominent barbs with straight base. Made of Dover chert.
Grover Bohannon col., museum quality, rare, valued $275-350.

• Motley from Hamilton co., TN. Blade 5 in. long, 2 1/8 in. wide, 1/8 in. thick. Symmetrical, thin, narrow, finely worked. Sharply serrated, uniform corner notches, beveled on one side of each face, straight base. Made of Dover chert.
Grover Bohannon col., museum quality, rare, valued $300-375.

• Motley from Hamilton co., TN. Point 2 1/3 in. long, 7/8 in. wide, 1/8 in. thick. Made of white pebble chert.
Priv. col., museum quality, valued $150-175.

• Motley from Hamilton co., TN. Blade 4 1/3 in. long, 2 in. wide, 1/4 in. thick. Made of marbled white tan chert.
Priv. col., museum quality, valued $250-350.

• Motley from Henderson co., KY. Blade 5 1/8 in. long, 2 1/2 in. wide, 1/8 in. thick. Excellent workmanship. Made of marbled brown white chert.
Priv. col., museum quality, valued $400-450.

• Motley from Henderson co., KY. Blade 4 2/3 in. long, 1 1/8 in. wide, 1/8 in. thick. Heat treated. Made of white tan chert.
Priv. col., excellent quality, valued $150-200.

• Motley from Henderson co., KY. Blade 4 1/3 in. long, 2 in. wide, 1/4 in. thick. Made of marbled white tan chert.
Priv. col., excellent quality, valued $200-225.

• Motley from Cumberland co., KY. Blade 4 7/8 in. long, 2 1/3 in. wide, 1/8 in. thick. Made of gray chert.
Priv. col., excellent quality, valued $200-275.

- Motley from Cumberland co., KY. Point 2 2/3 in. long, 1 1/16 in. wide, 1/8 in. thick. Made of gray pebble chert.
Priv. col., average quality, valued $50-75.

- Motley from Nart co., KY. Blade 4 11/16 in. long, 2 in. wide, 3/16 in. thick. Made of white pebble chert.
Priv. col., excellent quality, valued $225-250.

- Motley from Hamilton co., IL. Blade 5 in. long, 2 3/32 in. wide, 1/8 in. thick. Excellent workmanship, heat treated. Made of gray chert.
Priv. col., museum quality, valued $300-375.

- Motley from Hamilton co., IL. Point 2 2/3 in. long, 1 in. wide, 1/8 in. thick. Made of Mill Creek chert.
Priv. col., excellent quality, valued $150-175.

- Motley from Fulton co., KY. Blade 4 1/2 in. long, 1 1/2 in. wide, 3/16 in. thick. Made of grainy white tan chert.
Priv. col., average quality, valued $100-150.

- Motley from Fulton co., KY. Blade 4 7/8 in. long, 2 in. wide, 1/8 in. thick. Made of glossy brown chert.
Priv. col., museum quality, valued $300-350.

- Motley from Holt co., MO. Point 2 1/2 in. long, 1 1/16 in. wide, 1/8 in. thick. Made of white chert.
Priv. col., excellent quality, valued $125-150.

- Motley from Holt co., MO. Blade 5 1/3 in. long, 2 1/16 in. wide, 3/16 in. thick. Made of white chert.
Priv. col., museum quality, valued $350-400.

- Motley from Butler co., MO. Blade 4 5/8 in. long, 1 21/32 in. wide, 1/8 in. thick. Excellent workmanship. Made of streaked tan brown chert.
Priv. col., museum quality, valued $300-375.

- Motley from Harrison co., MO. Blade 5 1/8 in. long, 1 7/8 in. wide, 1/8 in. thick. Made of white tan pebble chert.
Priv. col., museum quality, valued $450-475.

- Motley from Harrison co., MO. Blade 4 2/3 in. long, 1 1/2 in. wide, 1/4 in. thick. Made of white tan chert.

Priv. col., museum quality, valued $350-450.

- Motley from Harrison co., MO. Blade 4 7/8 in. long, 2 3/32 in. wide, 1/8 in. thick. Made of porous chert.
Priv. col., average quality, valued $100-125.

New Market: 3,000-1,000 B.P. Woodland

Found predominantly in the Southeast. Small to medium sized point. Base is long and rounded, shoulders tapered. One shoulder is generally higher than the other.

◆ New Market from Hamilton co., TN. Point 2 in. long, 1/2 in. wide, 1/8 in. thick. Soft shoulders, rounded base, slight tip break. Made of brown chert.

Priv. col., average quality, valued $20-35.

- New Market from Hamilton co., TN. Point 2 1/3 in. long, 3/4 in. wide, 1/8 in. thick. Symmetrical, thin, narrow, sharply serrated. Soft shoulders, rounded base, slight tip break. Made of quartzite
Priv. col., average quality, valued $20-35.

- New Market from Cumberland co., TN. Point 1 7/8 in. long, 9/16 in. wide, 1/8 in. thick. Symmetrical, tapered shoulders, straight base, sharp serrated tip. Made of gray chert.
Priv. col., excellent quality, valued $60-85.

- New Market from Cumberland co., TN. Point 2 1/16 in. long, 2/3 in. wide, 3/16 in. thick. Symmetrical, barbed shoulders, straight base. Made of gray chert.
Priv. col., museum quality, valued $100-135.

- New Market from Cleborne co., AL. Point 1 1/8 in. long, 7/16 in. wide, 1/8 in. thick. Made of high grade quartzite.
Priv. col., average quality, valued $20-25.

- New Market from Cleburne co., AL. Point 2 in. long, 1/2 in. wide, 3/16 in. thick. Made of gray chert.
Priv. col., excellent quality, valued $80-85.

- New Market from Perry co., AL. Point 1 1/2 in. long, 5/8 in. wide, 5/16 in. thick. Made of quartzite.
Priv. col., average quality, valued $15-20.

- New Market from Perry co., AL. Point 1 3/8 in. long, 11/16 in. wide, 1/4 in. thick. Made of quartzite.
Priv. col., average quality, valued $20-25.

- New Market from Perry co., AL. Point 2 1/4 in. long, 7/8 in. wide, 3/16 in. thick. Made of brown chert.
Priv. col., excellent quality, valued $70-85.

- New Market from Perry co., AL. Point 1 1/3 in. long, 5/8 in. wide, 3/16 in. thick. Made of brown chert.
Priv. col., excellent quality, valued $75-80.

- New Market from Baker co., FL. Point 7/8 in. long, 7/16 in. wide, 1/8 in. thick. Made of white gray chert.
Priv. col., excellent quality, valued $50-65.

- New Market from Baker co., FL. Point 1 1/2 in. long, 5/8 in. wide, 3/16 in. thick. Made of gray pink chert.
Priv. col., excellent quality, valued $80-85.

- New Market from Baker co., FL. Point 1 1/4 in. long, 5/8 in. wide, 1/4 in. thick. Needle sharp tip. Made of rose quartz.
Priv. col., museum quality, valued $150-200.

- New Market from Benton co., MS. Point 1 3/8 in. long, 11/16 in. wide, 1/8 in. thick. Made of brown marbled slate.
Priv. col., excellent quality, valued $40-55.

- New Market from Benton co., MS. Point 2 1/3 in. long, 7/8 in. wide, 3/16 in. thick. Excellent workmanship, needle sharp tip. Made of gray chert.
Priv. col., museum quality, valued $100-125.

- New Market from Leake co., MS. Point 1 7/8 in. long, 2/3 in. wide, 7/16 in. thick. Made of quartzite.
Priv. col., average quality, valued $15-20.

- New Market from Glades co., FL. Point 1 5/8 in. long, 15/16 in. wide, 1/8 in. thick. Made of glossy brown chert.

Priv. col., excellent quality, valued $60-75.

- New Market from Glades co., FL. Point 2 1/32 in. long, 2/3 in. wide, 3/16 in. thick. Made of gray chert.
Priv. col., excellent quality, valued $80-85.

- New Market from Glades co., FL. Point 1 7/8 in. long, 5/8 in. wide, 1/4 in. thick. Poor workmanship. Made of gray chert.
Priv. col., average quality, valued $15-20.

- New Market from Citrus co., FL. Point 1 1/2 in. long, 9/16 in. wide, 1/8 in. thick. Made of quartzite.
Priv. col., average quality, valued $10-15.

- New Market from Citrus co., FL. Point 2 1/8 in. long, 1/2 in. wide, 3/16 in. thick. Made of gray marbled chert.
Priv. col., excellent quality, valued $40-55.

- New Market from Citrus co., FL. Point 1 2/3 in. long, 7/8 in. wide, 5/16 in. thick. Made of quartzite.
Priv. col., average quality, valued $15-20.

- New Market from Sharkey co., MS. Point 1 3/8 in. long, 11/16 in. wide, 1/8 in. thick. Made of quartzite.
Priv. col., average quality, valued $10-15.

- New Market from Sharkey co., MS. Point 2 1/3 in. long, 2/3 in. wide, 3/16 in. thick. Made of gray chert.
Priv. col., excellent quality, valued $50-65.

- New Market from Sharkey co., MS. Point 1 7/8 in. long, 5/8 in. wide, 3/16 in. thick. Made of milky quartz.
Priv. col., excellent quality, valued $65-80.

- New Market from Brooks co., GA. Point 3 1/8 in. long, 1 5/16 in. wide, 1/4 in. thick. Made of quartzite.
Priv. col., average quality, valued $20-25.

- New Market from Brooks co., GA. Point 2 1/8 in. long, 7/8 in. wide, 3/16 in. thick. Made of gray chert.
Priv. col., excellent quality, valued $60-65.

• New Market from Brooks co., GA. Point 1 1/3 in. long, 5/8 in. wide, 7/16 in. thick. Made of quartzite.
Priv. col., average quality, valued $15-20.

• New Market from Barrow co., GA. Point 1 5/8 in. long, 11/16 in. wide, 1/4 in. thick. Made of gray shale.
Priv. col., average quality, valued $20-25.

• New Market from Barrow co., GA. Point 2 1/8 in. long, 2/3 in. wide, 5/16 in. thick. Made of gray chert.
Priv. col., excellent quality, valued $50-65.

• New Market from Barrow co., GA. Point 1 13/16 in. long, 7/8 in. wide, 5/16 in. thick. Made of quartzite.
Priv. col., average quality, valued $15-20.

Nodena: 600-400 B.P. Mississippian to Historic

Found predominantly in the Midwest. A small to medium sized, narrow, thin, elliptical point. Base is generally rounded, occasionally snapped. Fine workmanship often parallel oblique flaked.

♦ Nodena from Boyd co., KY. Point 2 3/4 in. long, 1 1/8 in. wide, 3/8 in. thick. Symmetrical angular point, thin and finely serrated, very sharp tip and edges. Made of light gray chert.

Grover Bohannon col., excellent quality, valued $65-100.

♦ Nodena from Marshall co., TN. Point 2 1/8 in. long, 7/16 in. wide, 1/8 in. thick. Finely serrated, symmetrical, round base, sharp point tip. Made of milkly quartz.

Grover Bohannon col., museum quality, valued $125-165.

• Nodena from Butler co., KY. Point 2 1/8 in. long, 1 1/8 in. wide, 3/8 in. thick.

Symmetrical angular point, thin and finely serrated, very sharp tip and edges. Made of light gray chert.
Priv. col., excellent quality, valued $65-100.

- Nodena from Hawkins co., TN. Point 2 3/8 in. long, 5/16 in. wide, 1/4 in. thick. Wide sharp serrations, symmetrical, parallel oblique flaked. Snap base, sharp point tip. Made of oily black chert.
Priv. col., museum quality, valued $225-265.

- Nodena from Boyd co., KY. Point 2 3/4 in. long, 1 in. wide, 1/4 in. thick. Symmetrical angular point, widely serrated, thin and finely sharply serrated, very sharp tip and edges. Made of light gray chert.
Priv. col., excellent quality, valued $165-200.

- Nodena from Boyd co., KY. Point 1 7/8 in. long, 9/16 in. wide, 1/8 in. thick. Widely and finely serrated, symmetrical, round base, sharp point tip. Made of light gray chert.
Priv. col., museum quality, valued $150-185.

- Nodena from Boyd co., KY. Point 1 3/4 in. long, 1 1/16 in. wide, 1/8 in. thick. Symmetrical, wide, angular point, thin and finely serrated, very sharp tip and edges, snapped base. Made of light gray chert.
Priv. col., excellent quality, valued $85-120.

- Nodena from Marshall co., TN. Point 2 1/8 in. long, 11/16 in. wide, 1/8 in. thick. Thin, angular, finely serrated, symmetrical, round base, oblique parallel flaked. Made of Dover chert.
Priv. col., museum quality, rare, valued $250-300.

- Nodena from Fulton co., KY. Point 2 1/4 in. long, 1 in. wide, 3/8 in. thick. Symmetrical angular point, thick, widely and sharply serrated, very sharp tip and edges. Base is rounded and serrated. Made of light tan pebble chert.
Priv. col., museum quality, valued $185-230.

- Nodena from Fulton co., TN. Point 1 27/32 in. long, 5/16 in. wide, 1/8 in. thick. Thin, narrow, widely and sharply serrated, symmetrical. Oblique flaked, round base, sharp point tip. Made of light tan chert.
Priv. col., museum quality, valued $225-265.

- Nodena from Searcy co., AR. Point 7/8 in. long, 1/2 in. wide, 1/8 in. thick. Made of agate.
Priv. col., museum quality, rare, valued $50-65.

- Nodena from Searcy co., AR. Point 1 1/4 in. long, 11/16 in. wide, 1/8 in. thick. Made of translucent chert.
Priv. col., museum quality, valued $85-100.

- Nodena from Searcy co., AR. Point 2 in. long, 1 1/16 in. wide, 1/8 in. thick. Oblique parallel flaked. Made of Arkansas Brown chert.
Priv. col., museum quality, valued $200-220.

- Nodena from Searcy co., AR. Point 2 1/4 in. long, 1 1/32 in. wide, 1/8 in. thick. Made of tan pebble chert.
Priv. col., museum quality, valued $185-230.

- Nodena from Wheller co., OR. Point 1 1/8 in. long, 1/2 in. wide, 1/8 in. thick. Made of vein quartz.
Priv. col., museum quality, valued $150-200.

- Nodena from Wheller co., OR. Point 1 3/4 in. long, 1 1/16 in. wide, 1/8 in. thick. Made of vein quartz.
Priv. col., excellent quality, valued $125-150.

- Nodena from Wheeler co., OR. Point 7/8 in. long, 9/16 in. wide, 1/8 in. thick. Made of vein quartz.
Priv. col., museum quality, valued $150-200.

- Nodena from Spokane co., OR. Point 1 1/4 in. long, 5/8 in. wide, 3/16 in. thick. Needle sharp tip. Made of yellow quartz.
Juan Samudio col., museum quality, valued $175-250.

- Nodena from Polk co., OR. Point 1 7/8 in. long, 5/8 in. wide, 1/8 in. thick. Made of mauve chert.
Priv. col., museum quality, valued $150-185.

- Nodena from Polk co., OR. Point 1 1/4 in. long, 7/16 in. wide, 1/8 in. thick. Made of green pebble chert.
Priv. col., excellent quality, valued $85-120.

- Nodena from Polk co., OR. Point 2 7/8 in. long, 7/8 in. wide, 1/8 in. thick. Oblique parallel flaked. Made of gray purple pebble chert.
Priv. col., excellent quality, rare, valued $275-300.

- Nodena from Gillian co., OR. Point 2 1/4 in. long, 1 in. wide, 3/16 in. thick. Made of translucent pink chert.

Priv. col., museum quality, valued $200-250.

• Nodena from Gillian co., OR. Point 3 1/32 in. long, 13/16 in. wide, 1/8 in. thick. Made of pink green speckled pebble chert.
Priv. col., museum quality, valued $150-200.

• Nodena from Coosa co., AL. Point 1 3/4 in. long, 9/16 in. wide, 1/8 in. thick. Made of translucent gray chert.
Priv. col., excellent quality, valued $125-150.

• Nodena from Coosa co., AL. Point 2 3/8 in. long, 1 3/16 in. wide, 1/8 in. thick. Oblique parallel flaked, needle sharp tip. Made of white chert.
Priv. col., excellent quality, valued $85-100.

• Nodena from Calhoun co., AR. Point 2 3/4 in. long, 7/8 in. wide, 3/16 in. thick. Made of tan pebble chert.
Priv. col., museum quality, valued $185-230.

Nolan: 6,000-1,500 B.P. Mid-Archaic to Woodland

Found in the Midwest. A medium to large sized point or blade. Shoulders are tapered or rounded. Nolans exhibit needle sharp tips. The stem is steeply beveled on one side of each face. The base is either straight or convex.

♦ Nolan from Hardin co., KY. Point 2 7/8 in. long, 1 1/4 in. wide, 3/16 in. thick. Minute tip break, rounded shoulders. Stem is long and beveled on one side of each face. Base is expanded and straight. Made of a mauve high grade quartzite.

Grover Bohannon col., excellent quality, valued $85-125.

• Nolan from Hardin co., KY. Point 2 5/8 in. long, 1 1/3 in. wide, 3/16 in. thick. Stem is long beveled, heat treated. Base is expanded and straight. Made of white chert.
Grover Bohannon col., excellent quality, valued $65-85.

- Nolan from Hardin co., KY. Blade 3 7/8 in. long, 1 1/2 in. wide, 3/16 in. thick. Made of yellow tan chert.
Grover Bohannon col., excellent quality, valued $125-150.

- Nolan from Ballard co., KY. Blade 4 5/8 in. long, 1 1/2 in. wide, 3/16 in. thick. Made of brown white chert.
Priv. col., excellent quality, valued $100-125.

- Nolan from Hardin co., IL. Point 2 5/8 in. long, 1 5/8 in. wide, 3/16 in. thick. Made of gray chert.
Tim Rubbles col., excellent quality, valued $75-85.

- Nolan from Hardin co., IL. Point 2 7/8 in. long, 1 1/2 in. wide, 3/16 in. thick. Made of gray chert.
Priv. col., excellent quality, valued $100-125.

- Nolan from Hardin co., IL. Blade 4 1/8 in. long, 1 7/8 in. wide, 3/16 in. thick. Made of gray chert.
Priv. col., excellent quality, valued $200-225.

- Nolan from Hardin co., IL. Point 1 7/8 in. long, 1 1/16 in. wide, 3/16 in. thick. Made of brown white chert.
Priv. col., excellent quality, valued $65-85.

- Nolan from Hopkins co., KY. Blade 4 5/8 in. long, 1 2/3 in. wide, 3/16 in. thick. Made of yellow brown chert.
Priv. col., excellent quality, valued $150-175.

- Nolan from Hopkins co., KY. Blade 4 1/3 in. long, 1 7/8 in. wide, 3/16 in. thick. Made of cream white chert.
Priv. col., excellent quality, valued $100-125.

- Nolan from Marion co., KY. Point 2 7/8 in. long, 1 1/2 in. wide, 3/16 in. thick. Made of white gray chert.
Priv. col., excellent quality, valued $85-100.

- Nolan from Marion co., KY. Blade 4 3/8 in. long, 2 in. wide, 3/16 in. thick. Made of banded yellow tan chert.
Priv. col., excellent quality, valued $125-175.

- Nolan from Marion co., KY. Blade 4 1/8 in. long, 1 2/3 in. wide, 3/16 in. thick. Made of brown white chert.

Priv. col., excellent quality, valued $100-125.

Nootka: Historical

Points are found on the Vancouver Island coast. They are small to medium sized points. Points are beveled on one side of each face. Base is straight, the pont is generally and sharply serrated.

◆ Nootka from Vancouver Island. *Top:* 2 5/8 in. long, 2/3 in. wide, 3/16 in. thick. *Bottom:* 2 1/3 in. long, 1 1/8 in. wide, 1/4 in. thick. Both points beveled and serrated. Top point has slight tip break.

Southern IL Univ. col. Top: average quality, valued $40-70. Bottom: excellent quality, valued $65-90.

CHAPTER 12
OSCEOLA-PINE TREE

Osceola: 7,000-5,000 B.P. Early to Mid-Archaic

Found throughout the Midwest and southeastern states. Osceola are large points or blades, side notched, narrow, exhibiting fine quality workmanship. One of the most aesthetic points or blades of North America. Base is either notched, concave, or straight.

◆ Osceola from St. Louis co., MO. Blade 4 5/8 in. long, 1 3/16 in. wide, 1/4 in. thick. Heat treated, symmetrical, narrow, sharply serrated. Parallel side notches with concave base. Made of brown marbled chert.

Charles McCorkle col., museum quality, valued $450-600.

◆ Osceola from Union co., IL. Blade 3 3/4 in. long, 1 1/4 in. thick. Very symmetrical and finely serrated with uneven side notches. Parallel base sides, concave base. Made of local gray white chert.

Les Grubbe col., excellent quality, valued $275-350.

◆ Osceola from Union co., IL. Blade 3 7/8 in. long, 1 5/16 in. wide, 1/4 in. thick. Deep side notches, very symmetrical, concave base. Either irregularly serrated edges or a few worn nicks. Made of Mill Creek chert.

Les Grubbe col., excellent quality, valued $250-325.

◆ Osceola from Union co., IL. Point 2 3/4 in. long, 1 in. wide, 1/4 in. thick. Short for an Osceola, symmetrical, parallel notches with concave base. Made of light red chert.

Les Grubbe col., museum quality, valued $425-475.

◆ Osceolas from Grainger co., TN. *Left*: point 2 1/2 in. long, 1 1/8 in. wide, 3/16 in. thick. Concave edges, wide point with deep side notches and concave base. Made of Dover chert. *Right*: point 2 3/4 in. long, 1 3/16 in. wide, 1/4 in. thick. Heat treated, deep notches, left hand beveled. Made of Kaolin chert.

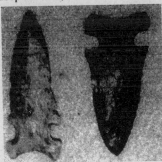

Les Grubbe col. Left: museum quality, valued $500-600. Right: museum quality, rare, valued $750-850.

◆ Osceola from Hamilton co., TN. Point 3 in. long, 1 1/4 in. wide, 1/4 in. thick. Concave edges and base, deep side notches, rounded tip. Made of Dover chert.

Les Grubbe col., excellent quality, valued $325-400.

◆ Osceola from Hamilton co., TN. Point 2 1/8 long, 1 1/8 in. wide, 3/16 in. thick. Very wide yet uniform side notches, edges sharp, symmetrical point. Concave base, sharp tip. Made of Dover chert.

Les Grubbe col., museum quality, valued $475-550.

◆ Osceola from Union co., IL. Point 2 5/8 in. long, 1 1/4 in. wide, 1/4 in. thick. Heat treated, symmetrical, deep side notches, concave base. Made of Dover chert.

Les Grubbe col., museum quality, valued $575-700.

◆ Osceola from Union co., IL. Point 2 3/4 in. long, 1 1/4 in. wide, 1/4 in. thick. Sides parallel to base, symmetrical, uniform side notches. Exceptional workmanship, sharply serrated, concave base. Made of Dover chert.

Les Grubbe col., museum quality, valued $750-850.

• Osceola from Hamilton co., TN. Blade 4 1/8 long, 1 5/8 in. wide, 5/16 in. thick. Narrow uniform side notches, edges sharp, symmetrical point, concave base. Made of gray chert.
Priv. col., excellent quality, valued $375-450.

• Osceola from Union co., IL. Blade 3 5/8 in. long, 1 3/4 in. wide, 1/4 in. thick. Heat treated, symmetrical, deep side notches, concave base. Made of Mill Creek chert.
Priv. col., museum quality, valued $425-600.

• Osceola from Union co., IL. Point 5 3/4 in. long, 2 1/4 in. wide, 1/4 in. thick. Heat treated, sides parallel to base, symmetrical, deep side notches. Sharply serrated, concave base. Made of Dover chert.
Priv. col., museum quality, valued $550-650.

- Osceola from St. Clair co., MO. Blade 4 3/8 in. long, 1 5/16 in. wide, 1/4 in. thick. Heat treated, symmetrical, sharp edge serration, concave base. Made of Mill Creek chert.
Priv. col., excellent quality, valued $250-300.

- Osceola from Union co., IL. Blade 5 3/4 in. long, 1 3/4 in. wide, 3/16 in. thick. Symmetrical, finely serrated, deep side notches. Good workmanship, long thin flaking, concave base. Made of Mill Creek chert.
Priv. col., excellent quality, valued $275-350.

- Osceola from Union co., IL. Blade 4 7/8 in. long, 1 1/2 in. wide, 1/4 in. thick. Deep side notches, heat treated, very symmetrical. Good workmanship, fine serrations, concave base. Made of Mill Creek chert.
Priv. col., excellent quality, valued $250-325.

- Osceola from Fentress co., TN. Blade 4 3/4 in. long, 1 2/3 in. wide, 1/4 in. thick. Symmetrical, parallel, deep side notches with concave base. Made of light gray chert.
Priv. col., excellent quality, valued $325-375.

- Osceola from Cannon co., TN. Point 2 1/4 in. long, 1 3/8 in. wide, 3/16 in. thick. Thin, wide point with deep narrow side notches, concave base. Made of tan pebble chert.
Priv. col., excellent quality, valued $200-250.

- Osceola from Fentress co., TN. Blade 4 3/4 in. long, 1 2/3 in. wide, 1/4 in. thick. Symmetrical, parallel, deep side notches with concave base. Made of light gray chert.
Priv. col., excellent quality, valued $325-375.

- Osceola from Fentress co., TN. Point 3 1/16 in. long, 1 3/4 in. wide, 1/8 in. thick. Thin, fine workmanship, wide point with deep, wide, side notches, straight base. Made of tan pebble chert.
Priv. col., museum quality, valued $275-350.

- Osceola from Fentress co., TN. Blade 4 3/8 in. long, 1 1/2 in. wide, 1/8 in. thick. Very thin finely worked piece with long thin flaking, sharp serrated edges and tip. Symmetrical, parallel, deep side notches with straight base. Made of light gray chert.
Priv. col., excellent quality, valued $350-425.

- ◆ Osceola from Union co., IL. Point 2 3/4 in. long, 1 7/8 in. wide, 1/4 in.

thick. Wide point, parallel oblique flaking, rounded tip. High quality workmanship, deep uneven side notches, concave base. Made of yellow quartz.

Les Grubbe col., museum quality, rare, valued $850-1,000.

• Osceola from Jackson co., IL. Blade 5 3/8 in. long, 2 in. wide, 1/4 in. thick. Made of Kaolin chert.
Priv. col., museum quality, rare, valued $1,250-1,500.

• Osceola from Jackson co., IL. Blade 6 1/4 in. long, 2 1/4 in. wide, 1/4 in. thick. Made of Mill Creek chert.
Priv. col., excellent quality, valued $575-650.

• Osceola from Jackson co., IL. Blade 4 7/8 in. long, 1 2/3 in. wide, 1/4 in. thick. Good workmanship. Made of Mill Creek chert.
Priv. col., excellent quality, valued $650-825.

• Osceola from Jackson co., IL. Blade 4 3/4 in. long, 2 1/3 in. wide, 1/4 in. thick. Made of Cobden chert.
Priv. col., museum quality, valued $725-875.

• Osceola from Schuyler co., IL. Blade 4 7/8 in. long, 1 5/16 in. wide, 1/4 in. thick. Made of gray white chert.
Priv. col., excellent quality, valued $250-300.

• Osceola from Schuyler co., IL. Blade 5 1/4 in. long, 1 7/8 in. wide, 3/16 in. thick. Made of white chert.
Priv. col., excellent quality, valued $275-350.

• Osceola from Schuyler co., IL. Blade 4 7/8 in. long, 1 1/2 in. wide, 1/4 in.

thick. Good workmanship. Made of gray chert.
Priv. col., excellent quality, valued $250-325.

• Osceola from Schuyler co., IL. Blade 4 3/8 in. long, 2 in. wide, 1/4 in. thick. Made of light gray chert.
Priv. col., excellent quality, valued $325-375.

- Osceola from Jackson co., IL. Blade 4 7/8 in. long, 1 2/3 in. wide, 1/4 in. thick. Good workmanship. Made of Mill Creek chert. *Priv. col., excellent quality, valued $650-825.*

- Osceola from Jackson co., IL. Blade 4 3/4 in. long, 2 1/3 in. wide, 1/4 in. thick. Made of Cobden chert. *Priv. col., museum quality, valued $725-875.*

- Osceola from Schuyler co., IL. Blade 4 7/8 in. long, 1 5/16 in. wide, 1/4 in. thick. Made of gray white chert. *Priv. col., excellent quality, valued $250-300.*

- Osceola from Saline co., IL. Blade 5 1/16 in. long, 1 5/8 in. wide, 3/16 in. thick. Good workmanship. Made of mauve chert. *Priv. col., museum quality, valued $1,375-1,550.*

- Osceola from Saline co., IL. Point 2 7/8 in. long, 2/3 in. wide, 1/4 in. thick. Good workmanship. Made of gray chert. *Priv. col., excellent quality, valued $250-275.*

- Osceola from Jasper co., IL. Blade 5 3/4 in. long, 2 1/32 in. wide, 3/16 in. thick. Excellent workmanship, heat treated. Made of green gray chert. *Priv. col., museum quality, valued $1,250-1,500.*

- Osceola from Coshocton co., OH. Blade 4 7/8 in. long, 1 11/16 in. wide, 1/4 in. thick. Good workmanship, fine thin flaking, symmetrical side notches. Base is parallel sided and straight. Made of Coshocton chert. *Priv. col., museum quality, valued $1,500-2,000.*

- Osceola from Darke co., OH. Blade 5 1/16 in. long, 1 7/8 in. wide, 5/16 in. thick. Made of white chert. *Priv. col., excellent quality, valued $375-450.*

- Osceola from Ashtabula co., OH. Blade 5 1/8 in. long, 2 1/16 in. wide, 3/16 in. thick. Good workmanship. Made of white chert. *Priv. col., museum quality, valued $850-1,000.*

- Osceola from Pickaway co., OH. Blade 4 1/2 in. long, 1 3/16 in. wide, 1/4 in. thick. Edges reworked, heat treated. Made of white chert. *Priv. col., average quality, valued $250-375.*

- Osceola from Wyandot co., OH. Blade 5 1/8 in. long, 1 7/16 in. wide, 1/4 in.

thick. Made of green chert.
Priv. col., excellent quality, valued $650-800.

- Osceola from Morrow co., OH. Blade 5 in. long, 1 7/8 in. wide, 1/8 in. thick. Excellent workmanship, heat treated, minutely serrated tip. Made of banded white brown chert.
Priv. col., museum quality, rare, valued $1,000-1,200.

- Osceola from Wabash co., IN. Blade 4 5/8 in. long, 1 1/3 in. wide, 3/18 in. thick. Good workmanship, heat treated. Made of local green chert.
Priv. col., museum quality, valued $750-875.

- Osceola from Adams co., IN. Blade 4 1/4 in. long, 2/3 in. wide, 1/4 in. thick. Very narrow. Made of white chert.
Priv. col., average quality, valued $225-275.

- Osceola from Payne co., OK. Blade 5 1/8 in. long, 2 1/4 in. wide, 1/4 in. thick. Excellent workmanship. Made of coal black flint.
Priv. col., museum quality, rare, valued $900-1,000.

- Osceola from Schuyler co., IL. Blade 6 1/2 in. long, 2 5/8 in. wide, 3/16 in. thick. Large even for an Osceola, excellent workmanship. Flaking is fine and thin, heat treated. Made of white chert.
Priv. col., museum quality, rare, valued $1,275-1,550.

- Osceola from Stokes co., NC. Blade 4 7/8 in. long, 1 3/4 in. wide, 1/4 in. thick. Good workmanship. Made of quartzite.
Priv. col., average quality, valued $250-325.

- Osceola from Jeff Davis co., TX. Blade 4 1/3 in. long, 2 1/2 in. wide, 1/4 in. thick. Made of porous gray chert.
Priv. col., average quality, valued $125-175.

- Osceola from Sabine co., TX. Blade 4 7/8 in. long, 1 9/16 in. wide, 1/2 in. thick. Heat treated, poor workmanship. Made of gray chert.
Priv. col., poor quality, valued $50-100.

- Osceola from Sabine co., IL. Blade 5 in. long, 2 1/8 in. wide, 3/16 in. thick. Made of gray chert.
Priv. col., average quality, valued $175-250.

- Osceola from Essex co., VA. Blade 4 3/8 in. long, 1 2/3 in. wide, 5/16 in. thick. Good workmanship. Made of quartzite.

Priv. col., average quality, valued $350-425.

• Osceola from Ohio co., WV. Blade 5 1/4 in. long, 2 1/8 in. wide, 1/4 in. thick. Made of pink quartzite.
Priv. col., excellent quality, valued $300-450.

• Osceola from Ohio co., WV. Blade 4 3/8 in. long, 1 11/16 in. wide, 1/4 in. thick. Made of white chert.
Priv. col., excellent quality, valued $250-300.

• Osceola from Asolin co., WV. Blade 4 1/4 in. long, 2 in. wide, 5/16 in. thick. Made of pink chert.
Priv. col., excellent quality, valued $275-350.

Palmer: 9,000-6,000 B.P. Mid to Late Archaic

Predominantly found in the Southeast. Palmer is a small point, triangular, corner notched, generally serrated. The base can be concave, convex, or straight ground base.

◆ Palmer from Crenshaw co., AL. Point 1 5/8 in. long, 1 in. wide, 1/8 in. thick. Highly serrated and sharp. Corner notched with slopping shoulders, sharp tip, ground tangs. Base is ground and concave. Made of pink pebble chert.

Grover Bohannon col., museum quality, valued $25-40.

• Palmer from Crenshaw co., AL. Point 1 1/8 in. long, 13/16 in. wide, 1/4 in. thick. Triangular, thick, corner notched, poorly serrated. The base is straight and ground. Made of pink pebble chert.
Grover Bohannon col., average quality, valued $10-15.

• Palmer from Crenshaw co., AL. Point 1 7/8 in. long, 1 in. wide, 1/8 in. thick. Symmetrical, highly serrated edges, pointed sharp tip. Corner notched, heat treated, ground tangs. Base is concave. Made of pink pebble chert.

Grover Bohannon col., museum quality, valued $35-50.

- Palmer from Sabine Parish, LA. Point 7/8 in. long, 7/16 in. wide, 3/16 in. thick. Symmetrical, uniformly triangular, corner notched, finely serrated, yet worn edges. The base is straight and ground. Made of quartzite.
Priv. col., average quality, valued $5-10.

- Palmer from Sabine Parish, LA. Point 1 1/16 in. long, 13/16 in. wide, 1/8 in. thick. Wide, symmetrically triangular, corner notched, serrated edges. The base is concave and ground. Good workmanship for the material. Made of quartzite.
Private col., excellent quality, valued $20-30.

- Palmer from Monroe co., AL. Point 1 3/8 in. long, 9/16 in. wide, 1/8 in. thick. Heat treated, symmetrical and narrow, highly serrated and sharp. Corner notched with straight shoulders, sharp tip, ground tangs. Base is ground and concave. Made of milky quartz.
Priv. col., museum quality, rare, valued $45-60.

- Palmer from Monroe co., AL. Point 1 1/8 in. long, 5/8 in. wide, 1/8 in. thick. Symmetrical, serrated and sharp edges. Corner notched with barbed shoulders, sharp tip. Base is ground and straight. Made of milky quartz.
Priv. col., excellent quality, valued $35-50.

- Palmer from Houston co., AL. Point 1 1/2 in. long, 7/8 in. long, 1/8 in. thick. Triangular, corner notched, crudely serrated. The base is convex and ground. Made of dark slate.
Priv. col., average quality, valued $10-15.

- Palmer from Houston co., AL. Point 1 7/8 in. long, 1 1/16 in. wide, 1/8 in. thick. Highly serrated and sharp edges. Corner notched, sharp tip, ground tangs. Base is ground and concave. Made of dark gray slate.
Priv. col., average quality, valued $20-25.

- Palmer from Houston co., AL. Point 1 2/3 in. long, 1 in. wide, 1/8 in. thick. Symmetrical, triangular, corner notched, parallel oblique flaked, highly serrated. The base is concave and ground. Made of dark gray slate.
Priv. col., average quality, valued $15-20.

- Palmer from Perry co., AL. Point 1 1/8 in. long, 11/16 in. wide, 1/8 in. thick. Corner notched, highly serrated, sharp tip, ground tangs. Base is ground and concave. Made of white pebble chert.
Priv. col., excellent quality, valued $25-35.

- Palmer from Saluda co., SC. Point 1 1/8 in. long, 9/16 in. wide, 3/16 in. thick. Broken tip, part of cache find. Made of banded slate.
Priv. col., average quality, valued $5-10.

- Palmer from Saluda co., SC. Point 1 5/16 in. long, 1/2 in. wide, 1/8 in. thick. Good workmanship, cache find. Made of banded slate.
Private col., excellent quality, valued $20-30.

- Palmer from Saluda co., SC. Point 1 3/8 in. long, 7/8 in. wide, 1/8 in. thick. Same cache find as above. Made of banded slate.
Priv. col., excellent quality, valued $10-20.

- Palmer from Saluda co., SC. Point 1 7/8 in. long, 1 3/16 in. wide, 3/16 in. thick. Cache point. Made of high grade quartzite.
Priv. col., excellent quality, valued $25-30.

- Palmer from Saluda co., SC. Point 1 5/16 in. long, 13/16 in. wide, 1/4 in. thick. Good workmanship, part of same cache find, heat treated. Made of banded slate.
Private col., museum quality, valued $40-45.

- Palmer from Geneva co., AL. Point 1 5/8 in. long, 1 in. wide, 1/8 in. thick. Excellent workmanship, heat treated. Made of milky quartz.
Priv. col., museum quality, rare, valued $45-60.

- Palmer from Geneva co., AL. Point 7/8 in. long, 3/4 in. wide, 1/4 in. thick. Made of quartztie.
Priv. col., average quality, valued $10-15.

- Palmer from Graham co., NC. Point 1 3/16 in. long, 13/16 in. wide, 1/3 in. thick. Good workmanship. Made of quartzite.
Private col., excellent quality, valued $20-30.

- Palmer from Hyde co., NC. Point 1 1/8 in. long, 5/8 in. wide, 1/8 in. thick. Made of gray flint.
Priv. col., museum quality, valued $25-30.

- Palmer from Marlboro co., SC. Point 1 in. long, 1/2 in. wide, 3/16 in. thick. Made of low grade quartzite.
Priv. col., average quality, valued $5-10.

- Palmer from Horry co., SC. Point 1 3/16 in. long, 11/16 in. wide, 3/16 in.

thick. Made of mauve quartzite.
Private col., excellent quality, valued $20-30.

• Palmer from Jasper co., SC. Point 1 1/8 in. long, 9/16 in. wide, 1/4 in. thick.
Made of milky quartz.
Priv. col., excellent quality, valued $25-30.

Palmillas: 6,000-3,000 B.P. Mid to Late Archaic

Found predominantly in the Midwest. Triangular points and blades, medium to large in size. Shoulders are barbed to horizontal. The stem of the base bulbous.

♦ Palmillas from Stewart co., TN. Point 2 3/8 in. long, 3/4 in. wide, 1/8 in.
thick. Uneven corner notches, deep random edge serrations, convex bulbous
stem. Made of Dover chert.

Grover Bohannon col., average quality, valued $8-12.

♦ Palmillas from Stewart co., TN. Point 2 3/8 in. long, 3/4 in. wide, 1/8 in.
thick. Uneven corner notches, deep random edge serrations, convex bulbous
stem. Made of Dover chert.

Grover Bohannon col., average quality, valued $8-12.

• Palmillas from Hamilton co., TN. Point 2 1/8 in. long, 1 in. wide, 3/16 in.
thick. Shoulders are horizontal, parallel corner notches. The stem of the base
bulbous. Made of gray chert.
Priv. col., excellent quality, valued $15-25.

• Palmillas from Hamilton co., TN. Point 2 5/8 in. long, 11/16 in. wide, 1/8 in.
thick. Barbed shoulders, parallel corner notches, deep, random, wide edge

serrations, concave bulbous base. Made of light tan chert.
Priv. col., excellent quality, valued $20-25.

• Palmillas from Humphreys co., TN. Point 1 13/16 in. long, 7/8 in. wide, 1/8 in. thick. Shoulders are barbed to horizontal. The stem of the base bulbous. Made of Dover chert.
Priv. col., museum quality, valued $30-40.

• Palmillas from Stewart co., TN. Point 2 1/4 in. long, 7/8 in. wide, 1/8 in. thick. Uneven corner notches, deep, random, sharp edge serrations, convex bulbous base. Made of Dover chert.
Grover Bohannon col., excellent quality, valued $30-40.

• Palmillas from Paul co., TX. Blade 3 7/8 in. long, 1 1/16 in. wide, 1/4 in. thick. Made of gray chert.
Priv. col., excellent quality, valued $25-30.

• Palmillas from Paul co., TX. Blade 4 1/8 in. long, 1 5/16 in. wide, 1/8 in. thick. Good workmanship. Made of gray chert.
Priv. col., museum quality, valued $40-45.

• Palmillas from Paul co., TX. Blade 3 13/16 in. long, 7/8 in. wide, 1/8 in. thick. Good workmanship, needle sharp tip. Made of white chert.
Priv. col., museum quality, valued $60-80.

• Palmillas from Andrews co., TX. Point 7/8 in. long, 11/16 in. wide, 1/4 in. thick. Made of quartzite.
Priv. col., poor quality, valued $2-5.

• Palmillas from Andrews co., TX. Point 2 in. long, 1 5/16 in. wide, 1/8 in. thick. Good workmanship. Made of gray chert.
Priv. col., museum quality, valued $40-45.

• Palmillas from Andrews co., TX. Blade 3 7/8 in. long, 1 3/8 in. wide, 1/8 in. thick. Good workmanship. Made of white chert.
Priv. col., excellent quality, valued $30-35.

• Palmillas from Bracken co., TX. Blade 4 in. long, 1 7/16 in. wide, 3/16 in. thick. Good workmanship. Made of porous white chert.
Priv. col., excellent quality, valued $20-25.

• Palmillas from Bracken co., TX. Point 2 3/16 in. long, 1 1/8 in. wide, 1/4 in. thick. Needle sharp tip. Made of dense white chert.

Priv. col., museum quality, valued $40-50.

- Palmillas from Harrison co., TX. Point 1 7/8 in. long, 13/16 in. wide, 1/4 in. thick. Made of quartzite.
Priv. col., average quality, valued $10-15.

- Palmillas from Harrison co., TX. Point 2 1/3 in. long, 1 5/16 in. wide, 3/16 in. thick. Made of banded gray chert.
Priv. col., museum quality, valued $50-55.

- Palmillas from Rowan co., KY. Blade 3 7/8 in. long, 1 1/2 in. wide, 1/4 in. thick. Made of yellow white chert.
Priv. col., excellent quality, valued $30-35.

- Palmillas from Rowan co., KY. Blade 4 1/32 in. long, 1 9/16 in. wide, 1/8 in. thick. Good workmanship. Made of banded gray chert.
Priv. col., museum quality, valued $40-45.

- Palmillas from Powell co., KY. Point 3 1/16 in. long, 1 1/8 in. wide, 1/8 in. thick. Good workmanship, heat treated, needle sharp tip. Made of white chert.
Priv. col., museum quality, valued $50-60.

- Palmillas from Bibb co., AL. Point 1 5/8 in. long, 1 in. wide, 1/4 in. thick. Made of quartzite.
Priv. col., average quality, valued $10-15.

- Palmillas from Bibb co., AL. Point 2 1/16 in. long, 1 1/2 in. wide, 1/4 in. thick. Made of quartzite.
Priv. col., average quality, valued $10-15.

- Palmillas from Calhoun co., AR. Blade 4 7/8 in. long, 2 1/16 in. wide, 3/16 in. thick. Good workmanship. Made of Arkansas brown chert.
Priv. col., museum quality, rare, valued $60-65.

- Palmillas from Somerville co., TX. Blade 4 3/8 in. long, 2 in. wide, 1/8 in. thick. Good workmanship, thin, needle sharp tip. Made of gray chert.
Priv. col., museum quality, valued $50-55.

- Palmillas from Somerville co., TX. Blade 3 15/16 in. long, 1 1/32 in. wide, 1/8 in. thick. Good workmanship, needle sharp tip. Made of white chert.
Priv. col., museum quality, valued $45-50.

- Palmillas from Midland co., TX. Point 2 7/8 in. long, 1 3/16 in. wide, 5/32 in. thick. Made of silver gray flint.
Priv. col., excellent quality, valued $20-25.

- Palmillas from Carroll co., TN. Point 2 1/4 in. long, 1 5/16 in. wide, 1/4 in. thick. Good workmanship. Made of glossy brown chert.
Priv. col., museum quality, valued $40-45.

- Palmillas from Carroll co., TN. Point 2 5/8 in. long, 1 3/8 in. wide, 1/4 in. thick. Made of tan white chert.
Priv. col., excellent quality, valued $30-35.

- Palmillas from Carroll co., TN. Blade 4 1/3 in. long, 2 1/16 in. wide, 1/3 in. thick. Made of gray chert.
Priv. col., excellent quality, valued $20-25.

- Palmillas from Carroll co., TN. Point 3 in. long, 1 1/8 in. wide, 1/8 in. thick. Good workmanship. Made of jasper.
Priv. col., museum quality, rare, valued $60-80.

- Palmillas from Franklin co., TN. Point 3 1/16 in. long, 1 5/16 in. wide, 1/4 in. thick. Broken tip. Made of Dover chert.
Priv. col., poor quality, valued $5-10.

- Palmillas from Jeff Davis co., TX. Point 2 7/8 in. long, 1 5/16 in. wide, 1/8 in. thick. Good workmanship. Made of gray chert.
Priv. col., excellent quality, valued $20-25.

- Palmillas from Jeff Davis co., TX. Blade 4 1/32 in. long, 1 1/2 in. wide, 1/8 in. thick. Good workmanship. Made of banded brown white chert.
Priv. col., excellent quality, valued $30-35.

Pandora: 4,000-1,000 B.P. Late Archaic to Woodland

Found in the midwestern states, medium to large size points and blades. Lanceolate points or blades. Edge or point blades are parallel or convex. The bases are generally straight.

- Pandora from Chester co., TN. Blade 4 1/2 in. long, 1 1/4 in. wide, 3/8 in. thick. Serrated, straight base, small tip break. Made of dark gray pebble chert.

Grover Bohannon col., excellent quality, valued $40-65.

• Pandora from Chester co., TN. Blade 4 7/8 in. long, 1 1/4 in. wide, 3/8 in. thick. Symmetrical, sharply serrated, straight base. Made of dark gray pebble chert.
Grover Bohannon col., museum quality, valued $60-85.

• Pandora from Cocke co., TN. Blade 4 1/16 in. long, 1 1/2 in. wide, 1/8 in. thick. Serrated, very thin, heat treated, good quality workmanship, straight base. Made of gray pink speckled pebble chert.
Priv. col, excellent quality, valued $45-65.

• Pandora from Cocke co., TN. Point 2 1/2 in. long, 3/4 in. wide, 3/8 in. thick. Serrated, narrow and symmetrical, heat treated, straight base. Made of gray pink speckled pebble chert.
Priv. col., excellent quality, valued $30-40.

• Pandora from Dade co., MO. Blade 3 7/8 in. long, 1 1/2 in. wide, 3/8 in. thick. Made of gray white pebble chert.
Priv. col., excellent quality, valued $50-55.

• Pandora from Dade co., MO. Blade 4 3/16 in. long, 1 3/4 in. wide, 1/8 in. thick. Made of gray pebble chert.
Priv. col, excellent quality, valued $45-65.

• Pandora from Dade co., MO. Blade 4 1/2 in. long, 2 in. wide, 1/4 in. thick. Made of white black speckled pebble chert.
Priv. col., excellent quality, valued $30-40.

• Pandora from Cleburne co., AL. Point 2 7/8 in. long, 1 1/4 in. wide, 3/8 in. thick. Made of quartzite.
Priv. col., average quality, valued $10-15.

• Pandora from Cleburne co., AL. Point 2 1/16 in. long, 1 1/2 in. wide, 1/8 in. thick. Good workmanship. Made of gray pink chert.
Priv. col, excellent quality, valued $25-35.

• Pandora from Cleburne co., AL. Point 3 1/32 in. long, 1 3/4 in. wide, 5/16 in. thick. Heat treated. Made of gray chert.
Priv. col., excellent quality, valued $30-40.

• Pandora from Cape Giradeau co., MO. Blade 4 in. long, 1 7/8 in. wide, 3/16 in. thick. Made of gray white chert.

Priv. col, excellent quality, valued $40-60.

• Pandora from Cape Giradeau co., MO. Blade 4 1/4 in. long, 2 1/16 in. wide, 1/4 in. thick. Made of white chert.
Priv. col., excellent quality, valued $35-40.

• Pandora from Cape Giradeau co., MO. Blade 3 7/8 in. long, 1 1/3 in. wide, 3/16 in. thick. Made of white chert.
Priv. col., excellent quality, valued $20-25.

• Pandora from Clay co., MO. Point 2 7/16 in. long, 1 1/2 in. wide, 1/8 in. thick. Good workmanship. Made of brown chert.
Priv. col, excellent quality, valued $25-35.

• Pandora from Calhoun co., AR. Point 2 11/32 in. long, 1 3/8 in. wide, 3/16 in. thick. Made of brown chert.
Priv. col., excellent quality, valued $30-40.

• Pandora from Ashley co., AR. Point 2 3/16 in. long, 1 1/4 in. wide, 3/16 in. thick. Made of gray pebble chert.
Priv. col, excellent quality, valued $25-35.

• Pandora from Ashley co., AR. Blade 4 1/3 in. long, 2 in. wide, 5/32 in. thick. Made of white pebble chert.
Priv. col., excellent quality, valued $30-40.

• Pandora from Ashley co., AR. Point 2 7/8 in. long, 1 1/4 in. wide, 1/4 in. thick. Made of gray shale.
Priv. col., average quality, valued $10-15.

• Pandora from Ashley co., AR. Point 2 7/16 in. long, 1 1/2 in. wide, 1/4 in. thick. Good workmanship. Made of quartzite.
Priv. col, average quality, valued $10-15.

• Pandora from Izard co., AR. Blade 3 21/32 in. long, 1 1/2 in. wide, 5/8 in. thick. Heat treated. Made of gray chert.
Priv. col., excellent quality, valued $30-35.

Pedernalis: 6,000-2,000 B.P. Mid-Archaic to Woodland

Predominantly a midwestern point or blade, medium to large in size. The stem is long, broad, and bifurcated. Pedernalis are generally barbed, edges are convex, concave, or recurved. Thin point or blade with high quality workmanship.

♦ Pedernalis from Meigs co., TN. Point 1 1/4 in. long, 3/4 in. wide, 3/16 in. thick. Very finely serrated edges and tip. Fluted bifurcated stem, sweeping tangs. Symmetrical, snapped base thinly ground.

Grover Bohannon col., museum quality, valued $45-65.

♦ Pedernalis from Lubbock, TX. Blade 3 1/4 in. long, 1 5/8 in. wide, 5/16 in. thick. Sharply barbed, thinly flaked, very sharp tip. Long bifurcated stem, two-thirds as wide as blade. Made of gray chert.

Grover Bohannon col., museum quality, valued $20-35.

• Pedernalis from Gallatin co., IL. Point 2 13/16 in. long, 11/16 in. wide, 1/8 in. thick. The stem is long, broad, and bifurcated. Barbed, edges are recurved. Thin point, high quality workmanship. Made of gray chert.
Priv. col, excellent quality, valued $25-40.

• Pedernalis from Gallatin co., IL. Blade 4 1/4 in. long, 2 1/8 in. wide, 1/8 in. thick. Thin, wide, sharply barbed, thinly flaked. Bifurcated stem, nearly as wide as blade. Made of gray chert.
Priv. col., excellent quality, valued $25-40.

• Pedernalis from Alexander co., IL. Blade 5 1/16 in. long, 1 7/8 in. wide, 1/4 in. thick. Long, narrow, symmetrical blade. Stem is long, broad, and bifurcated. Edges are recurved. Made of Mill Creek chert.
Priv. col., excellent quality, valued $55-75.

- Pedernalis from Alexander co., IL. Blade 3 3/4 in. long, 1 5/8 in. wide, 3/16 in. thick. Symmetrical, barbed, thinly flaked, very sharp tip. Long bifurcated stem. Made of Mill Creek chert.
Priv. col., excellent quality, valued $50-60.

- Pedernalis from Jackson co., IL. Point 3 in. long, 1 2/3 in. wide, 1/8 in. thick. The stem is long, broad and bifurcated. Barbed, edges are convex. Thin, symmetrical point, high quality workmanship. Made of Mill Creek chert.
Tim Rubbles col., excellent quality, valued $25-30.

- Pedernalis from Lubbock co., TX. Blade 4 1/32 in. long, 1 3/16 in. wide, 3/16 in. thick. Thin, narrow, symmetrical blade. Sharply barbed, thinly flaked, very sharp tip. Long bifurcated stem, nearly as wide the blade. Made of gray chert.
Grover Bohannon col., museum quality, valued $55-75.

- Pedernalis from Johnson co., TN. Point 1 1/2 in. long, 3/4 in. wide, 3/16 in. thick. Small, wide, symmetrical, fine point, sharp recurved edges. Fluted bifurcated stem with sweeping tangs. Symmetrical point, base snapped, thin, and ground. Made of Dover chert.
Grover Bohannon col., museum quality, valued $45-65.

- Pedernalis from Johnson co., TN. Point 2 1/8 in. long, 1 1/2 in. wide, 3/16 in. thick. Thin, wide, symmetrical, fine point, sharp edges. Bifurcated stem with snap tangs. Symmetrical, base snapped, thin, and ground. Made of tan to yellow chert.
Priv. col., museum quality, valued $40-55.

- Pedernalis from Lake co., TN. Blade 4 1/4 in. long, 2 3/4 in. wide, 1/4 in. thick. Symmetrical finely flaked, sharp tip and edges. Fluted bifurcated stem with snap tangs, heat treated. Base snapped, thin, with ground base tangs. Made of tan pebble chert.
Priv. col., excellent quality, valued $35-45.

- Pedernalis from Lake co., TN. Blade 3 7/8 in. long, 13/16 in. wide, 1/8 in. thick. Thin, symmetrically narrow, heat treated, good workmanship, pointed tip, sharp wide serrated edges. Fluted bifurcated stem with snap tangs. Base snapped, thin, and ground. Made of tan pebble chert.
Priv. col., excellent quality, valued $35-45.

- Pedernalis from Meigs co., TN. Blade 3 1/2 in. long, 1 3/4 in. wide, 5/16 in. thick. Point, sharp tip, wide serrated edges. Bifurcated stem with sweeping tangs. Symmetrical though wide blade, ground base. Made of a lightweight white

chert.
Grover Bohannon col., excellent quality, valued $50-60.

* Pedernalis from Meigs co., TN. Point 2 1/4 in. long, 1 1/4 in. wide, 3/16 in. thick. Fine worked point, sharp, serrated tip and edges. Fluted bifurcated stem with sweeping tangs. Base snapped and ground. Made of lightweight white chert. *Priv. col., museum quality, valued $65-85.*

* Pedernalis from Johnson co., TN. Point 1 7/8 in. long, 5/8 in. wide, 3/16 in. thick. Point, sharp serrated tip and edges. Fluted bifurcated stem with snap tangs. Symmetrical, narrow point, base snapped, thin, and ground. Made of gray pink speckled pebble chert.
Priv. col., excellent quality, valued $45-65.

* Pedernalis from Andrews co., TX. Blade 4 1/8 in. long, 2 1/32 in. wide, 1/8 in. thick. Good workmanship. Made of gray chert.
Priv. col., excellent quality, valued $45-60.

* Pedernalis from Andrews co., TX. Blade 5 5/16 in. long, 1 5/8 in. wide, 1/4 in. thick. Excellent workmanship. Made of glossy near translucent gray chert.
Priv. col., excellent quality, valued $55-75.

* Pedernalis from Hartley co., TX. Blade 3 2/3 in. long, 1 7/8 in. wide, 3/16 in. thick. Made of gray chert.
Priv. col., excellent quality, valued $40-50.

* Pedernalis from Kinney co., TX. Blade 4 1/32 in. long, 2 in. wide, 1/8 in. thick. Good workmanship, heat treated, part of cache. Made of gray chert.
Priv. col., excellent quality, valued $50-60.

* Pedernalis from Kinney co., TX. Blade 4 5/16 in. long, 1 7/8 in. wide, 1/4 in. thick. Excellent workmanship, heat treated, same cache. Made of gray chert.
Priv. col., excellent quality, valued $55-75.

* Pedernalis from Kinney co., TX. Blade 3 7/8 in. long, 1 5/8 in. wide, 1/8 in. thick. Good workmanship, heat treated, same cache. Made of gray chert.
Priv. col., excellent quality, valued $45-55.

* Pedernalis from Kinney co., TX. Blade 4 1/8 in. long, 1 21/32 in. wide, 1/8 in. thick. Good workmanship, same cache. Made of gray chert.
Priv. col., excellent quality, valued $45-60.

* Pedernalis from Titus co., TX. Blade 5 1/16 in. long, 1 7/8 in. wide, 1/4 in.

thick. Excellent workmanship. Made of glossy black flint.
Priv. col., museum quality, valued $95-120.

• Pedernalis from Payne co., OK. Blade 4 2/3 in. long, 2 1/8 in. wide, 3/16 in. thick. Made of yellow tan chert.
Priv. col., excellent quality, valued $50-60.

• Pedernalis from Payne co., OK. Blade 5 1/8 in. long, 2 1/16 in. wide, 1/8 in. thick. Excellent workmanship, heat treated. Made of white chert.
Priv. col., museum quality, valued $75-100.

• Pedernalis from Kiowa co., OK. Blade 4 9/16 in. long, 1 5/8 in. wide, 1/4 in. thick. Excellent workmanship. Made of dull gray chert.
Priv. col., museum quality, valued $75-85.

• Pedernalis from Kiowa co., OK. Point 3 17/32 in. long, 1 7/8 in. wide, 1/8 in. thick. Made of white chert.
Priv. col., excellent quality, valued $40-50.

Pelican: 10,000-6,000 B.P. Paleo-Transitional

Predominantly found in the midwestern states. Short, broad, usually auriculate small to medium sized point. Points are basal ground. Contracting stem, sometimes thinned or fluted tapered shoulders.

◆ Pelican from Hempstead co., AR. Point 2 1/4 in. long, 1 1/4 in. wide, 1/4 in. thick. Wide point, concave base, sharp tangs. Made of cream pebble chert.

Grover Bohannon col., average quality, valued $10-20.

• Pelican from Hempstead co., AR. Point 2 in. long, 1 5/8 in. wide, 1/4 in. thick. Random serrated edges, fluted on both sides, very sharp tip. Tapered shoulders, long contracting stem, ground base tangs. Made of Arkansas brown chert.
Grover Bohannon col., excellent quality, valued $25-40.

• Pelican from Hempstead co., AR. Point 2 1/2 in. long, 1 1/3 in. wide, 1/4 in. thick. Excellent workmanship. Made of Arkansas brown chert.
Grover Bohannon col., museum quality, valued $40-60.

• Pelican from Hempstead co., AR. Point 2 1/3 in. long, 1 3/8 in. wide, 3/16 in. thick. Distinct fluting. Made of Arkansas brown chert.
Grover Bohannon col., excellent quality, valued $25-40.

• Pelican from Martin co., IN. Point 2 in. long, 1 1/8 in. wide, 1/4 in. thick. Made of dense white chert.
Priv. col., excellent quality, valued $25-40.

• Pelican from Steuben co., IN. Point 2 3/8 in. long, 1 1/4 in. wide, 3/16 in. thick. Made of brown pebble chert.
Priv. col., average quality, valued $15-20.

• Pelican from St. Francis co., AR. Point 2 1/16 in. long, 1 1/3 in. wide, 1/4 in. thick. Made of grainy gray chert.
Priv. col., average quality, valued $20-25.

• Pelican from Lee co., AR. Point 2 1/3 in. long, 1 1/4 in. wide, 5/16 in. thick. Slight tip break. Made of Arkansas brown chert.
Priv. col., average quality, valued $10-20.

• Pelican from Ashley co., AR. Point 2 1/2 in. long, 1 1/2 in. wide, 1/4 in. thick. Made of quartzite.
Priv. col., average quality, valued $10-15.

• Pelican from Ashley co., AR. Point 2 2/3 in. long, 1 3/8 in. wide, 1/4 in. thick. Distinct fluting. Made of agate.
Priv. col., museum quality, rare, valued $55-75.

• Pelican from Boone co., MO. Point 2 1/2 in. long, 1 1/3 in. wide, 1/4 in. thick. Excellent workmanship. Made of glossy gray chert.
Priv. col., museum quality, valued $40-60.

• Pelican from Boone co., MO. Point 2 1/8 in. long, 1 1/2 in. wide, 3/16 in. thick. Made of brown tan chert.
Priv. col., excellent quality, valued $25-35.

• Pelican from Butler co., MO. Point 2 11/16 in. long, 1 1/3 in. wide, 1/4 in. thick. Excellent workmanship. Made of white chert.

Priv. col., excellent quality, valued $30-40.

- Pelican from Butler co., MO. Point 2 1/3 in. long, 1 3/8 in. wide, 5/16 in. thick. Thin based. Made of translucent gray chert.
Priv. col., museum quality, valued $45-50.

- Pelican from Wayne co., MO. Point 2 1/4 in. long, 1 2/3 in. wide, 1/4 in. thick. Made of white chert.
Priv. col., excellent quality, valued $30-40.

- Pelican from Wayne co., MO. Point 2 2/3 in. long, 1 5/8 in. wide, 5/16 in. thick. Made of white tan chert.
Priv. col., excellent quality, valued $25-40.

- Pelican from Bullock co., AL. Point 2 1/4 in. long, 1 1/2 in. wide, 1/4 in. thick. Made of quartzite.
Priv. col., average quality, valued $10-15.

- Pelican from Bullock co., AL. Point 2 3/8 in. long, 1 3/32 in. wide, 5/32 in. thick. Made of pink quartzite.
Priv. col., average quality, valued $15-20.

- Pelican from Bullock co., AL. Point 2 1/2 in. long, 1 9/16 in. wide, 1/4 in. thick. Excellent workmanship. Made of gray chert.
Priv. col., museum quality, valued $45-60.

- Pelican from Bullock co., AL. Point 2 1/2 in. long, 1 3/4 in. wide, 7/16 in. thick. Made of quartzite.
Priv. col., average quality, valued $15-20.

- Pelican from Alleghany co., NC. Point 2 1/3 in. long, 1 1/3 in. wide, 1/4 in. thick. Made of banded red slate.
Priv. col., excellent quality, valued $30-45.

- Pelican from Alleghanny co., NC. Point 2 1/3 in. long, 1 3/8 in. wide, 5/16 in. thick. Made of banded slate.
Priv. col., excellent quality, valued $25-35.

- Pelican from Davie co., NC. Point 2 11/16 in. long, 1 2/3 in. wide, 1/4 in. thick. Excellent workmanship. Made of high grade pink chert.
Priv. col., museum quality, valued $40-60.

• Pelican from Davie co., NC. Point 2 1/3 in. long, 1 5/8 in. wide, 5/16 in. thick. Distinct double fluting. Made of mauve chert.
Priv. col., museum quality, valued $45-60.

• Pelican from Yarkin co., NC. Point 3 in. long, 2 1/16 in. wide, 1/4 in. thick. Excellent workmanship. Made of white pebble chert.
Priv. col., excellent quality, valued $30-40.

• Pelican from Yarkin co., NC. Point 2 1/2 in. long, 1 1/2 in. wide, 1/4 in. thick. Made of brown tan chert.
Priv. col., excellent quality, valued $25-40.

Perdiz: 1,000-500 B.P. Mississippian

Found predominantly in the Midwest and into the western states. Perdiz is a small to medium point. They are triangular, narrow, with pointed barbs and sharp tips. Long, stems, convex, straight to rounded. This is an abundantly widespread point.

◆ Perdiz from Hempstead co., AR. Point 1 5/8 in. long, 3/4 in. wide, 1/8 in. thick. Fine workmanship, triangular, thin flaked, sharp tangs and stem. Made of mauve chert.

Grover Bohannon col., museum quality, valued $65-80.

• Perdiz from Izard co., AR. Point 1 2/3 in. long, 5/8 in. wide, 1/8 in. thick. Thin, good workmanship, sharply serrated edges, sharp tip and barbs. Deep corner notches, long stem, pointed base. Made of amber quartz.
Grover Bohannon col., museum quality, rare, valued $200-275.

• Perdiz from Hamilton co., TN. Point 2 in. long, 7/8 in. wide, 1/8 in. thick. Thin, sharply serrated edges, high quality workmanship, thinned tip. Deep corner notches, long stem, rounded base. Made of yellow quartz.
Grover Bohannon col., museum quality, valued $75-100.

• Perdiz from Kiowa co., OK. Point 1 in. long, 5/8 in. wide, 1/8 in. thick. Made

of gray chert.
Grover Bohannon col., excellent quality, valued $120-150.

- Perdiz from Kiowa co., OK. Point 2/3 in. long, 3/8 in. wide, 1/8 in. thick. Excellent quality. Made of white chert.
Grover Bohannon col., museum quality, valued $175-200.

- Perdiz from Kiowa co., OK. Point 1 1/16 in. long, 5/8 in. wide, 1/8 in. thick. Made of rose quartz.
Grover Bohannon col., museum quality, rare, valued $200-275.

- Perdiz from Craig co., OK. Point 7/8 in. long, 5/8 in. wide, 1/8 in. thick. Excellent workmanship. Made of yellow tan chert.
Grover Bohannon col., museum quality, valued $175-200.

- Perdiz from Dallas co., TX. Point 1 in. long, 5/8 in. wide, 1/8 in. thick. Made of gray flint.
Priv. col., excellent quality, valued $80-100.

- Perdiz from Dallas co., TX. Point 2/3 in. long, 3/8 in. wide, 1/8 in. thick. Excellent quality. Made of white chert.
Priv. col., excellent quality, valued $75-100.

- Perdiz from Webb co., TX. Point 1 1/8 in. long, 3/4 in. wide, 1/8 in. thick. Made of quartzite.
Grover Bohannon col., average quality, valued $25-50.

- Perdiz from Webb co., TX. Point 1 1/8 in. long, 2/3 in. wide, 1/8 in. thick. Excellent workmanship. Made of dull gray flint.
Grover Bohannon col., excellent quality, valued $65-85.

- Perdiz from Webb co., TX. Point 1 1/32 in. long, 3/4 in. wide, 1/8 in. thick. Made of gray chert.
Priv. col., excellent quality, valued $90-125.

- Perdiz from Kinney co., TX. Point 1 1/3 in. long, 7/8 in. wide, 1/8 in. thick. Excellent quality. Made of dense white chert.
Priv. col., museum quality, valued $150-200.

- Perdiz from Kinney co., TX. Point 1 3/16 in. long, 13/16 in. wide, 1/8 in. thick. Made of vein quartz.
Priv. col., excellent quality, valued $100-150.

- Perdiz from Somerville co., TX. Point 1 3/8 in. long, 1 in. wide, 1/8 in. thick. Excellent workmanship. Made of tan chert.
Priv. col., excellent quality, valued $100-125.

- Perdiz from Parker co., TX. Point 1 in. long, 5/8 in. wide, 3/16 in. thick. Made of gray chert.
Priv. col., excellent quality, valued $90-120.

- Perdiz from Midland co., TX. Point 1 1/3 in. long, 7/8 in. wide, 1/8 in. thick. Made of white chert.
Priv. col., excellent quality, valued $85-100.

- Perdiz from Midland co., TX. Point 1 5/16 in. long, 1 in. wide, 1/8 in. thick. Tip break. Made of white chert.
Priv. col., average quality, valued $35-50.

- Perdiz from Hopkins co., TX. Point 1 1/16 in. long, 7/8 in. wide, 1/8 in. thick. Made of grainy white tan chert.
Priv. col., average quality, valued $35-50.

- Perdiz from Hopkins co., TX. Point 1 5/32 in. long, 7/8 in. wide, 1/8 in. thick. Made of gray chert.
Priv. col., excellent quality, valued $100-120.

- Perdiz from Parker co., TX. Point 1 1/3 in. long, 1 in. wide, 1/8 in. thick. Excellent quality. Made of white chert.
Priv. col., excellent quality, valued $125-170.

- Perdiz from Parker co., TX. Point 1 3/32 in. long, 1 1/16 in. wide, 1/8 in. thick. Made of gray chert.
Priv. col., excellent quality, valued $150-175.

- Perdiz from Reagan co., TX. Point 1 1/8 in. long, 13/16 in. wide, 1/8 in. thick. Excellent workmanship. Made of banded tan chert.
Priv. col., museum quality, valued $225-300.

- Perdiz from Reagan co., TX. Point 1 3/16 in. long, 1 in. wide, 1/8 in. thick. Made of gray chert.
Priv. col., excellent quality, valued $120-140.

- Perdiz from Reagan co., TX. Point 1 1/3 in. long, 7/8 in. wide, 1/8 in. thick. Excellent quality. Made of red banded slate.

Priv. col., excellent quality, valued $125-150.

• Perdiz from Moyley co., TX. Point 1 3/16 in. long, 13/16 in. wide, 1/8 in. thick. Made of gray chert.
Priv. col., excellent quality, valued $100-125.

• Perdiz from Motley co., TX. Point 1 7/8 in. long, 1 1/16 in. wide, 1/8 in. thick. Excellent workmanship, large, needle sharp tip. Made of agate.
Priv. col., museum quality, rare, valued $275-380.

• Perdiz from Zapata co., TX. Point 1 in. long, 9/16 in. wide, 1/8 in. thick. Made of dull gray chert.
Priv. col., excellent quality, valued $120-150.

• Perdiz from Zapata co., TX. Point 13/16 in. long, 3/8 in. wide, 1/16 in. thick. Excellent workmanship, extremely thin. Made of white pink chert.
Priv. col., museum quality, valued $175-225.

• Perdiz from Sutton co., TX. Point 1 3/32 in. long, 11/16 in. wide, 1/8 in. thick. Made of quartzite.
Priv. col., average quality, valued $50-75.

• Perdiz from Sutton co., TX. Point 1 1/8 in. long, 7/8 in. wide, 1/8 in. thick. Made of quartzite.
Priv. col., average quality, valued $45-70.

• Perdiz from Sabine co., TX. Point 7/8 in. long, 5/8 in. wide, 1/8 in. thick. Made of gray chert.
Priv. col., excellent quality, valued $120-150.

• Perdiz from Sabine co., TX. Point 1 1/3 in. long, 1 in. wide, 1/8 in. thick. Made of quartzite.
Priv. col., average quality, valued $75-90.

• Perdiz from Sabine co., TX. Point 1 5/16 in. long, 7/8 in. wide, 1/8 in. thick. Made of quartzite.
Priv. col., average quality, valued $40-55.

• Perdiz from Sabine co., TX. Point 7/8 in. long, 5/8 in. wide, 3/16 in. thick. Made of tan chert.
Priv. col., excellent quality, valued $125-150.

• Perdiz from Sabine co., TX. Point 1 1/32 in. long, 13/16 in. wide, 1/8 in. thick. Made of gray chert.
Priv. col., excellent quality, valued $120-150.

• Perdiz from Jeff Davis co., TX. Point 11/16 in. long, 3/4 in. wide, 1/8 in. thick. Excellent quality. Made of white chert.
Priv. col., museum quality, valued $125-160.

• Perdiz from Jeff Davis co., TX. Point 1 1/32 in. long, 2/3 in. wide, 1/8 in. thick. Good workmanship. Made of gray chert.
Priv. col., excellent quality, valued $100-175.

• Perdiz from Jeff Davis co., TX. Point 7/8 in. long, 5/8 in. wide, 1/8 in. thick. Good workmanship. Made of gray chert.
Priv. col., excellent quality, valued $125-150.

Pickwick: 6,000-3,500 B.P. Mid to Late Archaic

Found throughout the Southeast. A medium to large point or blade. Stems are contracted or expanded. Sides are recurved, faces exhibit high quality secondary flaking, sharply serrated edges. May be beveled on one side of each face. Barbed shoulders above corner or side notches. Base convex, concave, straight, or rounded.

♦ Pickwick from Webster co., KY. Point 2 5/8 in. long, 1 1/2 in. wide, 3/16 in. thick. Finely serrated, upward flaring tangs. One tang shorter, very sharp; the other with slight break. Secondary flaking, contracting stem. Made of light gray chert.

Grover Bohannon col., excellent quality, valued $100-175.

♦ Pickwick from Hamilton co., TN. Blade 3 3/4 in. long, 1 1/2 in. wide, 1/4 in. thick. Sharply serrated edges, beveled on one side of each face. Parallel tangs, fine parallel flaked. Slightly recurved sides and expanded stem. Made of Dover

chert.

Grover Bohannon col., museum quality, valued $500-600.

• Pickwick from Abbevile co., SC. Blade 4 5/8 in. long, 1 7/8 in. wide, 3/16 in. thick. Made of white chert.
Grover Bohannon col., average quality, valued $40-75.

• Pickwick from Abbevile co., SC. Blade 4 1/4 in. long, 2 1/4 in. wide, 1/4 in. thick. Parallel flaked. Made of pinkish chert.
Grover Bohannon col., excellent quality, valued $150-200.

• Pickwick from Dillon co., SC. Point 2 7/8 in. long, 1 1/2 in. wide, 1/4 in. thick. Made of grainy gray chert.
Priv. col., excellent quality, valued $100-175.

• Pickwick from Dillon co., SC. Blade 5 1/4 in. long, 2 1/3 in. wide, 1/4 in. thick. Made of white black speckled chert.
Priv. col., average quality, valued $50-90.

• Pickwick from Humphreys co., TN. Blade 4 1/3 in. long, 2 1/8 in. wide, 1/4 in. thick. Made of Dover chert.
Priv. col., excellent quality, valued $250-300.

• Pickwick from Motley co., TX. Blade 4 7/8 in. long, 1 1/2 in. wide, 1/4 in. thick. Made of gray chert.
Priv. col., excellent quality, valued $200-275.

• Pickwick from Colbert co., AL. Blade 5 1/16 in. long, 2 1/4 in. wide, 1/4 in. thick. Made of white chert.
Priv. col., excellent quality, valued $350-400.

• Pickwick from Searcy co., AR. Blade 4 3/4 in. long, 2 1/32 in. wide, 5/16 in. thick. Made of brown chert.
Priv. col., excellent quality, valued $150-200.

• Pickwick from Searcy co., AR. Blade 3 7/8 in. long, 1 1/2 in. wide, 1/4 in.

420

thick. Made of gray chert.
Priv. col., average quality, valued $60-75.

• Pickwick from Searcy co., AR. Blade 5 in. long, 2 1/8 in. wide, 1/4 in. thick. Made of white chert.
Priv. col., average quality, valued $50-70.

• Pickwick from Henry co., KY. Blade 4 1/2 in. long, 2 in. wide, 1/4 in. thick. Made of tan white chert.
Priv. col., excellent quality, valued $150-220.

• Pickwick from Henry co., KY. Blade 4 7/8 in. long, 1 7/8 in. wide, 1/2 in. thick. Made of tan gray chert.
Priv. col., excellent quality, valued $200-250.

• Pickwick from Henry co., KY. Blade 5 1/32 in. long, 2 1/8 in. wide, 1/3 in. thick. Made of white pebble chert.
Priv. col., excellent quality, valued $350-390.

• Pickwick from Herny co., KY. Blade 4 3/4 in. long, 2 1/16 in. wide, 1/4 in. thick. Made of gray pinkish chert.
Priv. col., excellent quality, valued $225-300.

• Pickwick from Fulton co., KY. Point 2 3/8 in. long, 1 1/4 in. wide, 1/4 in. thick. Made of grainy gray chert.
Priv. col., excellent quality, valued $100-150.

• Pickwick from Fulton co., KY. Point 3 1/4 in. long, 1 1/3 in. wide, 1/4 in. thick. Made of grainy gray chert.
Priv. col., average quality, valued $50-60.

• Pickwick from Fulton co., KY. Point 3 in. long, 2 1/32 in. wide, 1/4 in. thick. Made of gray chert.
Priv. col., average quality, valued $50-70.

• Pickwick from Mercer co., KY. Point 2 3/8 in. long, 1 1/3 in. wide, 1/4 in. thick. Made of grainy white chert.
Priv. col., average quality, valued $40-75.

• Pickwick from Mercer co., KY. Point 3 1/4 in. long, 2 in. wide, 1/4 in. thick. Made of white tan chert.
Priv. col., average quality, valued $55-80.

• Pickwick from Mercer co., KY. Point 2 1/2 in. long, 1 3/4 in. wide, 1/4 in. thick. Made of white tan chert.
Priv. col., average quality, valued $50-70.

• Pickwick from Rowan co., KY. Point 2 5/8 in. long, 1 1/8 in. wide, 1/4 in. thick. Made of grainy tan gray chert.
Priv. col., average quality, valued $60-75.

• Pickwick from Rowan co., KY. Point 3 1/32 in. long, 1 1/2 in. wide, 1/4 in. thick. Made of white tan chert.
Priv. col., average quality, valued $50-80.

• Pickwick from Hamilton co., TN. Blade 5 1/8 in. long, 2 1/8 in. wide, 1/4 in. thick. Made of high grade pink chert.
Priv. col., excellent quality, valued $350-400.

• Pickwick from Hamilton co., TN. Blade 4 7/8 in. long, 1 1/3 in. wide, 1/4 in. thick. Made of brown chert.
Priv. col., excellent quality, valued $300-375.

• Pickwick from Hamilton co., TN. Blade 5 1/2 in. long, 2 1/8 in. wide, 1/4 in. thick. Made of brown chert.
Priv. col., excellent quality, valued $450-500.

• Pickwick from Johnson co., IL. Blade 4 3/4 in. long, 2 1/32 in. wide, 1/4 in. thick. Made of Mill Creek chert.
Priv. col., excellent quality, valued $175-250.

• Pickwick from Johnson co., IL. Blade 5 7/8 in. long, 2 1/8 in. wide, 1/4 in. thick. Made of Mill Creek chert.
Priv. col., excellent quality, valued $300-375.

• Pickwick from Union co., IL. Blade 5 1/32 in. long, 2 1/4 in. wide, 1/4 in. thick. Made of Cobden chert.
Priv. col., museum quality, valued $500-600.

• Pickwick from Union co., IL. Blade 5 1/32 in. long, 2 1/8 in. wide, 1/4 in. thick. Parallel flaked. Made of brown chert.
Priv. col., excellent quality, valued $350-400.

• Pickwick from Alexander co., IL. Blade 3 7/8 in. long, 1 1/2 in. wide, 1/4 in. thick. Made of gray chert.

Priv. col., excellent quality, valued $150-225.

• Pickwick from Alexander co., IL. Blade 5 in. long, 2 1/8 in. wide, 1/4 in. thick. Made of gray chert.
Priv. col., excellent quality, valued $250-300.

• Pickwick from Jackson co., IL. Blade 4 3/4 in. long, 2 1/4 in. wide, 1/4 in. thick. Made of white pebble chert.
Priv. col., excellent quality, valued $250-300.

• Pickwick from Jackson co., IL. Blade 4 7/8 in. long, 1 7/8 in. wide, 1/4 in. thick. Made of gray chert.
Priv. col., excellent quality, valued $300-375.

• Pickwick from Jackson co., IL. Blade 5 1/32 in. long, 2 1/3 in. wide, 1/4 in. thick. Made of gray chert.
Priv. col., excellent quality, valued $350-400.

Pine Tree: 8,500-4,500 B.P. Early Archaic

Pine Trees are usually considered a southeastern point or blade. From the number of Pine Tree points and blades recorded by the author, it would seem that they are often found in the Midwest. Points and blades are side notched, serrated, parallel flaked to center of piece. Bases are generally ground, convex, auriculate, straight or concave.

♦ Pine Tree from Dewitt co., IL. Blade 3 1/2 in. long, 1 1/4 in. wide, 1/4 in. thick. Exceptional workmanship, deep serrated edges, upper 1/4 sharply and finely serrated, needle sharp tip. Symmetrical, deep parallel corner notches, concave base. Made of dense white chert.

Priv. col., museum quality, valued $280-385.

♦ Pine Tree from Shelby co., TN. Point 1 1/8 in. long, 1/2 in. wide, 1/8 in. thick. Wide sharp serrations, convex base, uneven corner notches. Point has small tip break. Made of banded gray chert.

Grover Bohannon col., average quality, valued $25-35.

◆ Pine Tree from Greene co., IL. Blade 3 1/2 in. long, 1 1/2 in. wide, 1/4 in. thick. Heat treated, concave finely serrated edges. Deep parallel notches with concave base, very symmetrical. Made of brown chert.

Charles McCorkle, museum quality, valued $500-575.

◆ Pine Tree from Hamilton co., TN. Point 1 1/2 in. long, 1/2 in. wide, 1/8 in. thick. Unique tip, very sharp, deep and wide serrations. Long stem, convex base, very symmetrical. Made of white pebble chert.

Grover Bohannon col., museum quality, valued $225-275.

• Pine Tree from Humphreys co., IL. Blade 4 1/8 in. long, 1 7/8 in. wide, 1/4 in. thick. Made of Dover chert.
Grover Bohannon col., museum quality, valued $350-375.

• Pine Tree from Humphreys co., TN. Blade 5 1/32 in. long, 2 1/4 in. wide, 1/8 in. thick. Made of white pebble chert.
Grover Bohannon col., museum quality, valued $275-375.

• Pine Tree from Humphreys co., TN. Blade 3 7/8 in. long, 1 11/32 in. wide, 1/4 in. thick. Made of brown chert.
Priv. col., excellent quality, valued $300-350.

• Pine Tree from Humphreys co., TN. Blade 4 1/8 in. long, 1 1/2 in. wide, 1/8 in. thick. Made of brown chert.

Priv. col., excellent quality, valued $325-350.

• Pine Tree from Hamilton co., TN. Blade 3 2/3 in. long, 1 1/2 in. wide, 1/4 in. thick. Heat treated. Made of brown chert.
Priv. col., museum quality, valued $200-275.

• Pine Tree from Hamilton co., TN. Blade 4 in. long, 1 2/3 in. wide, 1/8 in. thick. Made of gray white pebble chert.
Priv. col., museum quality, valued $225-275.

• Pine Tree from Henderson co., TN. Point 2 7/8 in. long, 1 1/8 in. wide, 1/4 in. thick. Made of brown chert.
Priv. col., excellent quality, valued $150-200.

• Pine Tree from Henderson co., TN. Point 3 1/8 in. long, 1 1/32 in. wide, 3/16 in. thick. Made of marbled brown chert.
Priv. col., excellent quality, valued $125-150.

• Pine Tree from Henderson co., TN. Point 2 2/3 in. long, 1 1/2 in. wide, 1/4 in. thick. Made of marbled brown chert.
Priv. col., excellent quality, valued $120-150.

• Pine Tree from Henderson co., TN. Point 3 in. long, 1 1/3 in. wide, 3/16 in. thick. Heat treated. Made of banded gray white chert.
Priv. col., excellent quality, valued $125-175.

• Pine Tree from Chester co., TN. Point 2 7/8 in. long, 1 1/2 in. wide, 1/4 in. thick. Made of gray chert.
Priv. col., excellent quality, valued $100-125.

• Pine Tree from Chester co., TN. Point 2 1/8 in. long, 1 1/2 in. wide, 1/8 in. thick. Excellent workmanship. Made of banded brown chert.
Priv. col., museum quality, valued $225-250.

• Pine Tree from Chester co., TN. Point 1 2/3 in. long, 1 in. wide, 1/4 in. thick. Good workmanship. Made of banded brown chert.
Priv. col., museum quality, valued $100-150.

• Pine Tree from Chester co., TN. Point 2 1/16 in. long, 1 1/3 in. wide, 3/16 in. thick. Made of gray pebble chert.
Priv. col., excellent quality, valued $85-100.

• Pine Tree from Lewis co., TN. Point 1 7/8 in. long, 1 1/32 in. wide, 1/8 in. thick. Excellent workmanship. Made of brown white chert.
Priv. col., excellent quality, valued $100-150.

• Pine Tree from Lewis co., TN. Point 2 1/8 in. long, 1 1/2 in. wide, 1/4 in. thick. Made of gray chert.
Priv. col., excellent quality, valued $125-150.

• Pine Tree from Lewis co., TN. Point 1 2/3 in. long, 1 1/32 in. wide, 1/4 in. thick. Made of gray chert.
Priv. col., excellent quality, valued $100-125.

• Pine Tree from Lewis co., TN. Blade 2 1/8 in. long, 1 1/4 in. wide, 1/8 in. thick. Made of gray white chert.
Priv. col., excellent quality, valued $125-175.

• Pine Tree from Dyer co., TN. Blade 3 7/8 in. long, 1 1/3 in. wide, 1/4 in. thick. Excellent workmanship. Made of Buffalo River chert.
Priv. col., museum quality, valued $300-350.

• Pine Tree from Meade co., KY. Blade 4 1/32 in. long, 1 1/2 in. wide, 1/8 in. thick. Made of white pebble chert.
Priv. col., excellent quality, valued $225-250.

• Pine Tree from Meade co., KY. Blade 4 2/3 in. long, 1 1/2 in. wide, 1/4 in. thick. Heat treated. Made of white pebble chert.
Priv. col., average quality, valued $100-125.

• Pine Tree from Meade co., KY. Blade 4 1/3 in. long, 1 2/3 in. wide, 3/16 in. thick. Made of gray white chert.
Priv. col., excellent quality, valued $325-350.

• Pine Tree from Bath co., KY. Blade 3 13/16 in. long, 1 3/32 in. wide, 1/4 in. thick. Made of gray chert.
Priv. col., excellent quality, valued $200-250.

• Pine Tree from Bath co., KY. Blade 4 in. long, 1 1/8 in. wide, 1/8 in. thick. Made of brown chert.
Priv. col., excellent quality, valued $225-250.

• Pine Tree from Bath co., KY. Blade 3 27/32 in. long, 1 1/2 in. wide, 1/4 in. thick. Made of banded brown chert.

Priv. col., excellent quality, valued $150-175.

- Pine Tree from Harrison co., KY. Blade 4 1/3 in. long, 1 13/32 in. wide, 1/8 in. thick. Made of gray white chert.
Priv. col., excellent quality, valued $125-150.

- Pine Tree from Marion co., KY. Blade 4 1/8 in. long, 1 1/2 in. wide, 3/16 in. thick. Beveled on one side of each edge. Made of brown pink chert.
Priv. col., excellent quality, valued $250-350.

- Pine Tree from Marion co., KY. Blade 4 1/16 in. long, 1 1/2 in. wide, 1/4 in. thick. Made of lightweight gray chert.
Priv. col., excellent quality, valued $225-300.

- Pine Tree from Marion co., KY. Blade 3 13/16 in. long, 1 1/4 in. wide, 3/16 in. thick. Heat treated. Made of marbled brown chert.
Priv. col., museum quality, valued $220-275.

- Pine Tree from Marion co., KY. Blade 4 1/32 in. long, 1 1/3 in. wide, 1/4 in. thick. Made of gray white chert.
Priv. col., excellent quality, valued $125-175.

- Pine Tree from Powell co., KY. Point 2 7/8 in. long, 1 13/32 in. wide, 1/4 in. thick. Excellent workmanship. Made of gray chert.
Priv. col., excellent quality, valued $200-250.

- Pine Tree from Powell co., KY. Point 2 1/8 in. long, 1 1/8 in. wide, 1/8 in. thick. Made of white chert.
Priv. col., excellent quality, valued $125-150.

- Pine Tree from Powell co., KY. Blade 4 2/3 in. long, 2 1/2 in. wide, 1/4 in. thick. Heat treated, excellent workmanship. Made of Dover chert.
Priv. col., museum quality, valued $500-675.

- Pine Tree from Cumberland co., KY. Blade 5 in. long, 1 3/4 in. wide, 1/8 in. thick. Made of gray white chert.

Priv. col., museum quality, valued $225-275.

- Pine Tree from Cumberland co., KY. Blade 3 7/8 in. long, 1 1/4 in. wide, 1/4 in. thick. Made of brown chert.
Priv. col., excellent quality, valued $100-150.

- Pine Tree from Cumberland co., KY. Blade 4 1/4 in. long, 1 1/2 in. wide, 3/16 in. thick. Made of brown marbled chert.
Priv. col., excellent quality, valued $350-375.

- Pine Tree from Cumberland co., KY. Blade 3 13/16 in. long, 1 1/2 in. wide, 1/4 in. thick. Made of gray chert.
Priv. col., excellent quality, valued $200-275.

- Pine Tree from Cumberland co., KY. Blade 4 1/16 in. long, 1 3/4 in. wide, 3/16 in. thick. Made of white pebble chert.
Priv. col., excellent quality, valued $250-325.

- Pine Tree from Cumberland co., KY. Blade 3 7/8 in. long, 1 1/3 in. wide, 1/4 in. thick. Made of brown chert.
Priv. col., excellent quality, valued $300-350.

- Pine Tree from Cumberland co., KY. Blade 4 1/3 in. long, 1 1/2 in. wide, 1/4 in. thick. Made of gray chert.
Priv. col., excellent quality, valued $375-450.

- Pine Tree from Webster co., KY. Blade 3 7/8 in. long, 1 1/2 in. wide, 1/4 in. thick. Heat treated. Made of gray chert.
Priv. col., excellent quality, valued $120-155.

- Pine Tree from Webster co., KY. Point 2 1/4 in. long, 1 1/16 in. wide, 1/8 in. thick. Heat treated, beveled on side of face. Made of gray white pebble chert.
Priv. col., museum quality, valued $250-275.

- Pine Tree from Webster co., KY. Blade 4 7/8 in. long, 1 19/32 in. wide, 1/4 in. thick. Made of gray chert.
Priv. col., excellent quality, valued $325-350.

- Pine Tree from Webster co., KY. Blade 4 1/3 in. long, 1 1/2 in. wide, 3/16 in. thick. Made of brown marbled chert.
Priv. col., museum quality, valued $450-550.

- Pine Tree from Webster co., KY. Point 2 1/3 in. long, 1 1/2 in. wide, 1/4 in. thick. Heat treated. Made of marbled brown chert.
Priv. col., museum quality, valued $250-325.

- Pine Tree from Shelby co., KY. Blade 4 1/3 in. long, 1 1/3 in. wide, 3/16 in. thick. Made of gray white chert.

Priv. col., excellent quality, valued $175-225.

- Pine Tree from Shelby co., KY. Blade 3 7/8 in. long, 1 17/32 in. wide, 1/4 in. thick. Made of marbled brown chert.
Priv. col., excellent quality, valued $280-325.

- Pine Tree from Owen co., KY. Blade 4 3/8 in. long, 1 1/2 in. wide, 1/8 in. thick. Made of gray chert.
Priv. col., excellent quality, valued $225-250.

- Pine Tree from Owen co., KY. Point 3 1/3 in. long, 1 1/4 in. wide, 1/4 in. thick. Heat treated. Made of gray chert.
Priv. col., average quality, valued $80-125.

- Pine Tree from Owen co., KY. Point 2 7/8 in. long, 1 3/16 in. wide, 1/3 in. thick. Excellent workmanship. Made of gray white pebble chert.
Priv. col., museum quality, valued $250-300.

- Pine Tree from Hamilton co., TN. Blade 3 7/8 in. long, 1 1/2 in. wide, 1/4 in. thick. Good workmanship. Made of Dover chert.
Priv. col., excellent quality, valued $300-350.

- Pine Tree from Humphreys co., TN. Blade 4 3/8 in. long, 1 7/16 in. wide, 1/8 in. thick. Good workmanship. Made of Dover chert.
Priv. col., excellent quality, valued $350-375.

- Pine Tree from Hamilton co., TN. Blade 3 13/16 in. long, 1 1/2 in. wide, 1/4 in. thick. Heat treated. Made of tan brown chert.
Priv. col., museum quality, valued $200-275.

- Pine Tree from Hamilton co., TN. Blade 4 1/4 in. long, 1 7/32 in. wide, 1/8 in. thick. Made of gray white chert.
Priv. col., average quality, valued $100-125.

CHAPTER 13
REDSTONE-RUSSELL CAVE

<u>Redstone: 15,000-9,000 B.P. Paleo</u>

Found predominantly in the Southeast, medium to large point or blade, fluted. Thin pieces with convex edges, concave bases. Occasionally they are multiple fluted. Hafting areas are ground and distinct.

◆ Redstone from Murphysboro co., TN. Point 3 in. long, 1 1/8 in. wide, 1/4 in. thick. Multiple fluting, sharply serrated edges, slight left hand beveling. Deep concave ground base. Made of brown pebble chert.

Priv. col., museum quality, valued $1,250-1,750.

• Redstone from Murphysboro co., TN. Point 3 1/8 in. long, 1 1/4 in. wide, 1/4 in. thick. Multiple fluted, left hand beveling. Made of brown pebble chert.
Grover Bohannon col., average quality, valued $250-350.

• Redstone from Murphysboro co., TN. Point 2 7/8 in. long, 1 1/2 in. wide, 5/16 in. thick. Made of brown pebble chert.
Grover Bohannon col., average quality, valued $125-150.

• Redstone from Murphysboro co., TN. Point 2 3/8 in. long, 1 1/4 in. wide,

1/4 in. thick. Made of Dover chert.
Grover Bohannon col., average quality, valued $250-350.

- Redstone from Stewart co., TN. Blade 4 1/8 in. long, 1 1/2 in. wide, 5/16 in. thick. Made of brown pebble chert.
Priv. col., average quality, valued $125-175.

- Redstone from Bibb co., AL. Point 2 1/8 in. long, 1 1/16 in. wide, 1/4 in. thick. Good workmanship, multiple fluted. Made of pink pebble chert.
Priv. col., excellent quality, valued $750-850.

- Redstone from Bibb co., AL. Point 2 1/2 in. long, 1 1/3 in. wide, 7/16 in. thick. Good workmanship. Made of brown tan pebble chert.
Priv. col., excellent quality, valued $625-750.

- Redstone from Calhoun co., AR. Point 2 11/32 in. long, 1 1/4 in. wide, 1/4 in. thick. Made of Arkansas brown chert.
Priv. col., average quality, valued $250-350.

- Redstone from Bibb co., AL. Point 1 5/8 in. long, 1 1/32 in. wide, 5/16 in. thick. Made of white pebble chert.
Priv. col., average quality, valued $275-325.

- Redstone from Crenshaw co., AL. Point 3 in. long, 1 1/3 in. wide, 5/8 in. thick. Multiple fluting, good workmanship, left hand beveled. Made of high grade quartzite.
Priv. col., excellent quality, valued $450-650.

- Redstone from Crenshaw co., AL. Point 2 5/8 in. long, 1 11/16 in. wide, 5/16 in. thick. Made of brown pebble chert.
Priv. col., average quality, valued $175-250.

- Redstone from Allen Praish, LA. Point 2 1/2 in. long, 1 1/3 in. wide, 1/4 in. thick. Made of mauve chert.
Priv. col., excellent quality, valued $450-550.

- Redstone from Allen Praish, LA. Blade 4 in. long, 2 1/32 in. wide, 7/16 in. thick. Heat treated. Made of banded brown white chert.
Priv. col., excellent quality, valued $625-775.

- Redstone from Allen Praish, LA. Point 3 3/8 in. long, 1 1/2 in. wide, 1/2 in. thick. Made of white pebble chert.
Priv. col., average quality, valued $250-350.

• Redstone from Sabine Praish, LA. Point 2 3/8 in. long, 1 1/2 in. wide, 7/16 in. thick. Good workmanship. Made of pinkish white pebble chert. *Priv. col., excellent quality, valued $425-550.*

• Redstone from Sabine Praish, LA. Point 2 3/8 in. long, 1 1/4 in. wide, 1/4 in. thick. Made of yellow tan chert. *Priv. col., average quality, valued $250-350.*

• Redstone from Sabine Praish, LA. Blade 3 7/8 in. long, 1 3/4 in. wide, 9/16 in. thick. Excellent workmanship, beveled on all sides, double fluted with fine serrations. Made of brown chert. *Priv. col., museum quality, valued $1,250-1,500.*

• Redstone from Humphreys co., TN. Point 3 1/16 in. long, 2 in. wide, 1/2 in. thick. Multiple fluted, good workmanship. Made of gray chert. *Priv. col., excellent quality, valued $750-850.*

• Redstone from Benton co., MS. Point 2 17/32 in. long, 1 1/2 in. wide, 7/16 in. thick. Heat treated. Made of gray pebble chert. *Priv. col., average quality, valued $325-450.*

• Redstone from Benton co., MS. Point 2 7/8 in. long, 1 11/32 in. wide, 5/16 in. thick. Made of white chert. *Priv. col., average quality, valued $250-350.*

• Redstone from Benton co., MS. Point 2 1/8 in. long, 1 1/16 in. wide, 5/16 in. thick. Made of tan brown pebble chert. *Priv. col., average quality, valued $125-175.*

Reed: 1,500-350 B.P. Woodland through Mississippian into Historical

Found predominantly in the Midwest. Small, triangular, thin point. Side notched with straight base. Many Reed specimens are of excellent workmanship and material, though quite small.

◆ Reed from Wabash co., IN. Point 1 1/8 in. long, 1/2 in. wide, 1/8 in. thick. Finely serrated, sharp tip, symmetrical side notches, classic straight base. Made of jasper.

Grover Bohannon col., museum quality, rare, valued $45-50.

• Reed from Mills co., IA. Point 7/8 in. long, 5/16 in. wide, 1/16 in. thick. Good workmanship, thin, finely serrated, sharp tip, symmetrical, parallel side notches, classic straight base. Made of greenish gray chert.
Priv. col., museum quality, valued $30-35.

• Reed from Mills co., IA. Point 1 in. long, 11/32 in. wide, 1/8 in. thick. Finely serrated, thinned tip, symmetrical, deep parallel side notches, straight base. Made of white chert.
Priv. col., museum quality, valued $30-35.

• Reed from Mills co., IA. Point 11/16 in. long, 1/3 in. wide, 1/8 in. thick. Sharpley serrated, thin needle sharp tip, symmetrical, deep side notches, parallel sided straight base. Made of tan chert.
Priv. col., museum quality, valued $35-40.

• Reed from Cedar co., IA. Point 1 1/32 in. long, 1/2 in. wide, 3/16 in. thick. Thick, finely serrated, thinned tip, symmetrical, side notches, classic straight base. Made of glossy brown chert.
Priv. col., museum quality, valued $30-35.

• Reed from Kiowa co., OK. Point 1 1/32 in. long, 13/32 in. wide, 1/8 in. thick. Made of white tan chert.
Priv. col., excellent quality, valued $20-30.

• Reed from Texas co., OK. Point 15/16 in. long, 1/2 in. wide, 1/8 in. thick. Made of tan pebble chert.
Priv. col., excellent quality, valued $25-30.

• Reed from Texas co., OK. Point 1 3/16 in. long, 1/2 in. wide, 3/16 in. thick. Made of multi-tone brown chert.
Priv. col., museum quality, valued $30-35.

• Reed from Texas co., OK. Point 1 1/4 in. long, 1/2 in. wide, 1/8 in. thick. Made of dense white chert.
Priv. col., excellent quality, valued $25-30.

• Reed from Woods co., OK. Point 1 1/16 in. long, 9/16 in. wide, 1/8 in. thick. Made of yellow tan chert.
Priv. col., excellent quality, valued $25-30.

• Reed from Woods co., OK. Point 1 5/32 in. long, 5/8 in. wide, 5/16 in. thick.

Made of brown chert.
Priv. col., museum quality, valued $30-35.

- Reed from Andrews co., TX. Point 7/8 in. long, 9/32 in. wide, 1/8 in. thick.
Good field patina, heat treated. Made of dull white chert.
Priv. col., museum quality, valued $30-35.

- Reed from Andrews co., TX. Point 1 5/16 in. long, 1/2 in. wide, 1/8 in. thick.
Slight tip break. Made of gray chert.
Priv. col., average quality, valued $5-10.

- Reed from Cottle co., TX. Point 1 in. long, 7/16 in. wide, 5/32 in. thick. Made
of glossy red brown chert.
Priv. col., museum quality, valued $30-35.

- Reed from Cottle co., TX. Point 1 3/32 in. long, 23/32 in. wide, 3/16 in. thick.
Made of white chert.
Priv. col., excxellent quality, valued $25-30.

- Reed from Jeff Davis co., TX. Point 1 13/16 in. long, 5/8 in. wide, 1/8 in.
thick. Made of jasper.
Priv. col., museum quality, rare, valued $45-60.

- Reed from Jeff Davis co., TX. Point 1 1/32 in. long, 1/2 in. wide, 3/16 in.
thick. Several edge nicks. Made of glossy brown chert.
Priv. col., average quality, valued $10-15.

- Reed from Midland co., TX. Point 1 3/16 in. long, 19/32 in. wide, 1/8 in.
thick. Made of gray white chert.
Priv. col., museum quality, valued $25-30.

- Reed from Midland co., TX. Point 1 1/16 in. long, 1/2 in. wide, 1/8 in. thick.
Made of gray chert.
Priv. col., excellent quality, valued $30-35.

- Reed from Milland co., TX. Point 1 5/32 in. long, 5/8 in. wide, 3/16 in. thick.
Made of glossy brown chert.
Priv. col., museum quality, valued $40-45.

- Reed from Motley co., TX. Point 1 1/3 in. long, 19/32 in. wide, 1/8 in. thick.
Made of gray chert.
Priv. col., excellent quality, valued $25-30.

• Reed from Motley co., TX. Point 1 3/16 in. long, 1/2 in. wide, 1/8 in. thick. Made of tan brown chert.
Priv. col., excellent quality, valued $30-35.

• Reed from Motley co., TX. Point 1 5/32 in. long, 1/2 in. wide, 3/16 in. thick. Made of brown chert.
Priv. col., excellent quality, valued $20-25.

Rice: 9,000-5,000 B.P. Early Archaic

Found throughout the Midwest into the Northeast. Medium to large sized points or blades. Serrated edges, shallow bifurcated bases, sharp distinct shoulders, side or corner notched.

◆ Rice from Shelby co., TN. Point 1 1/4 in. long, 5/16 in. wide, 3/32 in. thick. Soft shouldered, transverse flaking, classic shallow bifurcated base. Minute tip break. Made of dark gray chert.

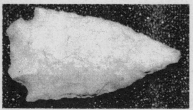

Grover Bohannon col., average quality, valued $15-25.

• Rice from Shelby co., TN. Point 3 1/16 in. long, 1 5/8 in. wide, 7/32 in. thick. Soft shouldered, transverse flaking, classic shallow bifurcated base, broken basal tang. Made of dark gray chert.
Grover Bohannon col., average quality, valued $15-25.

• Rice from Shelby co., TN. Point 2 1/2 in. long, 1 7/16 in. wide, 5/32 in. thick. Corner notched, thin random flaking, classic shallow bifurcated base, repaired tip. Made of dark gray chert.
Grover Bohannon col., average quality, valued $15-25.

• Rice from Shelby co., IN. Point 2 1/4 in. long, 1 5/16 in. wide, 3/32 in. thick. Distinct shoulders, several edge nicks, classic shallow bifurcated base. Made of dark green chert.
Priv. col., average quality, valued $15-25.

- Rice from Caldwell co., MO. Point 2 3/4 in. long, 1 5/16 in. wide, 7/32 in. thick. Distinct pointed shoulders, corner notched. Transverse flaking, classic shallow bifurcated base, needle sharp tip. Made of dull gray chert. *Priv. col., excellent quality, valued $45-65.*

- Rice from Seneca co., NY. Point 3 3/16 in. long, 1 7/8 in. wide, 5/32 in. thick. Made of red gray chert. *Priv. col., excellent quality, valued $35-45.*

- Rice from Seneca co., NY. Blade 4 1/2 in. long, 1 2/3 in. wide, 5/32 in. thick. Excellent workmanship. Made of banded red gray chert. *Priv. col., museum quality, valued $65-75.*

- Rice from Seneca co., NY. Blade 5 1/4 in. long, 1 15/16 in. wide, 5/32 in. thick. Made of pink green chert. *Priv. col., excellent quality, valued $50-65.*

- Rice from Seneca co., NY. Point 3 1/4 in. long, 1 9/16 in. wide, 5/16 in. thick. Transverse flaked, needle sharp tip. Made of gray pink chert. *Priv. col., excellent quality, valued $45-55.*

- Rice from Cortland co., NY. Point 3 3/16 in. long, 1 7/8 in. wide, 11/32 in. thick. Made of banded gray chert. *Priv. col., excellent quality, valued $15-25.*

- Rice from Cortland co., NY. Point 3 1/2 in. long, 1 13/16 in. wide, 7/32 in. thick. Repaired tip. Made of dark gray chert. *Priv. col., average quality, valued $20-25.*

- Rice from Ostego co., NY. Blade 4 1/3 in. long, 1 7/16 in. wide, 5/32 in. thick. Made of pink green chert. *Priv. col., excellent quality, valued $65-75.*

- Rice from Ostego co., NY. Point 2 5/8 in. long, 1 5/16 in. wide, 7/32 in. thick. Made of pink gray chert. *Priv. col., excellent quality, valued $40-50.*

- Rice from Bedford co., PA. Point 3 1/4 in. long, 1 1/2 in. wide, 1/4 in. thick. Made of pink chert. *Priv. col., excellent quality, valued $45-60.*

- Rice from Bedford co., PA. Point 2 3/4 in. long, 1 1/2 in. wide, 3/16 in. thick.

Made of gray chert.
Priv. col., excellent quality, valued $35-45.

• Rice from Bedford co., PA. Point 3 1/8 in. long, 1 3/16 in. wide, 7/32 in. thick.
Excellent workmanship. Made of pink to green chert.
Priv. col., museum quality, valued $85-100.

• Rice from Bedford co., PA. Blade 4 3/4 in. long, 1 7/8 in. wide, 1/3 in. thick.
Excellent transverse flaked. Made of gray chert.
Priv. col., museum quality, valued $75-90.

• Rice from Bedford co., PA. Point 4 3/16 in. long, 2 in. wide, 1/4 in. thick.
Made of gray chert.
Priv. col., excellent quality, valued $65-85.

• Rice from Snyder co., PA. Point 2 1/4 in. long, 1 1/16 in. wide, 1/4 in. thick.
Made of dark red slate.
Priv. col., excellent quality, valued $40-45.

• Rice from Snyder co., PA. Blade 5 1/4 in. long, 2 1/16 in. wide, 13/32 in.
thick. Made of banded pink black chert.
Priv. col., museum quality, valued $125-150.

• Rice from Snyder co., PA. Blade 5 1/3 in. long, 1 13/16 in. wide, 13/32 in.
thick. Needle sharp tip. Made of gray chert.
Priv. col., excellent quality, valued $70-85.

• Rice from Snyder co., PA. Blade 5 1/16 in. long, 1 7/8 in. wide, 1/3 in. thick.
Made of dark blue chert.
Priv. col., museum quality, rare, valued $150-250.

• Rice from Elk co., PA. Point 2 7/8 in. long, 1 5/16 in. wide, 1/4 in. thick.
Made of pink gray speckled chert.
Priv. col., excellent quality, valued $50-60.

• Rice from Elk co., PA. Point 2 3/4 in. long, 1 in. wide, 3/16 in. thick. Made of
greenish chert.
Priv. col., excellent quality, valued $45-65.

• Rice from Elk co., PA. Point 2 7/16 in. long, 1 5/16 in. wide, 1/8 in. thick.
Good workmanship. Made of gray chert.
Priv. col., museum quality, valued $70-90.

Rockwall: 1,500-900 B.P. Late Woodland

Small triangular point found throughout the Midwest and into the western states. Rockwalls are generally thin, corner notched, sharply serrated, beveled in a variety of forms. Shoulders are barbed, base is concave, convex, snapped or straight.

◆ Rockwall from Alexander co., IL. Point 1 in. long, 5/8 in. wide, 1/8 in. thick. Long shoulder tangs, finely serrated, very sharp tip, convex base. Made of jasper.

Priv. col., museum quality, rare, valued $85-120.

• Rockwall from Alexander co., IL. Point 7/8 in. long, 1/2 in. wide, 1/8 in. thick. Made of rose quartz.
Priv. col., museum quality, rare, valued $85-100.

• Rockwall from Alexander co., IL. Point 1 3/8 in. long, 5/8 in. wide, 1/8 in. thick. Made of Cobden chert.
Priv. col., museum quality, valued $75-90.

• Rockwall from Lake co., SD. Point 1 1/32 in. long, 1/2 in. wide, 1/8 in. thick. Made of blue white chert.
Priv. col., excellent quality, valued $65-80.

• Rockwall from Lake co., SD. Point 1 1/4 in. long, 7/8 in. wide, 1/8 in. thick. Made of false jasper.
Priv. col., excellent quality, valued $75-80.

• Rockwall from Lake co., SD. Point 1 in. long, 1/2 in. wide, 3/32 in. thick. Excellent workmanship. Made of marbled red tan chert.
Priv. col., museum quality, valued $85-100.

• Rockwall from Miner co., SD. Point 7/8 in. long, 1/3 in. wide, 1/8 in. thick. Made of vein quartz.
Priv. col., museum quality, valued $85-100.

• Rockwall from Miner co., SD. Point 1 3/32 in. long, 5/8 in. wide, 1/8 in.

thick. Excellent workmanship. Made of gray blue chert.
Priv. col., museum quality, valued $95-140.

• Rockwall from Miner co., SD. Point 1 5/32 in. long, 7/8 in. wide, 1/8 in. thick.
Heat treated. Made of blue white chert.
Priv. col., excellent quality, valued $75-85.

• Rockwall from Tripp co., SD. Point 1 1/8 in. long, 5/8 in. wide, 1/16 in. thick.
Thin, excellent workmanship. Made of black silver streaked chert.
Priv. col., museum quality, rare, valued $125-180.

• Rockwall from Tripp co., SD. Point 1 1/8 in. long, 1/2 in. wide, 5/32 in. thick.
Made of red brown chert.
Priv. col., excellent quality, valued $65-80.

• Rockwall from Wallace co., KS. Point 1 7/8 in. long, 1 in. wide, 1/8 in. thick.
Excellent workmanship, quite large for a Rockwall. Made of tan chert.
Priv. col., museum quality, valued $165-200.

• Rockwall from Wallace co., KS. Point 1 3/8 in. long, 15/16 in. wide, 1/8 in.
thick. Made of gray chert.
Priv. col., excellent quality, valued $65-80.

• Rockwall from Wallace co., KS. Point 1 in. long, 1/2 in. wide, 1/16 in. thick.
Good workmanship. Made of white chert.
Priv. col., excellent quality, valued $65-80.

• Rockwall from Dickinson co., KS. Point 1 1/32 in. long, 7/8 in. wide, 1/8 in.
thick. Made of gray chert.
Priv. col., excellent quality, valued $65-80.

• Rockwall from Dickinson co., KS. Point 1 1/3 in. long, 2/3 in. wide, 3/32 in.
thick. Made of tan chert.
Priv. col., excellent quality, valued $55-70.

• Rockwall from Dickinson co., KS. Point 1 1/8 in. long, 7/8 in. wide, 1/8 in.
thick. Made of tan chert.
Priv. col., excellent quality, valued $55-70.

• Rockwall from Grant co., NE. Point 1 1/16 in. long, 5/8 in. wide, 1/8 in. thick.
Made of gray chert.
Priv. col., excellent quality, valued $60-70.

- Rockwall from Grant co., NE. Point 1 1/32 in. long, 3/4 in. wide, 1/8 in. thick. Made of white chert.
Priv. col., excellent quality, valued $65-80.

- Rockwall from Grant co., NE. Point 1 1/3 in. long, 7/8 in. wide, 1/8 in. thick. Made of white chert.
Priv. col., excellent quality, valued $65-80.

- Rockwall from Grant co., NE. Point 1 1/32 in. long, 9/16 in. wide, 5/32 in. thick. Made of gray slate.
Priv. col., average quality, valued $45-50.

Rowan: 10,000-7,500 B.P. Paleo-Transitional

Found predominantly in the eastern states and into the Midwest. Medium to large sized point or blade. Side notched, generally crude workmanship. Base is often ground and as wide as or wider than point or blade face.

◆ Rowan from northeastern AR. Point 1 7/8 in. long, 1 1/16 in. wide, 1/4 in. thick. Typically crude point found further west than usual. Made of quartzite.

Priv. col., excellent quality, valued $10-15.

- Rowan from Murphysboro co., TN. Point 1 5/8 in. long, 1 in. wide, 3/16 in. thick. Made of gray chert.
Priv. col., excellent quality, valued $10-15.

- Rowan from Howell co., MO. Point 1 7/8 in. long, 1 1/16 in. wide, 1/4 in. thick. Made of white chert.
Priv. col., excellent quality, valued $10-15.

- Rowan from Howell co., MO. Point 2 5/8 in. long, 1 3/16 in. wide, 1/4 in.

thick. Made of white chert.
Priv. col., excellent quality, valued $20-25.

• Rowan from Marion co., MO. Point 3 1/8 in. long, 1 1/2 in. wide, 5/16 in. thick. Made of gray chert.
Priv. col., excellent quality, valued $25-35.

• Rowan from Marion co., MO. Point 2 7/8 in. long, 1 5/16 in. wide, 1/4 in. thick. Made of white chert.
Priv. col., excellent quality, valued $20-25.

• Rowan from Monroe co., MO. Point 3 3/8 in. long, 1 7/16 in. wide, 1/4 in. thick. Made of white tan chert.
Priv. col., excellent quality, valued $30-40.

• Rowan from Cocke co., TN. Point 3 1/3 in. long, 1 1/2 in. wide, 5/16 in. thick. Made of banded gray chert.
Priv. col., excellent quality, valued $40-45.

• Rowan from Cocke co., TN. Blade 3 7/8 in. long, 1 7/16 in. wide, 1/4 in. thick. Made of tan white chert.
Priv. col., excellent quality, valued $45-55.

• Rowan from Cocke co., TN. Blade 4 3/8 in. long, 1 11/16 in. wide, 1/4 in. thick. Made of gray white chert.
Priv. col., excellent quality, valued $50-55.

• Rowan from Montgomery co., TN. Blade 5 1/8 in. long, 2 1/16 in. wide, 7/16 in. thick. Excellent workmanship. Made of tan gray chert.
Priv. col., excellent quality, valued $50-65.

• Rowan from Montgomery co., TN. Blade 4 7/8 in. long, 1 1/2 in. wide, 1/4 in. thick. Made of tan white chert.
Priv. col., excellent quality, valued $50-65.

• Rowan from Perry co., TN. Blade 4 1/8 in. long, 1 5/8 in. wide, 1/4 in. thick. Made of white tan chert.
Priv. col., excellent quality, valued $50-55.

• Rowan from Perry co., TN. Blade 4 5/8 in. long, 2 in. wide, 5/16 in. thick. Made of dull gray chert.
Priv. col., excellent quality, valued $40-45.

- Rowan from Perry co., TN. Blade 5 1/8 in. long, 1 3/4 in. wide, 1/4 in. thick. Made of white tan chert.
Priv. col., excellent quality, valued $70-85.

- Rowan from Perry co., TN. Point 2 7/8 in. long, 1 7/16 in. wide, 1/4 in. thick. Made of white tan chert.
Priv. col., excellent quality, valued $30-35.

- Rowan from Perry co., TN. Point 2 1/4 in. long, 1 1/8 in. wide, 3/16 in. thick. Made of glossy gray chert.
Priv. col., excellent quality, valued $30-35.

- Rowan from Hamilton co., TN. Point 3 3/8 in. long, 1 1/4 in. wide, 1/4 in. thick. Made of gray white chert.
Priv. col., excellent quality, valued $50-55.

- Rowan from Hamilton co., TN. Blade 4 5/8 in. long, 1 7/16 in. wide, 1/4 in. thick. Good workmanship. Made of dense white chert.
Priv. col., excellent quality, valued $60-85.

- Rowan from Henry co., TN. Blade 4 1/8 in. long, 1 2/3 in. wide, 7/16 in. thick. Made of Dover chert.
Priv. col., museum quality, valued $80-95.

- Rowan from Henry co., TN. Blade 5 7/8 in. long, 1 13/16 in. wide, 1/4 in. thick. Made of tan white chert.
Priv. col., excellent quality, valued $80-85.

- Rowan from Henry co., TN. 4 3/8 in. long, 1 13/16 in. wide, 1/4 in. thick. Made of brown chert.
Priv. col., average quality, valued $20-25.

Russell Cave: 10,000-6,500 B.P. Paleo-Transitional into Early Archaic

Found predominantly in the Southeast. Medium sized point, serrated and beveled, triangular with weak shoulders. Shallow side notched, base concave to auriculate.

◆ Russell Cave from Hamilton co., TN. Point 2 1/2 in. long, 1 in. wide, 3/16 in. thick. Serrated and beveled on one side of each face. Classical notching and shoulders, concave base.

Priv. col., museum quality, valued $65-90.

• Russell Cave from Colleton co., SC. Point 2 2/3 in. long, 1 1/4 in. wide, 1/8 in. thick. Finely serrated and beveled on one side of each face. Side notched and weak shoulders, concave base. Made of greenish chert.
Priv. col., excellent quality, valued $45-50.

• Russell Cave from Colleton co., SC. Point 2 1/4 in. long, 1 1/16 in. wide, 3/16 in. thick. Serrated and beveled on one side of each face, concave base. Made of greenish chert.
Priv. col., excellent quality, valued $35-50.

• Russell Cave from Horry co., SC. Point 3 1/32 in. long, 1 1/3 in. wide, 1/4 in. thick. Made of banded red slate.
Priv. col., museum quality, valued $65-90.

• Russell Cave from Horry co., SC. Point 2 3/4 in. long, 1 1/4 in. wide, 1/8 in. thick. Finely serrated and beveled on one side of each face. Side notched and weak shoulders, concave base. Made of glossy brown chert.
Priv. col., excellent quality, valued $45-50.

• Russell Cave from Newberry co., SC. Point 2 1/2 in. long, 1 3/16 in. wide, 5/32 in. thick. Made of vein quartz.
Priv. col., excellent quality, valued $35-50.

• Russell Cave from Horry co., SC. Point 3 1/32 in. long, 1 1/3 in. wide, 1/4 in. thick. Made of banded slate.
Priv. col., museum quality, valued $65-90.

• Russell Cave from Colleton co., SC. Point 2 2/3 in. long, 1 1/4 in. wide, 1/8 in. thick. Finely serrated and beveled on one side of each face. Side notched and weak shoulders, concave base. Made of tan chert.
Priv. col., excellent quality, valued $45-50.

• Russell Cave from Colleton co., SC. Point 2 1/4 in. long, 1 1/16 in.

wide, 3/16 in. thick. Serrated and beveled on one side of each face, concave base.
Priv. col., excellent quality, valued $35-50.

• Russell Cave from Horry co., SC. Point 3 1/32 in. long, 1 1/3 in. wide, 1/4 in.
thick. Made of banded slate.
Priv. col., museum quality, valued $65-90.

• Russell Cave from Dixie co., FL. Point 3 in. long, 1 1/2 in. wide, 1/8 in. thick.
Good workmanship, very symmetrical. Made of quartzite.
Priv. col., average quality, valued $25-30.

• Russell Cave from Dixie co., FL. Point 2 7/16 in. long, 1 in. wide, 3/16 in.
thick. Made of quartzite.
Priv. col., average quality, valued $15-25.

• Russell Cave from Dixie co., FL. Point 3 5/32 in. long, 1 1/2 in. wide, 1/4 in.
thick. Made of quartzite.
Priv. col., museum quality, valued $15-20.

• Russell Cave from Citrus co., FL. Point 2 1/3 in. long, 1 1/4 in. wide, 1/8 in.
thick. Made of quartzite.
Priv. col., average quality, valued $25-30.

• Russell Cave from Citrus co., FL. Point 3 1/8 in. long, 1 7/16 in. wide,
3/16 in. thick. Made of pink chert.
Priv. col., excellent quality, valued $35-50.

• Russell Cave from Citrus co., FL. Point 3 1/32 in. long, 1 1/3 in. wide,
1/4 in. thick. Made of pink black speckled chert.
Priv. col., excellent quality, valued $45-50.

• Russell Cave from Gulf co., FL. Point 2 1/3 in. long, 1 1/4 in. wide, 3/16 in.
thick. Made of gray chert.
Priv. col., average quality, valued $15-20.

• Russell Cave from Gulf co., FL. Point 2 3/4 in. long, 1 3/8 in. wide, 1/8 in.
thick. Made of quartzite.
Priv. col., excellent quality, valued $25-35.

• Russell Cave from Gulf co., FL. Point 3 5/32 in. long, 1 2/3 in. wide, 1/4 in.
thick. Made of banded tan white chert.
Priv. col., museum quality, valued $65-80.

• Russell Cave from Bibb co., AL. Point 2 3/4 in. long, 1 1/8 in. wide, 1/8 in. thick. Made of gray chert.
Priv. col., excellent quality, valued $35-40.

• Russell Cave from Bibb co., AL. Point 2 1/4 in. long, 1 in. wide, 5/16 in. thick. Made of gray chert.
Priv. col., excellent quality, valued $35-40.

• Russell Cave from Bibb co., AL. Point 2 13/32 in. long, 1 1/2 in. wide, 1/4 in. thick. Made of gray slate.
Priv. col., average quality, valued $15-20.

CHAPTER 14
ST. CHARLES-SUMTER

St. Charles: 5,000-2,000 B.P. Late Archaic

Found throughout the Midwest and the eastern states. Medium to large sized point or blade. Generally broad, thin, exhibiting a high quality of workmanship. Blades are generally serrated, often beveled on one side of each face. Corner notched with dovetail type stem and base.

◆ St. Charles from Sauk co., WI. Point 3 1/8 in. long, 1 5/8 in. wide, 5/16 in. thick. Rounded tip, symmetrical, serrated edges. Heat treated, classic notching and base. Made of white to green marbled chert.

Priv. col., museum quality, valued $450-600.

◆ St. Charles from Union co., IL. Blade 4 in. long, 1 5/8 in. wide, 1/4 in. thick. Deep narrow corner notches, finely serrated tip and edges. Made of Mill Creek chert.

Priv. col., excellent quality, valued $300-400.

◆ St. Charles from Johnson co., IL. Blade 3 7/8 in. long, 1 3/8 in. wide, 1/4 in. thick. Finely serrated, excellent workmanship. Wide, long, symmetrical base. Made of Kaolin chert.

Priv. col., museum quality, rare, valued $675-800.

• St. Charles from Adams co., IN. Blade 4 1/8 in. long, 2 in. wide, 5/16 in. thick. Made of blue white chert.
Priv. col., museum quality, valued $350-400.

• St. Charles from Adams co., IN. Blade 4 1/3 in. long, 1 7/8 in. wide, 1/4 in. thick. Made of blue white chert.
Priv. col., excellent quality, valued $300-350.

• St. Charles from Adams co., IN. Blade 3 13/16 in. long, 1 1/4 in. wide, 1/4 in. thick. Excellent workmanship. Made of tan brown chert.
Priv. col., excellent quality, valued $275-325.

• St. Charles from Adams co., IN. Blade 4 1/8 in. long, 2 in. wide, 5/16 in. thick. Made of blue white chert.
Priv. col., museum quality, valued $350-400.

• St. Charles from Adams co., IN. Blade 4 1/2 in. long, 1 7/8 in. wide, 1/4 in. thick. Made of blue white chert.
Priv. col., excellent quality, valued $350-400.

• St. Charles from Adams co., IN. Blade 4 11/16 in. long, 1 1/2 in. wide, 1/4 in. thick. Made of tan brown chert.
Priv. col., excellent quality, valued $285-325.

• St. Charles from Adams co., IN. Blade 4 1/4 in. long, 2 1/32 in. wide, 5/16 in. thick. Made of blue white chert.
Priv. col., museum quality, valued $350-400.

• St. Charles from Adams co., IN. Blade 4 2/3 in. long, 1 7/8 in. wide, 1/4 in. thick. Made of white chert.
Priv. col., excellent quality, valued $350-375.

- St. Charles from Adams co., IN. Point 3 5/16 in. long, 1 1/4 in. wide, 1/4 in. thick. Good workmanship. Made of tan brown chert.
Priv. col., excellent quality, valued $225-250.

- St. Charles from Steuben co., IN. Blade 5 1/8 in. long, 2 in. wide, 7/32 in. thick. Heat treated, good workmanship. Made of white chert.
Priv. col., museum quality, valued $375-420.

- St. Charles from Steuben co., IN. Blade 5 in. long, 1 7/8 in. wide, 1/4 in. thick. Made of white chert.
Priv. col., excellent quality, valued $400-450.

- St. Charles from Steuben co., IN. Blade 4 3/16 in. long, 1 1/2 in. wide, 1/4 in. thick. Made of tan brown chert.
Priv. col., excellent quality, valued $325-375.

- St. Charles from Caldwell co., MO. Blade 4 5/8 in. long, 1 1/2 in. wide, 3/16 in. thick. Made of tan chert.
Priv. col., excellent quality, valued $350-375.

- St. Charles from Caldwell co., MO. Blade 5 1/3 in. long, 2 1/8 in. wide, 1/4 in. thick. Made of tan white chert.
Priv. col., excellent quality, valued $300-350.

- St. Charles from Caldwell co., MO. Blade 4 3/16 in. long, 1 1/3 in. wide, 1/4 in. thick. Made of tan brown chert.
Priv. col., excellent quality, valued $375-425.

- St. Charles from New Madrid co., MO. Blade 4 5/8 in. long, 1 1/2 in. wide, 5/16 in. thick. Several edge nicks. Made of white chert.
Priv. col., average quality, valued $50-80.

- St. Charles from New Madrid co., MO. Blade 4 2/3 in. long, 1 7/8 in. wide, 1/4 in. thick. Made of white chert.
Priv. col., excellent quality, valued $200-250.

- St. Charles from New Madrid co., MO. Blade 3 13/16 in. long, 1 1/4 in. wide, 1/4 in. thick. Made of tan chert.
Priv. col., excellent quality, valued $275-325.

- St. Charles from Osage co., MO. Blade 4 5/8 in. long, 2 in. wide, 3/16 in. thick. Made of brown chert.

Priv. col., excellent quality, valued $150-200.

• St. Charles from Osage co., MO. Blade 4 1/16 in. long, 1 7/8 in. wide, 1/4 in. thick. Made of brown white chert.
Priv. col., excellent quality, valued $280-350.

• St. Charles from Osage co., MO. Blade 4 1/3 in. long, 1 1/2 in. wide, 1/4 in. thick. Made of tan brown chert.
Priv. col., excellent quality, valued $275-325.

• St. Charles from Boone co., MO. Blade 5 in. long, 1 1/2 in. wide, 5/16 in. thick. Made of white chert.
Priv. col., excellent quality, valued $365-400.

• St. Charles from Boone co., MO. Blade 4 2/3 in. long, 1 7/8 in. wide, 1/3 in. thick. Made of white chert.
Priv. col., excellent quality, valued $300-350.

• St. Charles from Boone co., MO. Blade 4 in. long, 1 1/4 in. wide, 1/4 in. thick. Made of tan brown chert.
Priv. col., excellent quality, valued $275-325.

• St. Charles from Boone co., MO. Blade 4 1/8 in. long, 1 2/3 in. wide, 5/16 in. thick. Made of white chert.
Priv. col., excellent quality, valued $350-400.

• St. Charles from Stoddard co., MO. Blade 4 1/3 in. long, 1 7/8 in. wide, 1/4 in. thick. Made of white chert.
Priv. col., excellent quality, valued $300-350.

• St. Charles from Boone co., MO. Blade 3 15/16 in. long, 1 1/4 in. wide, 1/4 in. thick. Excellent workmanship, heat treated. Made of tan brown chert.
Priv. col., excellent quality, valued $275-325.

• St. Charles from Pike co., MO. Blade 4 1/4 in. long, 2 in. wide, 5/16 in. thick. Made of white chert.
Priv. col., excellent quality, valued $350-400.

• St. Charles from Pike co., MO. Blade 4 1/3 in. long, 1 5/8 in. wide, 1/4 in. thick. Made of white tan chert.
Priv. col., excellent quality, valued $300-350.

- St. Charles from Pike co., MO. Blade 4 3/16 in. long, 1 1/2 in. wide, 3/16 in. thick. Several edge nicks. Made of tan chert.
Priv. col., average quality, valued $75-125.

- St. Charles from Barton co., MO. Blade 4 1/8 in. long, 2 in. wide, 3/16 in. thick. Made of brown white chert.
Priv. col., excellent quality, valued $250-300.

- St. Charles from Barton co., MO. Blade 4 1/32 in. long, 1 7/8 in. wide, 3/16 in. thick. Made of brown white chert.
Priv. col., excellent quality, valued $300-350.

- St. Charles from Barton co., MO. Blade 5 13/16 in. long, 1 1/2 in. wide, 1/4 in. thick. Made of tan brown chert.
Priv. col., excellent quality, valued $250-275.

- St. Charles from Butler co., MO. Blade 4 1/32 in. long, 1 1/2 in. wide, 5/16 in. thick. Poor workmanship. Made of white chert.
Priv. col., averge quality, valued $50-80.

- St. Charles from Butler co., MO. Blade 4 1/2 in. long, 1 7/8 in. wide, 3/16 in. thick. Made of white chert.
Priv. col., excellent quality, valued $200-250.

- St. Charles from Butler co., MO. Point 2 13/16 in. long, 1 1/32 in. wide, 1/8 in. thick. Excellent workmanship, serrated on all four sides. Made of tan brown chert.
Priv. col., excellent quality, valued $275-325.

- St. Charles from Butler co., MO. Point 2 1/8 in. long, 1/2 in. wide, 3/16 in. thick. Part of same cache find as above. Serrated on all four sides, heat treated, needle sharp tip. Made of white chert.
Priv. col., museum quality, valued $250-300.

- St. Charles from Ballard co., KY. Point 2 1/3 in. long, 7/8 in. wide, 1/4 in. thick. Made of tan white chert.
Priv. col., excellent quality, valued $150-200.

- St. Charles from Ballard co., KY. Point 2 3/16 in. long, 3/4 in. wide, 1/8 in. thick. Excellent workmanship. Made of tan brown chert.
Priv. col., museum quality, valued $275-325.

Salish: 600 B.P. to Historical

Medium to large sized point or blade. Points found on the northwest coast of San Juan Islands and adjacent mainland. Made of San Juan Island flint or pebble chert. Wide variety in shape from triangular to leaf shaped. Side notched beveled with long convex stems.

◆ Salish from San Juan Islands. Blade 5 1/4 in. long, 2 1/8 in. wide, 3/16 in. thick. Round based, one edge beveled to tip. Made of black San Juan Island flint.

Southern IL Univ. col., museum quality, valued $200-250.

• Salish from San Juan Island. Blade 4 7/8 in. long, 2 1/8 in. wide, 1/4 in. thick. Round based blade finely parallel flaked with sharp edges. Made of black flint. *Southern IL Univ. Museum col., excellent quality, valued $120-180.*

◆ Salish from San Juan Island. Blade 3 7/8 in. long, 1 in. wide, 3/16 in. thick. Blade narrow, thin, triangular, straight based. Blade nicks and tip break. Made of San Juan Island black flint.

Southern IL Univ. Museum col., average quality, valued $35-45.

◆ Salish from the Fraser River. Blade 4 1/8 in. long, 1 5/8 in. wide, 1/4 in. thick. Side notched, long straight stem, angular, heat treated. Made of tan pebble chert.

Southern IL Univ. Museum col., excellent quality, valued $85-120.

San Patrice: 12,000-8,000 B.P. Mid to Late Paleo

Small midwestern point, generally thin. Usually serrated and side notched, often fluted, concave ground bases.

◆ San Patrice from Hamilton co., TN. Point 1 5/8 in. long, 1 1/4 in. wide, 1/4 in. thick. Serrated, side notched, ground concave base. Made of Dover chert.

Priv. col., excellent quality, valued $25-40.

• San Patrice from Hamilton co., TN. Point 1 5/8 in. long, 1 1/4 in. wide, 1/4 in. thick. Good workmanship. Made of Dover chert.
Priv. col., museum quality, valued $45-60.

• San Patrice from Hamilton co., TN. Point 1 3/8 in. long, 1 in. wide, 1/4 in. thick. Fluted on one face. Made of Dover chert.
Priv. col., excellent quality, valued $35-50.

• San Patrice from Hamilton co., TN. Point 1 5/8 in. long, 1 1/4 in. wide, 1/4 in. thick. Good workmanship. Made of Dover chert.
Priv. col., museum quality, valued $45-60.

• San Patrice from Hamilton co., TN. Point 1 3/8 in. long, 1 in. wide, 1/4 in. thick. Fluted on one face. Made of Dover chert.
Priv. col., excellent quality, valued $35-50.

• San Patrice from Alexander co., IL. Point 1 in. long, 1/2 in. wide, 1/8 in. thick. Made of Mill Creek chert.
Priv. col., excellent quality, valued $25-30.

• San Patrice from Alexander co., IL. Point 1 3/32 in. long, 7/8 in. wide, 3/16 in. thick. Made of Mill Creek chert.
Priv. col., excellent quality, valued $30-40.

• San Patrice from Alexander co., IL. Point 1 7/16 in. long, 3/4 in. wide, 1/8 in. thick. Good workmanship, thinly fluted. Made of Kaolin chert.
Priv. col., museum quality, rare, valued $55-70.

• San Patrice from Hardin co., IL. Point 1 5/32 in. long, 1 in. wide, 1/4 in. thick. Fluted, unique serrated edges. Made of gray chert.

Priv. col., excellent quality, valued $35-40.

• San Patrice from Hardin co., IL. Point 2 in. long, 1 1/16 in. wide, 1/4 in. thick. Made of gray chert.
Priv. col., excellent quality, valued $45-50.

• San Patrice from Hardin co., IL. Point 1 1/2 in. long, 7/8 in. wide, 1/4 in. thick. Fluted on one face. Made of Dover chert.
Priv. col., excellent quality, valued $35-45.

• San Patrice from Hardin co., IL. Point 1 7/8 in. long, 1 1/16 in. wide, 1/4 in. thick. Good workmanship. Made of tan chert.
Priv. col., excellent quality, valued $35-40.

• San Patrice from Hardin co., IL. Point 1 7/8 in. long, 1 in. wide, 1/32 in. thick. Fluted, heat treated. Made of tan brown chert.
Priv. col., excellent quality, valued $35-40.

• San Patrice from Hempstead co., AR. Point 1 7/8 in. long, 1 in. wide, 1/4 in. thick. Made of brown chert.
Priv. col., excellent quality, valued $40-50.

• San Patrice from Hempstead co., AR. Point 1 1/3 in. long, 1 in. wide, 3/16 in. thick. Made of brown chert.
Priv. col., excellent quality, valued $35-45.

• San Patrice from Izard co., AR. Point 2 in. long, 7/8 in. wide, 1/4 in. thick. Excellent workmanship. Made of Arkansas brown chert.
Priv. col., museum quality, valued $45-60.

• San Patrice from Izard co., AR. Point 1 5/8 in. long, 7/8 in. wide, 1/8 in. thick. Made of Arkansas brown chert.
Priv. col., excellent quality, valued $35-45.

• San Patrice from Izard co., AR. Point 2 in. long, 1 1/2 in. wide, 1/4 in. thick. Good workmanship. Made of Arkansas brown chert.
Priv. col., museum quality, valued $45-60.

• San Patrice from Izard co., AR. Point 1 7/8 in. long, 11/16 in. wide, 1/4 in. thick. Made of Arkansas brown chert.
Priv. col., excellent quality, valued $35-50.

- San Patrice from Harrison co., MO. Point 1 in. long, 1/2 in. wide, 1/8 in. thick. Excellent workmanship, thinly flaked, minutely and meticuiously serrated, thinned tip. Part of a cache find. Fluted, ground concave base. Made of jasper. *Priv. col., museum quality, rare, valued $65-80.*

- San Patrice from Harrison co., MO. Point 1 5/8 in. long, 7/8 in. wide, 1/8 in. thick. Made of white chert. *Priv. col., excellent quality, valued $35-45.*

- San Patrice from Harrison co., MO. Point 1 7/8 in. long, 1 in. wide, 1/4 in. thick. Good workmanship. Made of white chert. *Priv. col., excellent quality, valued $35-40.*

- San Patrice from Harrison co., MO. Point 1 1/2 in. long, 7/8 in. wide, 1/4 in. thick. Made of white tan chert. *Priv. col., excellent quality, valued $35-45.*

- San Patrice from Henderson co., KY. Point 1 7/8 in. long, 1 in. wide, 3/16 in. thick. Made of tan chert. *Priv. col., average quality, valued $25-30.*

- San Patrice from Henderson co., KY. Point 1 1/8 in. long, 13/16 in. wide, 3/16 in. thick. Made of tan white chert. *Priv. col., excellent quality, valued $35-40.*

- San Patrice from Henderson co., KY. Point 1 7/8 in. long, 1 1/16 in. wide, 1/4 in. thick. Made of tan white chert. *Priv. col., excellent quality, valued $35-40.*

- San Patrice from Henderson co., KY. Point 1 1/2 in. long, 31/32 in. wide, 1/4 in. thick. Made of tan white chert. *Priv. col., excellent quality, valued $25-40.*

- San Patrice from Holt co., MO. Point 7/8 in. long, 1/3 in. wide, 1/4 in. thick. Made of local white chert. *Priv. col., excellent quality, valued $35-40.*

- San Patrice from Holt co., MO. Point 1 1/8 in. long, 13/16 in. wide, 3/16 in. thick. Fluted, good workmanship. Made of local white chert. *Priv. col., excellent quality, valued $45-50.*

- San Patrice from Holt co., MO. Point 1 1/2 in. long, 3/4 in. wide, 1/8 in. thick.

Good workmanship. Made of tan white chert.
Priv. col., museum quality, valued $55-60.

• San Patrice from Holt co., MO. Point 1 3/4 in. long, 1 in. wide, 1/8 in. thick.
Fluted on one face, heat treated. Made of white pebble chert.
Priv. col., excellent quality, valued $55-60.

• San Patrice from Adams co., IN. Point 1 3/8 in. long, 3/4 in. wide, 1/4 in.
thick. Good workmanship, fluted on both faces. Made of local blue white chert.
Priv. col., museum quality, rare, valued $65-80.

• San Patrice from Adams co., IN. Point 1 7/8 in. long, 1 in. wide, 1/4 in. thick.
Fluted on both faces, finely flaked. Made of greenish chert.
Priv. col., excellent quality, valued $55-60.

• San Patrice from Adams co., IN. Point 2 in. long, 1 1/4 in. wide, 1/4 in. thick.
Good workmanship, large and symmetrical. Made of jasper.
Priv. col., museum quality, rare, valued $65-80.

• San Patrice from Jay co., IN. Point 1 1/2 in. long, 1 in. wide, 3/16 in. thick.
Made of gray pebble chert.
Priv. col., excellent quality, valued $35-50.

Sandia: 12,000-8,000 B.P. Paleo-Transitional

*Found from the Southeast into the western states. There is
considerable variety in the makeup of Sandia points and blades. They may be
narrow and elliptical with a concave base and one notch, they may be straight
based or deeply concave with fluting and drooping shoulders. Due to the variety
in Sandia it is difficult to categorize workmanship without some very subjective
standards.*

♦ Sandia from Hardin co., IL. Point 2 1/2 in. long, 1 1/2 in. wide, 3/16 in. thick.
Classic single notched with hafting marks. Fine sharp edges, straight base. Made
of pink white pebble chert.

Grover Bohannon col., museum quality, valued $225-300.

◆ Sandia from Shelby co., MO. Blade 3 3/4 in. long, 1 1/4 in. wide, 5/16 in. thick. Random flaked, finely serrated and sharp. Made of brown tan and pink chert.

Grover Bohannon col., average quality, valued $60-80.

• Sandia from Blaine co., NE. Point 2 5/8 in. long, 1 1/2 in. wide, 1/4 in. thick. Fine sharp edges, heat treated. Made of white porous pebble chert.
Priv. col., average quality, valued $125-180.

• Sandia from Blaine co., NE. Point 2 3/4 in. long, 1 1/3 in. wide, 3/16 in. thick. Made of dull flint.
Priv. col., average quality, valued $60-80.

• Sandia from Weston co., WY. Point 2 2/3 in. long, 1 1/4 in. wide, 3/16 in. thick. Made of gray pink chert.
Priv. col., excellent quality, valued $200-250.

• Sandia from Weston co., WY. Blade 4 1/2 in. long, 1 1/3 in. wide, 5/16 in. thick. Made of banded tan pink chert.
Priv. col., excellent quality, valued $60-80.

• Sandia from Weston co., WY. Point 2 2/3 in. long, 1 1/4 in. wide, 3/16 in. thick. Made of gray pink chert.
Priv. col., excellent quality, valued $200-250.

• Sandia from Natrona co., WY. Blade 4 1/32 in. long, 1 1/2 in. wide, 3/16 in. thick. Beveled on one side of each face, good workmanship. Made of banded red chert.
Priv. col., museum quality, valued $100-180.

• Sandia from Sublette co., WY. Point 3 in. long, 1 1/4 in. wide, 1/8 in. thick. Made of gray flint.
Priv. col., average quality, valued $80-100.

• Sandia from Sublette co., WY. Blade 6 1/2 in. long, 2 1/8 in. wide, 5/16 in. thick. Unusual blade, highly polished, distinct flaking and serrations. Made of

light gray chert.
Priv. col., museum quality, valued $650-850.

- Sandia from Sublette co., WY. Blade 4 2/3 in. long, 1 3/4 in. wide, 1/4 in. thick. Made of gray chert.
Priv. col., average quality, valued $100-150.

- Sandia from Converse co., WY. Blade 4 in. long, 1 2/3 in. wide, 3/16 in. thick. Made of flint.
Priv. col., average quality, valued $60-80.

- Sandia from Carter co., MT. Point 2 1/2 in. long, 1 1/4 in. wide, 3/8 in. thick. Good workmanship. Made of gray chert.
Priv. col., excellent quality, valued $200-250.

- Sandia from Carter co., MT. Blade 4 1/16 in. long, 1 1/2 in. wide, 7/16 in. thick. Made of tan chert.
Priv. col., excellent quality, valued $160-200.

- Sandia from Beaverhead co., MT. Point 2 3/4 in. long, 1 1/8 in. wide, 3/16 in. thick. Excellent workmanship. Made of pink black speckled chert.
Priv. col., excellent quality, valued $200-250.

- Sandia from Beaverhead co., MT. Point 3 1/32 in. long, 1 in. wide, 3/16 in. thick. Thin and narrow, good workmanship. Made of banded black to silver chert.
Priv. col., museum quality, valued $500-600.

- Sandia from Beaverhead co., MT. Point 2 3/4 in. long, 1 1/4 in. wide, 3/16 in. thick. Made of gray chert.
Priv. col., excellent quality, valued $200-250.

- Sandia from Beaverhead co., MT. Blade 5 1/16 in. long, 1 2/3 in. wide, 5/16 in. thick. Made of tan chert.
Priv. col., excellent quality, valued $450-500.

- Sandia from Treasure co., MT. Point 3 in. long, 1 1/2 in. wide, 3/16 in. thick. Made of gray chert.
Priv. col., excellent quality, valued $300-350.

- Sandia from Treasure co., MT. Blade 4 1/8 in. long, 1 1/2 in. wide, 1/4 in. thick. Made of white tan chert.
Priv. col., excellent quality, valued $260-300.

- Sandia from Treasure co., MT. Point 2 3/4 in. long, 1 1/8 in. wide, 3/16 in. thick. Made of gray chert.
Priv. col., excellent quality, valued $100-125.

- Sandia from Orleans co., NY. Blade 4 2/3 in. long, 1 1/2 in. wide, 5/16 in. thick. Made of high grade pink chert.
Priv. col., museum quality, valued $300-400.

- Sandia from Seneca co., NY. Blade 3 7/8 in. long, 1 1/4 in. wide, 7/16 in. thick. Made of quartzite.
Priv. col., average quality, valued $85-125.

- Sandia from Lewis co., NY. Blade 4 7/8 in. long, 1 2/3 in. wide, 5/16 in. thick. Made of yellow tan chert.
Priv. col., excellent quality, valued $360-420.

- Sandia from Lewis co., NY. Blade 4 2/3 in. long, 1 1/4 in. wide, 3/16 in. thick. Made of pink chert.
Priv. col., excellent quality, valued $200-250.

- Sandia from Cardin co., PA. Blade 4 1/4 in. long, 2 in. wide, 7/16 in. thick. Made of quartzite.
Priv. col., average quality, valued $100-120.

- Sandia from Cardin co., PA. Point 2 1/4 in. long, 1 3/8 in. wide, 7/16 in. thick. Made of black flint.
Priv. col., average quality, valued $80-100.

- Sandia from Perry co., PA. Blade 4 1/16 in. long, 1 1/2 in. wide, 5/16 in. thick. Made of banded slate.
Priv. col., excellent quality, valued $80-100.

- Sandia from Perry co., PA. Point 2 1/2 in. long, 1 1/8 in. wide, 3/16 in. thick. Made of multi-toned gray chert.
Priv. col., excellent quality, valued $200-250.

- Sandia from Perry co., PA. Blade 4 1/2 in. long, 1 1/4 in. wide, 1/4 in. thick. Made of tan white chert.
Priv. col., excellent quality, valued $160-180.

- Sandia from Tripp co., SD. Point 2 1/2 in. long, 1 1/16 in. wide, 3/16 in. thick. Made of gray chert.

Priv. col., excellent quality, valued $100-150.

- Sandia from Harkon co., SD. Blade 4 in. long, 1 1/2 in. wide, 3/16 in. thick. Made of tan chert.
Priv. col., excellent quality, valued $125-150.

- Sandia from Wheller co., OR. Point 3 in. long, 1 1/4 in. wide, 3/16 in. thick. Made of gray chert.
Priv. col., excellent quality, valued $200-250.

- Sandia from Polk co., OR. Blade 5 1/2 in. long, 1 1/3 in. wide, 5/16 in. thick. Large blade for the area. Made of coal back flint.
Priv. col., excellent quality, valued $60-80.

- Sandia from Madison co., ID. Blade 3 2/3 in. long, 1 1/32 in. wide, 3/16 in. thick. Good workmanship. Made of pink chert.
Priv. col., excellent quality, valued $200-250.

- Sandia from Elmore co., ID. Blade 4 1/32 in. long, 1 1/32 in. wide, 5/16 in. thick. Made of banded black pink chert.
Priv. col., excellent quality, valued $150-200.

- Sandia from Grady co., GA. Point 2 1/2 in. long, 1 in. wide, 1/4 in. thick. Made of gray chert.
Priv. col., excellent quality, valued $200-250.

- Sandia from Grady co., GA. Point 1 1/2 in. long, 3/4 in. wide, 5/16 in. thick. Good workmanship. Made of banded slate.
Priv. col., excellent quality, valued $80-100.

- Sandia from Franklin co., IA. Point 2 13/16 in. long, 1 1/4 in. wide, 3/16 in. thick. Made of pink chert.
Priv. col., excellent quality, valued $200-250.

- Sandia from Mills co., IA. Point 2 5/8 in. long, 1 1/3 in. wide, 5/16 in. thick. Made of banded red pink chert.
Priv. col., excellent quality, valued $120-180.

- Sandia from Butler co., IA. Point 2 1/3 in. long, 1 1/4 in. wide, 3/16 in. thick. Made of gray chert.
Priv. col., excellent quality, valued $200-250.

- Sandia from Butler co., IA. Blade 2 1/4 in. long, 1 3/16 in. wide, 1/4 in. thick. Made of tan yellow chert.
Priv. col., excellent quality, valued $150-225.

- Sandia from Pratt co., KS. Point 2 7/8 in. long, 1 1/4 in. wide, 3/16 in. thick. Made of white chert.
Priv. col., excellent quality, valued $200-250.

- Sandia from Pratt co., KS. Point 3 1/8 in. long, 1 1/3 in. wide, 5/16 in. thick. Made of white chert.
Priv. col., excellent quality, valued $150-200.

- Sandia from Pratt co., KS. Point 2 1/3 in. long, 1 1/16 in. wide, 3/16 in. thick. Made of gray chert.
Priv. col., excellent quality, valued $200-250.

- Sandia from Pratt co., KS. Point 2 1/2 in. long, 1 1/4 in. wide, 5/16 in. thick. Made of quartzite.
Priv. col., average quality, valued $40-50.

Scallorn: 1,500-400 B.P. Woodland through Mississippian to Historical

Predominantly a midwestern point. Small corner notches, generally serrated. Flaring stem with concave, convex, or straight base.

- Scallorn from Murphysboro co., TN. Point 1 1/4 in. long, 1/2 in. wide, 5/32 in. thick. Fine workmanship, sharply serrated tip and edges. Triangular and symmetrical. Made of gray chert.
Grover Bohannon col., museum quality, rare, valued $65-80.

- Scallorn from Hamilton co., TN. Point 1 in. long, 3/4 in. wide, 3/16 in. thick. Made of gray chert.
Grover Bohannon col., museum quality, valued $35-40.

- ◆ Scallorn from Hancock co., KY. Point 1 1/2 in. long, 5/8 in. wide, 1/4 in. thick. Good workmanship. Made of white chert.

Priv. col., excellent quality, valued $20-30.

- Scallorn from Hancock co., KY. Point 1 5/8 in. long, 2/3 in. wide, 7/32 in. thick. Made of white pebble chert.
Priv. col., excellent quality, valued $20-30.

- Scallorn from Hancock co., KY. Point 1 1/16 in. long, 3/4 in. wide, 1/8 in. thick. Made of gray chert.
Priv. col., excellent quality, valued $25-30.

- Scallorn from Hancock co., KY. Point 1 1/3 in. long, 7/8 in. wide, 1/4 in. thick. Made of white chert.
Priv. col., excellent quality, valued $20-30.

- Scallorn from Hancock co., KY. Point 1 3/8 in. long, 11/16 in. wide, 1/4 in. thick. Made of white pebble chert.
Priv. col., excellent quality, valued $20-30.

- Scallorn from Bullitt co., KY. Point 1 1/4 in. long, 7/8 in. wide, 3/16 in. thick. Made of gray chert.
Priv. col., excellent quality, valued $25-30.

- Scallorn from Bullitt co., KY. Point 1 1/16 in. long, 5/8 in. wide, 3/16 in. thick. Made of white pebble chert.
Priv. col., excellent quality, valued $20-30.

- Scallorn from Bullitt co., KY. Point 1 9/16 in. long, 13/16 in. wide, 5/16 in. thick. Made of white pebble chert.
Priv. col., excellent quality, valued $20-30.

- Scallorn from Hamilton co., IL. Point 1 3/16 in. long, 3/4 in. wide, 3/16 in. thick. Made of gray chert.
Priv. col., excellent quality, valued $35-40.

- Scallorn from Hamilton co., IL. Point 1 1/32 in. long, 5/8 in. wide, 1/4 in. thick. Made of white pebble chert.
Priv. col., excellent quality, valued $20-30.

- Scallorn from Hamilton co., IL. Point 1 3/8 in. long, 3/4 in. wide, 5/32 in. thick. Made of white pebble chert.
Priv. col., excellent quality, valued $20-30.

- Scallorn from Hamilton co., IL. Point 1 in. long, 1/2 in. wide, 3/16 in. thick. Made of gray multi-tone chert.

Priv. col., excellent quality, valued $30-40.

• Scallorn from Hamilton co., IL. Point 1 1/4 in. long, 5/8 in. wide, 3/16 in. thick. Made of white pebble chert.
Priv. col., excellent quality, valued $20-30.

• Scallorn from Hamilton co., IL. Point 1 7/8 in. long, 1 in. wide, 5/32 in. thick. Made of white pebble chert.
Priv. col., excellent quality, valued $20-30.

Scottsbluff: 10,000-6,500 B.P. Paleo-Transitional

Predominantly found in the Midwest. Medium to large sized point or blade. Weak shoulders, broad stemmed. Ground haftings are horizontal or oblique flaked. Side notched straight to slightly concave base.

◆ Scottsbluff from northeastern AR. Point 3 1/8 long, 1 1/2 in. 3/16 in. thick. Heat treated, parallel oblique flaked. Serrated edges, sharp tip. Made of light tan banded chert.

Priv. col., excellent quality, valued $45-65.

• Scottsbluff from Cape Giradeau co., MO. Blade 4 3/16 in. long, 1 7/8 in. wide, 1/4 in. thick. Horizontal tranverse flaked, sharply serrated, unique convex base. Made of Mill Creek chert.
Priv. col., excellent quality, valued $85-110.

• Scottsbluff from Cape Giradeau co., MO. Point 3 5/8 long, 1 1/3 in. wide, 3/16 in. thick. Made of light tan chert.
Priv. col., excellent quality, valued $50-55.

• Scottsbluff from Cape Giradeau co., MO. Blade 5 in. long, 1 7/8 in. wide, 1/4 in. thick. Made of gray chert.
Priv. col., excellent quality, valued $65-80.

- Scottsbluff from Lee co., AR. Point 3 5/8 long, 1 1/2 in. wide, 3/16 in. thick. Made of Arkansas brown chert.
Priv. col., excellent quality, valued $55-75.

- Scottsbluff from Lee co., AR. Blade 4 5/16 in. long, 1 7/8 in. wide, 1/4 in. thick. Made of gray chert.
Priv. col., excellent quality, valued $85-100.

- Scottsbluff from Lee co., AR. Point 3 7/8 long, 1 1/2 in. wide, 3/16 in. thick. Made of tan white chert.
Priv. col., excellent quality, valued $55-65.

- Scottsbluff from Lee co., AR. Blade 4 13/16 in. long, 1 7/8 in. wide,   1/4 in. thick. Made of tan yellow chert.
Priv. col., excellent quality, valued $85-100.

- Scottsbluff from Criaghead co., AR. Point 3 1/16 long, 1 1/4 in. wide, 3/16 in. thick. Made of light gray chert.
Priv. col., excellent quality, valued $45-65.

- Scottsbluff from Criaghead co., AR. Blade 4 7/16 in. long, 1 7/8 in. wide, 1/4 in. thick. Made of gray chert.
Priv. col., excellent quality, valued $65-80.

- Scottsbluff from Searcy co., AR. Point 3 long, 1 1/4 in. 3/16 in. thick. Made of tan chert.
Priv. col., excellent quality, valued $45-65.

- Scottsbluff from Searcy co., AR. Blade 4 7/16 in. long, 1 7/8 in. wide, 1/4 in. thick. Made of gray chert.
Priv. col., excellent quality, valued $65-80.

- Scottsbluff from Searcy co., AR. Point 3 1/4 long, 1 1/3 in. wide, 5/16 in. thick. Made of tan chert.
Priv. col., excellent quality, valued $45-65.

- Scottsbluff from Searcy co., AR. Blade 4 5/16 in. long, 1 7/8 in. wide, 1/4 in. thick. Made of brown chert.
Priv. col., excellent quality, valued $85-100.

- Scottsbluff from Drew co., AR. Point 3 1/8 long, 1 1/3 in. wide, 5/16 in. thick. Made of tan yellow chert.

Priv. col., excellent quality, valued $45-65.

• Scottsbluff from Drew co., AR. Blade 4 9/16 in. long, 1 7/8 in. wide, 3/16 in. thick. Made of gray chert.
Priv. col., excellent quality, valued $85-100.

Searcy: 7,500-4,500 B.P. Early to Mid-Archaic

Found throughout the Midwest. Small to medium point or blade. Points and blades are traditionally finely, deeply, and sharply serrated. Thin, narrow, hafting area is ground. Base is concave and ground.

◆ Searcy from Alexander co., IL. Blade 3 5/8 in. long, 3/4 in. wide, 1/4 in. thick. Deep, rounded serrations, slightly concave base. Made of pinkish quartzite, commonly called Arkansas quartz.

Priv. col., excellent quality, valued $40-55.

• Searcy from Monroe co., IL. Blade 4 3/8 in. long, 1 1/4 in. wide, 1/4 in. thick. Made of white pebble chert.
Priv. col., excellent quality, valued $40-50.

• Searcy from Monroe co., IL. Blade 4 7/8 in. long, 1 1/2 in. wide, 1/4 in. thick. Made of gray chert.
Priv. col., excellent quality, valued $50-60.

• Searcy from Monroe co., IL. Blade 4 5/16 in. long, 1 1/2 in. wide, 1/4 in. thick. Made of gray chert.
Priv. col., excellent quality, valued $40-50.

• Searcy from Monroe co., IL. Blade 4 1/16 in. long, 1 1/2 in. wide, 1/4 in. thick. Made of tan chert.
Priv. col., excellent quality, valued $40-50.

• Searcy from Monroe co., IL. Blade 4 3/8 in. long, 1 1/4 in. wide, 1/4 in. thick.

Made of white pebble chert.
Priv. col., excellent quality, valued $40-50.

• Searcy from Jefferson co., IL. Blade 4 in. long, 1 1/8 in. wide, 1/4 in. thick.
Made of white tan chert.
Priv. col., excellent quality, valued $40-50.

• Searcy from Emmet co., IA. Blade 4 3/4 in. long, 1 1/2 in. wide, 1/4 in. thick.
Made of gray chert.
Priv. col., excellent quality, valued $40-50.

• Searcy from Emmet co., IA. Blade 5 1/8 in. long, 1 1/2 in. wide, 1/4 in. thick.
Made of gray chert.
Priv. col., excellent quality, valued $40-50.

• Searcy from Osceola co., IA. Blade 4 1/8 in. long, 2 in. wide, 1/4 in. thick.
Made of banded red chert.
Priv. col., excellent quality, valued $40-50.

• Searcy from Osceola co., IA. Point 2 7/8 in. long, 1 1/32 in. wide, 1/4 in. thick.
Made of white yellow chert.
Priv. col., excellent quality, valued $40-50.

• Searcy from Osceola co., IA. Point 2 3/8 in. long, 1 in. wide, 1/4 in. thick.
Made of white yellow chert.
Priv. col., excellent quality, valued $40-50.

• Searcy from Cass co., IA. Point 2 1/8 in. long, 7/8 in. wide, 1/4 in. thick. Made
of white gray chert.
Priv. col., excellent quality, valued $40-45.

• Searcy from Cumberland co., IL. Point 3 1/8 in. long, 1 1/4 in. wide, 1/4 in.
thick. Made of white pebble chert.
Priv. col., excellent quality, valued $40-50.

• Searcy from Cumberland co., IL. Point 2 7/8 in. long, 1 in. wide, 1/4 in. thick.
Made of white pebble chert.
Priv. col., excellent quality, valued $40-50.

Sequoyan: 1,500-600 B.P. Mississippian

Found throughout the Midwest and into the northeastern states. A small point, narrow and thin. Deeply serrated edges, expanded bulbous stem.

♦ Sequoyan from Beaumont, TX. Point 1 1/2 in. long, 7/16 in. wide, 1/8 in.
thick. Deeply serrated in classic Sequoyan design. Sharp tip, bulbous stem, deep
side notched. Made of tan chert.

Priv. col., museum quality, valued $35-45.

• Sequoyan from Beaumont, TX. Point 1 11/16 in. long, 7/8 in. wide, 1/8 in.
thick. Made of tan chert.
Priv. col., excellent quality, valued $25-35.

• Sequoyan from Beaumont, TX. Point 1 1/3 in. long, 5/8 in. wide, 1/8 in. thick.
Made of tan chert.
Priv. col., excellent quality, valued $25-30.

• Sequoyan from Beaumont, TX. Point 1 1/2 in. long, 7/16 in. wide, 1/8 in.
thick. Made of white pebble chert.
Priv. col., excellent quality, valued $20-25.

• Sequoyan from Sabine co., TX. Point 1 1/16 in. long, 3/4 in. wide, 3/16 in.
thick. Made of quartzite.
Priv. col., average quality, valued $15-25.

• Sequoyan from Sabine co., TX. Point 1 1/8 in. long, 13/16 in. wide, 1/8 in.
thick. Made of pink quartzite.
Priv. col., average quality, valued $15-20.

• Sequoyan from Beaumont, TX. Point 1 1/4 in. long, 11/16 in. wide, 3/16 in.
thick. Made of white pebble chert.
Priv. col., excellent quality, valued $20-25.

• Sequoyan from Lampasas co., TX. Point 1 3/16 in. long, 7/8 in. wide, 5/32 in.
thick. Made of dull gray chert.
Priv. col., excellent quality, valued $20-25.

• Sequoyan from Lampasas co., TX. Point 1 1/8 in. long, 11/16 in. wide, 1/8 in.
thick. Made of dull gray chert.

Priv. col., excellent quality, valued $25-30.

• Sequoyan from Childress co., TX. Point 1 1/3 in. long, 7/8 in. wide, 1/8 in. thick. Made of white tan pebble chert.
Priv. col., excellent quality, valued $25-30.

• Sequoyan from Childress co., TX. Point 1 5/16 in. long, 7/8 in. wide, 1/8 in. thick. Made of banded tan chert.
Priv. col., excellent quality, valued $35-40.

• Sequoyan from Childress co., TX. Point 1 in. long, 5/8 in. wide, 1/8 in. thick. Made of quartzite.
Priv. col., average quality, valued $5-10.

• Sequoyan from Childress co., TX. Point 1 1/2 in. long, 7/8 in. wide, 1/8 in. thick. Made of porous white chert.
Priv. col., average quality, valued $10-15.

• Sequoyan from Brazos co., TX. Point 1 5/16 in. long, 7/8 in. wide, 3/32 in. thick. Made of gray chert.
Priv. col., excellent quality, valued $20-25.

• Sequoyan from Brazos co., TX. Point 1 in. long, 7/16 in. wide, 1/8 in. thick. Excellent workmanship. Made of gray chert.
Priv. col., museum quality, valued $35-40.

• Sequoyan from Brazos co., TX. Point 1 1/2 in. long, 7/8 in. wide, 1/8 in. thick. Made of white pebble chert.
Priv. col., excellent quality, valued $25-30.

• Sequoyan from Brazos co., TX. Point 1 9/16 in. long, 7/8 in. wide, 1/8 in. thick. Made of quartzite.
Priv. col., average quality, valued $15-20.

• Sequoyan from Lipscomb co., TX. Point 1 9/16 in. long, 7/8 in. wide, 5/32 in. thick. Made of gray chert.
Priv. col., excellent quality, valued $20-25.

• Sequoyan from Lipscomb co., TX. Point 1 1/8 in. long, 11/16 in. wide, 1/8 in. thick. Made of dull gray chert.
Priv. col., excellent quality, valued $25-30.

• Sequoyan from Crockett co., TX. Point 1 1/4 in. long, 7/8 in. wide, 1/8 in. thick. Made of tan pebble chert.
Priv. col., excellent quality, valued $25-30.

• Sequoyan from Crockett co., TX. Point 1 15/16 in. long, 7/8 in. wide, 1/8 in. thick. Made of marbled tan chert.
Priv. col., excellent quality, valued $35-40.

Simpson: 14,000-8,000 B.P. Late Paleo

Predominantly a far southeastern point or blade, small to medium in size. Lanceolate, recurved sided point or blade. Base similar to the Clovis unfluted. Deeply concave base with flaring ears, easily observed hafting areas.

◆ Simpson from Tampa, FL. Point 2 7/8 in. long, 1 1/4 in. wide, 1/4 in thick. Finely serrated point, sharp edges, rounded tip. Made of tan pebble chert.

Priv. col., excellent quality, valued $180-250.

• Simpson from Allen Parish, LA. Point 2 3/8 in. long, 1 1/16 in. wide, 1/4 in thick. Made of quartzite.
Priv. col., average quality, valued $55-70.

◆ Simpson from Savannah, GA. Point 2 1/4 in. long, 1 in. wide, 3/16 in. thick. Sharply serrated edges, pointed tip, typical concave base. Made of tan chert.

Grover Bohannon col., museum quality, valued $225-275.

- Simpson from Caddo Parish, LA. Point 2 1/8 in. long, 1 1/16 in. wide, 1/4 in thick. Made of pink quartzite.
Priv. col., excellent quality, valued $85-90.

- Simpson from Caddo Parish, LA. Point 2 1/8 in. long, 7/8 in. wide, 3/16 in. thick. Made of tan yellow chert.
Priv. col., excellent quality, valued $125-175.

- Simpson from Livingston Parish, LA. Point 2 in. long, 1 3/16 in. wide, 1/4 in thick. Made of quartzite.
Priv. col., average quality, valued $45-60.

- Simpson from Bullock co., AL. Point 2 1/16 in. long, 1 1/16 in. wide, 3/16 in. thick. Made of marbled tan chert.
Priv. col., museum quality, valued $200-225.

- Simpson from Bullock co., AL. Point 2 5/8 in. long, 1 3/16 in. wide, 1/4 in thick. Made of quartzite.
Priv. col., average quality, valued $45-60.

- Simpson from Abberville co., SC. Point 2 3/4 in. long, 1 1/2 in. wide, 3/16 in. thick. Excellent workmanship. Made of banded tan slate.
Priv. col., excellent quality, valued $150-200.

- Simpson from Jasper co., SC. Point 2 3/8 in. long, 1 5/16 in. wide, 1/4 in thick. Made of slate.
Priv. col., average quality, valued $50-60.

- Simpson from Dawson co., GA. Point 2 1/32 in. long, 1 in. wide, 1/8 in. thick. Made of brick red chert.
Priv. col., excellent quality, valued $125-175.

- Simpson from Dawson co., GA. Point 2 1/8 in. long, 1 3/16 in. wide, 1/4 in thick. Made of banded slate.
Priv. col., average quality, valued $55-70.

- Simpson from Dawson co., GA. Point 3 1/8 in. long, 1 1/3 in. wide, 3/16 in. thick. Made of tan yellow chert.
Priv. col., excellent quality, valued $175-225.

- Simpson from Brooks co., GA. Point 2 5/8 in. long, 1 3/16 in. wide, 5/32 in thick. Made of quartzite.

Priv. col., average quality, valued $55-70.

- Simpson from Brooks co., GA. Point 2 3/4 in. long, 1 1/8 in. wide, 3/16 in. thick. Made of gray chert.
Priv. col., excellent quality, valued $150-200.

- Simpson from Lanier co., GA. Point 2 1/8 in. long, 1 in. wide, 1/4 in. thick. Made of quartzite.
Priv. col., average quality, valued $50-60.

- Simpson from Lanier co., GA. Point 2 1/3 in. long, 7/8 in. wide, 3/16 in. thick. Made of tan slate.
Priv. col., excellent quality, valued $175-225.

- Simpson from Rabun co., GA. Point 2 5/16 in. long, 1 1/2 in. wide, 1/4 in. thick. Made of banded slate.
Priv. col., average quality, valued $65-80.

- Simpson from Rabun co., GA. Point 2 1/3 in. long, 1 1/16 in. wide, 3/16 in. thick. Made of tan yellow chert.
Priv. col., excellent quality, valued $200-225.

Smithsonia: 4,000-1,500 B.P. Late Archaic

Found predominantly in the southeastern states and into the eastern Midwest. A medium sized point, triangular, with barbed or tapered shoulders. Points generally symmetrical, long stemmed with a straight base.

◆ Smithsonia from Humphreys co., TN. Point 2 3/4 in. long, 1 1/2 in. wide, 1/4 in. thick. Finely serrated point, sharp tip, uniform shoulders and stem. Made of Horse chert.

Priv. col., excellent quality, valued $35-50.

- Smithsonia from Humphreys co., TN. Point 3 1/4 in. long, 1 2/3 in. wide,

1/4 in. thick. Made of Dover chert.
Priv. col., excellent quality, valued $45-60.

• Smithsonia from Humphreys co., TN. Point 2 7/8 in. long, 1 17/32 in. wide, 1/4 in. thick. Good workmanship. Made of Dover chert.
Priv. col., excellent quality, valued $50-60.

• Smithsonia from Clinton co., KY. Point 3 in. long, 1 3/4 in. wide, 1/4 in. thick. Made of gray chert.
Priv. col., excellent quality, valued $45-60.

• Smithsonia from Clinton co., KY. Point 2 7/8 in. long, 1 7/16 in. wide, 1/4 in. thick. Made of gray chert.
Priv. col., excellent quality, valued $50-60.

• Smithsonia from Fulton co., KY. Point 3 1/32 in. long, 1 2/3 in. wide, 3/16 in. thick. Made of white pebble chert.
Priv. col., excellent quality, valued $45-60.

• Smithsonia from Fulton co., KY. Point 2 5/8 in. long, 1 7/16 in. wide, 1/4 in. thick. Good workmanship. Made of greenish pebble chert.
Priv. col., excellent quality, valued $60-70.

• Smithsonia from Fulton co., KY. Point 3 in. long, 1 1/2 in. wide, 1/4 in. thick. Made of tan to white chert.
Priv. col., excellent quality, valued $45-60.

• Smithsonia from Fulton co., KY. Point 2 5/8 in. long, 1 5/32 in. wide, 1/4 in. thick. Made of tan yellow chert.
Priv. col., excellent quality, valued $50-60.

• Smithsonia from Henderson co., KY. Point 2 1/4 in. long, 1 1/16 in. wide, 1/4 in. thick. Made of gray chert.
Priv. col., excellent quality, valued $45-60.

• Smithsonia from Henderson co., KY. Point 2 3/8 in. long, 1 7/32 in. wide, 1/4 in. thick. Good workmanship. Made of dense white chert.
Priv. col., excellent quality, valued $50-60.

• Smithsonia from Pratt co., KS. Point 3 in. long, 1 1/2 in. wide, 1/4 in. thick. Uniquely symmetrical point. Made of white pebble chert.
Priv. col., excellent quality, valued $45-60.

- Smithsonia from Pratt co., KS. Point 2 1/8 in. long, 1 1/2 in. wide, 1/4 in. thick. Good workmanship. Made of gray chert. *Priv. col., excellent quality, valued $50-60.*

- Smithsonia from Hopkins co., KY. Point 3 1/16 in. long, 1 3/4 in. wide, 1/4 in. thick. Excellent workmanship. Made of Dover chert. *Priv. col., excellent quality, valued $50-60.*

- Smithsonia from Hopkins co., KY. Point 2 5/8 in. long, 1 11/32 in. wide, 3/16 in. thick. Good workmanship, slight tip break. Made of tan chert. *Priv. col., average quality, valued $25-30.*

- Smithsonia from Wallace co., KS. Point 2 1/4 in. long, 1 2/3 in. wide, 1/4 in. thick. Made of gray chert. *Priv. col., excellent quality, valued $40-50.*

- Smithsonia from Wallace co., KS. Point 2 7/8 in. long, 1 1/3 in. wide, 1/4 in. thick. Made of gray chert. *Priv. col., excellent quality, valued $45-50.*

- Smithsonia from Wallace co., KS. Point 3 1/16 in. long, 1 3/4 in. wide, 1/4 in. thick. Made of brown chert. *Priv. col., excellent quality, valued $45-60.*

- Smithsonia from Wallace co., KS. Point 2 3/8 in. long, 1 1/2 in. wide, 1/4 in. thick. Made of dull gray chert. *Priv. col., excellent quality, valued $50-60.*

Snyders: 2,500-1,500 B.P. Hopewell Woodland

Found throughout the Midwest and into the East. Point or blade medium to large in size. Generally quite broad, wide, deep corner notches, thin with high quality workmanship. Blade or point edges and stem convex.

◆ Snyders from Kent co., IL. Point 2 5/8 in. long, 1 7/16 in. wide, 1/4 in. thick. Unique point made of unusual chert of two different textures. Deep uniform notches, fractured base, sharp edges, sharp rounded tip. Made of unidentified chert.

Priv. col., excellent quality, valued $85-125.

♦ Snyders from Union co., IL. Point 2 in. long, 1 23/32 in. wide, 11/32 in. thick. Deep corner notches, convex base and edges. Edges finely serrated. Made of pink to rose chert.

Les Grubbe col., museum quality, valued $100-150.

♦ Snyders cache find from Union co., IL. *Left*: point 3 in. long, 1 7/8 in. wide, 1/4 in. thick. Made of Mill Creek chert. *Center*: blade 4 1/2 in. long, 3 1/8 in. wide, 1/2 in. thick. *Right*: blade 3 1/2 in. long, 1 5/8 in. wide, 1/4 in. thick. Made of Cobden Bullseye chert.

Les Grubbe col. Left: excellent quality, valued $50-75. Center: excellent quality, valued $150-200. Right: museum quality, valued $125-175.

♦ Snyders from Murphysboro co., TN. Blade 3 7/8 in. long, 2 1/4 in. wide, 1/4 in. thick. Exceptionally fine workmanship, minutely serrated edges, very sharp tip. Symmetrical blade, deep side notches with concave base. Made of rose white pebble chert.

Grover Bohannon col., museum quality, rare, valued $400-475.

♦ Snyders from Union co., IL. Point 2 1/4 in. long, 1 5/8 in. wide, 3/8 in. thick. Convex edges, one side sharper than the other, deep notches, convex base. Made of white pebble chert.

Priv. col., average quality, valued $65-90.

• Snyders from Union co., IL. Blade 4 7/8 in. long, 2 1/2 in. wide, 1/4 in. thick. Fine workmanship. Made of Mill Creek chert.
Tim Rubbles col., excellent quality, valued $200-250.

• Snyders from Union co., IL. Blade 4 1/4 in. long, 1 7/8 in. wide, 3/8 in. thick. Made of white gray pebble chert.
Priv. col., excellent quality, valued $150-200.

• Snyders from Union co., IL. Blade 5 in. long, 2 1/4 in. wide, 3/16 in. thick. Made of Cobden chert.
Priv. col., museum quality, valued $300-375.

• Snyders from Union co., IL. Blade 4 1/2 in. long, 2 1/8 in. wide, 3/16 in. thick. Excellent workmanship. Made of white pebble chert.
Priv. col., excellent quality, valued $165-200.

• Snyders from Union co., IL. Blade 3 7/8 in. long, 2 1/16 in. wide, 1/4 in. thick. Made of Mill Creek chert.

Tim Rubbles col., excellent quality, valued $200-250.

- Snyders from Union co., IL. Blade 4 1/4 in. long, 2 in. wide, 3/16 in. thick. Made of white gray pebble chert.
Tim Rubbles col., excellent quality, valued $150-200.

- Snyders from Union co., IL. Blade 5 1/4 in. long, 2 1/32 in. wide, 3/16 in. thick. Made of gray chert.
Priv. col., excellent quality, valued $250-300.

- Snyders from Jackson co., IL. Blade 4 1/8 in. long, 2 in. wide, 3/16 in. thick. Made of white pebble chert.
Priv. col., excellent quality, valued $150-200.

- Snyders from Jackson co., IL. Blade 4 3/8 in. long, 2 1/4 in. wide, 1/4 in. thick. Made of Mill Creek chert.
Priv. col., excellent quality, valued $200-250.

- Snyders from Alexander co., IL. Blade 4 1/3 in. long, 1 7/8 in. wide, 1/4 in. thick. Made of white gray pebble chert.
Priv. col., excellent quality, valued $150-200.

- Snyders from Hardin co., IL. Blade 4 in. long, 2 1/3 in. wide, 3/16 in. thick. Made of gray chert.
Priv. col., excellent quality, valued $200-225.

- Snyders from Gallatin co., IL. Blade 4 7/16 in. long, 2 1/8 in. wide, 3/16 in. thick. Excellent workmanship, needle sharp tip. Made of greenish pebble chert.
Priv. col., excellent quality, valued $150-200.

Stanfield: 10,000-8,000 B.P. Paleo-Transitional

Predominantly a southeastern point or blade medium to large in size. Lanceolate narrow blade or point, occasionally fluted with base.

- Stanfield from southeastern, KY. Blade 5 1/4 in. long, 2 3/8 in. wide, 1/2 in. thick. Fire treated with unique base. Blade seems to have been reworked in the past. Heavy field patina. Made of green to white chert.
Priv. col., excellent quality, valued $100-150.

- ◆ Stanfield from Hardin co., TN. Blade 8 1/4 in. long, 2 5/8 in. wide, 5/8 in.

thick. Heavy patina, parallel flaked, sharply serrated edges. Made of Mill Creek chert.

Grover Bohannon col., average quality, $25-40.

- Stanfield from Ballard co., KY. Blade 5 1/2 in. long, 2 1/8 in. wide, 1/2 in. thick. Made of white chert.
Priv. col., excellent quality, valued $100-150.

- Stanfield from Ballard co., KY. Blade 7 1/8 in. long, 2 in. wide, 7/16 in. thick. Made of tan brown chert.
Priv. col., excellent quality, $65-80.

- Stanfield from Metcalfe co., KY. Blade 6 1/4 in. long, 2 5/8 in. wide, 1/2 in. thick. Made of gray white chert.
Priv. col., excellent quality, valued $100-150.

- Stanfield from Metcalfe co., KY. Blade 8 in. long, 2 5/8 in. wide, 5/8 in. thick. Made of tan yellow chert.
Priv. col., excellent quality, $125-150.

- Stanfield from Rowan co., KY. Blade 5 1/4 in. long, 2 3/8 in. wide, 1/2 in. thick. Heat treated. Made of white chert.
Priv. col., excellent quality, valued $100-150.

- Stanfield from Harris co., GA. Blade 6 1/4 in. long, 3 in. wide, 5/8 in. thick. Made of quartzite.
Priv. col., average quality, $25-40.

- Stanfield from Harris co., GA. Blade 5 1/8 in. long, 2 1/8 in. wide, 1/2 in. thick. Made of banded slate.
Priv. col., excellent quality, valued $80-100.

- Stanfield from Harris co., GA. Blade 8 in. long, 3 1/32 in. wide, 5/8 in. thick. Good field patina. Made of pink chert.
Priv. col., excellent quality, $100-150.

• Stanfield from Rabun co., GA. Blade 5 1/4 in. long, 2 3/8 in. wide, 1/2 in. thick. Fluted base. Made of white chert.
Priv. col., excellent quality, valued $100-150.

• Stanfield from Rabun co., GA. Blade 7 1/32 in. long, 1 7/8 in. wide, 5/8 in. thick. Made of white pebble chert.
Priv. col., excellent quality, $75-100.

• Stanfield from Newberry co., SC. Blade 4 3/4 in. long, 2 1/8 in. wide, 1/2 in. thick. Made of pink chert.

Priv. col., excellent quality, valued $100-125.

• Stanfield from Newberry co., SC. Blade 8 1/3 in. long, 2 5/8 in. wide, 5/8 in. thick. Made of banded slate.
Priv. col., average quality, $45-60.

Stanley: 8,000-5,000 B.P. Early Archaic

Located in the South and Southeast. Small to medium sized point or blade, broad, shoulders tapered or weak. Shoulders on narrow blades are always narrow variety. Quality workmanship throughout Stanley points and blades. Most are serrated, with bifurcated stem.

♦ Stanley from Murphysboro co., TN. Blade 3 1/2 in. long, 15/16 in. wide, 1/4 in. thick. Long narrow variety of Stanley. Tapered shoulders, bifurcated stem. Made of quartzite.

Priv. col., average quality, valued $8-15.

♦ Stanley from Boone co., NC. Point 2 1/4 in. long, 1 3/4 in. wide, 1/4 in. thick. Broad, wide horizontal shoulders, one tang broken. Sharply serrated, very symmetrical, deeply bifurcated stem. Made of grainy white pebble chert.

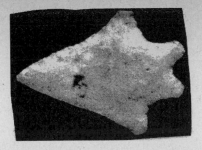

Priv. col., excellent quality, valued $25-35.

• Stanley from Murphysboro co., TN. Blade 3 7/8 in. long, 1 in. wide, 1/4 in. thick. Made of Dover chert.
Priv. col., museum quality, valued $35-45.

• Stanley from Cole co., TN. Blade 4 1/4 in. long, 1 7/8 in. wide, 1/4 in. thick. Made of gray pebble chert.
Priv. col., excellent quality, valued $25-35.

• Stanley from Cole co., TN. Blade 3 5/8 in. long, 1 1/16 in. wide, 1/4 in. thick. Made of gray chert.
Priv. col., excellent quality, valued $15-25.

• Stanley from Cole co., TN. Point 2 1/2 in. long, 1 1/3 in. wide, 1/4 in. thick. Good workmanship. Made of white chert.
Priv. col., excellent quality, valued $25-35.

• Stanley from Jefferson co., TN. Blade 3 11/16 in. long, 1 3/16 in. wide, 1/4 in. thick. Made of greenish pebble chert.
Priv. col., excellent quality, valued $30-35.

• Stanley from Ballard co., KY. Point 2 3/8 in. long, 1 1/4 in. wide, 3/16 in. thick. Made of white pebble chert.
Priv. col., excellent quality, valued $25-35.

• Stanley from Adair co., KY. Point 3 in. long, 1 1/16 in. wide, 1/4 in. thick. Made of gray chert.
Priv. col., excellent quality, valued $30-35.

• Stanley from Hyde co., NC. Point 2 1/2 in. long, 1 1/4 in. wide, 1/4 in. thick. Made of white pebble chert.
Priv. col., excellent quality, valued $25-35.

• Stanley from Hyde co., NC. Blade 3 3/4 in. long, 1 5/16 in. wide, 3/16 in. thick. Made of quartzite.
Priv. col., average quality, valued $8-15.

• Stanley from Hyde co., NC. Blade 4 1/4 in. long, 1 3/4 in. wide, 1/4 in. thick. Made of pink white pebble chert.
Priv. col., excellent quality, valued $25-35.

• Stanley from Stokes co., NC. Blade 3 1/2 in. long, 13/16 in. wide, 1/4 in. thick. Made of gray shale.
Priv. col., average quality, valued $8-15.

• Stanley from Stokes co., NC. Point 2 1/2 in. long, 1 3/4 in. wide, 1/4 in. thick. Made of gray white chert.
Priv. col., excellent quality, valued $25-35.

• Stanley from Graham co., NC. Blade 3 2/3 in. long, 1 3/16 in. wide, 1/4 in. thick. Made of quartzite.
Priv. col., average quality, valued $8-15.

• Stanley from Swain co., NC. Blade 4 in. long, 1 3/4 in. wide, 3/16 in. thick. Made of porous white chert.
Priv. col., average quality, valued $10-15.

Steuben: 2,000-1,000 B.P. Woodland

A medium to large sized point or blade. Found predominantly in the Midwest. Blade or point is narrow, stem long and expanded with straight to convex base. Shoulders are tapered weak to straight.

◆ Steuben from Murphysboro co., TN. Point 7/8 in. long, 1/4 in. wide, 1/8 in. thick. Very sharp, beveled on one side of each face. Finely serrated needle sharp tip. Made of a blue tan pebble chert.

Grover Bohannon col., excellent quality, valued $15-25.

• Steuben from Franklin co., TN. Point 1 3/8 in. long, 1/2 in. wide, 1/8 in. thick.

Made of tan pebble chert.
Grover Bohannon col., excellent quality, valued $15-25.

- Steuben from Franklin co., TN. Point 1 1/8 in. long, 1/2 in. wide, 1/8 in. thick. Made of tan pebble chert.
Grover Bohannon col., excellent quality, valued $15-25.

- Steuben from Davidson co., TN. Point 13/16 in. long, 1/3 in. wide, 1/8 in. thick. Made of white pebble chert.
Priv. col., excellent quality, valued $15-25.

- Steuben from Davidson co., TN. Point 1 1/8 in. long, 3/4 in. wide, 1/8 in. thick. Made of gray pebble chert.
Priv. col., excellent quality, valued $15-25.

- Steuben from Davidson co., TN. Point 1 5/8 in. long, 11/16 in. wide, 1/8 in. thick. Made of gray chert.
Priv. col., excellent quality, valued $15-25.

- Steuben from Davidson co., TN. Point 1 in. long, 1/2 in. wide, 1/8 in. thick. Made of tan yellow chert.
Grover Bohannon col., excellent quality, valued $15-25.

- Steuben from Franklin co., IL. Point 1 1/3 in. long, 5/8 in. wide, 1/8 in. thick. Made of Mill Creek chert.
Priv. col., excellent quality, valued $15-25.

- Steuben from Franklin co., IL. Point 1 1/8 in. long, 2/3 in. wide, 1/8 in. thick. Excellent workmanship. Made of Mill Creek chert.
Priv. col., excellent quality, valued $25-35.

- Steuben from Grangier co., TN. Point 1 1/3 in. long, 11/16 in. wide, 1/8 in. thick. Made of gray chert.
Priv. col., excellent quality, valued $15-25.

- Steuben from Grangier co., TN. Point 1 1/32 in. long, 1/2 in. wide, 1/8 in. thick. Made of yellow tan pebble chert.
Priv. col., excellent quality, valued $15-25.

- Steuben from Grangier co., TN. Point 1 1/4 in. long, 5/8 in. wide, 1/8 in. thick. Made of tan white chert.
Priv. col., excellent quality, valued $15-25.

- Steuben from Grangier co., TN. Point 1 1/32 in. long, 5/8 in. wide, 1/8 in. thick. Made of tan yellow chert.
Priv. col., excellent quality, valued $15-25.

- Steuben from Henderson co., TN. Point 1 1/8 in. long, 2/3 in. wide, 1/8 in. thick. Made of tan gray chert.
Priv. col., excellent quality, valued $15-25.

- Steuben from Henderson co., TN. Point 1 1/4 in. long, 7/8 in. wide, 1/8 in. thick. Made of tan yellow chert.
Priv. col., excellent quality, valued $15-25.

- Steuben from Giles co., TN. Point 1 1/2 in. long, 7/8 in. wide, 1/8 in. thick. Made of tan chert.
Priv. col., excellent quality, valued $15-25.

- Steuben from Giles co., TN. Point 1 1/3 in. long, 2/3 in. wide, 1/8 in. thick. Made of tan gray chert.
Priv. col., excellent quality, valued $15-25.

- Steuben from Giles co., TN. Point 1 3/8 in. long, 5/8 in. wide, 1/8 in. thick. Made of tan white chert.
Priv. col., excellent quality, valued $15-25.

- Steuben from Giles co., TN. Point 1 1/4 in. long, 11/16 in. wide, 1/8 in. thick. Made of white pebble chert.
Priv. col., excellent quality, valued $15-25.

- Steuben from Humphreys co., TN. Point 1 1/8 in. long, 5/8 in. wide, 1/8 in. thick. Made of tan yellow chert.
Priv. col., excellent quality, valued $15-25.

- Steuben from Humphreys co., TN. Point 1 in. long, 2/3 in. wide, 1/8 in. thick. Made of tan yellow chert.
Priv. col., excellent quality, valued $15-25.

- Steuben from Cooper co., TN. Point 1 1/3 in. long, 7/8 in. wide, 1/8 in. thick. Made of tan yellow chert.
Priv. col., excellent quality, valued $15-25.

- Steuben from Cooper co., TN. Point 1 1/32 in. long, 5/8 in. wide, 1/8 in. thick. Made of Dover chert.

Priv. col., museum quality, valued $25-35.

• Steuben from Hardin co., TN. Point 1 3/8 in. long, 1/2 in. wide, 1/8 in. thick. Made of tan pebble chert.
Priv. col., excellent quality, valued $15-25.

• Steuben from Hardin co., TN. Point 1 in. long, 5/8 in. wide, 1/8 in. thick. Made of tan gray chert.
Priv. col., excellent quality, valued $15-25.

Stillwell: 9,000-7,000 B.P. Early Archaic

Predominantly a midwestern point or blade. Corner notched points and blades, serrated edges. Barbed shoulders, concave ground base.

◆ Stillwell from Brown co., IL. Blade 3 3/4 in. long, 1 3/8 in. wide, 1/4 in. thick. Highly serrated, concave base, very sharp, deep corner notched. Made of white to blue chert.

Priv. col., museum quality, valued $250-325.

◆ Stillwell from Greene co., IN. Blade 3 1/2 in. long, 1 13/32 in. wide, 3/8 in. thick. Very thin, finely serrated blade. Made of Dover chert.

Priv. col., excellent quality, valued $150-200.

• Stillwell from Greene co., IL. Blade 4 1/3 in. long, 1 7/8 in. wide, 1/4 in. thick. Excellent workmanship. Made of white chert.
Priv. col., museum quality, valued $250-325.

• Stillwell from Greene co., IL. Blade 3 2/3 in. long, 1 1/2 in. wide, 1/4 in. thick. Made of Cobden chert.
Priv. col., excellent quality, valued $150-200.

• Stillwell from Coles co., IL. Blade 3 3/4 in. long, 1 1/3 in. wide, 1/4 in. thick. Made of white pebble chert.
Priv. col., excellent quality, valued $100-125.

• Stillwell from Coles co., IL. Blade 3 7/8 in. long, 1 9/32 in. wide, 3/16 in. thick. Made of green chert.
Priv. col., excellent quality, valued $150-200.

• Stillwell from Coles co., IL. Blade 4 3/4 in. long, 1 5/8 in. wide, 1/4 in. thick. Made of white chert.
Priv. col., excellent quality, valued $150-175.

• Stillwell from Coles co., IL. Blade 3 27/32 in. long, 1 3/32 in. wide, 3/8 in. thick. Made of green chert.
Priv. col., excellent quality, valued $150-200.

• Stillwell from Johnson co., IL. Blade 3 13/16 in. long, 1 5/8 in. wide, 1/4 in. thick. Made of Kaolin chert.
Priv. col., museum quality, rare, valued $275-350.

• Stillwell from Johnson co., IL. Blade 4 1/2 in. long, 1 13/32 in. wide, 3/8 in. thick. Excellent workmanship. Made of Mill Creek chert.
Priv. col., excellent quality, valued $150-200.

• Stillwell from Jackson co., IL. Blade 4 1/3 in. long, 2 in. wide, 1/4 in. thick. Made of white chert.
Priv. col., excellent quality, valued $150-175.

• Stillwell from Jackson co., IL. Blade 3 2/3 in. long, 1 3/8 in. wide, 3/8 in. thick. Made of gray chert.
Priv. col., excellent quality, valued $150-200.

• Stillwell from Johnson co., IL. Blade 4 3/16 in. long, 1 7/8 in. wide, 1/4 in. thick. Made of white gray chert.
Priv. col., excellent quality, valued $125-150.

• Stillwell from Johnson co., IL. Blade 4 1/16 in. long, 1 1/2 in. wide, 3/8 in. thick. Excellent workmanship. Made of Mill Creek chert.

Priv. col., excellent quality, valued $150-200.

• Stillwell from Jasper co., IL. Blade 4 3/32 in. long, 1 7/8 in. wide, 1/4 in. thick. Made of white pebble chert.
Priv. col., excellent quality, valued $150-175.

• Stillwell from Jasper co., IL. Blade 4 2/3 in. long, 1 13/32 in. wide, 3/16 in. thick. Excellent workmanship, needle sharp tip. Made of green chert.
Priv. col., museum quality, valued $200-250.

• Stillwell from Jasper co., IL. Blade 4 1/16 in. long, 2 1/8 in. wide, 1/4 in. thick. Excellent workmanship. Made of white chert.
Priv. col., museum quality, valued $175-250.

• Stillwell from Jasper co., IL. Blade 4 1/32 in. long, 1 13/16 in. wide, 3/8 in. thick. Made of green chert.
Priv. col., excellent quality, valued $150-200.

Sublet Ferry: 4,000-2,000 B.P. Woodland

Predominantly a small or medium sized point or blade from the southeastern United States. Side notched point with small base. Base is straight to slightly convex. Edges may be straight to convex and are traditionally serrated.

♦ Sublet Ferry from Bonneville, NC. Point 2 3/4 in. long, 3/4 in. wide, 3/16 in. thick. Finely serrated, symmetrical, side notched, concave base. Made of brown chert.

Grover Bohannon col., excellent quality, valued $45-65.

• Sublet Ferry from Catawaba co., NC. Point 2 1/2 in. long, 7/8 in. wide, 3/16 in. thick. Made of banded brown chert.
Grover Bohannon col., excellent quality, valued $45-65.

• Sublet Ferry from Catawaba co., NC. Point 2 1/4 in. long, 3/4 in. wide, 1/4 in.

thick. Made of brown chert.
Grover Bohannon col., excellent quality, valued $45-65.

• Sublet Ferry from Yarkin co., NC. Point 2 5/8 in. long, 2/3 in. wide, 3/16 in. thick. Made of red slate.
Grover Bohannon col., excellent quality, valued $45-65.

• Sublet Ferry from Yarkin co., NC. Point 2 1/3 in. long, 7/8 in. wide, 3/16 in. thick. Made of banded red slate.
Priv. col., excellent quality, valued $45-65.

• Sublet Ferry from Yarkin co., NC. Point 2 5/8 in. long, 1 in. wide, 1/4 in. thick. Made of gray chert.
Priv. col., excellent quality, valued $40-60.

• Sublet Ferry from Yarkin co., NC. Point 2 7/8 in. long, 7/8 in. wide, 3/16 in. thick. Made of banded red slate.
Priv. col., excellent quality, valued $45-65.

• Sublet Ferry from Swain co., NC. Point 3 1/4 in. long, 7/8 in. wide, 3/16 in. thick. Made of marbled tan brown chert.
Priv. col., excellent quality, valued $45-65.

• Sublet Ferry from Swain co., NC. Point 3 in. long, 3/4 in. wide, 1/4 in. thick. Made of brown chert.
Priv. col., excellent quality, valued $45-65.

• Sublet Ferry from Swain co., NC. Point 2 7/8 in. long, 1 in. wide, 3/16 in. thick. Made of marbled tan chert.
Priv. col., excellent quality, valued $45-65.

• Sublet Ferry from Coosa co., AL. Point 2 3/4 in. long, 7/8 in. wide, 1/8 in. thick. Made of brown chert.
Priv. col., excellent quality, valued $45-65.

• Sublet Ferry from Coosa co., AL. Point 2 1/2 in. long, 1 in. wide, 1/4 in. thick. Made of brown white chert.
Priv. col., excellent quality, valued $45-65.

• Sublet Ferry from Coosa co., AL. Point 2 1/8 in. long, 2/3 in. wide, 3/16 in. thick. Made of gray slate.
Priv. col., average quality, valued $25-35.

- Sublet Ferry from Crenshaw co., AL. Point 2 1/3 in. long, 7/8 in. wide, 1/8 in. thick. Made of brown white chert.
Priv. col., excellent quality, valued $35-55.

- Sublet Ferry from Crenshaw co., AL. Point 2 3/4 in. long, 1 1/16 in. wide, 1/4 in. thick. Made of gray brown chert.
Priv. col., excellent quality, valued $45-65.

- Sublet Ferry from Bullock co., AL. Blade 3 2/3 in. long, 1 1/8 in. wide, 3/16 in. thick. Made of quartzite.
Priv. col., average quality, valued $25-35.

- Sublet Ferry from Bullock co., AL. Point 2 1/2 in. long, 7/8 in. wide, 1/4 in. thick. Made of quartzite.
Priv. col., average quality, valued $15-25.

- Sublet Ferry from Bullock co., AL. Point 2 3/8 in. long, 1 in. wide, 3/16 in. thick. Made of quartzite.
Priv. col., average quality, valued $20-25.

- Sublet Ferry from Bullock co., AL. Point 2 7/8 in. long, 1 1/32 in. wide, 3/16 in. thick. Made of quartzite.
Priv. col., average quality, valued $25-35.

- Sublet Ferry from Allen Parish, LA. Point 2 1/3 in. long, 7/8 in. wide, 1/4 in. thick. Made of banded red chert.
Priv. col., excellent quality, valued $45-65.

- Sublet Ferry from Allen Parish, LA. Point 2 1/2 in. long, 1 1/8 in. wide, 1/4 in. thick. Made of quartzite.
Priv. col., excellent quality, valued $15-25.

- Sublet Ferry from Allen Parish, LA. Point 2 7/8 in. long, 1 1/3 in. wide, 3/16 in. thick. Made of gray chert.
Grover Bohannon col., excellent quality, valued $45-65.

- Sublet Ferry from Russell co., VA. Point 2 1/4 in. long, 7/8 in. wide, 1/8 in. thick. Made of brown chert.
Priv. col., excellent quality, valued $45-65.

- Sublet Ferry from Russell co., VA. Point 2 3/4 in. long, 1 in. wide, 1/4 in. thick. Made of gray chert.

Priv. col., excellent quality, valued $45-65.

• Sublet Ferry from Russell co., VA. Point 2 7/8 in. long, 1 1/8 in. wide, 3/16 in. thick. Made of pink quartzite.
Priv. col., excellent quality, valued $45-65.

• Sublet Ferry from Page co., VA. Point 2 1/3 in. long, 1 1/16 in. wide, 1/8 in. thick. Made of brown chert.
Priv. col., excellent quality, valued $35-45.

• Sublet Ferry from Page co., VA. Point 2 3/4 in. long, 1 1/8 in. wide, 1/4 in. thick. Made of brown chert.
Priv. col., excellent quality, valued $45-65.

• Sublet Ferry from Page co., VA. Point 2 5/8 in. long, 7/8 in. wide, 1/4 in. thick. Made of quartzite.
Priv. col., average quality, valued $25-35.

• Sublet Ferry from Halifax co., VA. Point 2 1/3 in. long, 7/8 in. wide, 3/16 in. thick. Made of brown chert.
Priv. col., excellent quality, valued $40-60.

• Sublet Ferry from Halifax co., VA. Point 2 1/2 in. long, 1 in. wide, 1/4 in. thick. Made of brown chert.
Priv. col., excellent quality, valued $45-65.

• Sublet Ferry from Halifax co., VA. Point 2 7/8 in. long, 1 1/3 in. wide, 3/16 in. thick. Made of quartzite.
Priv. col., excellent quality, valued $45-65.

• Sublet Ferry from Lewis co., WV. Point 2 2/3 in. long, 1 1/8 in. wide, 3/16 in. thick. Made of pink chert.
Priv. col., excellent quality, valued $45-65.

• Sublet Ferry from Lewis co., WV. Point 2 3/4 in. long, 1 in. wide, 1/4 in. thick. Made of brown chert.
Priv. col., excellent quality, valued $45-65.

• Sublet Ferry from Lewis co., WV. Point 2 7/8 in. long, 1 1/2 in. wide, 1/8 in. thick. Made of gray chert.
Priv. col., excellent quality, valued $45-65.

Sumter: 8,000-6,000 B.P. Early Archaic

Predominantly found in southeastern states. Medium to large sized point or blade. Broad, thick, with weak tapered shoulders and contracting stems.

♦ Sumter from Booneville, NC. Point 1 1/2 in. long, 1 1/4 in. wide, 1/4 in. thick. Classic Sumter. Made of quartzite.

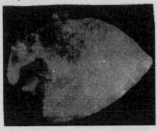

Grover Bohannon col., excellent quality, valued $5-10.

• Sumter from Ohio co., WV. Blade 4 1/2 in. long, 2 1/4 in. wide, 1/4 in. thick. Made of pink slate.
Priv. col., excellent quality, valued $35-40.

• Sumter from Ohio co., WV. Point 2 1/3 in. long, 1 3/4 in. wide, 1/4 in. thick. Made of quartzite.
Priv. col., average quality, valued $5-10.

• Sumter from Tyler co., WV. Blade 4 1/2 in. long, 2 1/4 in. wide, 1/4 in. thick. Made of pink slate.
Priv. col., excellent quality, valued $35-40.

• Sumter from Grayson co., VA. Blade 4 1/2 in. long, 2 1/4 in. wide, 1/4 in. thick. Made of pink chert.
Priv. col., excellent quality, valued $35-40.

• Sumter from Grayson co., VA. Blade 3 2/3 in. long, 1 3/4 in. wide, 1/4 in. thick. Made of gray chert.
Priv. col., average quality, valued $5-10.

• Sumter from Grayson co., VA. Blade 4 1/2 in. long, 2 1/4 in. wide, 1/4 in. thick. Made of gray chert.
Priv. col., excellent quality, valued $35-40.

- Sumter from Ben Hill co., GA. Blade 4 1/3 in. long, 2 1/2 in. wide, 1/4 in. thick. Made of pink black speckled chert.
Priv. col., excellent quality, valued $35-40.

- Sumter from Ben Hill co., GA. Blade 4 1/16 in. long, 1 1/2 in. wide, 1/4 in. thick. Made of quartzite.
Priv. col., average quality, valued $15-20.

- Sumter from Ben Hill co., GA. Blade 4 1/2 in. long, 2 1/4 in. wide, 1/4 in. thick. Made of gray chert.
Priv. col., excellent quality, valued $35-40.

- Sumter from Dawson co., GA. Blade 4 1/16 in. long, 2 1/3 in. wide, 1/4 in. thick. Made of pink chert.
Priv. col., excellent quality, valued $35-40.

- Sumter from Dawson co., GA. Blade 3 7/8 in. long, 1 3/4 in. wide, 1/4 in. thick. Made of quartzite.
Priv. col., average quality, valued $10-15.

- Sumter from Dawson co., GA. Blade 4 1/32 in. long, 2 1/8 in. wide, 1/4 in. thick. Made of gray chert.
Priv. col., excellent quality, valued $35-40.

- Sumter from Dawson co., GA. Blade 4 in. long, 2 1/16 in. wide, 1/4 in. thick. Made of pink slate.
Priv. col., average quality, valued $20-30.

- Sumter from Wheeler co., GA. Point 2 2/3 in. long, 1 3/4 in. wide, 1/4 in. thick. Made of quartzite.
Priv. col., average quality, valued $5-10.

- Sumter from Wheeler co., GA. Blade 4 1/32 in. long, 2 1/8 in. wide, 1/4 in. thick. Made of quartzite.
Priv. col., average quality, valued $15-20.

- Sumter from Wheeler co., GA. Blade 4 1/4 in. long, 2 1/3 in. wide, 1/4 in. thick. Made of pink black speckled chert.
Priv. col., excellent quality, valued $35-40.

- Sumter from Wheeler co., GA. Point 2 1/3 in. long, 1 3/4 in. wide, 1/4 in. thick. Made of quartzite.
Priv. col., average quality, valued $5-10.

- Sumter from Wheeler co., GA. Point 3 1/32 in. long, 2 1/8 in. wide, 1/4 in. thick. Made of greenish chert.
Priv. col., excellent quality, valued $35-40.

- Sumter from Wheeler co., GA. Blade 4 in. long, 1 7/8 in. wide, 1/4 in. thick. Made of pink white chert.
Priv. col., excellent quality, valued $35-40.

- Sumter from Wilkes co., GA. Point 2 2/3 in. long, 1 3/4 in. wide, 1/4 in. thick. Made of quartzite.
Priv. col., average quality, valued $5-10.

- Sumter from Wilkes co., GA. Point 2 1/2 in. long, 2 in. wide, 1/4 in. thick. Made of white pebble chert.
Priv. col., excellent quality, valued $35-40.

- Sumter from Coffee co., GA. Blade 4 in. long, 1 7/8 in. wide, 1/4 in. thick. Made of marble tan chert.
Priv. col., excellent quality, valued $35-40.

- Sumter from Coffee co., GA. Blade 4 1/3 in. long, 1 3/4 in. wide, 1/4 in. thick. Made of tan chert.
Priv. col., average quality, valued $5-10.

- Sumter from Coffee co., GA. Blade 4 1/2 in. long, 2 in. wide, 1/4 in. thick. Made of gray slate.
Priv. col., excellent quality, valued $35-40.

- Sumter from Coffee co., GA. Blade 4 1/4 in. long, 1 3/4 in. wide, 1/4 in. thick. Made of gray slate.
Priv. col., excellent quality, valued $35-40.

- Sumter from Effingham co., GA. Point 2 1/3 in. long, 1 1/4 in. wide, 1/4 in. thick. Made of quartzite.
Priv. col., average quality, valued $5-10.

- Sumter from Effingham co., GA. Point 2 1/2 in. long, 1 1/4 in. wide, 1/8 in. thick. Made of dull gray slate.
Priv. col., excellent quality, valued $35-40.

CHAPTER 15
TABLE ROCK-TURKYETAIL

Table Rock: 4,000-3,000 B.P. Late Archaic

Found thoughout the Midwest and into the Northeast. A medium to large sized point or blade. Expanded pieces with straight to tapered shoulders. Usually sharp edged points.

♦ Table Rock from northeastern AR. Point 2 1/8 in. long, 1 in. wide, 1/8 in. thick. Parallel stem, convex base, straight sharp shoulders. Sharp edge, and sharp pointed tip. Made of pink marbled chert.

Priv. col., museum quality, valued $15-25.

• Table Rock from St. Francis co., AR. Point 2 7/8 in. long, 1 1/4 in. wide, 1/8 in. thick. Made of gray chert.
Priv. col., excellent quality, valued $15-25.

• Table Rock from St. Francis co., AR. Point 2 1/2 in. long, 7/8 in. wide, 1/8 in. thick. Made of gray chert.
Priv. col., excellent quality, valued $15-25.

• Table Rock from Ashley co., AR. Point 3 1/8 in. long, 1 1/3 in. wide,

1/8 in. thick. Made of Arkansas brown chert.
Priv. col., museum quality, valued $25-35.

- Table Rock from Adams co., IN. Point 3 1/16 in. long, 1 1/2 in. wide, 1/8 in. thick. Made of greenish white chert.
Priv. col., museum quality, valued $20-30.

- Table Rock from Adams co., IN. Point 3 1/2 in. long, 1 3/8 in. wide, 1/8 in. thick. Made of gray chert.
Priv. col., excellent quality, valued $15-25.

- Table Rock from Adams co., IN. Point 3 1/8 in. long, 1 1/3 in. wide, 1/8 in. thick. Made of white pebble chert.
Priv. col., excellent quality, valued $25-35.

- Table Rock from Adams co., IN. Point 2 3/16 in. long, 1 1/32 in. wide, 1/8 in. thick. Made of white chert.
Priv. col., excellent quality, valued $15-20.

- Table Rock from St. Clair co., MO. Blade 4 1/2 in. long, 2 in. wide, 1/4 in. thick. Made of white chert.
Priv. col., excellent quality, valued $35-45.

- Table Rock from St. Clair co., MO. Blade 4 1/8 in. long, 1 2/3 in. wide, 1/3 in. thick. Excellent workmanship, heat treated. Made of Mill Creek chert.
Priv. col., museum quality, valued $35-50.

- Table Rock from New Madrid co., MO. Point 3 in. long, 1 13/32 in. wide, 1/8 in. thick. Made of gray chert.
Tim Rubbles col., excellent quality, valued $20-30.

- Table Rock from New Madrid co., MO. Point 2 7/16 in. long, 1 3/8 in. wide, 3/16 in. thick. Made of gray white chert.
Priv. col., excellent quality, valued $15-25.

- Table Rock from New Madrid co., MO. Point 3 1/16 in. long, 1 2/3 in. wide, 1/4 in. thick. Poor workmanship. Made of brown chert.
Priv. col., average quality, valued $5-10.

• Table Rock from Dade co., MO. Blade 5 1/16 in. long, 2 in. wide, 1/8 in. thick. Excellent workmanship. Made of pinkish white chert.
Priv. col., museum quality, valued $50-70.

• Table Rock from St. Clair co., MO. Blade 5 1/2 in. long, 1 7/8 in. wide, 1/8 in. thick. Good workmanship. Made of gray chert.
Priv. col., excellent quality, valued $35-45.

• Table Rock from Holt co., MO. Blade 4 3/8 in. long, 1 2/3 in. wide, 1/8 in. thick. Made of gray chert.
Priv. col., excellent quality, valued $35-45.

• Table Rock from Jasper co., IL. Point 2 9/16 in. long, 1 1/4 in. wide, 1/8 in. thick. Made of greenish white chert.
Priv. col., excellent quality, valued $20-30.

• Table Rock from Alexander co., IL. Point 2 1/2 in. long, 1 3/32 in. wide, 1/8 in. thick. Made of gray chert.
Priv. col., excellent quality, valued $15-25.

• Table Rock from Alexander co., IL. Point 3 1/4 in. long, 1 1/2 in. wide, 1/8 in. thick. Made of Mill Creek chert.
Priv. col., excellent quality, valued $25-35.

• Table Rock from Alexander co., IL. Point 3 5/16 in. long, 1 1/2 in. wide, 1/8 in. thick. Made of gray white chert.
Priv. col., excellent quality, valued $10-20.

• Table Rock from Johnson co., IL. Blade 4 1/2 in. long, 1 7/8 in. wide, 3/16 in. thick. Made of gray chert.
Priv. col., excellent quality, valued $25-35.

• Table Rock from Johnson co., IL. Point 3 5/8 in. long, 1 3/4 in. wide, 1/8 in. thick. Made of Mill Creek chert.
Priv. col., excellent quality, valued $25-35.

• Table Rock from Johnson co., IL. Blade 5 1/16 in. long, 2 1/16 in. wide, 1/8 in. thick. Excellent workmanship. Made of Mill Creek chert.
Priv. col., museum quality, valued $50-60.

Talco: 800-500 B.P. Mississippian to Historic

Predominantly found in the midwestern states. Small to medium sized point. Triangular point, narrow, finely serrated edges, concave base.

♦ Talco from Hamilton co., TN. Point 1 1/4 in. long, 3/4 in. wide, 1/8 in. thick. Small triangular, slight tip break, one edge finely serrated. Made of milky quartz.

Grover Bohannon col., average quality, valued $10-15.

♦ Talco from Hamilton co., TN. Point 1 1/8 in. long, 1/2 in. wide, 1/8 in. thick. Finely, sharply serrated, very fine and sharp tip. Concave base. Made of gray chert.

Grover Bohannon col., museum quality, $30-40.

• Talco from Hamilton co., TN. Point 1 3/4 in. long, 3/4 in. wide, 3/16 in. thick. Made of gray chert.
Priv. col., excellent quality, valued $15-25.

• Talco from Hamilton co., TN. Point 1 1/3 in. long, 5/8 in. wide, 1/8 in. thick. Concave base. Made of gray chert.
Grover Bohannon col., excellent quality, $20-30.

• Talco from Overton co., TN. Point 1 1/2 in. long, 13/16 in. wide, 1/8 in. thick. Made of quartzite.
Grover Bohannon col., average quality, valued $10-15.

• Talco from Chester co., TN. Point 1 in. long, 1/2 in. wide, 1/8 in. thick. Made of gray chert.
Priv. col., excellent quality, $20-30.

• Talco from Sevier co., TN. Point 1 1/4 in. long, 5/8 in. wide, 1/8 in. thick. Made of milky quartz.

Priv. col., museum quality, valued $40-45.

• Talco from Sevier co., TN. Point 1 3/8 in. long, 7/8 in. wide, 1/8 in. thick. Excellent workmanship. Made of jasper.
Priv. col., museum quality, $50-70.

• Talco from Davidson co., TN. Point 2 1/4 in. long, 7/8 in. wide, 3/16 in. thick. Made of gray chert.
Priv. col., excellent quality, valued $15-25.

• Talco from Stewart co., TN. Point 1 3/4 in. long, 2/3 in. wide, 1/8 in. thick. Made of gray chert.
Priv. col., excellent quality, $20-30.

• Talco from Greene co., TN. Point 2 1/2 in. long, 1 1/16 in. wide, 1/8 in. thick. Made of Dover chert.
Priv. col., museum quality, valued $40-45.

• Talco from Giles co., TN. Point 1 7/8 in. long, 2/3 in. wide, 3/16 in. thick. Made of gray chert.
Priv. col., excellent quality, valued $30-35.

• Talco from Henderson co., KY. Point 2 1/4 in. long, 7/8 in. wide, 3/16 in. thick. Made of tan chert.
Priv. col., excellent quality, valued $25-35.

• Talco from Hopkins co., KY. Point 1 1/2 in. long, 11/16 in. wide, 3/16 in. thick. Made of marbled gray chert.
Priv. col., excellent quality, $20-30.

• Talco from Lawrence co., KY. Point 1 1/2 in. long, 1 5/16 in. wide, 1/4 in. thick. Very broad, poor workmanship. Made of quartzite.
Priv. col., poor quality, valued $2-5.

• Talco from Cumberland co., KY. Point 7/8 in. long, 7/16 in. wide, 1/8 in. thick. Excellent workmanship, finely serrated and flaked. Made of oily gray chert.
Priv. col., museum quality, valued $40-50.

• Talco from Bullitt co., KY. Point 1 2/3 in. long, 3/4 in. wide, 3/16 in. thick. Made of gray chert.
Priv. col., excellent quality, valued $15-25.

• Talco from Cardin co., PA. Point 1 1/2 in. long, 13/16 in. wide, 1/8 in. thick. Made of gray chert.
Priv. col., excellent quality, $20-30.

• Talco from Snyder co., PA. Point 1 2/3 in. long, 1 in. wide, 1/8 in. thick. Made of green chert.
Priv. col., excellent quality, valued $20-25.

• Talco from Bedford co., PA. Point 1 7/8 in. long, 11/16 in. wide, 1/8 in. thick. Made of gray chert.
Priv. col., excellent quality, valued $35-55.

• Talco from Bedford co., PA. Point 1 3/4 in. long, 7/8 in. wide, 3/16 in. thick. Made of banded slate.
Priv. col., excellent quality, valued $15-25.

• Talco from Bedford co., PA. Point 1 1/2 in. long, 7/8 in. wide, 1/8 in. thick. Made of banded slate.
Priv. col., excellent quality, $20-30.

• Talco from Mercer co., OH. Point 2 in. long, 1 3/16 in. wide, 1/8 in. thick. Made of banded slate.
Priv. col., average quality, valued $10-15.

• Talco from Morrow co., OH. Point 1 1/3 in. long, 7/8 in. wide, 1/8 in. thick. Made of dense white chert.
Priv. col., excellent quality, valued $20-30.

Texas Blade: 4,000-1,000 B.P. Late Archaic to Woodland

Found almost exclusively in Texas. Medium to large point or blade. Often beveled, convex to straight base, broad lanceolate point or blade.

◆ Texas Blade from Lubbock co., Texas. Blade 3 3/4 in. long, 2 1/8 in. wide, 3/16 in. thick. Beveled on one side of both edges and highly serrated. Blade once broken and repaired. Made of gray chert.

Grover Bohannon col., average quality, valued $25-40.

• Texas Point from Littlerock, AR. Point 2 !/4 in. long, 1 1/2 in. wide, 1/4 in. thick. Sharp tip, edges gradually beveled, convex base. Made of black flint. *Grover Bohannon col., excellent quality, valued $40-55.*

• Texas Blade from Lubbock co., TX. Blade 4 3/4 in. long, 2 in. wide, 1/4 in. thick. Made of gray chert. *Grover Bohannon col., excellent quality, valued $25-40.*

• Texas Point from Lubbock co., TX. Blade 5 1/4 in. long, 2 1/4 in. wide, 1/4 in. thick. Made of dull gray chert. *Grover Bohannon col., excellent quality, valued $40-55.*

• Texas Blade from Lubbock co., TX. Blade 5 1/2 in. long, 2 1/8 in. wide, 3/16 in. thick. Made of gray chert. *Priv. col., excellent quality, valued $35-40.*

• Texas Point from Reagan co., TX. Point 2 1/2 in. long, 1 1/32 in. wide, 1/8 in. thick. Made of gray chert. *Priv. col., excellent quality, valued $40-50.*

• Texas Blade from Reagan co., TX. Blade 4 7/8 in. long, 2 in. wide, 3/16 in. thick. Made of gray chert. *Priv. col., excellent quality, valued $30-40.*

• Texas Point from Reagan co., TX. Point 3 1/3 in. long, 1 1/4 in. wide, 3/16 in. thick. Edges reworked. Made of white chert. *Priv. col., excellent quality, valued $40-45.*

• Texas Point from Midland co., TX. Blade 4 1/4 in. long, 1 7/8 in. wide, 1/4 in. thick. Made of dull gray chert. *Priv. col., excellent quality, valued $45-50.*

- Texas Blade from Midland co., TX. Blade 4 7/8 in. long, 2 1/8 in. wide, 3/16 in. thick. Made of gray chert.
Priv. col., excellent quality, valued $30-40.

- Texas Point from Midland co., TX. Blade 3 31/32 in. long, 1 1/2 in. wide, 3/16 in. thick. Made of tan white chert.
Priv. col., excellent quality, valued $40-55.

- Texas Point from Sutton co., TX. Blade 5 1/2 in. long, 2 1/2 in. wide, 1/4 in. thick. Excellent workmanship, steeply beveled on all four sides. Made of dull gray chert.
Priv. col., museum quality, valued $60-75.

- Texas Blade from Sutton co., TX. Blade 3 7/8 in. long, 1 7/16 in. wide, 3/16 in. thick. Made of gray chert.
Priv. col., excellent quality, valued $30-40.

- Texas Point from Sutton co., TX. Point 3 1/16 in. long, 1 5/8 in. wide, 3/16 in. thick. Made of tan chert.
Priv. col., excellent quality, valued $40-50.

- Texas Point from Crockett co., TX. Point 2 5/8 in. long, 1 1/8 in. wide, 1/4 in. thick. Made of gray flint.
Priv. col., excellent quality, valued $30-35.

- Texas Blade from Crockett co., TX. Point 3 1/8 in. long, 1 7/8 in. wide, 1/4 in. thick. Made of gray flint.
Priv. col., excellent quality, valued $30-40.

- Texas Point from Parker co., TX. Point 3 1/3 in. long, 1 7/16 in. wide, 1/4 in. thick. Good workmanship. Made of quartzite.
Priv. col., average quality, valued $20-25.

- Texas Point from Webb co., TX. Point 2 3/8 in. long, 1 1/4 in. wide, 1/4 in. thick. Made of silver gray flint.
Priv. col., excellent quality, valued $30-35.

- Texas Blade from Webb co., TX. Blade 4 7/8 in. long, 2 1/8 in. wide, 3/16 in. thick. Made of tan white chert.
Priv. col., excellent quality, valued $30-40.

• Texas Point from Webb co., TX. Point 3 3/32 in. long, 1 5/8 in. wide, 3/16 in. thick. Made of tan white chert.
Priv. col., excellent quality, valued $30-35.

• Texas Point from Webb co., TX. Point 2 7/8 in. long, 1 1/8 in. wide, 1/4 in. thick. Made of dull gray flint.
Priv. col., excellent quality, valued $40-55.

• Texas Blade from Kimble co., TX. Point 3 1/8 in. long, 1 1/2 in. wide, 3/16 in. thick. Made of gray chert.
Priv. col., excellent quality, valued $30-40.

• Texas Point from Childress co., TX. Point 3 1/2 in. long, 1 1/2 in. wide, 1/4 in. thick. Made of yellow chert.
Priv. col., excellent quality, valued $30-45.

Thebes: 10,000-8,000 B.P. Early Archaic

Predominantly found in the Midwest. Medium to large size point or blade. Deeply side notched, highly serrated edges. Many examples are beveled and reworked. Bases are broad and parallel, straight or concave and ground.

♦ Thebes from Galesburg, IL. Point 3 in. long, 2 in. wide, 1/4 in. thick. Deeply notched, highly serrated angular point. Beveled on one side of each face. Concave base with flaring tangs. Made of blue white chert.

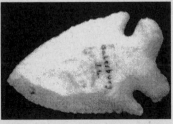

Priv. col., excellent quality, valued $325-450.

♦ Thebes from Green co., IL. Blade 5 1/2 in. long, 2 3/16 in. wide, 1/4 in. thick. Deep corner notches, straight base, highly serrated edges. Very sharp, heavy field patina, slight tip break. Made of white pebble chert.

Tim Crawford col., average quality, valued $125-175.

♦ Thebes from Greene co., IL. Blade 5 1/2 in. long, 2 in. wide, 1/4 in. thick. Deeply corner notched, triangular blade, highly serrated sharp edges. High quality workmanship, heavy field patina. Made of Mill Creek chert.

Tim Crawford col., museum quality, valued $2,300-2,500.

♦ Thebes from Union co., IL. Blade 5 5/8 in. long, 2 1/8 in. wide, 1/4 in. thick. Deep angled side notches, beveled on one side of each face. Heat treated, sharply and finely serrated. Parallel sided with concave base. Made of Mill Creek chert.

Priv. col., excellent quality, valued $200-250.

♦ Thebes from Union co., IL. Blade 5 1/8 in. long, 1 5/8 in. wide, 1/4 in. thick. Heat treated blade very symmetrical with uniform base and notches. Highly serrated with several blade nicks and tip break. Made of Mill Creek chert.

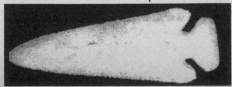

Priv. col., excellent quality, valued $450-600.

◆ Thebes from Jackson co., IL. Blade beveled on one side of each face, finely and sharply serrated. Exceptional workmanship, very symmetrical, triangular blade. Made of Mill Creek chert.

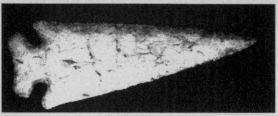

Priv. col., museum quality, valued $1,250-1,450.

◆ Thebes from Jackson co., IL. Point 2 1/8 in. long, 1 1/4 in. wide, 3/16 in. thick. Extremely fine workmanship, finely flaked and sharply serrated. Deep angular notches, wide uniform staight base. Heat treated and beveled on one edge of each side. Made of white chert.

Priv. col., museum quality, rare, valued $300-425.

◆ Thebes from Chapman River, KY. Blade 4 1/2 in. long, 1 1/2 in. wide, 1/4 in. thick. Symmetrical, rounded tip blade, quite sharp, long blade tang for a Thebes. Deep notches, uniform straight base. Made of Dover chert.

Priv. col., excellent quality, valued $85-125.

◆ Thebes from Toledo, OH. Blade 5 in. long, 1 1/2 in. wide, 1/4 in. thick. Heat treated, concave, beveled sides. Large angled straight stem very symmetrical. Made of rose colored chert.

Priv. col., excellent quality, valued $150-200.

◆ Thebes from northern OH. Point 2 1/4 in. long, 1 1/4 in. wide, 3/16 in. thick. Wide concave base, deeply notched. Beveled on one side of each face, finely serrated, distinct markings. Made of Cochocton chert.

Priv. col., excellent quality, valued $150-185.

• Thebes from Union co., IL. Blade 3 5/8 in. long, 1 1/4 in. wide, 1/4 in. thick. Heavly beveled on all four edges. Heat treated with unique near rectangular ground base. Deep uniform side notches, sharply serrated. Made of Kaolin chert *Les Grubbe col., museum quality, rare, valued $1,280-1,520.*

• Thebes from central IL. Blade 5 1/4 in. long, 2 1/4 wide, 3/16 in. thick. Fine workmanship, long, triagular, thin, finely flaked and serrated. Heavy field patina, concave base. Made of very lightweight white chert. *Les Grubbe col., museum quality, valued $1,800-2,200.*

• Thebes from Miami co., IN. Point 2 3/4 in. long, 1 1/32 in. wide, 3/16 in. thick. Heat treated. Same cache. Made of blue white chert. *Priv. col., excellent quality, valued $250-300.*

◆ Thebes from Union co., IL. Blade 4 in. long, 2 1/4 in. wide, 1/4 in. thick. Broad, rounded tip, sharply serrated. Deep side notches, anchor notched based. Made of Mill Creek chert.

Les Grubbe col., museum quality, valued $1,500-1,850.

◆ Thebes from Union co., IL. Point 3 in. long, 2 1/4 in. wide, 1/4 in. thick. Sharply serrrated edges, beveled on one side of each face. Deeply notched with thin concave base. Made of Mill Creek chert.

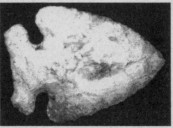

Les Grubbe col., excellent quality, valued $380-450.

◆ Thebes from Union co., IL. Point 2 1/2 in. long, 2 3/16 in. wide, 5/8 in. thick. Nicely beveled on one side of each face. Symmetrical point with rectangular concave base. Made of quartz.

Les Grubbe col., average quality, valued $75-125.

• Thebes from Union co., IL. Blade 3 3/4 in. long, 1 5/16 in. wide, 1/4 in. thick. Long angular blade, deeply notched, small slightly rectangular concave base. Made of Kaolin chert.
Les Grubbe col., average quality, rare, $260-325.

◆ Thebes from Union co., IL. Point 3 in. long, 1 1/2 in. wide, 1/4 in. thick. Wide, sharp point highly serrated, extremely sharp tip. Parallel shoulders with concave stem and base, heavy field patina. Made of Mill Creek chert.

Les Grubbe col., museum quality, valued $345-400.

◆ Thebes from Johnson co., IL. Blade 3 3/4 in. long, 2 1/4 in. wide, 3/16 in. thick. Wide, lightweight, deeply notched, several edge nicks, concave base.

Les Grubbe col., excellent quality, valued $200-250.

• Thebes from Stewart co., TN. Point 1 5/16 in. long, 3/4 in. wide, 3/16 in. thick. Wide sharp serrations, beveled on one side of each face. Made of Cobden Hornstone chert.
Grover Bohannon col., museum quality, valued $650-800.

◆ Thebes from Johnson co., IL. Point 2 1/16 in. long, 1 1/2 in. wide, 3/16 in. thick. Steeply beveled, deeply notched, very rounded base, convex. Made of white chert.

Les Grubbe col., museum quality, valued $325-400.

• Thebes from Union co., IL. Blade 4 2/3 in. long, 2 1/4 in. wide, 1/4 in. thick. Excellent workmanship. Made of Kaolin chert.
Priv. col., museum quality, rare, valued $1,500-1,850.

• Thebes from Union co., IL. Point 3 1/2 in. long, 1 7/8 in. wide, 3/16 in. thick. Excellent workmanship. Made of Cobden chert.
Priv. col., museum quality, valued $800-950.

• Thebes from Union co., IL. Point 2 2/3 in. long, 2 3/16 in. wide 5/8 in. thick. Made of Cobden chert.
Priv. col., excellent quality, valued $175-225.

• Thebes from Jackson co., IL. Point 3 1/4 in. long, 1 1/16 in. wide, 1/4 in. thick. Made of Kaolin chert.
Les Grubbe col., excellent quality, rare, $300-350.

• Thebes from Jackson co., IL. Point 3 1/2 in. long, 1 1/2 in. wide, 3/16 in. thick. Made of gray white pebble chert.
Tim Rubbles col., excellent quality, valued $150-200.

• Thebes from Miami co., IN. Blade 4 1/8 in. long, 2 in. wide, 1/4 in. thick. Heat treated. Part of cache find. Made of greenish chert.
Priv. col., excellent quality, valued $500-650.

• Thebes from Miami co., IN. Point 3 1/3 in. long, 1 7/8 in. wide, 3/16 in. thick. Excellent workmanship, heat treated. Same cache. Made of green speckled chert.
Priv. col., museum quality, valued $600-750.

• Thebes from Miami co., IN. Point 2 1/2 in. long, 1 3/16 in. wide 3/8 in. thick. Material generally found in the Wabash Valley. Heat treated. Same cache. Made of white blue chert.
Priv. col., excellent quality, valued $275-350.

• Thebes from Miami co., IN. Point 3 1/32 in. long, 1 1/8 in. wide, 3/16 in. thick. Heat treated. Same cache. Made of white pebble chert.
Priv. col., excellent quality, $300-375.

• Thebes from Davies co., MO. Blade 4 1/2 in. long, 2 1/32 in. wide, 3/16 in. thick. Good workmanship. Made of white pebble chert.
Priv. col., excellent quality, valued $300-350.

• Thebes from Davies co., MO. Blade 4 1/2 in. long, 1 7/8 in. wide, 3/8 in. thick. Good workmanship. Made of tan yellow chert.
Priv. col., excellent quality, valued $400-450.

• Thebes from Cape Giradeau co., MO. Point 2 7/16 in. long, 2 in. wide, 7/16 in. thick. Made of quartzite.
Priv. col., average quality, valued $75-100.

• Thebes from Cape Giradeau co., MO. Point 3 in. long, 1 3/16 in. wide, 1/4 in. thick. Made of local white chert.
Priv. col., excellent quality, $300-350.

• Thebes from Cape Giradeau co., MO. Point 2 13/32 in. long, 1 1/2 in. wide, 3/16 in. thick. Made of local white chert.
Priv. col., excellent quality, valued $150-200.

• Thebes from Searcy co., AR. Blade 4 7/8 in. long, 2 in. wide, 1/4 in. thick. Excellent workmanship, steeply beveled, reworked edges. Made of Arkansas brown chert.
Priv. col., museum quality, valued $1,000-1,250.

• Thebes from Lee co., AR. Blade 5 1/2 in. long, 2 5/8 in. wide, 1/8 in. thick. Excellent workmanship, thinly flaked. Made of black flint.
Priv. col., museum quality, valued $600-650.

• Thebes from Hempstead co., AR. Blade 3 27/32 in. long, 1 5/16 in. wide, 7/16 in. thick. Made of quartzite.
Priv. col., average quality, valued $75-125.

• Thebes from Calhoun co., AR. Blade 5 1/4 in. long, 1 7/16 in. wide, 1/4 in. thick. Narrow, heat treated with highly serrated reworked edges. Made of Arkansas brown chert.
Priv. col., excellent quality, rare, $1,300-1,450.

• Thebes from Calhoun co., AR. Point 3 1/4 in. long, 1 1/2 in. wide, 3/16 in. thick. Made of white pink black speckled pebble chert.
Priv. col., excellent quality, valued $250-300.

Tortugas: 6,000-1,000 B.P. Mid-Archaic to Woodland

Predominantly a midwestern point found into the Southeast. Medium sized, thickly triangular point. Straight to concave, convex base, generally thinned. May be beveled on one side of each face.

◆ Tortugas from Stewart co., TN. Point 1 3/4 in. long, 1 1/4 in. wide, 1/4 in. thick. Point broad, thick, roughly serrated, concave base. Made of pink pebble chert.

Priv. col., average quality, valued $5-10.

◆ Tortugas from Hardin co., IL. Point 1 5/16 in. long, 7/16 in. wide, 1/4 in. thick. Sharply beveled on one side of each face. Slightly concave base, sharply serrated edges. Made of white quartz.

Grover Bohannon col., excellent quality, valued $15-25.

• Tortugas from Hamilton co., TN. Blade 3 1/8 in. long, 1 7/16 in. wide, 5/16 in. thick. Slight tip break. Finely serrated, thinned straight base. Made of black flint.
Grover Bohannon col., poor quality, valued $2-5.

• Tortugas from Stewart co., TN. Point 2 1/4 in. long, 1 1/4 in. wide, 3/16 in. thick. Made of quartzite.
Grover Bohannon col., average quality, valued $5-10.

• Tortugas from Stewart co., TN. Point 1 15/16 in. long, 11/16 in. wide, 1/4 in. thick. Made of Dover chert.
Grover Bohannon col., museum quality, valued $25-35.

• Tortugas from Henderson co., TN. Blade 3 7/8 in. long, 2 1/16 in. wide, 5/32 in. thick. Made of banded brown chert.
Grover Bohannon col., excellent quality, valued $30-35.

• Tortugas from Monroe co., MO. Point 2 3/4 in. long, 1 1/4 in. wide, 3/16 in. thick. Made of white chert.
Priv. col., average quality, valued $5-10.

• Tortugas from Monroe co., MO. Point 2 5/16 in. long, 1 1/16 in. wide, 5/32 in. thick. Made of Mill Creek chert.
Priv. col., excellent quality, valued $20-30.

• Tortugas from Monroe co., MO. Blade 4 7/8 in. long, 2 5/16 in. wide, 5/16 in. thick. Made of marbled brown white chert.
Priv. col., excellent quality, valued $30-35.

- Tortugas from Clay co., MO. Point 2 1/2 in. long, 1 1/3 in. wide, 3/16 in. thick. Made of pink quartzite.
Tim Rubbles col., average quality, valued $5-10.

- Tortugas from Clay co., MO. Point 1 11/16 in. long, 5/8 in. wide, 1/4 in. thick. Excellent workmanship. Made of dense white chert.
Tim Rubbles col., museum quality, valued $25-35.

- Tortugas from Bolinger co., MO. Blade 4 3/8 in. long, 2 3/16 in. wide, 3/16 in. thick. Made of tan chert.
Tim Rubbles col., excellent quality, valued $30-35.

- Tortugas from Wabash co., IN. Point 2 1/3 in. long, 1 1/4 in. wide, 3/16 in. thick. Beveled, highly serrated, excellent workmanship. Made of local green chert.
Priv. col., museum quality, valued $45-60.

- Tortugas from Wabash co., IN. Point 2 11/16 in. long, 13/16 in. wide, 5/32 in. thick. Excellent workmanship. Made of green chert.
Priv. col., museum quality, valued $45-55.

- Tortugas from Wabash co., IN. Blade 4 1/8 in. long, 2 3/16 in. wide, 5/32 in. thick. Excellent workmanship, minutely serrated edges. Made of local green chert.
Priv. col., museum quality, valued $50-55.

- Tortugas from Wabash co., IN. Blade 3 15/16 in. long, 1 1/4 in. wide, 3/16 in. thick. Good workmanship. Made of white pebble chert.
Priv. col., museum quality, valued $35-40.

- Tortugas from Bibb co., AL. Point 2 5/16 in. long, 1 1/16 in. wide, 1/4 in. thick. Made of quartzite.
Priv. col., average quality, valued $5-15.

- Tortugas from Bibb co., AL. Blade 4 5/8 in. long, 2 1/8 in. wide, 1/8 in. thick. Finely flaked, excellent workmanship. Made of banded red white chert.
Priv. col., museum quality, valued $50-65.

- Tortugas from Bibb co., AL. Point 2 2/3 in. long, 1 5/32 in. wide, 3/16 in. thick. Made of quartzite.
Priv. col., average quality, valued $5-10.

- Tortugas from Coosa co., AL. Point 2 in. long, 1 1/16 in. wide, 1/4 in. thick. Made of high grade quartzite.
Priv. col., excellent quality, valued $25-35.

- Tortugas from Bullock co., AL. Blade 3 31/32 in. long, 2 in. wide, 3/32 in. thick. Excellent workmanship. Made of banded red brown chert.
Priv. col., excellent quality, valued $30-35.

Turkeytail: 4,500-2,500 B.P. Late Archaic to Woodland

Predominantly midwestern, also found into the Southeast. Medium to large sized point or blade. Commonly elliptical, shallow side notches. Very unique and distinct stem, convex, occasional straight base tip.

◆ Turkeytail from Murphysboro co., TN. Blade 4 5/8 in. long, 1 1/2 in. wide, 1/4 in. thick. Blade narrow, deeply serrated, multiple flaking levels, slight tip break. Classic stem, straight snap tip base. Made of light gray chert.

Grover Bohannon col., average quality, valued $300-375.

◆ Turkeytail from Hamilton co., TN. Point 3 5/16 in. long, 1 5/8 in. wide, 1/8 in. thick. Thin, sharply serrated, random flaked, sharp pointed tip. Rounded turkeytail base below shallow corner notches. Made of Dover chert.

Grover Grover col., museum quality, rare, valued $650-800.

- Turkeytail from Harrison co., MO. Blade 5 3/16 in. long, 2 5/8 in. wide, 1/8 in. thick. Excellent workmanship, classical tail. Made of pink chert. *Priv. col., museum quality, valued $500-600.*

- Turkeytail from Effingham co., IL. Blade 4 7/8 in. long, 1 11/16 in. wide, 1/4 in. thick. Made of gray chert. *Priv. col., excellent quality, valued $300-375.*

- Turkeytail from Hamilton co., IL. Point 3 5/32 in. long, 1 1/2 in. wide, 1/8 in. thick. Good workmanship. Made of Mill Creek chert. *Priv. col., excellent quality, valued $250-300.*

- Turkeytail from Hamilton co., IL. Blade 5 1/16 in. long, 2 3/8 in. wide, 3/32 in. thick. Excellent workmanship. Made of pink black speckled chert. *Priv. col., museum quality, valued $575-650.*

- Turkeytail from Effingham co., GA. Blade 5 7/8 in. long, 2 7/16 in. wide, 1/4 in. thick. Made of gray chert. *Priv. col., excellent quality, valued $300-375.*

- Turkeytail from Harris co., GA. Blade 6 15/32 in. long, 2 2/3 in. wide, 1/8 in. thick. Excellent workmanship. Made of banded slate. *Priv. col., museum quality, valued $850-1,000.*

- Turkeytail from Harris co., GA. Blade 5 7/16 in. long, 2 5/8 in. wide, 5/32 in. thick. Excellent workmanship. Made of blue white chert. *Priv. col., museum quality, valued $750-850.*

- Turkeytail from Echols co., GA. Blade 5 7/8 in. long, 2 1/16 in. wide, 1/4 in. thick. Made of gray chert. *Priv. col., excellent quality, valued $300-375.*

- Turkeytail from Rabun co., GA. Point 3 in. long, 1 1/4 in. wide, 1/8 in. thick. Good workmanship. Made of green gray slate. *Priv. col., excellent quality, valued $250-300.*

- Turkeytail from Rabun co., GA. Blade 4 3/16 in. long, 2 1/4 in. wide, 5/32 in. thick. Excellent workmanship. Made of white pebble chert. *Priv. col., museum quality, valued $500-600.*

- Turkeytail from Adair co., IA. Blade 4 3/8 in. long, 1 9/16 in. wide, 1/4 in. thick. Made of gray chert.
Priv. col., excellent quality, valued $300-350.

- Turkeytail from Cedar co., IA. Point 3 in. long, 1 1/2 in. wide, 1/8 in. thick. Good workmanship, uniquely symmetrical. Made of white red marbled chert.
Priv. col., museum quality, valued $450-600.

- Turkeytail from Cedar co., IA. Blade 5 3/16 in. long, 2 1/3 in. wide, 3/16 in. thick. Made of beige chert.
Priv. col., excellent quality, valued $475-550.

- Turkeytail from Clarke co., VA. Blade 4 1/8 in. long, 2 1/16 in. wide, 1/4 in. thick. Made of gray chert.
Priv. col., excellent quality, valued $300-375.

- Turkeytail from Russell co., VA. Point 3 3/32 in. long, 1 1/3 in. wide, 3/16 in. thick. Good workmanship. Made of gray shale.
Priv. col., excellent quality, valued $150-200.

- Turkeytail from Russell co., VA. Blade 5 3/16 in. long, 2 1/8 in. wide, 5/32 in. thick. Excellent workmanship. Made of gray shale.
Priv. col., excellent quality, valued $375-450.

- Turkeytail from Iberville Parish, LA. Blade 4 5/8 in. long, 3 in. wide, 1/4 in. thick. Made of high grade quartzite.
Priv. col., excellent quality, valued $300-375.

- Turkeytail from Iberville Parish, LA. Point 3 1/2 in. long, 1 1/2 in. wide, 1/8 in. thick. Made of Bullseye chert.
Priv. col., excellent quality, valued $250-300.

- Turkeytail from Iberville Parish, LA. Blade 5 9/16 in. long, 2 7/8 in. wide, 5/32 in. thick. Excellent workmanship. Made of pinkish gray chert.
Priv. col., museum quality, valued $675-850.

- Turkeytail from Greenbrier co., WV. Blade 4 1/8 in. long, 1 13/16 in. wide, 1/4 in. thick. Made of gray flint.
Priv. col., excellent quality, valued $200-275.

- Turkeytail from Tyler co., WV. Point 3 17/32 in. long, 1 1/2 in. wide, 1/8 in. thick. Good workmanship. Made of multi-toned brown chert. *Priv. col., excellent quality, valued $350-400.*

- Turkeytail from Tyler co., WV. Blade 5 in. long, 2 3/4 in. wide, 5/32 in. thick. Made of pink pebble chert. *Priv. col., museum quality, valued $675-750.*

- Turkeytail from Livingston Parish, LA. Blade 4 3/8 in. long, 1 1/16 in. wide, 1/4 in. thick. Part of a cache find. Made of gray chert. *Priv. col., excellent quality, valued $300-375.*

- Turkeytail from Livingston Parish, LA. Point 3 15/32 in. long, 1 1/2 in. wide, 1/8 in. thick. Made of quartzite. *Priv. col., excellent quality, valued $250-300.*

- Turkeytail from Livingston Parish, LA. Blade 5 in. long, 2 1/4 in. wide, 5/32 in. thick. Made of pink chert. *Priv. col., excellent quality, valued $375-450.*

- Turkeytail from Caldwell Parish, LA. Blade 4 3/8 in. long, 1 7/16 in. wide, 1/4 in. thick. Made of gray chert. *Priv. col., excellent quality, valued $350-425.*

- Turkeytail from Caldwell Parish, LA. Point 3 13/32 in. long, 1 1/4 in. wide, 1/8 in. thick. Good workmanship. Made of gray banded chert. *Priv. col., excellent quality, valued $450-600.*

- Turkeytail from Caldwell Parish, LA. Blade 4 3/16 in. long, 2 1/8 in. wide, 7/32 in. thick. Excellent workmanship. Made of pink gray chert. *Priv. col., museum quality, valued $675-850.*

CHAPTER 16
UVALADE-ZORRA

Uvalade: 6,500-1,000 B.P. Mid-Archaic to Woodland

Predominantly midwestern found into the Southeast. Medium sized point with barbed to tapered shoulders, side notched. Often serrated, generally narrow, bifurcated base.

♦ Uvalade from Jackson co., IL. Point 2 3/4 in. long, 1 1/16 in. wide, 1/8 in. thick. Classic design, sharply serrated, bifurcated stem, side notched, barbed shoulders. Made of mauve chert.

Jim Smith col., museum quality, valued $40-60.

• Uvalade from Effingham co., IL. Point 2 7/8 in. long, 1 5/16 in. wide, 1/4 in. thick. Made of greenish gray chert.
Priv. col., excellent quality, valued $30-45.

• Uvalade from Effingham co., IL. Point 3 in. long, 1 1/4 in. wide, 1/8 in. thick. Made of white chert.
Priv. col., excellent quality, valued $35-50.

• Uvalade from Hamilton co., IL. Point 3 1/16 in. long, 2 1/8 in. wide, 5/32 in.

thick. Excellent workmanship. Made of Mill Creek chert.
Priv. col., museum quality, valued $55-65.

- Uvalade from Effingham co., IL. Point 2 7/8 in. long, 1 5/16 in. wide, 1/4 in. thick. Made of greenish gray chert.
Priv. col., excellent quality, valued $30-45.

- Uvalade from Effingham co., IL. Point 3 in. long, 1 1/4 in. wide, 1/8 in. thick. Made of white chert.
Priv. col., excellent quality, valued $35-50.

- Uvalade from Hamilton co., IL. Point 3 1/16 in. long, 2 1/8 in. wide, 5/32 in. thick. Excellent workmanship. Made of Mill Creek chert.
Priv. col., museum quality, valued $55-65.

- Uvalade from Amelia co., VA. Point 2 3/8 in. long, 1 7/16 in. wide, 1/4 in. thick. Made of gray chert.
Priv. col., excellent quality, valued $30-35.

- Uvalade from Amelia co., VA. Point 3 in. long, 1 1/3 in. wide, 1/8 in. thick. Made of white pebble chert.
Priv. col., excellent quality, valued $35-50.

- Uvalade from Amelia co., VA. Point 2 7/16 in. long, 1 3/8 in. wide, 3/16 in. thick. Made of quartzite.
Priv. col., excellent quality, valued $35-45.

- Uvalade from Essex co., VA. Point 2 5/8 in. long, 1 1/4 in. wide, 1/3 in. thick. Made of quartzite.
Priv. col., average quality, valued $10-15.

- Uvalade from Essex co., VA. Point 3 1/8 in. long, 1 1/3 in. wide, 1/8 in. thick. Made of white chert.
Priv. col., excellent quality, valued $35-45.

- Uvalade from Essex co., VA. Point 3 3/16 in. long, 2 1/8 in. wide, 5/32 in. thick. Made of flint.
Priv. col., average quality, valued $25-35.

- Uvalade from Kiowa co., OK. Point 2 5/8 in. long, 1 7/16 in. wide, 1/4 in. thick. Made of gray chert.

Priv. col., excellent quality, valued $30-35.

• Uvalade from Woods co., OK. Point 3 1/32 in. long, 1 5/8 in. wide, 1/8 in. thick. Made of white pebble chert.
Priv. col., excellent quality, valued $35-45.

• Uvalade from Woods co., OK. Point 3 5/16 in. long, 2 in. wide, 5/32 in. thick. Excellent workmanship. Made of gray chert.
Priv. col., museum quality, valued $45-55.

• Uvalade from Payne co., OK. Point 2 1/2 in. long, 1 5/32 in. wide, 1/4 in. thick. Made of gray chert.
Priv. col., excellent quality, valued $30-45.

• Uvalade from Payne co., OK. Point 2 2/3 in. long, 1 1/2 in. wide, 1/8 in. thick. Made of white tan chert.
Priv. col., excellent quality, valued $35-45.

• Uvalade from Payne co., OK. Point 3 3/16 in. long, 2 1/32 in. wide, 3/16 in. thick. Made of gray chert.
Priv. col., excellent quality, valued $45-55.

Wade: 4,500-2,500 B.P. Late Archaic to Woodland

Predominantly a southeastern point or blade, medium to large sized. Broad, corner notched, predominantly barbed point or blade. Barbs may reach to a straight, concave, convex, or sharp base.

◆ Wade from Fort Lauderdale, FL. Point 2 in. long, 1 5/16 in. wide, 1/8 in. thick. Thin finely serrated, medium length barbed tangs, bifurcated base. Made of glossy gray chert.

Priv. col., museum quality, valued $35-45.

- Wade from Fort Dixie co., FL. Point 2 1/4 in. long, 1 7/16 in. wide, 1/8 in. thick. Made of glossy gray chert.
Priv. col., museum quality, valued $35-40.

- Wade from Citrus co., FL. Point 2 1/8 in. long, 1 5/16 in. wide, 1/8 in. thick. Made of gray chert.
Priv. col., excellent quality, valued $30-40.

- Wade from Citrus co., FL. Point 2 1/4 in. long, 1 5/16 in. wide, 1/8 in. thick. Made of gray chert.
Priv. col., excellent quality, valued $35-40.

- Wade from Citrus co., FL. Point 2 1/8 in. long, 1 3/16 in. wide, 1/8 in. thick. Made of quartz.
Priv. col., excellent quality, valued $30-40.

- Wade from Gulf co., FL. Point 2 1/2 in. long, 1 5/16 in. wide, 1/8 in. thick. Made of glossy pink chert.
Priv. col., museum quality, valued $35-40.

- Wade from Gulf co., FL. Point 2 3/8 in. long, 1 5/16 in. wide, 1/8 in. thick. Made of gray multi-tone chert.
Priv. col., excellent quality, valued $30-40.

- Wade from Gilchrist co., FL. Point 2 1/2 in. long, 1 7/16 in. wide, 1/8 in. thick. Made of gray chert.
Priv. col., excellent quality, valued $35-40.

- Wade from Gilchrist co., FL. Point 2 3/8 in. long, 1 5/16 in. wide, 1/8 in. thick. Made of gray chert.
Priv. col., excellent quality, valued $30-40.

- Wade from Baker co., FL. Point 2 11/32 in. long, 1 5/16 in. wide, 1/8 in. thick. Made of quartzite.
Priv. col., average quality, valued $10-20.

- Wade from Baker co., FL. Point 2 5/8 in. long, 1 3/16 in. wide, 1/8 in. thick. Made of gray chert.
Priv. col., excellent quality, valued $30-40.

• Wade from Baker co., FL. Point 2 1/3 in. long, 1 5/16 in. wide, 1/8 in. thick. Made of gray chert.
Priv. col., excellent quality, valued $35-40.

• Wade from Baker co., FL. Point 2 7/8 in. long, 1 1/2 in. wide, 1/8 in. thick. Made of dull gray chert.
Priv. col., excellent quality, valued $30-40.

• Wade from Baker co., FL. Point 3 1/8 in. long, 1 5/16 in. wide, 1/8 in. thick. Made of banded brown chert.
Priv. col., museum quality, valued $35-45.

• Wade from Holmes co., FL. Point 2 7/8 in. long, 1 3/16 in. wide, 1/8 in. thick. Made of gray chert.
Priv. col., excellent quality, valued $30-40.

• Wade from Holmes co., FL. Point 2 1/3 in. long, 1 1/2 in. wide, 1/8 in. thick. Made of gray chert.
Priv. col., excellent quality, valued $35-40.

• Wade from Holmes co., FL. Point 2 5/8 in. long, 1 1/4 in. wide, 1/8 in. thick. Made of gray chert.
Priv. col., excellent quality, valued $30-40.

• Wade from Glades co., FL. Point 2 1/16 in. long, 1 3/8 in. wide, 1/8 in. thick. Made of glossy brown chert.
Priv. col., museum quality, valued $35-40.

• Wade from Glades co., FL. Point 2 3/8 in. long, 1 7/16 in. wide, 1/8 in. thick. Made of gray multi-tone chert.
Priv. col., excellent quality, valued $30-40.

• Wade from Glades co., FL. Point 2 1/3 in. long, 1 5/8 in. wide, 1/8 in. thick. Made of gray chert.
Priv. col., excellent quality, valued $35-40.

• Wade from Glades co., FL. Point 2 5/8 in. long, 1 5/32 in. wide, 1/8 in. thick. Made of gray chert.
Priv. col., excellent quality, valued $30-40.

Wheeler: 10,000-8,000 B.P. Paleo-Transitional

Found throughout the Southeast. Lanceolate, small to medium sized point or blade. May be fluted, collateral flaking, fine workmanship, sharply serrated. Base is concave and beveled.

Wheeler Excuvate is a small to medium sized point. Lanceolate point often fluted, deeply beveled, finely serrated, collateral flaking.

Wheeler Expanded Base is a small to medium point. Lanceolate with expanding base ears, base deeply concave, very scarce point type.

◆ Wheeler Excuvate from Livingston co., KY. Point 3 in. long, 1 1/32 in. wide, 1/4 in. thick. Steeply beveled and sharply serrated. Made of gray to white.

Priv. col., museum quality, valued $250-325.

◆ Wheeler Excuvate from Hamilton co., TN. Point 2 5/16 in. long, 3/4 in. wide, 3/16 in. thick. Collateral flaked. Made of Dover chert.

Priv. col., museum quality, valued $200-300.

• Wheeler Excuvate from Clay co., NC. Point 2 1/4 in. long, 1 5/16 in. wide, 1/8 in. thick. Excellent workmanship. Made of pink chert.
Priv. col., museum quality, valued $35-40.

• Wheeler Excuvate from Clay co., NC. Point 1 7/8 in. long, 1 5/16 in. wide, 1/8 in. thick. Made of brown multi-tone chert.
Priv. col., excellent quality, valued $30-40.

• Wheeler Excuvate from Clay co., NC. Point 2 1/3 in. long, 1 3/8 in. wide, 1/8 in. thick. Made of quartzite.

Priv. col., average quality, valued $25-30.

- Wheeler Excuvate from Clay co., NC. Point 2 1/3 in. long, 1 1/16 in. wide, 1/8 in. thick. Made of quartzite.
Priv. col., average quality, valued $10-20.

- Wheeler Excuvate from Hyde co., NC. Point 2 3/4 in. long, 1 1/4 in. wide, 1/8 in. thick. Made of quartzite.
Priv. col., average quality, valued $15-20.

- Wheeler Excuvate from Hyde co., NC. Point 1 5/8 in. long, 1 in. wide, 1/8 in. thick. Made of brown chert.
Priv. col., excellent quality, valued $30-40.

- Wheeler Excuvate from Hyde co., NC. Point 2 2/3 in. long, 1 3/32 in. wide, 3/16 in. thick. Made of banded slate.
Priv. col., excellent quality, valued $35-40.

- Wheeler Excuvate from Hyde co., NC. Point 1 2/3 in. long, 11/16 in. wide, 1/8 in. thick. Made of brown chert.
Priv. col., excellent quality, valued $30-40.

- Wheeler Excuvate from Catawaba co., NC. Point 2 1/8 in. long, 1 5/16 in. wide, 1/8 in. thick. Made of banded brown slate.
Priv. col., museum quality, valued $35-40.

- Wheeler Excuvate from Catawaba co., NC. Point 1 5/8 in. long, 7/8 in. wide, 1/8 in. thick. Made of brown chert.
Priv. col., excellent quality, valued $30-40.

- Wheeler Excuvate from Catawaba co., NC. Point 1 2/3 in. long, 1 in. wide, 1/8 in. thick. Made of pink quartzite.
Priv. col., excellent quality, valued $35-45.

- Wheeler Excuvate from Yarkin co., NC. Point 2 1/4 in. long, 13/16 in. wide, 1/8 in. thick. Made of quartzite.
Priv. col., average quality, valued $10-20.

- Wheeler Excuvate from Yarkin co., NC. Point 2 1/4 in. long, 1 5/16 in. wide, 1/8 in. thick. Excellent workmanship. Made of gray chert.
Priv. col., museum quality, valued $35-40.

• Wheeler Excuvate from Onslow co., NC. Point 1 7/8 in. long, 1 1/16 in. wide,
1/8 in. thick. Made of tan multi-tone chert.
Priv. col., excellent quality, valued $30-40.

• Wheeler Excuvate from Onslow co., NC. Point 2 1/3 in. long, 1 3/8 in. wide,
1/8 in. thick. Made of tan chert.
Priv. col., average quality, valued $25-30.

• Wheeler Excuvate from Onslow co., NC. Point 2 1/3 in. long, 1 1/16 in. wide,
1/8 in. thick. Made of quartzite.
Priv. col., average quality, valued $10-20.

◆ Wheeler Triangular from Yadkin co., NC. Point 1 3/4 in. long, 7/8 in. wide,
1/8 in. thick. Heat treated, sharply serrated edges and tip. Made of pink white
chert.

Priv. col., excellent quality, valued $65-80.

• Wheeler Triangular from Yadkin co., NC. Point 2 1/4 in. long, 1 1/8 in. wide,
1/8 in. thick. Made of white chert.
Priv. col., excellent quality, valued $65-80.

• Wheeler Triangular from Swain co., NC. Point 1 7/8 in. long, 1 1/8 in. wide,
1/4 in. thick. Made of pink white chert.
Priv. col., excellent quality, valued $65-80.

• Wheeler Triangular from Swain co., NC. Point 2 1/2 in. long, 1 1/16 in. wide,
3/16 in. thick. Made of white brown slate.
Priv. col., excellent quality, valued $45-60.

• Wheeler Triangular from Swain co., NC. Point 2 7/8 in. long, 1 1/4 in. wide,
1/4 in. thick. Made of pink quartz.
Priv. col., excellent quality, valued $65-80.

• Wheeler Triangular from Wataga co., NC. Point 2 3/4 in. long, 1 1/3 in. wide,

3/16 in. thick. Made of white tan chert.
Priv. col., excellent quality, valued $45-60.

- Wheeler Triangular from Wataga co., NC. Point 1 5/8 in. long, 1 1/32 in. wide, 1/4 in. thick. Made of pink white chert.
Priv. col., excellent quality, valued $65-80.

- Wheeler Triangular from Stokes co., NC. Point 2 1/3 in. long, 1 1/8 in. wide, 1/8 in. thick. Made of tan chert.
Priv. col., excellent quality, valued $60-70.

- Wheeler Triangular from Stokes co., NC. Point 2 in. long, 1 1/8 in. wide, 1/4 in. thick. Made of white pebble chert.
Priv. col., excellent quality, valued $65-75.

- Wheeler Triangular from Stokes co., NC. Point 3 1/4 in. long, 1 1/3 in. wide, 1/4 in. thick. Made of gray chert.
Priv. col., excellent quality, valued $50-60.

- Wheeler Triangular from Stokes co., NC. Point 2 1/8 in. long, 1 5/32 in. wide, 1/4 in. thick. Made of porous white chert.
Priv. col., average quality, valued $35-40.

- Wheeler Triangular from Stokes co., NC. Point 2 1/2 in. long, 1 1/16 in. wide, 1/8 in. thick. Made of porous white chert.
Priv. col., excellent quality, valued $45-60.

- Wheeler Triangular from Stokes co., NC. Point 3 1/8 in. long, 1 3/8 in. wide, 1/4 in. thick. Excellent quality. Made of high grade pink chert.
Priv. col., museum quality, valued $85-100.

- Wheeler Triangular from Richmond co., NC. Point 2 1/3 in. long, 1 1/4 in. wide, 3/16 in. thick. Made of banded white tan chert.
Priv. col., excellent quality, valued $55-65.

- Wheeler Triangular from Richmond co., NC. Point 1 7/8 in. long, 7/8 in. wide, 1/8 in. thick. Made of blue white chert.
Priv. col., excellent quality, valued $65-80.

- Wheeler Triangular from Richmond co., NC. Point 3 in. long, 1 5/32 in. wide, 1/8 in. thick. Made of gray slate.

Priv. col., excellent quality, valued $55-70.

• Wheeler Triangular from Richmond co., NC. Point 2 5/8 in. long, 1 1/8 in. wide, 1/4 in. thick. Made of brown slate.
Priv. col., excellent quality, valued $45-60.

• Wheeler Triangular from Gates co., NC. Point 2 3/32 in. long, 1 1/8 in. wide, 3/16 in. thick. Made of white tan chert.
Priv. col., excellent quality, valued $45-60.

• Wheeler Triangular from Gates co., NC. Point 1 7/8 in. long, 1 5/32 in. wide, 1/4 in. thick. Made of pink white marbled chert.
Priv. col., excellent quality, valued $65-80.

• Wheeler Triangular from Alleghany co., NC. Point 2 1/4 in. long, 1 1/8 in. wide, 1/8 in. thick. Made of white chert.
Priv. col., excellent quality, valued $65-80.

• Wheeler Triangular from Alleghany co., NC. Point 2 in. long, 7/8 in. wide, 1/4 in. thick. Made of light gray slate.
Priv. col., excellent quality, valued $45-60.

• Wheeler Triangular from Graham co., NC. Point 2 3/32 in. long, 1 1/32 in. wide, 1/8 in. thick. Made of white tan chert.
Priv. col., excellent quality, valued $45-60.

• Wheeler Triangular from Graham co., NC. Point 2 5/8 in. long, 1 1/2 in. wide, 1/4 in. thick. Made of gray chert.
Priv. col., excellent quality, valued $75-85.

• Wheeler Triangular from Avery co., NC. Point 2 1/3 in. long, 1 1/16 in. wide, 1/4 in. thick. Made of gray slate.
Priv. col., excellent quality, valued $65-80.

• Wheeler Triangular from Avery co., NC. Point 1 1/8 in. long, 5/8 in. wide, 1/4 in. thick. Excellent workmanship. Made of white chert.
Priv. col., excellent quality, valued $65-80.

White Springs: 8,000-6,000 B.P. Early to Mid-Archaic

Found predominantly in the Southeast into the Midwest. Medium sized point or blade, triangular. Wide short stem, square shoulders, or concave base.

- White Springs from Humphreys co., TN. Point 2 9/16 in. long, 1 3/4 in. wide, 5/8 in. thick. Poor workmanship and material. Made of conglomerate brown chert.
Priv. col., poor quality, valued $5-10.

- ◆ White Springs from Madison co., AL. Point 2 31/32 in. long, 1 1/4 in. wide, 3/16 in. thick. Made of porous pink chert.

Priv. col., excellent quality, valued $30-40.

- ◆ White Springs from Stewart co., TN. Point 1 1/2 in. long, 1 in. wide, 1/4 in. thick. Made of glossy black flint.

Priv. col., museum quality, valued $45-60.

- White Springs from New Madrid co., MO. Point 3 1/2 in. long, 1 1/2 in. wide, 3/16 in. thick. Made of pink chert.
Priv. col., excellent quality, valued $30-40.

- White Springs from New Madrid co., MO. Blade 5 1/3 in. long, 2 5/8 in. wide, 1/4 in. thick. Excellent workmanship, heat treated. Made of white chert.
Priv. col., museum quality, valued $125-150.

- White Springs from New Madrid co., MO. Point 3 1/4 in. long, 1 3/4 in. wide, 1/4 in. thick. Made of Mill Creek chert.

Priv. col., excellent quality, valued $45-60.

• White Springs from New Madrid co., MO. Point 2 1/2 in. long, 1 1/8 in. wide, 3/16 in. thick. Made of tan chert.
Priv. col., excellent quality, valued $30-40.

• White Springs from Wayne co., MO. Blade 5 1/32 in. long, 2 3/8 in. wide, 1/4 in. thick. Made of brown chert.
Priv. col., museum quality, valued $75-100.

• White Springs from Wayne co., MO. Blade 4 2/3 in. long, 1 7/8 in. wide, 3/16 in. thick. Made of banded tan chert.
Priv. col., excellent quality, valued $55-65.

• White Springs from Johnson co., IL. Point 3 1/8 in. long, 1 1/2 in. wide, 1/8 in. thick. Excellent workmanship. Made of white pebble chert.
Priv. col., excellent quality, valued $50-60.

• White Springs from Johnson co., IL. Blade 4 2/3 in. long, 1 7/8 in. wide, 3/16 in. thick. Made of mauve pebble chert.
Priv. col., museum quality, valued $75-85.

Williams: 6,500-1,000 B.P. Mid-Archaic to Woodland

Midwestern point or blade, medium to large sized. Side notched or corner notched, wide, long stem, tapered or barbed shoulders, convex base.

◆ Williams from Hamilton co., IL. Point 2 11/16 in. long, 1 3/4 in. wide, 3/16 in. thick. Heat treated classical design. Made of Mill Creek chert.

Priv. col., excellent quality, valued $55-75.

◆ Williams from Stokes co., NC. Point 2 3/4 in. long, 1 9/16 in. wide, 3/16 in. thick. Good workmanship. Made of pink quartz.

Priv. col., museum quality, valued $200-250.

• Williams from Johnson co., IL. Point 2 5/16 in. long, 1 1/4 in. wide, 3/16 in. thick. Heat treated, good workmanship. Made of Mill Creek chert.
Priv. col., excellent quality, valued $100-125.

• Williams from Johnson co., IL. Point 2 7/8 in. long, 1 7/16 in. wide, 3/16 in. thick. Made of gray chert.
Priv. col., excellent quality, valued $80-100.

• Williams from Jasper co., IL. Point 3 in. long, 1 3/4 in. wide, 3/16 in. thick. Made of green chert.
Priv. col., excellent quality, valued $65-75.

• Williams from Jasper co., IL. Point 2 7/8 in. long, 1 1/2 in. wide, 3/16 in. thick. Good workmanship. Made of white pebble chert.
Priv. col., museum quality, valued $150-200.

• Williams from Gallatin co., IL. Point 3 3/16 in. long, 1 5/8 in. wide, 3/16 in. thick. Heat treated. Made of gray chert.
Priv. col., excellent quality, valued $65-75.

• Williams from Gallatin co., IL. Blade 3 3/4 in. long, 1 5/8 in. wide, 3/16 in. thick. Good workmanship. Made of gray chert.
Priv. col., excellent quality, valued $150-200.

• Williams from Gallatin co., IL. Blade 4 1/16 in. long, 1 7/8 in. wide, 3/16 in. thick. Made of gray chert.
Priv. col., excellent quality, valued $85-100.

• Williams from Gallatin co., IL. Blade 2 3/4 in. long, 1 9/16 in. wide, 3/16 in. thick. Excellent workmanship. Made of gray chert. *Priv. col., museum quality, valued $200-250.*

Yarkin: 2,500-400 B.P. Woodland, Mississippian to Historic

Found thoughout the Southeast and East. Small to medium sized point. Thick, broad, and triangular, deep concave base, generally flaring tangs.

♦ Yarkin from Richmond co., NC. Point 2 5/16 in. long, 1 3/16 in. wide, 1/8 in. thick. Made of mauve chert.

Priv. col., museum quality, valued $100-125.

• Yarkin from Richmond co., NC. Point 2 15/16 in. long, 1 3/8 in. wide, 1/8 in. thick. Made of red banded slate. *Priv. col., excellent quality, valued $80-100.*

• Yarkin from Richmond co., NC. Point 1 11/16 in. long, 13/16 in. wide, 1/8 in. thick. Made of flint. *Priv. col. average quality, valued $40-45.*

• Yarkin from Bibb co., AL. Point 2 3/16 in. long, 1 in. wide, 1/8 in. thick. Made of quartzite. *Priv. col., average quality, valued $30-40.*

• Yarkin from Lamar co., AL. Point 1 1/2 in. long, 5/8 in. wide, 1/8 in. thick. Made of quartzite. *Priv. col. average quality, valued $35-45.*

- Yarkin from Lamar co., AL. Point 2 in. long, 7/8 in. wide, 3/16 in. thick. Made of gray slate.
Priv. col., excellent quality, valued $60-80.

- Yarkin from Coosa co., AL. Point 1 5/16 in. long, 11/16 in. wide, 1/8 in. thick. Made of pink quartzite.
Priv. col., average quality, valued $40-45.

- Yarkin from Perry co., AL. Point 1 13/16 in. long, 1 1/8 in. wide, 1/8 in. thick. Wide, poor workmanship. Made of quartzite.
Priv. col., average quality, valued $40-60.

- Yarkin from Colbert co., AL. Point 1 1/16 in. long, 5/8 in. wide, 3/32 in. thick. Excellent workmanship. Made of jasper.
Priv. col., museum quality, rare, valued $100-125.

- Yarkin from Drew co., AR. Point 2 in. long, 7/8 in. wide, 1/8 in. thick. Made of dull gray flint.
Priv. col., excellent quality, valued $60-80.

- Yarkin from Craighead co., AR. Point 1 5/8 in. long, 11/16 in. wide, 1/8 in. thick. Made of black silver streaked flint.
Priv. col., excellent quality, valued $70-85.

- Yarkin from Perry co., PA. Point 1 1/32 in. long, 1 3/4 in. wide, 1/8 in. thick. Made of pink green black speckled chert.
Priv. col., excellent quality, valued $80-100.

- Yarkin from Bedford co., PA. Point 1 9/16 in. long, 2/3 in. wide, 1/8 in. thick. Made of banded black white chert.
Priv. col., excellent quality, valued $60-75.

- Yarkin from Bedford co., PA. Point 1 15/16 in. long, 1 1/32 in. wide, 1/8 in. thick. Good workmanship. Made of gray chert.
Priv. col., excellent quality, valued $80-100.

- Yarkin from Seneca co., NY. Point 2 1/16 in. long, 13/16 in. wide, 3/16 in. thick. Cache find. Made of pink gray chert.
Priv. col., excellent quality, valued $70-85.

- Yarkin from Seneca co., NY. Point 2 5/16 in. long, 1 1/8 in. wide, 1/8 in. thick. Good workmanship. Same cache find. Made of pink gray chert. *Priv. col., excellent quality, valued $80-100.*

- Yarkin from Seneca co., NY. Point 1 13/16 in. long, 11/16 in. wide, 1/8 in. thick. Cache find. Made of pink gray chert. *Priv. col., average quality, valued $40-45.*

- Yarkin from Seneca co., NY. Point 2 5/8 in. long, 1 1/2 in. wide, 3/16 in. thick. Good workmanship, cache find. Made of pink gray chert. *Priv. col., excellent quality, valued $80-100.*

- Yarkin from Seneca co., NY. Point 2 3/16 in. long, 9/16 in. wide, 1/8 in. thick. Cache find, slight tip break, good workmanship. Made of pink gray chert. *Priv. col., average quality, valued $40-45.*

Zorra: 6,000-4,000 B.P. Mid-Archaic

Midwestern point or blade. Tapered shoulders, long tapered stem, stem generally flat on one face. Stem also beveled on one side of each face. High quality workmanship, finely flaked and serrated. Needle sharp tips with straight base.

◆ Zorra from Greer co., OK. Blade 4 in. long, 1 1/4 in. wide, 1/8 in. thick. Good workmanship, needle sharp tip. Made of white chert.

Priv. col., excellent quality, valued $80-120.

- Zorra from Greer co., OK. Blade 4 3/8 in. long, 1 1/3 in. wide, 3/16 in. thick. Good workmanship, needle sharp tip, fine flaking, beveled on one side of each edge and stem face. Made of white tan chert. *Priv. col., museum quality, valued $150-200.*

- Zorra from Greer co., OK. Blade 4 1/2 in. long, 1 1/8 in. wide, 1/8 in. thick. Good workmanship, needle sharp tip, edges reworked. Made of white chert. *Priv. col., excellent quality, valued $80-120.*

- Zorra from Greer co., OK. Blade 5 1/32 in. long, 1 3/4 in. wide, 1/4 in. thick. Good workmanship, needle sharp tip. Made of gray flint. *Priv. col., excellent quality, valued $80-100.*

- Zorra from Payne co., OK. Blade 4 7/8 in. long, 1 5/8 in. wide, 1/8 in. thick. Good workmanship, needle sharp tip, heat treated. Made of white yellow chert. *Priv. col., excellent quality, valued $90-125.*

- Zorra from Payne co., OK. Blade 4 3/4 in. long, 1 1/2 in. wide, 3/16 in. thick. Good workmanship, rounded, serrated tip. Made of tan chert. *Priv. col., excellent quality, valued $100-150.*

- Zorra from Payne co., OK. Blade 4 1/32 in. long, 1 1/8 in. wide, 3/16 in. thick. Made of gray flint. *Priv. col., excellent quality, valued $50-70.*

- Zorra from Sioux co., NB. Blade 5 1/2 in. long, 2 1/4 in. wide, 1/3 in. thick. Good workmanship. Made of gray flint. *Priv. col., excellent quality, valued $70-80.*

- Zorra from Sioux co., OK. Blade 3 7/8 in. long, 1 1/8 in. wide, 3/32 in. thick. Good workmanship, needle sharp tip. Made of white black speckled pebble chert. *Priv. col., excellent quality, valued $80-100.*

CHAPTER 17
CASE COLLECTIONS

Most collectors take very good care of their artifacts. They are usually stored in quality wood and glass cases. Following are a few case examples and their estimated values. I leave it to the reader to identify the individual pieces from the preceding work of this book.

◆ Case collection pieces from Union co., IL. All museum quality pieces and tooth necklace from Union co., IL. Cache find.

Les Grubbe col., museum quality, valued $4,500-6,000.

◆ Case collection of Bob Mapples. All museum quality. Location sites vary. Most pieces of high grade Dover chert.

Priv. col., museum quality pieces, valued $5,000- 7,500.

◆ Case collection representing Snyders, Thebes, Adena, Cobbs, and Clovis. Bone sewing tools part of a cache find. Other than the bone collection, which is museum quality, the pieces are of excellent quality. Heat treated.

Les Grubbe col., excelent to museum quality, valued $3,500-4,500.

• Cahokia case with a variety of Cahokia type points. Nearly all were found in Johnson and Union co., IL. Some of the points have been fire treated, also in the case a number of bone tools and beads. All points made of Mill Creek chert. *Les Grubbe col., average-museum quality, case valued $650-800.*

CHAPTER 18
STONE TOOLS IN BRIEF

There are numerous other types of stone tools and artifacts designed by the indigenous populations of the Americas. The beauty of some of these pieces rivals the fine works of Chinese, Peruvian, Mayan, and Euopean treasures. In addition there also numerous artifacts and items produced by the Amerind of bone, metal, leather, wood, textiles, and more. As you can easily see, a single work covering all these collectibles would be a difficult and cumbersome volume to carry. Except for a few items, collectibles will be identified and priced in my next work on American Indian collectibles, to be released by Ballantine's House of Collectibles in the near future.

In this last chapter I have chosen to give example of Adzes, Awls, Axes, Banner Stones, Celts, Discordals, Drills, Hoes, Plows, Scrapers, and Spatulas.

Adzes:

Adzes are recognized as woodworking tools, prestige symbols, and ceremonial pieces. The quality, material, and workmanship of adzes varies greatly. The following listings include granite, chert, and hematite adzes.

♦ Adze from northern WI. Adze 7 3/4 in. long, 3 1/2 in. wide, 1 1/8 in. thick, weight approx. 3 1/2 lbs. Finely ground with sand and water. The edge is deceivingly sharp for such a large, thick, and heavy piece. Made of a brown rose granite.

Priv. col., excellent quality, valued $80-100.

◆ Adze from Frazier River, Salish Culture. Adze 4 1/4 in. long, 2 1/8 in. wide, 1 1/2 in. thick, approx. weight 3/4 lbs. Made of molted green nephrite.

Southern IL Univ. col., excellent quality, valued $180-250.

◆ Adze from Frazier River, Interior Salish Culture. Adze 4 3/16 in. long, 2 1/2 in. wide, 1 1/8 in. thick, approx. weight 1 1/3 lbs. Excellent workmanship, finely worked and sharp blade edge. Made of heavy, dense, black stone.

Southern IL Univ. col., museum quality, valued $450-600.

Awls:

Awls are also referred to as "punches" and occasionally "drills". In many ways they served the same functions. Awls were used extensively in leather and woodworking. It is often a difficult task to distinguish between awls and drills. However, the wear of an awls' tip and the lack of serrations are good indicators. Many times only an indepth analysis can truly separate one from the other.

◆ Awl from Hamilton co., TN. Awl 3 5/16 in. long, 1 3/16 in. wide at base, 1/4 in. thick. Well worn tip. Apparently originally designed as an awl rather than a reworked point or blade. Made of Dover chert.

Priv. col., excellent quality, valued $25-40.

◆ Awl from Hamilton co., IL. Awl 1 1/16 in. long, 1/2 in. wide at base, 1/4 in. thick. Rounded worn tip, concave base, slight fluting. Likely a reworked Clovis or related style piece. Made of jasper.

Priv. col., average quality, rare, valued $10-15.

◆ Awl from Jackson co., IL. Awl 1 1/2 in. long, 1 in. wide, 5/16 in. thick. Heat treated, sharp yet worn tip. Made of jasper.

Tim Rubbles col., excellent quality, rare, valued $35-45.

◆ Awl from the Tennessee River. Awl 2 5/8 in. long, 1 in. wide, 1/2 in. thick. Awl displays excellent workmanship, beveled sides, and sharp tip. A pollen analysis test was done on this piece by the author to help determine if piece was an awl or drill. The smooth, oily tip and residue of fauna material leads one to believe it is an awl rather than drill. Reworked from a Baker point. Made of tan pebble chert.

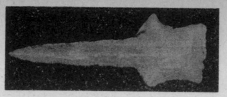

Tony Clinton col., museum quality, valued $45-65.

Axes:

Axes are working, fighting, ceremonial, and prestige artifacts. They vary greatly in quality of workmanship and material. Their size variation is somewhat mind boggling. Axes always display one of several varieties of hafting areas.

◆ Barbed Axe from northern Piatt or Mackinac co., MI. Axe 11 in. long, 4 1/2 in. wide, 3/4 in. hafting groove, 2 in. thick, weight 5 1/4 lbs. Despite the size of the piece, the edge is finely thinned, still carrying a fine edge. Made of conglomerate stone.

Joe Lift col., museum quality, rare, valued $850-1,200.

◆ Axe from central IL. Axe 4 3/4 in. long, 2 1/2 in. wide, 1 1/3 in. thick, weight 3 1/2 lbs. Excellent workmanship, full grooved hafting area, highly polished from workmanship and wear. Made of laminite.

Joe Lift col., museum quality, valued $750-1,000.

♦ Axe from St. Clair co., IL. Axe 3 5/8 in. long, 2 3/8 in. wide, 1 1/2 in. thick, weight 2 1/3 lbs. Hafting groove is a three-quarters type groove 1 in. wide. Considering its dimensions it was likely reworked from a large axe to its current size. Edge is in fine condition and worked to a high dark, oily sheen. Made of pink gray quartz.

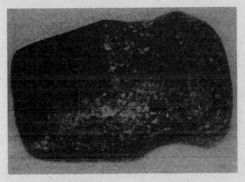

Fred Suite col., excellent quality, valued $85-120.

Banner Stones:

Banner stones are considered to be strictly ceremonial. Considering their design and the quality of their workmanship and material, this is a reasonable assumption. However, the possibility of other usages needs to be kept open. Regardless of their usage, Banner stones are some of the most aesthetic pieces of worked stone to be found. Originals are always different diameters at opposite ends of mounting holes.

♦ Banner stone from Davies co., IN. Banner stone 3 7/8 in. long, blade 2 1/2 in. wide, 1 1/2 in. thick blades, 7/8 in. thick center. One end of mounting hole is 1/3 in. in diameter, the other 5/16 in. Very symmetrical piece. Made of high grade rose quartz.

Chuck Sears col., museum quality, rare, valued $2,500-3,500.

◆ Banner stone from St. Louis co., MO. Banner stone 5 in. long, one blade 3 1/2 in., the other 3 1/4 in. Mounting hole 10mm at one end, 12mm at the other. Excellent workmanship, finely ground to a smooth gloss, heat treated. Made of milky quartz.

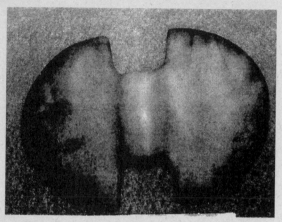

Lenord Johnson col., museum quality, valued $4,500-5,500.

Celts:

Celts, like Banner stones, are generally considered by collectors to be ceremonial pieces. Celts, however, have been found to be associated with fine woodworking. They vary considerably in size and are identified as Celts and Mini Celts. They are generally well designed and well worked pieces of good material.

◆ Celt from Union co., IL. Mini Celt 2 3/4 in. long, 2 in. wide, 3/4 in. thick. Still retains a fine, sharp (for the material) edge. Made of pink, gray, and black speckled granite.

Les Grubbe col., excellent quality, valued $125-175.

◆ Celt from northwestern TN. Celt 2 3/8 in. long, 1 1/2 in. wide, 7/8 in. thick. Mini Celt with sharp edge exhibiting a 3/4 in. bevel, weight 1 2/3 lbs. Excellent workmanship. Made of hematite.

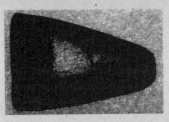

Les Grubbe col., excellent quality, valued $160-200.

Discordals:

Discordals servred a variety of functions from the utilitarian, magical, symbolic, and ceremonial. They were used for the grinding, a numerous variety of grains, herbs, and other organic and mineral material.

◆ Discordal from Pike co., IL. Discordal 3 in. diameter, 1 /1/3 in. thick, indentation 5/16 in. deep, weight approx. 1 1/4 lbs. Commonly called a Bisket Discordal. Excellent workmanship, smoothly ground. Made of pink black speckled granite.

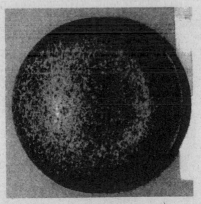

Tom Bryden col., museum quality, valued $750-900.

◆ Discordal from Calhoun co., IL. Discordal 3 1/4 in. diameter, 2 1/16 in. thick. Indentation 1/4 in. deep, 1 1/8 in. diameter. Commonly called a Bisket Discordal. Made of quartzite.

Fred Suite col., average quality, valued $100-150.

Drills:

     Drills are commonly expended points reworked. Their functions vary a great deal. They serve some of the same functions as awls and often punches, as well as serving as wood, metal, and leather drills. Due to their usage, drill tips often are heat treated and extremely sharp.

◆ Drill from Union co., IL. Drill 4 1/8 in. long, 7/8 in. wide at base, 5/16 in. thick. Excellent reworked dovetail piece. Made of Mill Creek chert.

Priv. col., excellent quality, valued $40-60.

◆ Drill from Livingston co., KY. Drill 2 1/4 in. long, 3/4 in. wide, 1/2 in. thick. Heat treated base and tip. Reworked from a Big Sandy point. Made of cream pebble chert.

Tony Clinton col., museum quality, valued $65-80.

◆ Drill from Murphysboro co., TN. Drill 4 1/3 in. long, 3/4 in. wide base, 7/16 in. thick. Heat treated, worn tip, good field patina. Made of Dover chert.

Priv. col., museum quality, valued $50-60.

Hoes or Spades:

Hoes or spades are stone tools used in horticulture, virtual predecessors to their modern counterparts. Hoes are hafted tools on a long wooden shaft, used to turn, hoe, and weed horticultural areas. They were also used as digging tools.

◆ Hoe from Union co., IL. Hoe 6 in. long, 2 in. shaft, 4 in. base, 1 in. thick. Heat treated, excellent field patina, edge well worked and smooth. Made of Mill Creek chert.

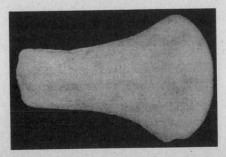

Les Grubbe col., museum quality, valued $200-300.

♦ Hoe from Mt. Vernon, IL. Hoe 9 3/4 in. long, 4 1/2 in. wide, 1 in. thick. Authentic piece, polished at edge from use. Made of white chert.

Dales Resale and Reproductions, average quality, valued $60-80.

Plows:

Plows are larger horticultural tools used for turning relatively large areas of soil to be planted. Like hoes, plows also served as digging implements, acting in their secondary function as shovels. There are a great number of early Amerind plows in existence, however those in complete condition are infrequent and quite valuable. Don May has the most complete plow and hoe collection in the entire Midwest. Don would be extremely hard pressed to part with one of his prizes. I have traveled hundreds of miles to see this outstanding collection, as have thousands of others who enjoy viewing exceptional and large collections each year.
.

♦ Plow from St. Clair co., IL. Plow 14 1/2 in. long, 5 1/2 in. wide, 7/8 in. thick. Heat treated, once part of the H. M. Whelkley Collection. This piece is exceptionally thin for its type. Made of Mill Creek chert.

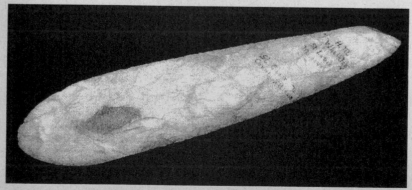

Don May col., museum quality, valued $1,200-1,500.

♦ Plow from Madison co., IL. Plow 14 5/8 in. long, 5 1/4 in. wide, 1/2 in. thick. Heat treated, thin, smooth from work. Made of Mill Creek chert.

Don May col., excellent quality, valued $850-1,000.

Scrapers:

Scrapers, like the majority of stone tools, served a variety of functions. Their use is fairly self explanatory. The variety of scrapers is immense. There are those that are hand held, or held in the hand with something between the hand and scraper, and there is a large variety of hafting designs for specific functions. Scrapers are possibly the most numerous of stone artifacts.

♦ Scraper from Jackson co., IL. Scraper 2 1/16 in. long, 1 5/8 in. wide, 1/4 in. thick. Teardrop shaped scraper, the wide end showing more frequent usage. A test by the author showed heavy fauna residue. Made of Cobden Hornstone chert.

Tim Rubbles col., museum quality, valued $20-25.

♦ Scraper from Hamilton co., IL. Scraper 3 1/2 in. long, 1 1/2 in. wide, 1/4 in. thick. Tip rounded and beveled on one face, very sharp. Good field patina, heat treated, nodule skin still on straight base. Made of Dover chert.

Grover Bohannon col., museum quality, valued $25-30.

◆ Scraper from Stewart co., IL. Scraper 2 1/4 in. long, 1 1/4 in. wide, 3/8 in. thick. Short snap base stem, beveled on one face, very sharp. Poor workmanship, random flaked. Made of black flint.

Grover Bohannon col., average quality, valued $5-10.

◆ Scraper from Murpysboro co., TN. Scraper 2 9/16 in. long, 1 2/3 in. wide, 5/32 in. thick. Thin,finely beveled and rounded edge. Made of multi-toned brown chert.

Grover Bohannon col., museum quality, valued $25-30.

Spatulas:

Spatulas are tools that vary in size according to their use. Predominantly a cooking and servining utinsil.

◆ Spatula from Pike co., IL. Spatula 9 1/3 in. long, 4 in. wide spoon, stem 1 1/4 in. thick and 1 3/8 in. wide, approx. weight 2 lbs. Excellent workmanship. Made of banded slate.

R. Quinn col., museum quality, valued $200-250.

♦ Spatula from Adams co., IL. Spatula 8 1/4 in. long, 3 in. wide, 1 5/8 in. thick. Angular stem. Has been in considerable heat and oils. Made of black slate.

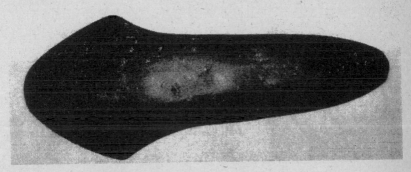

R. Quinn col., excellent quality, valued $125-175.

GLOSSARY

A

Adze: A woodworking tool in the axe family.
Agate: Fossilized semi-precious stone.
Armerind: The indigenous peoples of the Americas.
Artifact: Any object made by human hands.
Asymmetrical: Points or blades of different form on opposing faces.
Atlatl: Spear thrower.
Auriculate: Rounded or pointed stem or base ears.
Awl: A point of bone, stone, or metal used for piercing holes.
Axe: Metal or stone cutting tool perforated for a handle.

B

Barb: A pointed shoulder or wing.
Basal Edge: The bottom of a point or blade.
Basal Grinding: Smooth hafting areas designed to avoid damage to hafting material.
Basal Notched: When the base of a point or blade is notched.
Base: The bottom portion of a point or blade, often used for hafting.
Beveling: The sloping of a blade's or point's edges.
Bifurcated: A central notch splitting a stem into two ears.
Blade: Also called the face of the point or blade.
B.P.: Before present (present being 1950).
Buffalo River Chert: A middle Tennessee chert, speckled, banded mutli-tone.
Bulbous: Having a circular or rounded stem base.
Burlington Chert: A quartz chert found in Illinois and Missouri.

C

Cache: A single deposit find of a group of artifacts.
Carter Cave Chert: Found in Kentucky, reddish orange.
Celt: A form of Adze attached to a staff.
Ceremonial: An artifact designed for use in religious and cultural rounds.
Chert: A stone softer and denser than flint or quartz. Varies greatly in quality,

color, and size.

Classic: Representative of the ideal in a particular design.

Clipped: A particular type of fracture of the wing or shoulder of a point or blade.

Collateral: Parallel flaking that meets in the center of point or blade.

Concave: Inward.

Conglomerate: A metamorphic rock of clay, mud, and small stones and pebbles.

Contracting: The narrowing of the width of a point or blade.

Convex: Outward.

Corner Notched: Basal corner notched for hafting.

Corner Tang: A single tang on a basal corner.

Coshocton Chert: A central and southern Ohio chert, gray blue black in color.

D

Discordal: A disk shaped stone artifact.

Dovetail: A particular base type.

Dover Chert: High grade chert from near Dover, Tennessee; brown, marbled, banded to black.

E

Ears: Projections from the tip of a base.

Early Archaic: Cultural period from 12,500-8,500 B.P.

Edge: The line at which a surface ends.

Expanding: The width of a point or blade expanding.

F

Fishtail: A point or blade with an auriculate stem.

Flaking: The chipping of a point or blade.

Flint: A silica type high quality stone.

Flint Ridge Chert: High quality multi-tone chert from near Columbus, Ohio.

Fluted: Having a grooved channel in a point or blade.

Fort Payne Chert: A multi-toned Alabama chert.

H

Heat Treated: Material exposed to temperatures over 500 degrees Fahrenheit for several days.

Historic: The cultural period when Amerinds came in contact with Europeans.

Hoe: Stone farming implement.

Horizontal Transverse: Parallel horizontal flaking from one edge of the point or blade to the other.

Hornstone: A bluish to gray chert found in Kentucky, Indiana, and Illinois.

Horse Creek Chert: From western Tennessee; red, yellow, and blue colored.

J

Jasper: A very high grade chert, red to yellow.

L
Lanceolate: Having a stemless point or blade.
Late Archaic: Cultural period from 4,500-2,500 B.P.
Late Paleo: Cultural period from 16,500-8,500 B.P.
Lobbed: Rounded base ears meeting as two circles.

M
Mississippian: Cultural period from between 1,500-400 B.P.
Mid-Archaic: Cultural period from 7,500-4,000 B.P.

N
Nodule: A formation of chert, flint, jasper, and numerous other materials used in artifact manufacture found in limestone.

O
Oblique Transverse: Refers to an oblique parallel flaking style.
Obsidian: A black, volcanic rock.
Opaque: Does not allow light to pass through.

P
Paleo: The earlirest archaeological period in the Americas; 48,000-12,000.
Paleo Transitional: The cultural period between 15,000-9,000 B.P.
Patina: A coating caused by oxidization, chemically treated to oxide exposure.
Percussion flaking: The first stage of point or blade flaking. Flaking by striking with a blunt object.
Pressure Flaking: The final stage of flaking. Flaking by pressure.
Prestige Point: A point designed as a status or role symbol.
Projectile point: A point designed to be propelled in a variety of ways.

Q
Quartz: A mineral composed of silicon and oxygen.
Quartzite: A rock consisting of interlocking quartz grains.

R
Reproduction: The modern representation of an original artifact.

S
Scraper: A tool used to scrap hides, wood, and other products, often made from broken points.
Serrating: The degree of sawtooth work on point or blade edges.
Shoulder: The area of a point or blade that separates the blade and stem.
Side Notched: Having a notch in the side of a point or blade for decoration or hafting.

Slate: A metamorphic sedimentary material.
Snap Base: The base has been intentionally snapped.
Snap Tangs: The tangs have been intentionally snapped.
Spatulas: Used as spoons, ladles, or scrapers; used in a large variety of utilitarian functions.
Stem: The area of a point or blade below the shoulders.
Symmetrical: A measurement of the excellence of proportion and balance of an artifact.

T

Tangs: A projection from the base or shoulders of a point or blade.
Transitional: A period between distinct cultural periods.
Translucent: Allows light to pass through.
Transverse Flaking: Flaking which extends to the edge horizontally from the center of a point or blade.
Turkeytail: An Adena family point with a triangular stem.

U

Unfluted: An identification statement for which a point or blade that is usually fluted, but lacks the flute(s).

W

War Point: Self explanatory, identified in style through their being found in the bodies of Amerinds.
Wing: Same as barb.
Woodland: Cultural period from 3,500-1,250 B.P.

RESOURCES

Auctions and Auctioneers:

Bob Sleeper Auction Center, 920 Elm, Higgnisville, MO 64037. Phone: (816)587-0019.

Gene Johns Auction Service, Box 182, Nebo, IL 62355. Phone: (217)734-2010.

Hesse Galleries, 53 Main Street, Otego, NY 13825. Phone: (607)988-6322.

Lolli Brothers, Jim, Dominic, Frankie, and Tim, Hwy. 63 South, Macon, MO 63552. Phone: (816)385-2516.

Michael Steele, 5665 Oak St., Rt. 605, Westerville, OH 43081. Call after 5pm. Phone: (614)985-4612.

The Nashville Auction and Opryland Show, Richard Redenbaugh, Loudon, TN 37774. Phone: (615)988-0004. Fax:(615)988-0117.

Painter Creek Auction Service, Jon Sorgenfrei, Quincy Motor Inn, 200 Main Street, Quincy, Il 62301.

Robert N. Converse, Inc., 199 Converse Drive, Plain City, OH 43064. Phone: (614)873-5471.

Collectors:

Lannie Abrams, Rumsey, KY 42371. Phone: (502)273-3851.

Ray Acra, 323 Thomas Lane, Harrison, OH 45030. Phone: (513)367-1744.

Grover Bohannon, Memphis, TN. Phone: (901)353-1016.

Tony Clinton, 3242 Adams, Paducah, KY 42001.

Tim Crawford, 114 W. Prarie, Roadhouse, IL 62082. Phone: (217)589-5090.

Col. Phil Cummins, 219 Main Street, Augusta, KY 41002. Chief of Augusta Police Dept. Phone: (606)756-3296.

Larry Dyer, 11175 S. 100 W. Columbus, IN 47201. Phone:(812)342-6398.

Les Grubbe, Union Co., IL. Phone: (618)833-3445.

Kenneth Hamilton, 416 South Walnut, Harrison, AK 72601. Phone: (501)743-2175.

Ricky L. Henson, Rt. 7, Box 325, Benton, KY 42035. Phone: (502)527-0841.

Mike Kirtz, Oblong, IL. Phone: (618)592-3966.

Joe Lift, 3616 Platte Court, Lafayette, IN 47905. Phone: (317)447-2307.

Bobby and Pat Maples, Rt. 4, Box 990, Waynesboro, TN 38485. Phone: (615)722-5981.

Ed Meiners, 219 Westwood, East Alton, IL 62024-1642. One of the largest collectors in the U.S. Phone: (618)259-3764.

Roy Mitchell, 3104 Glenmere Place, S.W. Decatur, AL 35603. Phone: (205)350-3103.

Bob Morast and Faye Morast, 128 Fairmount Hwy, Calhoun, GA 30701. Phone: (404)625-4840.

Floyd Ritter, East St. Louis, IL. Phone: (618)345-9814.

Robert J. Schlapp, 54 Royce Drive, Oswego, IL 60543. Phone: (708)554-8140.

Ralph Strope, P.O. Box 952, Pekin, IL 61554. Phone: (309)347-2570.

Dan Stroud, 123 East Seventh Street, Chattanooga, TN 37402. Phone: (615)757-2545.

Dave Zinkie, Howe, IN. Phone: (219)562-2415.

Dealers:

American Indian Artifacts, P.O. Box 89, Paso Robles, CA 93447. Phone: (805)238-6129.

Ancient Art, Brian H. Gibson, 114 Farragot Road, Cincinnati, OH 45218. Phone: (513)851-6557.

Back to Earth, Larry Garvin, 17 North LaSalle Drive, South Zanesville, OH 43701. Phone: (614)454-0874.

Bruce Cantrell, 1223 Blossom Lane, Kingston, TN 37763. Phone: (615)376-6451.

Kevin Cordeiro, P.O. Box 579, Somerset, MO 02726. Phone: (508)675-4886.

Dale's Resale Shop, Jim Poe or Cindy Boyer, 2501 Washington Ave., Granite City, IL 62040. Phone: (618)451-2354.

First Mesa, Larry A. Lentz, P.O. Box 1256, South Bend, IN 46624. Phone: (219)232-2095.

Ron Helman, 1993 Dingman Slage Rd., Sidney, OH 45365. Phone: (513)492-2923.

Indian Relics, Roy Mitchell, 3104 Glenmere Place, S.W. Decatur, AL 35603. Phone: (205)350-3103.

JG Indian Artifacts, Bill Jackson, Main Street, Sharpsburg, KY 40374. Phone: (606)247-2701.

Mac-O-Chee Trading Co., W.B. Baughman, 301 S. Taylor St., West Liberty, OH 43357. Phone: (513)465-4001.

Gary Mumaw, 549 East Main St., Versailles, OH 45380. Phone: (513)526-5687.

W.T. Pinkston, 466 W. Office St., Harrodsburg, KY 40330. Phone: (606)734-4213.

Pocotaug Trading Post, John and Allan Atkins, 109 Windshire Drive, South Windsor, CT 06074. Phone: (203)644-4476.

Prehistoric Points, J.W. Bailey, P.O. Box 328, Cookeville, TN 38503. Phone: (615)526-2256.

Quality Indian Artifacts, Jim Justice and Mike Nelson, 246 W. Ottawa St., Richwood, OH 43344.

Ray Stanford Fine Art and Antiquities, P.O. Box 599, College Park, MD 20740.

Ralph Sentell Jr. Phone: (901)584-8718.

Greg Shipley, 6672 Maple St., Rt. 36, Cable, OH 43009. Phone: (513)652-3020.

Duke Snyder, P.O. Box 362, Bethel, OH 45106. Open after 6pm. Phone: (513)734-3119.

The Solid Rock, Jerry Dickey, 1743 W. Broadway, Suite 171, Maryville, TN 37701. Phone: (619)982-0805.

Tomarack Trading Co., Jerry Gaither, 2785 Pacific Coast Highway, Suite E-333, Torrance, CA 90505. Phone: (310)832-8996.

Tom Davis Artifacts, Box 386-272, Airport Road, Stanton, KY 40380. Phone: (606)663-9871.

Len Weidner, 13706 Robbins Road, Westerville, OH 43081. Phone: (614)965-2868.

Organizations:

Illinois State Archaelogical Society, Tommy W. Bryden, Secretary and Treasurer, R.R.8, Box 114, Springfield, IL 62707. Phone: (217)529-8691.

Indiana Archaelogical Society, David Lutz (812)833-8344 or Bill Clark (812)897-2417.

Indiana Archaeological Society Inc., Mark Clapp, R.R. 1, Box 74, New Richmond, IN 47967.

Piedmont Archaeological Society, Officers Lee and Tracie Altman (803)585-5764, Jim Maus (919)998-2461, Rodney Peck (704)786-6294, 2438 Scott Street, Spartansburg, SC 29303.

Prehistoric Antiquities Quarterly, Bill Balinger, President. Phone: (513)747-2225.

Periodicals:

Archaeology Monthly Periodical. 135 William Street, New York, NY 10038.

Central States Archaeological Journal. 731 Thames Dr., Schaumburg, IL 60193.

Indian Artifact Magazine. Rd. 1, Box 240, Dept. P, Turboville, PA 17792.

Prehistoric Antiquities Quarterly. Box 53, North Lewisburg, OH 43060.

Reproductions and Restorations:

Jerry Jenkins, Rt. 5, Box 472, Cynthiana, KY 41031. Phone: (606)234-3350.

Old Barn Auction, 10040 Mill St., Rt. 224 West, Findlay, OH 45840. Phone: (419)422-8531.

Prehistoric Beauty, Charles F. Wood, P.O. Box 504, Wellston, OH 45692. Phone: (614)384-6551.

Quality Restoration, Dennis Bushley, 113 Pine Forest Drive, Selena, AL 36701. Phone: (205)875-5299.

Taylor Studios, P.O. Box 1063, Mammoth, IL 61833. Phone: (217)586-2047.

Shows and Events:

CSAJ (Central States Archaeological Journal) events:
    Allen, MI Show
    Anderson, IN Show
    Athens, AL Show
    Aztalan, WI Show
    Baraboo, WI Show
    Baxter, TN Show
    Boonville, IN Show
    Bridgeton, MO Show
    Camden, SC Show
    Cartersville, GA Show
    Cleveland, AL Show
    Cleveland, GA Show
    Collinsville, IL Show
    Constantine, MI Show
    Crawfordsville, IN Show

Davenport, IA Show
Fayetteville, AR Show
Gilbertsville, KY Show
Harrison, AR Show
Huntington, IN Show
Indianola, IA Show
Jackson, AL Show
Jackson, TN Show
Jefferson City, MO Show
Kankakee, IL Show
Keosanque, IA Show
LaCrosse, WI Show
Lansing, MI Show
Lexington, KY Show
Lineville, AL Show
Lucas, KY Show
Marietta, GA Show
McMinnville, TN Show
Monticello, WI Show
Mt. Pleasant, IA Show
Nashville, TN Show
Olive Branch, IL Show
Owensboro, KY Show
Paoli, IN Show
Prattville, AL Show
Richfield, WI Show
Sheffield, AL Show
Sikeston, MO Show
Springfield, IL Show
St. Louis County, MO Show
Swainsboro, GA Show
Terre, MO Show
Thomson, GA Show
Ullin, IL Show
Utica, IL Show
Waverly, TN Show
Waynesboro, TN Show
West Olive, MI Show

G.S.L.A.S. (Greater St. Louis Archaeological Society), Relic Shows Contact Mr. John Beyes, 11552 Patty Ann Dr., St. Louis, MO 63146.

Illinois State Archaeological Society, Tommy Bryden. Phone: (217)529-8691.

The Owensboro Show; Owensboro, Kentucky Indian Art Shows Inc., P.O.Box 7, Tell City, IN 47586. Phone: (812)547-4881.

S.D.P.A. (The Society for the Documentation of Prehistoric Artifacts), Floyd Ritter. Phone: (618)345-9814.

ABOUT THE AUTHOR

JOHN L. STIVERS has an A.S. and a BA in Anthropology, and a MS Ed. in Higher Education/Anthropology. He has worked at twelve archaeological digs and has over three years archaeological lab experience in identifications. Mr. Stivers was the Assistant Registrar at Southern Illinois University Museum during 1981–1982, during which time he also conducted 18 months of field research.

A former Marine of the Vietnam era, Mr. Stivers is also the father of three daughters and currently resides in a Central American country.